T0178264

Lecture Notes in Computer Science 13324

More information about this series at https://link.springer.com/bookseries/558

Matthias Rauterberg (Ed.)

Culture and Computing

10th International Conference, C&C 2022
Held as Part of the 24th HCI International Conference, HCII 2022
Virtual Event, June 26 – July 1, 2022
Proceedings

 Springer

Editor
Matthias Rauterberg
Eindhoven University of Technology
Eindhoven, The Netherlands

ISSN 0302-9743   ISSN 1611-3349 (electronic)
Lecture Notes in Computer Science
ISBN 978-3-031-05433-4   ISBN 978-3-031-05434-1 (eBook)
https://doi.org/10.1007/978-3-031-05434-1

This Springer imprint is published by the registered company Springer Nature Switzerland AG
The registered company address is: Gewerbestrasse 11, 6330 Cham, Switzerland

Foreword

Human-computer interaction (HCI) is acquiring an ever-increasing scientific and industrial importance, as well as having more impact on people's everyday life, as an ever-growing number of human activities are progressively moving from the physical to the digital world. This process, which has been ongoing for some time now, has been dramatically accelerated by the COVID-19 pandemic. The HCI International (HCII) conference series, held yearly, aims to respond to the compelling need to advance the exchange of knowledge and research and development efforts on the human aspects of design and use of computing systems.

The 24th International Conference on Human-Computer Interaction, HCI International 2022 (HCII 2022), was planned to be held at the Gothia Towers Hotel and Swedish Exhibition & Congress Centre, Göteborg, Sweden, during June 26 to July 1, 2022. Due to the COVID-19 pandemic and with everyone's health and safety in mind, HCII 2022 was organized and run as a virtual conference. It incorporated the 21 thematic areas and affiliated conferences listed on the following page.

A total of 5583 individuals from academia, research institutes, industry, and governmental agencies from 88 countries submitted contributions, and 1276 papers and 275 posters were included in the proceedings to appear just before the start of the conference. The contributions thoroughly cover the entire field of human-computer interaction, addressing major advances in knowledge and effective use of computers in a variety of application areas. These papers provide academics, researchers, engineers, scientists, practitioners, and students with state-of-the-art information on the most recent advances in HCI. The volumes constituting the set of proceedings to appear before the start of the conference are listed in the following pages.

The HCI International (HCII) conference also offers the option of 'Late Breaking Work' which applies both for papers and posters, and the corresponding volume(s) of the proceedings will appear after the conference. Full papers will be included in the 'HCII 2022 - Late Breaking Papers' volumes of the proceedings to be published in the Springer LNCS series, while 'Poster Extended Abstracts' will be included as short research papers in the 'HCII 2022 - Late Breaking Posters' volumes to be published in the Springer CCIS series.

I would like to thank the Program Board Chairs and the members of the Program Boards of all thematic areas and affiliated conferences for their contribution and support towards the highest scientific quality and overall success of the HCI International 2022 conference; they have helped in so many ways, including session organization, paper reviewing (single-blind review process, with a minimum of two reviews per submission) and, more generally, acting as goodwill ambassadors for the HCII conference.

This conference would not have been possible without the continuous and unwavering support and advice of Gavriel Salvendy, founder, General Chair Emeritus, and Scientific Advisor. For his outstanding efforts, I would like to express my appreciation to Abbas Moallem, Communications Chair and Editor of HCI International News.

June 2022   Constantine Stephanidis

HCI International 2022 Thematic Areas and Affiliated Conferences

Thematic Areas

- HCI: Human-Computer Interaction
- HIMI: Human Interface and the Management of Information

Affiliated Conferences

- EPCE: 19th International Conference on Engineering Psychology and Cognitive Ergonomics
- AC: 16th International Conference on Augmented Cognition
- UAHCI: 16th International Conference on Universal Access in Human-Computer Interaction
- CCD: 14th International Conference on Cross-Cultural Design
- SCSM: 14th International Conference on Social Computing and Social Media
- VAMR: 14th International Conference on Virtual, Augmented and Mixed Reality
- DHM: 13th International Conference on Digital Human Modeling and Applications in Health, Safety, Ergonomics and Risk Management
- DUXU: 11th International Conference on Design, User Experience and Usability
- C&C: 10th International Conference on Culture and Computing
- DAPI: 10th International Conference on Distributed, Ambient and Pervasive Interactions
- HCIBGO: 9th International Conference on HCI in Business, Government and Organizations
- LCT: 9th International Conference on Learning and Collaboration Technologies
- ITAP: 8th International Conference on Human Aspects of IT for the Aged Population
- AIS: 4th International Conference on Adaptive Instructional Systems
- HCI-CPT: 4th International Conference on HCI for Cybersecurity, Privacy and Trust
- HCI-Games: 4th International Conference on HCI in Games
- MobiTAS: 4th International Conference on HCI in Mobility, Transport and Automotive Systems
- AI-HCI: 3rd International Conference on Artificial Intelligence in HCI
- MOBILE: 3rd International Conference on Design, Operation and Evaluation of Mobile Communications

List of Conference Proceedings Volumes Appearing Before the Conference

1. LNCS 13302, Human-Computer Interaction: Theoretical Approaches and Design Methods (Part I), edited by Masaaki Kurosu
2. LNCS 13303, Human-Computer Interaction: Technological Innovation (Part II), edited by Masaaki Kurosu
3. LNCS 13304, Human-Computer Interaction: User Experience and Behavior (Part III), edited by Masaaki Kurosu
4. LNCS 13305, Human Interface and the Management of Information: Visual and Information Design (Part I), edited by Sakae Yamamoto and Hirohiko Mori
5. LNCS 13306, Human Interface and the Management of Information: Applications in Complex Technological Environments (Part II), edited by Sakae Yamamoto and Hirohiko Mori
6. LNAI 13307, Engineering Psychology and Cognitive Ergonomics, edited by Don Harris and Wen-Chin Li
7. LNCS 13308, Universal Access in Human-Computer Interaction: Novel Design Approaches and Technologies (Part I), edited by Margherita Antona and Constantine Stephanidis
8. LNCS 13309, Universal Access in Human-Computer Interaction: User and Context Diversity (Part II), edited by Margherita Antona and Constantine Stephanidis
9. LNAI 13310, Augmented Cognition, edited by Dylan D. Schmorrow and Cali M. Fidopiastis
10. LNCS 13311, Cross-Cultural Design: Interaction Design Across Cultures (Part I), edited by Pei-Luen Patrick Rau
11. LNCS 13312, Cross-Cultural Design: Applications in Learning, Arts, Cultural Heritage, Creative Industries, and Virtual Reality (Part II), edited by Pei-Luen Patrick Rau
12. LNCS 13313, Cross-Cultural Design: Applications in Business, Communication, Health, Well-being, and Inclusiveness (Part III), edited by Pei-Luen Patrick Rau
13. LNCS 13314, Cross-Cultural Design: Product and Service Design, Mobility and Automotive Design, Cities, Urban Areas, and Intelligent Environments Design (Part IV), edited by Pei-Luen Patrick Rau
14. LNCS 13315, Social Computing and Social Media: Design, User Experience and Impact (Part I), edited by Gabriele Meiselwitz
15. LNCS 13316, Social Computing and Social Media: Applications in Education and Commerce (Part II), edited by Gabriele Meiselwitz
16. LNCS 13317, Virtual, Augmented and Mixed Reality: Design and Development (Part I), edited by Jessie Y. C. Chen and Gino Fragomeni
17. LNCS 13318, Virtual, Augmented and Mixed Reality: Applications in Education, Aviation and Industry (Part II), edited by Jessie Y. C. Chen and Gino Fragomeni

39. CCIS 1582, HCI International 2022 Posters - Part III, edited by Constantine Stephanidis, Margherita Antona and Stavroula Ntoa
40. CCIS 1583, HCI International 2022 Posters - Part IV, edited by Constantine Stephanidis, Margherita Antona and Stavroula Ntoa

http://2022.hci.international/proceedings

Preface

Culture and computing is an important research area which aims to address the human-centered design of interactive technologies for the production, curation, preservation, and fruition of cultural heritage, as well as developing and shaping future cultures. There are various research directions in the relations between culture and computing: to preserve, disseminate, and create cultural heritages via ICT (e.g., digital archives), to empower humanities research via ICT (i.e., digital humanities), to create art and expressions via ICT (i.e., media art), to support interactive cultural heritage experiences (e.g., rituals), and to understand new cultures born on the Internet (e.g., net culture, social media, games).

The International Conference on Culture and Computing (C&C), an affiliated conference of the HCI International (HCII) conference, arrived at its 10th edition and provided an opportunity to share research issues and discuss the future of culture and computing. One volume of the HCII 2022 proceedings is dedicated to this year's edition of the C&C conference and focuses on topics related to user experience, culture, and technology; interactions with tangible and intangible cultural heritage; culture and computing in arts and music; and reflections on ICT and culture.

Computer-based interactive art influences society by changing opinions, instilling values, and translating experiences across space and time. Research presented in this volume shows that cultural artifacts affect the fundamental sense of self. Cultural artifacts like intangible heritage, light, literature, music, painting, sculpture, and the other arts are often considered to be the repository of a society's collective memory. The artistic part of cultural heritage preserves what fact-based historical records cannot: how it felt to exist in a particular place at a particular time. Art in this sense is communication; it allows people from different cultures and different times to communicate with each other via images, interactive art, sounds, and stories. Cultural artifacts are often a vehicle for social change. It can give voice to the politically or socially disenfranchised. A song, film, or novel can rouse emotions in those who encounter it, inspiring them to rally for change. Cultural artifacts also have utilitarian influences on society. Each presented paper explores different themes from a comparative and global perspective and offers a broad range of topics, allowing the reader to get familiar with the current state of the art. I encourage every reader to enjoy the academic topics they are passionate about.

Papers of this volume are included for publication after a minimum of two single-blind reviews from the members of the C&C Program Board or, in some cases, from members of the Program Boards of other affiliated conferences. I would like to thank all of them for their invaluable contribution, support, and efforts.

June 2022   Matthias Rauterberg

10th International Conference on Culture and Computing (C&C 2022)

Program Board Chair: **Matthias Rauterberg,** Eindhoven University of Technology, The Netherlands

- Emmanuel G. Blanchard, IDU Interactive Inc., Canada
- Erik Champion, University of Western Australia, Australia
- Philippe Codognet, CNRS and Sorbonne University, France/University of Tokyo, Japan
- Nick Degens, Hanze University of Applied Sciences, The Netherlands
- Maria Economou, University of Glasgow, UK
- Jean Gabriel Ganascia, Sorbonne University, France
- Halina Gottlieb, Digital Heritage Center Sweden AB, Sweden
- Susan Hazan, Digital Heritage Israel, Israel
- Rüdiger Heimgärtner, Intercultural User Interface Consulting, Germany
- Gert Jan Hofstede, Wageningen University, The Netherlands
- Yiyuan Huang, Beijing Institute of Graphic Communication, China
- Isto Huvila, Uppsala University, Sweden
- Toru Ishida, Waseda University, Japan
- Katerina Kabassi, Ionian University, Greece
- Gertraud Koch, University of Hamburg, Germany
- Donghui Lin, Kyoto University, Japan
- Yohei Murakami, Ritsumeikan University, Japan
- Ryohei Nakatsu, Kyoto University, Japan
- Susan Nugent, Wrexham Glyndwr University, UK
- Seth Oppong, University of Botswana, Botswana
- Jong-Il Park, Hanyang University, South Korea
- Antonio Rodà, University of Padua, Italy
- Kasper Rodil, Aalborg University, Denmark
- Pertti Saariluoma, University of Jyväskylä, Finland
- Hooman Samani, University of Plymouth, UK
- Vibeke Sørensen, Stanford University, USA
- Maria Shehade, CYENS Centre of Excellence, Cyprus
- Theopisti Stylianou-Lambert, Cyprus University of Technology and CYENS Centre of Excellence, Cyprus
- William Swartout, University of Southern California, Los Angeles, USA
- Daniel Thalmann, École Polytechnique Fédérale de Lausanne, Switzerland
- Claudia Trillo, University of Salford, UK
- Michael Walsh, Nanyang Technological University Singapore, Singapore
- Jianjiang Wang, Shanghai Normal University, China
- Lin Zhang, Communication University of China, China

The full list with the Program Board Chairs and the members of the Program Boards of all thematic areas and affiliated conferences is available online at

http://www.hci.international/board-members-2022.php

HCI International 2023

The 25th International Conference on Human-Computer Interaction, HCI International 2023, will be held jointly with the affiliated conferences at the AC Bella Sky Hotel and Bella Center, Copenhagen, Denmark, 23–28 July 2023. It will cover a broad spectrum of themes related to human-computer interaction, including theoretical issues, methods, tools, processes, and case studies in HCI design, as well as novel interaction techniques, interfaces, and applications. The proceedings will be published by Springer. More information will be available on the conference website: http://2023.hci.international/.

General Chair
Constantine Stephanidis
University of Crete and ICS-FORTH
Heraklion, Crete, Greece
Email: general_chair@hcii2023.org

http://2023.hci.international/

Contents

Reflections on ICT and Culture

User Experience, Culture, and Technology

Putting Users in the Loop: How User Research Can Guide AI Development for a Consumer-Oriented Self-service Portal

Frank Binder[1]([⊠]) [iD], Jana Diels[2], Julian Balling[1,3], Oliver Albrecht[4],
Robert Sachunsky[3], J. Nathanael Philipp[3], Yvonne Scheurer[4], Marlene Münsch[2],
Markus Otto[5], Andreas Niekler[3], Gerhard Heyer[1,3], and Christian Thorun[2]

[1] Institute for Applied Informatics at Leipzig University (InfAI), Leipzig, Germany
{binder,balling}@infai.org
[2] ConPolicy GmbH - Institute for Consumer Policy, 10827 Berlin, Germany
{j.diels,m.muensch,c.thorun}@conpolicy.de
[3] Natural Language Processing Group, Leipzig University, Leipzig, Germany
{sachunsky,aniekler,heyer}@informatik.uni-leipzig.de,
jonas_nathanael.philipp@uni-leipzig.de
[4] co2online gGmbH, Hochkirchstr. 9, 10829 Berlin, Germany
{oliver.albrecht.extern,yvonne.scheurer}@co2online.de
[5] SEnerCon GmbH, Hochkirchstr. 11, 10829 Berlin, Germany
markus.otto@senercon.de

Abstract. This study investigates three challenges for developing machine learning-based self-service web apps for consumers. First, we argue that user research must accompany the development of ML-based products so that they better serve users' needs at all stages of development. Second, we discuss the data sourcing dilemma in developing consumer-oriented ML-based apps and propose a way to solve it by implementing an interaction design that balances the workload between users and computers according to the ML component's performance. To dynamically define the role of the user-in-the-loop, we monitor user success and ML performance over time. Finally, we propose a lightweight typology of ML-based systems to assess the generalizability of our findings to other ML use cases.

Our case study uses a newly developed web application that allows consumers to analyze their heating bills for potential energy and cost savings. Based on domain-specific data values extracted from user-provided document images, an assessment of potential savings is derived and reported back to the user.

Keywords: HCI · Machine learning · User research · Interaction design

© The Author(s), under exclusive license to Springer Nature Switzerland AG 2022
M. Rauterberg (Ed.): HCII 2022, LNCS 13324, pp. 3–19, 2022.
https://doi.org/10.1007/978-3-031-05434-1_1

1 Introduction

With the rise of artificial intelligence (AI) and machine learning (ML), many consumer-oriented applications have entered the market that leverage AI and ML for assisting consumers in various settings (e.g., recommendation systems, natural language-based interactions with smart assistants, face recognition in photo collections, or text recognition from document images).

However, many small and medium-sized enterprises and especially the public sector are still struggling to provide ML-based products and services that really satisfy their users' needs and successfully assert themselves on the market [17][1]. One reason for this can be seen in the often one-sided focus only to optimize the technical power of the respective service while treating consumer aspects subordinately. Consequently, estimates range from 60% to 85% project failure rates for AI-, ML-, and data-driven implementations [30]. While other surveys show a brighter picture (e.g., [27]), the bottom line still holds: Many AI projects fail, as ML models do not transition successfully from research and development into market stages.

Using the example of a smart consumer application, we pursue the question of where and how users and user research can be brought in the loop of AI research and development to increase acceptance and, thereby, increase the chances of market success of ML-based products and services.

The paper is structured as follows: Sect. 2 sheds light on the context and motivation of this study. Section 3 elaborates on the terminology and the different roles that we perceive for humans to take "in the loop", before it presents a lightweight ad-hoc typology of ML-based systems in order to provide guidance regarding the potential and limitations in generalizing our method and findings to other (types of) ML-based systems. Section 4 presents our case study and introduces our ML-based prototype of a "smart" web app for consumers to have their heating bills analyzed and checked for potential energy and cost savings. It also identifies the methods we used for qualitative user research and for quantifying user success and the overall performance of our ML-based system. The remaining sessions provide results and discussion, as well as our conclusion and outlook.

2 Motivation

It has long been general scientific practice to evaluate the quality of an ML-based service merely by judging how accurate (and how fast) it can process provided data and deliver results. This approach might be adequate for scientific use cases or lab settings, such as the ubiquitous shared tasks. However, these assessment standards frequently fall short in production settings, especially when assessing ML-based applications tailored for end users.

This is because consumers do not only consider the analytic power of the underlying AI when evaluating an application. Instead, in line with existing research on user experience and interface design [7, 20, 22, 23, 33], they can be deemed to place (at least) equal

---

[1] We use the term machine-learning-based systems, or ML-based systems, as software systems that include "one or more components that learn how to perform a task from a given data set" [29]. See Sect. 3 for further terminological considerations.

importance on factors such as overall functionality, user friendliness, or data protection standards. Hence, and in accordance with Auer and Felderer [2], evaluation and quality assurance of ML-based systems need to move from lab settings to live or production environments. Consequently, research and development of user-centered ML-based services should not only focus on the ML components' quality (and possibly efficiency). Instead, they need to be complemented by research on user experience and the respective acceptance criteria.

Further, typical scientific evaluation paradigms adapt to cases with relatively easy access to structured data or rely on publicly shared special-purpose data sets and collections to train and operate the ML components. However, this is often not feasible when developing consumer-oriented services in market settings (as opposed to lab settings). Here, users themselves need to supply the required data. This approach, in turn, implies that, especially in early development stages, only little data is available. The accuracy and analytical power of the ML component only evolve as the number of user interactions increases. Those applications face the challenge of winning and keeping users despite the restricted functionality of the integrated ML component in its early stages of development. Accordingly, the quality assessment of a user-centered ML-based service should be understood and designed as a fluent process, during which its accuracy incrementally increases in codependence with continuous user interaction.

Consequently, accuracy and efficiency of ML-based applications cannot be regarded as ends to themselves. Instead, in real market settings for consumer-oriented applications, AI quality and user acceptance are interlinked and need to be treated as mutually interdependent throughout the respective development process. As such, putting users in the loop of AI development becomes mandatory.

Finally, much of the research in AI and ML appears to evolve around specific challenges and benchmarks, such as shared tasks[2]. The discussions of related ML practices are frequently tied to a particular use case and rarely explicitly reflect on the greater variety of ML-based systems or potentially related cases and their distinctions. Therefore, it is difficult to assess if findings and "best practices" derived from such settings are applicable in general to (the research and development of) other kinds of ML-based systems, or rather, if appropriate restrictions apply.

By and large, this research's goal is threefold: First, it aims to design and test a development process for a consumer-oriented ML-based self-service application that explicitly puts users in the loop and includes user acceptance criteria as evaluation standards. Second, it tries to overcome the data sourcing dilemma for an application that requires frequent (and successful) user interaction to collect data items for improving its ML component, even though this component is of only limited use at early stages of development. Lastly, we reflect on the generalizability of our findings. To this end, we propose and apply a lightweight ad-hoc typology of ML-based systems, which attempts

---

[2] Shared tasks, such as the table detection and recognition challenges of the ICDAR conference series [10, 11], are a ubiquitous means within machine learning communities. They usually focus on solving or improving a specific ML use case by applying and fine-tuning (highly specialized) machine-learning techniques towards a predefined, shared goal. While a helpful motivation and illustration for the specific tasks and the applicable techniques, there is usually no need to further contextualize or generalize beyond the specific setting of the task at hand.

to provide a first step towards a more consistent view on the heterogeneity of machine learning projects and ML-based products. We also comment on the presumed paradigm shift from "humans in the loop" towards "AI in the loop", where humans leave their role of data annotators behind and primarily leverage the ML component for their analysis and decision making.

3   Preliminary and Terminological Considerations

3.1   Machine Learning-Based Systems and "The Loop"

For our study, we adopt the definition of machine-learning-based systems, or ML-based systems, as software systems that include "one or more components that learn how to perform a task from a given data set" [29]. Similarly, we use "ML-based service" to denote a digitally provided application or service that assists users in reaching a particular goal by using the respective ML-based system. We use the term ML component to refer to the specific machine learning component that is part of the respective system or service in its production setting. The ML component is usually integrated via an API that allows the other system components to request predictions from the contained ML model when provided with (novel) data points. While the users interact with a front-end component, their provided data is forwarded to the ML component for processing, usually for classification or prediction tasks.

The ML model is the central part of the ML component, which captures the "acquired knowledge" that the ML component needs to perform its respective task. The model itself is usually based on a pre-trained and fine-tuned backbone or backbone variant selected from literature and available implementations to fit the task at hand. Models, specifically their internal weights, are regularly updated in training iterations that usually take place in separated lab settings, based on newly assembled or substantially revised training data or on other hypotheses for potential improvements in accuracy or processing time. Such a newly fine-tuned or re-trained model to be deployed to production is denoted as an "ML model increment".

The iterative process of developing and maintaining ML-based systems is what we perceive to be "the loop". It consists of the following steps:

1. Collecting and curating new revisions of the data set;
2. Taking an ML model - possibly from the production setting - and submitting it to re-training or fine-tuning by leveraging this newly compiled data set for model training;
3. Evaluating the model's performance with regard to accuracy and processing speed (or computing resources used);
4. In case of significant improvements, re-deploying the newly created ML model increment to the production setting.

The data set used to train the ML model in our case, as in many others[3], is derived from user interactions with the overall ML-based system or a non-ML-based predecessor. More specifically, in the present case study, the data set comprises user-provided

---

[3] See Sect. 3.3 for a brief typology of ML use cases.

document page images and corresponding data points, which the ML-based system is designed to automatically extract from the documents once it is in production. Part of the data set is usually collected automatically and in large quantities from user interactions, such as the user-provided document images. In contrast, other parts, namely the data that the ML component is supposed to extract, must be curated manually for training and (pre-) evaluation of the respective ML model increment. This manual data annotation or curation step is where humans take their turn within the loop.

3.2 Different Roles within the Loop

The exact role of humans in the loop can be differentiated (a) with respect to the humans' relation towards the ML-based system and (b) according to their level of expertise regarding the task at hand. First, we distinguish humans who are users of the ML-based systems in its production setting "on stage" from those primarily involved "behind the scenes", i.e., when curating data for training ML models. Both roles can be part of the loop. Table 1 illustrates possible combinations of these distinctions with some widespread (and some perceivable) use cases for ML-based systems[4].

Table 1. Example machine learning use cases with humans-in-the-loop providing data for the ML-based systems while in different roles and with different levels of (human) expertise

Role of the human-in-the-loop	Required skill level	Exemplary ML use cases
Data annotator ("behind the scenes")	Low	(Internally or externally) crowd-sourced data annotations such as general-purpose audio transcription or object annotations in photo collections
	High	Data annotation for ML-based medical systems, such as medical imaging, clinical decision support etc. in development settings
User ("on stage")	Low	Using general web search engines and providing feedback to the system by deciding (not) to click on recommended links; Consuming news or video feeds; Correcting typing suggestions in virtual keyboards; Pushing a "Report as spam" button for incoming spam mails that have not (yet) been automatically marked as such
	High	Medical doctors documenting their decisions in ML-assisted clinical decision support software, or live correcting their case-related voice transcriptions; A driver of an autonomous car actively counteracting the car's actions or recommendations

While traditionally the latter role of data annotators "behind the scenes" is more typically referred to as "humans-in-the-loop", in many types of ML-based systems, it is in fact users "on stage" who provide the (complete) training data for the next model increment - merely by interacting with the ML-based system. For example, users

---

[4] Further examples and perspectives on human-in-the-loop approaches can be found in [14, 21, 35]. Examples of domain-specific roles for humans include the doctor-in-the-loop [15] and the analyst-in-the-loop [6].

consume news feeds or media streaming recommendations with respective attention spans, reading times, or even (streaming) fees, they decide (not) to click on search result links and thereby implicitly mark them as more (or less) relevant. Users may also browse and select items from interactive online catalogues and shopping websites, and in doing so provide valuable data for the integrated ML-based recommendation engines and their next training iteration.

The second distinction focuses on the level of competency or expertise regarding the task at hand - which is, however, to be taken very carefully. Today, in knowledge-based settings, trained and qualified humans make informed decisions. ML-based systems can assist or - technically speaking - potentially take over the human part with performance levels that equal or exceed human capabilities, both in terms of speed and accuracy. Such scenarios become even more intriguing when considering tasks that are otherwise exclusively performed by highly qualified professionals, such as judges in court or medical doctors in hospitals.

On the other hand, the development of the ML components, and the training of their models, require large quantities of sophistically collected (and usually manually curated and annotated) data. For some tasks, non-experts might perform data. Other cases might require high levels of academic qualification, such as labeling cancer cells in images of tissue. However, even such cases can sometimes be performed by specialized annotators after sufficient training. Hence, one must be careful not to mix competence with authority and beware of narrow versus broad fields of competence of the humans-in-the-loop.

Another highly relevant distinction in our study concerns the motivation (or incentives) of the humans-in-the-loop. While annotators "behind the scenes" are usually motivated through material compensations or payments (possibly depending on the quality of their deliverables), users "on stage" primarily intend to achieve a "successful interaction" with the system to reach some use case-specific goal(s)[5]. Hence, in "on stage" settings, users implicitly provide data for training iterations merely by using a particular ML-based system[6].

3.3   A Lightweight Typology of ML-Based Systems

Each ML-based system and its creation is a unique project in terms of goals, context, and conditions. To better understand the individual project's challenges and assess the transferability of lessons learnt in the development process to other cases, it helps to characterize the respective ML-based system with regard to certain common aspects. We propose to consider the following common aspects inspired by [25, 27]: (a) target group, (b) type of data, (c) data set size and (c) type of use case. Table 2 lists these aspects along with their categories.

---

[5] Note that there is at least one famous class of "behind the scenes" data annotation scenarios, where users are motivated merely by their will to successfully interact with the annotation tool in order to pass a specific test: ReCaptcha requires web users to "voluntarily" perform (partly difficult) annotation tasks of (sections of) scans or photos from extensive image collections in order to authenticate themselves as humans [34].

[6] It is precisely those "on stage" settings, where the paradigm shift, that is referred to in the invitation to this panel, can be expected to be successfully implemented.

Table 2. A lightweight typology of ML-based systems based on aspects discussed in [25] and [27]. Categories that apply to our case are highlighted in bold.

Aspect	Categories
Target group	**Consumers**, businesses, educational institutions, public administration, etc
Type of data	**Unstructured data**, structured data
Size of data set	**Small data set**, large data set
Type of use case	Quality assurance in production; chatbots; error reduction, route optimization; process automation; predictive maintenance; **automated transaction processing** (damage notification or similar); **customer self-service;** supply chain optimization; intelligent/smart product development

4 Case Study and Method

We use a case study to investigate our research goals. Specifically, we open the discussion on how to "put *users* in the loop" by integrating them in the development process of consumer-oriented ML-based self-service systems. Second, we try to overcome the data sourcing dilemma in the case of an ML-based consumer-oriented self-service application by leveraging the data from user interactions to iteratively retrain and incrementally optimize the ML model.

In the following, we first describe the Smart_HEC application and its technical underpinnings. Subsequently, we report on our user research and how we monitor user success and ML performance over time.

4.1 The "Smart_HEC" Web App for Analyzing Heating Bills[7]

Our case study builds on a newly developed web application that allows consumers to analyze their heating bills for potential energy and cost savings. Users can upload scans or photos of their heating bills to the so-called "Smart_HEC" application. Then, specific data values ("target values") are extracted from these user-supplied document images by a highly customized open-source machine learning component for visual document analysis. Based on the extracted values, an assessment of potential savings is derived and reported back to the user.

Applying the typology for ML use cases presented in Sect. 3.3 above, we can position our case as follows: We present a consumer-oriented use case at the intersection of (document-based) process automation and customer self-service. The system is operating on unstructured data and the data set is of small size, cf. Table 2.

---

[7] The technical description of the Smart_HEC web app and its ML component is adopted from the corresponding project's final report [31].

We use the publicly-funded open-source framework OCR-D [9, 24] for layout analysis, text recognition, and data extraction. OCR-D follows a modular approach, i.e., it provides interfaces for existing tools or develops its own. Modules, called processors, are executed sequentially in a workflow pipeline. Each processing step can make use of the results of the previous one. The processing pipeline in our web app backend uses existing processors for binarization, noise removal, deskewing, cropping, segmentation, and OCR. The latter uses the open-source optical character recognition engine Tesseract [32]. Finally, the extracted target values are automatically post-corrected by passing Tesseract's OCR hypotheses through a regular-expression-based decoder[8].

In order to cater for the highly heterogenous layouts of heating bills, custom extensions were integrated that use a variant of Mask R-CNN [1, 12] as the core ML component in our processing pipeline. Mask R-CNN is a particular implementation of a region-based convolutional neural network for object recognition on image data. In our case, it aims to detect the regions of up to 34 relevant domain-specific characteristic (target) values for each heating bill. It does so by following a "visual lookup approach" over document page images: The target values' positioning on the document pages is unknown in advance and only indicated by corresponding context terms. These context terms serve as cues in the lookup, as they appear in horizontal or vertical proximity to the target values, but in an overall free-floating tabular-like layout without strict tabular relations[9].

For training, i.e., fine-tuning and evaluating the Mask R-CNN in the development stage, a data basis, the so-called ground truth, was created by manually annotating context regions and target regions for up to 34 characteristic values on a total of 495 heating bills using the LAREX annotation tool [28]. Annotators and ML engineers can inspect the training results of the neural network using the COCO Explorer [19]. All required tools and the AI module are provided as Docker containers and are available as open-source software for further use and development. Comprehensive documentation for training and evaluating the applied neural networks are publicly available.

4.2 Applying User Research to Guide the ML Development Process

Given the assumption that the acceptance of the Smart_HEC application does not depend on the performance and accuracy of the underlying ML component alone, a second stream of research was integrated into the development process. Specifically, user experience and user acceptance studies were amalgamated with the technical development of the Smart_HEC application and findings of one domain were integrated into further developing the other. As such, the two pillars of research were refined interdependently with the mutual goal to create a service that was (1) technically powerful and (2) accepted by its users.

---

[8] Note that we do not perform any fine-tuning of language models for OCR. We use Tesseract's pre-trained models for contemporary German as provided. Once the correct ROIs for the target values are identified by the Mask R-CNN, our lever for improving the OCR results lies mainly with ranking and filtering Tesseract's hypotheses through pattern matching in the post-decoder.

[9] This highly dynamic layout with unknown positionings of the target values does not allow for classical form data extraction or otherwise useful table detection heuristics, cf. a similar discussion in [5]. Hence, our ML-based approach attempts to mimic a human visual lookup strategy for finding the required target values on the document page images.

Based on the evolving performance level of the ML component and the respective research questions, different forms of qualitative and quantitative user research were applied [3, 8, 16, 22]. The overarching goal was to create a service that meets user expectations regarding user friendliness and navigation, comprehensibility, and data protection standards. The user research process can be divided into three stages that served different research goals and, hence, were tackled with different research methods:

Preparatory Stage: Understanding User Expectations and Needs. The preparatory stage kicked off with an internal *User Story Mapping Workshop*. Its goal was to depict exemplary user groups by means of personas and to outline their individual needs, expectations, and possible challenges [26]. These personas were meant to give an orientation when developing the ML-based service and its interface.

Based on the personas, first mock-ups of the Smart_HEC application were developed. Subsequently, these mock-ups were tested and discussed in two *explorative (online) focus groups* with nine participants each. The focus groups aimed at understanding motivational levers and expectations. Also, they were meant to shed light on necessary prerequisites for consumers to use a smart heating check, their attitudes and concerns about AI and the preferred interaction style (i.e., chatbot versus smart questions). Some of the attained qualitative results were then quantitatively confirmed by an online survey with 267 participants. Also, another *large-scale quantitative online survey* with 217 participants was conducted to understand user expectations and concerns regarding data protection standards. Specifically, with the help of mock-ups, this research tried to carve out how to win consumers' trust in an application and its processing of personal data.

All attained results of the preparatory stage fed back into the further technical development process of the ML-based heating bill check.

Stage 1: Optimization of Initial Implementations Based on User Interaction.
User research stage 1 already relied on a first prototype of the Smart_HEC application. Hence, it was possible to test user interaction more realistically and directly derive avenues for optimizing the service, its functionality, and its interface.

At first, five *UX tests* applying the *Thinking Aloud Approach* [18] were carried out: Test persons were asked to freely articulate their thoughts, associations and points of criticism while navigating through the prototype application. The goal of the UX tests was to gain specific insights on users' understanding of the different page elements and their evaluation of the application's user guidance, navigation, and functionality. Also, behavioral barriers, misconceptions as well as deficiencies within the navigation were expected to show during the tests.

Next, four more *online focus groups* (with four participants each) were carried out. These focus groups aimed at understanding if users see an added value in the Smart_HEC service, its results, and the results' graphical representation. Again, this perspective is crucial since an ML-based service that does not meet user needs and expectations can be assumed to fail in the market despite a possibly perfectly functional ML component.

Stage 2: Analysis of User Acceptance and Conversion. The applied user tests in stage 2 could already resort to a live beta-version of the Smart_HEC application and, hence, observe users live interaction with the service. Against this background, seven *UX tests* were performed using the *Thinking Aloud Method*. The specific goal of these tests was to monitor if users could pass through the entire service and detect critical points with a high likelihood of abandonment. Digital natives were tested against non-natives to carve out possible differences due to different experience levels in using and navigating web apps.

4.3 Measuring User Success and ML Performance

Our user research made us aware that we would need a sophisticated interaction design to overcome our data sourcing dilemma. In our case, it guided us, first, to offer users to choose between a (possibly immature) ML-assisted path and a path of manual data entry. Secondly, as the automatic data extraction is still volatile, we present the extracted data for review and correction by the user. This approach allows us to shift increasingly larger proportions of the workflow from the user to the ML component when the ML results become more and more dependable with each new model increment.

To measure the success of our approach, we used several KPIs from the live setting to approximate user success and ML performance. All KPIs were determined per user session. Each such session is characterized either by uploading one or more document page images of a single heating bill for ML-assisted processing, or by manually filling out a comprehensive web form that collects all the necessary data values from that singular heating bill.

We consider a user session successful if the user duly performs every necessary step until the result page has been reached and shown to the user. Similar to measuring success in online sales, we denote a successful user session as *conversion*. The *conversion rate*, i.e., the ratio of conversions over all user sessions, is our central key performance indicator for approximating user success.

We measured the performance of the ML component in two ways whenever users choose the ML-assisted path over manual form filling. First, we counted the number of target regions, or regions of interest (ROIs), that the ML module identifies. This indicator is, however, potentially misleading, as one cannot tell whether the identified ROIs are, in fact, correct without labelling each novel data item, which was not feasible. It is clear, however, that identifying a certain number of ROIs is a prerequisite for extracting the target values from these regions, and as such, for delivering the data required for analyzing the heating bill. Hence, this indicator can be seen as an upper limit to estimate the performance of the underlying ML model and the overall data extraction.

Secondly, even in the ML-enabled mode, the user was presented with a submission form containing fields for all target values required to analyze the heating bill. However, all form fields were pre-filled with the values that the integrated OCR engine extracted from the identified ROIs. The users were asked to review and correct the data if necessary. We then compared the OCR results from the identified ROIs with the submitted data from the corresponding form fields. This allowed for calculating the number of correctly automatically extracted target values per submitted heating bill. This number serves as the prime indicator of ML performance and the end-to-end evaluation of the live system in the final prototype stage.

In order to investigate the performance development of our ML-based service over time, we grouped the total amount of user sessions in two ways. Firstly, we consider two consecutive stages of development: Stage 1, also denoted "beta stage", comprises all user interactions during a 17-week time span. A first stable and productive version of the ML component was in use during that period. Stage 2 comprises all user sessions from nine subsequent weeks after a significantly improved version of the ML component had been deployed[10]. That second stage is denoted "final prototype stage".

The second distinction with respect to the conversion rate across user sessions concerns the interaction scenario chosen by the user: It is either the *ML-supported path* of uploading document images or the *manual path*, where users themselves look up and type in the required target values from their heating bills. We compare conversion rates between these groupings.

5   Empirical Results

5.1   Integration of User Research

Accompanying the technical development of the Smart_HEC application with different forms of quantitative and qualitative user research led to an agile process in which the respective empirical results at each stage directly guided the following iterations. Apart from smaller adjustments, there were three major findings that put the whole application development under scrutiny, and which would not have been detected without sound user research.

Specifically, the first UX tests revealed that users ran into several problems of understanding and struggled with uploading or inserting data. As this, however, is crucial for the ML-based system to operate and learn, the interface and user navigation and the data uploading process were revised from scratch.

Moreover, the focus groups showed that test persons did not fully understand the results of the heating check, quickly lost interest in the result representation, and could not be motivated to further engage with the results. These findings were taken as a reason to entirely overhaul the result section to create a service that is relevant for its users.

The UX tests of the prototype showed that digital natives place high demands both on the AI and its effectiveness as well as the general user interface. Whenever one of these two aspects did not perform as expected, digital natives were likely to leave the service. On the other hand, the digital non-natives were confused and insecure when either the AI was slow or only recognized a few values or when they did not understand what to do next. This group also showed a high likelihood to quit at these critical points. Despite the different underlying reasons, it became evident that for consumer-oriented services, AI-effectiveness and good user interface design are no independent variables and, thus, need to be intertwined when developing a successful service for consumers.

---

[10] Improvements between the two stages were mainly achieved by re-annotating large numbers of ROIs in the ground truth and re-training the Mask R-CNN, after systematic problems with the previous annotations had been discovered.

5.2 User Success and Incremental ML Improvement

As explained above, we collected data for estimating user success and ML performance by tracking user sessions and their results for two interaction modes and across two time periods. Stage 1 ("beta stage") yielded 101 ML-enabled user sessions and 116 manual data extraction sessions for this first period. The consecutive 2nd stage ("final prototype stage") produced 109 ML-supported sessions and 252 sessions with manual data extraction. The descriptive statistics for these groups are summarized in Table 3.

Regarding user success, the calculated conversion rate for the ML-enabled path remained constant at 0.48 across both periods, while the conversion rate without ML support decreased from 0.47 in stage one to 0.23 in stage two. Although the conversion rates seem comparable, we discuss pitfalls in their interpretation in the next section. At least, we can say that choosing the ML-enabled path did not seem to have a negative impact on conversions, i.e., on user success, even though the ML component performed poorly, especially in the early stages of development.

The number of regions of interest identified by the ML component increased significantly from an average of 7.4 in stage 1 to 14.0 in stage 2. However, the performance of the ML-component is apparently degraded by the following OCR-driven data extraction step, which only correctly extracts an average of 2.96 and 4.68 target values, respectively[11]. Nevertheless, by comparing the boxplots of the two periods in Fig. 1, we see an increase of the statistical location parameters, like median, quantiles and even the average, between the two stages for the ML performance indicators. Thus, we were able to increase ML performance while keeping the user success at a constant level, despite the limitations of the overall performance of our ML-based system prototype.

Table 3. Descriptive statistics for our KPIs to estimate user success and ML capabilities

Variable	Group	Group size	Minimum	1st Quantile	Median	Mean	3rd Quantile	Maximum
1. Identified regions per heating bill	Stage 1	101	1	4	8	7.4	11	17
	Stage 2	109	1	9	15	14.0	18	28
2. Correctly extracted values per heating bill	Stage 1	101	0	0	2	2.96	5.0	11
	Stage 2	109	0	0	4	4.68	8	20
3. Conversion rate with ML support	Stage 1	101	–	–	–	0.48	–	–
	Stage 2	109	–	–	–	0.48	–	–
4. Conversion rate without ML support	Stage 1	116	–	–	–	0.47	–	–
	Stage 2	252	–	–	–	0.23	–	–
	Overall	368	–	–	–	0.30	–	–

---

[11] These results could also indicate problems with the exact locations of the identified ROIs in the production environment. Such problems were, however, not observed in the lab setting.

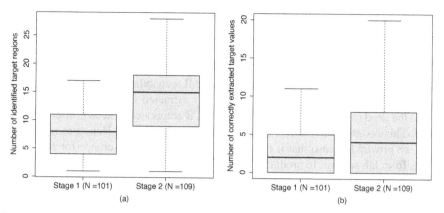

Fig. 1. Boxplots comparing two stages of ML model development on novel data with no available ground truth: (a) Number of identified target regions (Mask R-CNN) as an upper limit to the number of *correctly* identified target regions, (b) Number of correctly extracted values end-to-end (Mask-R CNN + OCR), i.e., the number of extracted values that were not altered by the users in the post-correction review form

5.3   Discussion and Limitations

As depicted above, the case study generated some fruitful insights on how to put users in the loop of development processes of ML-based consumer services. Specifically, our results challenge the general scientific practice to merely consider the technical power of an ML-based system when assessing its quality. On the contrary, we were able to show that for the case of consumer-oriented ML-based applications, AI efficiency and adequate user interface design are no independent variables. In fact, the most powerful ML component is useless whenever the respective application does not meet its users' demands in other aspects. Likewise, optimized interface design cannot make up for a malfunctioning AI. Consequently, both aspects must be integrated in order to create a successful consumer service. Our results support the hypotheses that users need to be taken into the loop of AI development.

However, there are limitations to the interpretability of our results. First, our study had to rely on a relatively small sample of interactions due to the ongoing development process of the application. Second, test persons within the user research were incentivized, so that their behavior might be biased and, hence, differ from users in later stages of the product life cycle. In principle, the users' post-correction of target values cannot be trusted when offering users incentives to participate in the evaluation of the system. While it increases the number of attendees, some users rush through the correction process and submit wrong data corrections. Therefore, a second plausibility check needs to be implemented and reviewed before integrating the collected data into the training data for the next model increment.

6   Conclusion and Outlook

Our study showed that user research can substantially aid in developing ML-based services and that the evaluation of ML-based systems must take place in live settings. In our case, user research led us to an interaction design that allows us to track user success and ML performance over time and adjust our focus accordingly. Especially during stage 1 of our study, a primary effort was to create and integrate more high-quality training data in order to improve the results of the "visual lookup approach" and its detection of ROIs on the document page images. Only by tracking ML capabilities in the live setting "on stage", i.e., by calculating the number of correctly extracted values per heating bill, we realized the need to shift our focus towards the OCR component and its post-corrections instead. This insight would not have been gained in a lab setting. Hence, as mentioned above, we proved the case that it is essential to shift quality assurance for ML-based systems from lab settings to production environments [2, 4].

In our case study, users were both in the loop of improving the ML component as well as in the loop for improving the overall interaction design. This involvement, arguably, showed the users our appreciation for their engagement and kept them engaged, enabling us to overcome the data sourcing dilemma for consumer-oriented ML-based services that require frequent (and successful) user interaction to collect data items for the training of the ML component.

Although in our prototype, the model does not learn directly from user interactions, the evaluation of the users' corrections guided our focus for technical improvements as well as the preparation of further training data. For this purpose, in cases where the data extraction fails due to missing or incorrect ROIs, the affected documents can be used for training the Mask RCNN after annotating the correct ROIs. Without the users' corrections, we would not be able to extend the training data in such a targeted way. As such, our prototype comprises elements "of both machine-learning-assisted humans and human-assisted machine learning" [21] and allows for iteratively redefining the role of the human "in our loop" as ML performance improves.

From our perspective, the paradigm shift from "humans in the loop" towards "AI in the loop" depends on the individual maturation of any ML-based system. We believe that it does not occur as a singularity. Rather, by implementing a suitable interaction design, this shift can be managed gradually, and its potential can be harnessed at earlier stages of development than previously expected[12]. Hence, future incarnations of our self-service web app may not only allow us to balance the workload between AI and users, but to automatically adjust that balance according to AI capabilities in real-time and at each user interaction. This progress might lead to ML components that are self-aware of their capabilities (or lack thereof) and can adjust their interactions accordingly.

Our findings may contribute to the methodology of engineering ML-based systems, which is only just being established [13]. A typology of ML-based systems, possibly similar to our lightweight approach, may help assess the generalizability of our findings and the related methodological considerations.

Future interaction designs, leveraging more efficient ML components, may entirely shift the analysis of user-provided documents to the consumers' (mobile) devices, even for such highly domain-specific use cases as ours. In that case, by default, no further

---

[12] For instance, in our case, it might be possible to reduce the human annotation workload through automatically pre-labelling potential ROIs by locating the users' corrected target values on the corresponding document images.

training data will be collected during the operation of the ML-based system. To incrementally improve such services, different interaction designs will be required once again, such as asking the users to upload their document images if the automatic data extraction performed poorly on the user's device, hence, explicitly asking the users to help collect challenging data for developing the next generation of machine learning models.

Acknowledgments. This research was supported by the German Federal Ministry of Justice and Consumer Protection (BMJV) under grants no. 28V2304A19, 28V2304B19, 28V2304C19, 28V2304D19. Partial contributions were funded by the German Federal Ministry of Education and Research (BMBF) under grant no. 01IS20091B, and by the Development Bank of Saxony (SAB) under project number 100335729.

References

1. Abdulla, W.: Mask R-CNN for object detection and instance segmentation on Keras and TensorFlow. https://github.com/matterport/Mask_RCNN. Accessed 11 Feb 2022
2. Auer, F., Felderer, M.: Shifting quality assurance of machine learning algorithms to live systems. In: Tichy, M., Bodden, E., Kuhrmann, M., Wagner, S., Steghöfer, J.-P. (eds.) Software Engineering und Software Management 2018, pp. 211–212. Gesellschaft für Informatik, Bonn (2018)
3. Baur, N., Blasius, J. (eds.): Handbuch Methoden der empirischen Sozialforschung. Springer, Wiesbaden (2014). https://doi.org/10.1007/978-3-531-18939-0
4. Beede, E., et al.: A human-centered evaluation of a deep learning system deployed in clinics for the detection of diabetic retinopathy. In: Proceedings of the 2020 CHI Conference on Human Factors in Computing Systems, Honolulu, HI, USA, pp. 1–12. ACM (2020). https://doi.org/10.1145/3313831.3376718
5. Bürgl, K., Reinhardt, L., Binder, F., Müller, L., Niekler, A.: Digitizing Drilling Logs - Challenges of typewritten forms. In: Gesellschaft für Informatik (ed.) 51. Jahrestagung der Gesellschaft für Informatik, INFORMATIK 2021 - Computer Science & Sustainability, Berlin, pp. 709–718. Gesellschaft für Informatik, Bonn (2021). https://doi.org/10.18420/informatik2021-059
6. Chegini, M., et al.: Interactive visual labelling versus active learning: an experimental comparison. Front. Inf. Technol. Electron. Eng. **21**, 524–535 (2020). https://doi.org/10.1631/FITEE.1900549
7. Davis, F.D.: Perceived usefulness, perceived ease of use, and user acceptance of information technology. MIS Q. 319–340 (1989)
8. Dietrich, T., Trischler, J., Schuster, L., Rundle-Thiele, S.: Co-designing services with vulnerable consumers. J. Serv. Theory Pract. **27**, 663–688 (2017). https://doi.org/10.1108/jstp-02-2016-0036
9. Engl, E.: OCR-D kompakt: Ergebnisse und Stand der Forschung in der Förderinitiative. Bibliothek Forschung und Praxis (44), 218–230 (2020). https://doi.org/10.1515/bfp-2020-0024
10. Gao, L., et al.: ICDAR 2019 competition on table detection and recognition (cTDaR). In: 2019 International Conference on Document Analysis and Recognition (ICDAR), pp. 1510–1515 (2019). https://doi.org/10.1109/ICDAR.2019.00243
11. Göbel, M., Hassan, T., Oro, E., Orsi, G.: ICDAR 2013 table competition. In: 12th International Conference on Document Analysis and Recognition, pp. 1449–1453 (2013). https://doi.org/10.1109/ICDAR.2013.292

12. He, K., Gkioxari, G., Dollár, P., Girshick, R.B.: Mask R-CNN. In: 2017 IEEE International Conference on Computer Vision (ICCV), pp. 2980–2988 (2017). https://doi.org/10.1109/ICCV.2017.322
13. Hesenius, M., Schwenzfeier, N., Meyer, O., Koop, W., Gruhn, V.: Towards a software engineering process for developing data-driven applications. In: 2019 IEEE/ACM 7th International Workshop on Realizing Artificial Intelligence Synergies in Software Engineering (RAISE), pp. 35–41. IEEE (2019). https://doi.org/10.1109/raise.2019.00014
14. Holzinger, A.: Interactive machine learning for health informatics: when do we need the human-in-the-loop? Brain Inform. **3**(2), 119–131 (2016). https://doi.org/10.1007/s40708-016-0042-6
15. Holzinger, A., Valdez, A.C., Ziefle, M.: Towards interactive recommender systems with the doctor-in-the-loop. In: Weyers, B., Dittmar, A. (eds.) Mensch und Computer 2016 - Workshopband. Gesellschaft für Informatik e.V., Aachen (2016). https://doi.org/10.18420/MUC2016-WS11-0001
16. Kettner, S.E., Thorun, C.: Verbraucherstudie 2019: Wie erreicht man Verbraucherin- nen und Verbraucher im Zeitalter digitaler Informationsangebote. Final report. ConPolicy GmbH, Berlin (2019)
17. Lell, O., Kettner, S.E., Thorun, C., Bendig, T.: Verbraucherschutz digital neu denken: Consumer Protection Technologies - Politische Relevanz, Potential und Handlungsbedarf. ConPolicy GmbH, Berlin (2021)
18. Lewis, C.: Using the "thinking-aloud" method in cognitive interface design. IBM TJ Watson Research Center, Yorktown Heights (1982)
19. Lin, T.-Y., et al.: Microsoft COCO: common objects in context. In: Fleet, D., Pajdla, T., Schiele, B., Tuytelaars, T. (eds.) ECCV 2014. LNCS, vol. 8693, pp. 740–755. Springer, Cham (2014). https://doi.org/10.1007/978-3-319-10602-1_48
20. Mahlke, S.: Factors influencing the experience of website usage. In: Extended Abstracts on Human Factors in Computing Systems, CHI 2002, pp. 846–847 (2002)
21. Monarch, R.: Human-in-the-Loop Machine Learning. Manning Publications, New York (2021)
22. Morville, P.: User experience design. https://semanticstudios.com/user_experience_design/. Accessed 11 Feb 2022
23. Moser, C.: User Experience Design. Springer, Heidelberg (2012). https://doi.org/10.1007/978-3-642-13363-3
24. Neudecker, C., et al.: OCR-D: an end-to-end open source OCR framework for historical printed documents. In: Proceedings of the 3rd International Conference on Digital Access to Textual Cultural Heritage, Brussels, pp. 53–58. ACM (2019). https://doi.org/10.1145/3322905.3322917
25. Ng, A.: Structured and Unstructured Data: Implications for AI Development. The Batch. https://read.deeplearning.ai/the-batch/structured-and-unstructured-data-implications-for-ai-development/. Accessed 05 Nov 2021
26. Patton, J., Economy, P.: User Story Mapping: Discover the Whole Story, Build the Right Product. 1st edn. O'Reilly Media Inc. (2014)
27. Reder, B.: Machine Learning 2021. IDG Business Media GmbH, München (2021)
28. Reul, C., Springmann, U., Puppe, F.: LAREX: a semi-automatic open-source tool for layout analysis and region extraction on early printed books. In: Proceedings of the 2nd International Conference on Digital Access to Textual Cultural Heritage, Göttingen, pp. 137–142. Association for Computing Machinery (2017). https://doi.org/10.1145/3078081.3078097
29. Riccio, V., Jahangirova, G., Stocco, A., Humbatova, N., Weiss, M., Tonella, P.: Testing machine learning based systems: a systematic mapping. Empir. Softw. Eng. **25**(6), 5193–5254 (2020). https://doi.org/10.1007/s10664-020-09881-0

30. Roberts, L.: The value of AI: now and the future (PART 2) AI Failures, Pitfalls, Key Learnings and Success. https://www.linkedin.com/pulse/value-ai-now-future-part-2-failures-pitfalls-key-success-roberts/. Accessed 05 Nov 2021

31. Scheurer, Y., et al.: Abschlussbericht Smart_HEC (Kurzfassung). co2online gGmbH, Berlin (2021)

32. Smith, R.: An overview of the tesseract OCR engine. In: Ninth International Conference on Document Analysis and Recognition (ICDAR 2007), pp. 629–633 (2007). https://doi.org/10.1109/ICDAR.2007.4376991

33. Thielsch, M.T., Blotenberg, I., Jaron, R.: User evaluation of websites: from first impression to recommendation. Interact. Comput. **26**(1), 89–102 (2014)

34. von Ahn, L., Maurer, B., McMillen, C., Abraham, D., Blum, M.: reCAPTCHA: human-based character recognition via web security measures. Science **321**, 1465–1468 (2008). https://doi.org/10.1126/science.1160379

35. Yimam, S.M., Biemann, C., Majnaric, L., Šabanović, Š, Holzinger, A.: An adaptive annotation approach for biomedical entity and relation recognition. Brain Inform. **3**(3), 157–168 (2016). https://doi.org/10.1007/s40708-016-0036-4

The "Onion Model of Human Factors": A Theoretical Framework for Cross-Cultural Design

Zhi Guo[1,2], Pei-Luen Patrick Rau[1(✉)], and Rüdiger Heimgärtner[3]

[1] Tsinghua University, Beijing, Republic of China
rpl@mail.tsinghua.edu.cn
[2] State University of New York at Buffalo, Buffalo, NY, USA
zhiguo@buffalo.edu
[3] Intercultural User Interface Consulting (IUIC), Lehderstraße 71, 13086 Berlin, Germany
ruediger.heimgaertner@iuic.de

Abstract. Needs and preferences are two critical elements for starting a user-centered design. Nevertheless, there is a gap between the link of needs and preferences of user interface/experience. It is very difficult to find out why such a need could be transferred into a design preference. The exploration of dimensions in human factors could provide a theoretical foundation for the gap. Based on cultural "onion and iceberg" models and the dimensions of human factors, the present paper proposed the "onion model" of human factors as a framework to guide related activities of cross-cultural design. The dimensions from the core layer to the surface layer include motivation and preference, needs, values/beliefs/attitudes, identity (social role and self-image), cognition (from sensation to action selection), language, and behavior patterns. Besides the mentioned dimensions, emotion has an interaction across the layers. The distance between the center of a circle and the origin point of the "hidden" word shows the degree of the core. The core layers directly influence the nearest surface layer and indirectly influence the other surface layers. The onion model of human factors provides a theoretical framework for design-related activities, like evaluating existing interfaces in different cultures. The paper takes the differences of mobile apps in the U.S. and China as examples to illustrate that the onion model of human factors could provide the potential reasonable link between these differences and their possible explanations in a holistic perspective.

Keywords: Human factors · Onion model · Cross-cultural design · Mobile app

1 Introduction

Personas are important at the early stage of design and typically used to describe the user on a personal level, with their needs, preferences and habits [1]. They are also helpful to conduct user testing, evaluate new features, align with business strategy, facilitate analysis, and allow the product group to work at the same page [1, 2].

© The Author(s), under exclusive license to Springer Nature Switzerland AG 2022
M. Rauterberg (Ed.): HCII 2022, LNCS 13324, pp. 20–33, 2022.
https://doi.org/10.1007/978-3-031-05434-1_2

But the method of personas has its limitations. The designers must commit themselves to the personas and trust in them to take fully advantage of them during the design process as there is a gap between the needs and the preference in design elements. For example, the methods to create a persona, such as interview or survey, are subjective and needs more expertise to support [3, 4]. Even the designers with rich experience think personas do not include enough information, and consequently would not be helpful in the design process [5]. Hence, it is necessary to propose an overall framework of human factors to guide the user-centered design process.

Moreover, personas are not suitable to be used in cross-cultural design. As we know, personas are created based on specific target group or small population levels [2, 4, 5]. But cross-cultural design generally would involve a large-scale population or group of persons, like different nations. So, a persona provides less information in cross-cultural design than in the situation personas were used in a traditional way. Some researchers have tried to use cultural models to get a link between cultural dimensions and interface differences among nations. For example, Singh and Matsuo [6] conducted a content analytic study of U.S. and Japanese web sites using the dimensions of Hofstede's cultural values to propose a framework as a guide for developing cultural congruent websites. Callahan [7] also analyzed the cultural differences and similarities in design of university websites from Malaysia, Austria, the United States, Ecuador, Japan, Sweden, Greece and Denmark based on Hofstede's model of cultural dimensions. But there's still a gap between the values of humans and using graphical elements.

Therefore, the present study aims to develop a holistic framework of human factors with multiple dimensions for cross-cultural design.

2 Human Factors in Culture

In terms of intercultural user interface design (IUID), Heimgärtner [8] proposed a toolbox for IUID consisting of the IUID method-mix, which provides a methodology to create the link between cultural dimensions and HCI dimensions as well as user interface characteristics. The IUID toolbox uses a hybrid approach integrating a combined use of the following concepts ("IUID Method-Mix" for short) to derive cultural HCI indicators relevant for the derivation of recommendations for IUID: HCI dimensions, cultural dimensions, intercultural variables, user interface characteristics, the culture dependent HCI model and finally the method of culture-oriented design. In the toolbox, Heimgärtner proposed the relationship between cultural dimensions (i.e. Hofstede's model of cultural dimensions: individualism vs. collectivism, uncertainty avoidance, long term orientation and masculinity vs. femininity [9]) and HCI dimensions (i.e. information density, information frequency, interaction speed and frequency [10]). Heimgärtner stated the cultural dimensions alone are too rough for intercultural user interface design and additional cultural variables are necessary to be included in a theoretical framework for IUID.

2.1 Models of Cultural Dimensions

In the past many different studies are conducted to show how national culture influences information systems [11]. The different cultural models are clustered into three types based on the amount of cultural dimensions taken into account: historical-social models, single, and multiple dimension models are used in the literature [12]. Historical-social models evaluate cultures based on historical evolution and social heritage at a regional level. Single dimension models categorize cultures into one dimension with two contradicting values. For example, these values can be low and high context [13, 14], or polymorphic and monochromic [15]. In contrast to single dimension models, the multiply dimensions' models consider more than one facet of a culture, as for instance the six-dimensions' model of Hofstede.

Hofstede's Six-Dimension Model. In terms of values and attitudes, Hofstede's cultural model has been widely accepted by researchers and practitioners [16–18]. The model consists of the following six cultural dimensions: power distance, individualism, masculinity, uncertainty avoidance, long-term orientation and indulgence [9, 19, 20]. Each country is graded within these six dimensions with values ranging from 0 to 100. The higher the number, the more the characteristics described by the dimension is true for a culture.

Power Distance (PD): acceptance of class differences in a particular culture.

Individualism (vs. collectivism): the degree to which individuals feel they are "on their own" rather than part of a larger group identity.

Masculinity (vs. Feminist): the degree to which a culture emphasizes competition, achievement, and "getting ahead".

Uncertainty avoidance (UA): intolerance for ambiguity and risk.

Long term orientation (vs. short term orientation): the degree to which a culture focuses on the future.

Hofstede [19] and Cyr [21] both found Chinese and German had significant scores on power distance, individualism, and has a slight difference on indulgence. Uncertainty avoidance, long-term orientation and indulgence are just significant in one of the two studies.

Hall's Single Dimension Model. Hall [13, 14] defines culture as the way of life of a people: the sum of their learned behavior patterns, attitudes and material things. Hall stated the categorization of culture into high context versus low context cultures to understand their basic differences in communication style in different cultures. Researcher stated that individualism-collectivism has a direct effect and an indirect effect via self-construal on communication style - especially self-construal predicts the communication style better [22]. A person with independent self in an individualistic culture uses low-context communication, focusing more on self or topic itself, whereas a person with interdependent self-construal in a collectivistic culture applies high-context communication.

High context communication is implicit, indirect, ambiguous, harmonious, reserved and understated, which involves more of the information in the physical context or internalized in the person, which provides greater confidence in nonverbal clues of communication than the verbal aspects [13, 14, 22]. This is typical in Asian countries and reactive cultures.

Low context communication is explicitly stated through direct and precise language based on true intentions [13, 14, 22], which is typical in German-speaking countries and linear-active cultures [23]. Moreover, members from linear-active cultures are factual and decisive planners who are task-oriented, highly organized and prefer doing one thing at a time, termed monochronic [24]. In monochronic cultures, people take time commitments (deadlines, schedules) seriously, and they adhere strictly to plans [25].

In contrast, members of reactive cultures would like to be courteous, outwardly amiable, are accommodating and compromising, use silence and thinking in silence and are good listeners who combine their own and other's opinions. People from reactive cultures rather like to do multiple tasks at a time, termed polychronic [24]. People from polychronic cultures rank personal involvement and completion of tasks above the demands of the pre-set schedules, and they change plans often and easily, and have a more relaxed approach to punctuality [25].

2.2 Iceberg Model of Human Competence

Two prominent ways to illustrate the concept of culture are the onion model (see Fig. 1a) and the iceberg model (see Fig. 1b) [26–29]. The onion model is used to show the depth of different ways to embody culture. The inner layer is more invisible than the outer layers.

As to the iceberg model, the competence model from individual perspective could provide a detailed description about the stratified representation of culture-related dimensions in human factors. Human factors design is understanding human capabilities or limitations and applying this knowledge to system or interface design. Therefore, it is necessary to learn about the human competence model to get insights into the framework of human capabilities.

McClelland, the father of the competency movement, introduced the competency approach to describe the characteristics underlying superior performance [27, 28]. He compared competencies to an iceberg with motives, traits, self-image, values, attitudes and social role, knowledge, and behavior (see Fig. 1b). Behavior, knowledge and skills are at the tip of iceberg, which are more observable. Values, attitudes, social roles, self-image, traits, and motives are the underlying elements, which are not easy to identify. Hence, the iceberg model of human competence overlaps with the onion model of culture, see Fig. 1a [19, 26, 29].

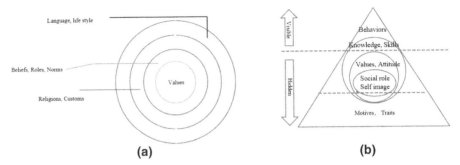

Fig. 1. The onion model of culture (a, left) and the iceberg model of human competence (b, right)

3   The Onion Model of Human Factors in Culture

Human factors are the applications of psychological and physiological principles to the engineering and design of products, processes, and systems [30] to make people use system or machine efficiently, safely, and comfortably. Human factors involve human cognition, emotion, and behavior patterns [31] as well as physiological and biomechanical characteristics related to physical activity [32]. Cognition includes consciousness, imagination, perception, thinking, judgement, language, and memory. Combined with the onion model and iceberg model of culture, the "onion model of human factors" was developed in the present study, see Fig. 2. The concepts in the onion model of human factors and their relationships are described in this paper based on the literature review.

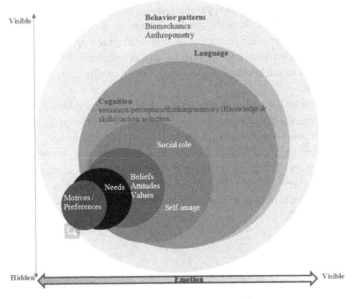

Fig. 2. The onion model of human factors

The dimensions from the core layer to the surface layer include motivation and preference, needs, values/beliefs/attitudes, identity (social role and self-image), cognition (from sensation to action selection), language, and behavior patterns. Besides the mentioned dimensions, emotion has an interaction across all layers (see the Fig. 2). The distance between the center of a circle and the origin point of the "hidden" word shows the degree of core: the closer the distance of a layer away from the origin point labeled hidden is, the more core and important the concept of layer is. The more core layers have a direct effect on the layer closest to it and indirect effects on the remaining outer layers.

3.1 Motivation/Preferences and Needs

Motivation and preferences are at the same level, the most core level. Motivation is willingness of action or behavior, including need-based motivation [33, 34] and reward-based motivation that is related to emotion [35]. Preference is the selection of one thing or person over others. It is akin to the notion of want. The thing or object a human prefer is something that he/she desires to have, whether he/she needs it. Some preferences are related to goals or intentions, which are conscious. But some are unconscious human experiences, which are influenced by culture.

The next layer is needs as motivation includes a need-based motivation, and some preferences are related to goals or intentions. Needs are related to how live a recognizably human life. The thing or object of a human need is something, which he/she must have in their life, involving basic needs and psychological needs. Needs are influenced by culture and responsible for most of the behavior.

The relationship between motives/preferences and needs is shown in Fig. 3. Psychological needs and some unconscious human preferences related to reward-based or emotion-based motivation are influenced by culture. For example, culture shapes people's preferences for approach versus avoidance motivation. Approach motivation is that the energization or the direction of behavior was motived by positive stimuli (i.e. gain); whereas avoidance motivation is that the energization or direction of behavior was triggered by negative stimuli (i.e. loss). Chinese or Japanese prefer avoidance goals while people in German or US prefer approach goals [36, 37]. Americans were better at recalling positive events that either had or had not been happened (e.g., I found a 20-dollar bill? Or the movie I wanted to watch was not playing anymore?), whereas Japanese were better at recalling negative events that had or had not been happened (e.g., I found a zit on my nose? Or my least favorite class got cancelled).

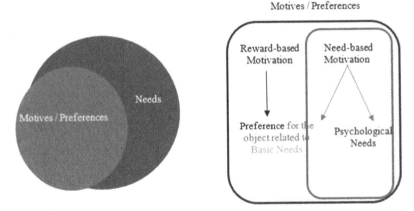

Fig. 3. The onion part (left) and the scale part (right) of motivation and needs

3.2 Values and Identity

Values are enduring beliefs that a specific mode of conduct/behavior is personally or socially preferable to an opposite mode of conduct/behavior, i.e., family, successful career, money, power, wisdom, love, skill, morality, and pleasure, which are influenced by culture.

Meaning in life or purpose is related to values and motivations [38]. Sometimes an individual is motivated by his/her values to achieve a sense of meaning in life. Values and needs are also closely linked and have an overlap [39]. Needs are basic, dynamic and contextual, while values are long-term oriented and core. In consciousness, values guide a person's psychological needs. As needs are filled for an individual but values are fulfilled by the individual, values are more close to choice, action, and behavior [40]. We can use our values to guide us in making choices about the most meaningful ways of having our needs met.

Identity is the term what and how an individual thinks about himself/herself, the sum of our knowledge and understanding of ourselves, including self-identity (i.e., self-image) and social identity (i.e., social roles). It is influenced by values. Carl Rogers [41], a humanistic psychologist, states that self-image is the view we have of ourselves, like independent self and interdependent self [42]. Chinese are more likely to think themselves as interdependent self, while people in Western countries are independent selves. Social roles are how we see ourselves in society (i.e., parent, son, friends, student, teacher), which affects what we think, we should do in a particular role, and the things that we consider to be important. So, the common values, attitudes, and beliefs have an influence on the individual's identity. Self-image and social roles are a powerful driver of cognition and behavior [43]. Therefore, its layer is located at the one between values/beliefs/attitudes and cognition. The relationships among needs, values, and identity are shown in Fig. 4.

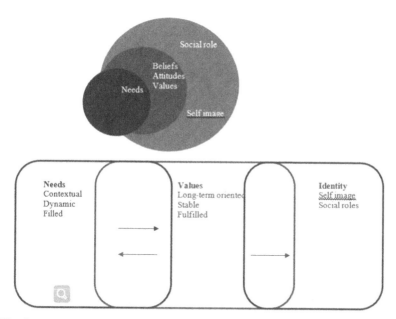

Fig. 4. The onion part (top) and the scale part (bottom) of needs, values, and identity

3.3 Cognition, Language and Behavior

Values and identity influence the cognitive or psychological processing. Cognition is a term referring to the mental processes involved in gaining knowledge and comprehension. It contains attention, perception, memory, thinking, decision-making, learning, and language [44, 45]. The theory of cognitive dissonance [46] proposes that people have a motivational drive to reduce the dissonance by changing, justifying, or rationalizing their attitudes, beliefs, and behaviors. Therefore, cognition is between values/beliefs/attitudes, and behavior, and based on the layer of identity. Cognition is finally located at the layer between identity and behavior (see Fig. 5). And, also cognition and communication style is influenced by culture. For example, Asians tend to engage in context-dependent and holistic perceptual processes by attending to the relationship between the object and the context in which the object is located, while Westerners tend to engage in context-independent and analytic perceptual processes by focusing on a salient object independently of its context [47]. Chinese prefer high-context communication, but people in Western countries prefer low-context communication [13, 14]. The study of Rau et al. [48] showed that Chinese individuals preferred and trusted the implicit style and were more likely to accept the implicit recommendations, while German preferred and trusted the explicit style and were more likely to accept the explicit recommendations.

Language concerns about descriptions of abstract thoughts, situations, objects, and sounds. The interaction between language and cognition remains an unsolved scientific challenge. But it is sure that they are linked to each other. Language helps us to develop cognition, but cognition does not entirely rely on language as evidenced by hearing-disabled persons [49]. Language is a communication tool, which transmits cultural knowledge and influences social behavior [50]. It is implicated in most of the

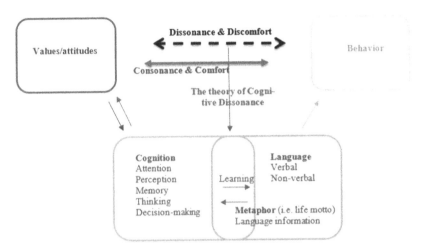

Fig. 5. The relationship among values/attitudes, cognition, language, and behavior

phenomena that lie at the core of social psychology: attitude change, social perception, personal identity, social interaction, intergroup bias and stereotyping, attribution, and so on.

Emotion is a conscious and unconscious mental reaction subjectively experienced as strong feeling usually directed towards a specific object/thing/person and typically accompanied by physiological and behavioral changes in the body. It is associated with thoughts, feelings, and behavioral responses. It is across the whole process ranging from motivation to behavior and mutual interaction with and within the whole process. For example, the sound of music drives us emotionally, and emotion reversely influences the choice of music songs [49]. Emotion is also culturally influenced. For instance, Frijda & Sundararajan [51] stated harmony-based savoring as a unique Chinese emotion.

4   The Application of Onion Model of Human Factors

The implication of the onion model of human factors is that it provides potential or even verified explanations for cross-cultural design. Here we take the interface differences of mobile apps in China and in the US as examples to illustrate how to propose explanations for the differences. We used the IUID mixed method to find the examples of cultural differences in mobile app design, including apps for maps, music, shopping, service, and communication in China and in the US.

4.1   Scenario-Based vs. Function-Based Design

Both mobile map and service apps show that mobile apps in China are designed based on scenarios or contexts whereas those in US are designed based on functions or attributes (see Fig. 6). For example, Baidu map and AutoNavi map in China provide covid-19 info (i.e., numbers of cases and the update regulation or notification) on the main page of the map. Google map has not included the related info on the main page at all. Besides this difference, map apps in China use the scenario (i.e., Commuting scenario) to be as the label of menu items, which does not occur in American map apps.

According to user interface elements identified by Marcus [17], this kind of difference belongs to the mental model dimension, which is related to categories in human cognition. In terms of the onion model of human factor, these UI elements are related to attention, perception, and memory parts, which are embodied by cognitive style. Nisbett [47] found that Chinese tend to put relevant activities together (holistic thinking) whereas Western users are likely to concentrate on completing specific activities individually (analytic thinking). In terms of the relationships of the layers, we could link the difference in cognitive style to that in motivation, need, and values as these three dimensions have direct and indirect effects on cognitive style. Chinese preference for holistic thinking is related to avoidance loss in motivation, relatedness need, and collectivism and long-term orientation values [53]. Avoidance loss, especially loss of face, make people be more concerned about others (i.e. needs and judgements), and finally cultivate the relatedness need and more collectivistic culture within a group. People with holistic thinking are more likely to have the high-context communication and polychromic time management style. But approach goal or benefits in motivation, autonomy need, individualism and short-term orientation, low-context communication, and monochromic time management style are related to analytic thinking.

Hence, our model provides more detailed information to help designers or practitioners to understand why there is such a difference (see Fig. 6). It is more concrete than persona-based approach, and could help researchers to find specific evidence by literature review in terms of these dimensions and their features and form a hypothesis even though there is no related study on the needed topics.

Fig. 6. Different user interface characteristics of map apps in China (the two left) and in the US (the one right)

4.2 Strong Social Connection Design in China

Map, music, and service apps in China would like to make user have a strong social connection with friends and strangers (i.e., nearby) by gamification (i.e., ranking). For example, Fig. 7 shows that the AutoNavi map app displays the info "You defeated 5.2% of users!", but Google map shows "let friends know where you are" and does not involve the info of unknown users. It is related to the avoidance loss (face is important, I cannot lose my face), status self-identify need, power distance value, high context, and harmony-based savoring emotion. Ranking could realize the user's status self-identity needs and power distance value. It is gamified not in a real world, which would align with the Chinese preference for harmony-based savoring in high context communication. They need to pay attention to the balance of others and themselves as Chinese are interdependent self-construal and their thoughts, feelings, and motivations are embedded in relationships and in specific context, settings, and roles [42].

AutoNavi Map   Google Map

Fig. 7. The difference between AutoNavi map and Google map in the social connection by gamification

4.3   Passive Error-Tolerance Interaction vs. Proactive Error Avoidance

Mobile apps in China show a simple setting choice, whereas mobile apps in the US provide multiple choices for setting a feature. For example, Fig. 8 shows WeChat, a communication app in China, just enabling binary choices for setting a feature, like either "on" or "off". In contrast, Messenger provides five choices for users to complete their settings. This is related to error or risk tolerance. In the onion model of human factors, it is corresponding to low uncertainty avoidance in China but high uncertainty avoidance in Western cultures. It is also related to security needs. It might be different requirements to satisfy the security needs for Chinese and American users. Sauer, Mertens, Groß, Heitland, and Nitsch [52] found that Chinese trust passive safety more than Americans.

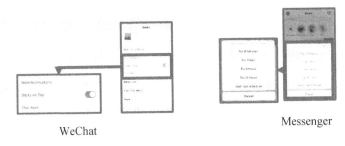

WeChat   Messenger

Fig. 8. The differences in setting up a feature in WeChat and in Messenger

5 Conclusion

The onion model of human factors provides a holistic framework for cross-cultural design. The dimensions from the core to the surface layer include motivation and preference, needs, values/beliefs/attitudes, identity (social role and self-image), cognition (from sensation to action selection), language, and behavior patterns. Besides the mentioned dimensions, emotion comes into play across the layers. The multiple dimensions related to culture and the relationship among the dimensions in the onion model of human factors allows researchers, designers and practitioners to gather more detailed information for further research or deriving reasonable activities for intercultural user interface design as it provides theoretical explanations for cross-cultural differences.

References

1. Henka, A., Zimmermann, G.: Persona based accessibility testing. In: Stephanidis, C. (ed.) HCI 2014. CCIS, vol. 435, pp. 226–231. Springer, Cham (2014). https://doi.org/10.1007/978-3-319-07854-0_40
2. Negru, S., Buraga, S.: A knowledge-based approach to the user-centered design process. In: Fred, A., Dietz, J.L.G., Liu, K., Filipe, J. (eds.) IC3K 2012. CCIS, vol. 415, pp. 165–178. Springer, Heidelberg (2013). https://doi.org/10.1007/978-3-642-54105-6_11
3. Chapman, C.N., Milham, R.P.: The personas' new clothes: methodological and practical arguments against a popular method. In: Proceedings of the Human Factors and Ergonomics Society Annual Meeting. SAGE Publications, Los Angeles (2006)
4. Pruitt, J., Adlin, T.: The Persona Lifecycle: Keeping People in Mind throughout Product Design. Elsevier (2010)
5. Viana, G., Robert, J.-M.: The practitioners' points of view on the creation and use of personas for user interface design. In: Kurosu, M. (ed.) HCI 2016. LNCS, vol. 9731, pp. 233–244. Springer, Cham (2016). https://doi.org/10.1007/978-3-319-39510-4_22
6. Singh, N., Matsuo, H.: Measuring cultural adaptation on the web: a content analytic study of US and Japanese Web sites. J. Bus. Res. 57(8), 864–872 (2004)
7. Callahan, E.: Cultural similarities and differences in the design of university web sites. J. Comput.-Mediat. Commun. 11(1), 239–273 (2005)
8. Heimgärtner, R.: Towards a toolbox for intercultural user interface design. In: CHIRA (2019)
9. Hofstede, G., Hofstede, G.J., Minkov, M.: Cultures and Organizations: Software of the Mind, vol. 2. Mcgraw-Hill, New York (2005)
10. Heimgärtner, R.: Reflections on a model of culturally influenced human–computer interaction to cover cultural contexts in HCI design. Int. J. Hum.-Comput. Interact. 29(4), 205–219 (2013)
11. Myers, M.D., Tan, F.B.: Beyond models of national culture in information systems research. In: Human Factors in Information Systems, pp. 1–19. IGI Global (2002)
12. Morden, T.: Models of national culture–a management review. Cross Cult. Manag. Int. J. (1999)
13. Hall, E.T.: The silent language in overseas business. Harv. Bus. Rev. 38(3), 87–96 (1960)
14. Hall, E.T.: Beyond Culture. Anchor (1989)
15. Bottger, P.C., Hallein, I.H., Yetton, P.W.: A cross-national study of leadership: participation as a function of problem structure and leader power. J. Manag. Stud. 22(4), 358–368 (1985)
16. Khan, T., Pitts, M., Williams, M.A.: Cross-cultural differences in automotive HMI design: a comparative study between UK and Indian users' design preferences. J. Usability Stud. 11(2), 45–65 (2016)

17. Marcus, A.: Cross-cultural user-interface design for work, home, play, and on the way. In: ACM SIGGRAPH ASIA 2010 Courses, pp. 1–160 (2010)
18. Morling, B., Lee, J.M.: Culture and motivation. In: The Praeger Handbook of Personality Across Cultures: Culture and Characteristic Adaptations, vol. 2, pp. 61–89. Praeger/ABC-CLIO: Santa Barbara (2017)
19. Hofstede, G.: Culture's recent consequences: using dimension scores in theory and research. Int. J. Cross Cult. Manag. **1**(1), 11–17 (2001)
20. Hofstede, G.: Dimensionalizing cultures: the Hofstede model in context. Online Readings Psychol. Cult. **2**(1), 2307–0919.1014 (2011)
21. Cyr, D.: Modeling web site design across cultures: relationships to trust, satisfaction, and e-loyalty. J. Manag. Inf. Syst. **24**(4), 47–72 (2008)
22. Gudykunst, W.B., et al.: The influence of cultural individualism-collectivism, self construals, and individual values on communication styles across cultures. Hum. Commun. Res. **22**(4), 510–543 (1996)
23. Lewis, R.: When Cultures Collide: Leading Across Cultures. Nicholas Brealey International (2010)
24. Hall, E.T.: Monochronic and polychronic time. Intercultural Commun. Reader **9**, 280–286 (2000)
25. Migdał, A.M.: 5 Time Perception. Reader on Sensitive Zones, p. 29 (2020)
26. Ciascai, L.: Using graphic organizers in intercultural education. Acta Didactica Napocensia **2**(1), 9–18 (2009)
27. Lin, W., Shan, C., Yu, S.: The harmonization of professional teaching and professional-competency training in financial management. Chin. Stud. **3**(04), 165 (2014)
28. McClelland, D.C.: Testing for competencies rather than intelligence American Psychologist (1973). Internet. Consultado el 03 de diciembre del 2018. Disponible en: https://rieoei.org/historico/deloslectores/Maura.PDF
29. Straub, D., et al.: Toward a theory-based measurement of culture. J. Glob. Inf. Manag. (JGIM) **10**(1), 13–23 (2002)
30. Wickens, C.D., et al.: An Introduction to Human Factors Engineering, vol. 2. Pearson Prentice Hall, Upper Saddle River (2004)
31. Gerrig, R., et al.: Psychology and Life, vol. 20, Pearson, Boston (2010)
32. International Ergonomics Association: Human Factors/Ergonomics (HF/E) (2020)
33. Maslow, A.H.: A Theory of Human Motivation. General Press (2019)
34. McClelland, D.C., Burnham, D.H.: Power is the Great Motivator. Harvard Business Review Press (2008)
35. Reeve, J., Lee, W.: A neuroscientific perspective on basic psychological needs. J. Pers. **87**(1), 102–114 (2019)
36. Yu, A.-B.: Ultimate life concerns, self, and Chinese achievement motivation (1996)
37. Bond, M.H.: The Oxford Handbook of Chinese Psychology. Oxford Library of Psychology (2010)
38. Siwek, Z., Oleszkowicz, A., Słowińska, A.: Values realized in personal strivings and motivation, and meaning in life in polish university students. J. Happiness Stud. **18**(2), 549–573 (2017)
39. Breitsprecher, B.: Values, Needs, Wants (2016). https://www.slideshare.net/bogeybear/values-needs-and-wants
40. Devoe, D.: Viktor Frankl's logotherapy: the search for purpose and meaning. Inquiries J. **4**(07) (2012)
41. Rogers, C.R.: A Theory of Therapy, Personality, and Interpersonal Relationships: As Developed in the Client-Centered Framework, vol. 3. McGraw-Hill, New York (1959)
42. Swann, W.B., Jr., et al.: When group membership gets personal: a theory of identity fusion. Psychol. Rev. **119**(3), 441 (2012)

43. Lynch, K.D.: Modeling role enactment: linking role theory and social cognition. J. Theory Soc. Behav. **37**(4), 379–399 (2007)
44. Eysenck, M.W., Keane, M.T.: Cognitive Psychology: A Student' Handbook. Psychology Press (2015)
45. Solso, R.L., MacLin, M.K., MacLin, O.H.: Cognitive Psychology. Pearson Education, New Zealand (2005)
46. Festinger, L.: A Theory of Cognitive Dissonance, vol. 2. Stanford University Press (1962)
47. Nisbett, R.E.: The Geography of Thought: How Asians and Westerners Think Differently and Why. Simon and Schuster, New York (2004)
48. Rau, P.P., Li, Y., Li, D.: Effects of communication style and culture on ability to accept recommendations from robots. Comput. Hum. Behav. **25**(2), 587–595 (2009)
49. Perlovsky, L.: Language and cognition interaction neural mechanisms. Comput. Intell. Neurosci. (2011)
50. Krauss, R.M., Chiu, C.Y.: Language and social behaviour. In: Gilbert, S.F.D., Lindsey, G. (eds.) Handbook of Social Psychology, pp. 41–88. McGraw-Hill, Boston (1998)
51. Frijda, N.H., Sundararajan, L.: Emotion refinement: a theory inspired by Chinese poetics. Perspect. Psychol. Sci. **2**(3), 227–241 (2007)
52. Sauer, V., Mertens, A., Groß, S., Heitland, J., Nitsch, V.: Designing automated Vehicle interiors for different cultures: evidence from China, Germany, and the United States. Ergon. Des. (2020)
53. Scarborough, J.: Comparing Chinese and western cultural roots: why "east is east and...". Bus. Horiz. **41**(6), 15 (1998)

From Online Games to "Metaverse": The Expanding Impact of Virtual Reality in Daily Life

Shengyu Jian[✉], Xin Chen, and Jiaping Yan

School of Fine Arts and Design, Yangzhou University, Yangzhou 225009,
People's Republic of China
474677690@qq.com

Abstract. Due to its wider and wider range of applications, virtual reality technology plays a very important role in expanding the field of human existence. From traditional video games to online games to "Metaverse", human beings have made virtual reality more refined and comprehensive. Technical entertainment based on virtual reality has also caused social problems such as addictive dependence and escapism. "Metaverse", or the so-called "virtual reality Internet", as a representative of the next generation of Internet, contains both risks and opportunities.

Keywords: Virtual reality · Online games · Metaverse · Internet · Artificial intelligence

1 Introduction

From a spatial perspective, the development of society is the process by which human beings continue to broaden their field of activity. Human beings are not willing to live only in the real world, but actively use their imagination to develop a virtual world. As a result, people began to gradually enrich "games", a practical method that allows people to use their imagination. "Games" in a broad sense encompasses forms ranging from play and painting to more sophisticated artistic and literary creations. The emergence of digital games is an important node of this practice. It externalizes human imagination from a subjective existence to an objective existence. From then on, virtual reality has a physical support from technology.

In the 2020s, as Virtual Reality technology continued to be iteratively upgraded and continued to be used in daily scenes. "Metaverse", a term that was proposed in science fiction in 1992, became popular because of Zuckerberg's advocacy. Although the relevant technologies involved in the "Metaverse" are not yet mature, and the specific plans related to its future development are not yet clear, the post-human era characterized by the construction of "virtual reality" has arrived. From video games to online games, and then to "Metaverse", Human subjective imagination has evolved into the objective form of virtual reality. More refined and comprehensive virtual reality is created. The

M. Rauterberg (Ed.): HCII 2022, LNCS 13324, pp. 34–43, 2022.
https://doi.org/10.1007/978-3-031-05434-1_3

concept of "Metaverse" comes from human technical entertainment activities, but it has surpassed the original "entertainment" attributes and evolved into a large-scale data ecosystem, that is, a virtual world.

Some scholars reminded: "Pseudo-modernity is integrated into modern civilization through computer technology, artificial intelligence technology and other high-tech technologies, and poses a threat to modern human civilization" [1]. Therefore, as we advance the process of virtual reality technology, we must pay attention to its negative effects, promptly criticize and correct them, and also study its positive effects and analyze what important changes it will bring to human society.

2 Technological Entertainment: Virtual Reality Moves to the Foreground of History

The cultural products produced in modern society do not necessarily have the spiritual qualities that promote the development of "modernity" in this era. The end of the 20th century to the beginning of the 21st century was a highly complex period of rapid expansion of human society. On the one hand, the public enjoys unprecedented rich material and spiritual products; on the other hand, technology brings more psychological problems such as frustration and confusion to people. In fact, technological entertainment, including online games, is a typical representative of this modern complexity.

The desire to play is rooted in human nature. Due to its simulation characteristics, online games often require players to be immersed in them to operate. This has caused it to actually become a type of entertainment that consumes more players' time and energy. After all, games create a fascinating "second world" outside of reality. As far as the current situation in society is concerned, online entertainment, which is dominated by online games, has increasingly become the mainstream entertainment method for young people. In public areas such as waiting stations and subways, technological entertainment based on online games has become the core pastime for young people in the era of fragmentation.

The news events that once swept the screen in China at the end of 2021 included the Chinese EDG team winning the "League of Legends" S11 global finals on November 6. This victory prompted many students from various universities in China to organize a group carnival for this, as if they were spending a grand traditional festival. In fact, about ten years ago, online games were considered by academia to be an "exclusive" entertainment project for a specific group of students who were so-called "playful" and "lack of desire to learn". In contrast, students who are interested in professional learning rarely use online games as their entertainment options.

Since the 21st century, online games have gradually got rid of their original marginal status and have begun to become an important form of entertainment on the contemporary historical stage. And also during this time, the interaction between online games and movies has become more and more frequent. Many online games have begun to have the high-definition picture quality of movies and the narrative techniques of movies, allowing players to participate in the game as if they are in the movie as a movie character. And as this kind of interaction breaks the boundaries of traditional media, online games will most likely become the strongest "new king" among all forms of entertainment in the next few decades.

In terms of the scope of this college student carnival, we can already speculate that the number of game players in Chinese universities is already quite large. The younger generation has been living in a networked and digitalized technological era since childhood. Their conceptual acceptance of online entertainment, including online games, is much higher than that of their predecessors. This is a large and growing group, and in the next few decades, these current young people will gradually take over from their parents in various positions and become the backbone of society. As a result, the online entertainment habits of many of them will also affect the future development of society to varying degrees. So when Facebook founder and CEO Mark Elliot Zuckerberg came up with the "Metaverse" concept, it will cause such a big response on a global scale. If his move can come true, then the entire Internet development will open a new page under the drive of his enterprise. However, problems also follow. For the online entertainment discussed in this article, which is based on online games, the arrival of the "Metaverse" era based on virtual reality technology will also push the problem of Internet addiction to a new level.

Unlike previous video games, which are displayed with a flat interface, the upcoming "Metaverse" will strive to create sensory experiences such as realism and immersion in front of players. So they pay special attention to the use of virtual reality wearable devices. This means that as the form of online games becomes more and more advanced, and the corresponding supporting equipment becomes more and more advanced, the so-called virtual world addiction problem that people are addicted to technological entertainment will also become more serious. These problems that are about to occur in the mature stage of virtual reality can already be seen in the current online game addiction problem. Therefore, while cheering the arrival of the "Metaverse" era, the public must also realize that these capital giants may be planning to build three-dimensional, fully simulated large-scale video games in the name of "Metaverse", rather than building A colorful virtual world.

3   Addictive Dependence: Virtual Reality Brings Negative Effects

The continuous emergence of new technologies brings new entertainment, spiritual experience and material empowerment, but also brings many structural social problems. Virtual world addiction is one of the more prominent problems of this kind. If you look at the current online game addiction problem, you can get a glimpse of the real dangers that will emerge after the next virtual reality technology (such as "Metaverse") gradually matures. Because of their open-ended interaction and psychological immersion, online games can be considered a form of preview before the official arrival of Metaverse.

Games are generally regarded as the decompression valve of reality, allowing people to vent and relax. Online games are also one of the many types of games invented by humans. Some people in society denounce online games as "mental opium" and "electronic drugs" from the moral level. Although this statement has been criticized as an exaggeration because it over-exaggerates the negative effects of online games, compared with other forms of entertainment, online games do have their own particularities, that is, their high addiction. Although the Metaverse still does not appear in our daily life, we should also be moderately vigilant considering that the current online games have caused the problem of addiction symptoms.

The academic community has long been naming the addiction symptoms brought about by this technological entertainment from the medical level. There are naming around the online game itself, such as "Internet Gaming Disorder" (IGD), or from the broader Internet itself, such as "Internet addiction disorder" (IAD).

Some scholars have started to study and analyze the brain activity of addicts from functional magnetic resonance imaging technology. After comparison, they have concluded that there are many differences in brain response areas between online game addicts and traditional drug addicts, which should not be confused. However, there are indeed some similarities between the two in that the activity of the brain reward system is induced to increase [2]. Other studies have shown that the brain activation state of patients with online game addiction is quite similar to those of patients with substance addiction or pathological gambling [3]. In other words, online games do have the attribute of "quasi-drugs". At least they are as dangerous as drugs in terms of their addictive effects on the brains of patients. If online games are allowed to develop unrestrictedly, it is likely to have various adverse effects on social development. In addition, Internet addiction can also cause physical damage to addicts, such as withdrawal symptoms, circadian clock disorders, neurasthenia, joint inflammation, vision loss, anxiety and depression, and impaired social function. This shows that the virtual world can bring substantial harm to people (Table 1).

Table 1. FMRI manifestations of patients with "IGD" (Internet Gaming Disorder) [4, 5].

Activated areas of the brain	Inhibited areas of the brain
The prefrontal cortex, the right orbital frontal cortex, the right dorsolateral prefrontal cortex, the bilateral anterior cingulate cortex, the right caudate nucleus, and the right nucleus accumbens are activated very significantly These may indicate that the part of the patient's brain involved in the desire for rewards is overactive	The gray matter volume of the anterior cingulate gyrus, orbitofrontal lobe, dorsolateral prefrontal lobe, and premotor cortex decreased These may indicate that the part of the patient's brain involved in cognitive control and decision-making abilities is showing an impaired state

The above FMRI observations of patients show that the parts of their brains related to rational judgment (cognition, decision-making) are inhibited or even damaged, while the parts related to perceptual judgment (emotion, desire, volition) are overactivated.

The current video game adopts this approach at a macro level: on the one hand, the pleasure of being a positive stimulus allows the player to enjoy it, on the other hand, the constant anxiety as a negative stimulus makes the player worry about gains and losses, and become more and more addicted to it. In order to indulge players, game designers often make certain technical settings for the difficulty of the game. For example, strictly control the speed and rhythm of the game, try to keep players in a state of alternating between excitement and relaxation, so as to prevent players from reducing online time due to diminishing freshness. For example, the difficulty of the game encountered by the player is set to be slightly higher than the current level of the player, and the player is tempted to constantly try to upgrade through the level.

Especially at present, game designers are beginning to introduce functional artificial intelligence into game programs. The program sometimes reduces the difficulty to give the player the thrill of excitement, and sometimes increases the difficulty so that the player is controlled by anxiety and anxiety in frustration, and is unwilling to stop the game. Players are unable to extricate themselves in such a polarized state, slowly becoming insensitive to the physical world in real life, but at the same time constantly increasing their online time. Online games have always tried to give players an illusory sense of control, but in fact, the master control of the game has always been firmly controlled by the merchants.

Large companies such as Facebook are now designing and building "Metaverse" for profit. Who can guarantee that they will not adopt these strategies to control players mentally? No matter how beautiful the online games in the virtual world are, we can't help but feel anxious when we think of the number of children playing games in the "Metaverse" in the future than the number of children playing football on the playground.

The current academic research on the problem of addiction to online games is mainly centered on young people who are mentally unsound, as if adults are acquiesced to be a kind of soundness who can consciously use rational thinking and self-control to resist addiction when facing online games. But in fact, when adults face their mental addiction, their performance is no better than teenagers. Because the addiction of adolescents is often just a staged behavior prompted by curiosity, while the addiction of adults is likely to be a long-term behavior that actively seeks comfort and escapes from reality.

According to psychologist Mihaly Csikszentmihalyi, those behaviors that can bring "rewarding experience" can allow practitioners to gain an experience of enjoyment and immerse themselves in it. His statement can be used to explain how online games cause the audience to become addicted, and it can even be used to speculate how "Metaverse" will produce corresponding "cyber addicts" in the future.

The reason why a considerable number of players indulge in online games is precisely because they enjoy the sense of belonging they can't get in real life. In the same way, "Metaverse" is likely to push the current online games to bring such online immersion and addiction to a higher level. When players have completed the transformation of reshaping their self-identity in virtual reality and become accustomed to the new life in it, they will have a sense of strangeness and rejection of real life. In this process, many social problems of adults will emerge, such as self-identity barriers and interpersonal communication barriers.

The reason why academia is uneasy when capital giants hype the concept of "Metaverse" is that the construction of "Metaverse" is currently promoted by profit-oriented companies, such as social media companies and online game companies. The public is concerned about the following: "Metaverse" is supposed to mean "online virtual reality", but it may be narrowed down to a "big online virtual game" by profit-oriented companies.

4 Escape from Reality: When Virtual Reality Becomes a Way of Life

Whether it is "Internet Gaming Disorder" or "Internet addiction disorder" (including various Internet-based recreational services, such as browsing short videos, watching gossip news, etc.), its essence is derived from the "boringness" of the individual. According to relevant research, the individual's tendency to be bored is closely related to the tendency to addiction to online games. People with high boring tendencies are more likely to seek stimulating experiences in online games driven by negative emotions, thereby obtaining a sense of satisfaction [6]. Such problems will likely intensify in the future "Metaverse" with the characteristics of "virtual reality".

An senior investor once criticized that some young people now lack competitive ambitions and waste too much time on the beach. In fact, with the advancement of commercial projects such as "Metaverse", perhaps he will witness a worse situation than basking on the beach: a large number of cyber addicts appear in the virtual world. Because of the highly addictive nature of "Metaverse", people who enjoy immersive experiences may fall into a fascination with the virtual world.

Strictly speaking, "boredom" can be divided into "individual boredom" and "social boredom". The so-called "individual boredom" refers to the mental state of the individual lacking external stimuli. This kind of "individual boredom" is a state that everyone will often appear in daily life. Driven by boring emotions, he will actively look for objects that can make oneself interested and relieve boredom. At this time, for recreational purposes, Internet services, including online games, are excellent choices.

But in addition, there is a more structural and deep-seated boredom that plagues the public: "social boredom." The so-called "social boredom" refers to the fact that individuals cannot normally obtain material and spiritual support from social identity, and thus fall into a negative emotion that feels that they are isolated. For example, if someone is at the bottom of society and feels painful for it, but in reality he has no resources to get rid of this state, so at this time he will have "social boredom". Once this negative emotion continues for a long time, it will become a negative mental state that has a profound impact on the person.

Generally speaking, an individual with healthy behavior habits and appropriate social identity support will only be in a transient state of boredom. He seeks relief from the object of his pastime in order to better re-engage in his work afterwards. But if this person has the problem of "social boredom", which stems from his inability to realize self-worth in work and life, then he will compensate for the sense of accomplishment and satisfaction from other places. Under such circumstances, indulging in digital entertainment in the virtual world will become one of his options, and it is likely to be the first option.

In the process of efficiently improving social efficiency, the market economy is also producing many interlocking and structural social problems. This kind of problem will become more common, serious and diverse after the speed of science and technology is greater than the speed that humans can adapt.

Will the future human society enter the so-called "combination of low-quality life and advanced technology" often described in those "cyberpunk" movies? With the continuous development of science and technology, artificial intelligence equipment will inevitably replace the slower and less cost-effective human skilled workers in various positions in the society. If countries around the world fail to take timely countermeasures, such uncoordinated technological progress may lead to the emergence of a large number of "surplus" labor at the bottom of society in the future.

The movie "Ready Player One" (2018) shows and criticizes this so-called "cyberpunk" future life. These "redundant people" who feel that there is no way out are likely to fall into the bad mental state of "social boredom". At that time, the virtual world may become the best containment for them to escape the negative emotions caused by the pain and helplessness of reality. If the function of "Metaverse" is powerful enough by then, it is very likely to be used by many "superfluous people" in society as the primary option to abandon real life and switch to virtual life. This is why it is said that only when the people have equal rights to development can society develop in a positive direction. If the prosperity brought about by technological progress cannot benefit most people in the society, then this prosperity will eventually be destroyed by social conflicts caused by the polarization of social groups.

The real world is a comprehensive world, and people must have more comprehensive skills to obtain their own living space. In contrast, the virtual world is a one-sided world, as long as individuals have some special game abilities, they can achieve success in the virtual world. The one-sided life of the virtual world makes it easy to indulge people who live unsatisfactorily in the real world. It is alarming that if the individual is in a state of singular information reception for a long time, then his ideological form will inevitably be distorted.

Assuming such a scene, someone is just a marginal person with low social status and neglected in the real world, but he is a player who can gallop freely and let himself go in the virtual world. Especially if this video game allows him to earn virtual currency (such as Bitcoin, etc.) that can be used in his real life. It is estimated that he is more willing to stay away from the real world that makes him feel pain, disgust and anxiety, and hides in this virtual structure, so that he can enjoy his illusory happy life in it for a long time.

This means that the virtual world, especially the "Metaverse", is likely to cultivate a group of unilaterally developed mentally deformed people in batches, who are addicted to cyberspace. Individuals' excessive immersion in the virtual world is often accompanied by their alienation from the real world. Like technical entertainment such as online games, the most worrying thing about "Metaverse" is the problem of indulging in the virtual world and escaping from real life.

Science fiction writer Liu Cixin is a firm critic of the virtual world of "Metaverse". According to his point of view, the future of human beings has two development directions. One is the outward expansion type, that is, the development of advanced technology for interstellar exploration. Human beings will eventually go out of the earth, march into the universe, and become a space civilization; the second is the involution type, that is, development around Introverted technology developed by "virtual reality", human beings are reduced to virtual civilization due to the comfort and joy brought by the virtual world. And if human beings have developed virtual technology to a highly developed level before the expansion of interstellar exploration technology has been developed, so that humans can enjoy highly realistic virtual life without leaving the earth, then this technological situation is for humans civilization will be a disaster rather than a gospel.

Objectively speaking, Liu Cixin's view may be too pessimistic. In fact, the exploration of outer space and the inner exploration of the "metaverse" are not an either-or choice. Instead, the two explorations can be combined and developed together. For example, before conducting real outer space exploration, scientists can conduct simulation experiments in virtual inner exploration. In the long journey of space, astronauts can also use the technical entertainment provided by virtual technology to carry out recreational activities.

5 Possible Advantages: Development Prospects Brought by "Metaverse"

In the previous discussion, we talked about the risks brought by the "Metaverse", but in fact it also contains important historical opportunities to promote human progress. The reason why the concept of "Metaverse" can suddenly become a hot spot at the end of 2021 is because it meets the public's eager expectations for the next generation of the Internet.

After all, in accordance with the logic of the development of Internet technology, the "virtual reality Internet" has reached the stage where it is ready to emerge. Therefore, Zuckerberg's declaration on behalf of Facebook has ignited the long-saved enthusiasm of the public and even the capital market like a match, and this kind of attention has been released on the concept of "Metaverse". From online games to "Metaverse", technological entertainment has gradually evolved from a relatively simple and rough form to a highly informative and exquisite form of virtual reality. The public can not only play digital games on the Internet, but also make their lives a part of the virtual world (Table 2).

Table 2. The history of the Internet from its appearance to its evolution to the present can be roughly divided into three stages.

Different stages	Characteristics
The "PC Internet" era	At this stage, the Internet era was started by relying on the way the computer was connected to the network
"Mobile Internet" era	At this stage, people no longer only use computers to surf the Internet at a fixed location, but can use mobile devices such as mobile phones to freely access the Internet anytime and anywhere
"Virtual reality Internet" era	At this stage, the Internet that people visit is no longer just the traditional two-dimensional Internet, but a three-dimensional virtual reality Internet

The development process of the Internet from the first to the third stage is the process of its gradual physicalization: the Internet has gradually become an inseparable part of human life, and it has also begun to become a part of the body through various network access devices.

It can even be said that the access terminals including smart phones, tablet computers, etc., and the following virtual reality devices (VR) and augmented reality devices (AR) have become human "artificial organs". Technological sensations such as network perception and virtual perception have also become new human perceptions after the five natural sensations like vision and hearing and so on. In addition to being able to "see", "hear", "smell", "touch" and "taste" external objects with natural organs, we can also perceive new objects that appear in the virtual reality field through "artificial organs".

Although the underlying technical infrastructure of "Metaverse" is still immature, the public's conceptual acceptance of it is basically complete. In the first 20 years of the 21st century, the widespread use of various technologies including mobile Internet and virtual reality in daily life has allowed the public to live in a dual world composed of reality and the Internet. The arrival of the "Metaverse" is nothing more than bringing cyberspace to the stage of virtual reality.

The emergence of the COVID-19 epidemic at the end of 2019 is also prompting Human beings to build a "virtual reality Internet" earlier. The epidemic has brought the world into a social era of "non-physical contact" suddenly. The traditional model of "face-to-face" that people take for granted in daily life has been severely impacted. Under forced physical isolation, social activities of "de-incarnation" began to be widely used in social practice, and even gradually became a common trend.

Due to its cross-regional and non-contact advantages, online meetings have gradually become a mainstream option for holding meetings; Technological entertainment methods, such as online games and cloud visits to museums, that you can participate in without stepping out of your home, have gradually become popular in the process; In countries where mobile payment is developed, such as China, such payment methods that do not need to touch physical banknotes are also likely to replace traditional cash payments.

In short, COVID-19 has accelerated the virtualization of global human activities in this process. Various signs indicate that Human beings has begun to need to add a relatively independent, complete and content-rich large-scale data ecosystem that can support human virtual social life in addition to reality. Facebook and other companies are betting on the "Metaverse" project, which is actually trying to conform to the changing trend of the Internet in the 21st century.

The construction of a virtual world is an important event in human history, marking a big step forward for human beings in exploring the expansion of their own living space. People's spiritual life will not be limited to the real field defined by the material world, but will further extend to the virtual field constructed freely by human beings themselves. In this virtual new world, what restricts human activities will no longer be the various rules in the physical world, but only the imagination and creativity of human beings.

For example, the visual information of the virtual world has foldable and expandable hyperlink functions that the real world does not have; images can be zoomed in or out, and similar searches can be performed; 3D layers of modeling can be stereoscopically perspective, etc.. Such forms are not present in the real world, but belong to the virtual world alone. In such a virtual environment, individuals naturally have multi-tasking and beyond-horizon scheduling capabilities. The suitability of his working conditions will surpass the traditional real world, and his work efficiency and output will also be improved.

Outstanding figures in every era need the technological products of this era as their stage. Kevin Kelly once asked, how many high-level geniuses in this world did not encounter the technical opportunities that allowed them to display their talents in their own time? For example, if before Mozart died, piano and symphony had not yet appeared; if Van Gogh came to the world, cheap oil painting technology had not yet come out; and if Hitchcock and Chaplin had not encountered the era of popularization of film technology. Then these great artistic geniuses in history are likely to be silently buried in the pages of history.

Similarly, if a virtual reality technology platform such as "Metaverse" is built, it may allow many undiscovered geniuses to gain space and add new brilliance to human history. Imagine that characters such as three-dimensional graffiti artists, three-dimensional sound effects editors, etc., can truly realize their full potential only after the emergence of "virtual reality" scenes such as "Metaverse".

Virtual reality is having a profound impact on human daily life. In terms of negative effects, it will bring problems such as Internet addiction, and it will also make some people escape from reality through the virtual world and deepen their self-enclosed state. But at the same time, virtual reality also opens up new space for human beings in addition to physical space, thereby expanding the scope of human activities. Perhaps, as a new space for human survival, the "virtual reality Internet" itself does not have the attributes of good and evil, the key is how humans use it. As an integrated body with the most cutting-edge and top technology in the future history, the virtual reality Internet needs to integrate intelligent resources from various disciplines, involving a series of interrelated fields: big data, blockchain, 5G network, artificial intelligence, Human-machine docking, brain science and neuroscience, etc. In order to build it, Human beings will continue to challenge the limits of existing technology, and continue to optimize the combination of resources in all aspects, in the process to push the progress of science and technology to a new peak.

References

1. Wang, J., Chen, H.: Bie-modernism and cultural computing. In: Rauterberg, M. (ed.) HCII 2021. LNCS, vol. 12795, pp. 474–489. Springer, Cham (2021). https://doi.org/10.1007/978-3-030-77431-8_30
2. Ma, N., et al.: Preliminary fMRI comparative study on the reward system of game addiction and drug addicts. In: Proceedings of the Fourth Member Congress of the Chinese Society of Neuroscience and the Eighth National Academic Conference, pp. 76–77 (2009)
3. Wang, Z., Zhao, M.: The current status of intervention research on adolescents' online game addiction. Neural Dis. Mental Hyg. **10**, 731–735 (2018)
4. Lin, X., Jia, X., Zang, Y.F., et al.: Frequency-dependent changes in the amplitude of low-frequency fluctuations in internet gaming disorder. Front. Psychol. **6**, 1471 (2015)
5. Yao, Y.W., Liu, L., Ma, S.S., et al.: Functional and structural neural alterations in Internet gaming disorder: a systematic review and meta-analysis. Neurosci. Biobehav. Rev. **83**, 313–324 (2017)
6. An, H.: The influence of boredom on online game addiction: the mediating role of online game cognitive bias. Educ. Theory Pract. **15**, 42–44 (2020)

Virtual Reality Interaction Toward the Replacement of Real Clinical Nursing Education

Chanhee Kim[1] , Hyeongil Nam[1] , Ji-Young Yeo[2(✉)] , and Jong-Il Park[1(✉)]

[1] Computer Science, Hanyang University, Seongdong-gu, Seoul, Republic of Korea
{dearchan,skagusrlf,jipark}@hanyang.ac.kr
[2] School of Nursing, Hanyang University, Seongdong-gu, Seoul, Republic of Korea
shine73@hanyang.ac.kr

Abstract. Due to time and space constraints and limited resources, clinical nursing education in real-life environments has limitations for sufficient learning. In this paper, we propose a novel interaction method for immersive virtual simulations in clinical nursing that considers the characteristics and process of each to enable learners to learn and perform realistic nursing skills. First, (1) hand gestures and speech modalities can be used as input modalities according to each type of skill, and nursing skills can be performed while the degree of behavioral freedom is ensured. (2) The timing and method of evaluating the interaction of the skills to be learned vary depending on how they are performed through the analysis of hand gestures and speech input. (3) In addition, depending on the evaluation, this method can provide immediate feedback (e.g., audio-visual feedback) as well as feedback about accumulated nursing skills interaction, which can maximize the learning effects (e.g., additional quizzes and final clinical nursing results). With the actual nursing skill implemented by the proposed method, the feasibility of immersive VR nursing practice based on the pediatric pneumonia scenario was verified through a pilot study. As a result, high scores were obtained in a simple questionnaire evaluation, and the feasibility was confirmed through an interview evaluation of both learners and instructors. With the proposed method, it is expected that the quality of clinical nursing education can be improved while learning the details and the overall flow of nursing skills through realistic interactions.

Keywords: Nursing education · Virtual reality · Multimodal interaction

1 Introduction

Recently, nursing education for clinical practice that utilizes the application of simulations has been increasing to solve issues of insufficient practical training and difficult practice conditions [1–3]. Moreover, simulation-based education is being applied to nursing due to the advantage of being able to convert acquired theoretical knowledge into the practical knowledge required in the nursing field [4]. Clinical practice can be carried out in a safe environment, and possible problems faced in clinical situations can

M. Rauterberg (Ed.): HCII 2022, LNCS 13324, pp. 44–67, 2022.
https://doi.org/10.1007/978-3-031-05434-1_4

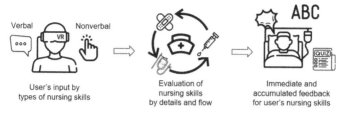

Fig. 1. Concept of nursing skill in immersive virtual reality.

be directly solved through simulation-based education [5]. Also, students who still lack practical knowledge can practice nursing skills without the risk of harming real patients, thereby reducing the psychological burden on the safety of patients and enabling repeated learning through various trial-and-error processes [6] (Fig. 1).

In recent years, research using natural user interfaces (NUIs), such as hand gestures in immersive virtual reality (VR) in nursing education, has been conducted [7]. However, simulations using a controller are still dominant in nursing practice sites [8]. Using a controller easily builds up fatigue, causes discomfort, reduces naturalness, and can negatively affect learners [9, 10]. On the other hand, when interactions are conducted using a person's bare hands, students can participate directly, thereby honing their nursing skills and helping them become familiar with a VR environment in which they may have limited experience [11, 12]. Thus, since verbal expression in the nursing skill learning process is included as an important skill element, it is necessary to reflect speech input [13]. Therefore, in this study, nursing skills, including both non-verbal and verbal activities, can be learned using both hand gestures and speech input in immersive VR. Based on these realistic interactions, learners can be provided with a feeling of being in a real environment, which can derive more effective learning outcomes [11, 12].

In addition, to provide an appropriate environment for education through VR sim-ulation, it is necessary to determine whether the conditions necessary to acquire each skill are met by focusing on 'how' learners perform, rather than focusing only on 'what' they do. Most of the previous studies have mainly evaluated the applicability of VR in nursing education, such as acquiring simple skills like administering an intravenous injection [14]. Therefore, this study seeks to propose a nursing skill evaluation method that can reflect the characteristics and objectives of each nursing skill, without being limited to learning only specific skills in immersive VR, as was done in a previous study [14]. More specifically, it considers how to determine the interactions in nursing skills performance using the non-verbal and verbal learning items required for nursing skills to be learned. Furthermore, by applying different points of time when the interactions in nursing skills performance were evaluated according to the importance of the learning objective, such as the order and the details of the performed nursing skills, the proposed method sought to improve the effectiveness of learning.

Also, while clinical nursing practice using VR simulation is increasing, research on the interaction input method to provide an optimal environment to learners, and on the technical method to evaluate performance competency and provide feedback on it, has thus far been inadequate. Therefore, to maximize the effectiveness of training, the feedback method in this study was diversified into virtual nursing supplies or patient and guardian's response feedback in the virtual space. Additional missions or quizzes related to the specific nursing skills that learners were performing were also available. Differentiation was also made at the time of feedback, such as showing the effect immediately or showing the effect of accumulated skills.

A pilot study was conducted to verify the feasibility of complementing actual clinical nursing practice with the proposed interaction method. Positive results were confirmed through a questionnaire evaluation conducted after the simulation experience and a qualitative evaluation conducted in the form of an interview.

This study is meaningful as a basic study of an interaction method that can effectively teach various nursing skills with a sense of realism using learner's hand gestures and speech input in immersive VR. Furthermore, depending on the nursing skill that needs to be learned, we show that if more input modalities are used or various types of feedback are provided, this method can be widely applied to various forms of nursing practice education.

This study proposes an interaction method for clinical nursing skill education with telepresence using multimodal inputs in immersive VR. The detailed contributions are as follows:

1. Improve the sense of realism by using the learner's multimodal (hand gestures and speech) inputs with a high degree of freedom for learning clinical nursing skills.
2. Analyze the learner's verbal or non-verbal expressions in detail by focusing not only on the flow of nursing skills but also on the details of the performance process; this is done to establish the evaluation method and timing of the interactions performance for the nursing skills depending on the learning objectives.
3. Seek to improve the learning effect by providing not only immediate feedback, but also accumulated feedback (e.g., quizzes or additional missions).

The structure of this study is as follows. First, Sect. 2 confirms related prior research, while Sect. 3 explains the interaction method for the proposed clinical nursing practice simulation. Experiments and evaluations using the proposed interaction method are described in Sect. 4. Section 5 draws a conclusion.

2   Related Works

2.1   Realistic Interaction Input

There are many technologies and studies using VR to teach practical nursing skills [2, 3]. Chen's study showed that only 'Knowledge' among a learner's Knowledge, Skills, Satisfaction, Confidence, and Performance Time was effective in nursing education using VR, but 'Skills' was not effective [3]. The reason is considered to be that the situation and environment in VR did not successfully emulate reality when performing 'Skills' [3]. Therefore, to learn subdivided nursing skills in immersive VR, interaction with an environment closer to the real environment is required, and it is important that the learner's inputs are similar to ones used in reality. In this case, to learn detailed nursing skills, both non-verbal and verbal expressions (e.g., conveying information and explaining prescriptions to patients) should be made so that nursing supplies can be utilized or contact with patients can be experienced [15, 16].

In Ubisim's immersive VR, learners can actually select a scenario to learn non-verbal skills, and a platform has been developed to allow learners to enter clinical situations to perform interactions using controllers within a safe and standardized environment [2, 17]. However, in this technology, even if a VR controller is used only to approach a virtual object, hand gestures are arbitrarily changed to suit the relevant skill, and the interaction is often performed as it is. In this case, the sense of realism of the input itself when using a controller decreases, and it is limited for detailed learning, such as hand gestures [17]. Next, it is necessary to conduct verbal training for communication with patients and guardians; this is a soft skill that must be covered when teaching nursing skills [8, 16].

Therefore, in this study, unlike in previous studies, learners' NUIs are used as multi-modal inputs to make non-verbal and verbal training similar to a real-life environment. Specifically, learners use their bare hands to make contact with virtual patients in VR. Moreover, a non-verbal interaction input is used to learn detailed parts, such as hand gestures and speed, when holding virtual objects. Furthermore, using speech as an input enables verbal learning, such as explaining nursing skills to patients and explaining a patient's current condition. Additionally, to make it more similar to real clinical nursing situations, each input modality is not forced to proceed only sequentially when nursing skills are in progress; instead, learners have the freedom to use interactive inputs (within boundaries that do not exceed learning errors).

2.2 Nursing Skill Performance Evaluation

This paper seeks to improve the learning effect by differentiating the evaluation method and timing of the nursing skill performance according to the learning subject and purpose of nursing skills. Specifically, according to Radianti's study, when creating content for education using immersive VR, a gap is formed when mapping between a theoretical learning subject and the actual skills-based application of that knowledge [18]. In particular, it is necessary to reduce this difference when creating educational programs for areas that require learning various non-verbal and linguistic elements, such as nursing education. Therefore, in this paper, considering all the non-verbal and verbal matters required for learning nursing skills, a method for determining the nursing skill performance was applied. Accordingly, it sought to reduce the difference between the subjects to be theoretically learned and the nursing skills that the learner would actually perform in VR.

Regarding the timing of the evaluation of the nursing skill performance, a study by Bjørk et al. confirmed that, when providing patients with information about the nursing skills being performed, the fact that they have been provided this information is not the only important matter; the timing at which such information is provided to patients is also important [19]. This means that the point at which the learner recognizes that they have performed nursing skills differs depending on the subject to be learned for each nursing skill. Additionally, according to a study by Dubovi et al., not only the overall flow but also the step-by-step details were considered important conditions for successful nursing skill performance [20]. Therefore, in this paper, the learner's nursing skill performance was evaluated by focusing on the overall flow or details of each skill, according to the learning objectives, instead of simply looking at whether or not the learner accomplished their goal.

2.3 Feedback of Nursing Skills

Prior research that evaluated the effectiveness of training using VR emphasized the need for feedback that is similar to a real environment, which can be achieved by combining various forms of feedback (e.g., visual and auditory feedback) to learners on the VR training platform [21]. It also implies that, with VR education, more in-depth learning is possible by examining the actions performed by learners themselves (either auditory or visual actions) [21]. This training method serves not only as a training evaluation method of VR-based simulations for learners, but also provides additional learning opportunities for them [21].

The study by Hara et al. provides feedback on learners' behavior by changing the overall background color [22]. In the case of a wrong behavior, the background color is adjusted to a red color to inform learners of their mistakes [22]. However, those who participated in the preceding studies responded that such feedback made it difficult for them to recognize their own mistakes and that it lacked a sense of realism [22]. Also, there was an opinion from participants that the patient avatar should speak out and exhibit a response [22]. Therefore, in this paper, objects that learners interact with (e.g., virtual patients and virtual nursing supplies) provide direct feedback to increase the sense of realism and allow learners to experience realistic results.

Tan et al.'s study further tests learners' knowledge and problem-solving skills by providing them with several mini-games. Games related to the situation are provided so that learners can focus on the situation at hand (e.g., selecting the appropriate equipment to proceed with a transfusion) [23]. Learners must present the correct answer in the game to proceed to the next nursing skill level [23]. The results according to the learners' correct answers are provided as immediate feedback (e.g., in a game about reporting a blood transfusion reaction, feedback on an appropriate communication structure with the doctor is provided) [23]. However, in the preceding study, since the nursing skills learners used to conduct simulations were game-based, the learners' degree of freedom was low and there was a limit to self-learning the overall flow. To optimize clinical competency, additional missions (e.g., mini-games and practical simulations) should be used in tandem appropriately [23]. Therefore, this paper proposes an interaction method in which learners can learn all the overall flow and details while performing their own skills. This further enhances problem-solving skills through additional mission and increases understanding through repetitive learning.

3 Method

3.1 Overview

The overall structure required for making an interaction method for clinical nursing education, as proposed in this study, is shown in Fig. 2. The unit of the proposed interaction method is largely composed of a series of flows that determines the method and timing of evaluating the learner's nursing skill performance (sub-activity recognizer, nursing skill performance evaluator). This series depends on the learner's input type and learning objectives according to the type of nursing skills and feedback (feedback generator). At this time, the individual nursing skill described in this paper is not only made up of a learner's single speech input or hand gesture (sub-activity), but it also consists of several speech inputs and natural hand gestures in time sequence (similar to the experience at a real clinical site) to evaluate the nursing skill performance (activity).

Fig. 2. Overview of the nursing skill method (white box: data state, gray box: processing module).

3.2   Realistic Interaction Input

For learners to learn nursing skills in immersive VR with a sense of realism, input methods like emotional support, information delivery, and nursing intervention were selected. To learn nursing skills, it is important that both verbal and non-verbal inputs are made [13, 24]. To achieve this, hand gestures that enable the use of nursing supplies and direct care for patients are used in this study to maximize the similarity with real clinical trials and to perform non-verbal nursing skills. Additionally, when performing verbal nursing skills, speech input that can intuitively pass information or provide emotional support is used.

To use hand gestures as a form of non-verbal input, collisions are specifically placed at each finger joint of a virtual object. Events following hand gestures are recognized by making contact with the corresponding nursing supplies or by collisions with a patient when using a certain pose of the fingers. At this time, fatigue increases if the learner has to learn the interaction for complicated hand gestures in advance [25]. In this study, to make realistic interactions possible while supplementing these points, hand gestures are composed of pinching and touching when interacting with virtual objects, such as virtual nursing supplies.

Linguistically, to remove noise and other elements that are unrelated to the learner's intention, the start and end of the speech input are specified with hand gestures so that the learner can determine when they want to speak.

3.3   Evaluation of Nursing Skill Performance (Sub-activity Recognizer, Nursing Skill Evaluator)

Selection of Method for Determining Nursing Skill Performance
Depending on the training purpose, the process of performing nursing skills can be analyzed according to the verbal and non-verbal behavior received from learners. Specifically, the learner's verbal and non-verbal inputs are recognized with the concept of a

sub-activity, which is a detailed action (e.g., a single hand gesture or a speech sentence) as outlined in Fig. 3. Furthermore, the learner's verbal and non-verbal behavioral units (i.e., sub-activities) are arranged in a nursing skill list (activity list) that is analyzed sequentially for nursing skill performance evaluation. Additionally, the evaluation result is derived as shown in Fig. 4.

Learning Non-verbal Nursing Skills. Both contact and hand gestures with virtual objects generated in the process of performing nursing skills directly on a patient using a nursing supply or indirectly through a caregiver are included and recorded. For example, [nursing skill] when a drug needs to be mixed in the process of inserting a catheter into a patient, [sub-activity] the process also includes the contact between virtual objects, such as when picking up a virtual drug reagent and taking it to the catheter.

Learning Verbal Nursing Skills. To determine whether verbal nursing skills are performed, there is a limit to organizing all the words in the sentences spoken by the learner for a certain period of time in the nursing skill list. For this reason, the information provided to the patient or caregiver goes through a delivery parser (database of information) and a parser that can analyze emotional support (database of emotional support). The recognized data (sub-activity) is sequentially organized in the nursing skill list (activity list). When verbal nursing skills, such as the analysis of emotional support and delivery of nursing information, were performed intuitively, a word-based recognition method was applied to the speech inputs to enhance the sense of realism, making it closer to real clinical nursing. In this way, it is possible to accurately convey the nursing situation and the name of the nursing supply for accurate delivery of information, or to classify and evaluate expressions indicating emotional support. Specifically, by analyzing the sentences of the speech input spoken by the learner in units of words, the words for delivering information required for the relevant skill and the word module representing the expression of emotional support are divided to evaluate whether successful performance has taken place. For example, [nursing skill] in the process of explaining the prescribed drug to a patient, [sub-activity] we can assume a situation where the learner says to a virtual patient, "This drug is an antibiotic. Have your child take this drug three times a day after meals. You can do well, so you don't have to be anxious." At this time, words such as "antibiotics" and "three times a day after meals" are understood as performing the delivery of information (subdivided into drug explanation and dosage method) through the information delivery parser. In contrast, words such as "well" and "anxious" are analyzed as the performance of emotional support through the parser that determines the type of emotional support.

Selection of Timing for Evaluating Nursing Skill Performance

Since the elements that need to be focused on are different for each skill, the timing of the nursing skill performance evaluation was divided into two types according to the characteristics of the skill. There are skills in which it is important to understand the overall flow, and there are also cases where details such as drug dose and injection angle are the purpose of the training when performing a skill [19, 20]. Therefore, to equip learners with the appropriate clinical nursing skills, this study evaluates whether the

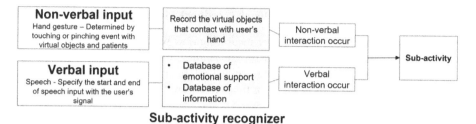

Sub-activity recognizer

Fig. 3. Method of the sub-activity recognizer.

nursing skills have been correctly performed by varying the timing of the evaluation of the nursing skill according to the training objective of each nursing skill.

Learning the Flow of Skills. For nursing skills where learners' understanding of the overall process is important, the timing of the evaluation is determined when learners have finished inputting all interactions. Here, the evaluation checks if the order of the sub-activities received as input is incorrect or if sub-activities that should not have been performed are included. For instance, [nursing skill] when learners are learning skills such as how to turn off the infusion pump (add sub-activities to activity list), the evaluation ensures that they have become familiar with the overall flow (analysis of activity list), from turning off the power button (sub-activity 1) to closing the 3-way stopcock (sub-activity 2) and clamp (sub-activity 3).

Learning the Details of Skills. When learners need to learn the details of a given skill, it is necessary to evaluate whether the interactions (sub-activity) taking place to perform one skill are correct every time they are inputted. For [nursing skill] intravenous injection, [sub-activity] for which the injection angle is important (analysis of sub-activity), it is necessary to determine whether the injection area is disinfected with an alcohol swab and also evaluate (simple action) whether the injection needle (IV catheter) is correctly inserted at an angle of 30° or less (detail of nursing skill).

The overall description of the evaluation of nursing skill performance can be seen in Fig. 4.

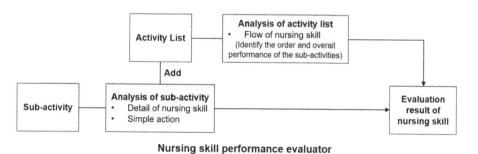

Nursing skill performance evaluator

Fig. 4. Method of the nursing skill performance evaluator.

3.4   Nursing Skill Performance Feedback (Feedback Generator)

By providing appropriate feedback after measuring how well the learner achieved the learning objectives in clinical nursing skills education, the student's learning effect can be improved to achieve a deeper level of learning [26]. In this regard, this paper provides feedback in appropriate ways at the right times to ensure that the learners perform the nursing skills correctly.

Feedback Method

Feedback Through Nursing Supplies, Patient and Caregiver's Reaction. When   a learner performs a nursing skill on virtual patient using virtual nursing supplies, feedback on the applicable performance is provided through the subject to which the learners are applying the interaction. For example, [nursing skill] in turning off an infusion pump and IV catheter removal, [sub-activity] when removing a tape to fix the catheter, if learners do not support it using both hands or if they remove it too quickly, they are provided with a warning sound that this is not the correct action. Additionally, they may receive feedback through the virtual patient's reaction (for instance, screaming). Also, if the learner presses onto the patient's body, changes in skin color can be seen.

Feedback Through Additional Missions. Additional missions are given when the learner needs to verify critical knowledge before performing nursing skills, or when the details of an individual skill are important. During additional missions, the learner repeatedly performs nursing skills and retraces their learning content to make sure it stays in the learner's memory longer. For example, [nursing skill] in antibiotic skin test (AST) preparation and testing, [sub-activity] when mixing a drug for AST or determining the exact dose, learners are required to perform additional learning through missions such as pop-up quizzes, as shown in Fig. 5(a).

Feedback on Confirmation of Performance via Text. In clinical nursing practice with immersive VR simulation, text is displayed to intuitively show the results of nursing skills performed by the learners, as shown in Fig. 5(b). Information that learners need to recognize (such as the elapsed time, patient call, interaction with a virtual object, etc.) can be easily and accurately recognized through text.

Feedback Timing

Feedback on Prompt Skills. Feedback is provided to learners when the immersive VR simulation is in progress so that they can correct mistakes and see the results of their nursing skill in real time. For example, after providing the learners with the dosage of the drug while dispensing the drug and the infusion pump's hourly infusion rate, etc. in the form of a pop-up quiz, feedback on the selected answer is immediately provided. This allows the learners to engage in repeated learning. In addition, by immediately providing feedback that is generated differently depending on the skill performed by the learners, learners can see the results of the nursing skills that they select.

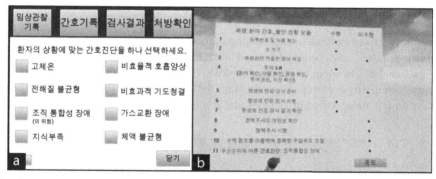

Fig. 5. Example of the feedback method. (a) Additional quiz and (b) performance checklist via text.

Feedback on the Accumulated Skills. By having learners accumulate nursing skills through the immersive VR simulation, they can experience a range of possible results. For example, in the process of drug administration to a patient according to a prescription, if an unexpected situation occurs (such as IV site swelling), the existing IV catheter can be removed from the patient. After the patient rests with an ice pack, the intravenous injection can be performed again according to how each accumulated nursing skill was performed. The learner experiences the swelling state of the patient's arm as final type of feedback. Through this, the learners can naturally learn the influence not only the influence among individual actions (sub-activities) but also the influence among accumulated nursing skills (activities). After completing all nursing interventions, feedback is provided on the most important key points within individual scenarios. By pointing out essential skills that the learners missed, learners can reflect on their clinical nursing performance and engage in self-directed learning.

The overall description of the determination of nursing skill performance feedback can be seen in Fig. 6.

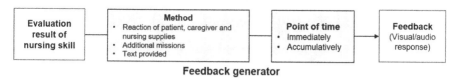

Fig. 6. Feedback generator for nursing skill.

3.5 Nursing Skill Implementation

Using the proposed method, several nursing skills were selected to implement as example interactions. The scenes being performed in the immersive VR for each skill are shown in Figs. 7 and 8. The input of the nursing skills, the method and timing of determining activity for nursing performance evaluation, the explanation of the feedback method, and the timing are specified in Tables 1 and 2.

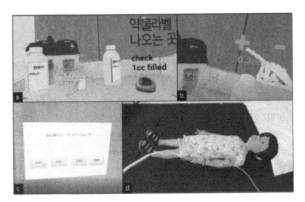

Fig. 7. Implementation of antibiotic skin tests (AST), (a) Sub-activity of dissolving antibiotics with normal saline, (b) sub-activity of filling a syringe to dilute antibiotics and normal saline according to the dose, (c) Quiz of the time lag between testing and interpretation, and (d) sub-activity of examination of the results on the AST (the volar forearm of the patient).

Fig. 8. Implementation of turning off the infusion pump and removing the IV catheter. (a) Sub-activity of stop IV infusion with clamp, (b) sub-activity of turning off the infusion pump, (c) sub-activity of disinfecting IV site, and (d) quiz for explaining the procedure to patient and caregiver.

Table 1. Implementation of preparations for antibiotic skin tests (ASTs).

Preparations for antibiotic skin tests (AST) & Performing an antibiotic skin tests (AST)					
Sub-activity	Input	Evaluation of **detailed activity or simple activity	Feedback on sub-activity (V: Visual response, A: Audio response)	Nursing skill evaluation	Nursing skill feedback
Perform hand hygiene	Hand disinfectant or basin touch	Acknowledge performance as soon as it is touched	V: Show text and water flows from the faucet	Evaluation of the overall flow	Proceed to the next detailed sub-activity through sequential progress
Dissolve antibiotics with normal saline	Pick up a syringe with a pinch gesture and overlap with saline solution and antibiotics	Acknowledge performance when in contact with a virtual object	V: Show text and dilution effects for each contact between objects		
Fill with syringe to dilute antibiotics and normal saline according to the dose	Adjust the amount of reagent solution by pressing a button	Touching "+" and "−" buttons related to the amount of antibiotics	V: Show an adjusted amount with the number		
		**Approve if antibiotics and normal saline solution are adjusted to a certain amount	V: Show performance completion status by text		
Adjust the drug concentration in the syringe for the test	Control by pressing a button to empty the syringe	Acknowledge when touching "+", "−" buttons to adjust the amount	V: Show an adjusted amount with the number		
		**Acknowledge performance when the drug concentration in the syringe for the test is properly adjusted	V: Show performance completion status by text		

(continued)

Table 1. (*continued*)

Preparations for antibiotic skin tests (AST) & Performing an antibiotic skin tests (AST)

Sub-activity	Input	Evaluation of **detailed activity or simple activity	Feedback on sub-activity (V: Visual response, A: Audio response)	Nursing skill evaluation	Nursing skill feedback
Identify patient	Use speech input to ask the patient for two identifiers (patient name and medical identification number), Compare the patient information on the AST order to the patient's ID band;	**Acknowledge when including the words associated with the name and medical identification number, and when touching the patient's ID band	A: Provide patient name and registration number from virtual patient V: Present patient information as patient ID band expand		
Provide information and emotional support related to AST	Explain the reason for the AST	**Acknowledge when including words related to the AST explanation	A: Provide the further questions or express understanding from the virtual caregiver		
	Provide emotional support to relieve anxiety for patient and caregiver	**Acknowledge when including words related to emotional support	A: Provide the answer from virtual caregiver		

Table 1. (*continued*)

Preparations for antibiotic skin tests (AST) & Performing an antibiotic skin tests (AST)					
Sub-activity	Input	Evaluation of **detailed activity or simple activity	Feedback on sub-activity (V: Visual response, A: Audio response)	Nursing skill evaluation	Nursing skill feedback
Re-confirm the patient information	Re-confirm patient information by speech and hand gesture	**Acknowledge if words include patient name and registration number	A: Provide the answer from the virtual patient V: Present the patient information as the patient ID band expand		
Complete intradermal injection	Disinfect the area with an alcohol swab	Contact the patient's arm with an alcohol swab	V: Show text		
	Inserting an IV catheter at the tip of a syringe into the skin	**Insert an IV catheter at the tip of a syringe into the patient's arm within 30°	V or A: If the insertion angle is within 30°, the completion text is presented; otherwise, Patient's screams is provided		
Communicate about precautions the AST	Explain the condition after the AST	**Acknowledge if words include appropriate explanation related to the conditions after the AST	A: Provide the answer from virtual caregiver & V: quiz of the time lag between testing and interpretation		

Table 2. Implementation of turning off an infusion pump and IV catheter removal

Turning off an infusion pump and IV catheter removal

Sub-activity	Input	Evaluation of **detailed activity or simple activity	Feedback on sub-activity (V: Visual response, A: Audio response)	Nursing skill evaluation	Nursing skill feedback
Provide information of the procedure to the patient and the caregiver	Use speech input to explain the procedure of the nursing skill	**Acknowledge if speech includes words like "injection", "I will remove", and other precautions after removing the injection	A: Provide the answer from the virtual patient	Evaluation of the overall flow	Text and beep to notify that the sequence is not correct if the sequence is not followed
Turn infusion pump off	Touch the power button on the infusion pump	Acknowledge performance when the learner's hand is in contact with a virtual object	A: Provide sound feedback when the correct location is touched		
stop IV infusion with clamp	Touch the clamp of the IV tubing	Acknowledge when the learner's hands are in contact with a virtual object	V: Reposition the pulley wheel when the clamp is touched in the correct direction		
Remove IV fixation tape	Lift by overlapping with the fixing tape and using a pinching gesture	Acknowledge when the IV fixation tape is no longer in contact with the virtual patient	V: Virtual tape removal		

(*continued*)

Table 2. (*continued*)

Turning off an infusion pump and IV catheter removal

Sub-activity	Input	Evaluation of **detailed activity or simple activity	Feedback on sub-activity (V: Visual response, A: Audio response)	Nursing skill evaluation	Nursing skill feedback
		**If it is above a certain speed, it is evaluated to be too fast	A: If it is evaluated to be too fast, a warning sound and sounds of a screaming patient are provided		
		**Acknowledge if the other hand of the learner overlaps with the patient's arm when one hand of the learner pinches the virtual tape	A: Warning sound is provided if not supported by both hands		
Prepare for IV catheter removal	Pinch alcohol swab and place it at the IV site	Acknowledge performance when virtual alcohol swab is in contact with the virtual patient's arm			
Remove the IV catheter	Pinch the catheter and remove it	Acknowledge performance when the virtual catheter is no longer in contact with the virtual patient	V: Remove the catheter that was fixed to the patient's arm		

(*continued*)

Table 2. (*continued*)

Turning off an infusion pump and IV catheter removal

Sub-activity	Input	Evaluation of **detailed activity or simple activity	Feedback on sub-activity (V: Visual response, A: Audio response)	Nursing skill evaluation	Nursing skill feedback
		**If it is above a certain speed, it is evaluated to be too fast	A: If it is evaluated to be too fast, a warning sound and a screaming of the patient are provided		
Compress IV removal site	After pinching the alcohol swab, press the IV removal site	Acknowledge performance when virtual alcohol swab is in contact with the virtual patient's arm			
Attach the bandage	Pinch the bandage and attach it at the IV removal site	Acknowledge performance when in contact with the virtual bandage and the virtual patient's arm	V: Fix the virtual bandage on the patient's arm		

4 Experiments

4.1 Pilot Study

To confirm the effect of when the learner studied nursing skills in immersive VR using the method proposed in this study, a pilot study was conducted. This pilot study was conducted while wearing an HTC Vive Pro and implementing a clinical nursing practice simulation in an immersive virtual environment with Unreal Engine 4. The user's direct hand movements received images from the camera on the front of the HTC Vive Pro, and hand pose information was acquired in the user's first-person view using HTC Vive's Hand Tracking SDK. The speech was analyzed using the deep learning-based Google Speech to Text API after receiving the user's speech input through the Google Speech Kit. Further, using the Text to Speech API, the audio of the virtual object was provided to the learners. User evaluation is one method that can be used to check whether the developed interaction method should be applied to actual nursing education. In this way, the possibility of generalization can be identified. Also, it can verify the utility of the design and implementation of the simulation content developed by this research for nursing practice.

Therefore, experiments were conducted on nursing students to understand the nature and limitations of the nursing simulation content and to provide an actual response. In the experiment, a scenario-based program was implemented so that learners could understand the patient's current condition and overall situation. The scenario involves the hospitalized children with pneumonia, and the scene is organized to show the status and prescription information of the patients. The scenario includes, "preparation and testing of antibiotic skin test (AST)" and "turning off an infusion pump and IV catheter removal", as the main skills. Study participants experience multi-modal interactions through 'audio response and hand movements' in the virtual ward as they speak to virtual patient and caregiver and perform nursing skills. The experiment was conducted with a total of eight people (five learners and three instructors) who had a Korean nurse certificate. All study participants performed a simulation including the relevant nursing skills after experiencing sufficient practice in VR for more than one hour. A brief survey and interview for the technical evaluation and learning effects were conducted after the experiment. The survey questions were constructed with reference to previous studies [27–29]; these are shown in Table 4. After completing the simulation, learners and instructors responded to the questions on a Likert 7-point scale for Q1 to Q4 and a Likert 9-point scale for Q5 in Table 4. Next, an interview about the simulation was conducted. In the case of instructors, to ensure that respondents had well-informed professional opinions, those who majored in nursing and had more than five years of educational career experience were selected. Semi-structured interviews were conducted with instructors and learners about the advantages, disadvantages, and improvement points of the proposed method. In the case of qualitative interviews, to confirm the practical strengths, weaknesses, and points of improvement of the developed VR content, the four open-ended questions used by Servotte et al. (2020) in their VR simulation study were revised and used; these are shown in Table 3 [30].

Table 3. Experimental interview statements.

Q1	What were your first impressions, thoughts, and feelings about the VR simulation experience?
Q2	What did you enjoy while experiencing VR simulation? What do you think is its strength?
Q3	What was the inconvenience while experiencing the VR simulation? What do you think is its weakness?
Q4	What could be improved in the future?

4.2 Results

Survey Evaluation

The results of the survey, related to the immersive VR simulation using the interaction method for clinical nursing practice suggested in this paper, are as shown in Table 4. The average of the all questions, respectively, were showing fairly high scores close to the each of the total scores. From this, we judged that the interaction method proposed in this paper worked good to the learners in VR clinical nursing practice. However, it was considered that the reason for the relatively low score compared to the rest of the questions was that the audio response of virtual patients and caregiver through text-to-speech may have felt unnatural. In the future, this will be improved by using pre-recorded voices of actual people for audio responses of virtual patients and caregivers.

Table 4. Experimental survey statements and results

	Questions	Mean(std)/total score
Q1	Were you able to predict what reaction would display depending on the sub-activity you performed?	5.42(1.50)/7
Q2	By the end of the virtual experience, how competent have you become in moving and interacting?	4.79(1.53)/7
Q3	Did the proposed solution provide a problem-solving opportunity?	5.33(1.23)/7
Q4	Is the feedback provided by the proposed method useful for patient care?	5.58(1.51)/7
Q5	Was the interaction between the sub-activity performed and the audio response appropriate?	4.63(2.32)/9

Instructor's Quality Evaluation

To the three instructors, the scenarios and main feedback functions for the proposed interaction method of the VR simulation content were explained. After experiencing the simulation using the HMD, the instructors provided feedback about the strengths, weaknesses, and potential improvement areas (by answering the questions in Table 3) of the interaction method; these results are shown in Table 5. As for strengths, there were opinions that by providing an experience similar to reality, it was possible to directly implement nursing skills and to experience communication with patients, caregivers and doctors. In addition, there were opinions that it was good to experience the results of the scenario differently and to receive feedback depending on the level of a learner's performance. Through this, it could be confirmed that, unlike preceding research that provided feedback outside the simulation or focused only on immediate response changes from the instructor's point of view, the quality of education can be improved by showing various types of feedback to learners according to the learning objectives [14]. As for areas for improvement, there were opinions about the lack of convenience of using the widget menu, although these could be addressed by providing more pre-practice time to participants who were not familiar with VR. The ability to operate individual virtual objects could be improved to allow the user to grasp or select objects in a variety of ways, which could be optimized according to individual preferences.

Table 5. Instructor's evaluation of the proposed method.

Division	Key opinion	Frequency (n = 3)
Strength	Providing opportunities for indirect experiences similar to reality	3
	Able to experience various communication experiences such as with guardians, patients, and doctors	3
	Hands-on nursing skills can be directly conducted	2
	No risk of patient safety in the event of a mistake	2
	The results of the scenario differ depending on the level of learner performance	3
	Nursing performance results can be viewed through the feedback window	2
Weakness	Difficult to operate hand movements	2
	Error in speech recognition	2
	The proportion of virtual objects in the virtual space is not correct	1
Areas of improvement	Conduct sufficient orientation and pre-practice on virtual object operation	3
	Secure a safe practice environment	2
	Improved convenience of using the widget menu	2

Learner's Qualitative Evaluation

The VR experience was conducted for a total of five learners. All of the learners were nursing students who graduated from nursing school in February 2021. The learner's qualitative evaluation results (Table 6) of the proposed method have been organized in terms of strengths, weaknesses, and improvements. The advantages suggested by the learners matched those of the instructors' qualitative evaluation. Learners felt they could perform nursing skills directly by hand and experience the whole process. There was also a majority opinion that the clinical site was well-implemented in a virtual environment, that it was possible to interact with a virtual guardian, and that additional questions or quizzes increased engagement. Through this, it was confirmed that it was possible to understand the details and the overall flow of the skills, going beyond learning only the overall flow, which was done in preceding research [17]. As for weaknesses and areas of improvement, similar to the results of the survey, there were opinions that it would be good to diversify the object's response and provide more realistic emotional audio feedback, as opposed to text-to-speech audio. There were also opinions about the difficulty of conducting interactions in VR. However, it is judged that this can be solved by providing sufficient practice for interaction, depending on the individual's VR skill level, before the learner directly carries out the immersive VR simulation.

Table 6. Learner's evaluation of the proposed method.

Division	Key opinions	Frequency (n = 5)
Strength	Performing nursing skills by hand and experiencing procedures firsthand	5
	An environment similar to a clinical site is well realized visually	4
	Being able to interact with virtual guardians	4
	Questions or quizzes of virtual objects increase engagement	3
	Feedback allows learners to take the performance assessment instantly	2
Weakness	Difficulty in manipulating virtual objects	4
	Focusing on the operation makes it difficult to concentrate on the practice contents	2
	Poor readability of communication text	1
Areas of improvement	Diversification of the response of virtual objects	4
	It would be nice if the audio of the virtual object could express emotions like a human	2

The proposed interaction method, which utilizes immersive VR for clinical nursing education, was implemented in an environment similar to an actual clinical site. According to the opinions of instructors and learners about the strengths of this method, nursing skills can be learned through VR experiences that are similar to real ones. Therefore, it is determined that the interaction method proposed in this study has high applicability to actual education settings.

5 Conclusion

In this study, an interaction method that allows learners to develop nursing skills by using hand movements and speech inputs in immersive VR is proposed. Unlike preceding research, learners interact and learn using NUI for both non-verbal and verbal inputs, depending on the target nursing skill they're trying to learn. The interaction is made possible by assigning degrees of freedom to the use of hand movements and speech modes, similar to those found in an actual clinical nursing environment. In addition, according to the purpose of the nursing skill training, the performance evaluation method of each nursing skill is determined. Furthermore, the corresponding performance evaluation timing is also suggested so that the overall skill flow can be grasped and details of the skill can be learned. Finally, feedback on nursing skills can be provided at an appropriate time (immediately or cumulatively), and the feedback method can be diversified to enhance the learning effect by providing additional missions, quizzes, and text results, as well as nursing supplies or patient and caregiver's responses. To confirm the effect of the proposed nursing skill method, from the learner's input to the feedback according to the nursing skill performance, different nursing skills were assessed. To do this, "antibiotic skin test (AST) preparation and testing" and "turning off an infusion pump and IV catheter removal" tests were implemented and analyzed in a pilot study. The applicability of the proposed method to actual education settings was also confirmed by conducting a brief questionnaire evaluation and qualitative interviews with both learners and instructors. Through this, it is judged that in the process of simulating nursing skills through immersive VR, it is possible to learn both the flow and the details of verbal/non-verbal nursing skills with a sense of realism, and to experience various forms of feedback within VR. In addition, it is believed that the proposed method can increase the learning effect by providing a sufficient environment for education, such as experiencing real-life results, without any physical or time restrictions for learners. However, there are still limitations (e.g. the response of virtual objects may feel unnatural and carrying out the training simulation may be difficult depending on the user's VR proficiency). Nonetheless, we believe that effective interaction in virtual space for nursing education will be possible by addressing these limitations in future.

Acknowledgments. This work was supported by the National Research Foundation of Korea (NRF) grant funded by the Korea government (MSIT; Ministry of Science and ICT) (No. 2020R1G1A1102709). This work was supported by the National Research Foundation of Korea (NRF) grant funded by the Korea government (MSIT) (NRF-2019R1A4A1029800).

References

1. Lim, K.C.: Directions of simulation-based learning in nursing practice education: a systematic review. J. Korean Acad. Soc. Nurs. Educ. **17**(2), 246–256 (2011)
2. https://www.ubisimvr.com/
3. Chen, F.-Q., et al.: Effectiveness of virtual reality in nursing education: meta-analysis. J. Med. Internet Res. **22**(9), e18290 (2020)
4. Medley, C.F., Horne, C.: Using simulation technology for undergraduate nursing education. J. Nurs. Educ. **44**(1), 31–34 (2005)

5. Bond, W.F., Spillane, L.: CORD core competencies simulation group. The use of simulation for emergency medicine resident assessment. Acad. Emerg. Med. **9**(11), 1295–1299 (2002)
6. Turcato, N., Robertson, C., Covert, K.: Simulation-based education: what's in it for nurse anesthesia educators? AANA J. **76**, 257–262 (2008)
7. Yu, M., Yang, M., Ku, B., Mann, J.S.: Effects of virtual reality simulation program regarding high-risk neonatal infection control on nursing students. Asian Nurs. Res. **15**(3), 189–196 (2021)
8. Plotzky, C., et al.: Virtual reality simulations in nurse education: a systematic mapping review. Nurse Educ. Today **101**, 104868 (2021)
9. Li, Y., Huang, J., Tian, F., Wang, H.-A., Dai, G.-Z.: Gesture interaction in virtual reality. Virtual Reality Intell. Hardw. **1**(1), 84–112 (2019)
10. Höll, M., Oberweger, M., Arth, C., Lepetit, V.: Efficient physics-based implementation for realistic hand-object interaction in virtual reality. In: 2018 IEEE Conference on Virtual Reality and 3D User Interfaces (VR), pp. 175–182 (2018)
11. Johnson-Glenberg, M.C.: Immersive VR and education: embodied design principles that include gesture and hand controls. Front Robot AI **5**, 81 (2018)
12. Breitkreuz, K.R., et al.: Nursing faculty perceptions of a virtual reality catheter insertion game: a multisite international study. Clin. Simul. Nurs. **53**, 49–58 (2021)
13. Chambers, S.: Use of non-verbal communication skills to improve nursing care. Br. J. Nurs. **12**(14), 874–878 (2003)
14. Bayram, S.B., Caliskan, N.: The use of virtual reality simulations in nursing education, and patient safety. In: Contemporary Topics in Patient Safety, vol. 1. IntechOpen (2020)
15. Weiss, S., et al.: Applications of immersive virtual reality in nursing education—a review. Clusterkonferenz Zukunft der Pflege—Innovative Technologien für die Praxis, Oldenburg (2018)
16. Kim, Y.-J., Ahn, S.-Y.: Factors influencing nursing students' immersive virtual reality media technology-based learning. Sensors **21**(23), 8088 (2021)
17. Choi, K.-S.: Virtual reality wound care training for clinical nursing education: an initial user study. In: 2019 IEEE Conference on Virtual Reality and 3D User Interfaces (VR), pp. 882–883 (2019)
18. Radianti, J., et al.: A systematic review of immersive virtual reality applications for higher education: design elements, lessons learned, and research agenda. Comput. Educ. **147**, 103778 (2020)
19. Bjørk, I.T., Kirkevold, M.: From simplicity to complexity: developing a model of practical skill performance in nursing. J. Clin. Nurs. **9**(4), 620–631 (2000)
20. Dubovi, I., Levy, S.T., Dagan, E.: Now I know how! The learning process of medication administration among nursing students with non-immersive desktop virtual reality simulation. Comput. Educ. **113**, 16–27 (2017)
21. Xie, B., et al.: A review on virtual reality skill training applications. Front. Virtual Reality **2**, 49 (2021)
22. Hara, C.Y.N., et al.: Design and evaluation of a 3D serious game for communication learning in nursing education. Nurse Educ. Today **100**, 104846 (2021)
23. Tan, A.J.Q., et al.: Designing and evaluating the effectiveness of a serious game for safe administration of blood transfusion: a randomized controlled trial. Nurse Educ. Today **55**, 38–44 (2017)
24. Nishizawa, Y., et al.: The non-verbal communication skills of nursing students: analysis of interpersonal behavior using videotaped recordings in a 5-minute interaction with a simulated patient. Japan J. Nurs. Sci. **3**(1), 15–22 (2006)
25. Cheema, N., et al.: Predicting mid-air interaction movements and fatigue using deep reinforcement learning. In: Proceedings of the 2020 CHI Conference on Human Factors in Computing Systems, pp. 1–13 (2020)

26. Chang, Y.M., Lai, C.L.: Exploring the experiences of nursing students in using immersive virtual reality to learn nursing skills. Nurse Educ. Today **97**, 104670 (2021)
27. Witmer, B.G., Singer, M.J.: Measuring presence in virtual environments: a presence questionnaire. Presence **7**(3), 225–240 (1998)
28. Wotton, K., et al.: Third-year undergraduate nursing students' perceptions of high-fidelity simulation. J. Nurs. Educ. **49**(11), 632–639 (2010)
29. Grierson, L., et al.: Simulation-based education and the challenge of transfer. In: Clinical Simulation, pp. 115–127. Academic Press (2019)
30. Servotte, J.C., et al.: Virtual reality experience: immersion, sense of presence, and cybersickness. Clin. Simul. Nurs. **38**, 35–43 (2020)

D-WISE Tool Suite for the Sociology of Knowledge Approach to Discourse

Gertraud Koch[1] 📍, Chris Biemann[2] 📍, Isabel Eiser[1(✉)] 📍, Tim Fischer[2] 📍,
Florian Schneider[2] 📍, Teresa Stumpf[1] 📍, and Alejandra Tijerina García[1] 📍

[1] Institute of Anthropological Studies in Culture and History, University of Hamburg,
Grindelallee 46, 20146 Hamburg, Germany
{gertraud.koch,isabel.eiser,teresa.strumpf,
alejandra.tijerina.garcia}@uni-hamburg.de
[2] Department of Informatics, Language Technology Group (LT), University of Hamburg,
Vogt-Kölln-Straße 30, 22527 Hamburg, Germany
{chris.biemann,tim.fischer,florian.schneider-1}@uni-hamburg.de

Abstract. Under the umbrella of the D-WISE project, manual and digital
approaches to discourse analysis are combined to develop a prototypical working
environment for digital qualitative discourse analysis. This new qualitative data
analysis tool, called D-WISE Tool Suite, is built up in a process of close exchange
by the two teams from humanities and informatics and focuses on developing
central innovations regarding the availability of relevant Digital Humanities (DH)
applications. Bridging the gap between structural patterns detected with digital
methods and interpretative processes of human meaning making is at the core
of the collaborative approach of anthropological studies and computer linguistics
in the D-WISE project, which innovates both informatics technology of context-
oriented embedding representations and hermeneutic methodologies for discourse
analysis in the Sociology of Knowledge Approach to Discourse (SKAD). In this
paper, the intertwining of the two paradigms Human-in-the-loop and AI-in-the-
loop will be presented by outlining the concept of Human Computer Interaction
(HCI) in the D-WISE Tool Suite with its AI-empowered features and established
modes of feedback-loops and the supported functions for facilitating SKAD.

Keywords: Human Computer Interaction · Discourse analysis ·
Human-in-the-loop · AI-in-the-loop · User stories

1 Introduction

The research project D-WISE is a close collaboration of an interdisciplinary team of
researchers with the humanities represented by the Institute of Anthropological Studies in Culture and History and Information Technologies represented by the Language
Technology Group at the Department of Informatics at the University of Hamburg.
Started in May 2021, the project aims to develop central innovations to address challenges researchers are facing with regard to methodological approaches from Digital
Humanities (DH) and discourse analysis and the increasing dealing with open corpora,

M. Rauterberg (Ed.): HCII 2022, LNCS 13324, pp. 68–83, 2022.
https://doi.org/10.1007/978-3-031-05434-1_5

consisting of heterogeneous, multimodal, and big data. To address these goals, under the umbrella of the D-WISE project, manual and digital approaches to discourse analysis are combined to develop a prototypical working environment for digital qualitative discourse analysis. This new qualitative data analysis tool, called D-WISE Tool Suite, is built up in a process of close exchange by the two teams from the humanities and informatics and focuses on developing central innovations regarding the availability of relevant DH applications. For improved modelling of the plurality of meaning and the integrated processing of multimodal data, contextualized embeddings are developed to expand the existing range of DH methods and support and enhance the research process via artificial intelligence (AI) supported functionalities and semi-automated processes. In a constant combination of manual analyses by human agents and its provided feedback loops, digital automated functions are simultaneously developed to the needs of the human scientists and the detected shortcomings in comparative critical analyses of existing tools. This methodological approach, called user stories, enable a constant exchange and trouble-free interdisciplinary collaboration, as well as reflexive, hermeneutic processes, and documentation of the discourse analysis. This interactive working mode manifested in the development of the D-WISE Tool Suite will be presented here as a methodological approach to combine manual and digital analytical methods in qualitative and quantitative social and cultural research facilitating also the epistemological reflection on relevance and validity of the gathered data and the hermeneutic processes. Therefore, while the approach focuses in a first step traditionally on Human-in-the-loop, in a later step AI-in-the-loop will be brought into focus again to support the user and the process of discourse analysis with digital solutions, algorithms, and AI. Originated directly in the research process, this circulation of agency in human and computer interaction and the mutual backing, the enhancement of technical functionalities, and training abilities of the AI by humans, as well as the improvement of qualitative research processes of the humans by the AI-supported digital work environment, lays ground for a new approach of reciprocal influence, enhancement, and reflective processes.

For this paper, the intertwining of the two paradigms Human-in-the-loop and AI-in-the-loop will be presented by outlining the concept of Human Computer Interaction (HCI) in the D-WISE Tool Suite with its AI-empowered features and diverse modes of feedback-loops and the supported functions for facilitating the methodological approach of the Sociology of Knowledge Approach to Discourse Analysis (SKAD) (Keller et al. 2018). The alignment of this methodological and technical innovation is based on the epistemological principles of Grounded Theory (GT) as a methodology for reducing the fast complexity of social settings in hermeneutic research and advances in informatics. Powered by state-of-the-art NLP models (natural language processing models), the D-WISE Tool Suite is designed with multimodal media as its core. AI-in-the-loop is considered a core principle when developing features, to allow for a novel AI-aided hermeneutic process where humans and machines benefit and learn from each other.

2   Project Overview

The D-WISE project aims to address the lack of digital solutions for multimodal discourse analyses with the capacity to cope with the multimodality of materials, the plurality and ambiguity of meanings, which all provide multiple challenges and complexities for digital solutions. Seeking to bridge the gap between structural patterns detected through digital methods and interpretative processes of human meaning making is at the heart of the collaborative approach of anthropological studies and computer linguistics in the project, which innovates both informatics technology of context-oriented embedding representations and hermeneutic methodologies for discourse analysis in SKAD. The D-WISE approach centers human-algorithm interactions, to improve AI research systems, which have an impact on the human research process and outcome. At the same time, SKAD addresses the challenge of coping with an ever-increasing number of digital materials on the Internet and beyond by enhancing the methodology through digital methods.

The epistemological reflection and further development of hermeneutic methodology in the use of semi-automated procedures is an integral part of the projects' elaboration on how automation can be usefully integrated into qualitative discourse-analytical approaches. Relevant tools for automated analyses are made available in a newly developed work environment that focuses methodologically on the SKAD discourse analytical approach and form a heterogeneous and multimodal material basis from different research contexts of the humanities. In the course of the project, the range of methods will be broadened by developing contextualized embeddings for improved modeling of meaning plurality and integrated processing of multimodal data. Methodological and technical innovations and reflection, combined with discourse analysis and GT as a hermeneutic methodology are aligned through constant and close collaborative exchange between the two teams from cultural anthropology and language technology.

2.1 Augmenting Capabilities: Of Humans and AI in the Loop

A major interest of the project is to contribute to a human-centered approach, which is a sign in AI development becoming stronger (Li and Hilliges 2021)[1]. In the center of this development, key questions are how humans and AI interact and in which way does this interaction aid human needs. One of the crucial places where this issue resides and the question determines if AI approaches are human-centered is "the loop," a most important component of learning systems. Loops are implemented for providing feedback, hence they are essential for learning by giving opportunity to correct, improve, and evaluate results in AI, as well as for human learning, for developing further information technologies and for humanities research.

Human-in-the-Loop. The Human-in-the-loop paradigm is closely linked to the concept of Interactive Machine Learning (IML), which can be defined as "algorithms that can interact with agents and can optimize their learnings behavior through these interactions, where the agents can also be human" (Holzinger 2016, p. 119). Even though interactions with both computational and human agents are important for optimizing the learning behavior of machines, it is mostly human expertise and the heuristic selections made through these interactions that supports automated processes. This is crucial in solving computational problems by giving feedback, through which the creation of training

---

[1] Li and Hilleges (2021, vi) point this out in their introduction with reference to the foundation of new institutes in Stanford, Maryland, Utrecht and the Technical University in Denmark.

materials for learning and occasionally for the development of so-called Gold Standard materials takes place. While most algorithm-in-the-loop settings still rely on a human decision maker to interpret and incorporate information, prioritizing the human's decision over the algorithms are processed as the most important outcome (Green and Chen 2019, p. 9). However, giving feedback to learning AI systems is mostly a repetitive, boring, and often unpaid task for human minds; solving Captchas queries for training image recognition, monitoring tags of automated annotations or automatically selected patterns to feed the data hunger of AI systems and give important feedback to the machine, offer but hardly any benefit for people performing these tasks. At best, the benefits for humans in human-in the-loop approaches come indirectly (Krishna et al. 2021) or in a figurative sense of efficiently working AI systems. However, the Human-in-the-loop paradigm is not synonymous with human-centered AI as we can observe through the example of the autonomous vehicle; in real-life situations bringing humans-**out**-of-the-loop is essential for saving lives, even though a very challenging undertaking (Holzinger 2016, p. 120).

AI-in-the-Loop. The second way of organizing feedback for learning puts AI-systems in the loop of human learning and thus shifts human-machine-interaction towards a paradigm of hybrid intelligent systems. "We define hybrid intelligence (HI) as the combination of human and machine intelligence, augmenting human intellect, and capabilities instead of replacing them and achieving goals that were unreachable by either humans or machines" (Akata et al. 2020, p. 18). Including AI-in-the-loop for giving feedback to human research and knowledge production alongside the established Human-in-the-loop paradigm, we get a hybrid knowledge system by organizing iterative feedback processes, which allow for mutual benefit for both humans and AI systems (Oeste-Reiß et al. 2021) (Fig. 1).

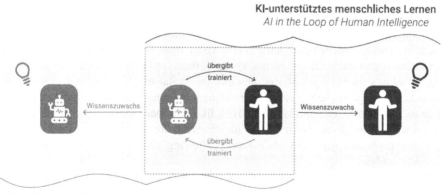

Fig. 1. Hybrid knowledge production system; Source: Oeste-Reiß et al. 2021, 149.

2.2   Prototype

The D-WISE Tool Suite is currently implemented as a web-based server architecture on the basis of already successfully established DH methods and the parallel processing by researchers from humanities and informatics, and will be accessible in open access. As a web-based annotation tool with machine learning components, the D-WISE Tool Suite offers a process that is "interactive, as it suggests annotations that can be accepted, rejected or corrected by the annotator, whereby machine learning gets better in time" (Yimam et al. 2017). The Tool Suite supports all SKAD steps – from the specification of the research phenomenon to the evaluation and its documentation. This research process is technically developed as a cyclic process, adaptable, and reusable, therefore corresponding to a hermeneutic circle, which, with repeated questioning and constant expansion of the state of knowledge, leads in repeat to new questions, insights, and, as a consequence, to a deeper understanding of the phenomenon.

As a prototype, the D-WISE Tool Suite will initially be implemented with a SKAD of current discourses on digitization in the healthcare sector and the associated data protection issues. The discourses in the course of new legal regulations will be examined with regard to the actors and groups of actors involved, in particular patients, physicians, clinics, health insurance companies, companies, interest groups, and politics. For this purpose, represented discourse positions will be analyzed on the basis of information available online and supplementary ethnographically collected data. Based on this, the usability of the D-WISE Tool Suite for scientists from different disciplines will be evaluated and further developed within the framework of a fellow program.

2.3   Digital Tools and Hermeneutics in SKAD

Digital tools for organizing and annotating research data, such as Excel in the simplest form, or data analysis programs such as MaxQDA Atlas.ti, NVivo, or CATMA, can offer a useful and supportive addition in discourse analysis, in quantitative and especially qualitative data analysis and data coding following GT: the discovery of social structures or describing cultural phenomena in the social world through coding processes, which in turn should reveal theoretical concepts, visualize them, and thus make them understandable. Moreover, in the light of vast amounts of digital materials, digital tools invite researchers to explore their capacity by offering additional tool functions for structural analyses and distant reading (Moretti 2013), like sentiment analysis, visualizations of word distributions, discursive trends as identified by the 'topic finder,' word frequencies, word co-occurrences, and others more – allowing new possibilities for insights in discourse analysis.

With the integration of IT tools and infrastructures into the knowledge production in the humanities, ontological changes take place in the knowledge production; new social, ethical, and political constellations are consolidated, disturbed, or created (Koch 2018, p. 71). Complex human-computer interaction become part of research processes, which may only be understood sufficiently in phenomenological-descriptive and ethical-normative respects (Fritz et al. 2020, p. 3). Moreover, a challenge of digital approaches still is, that "[c]reativity is supposedly reduced to choices of possibilities selected by programs, causing independent new creations to disappear from the horizon of possi-bilities in the humanities production of insight" (Koch 2018, p. 69)[2]. The integration of structural approaches into the qualitative hermeneutical approach of SKAD can be understood as an infrastructuring for social and cultural research, and thus has the prob-lematic aspect that "people's discursive and work practices get hustled into standard form" (Koch 2018, p. 70)[3]. It also raises methodological and epistemological issues in studying social reality, which will be addressed and embedded into the development of the D-WISE Tool Suite.

The SKAD works in circular processes or hermeneutic circles of search, selection, analysis, and interpretation of research data, supported by literature work, performed iteratively until the research question is answered (Carter et al. 2020, pp. 255–256)[4]. These basic operations prepare the ground for the intertwining of hermeneutic epistemic processes of SKAD with the structural methods provided by digital tools assembled in the D-WISE Tool Suite.

The HCI-concept in D-WISE seeks to bridge the gap between the manual hermeneu-tic process and an AI-guided research process enhancing the human hermeneutic process.

3 The HCI Concept in D-WISE

By focusing on building a working environment for integrating digital methods into discourse analysis through an approach in which scholars have an active say in the creation of specific features, can integrate their ways of thinking, and doing discourse analysis, the creation of the D-WISE Tool Suite goes beyond tailoring its features and usability to researchers in the humanities by adapting it to different styles of doing SKADs. The consideration of a variety of styles is a particularly challenging task for HCI design; epistemological specifics, different levels of practice and experience matter. The bandwidth of varying requirements will be tackled in the project's development through continuous feedback loop mechanisms from different angles.

Bringing not only the human but also AI in the loop alternately in the loop, means that human research processes of data acquisition, analysis, and interpretation can be enhanced by AI as well as AI processes can be enhanced by human interaction in combi-nation with machine learning processes. The mutual assistance between human actors as well as AI can act as an ethical control body to avoid the use and development of biased features that lead to stereotypical or discriminatory use and outcome in process of data analysis. Centering Human-in-the-loop and approaching the tool suite development via a) the user stories and b) the fellow program as a link between qualitative and quanti-tative research, between manual and digital research, can help gaining a more nuanced understanding of relationships and connections, of infrastructures between human and technological components (Koch 2018: 71).

---

[2] Koch points this out with reference to Evans 2012.

[3] Koch is referring to Bowker and Star 2004.

[4] Carter et al. on hermeneutic literature review, here with reference to Boell & Cecez-Kecmanovic, 2014.

While the user stories are mainly implemented to support the software development, the following fellow program is created to support the development process as well as the research process after successful implementation of the tool. In a testing phase before and while the fellow program is going on, tutorials and questionnaires will be implemented to not only guide the human through the analysis process, but to similarly reflect the individual user experience and enhance not the user's analysis. By using the tutorials and questionnaires, the human in contrast improves the AI's guiding characteristics, as the machine will learn through these tutorials and about the priorities the researcher sets for the individual research project.

The following sections will guide through the HCI Concept in D-WISE, acknowledging first the human in D-WISE followed by a focus on the strategies putting AI-in-the-loop in the D-WISE project. The latter will give a more practical insight into development process, working mode, and tool features of the Tool Suite, focusing on semi-automated processes of filtering.

3.1   The Human in D-WISE

With the methodological approach of the user stories the D-WISE project cross-disciplinary and collaboratively analyses what the existing tools lack in functions and functionalities and what must be improved to improve the working experience and outcome.

Several Qualitative Text Analysis Tools are available but are often neglected by users. Many tools cannot cope with big data without getting cluttered, because data management systems lack functionality and clarity. Furthermore, users need an extensive technical understanding not only of digital tools in general but especially for the individual tool in use. Workshops, Tutorials and Labs must be studied to get to understand the possibilities of the individual work. Important functionalities are hidden and not transparent in their implementation, what stops many scientists to use them, while it is not possible to describe the process of the digital research and its outcomes and therefore to assure scientific standards.

Even in the process of a critical as well as uncritical user experience or analysis of the usage of a qualitative analysis tool, an improvement and sharpening of the research question and process is happening. The same way a focused or changing research question changes the perspective, reading and outcome of text work and research, in a similar way AI exercises influence on the researcher and the research process. While AI can have a deep impact on manual research, this impact can be experienced both positively as well as negatively[5]. By adapting and improving selected features by building a new web-based tool suite, user stories are implemented in the research process. While there is still the user in the loop, which is the dominant paradigm in AI development, in the D-WISE concept the actors in the loop are switching, so that in a next step thus the AI will be in the loop.

User Stories. Existing Qualitative Data Analysis (QDA) software offer a reference frame for further development of QDA functionalities and tools. They give insight into

---

[5] How do computers influence its users by its categorization, stereotypically, gender disparate or even racist presets via biased trainings by humans? See Rodwell in this panel (preprint).

technical possibilities, which functions have proven as useful and demanded and which trends are followed (Schäffer et al. 2021, p. 3)[6].

A key strategy to put the human in the center and to develop the DWTS in a cross-field approach is the applied model of user stories, which furthermore enables the link between manual and digital analysis and as link between quantitative and qualitative analysis. Guided questions are designed to ensure users attention and enhance the reflection process. The template structure for creating user stories follows three key elements: the who, the what, and the why; these fundamental dimensions are then spelled out as "*As a <role>, I want <goal> so that <benefit>*" (Wautelet et al. 2014, pp. 211–212). To articulate informed and productive user stories, comparative, critical analysis and reflection of work experience with existing QDA tools and their missing or insufficient functionalities represents a key element and initial step. Having tested other digital platforms available, both commercially (e.g. MAXQDA, atlas.ti) and open source (e.g. CATMA, WebAnno), different functions and features that could be of interest where listed and categorized. The categories currently in use are general, search, acquisition, coding, reflection, and analysis – all key elements when applying discourse analytical methodology. A few examples of these are:

Category: Acquisition – I would also like to add social media input into my corpus, for example tweets
Category: Reflection – I would like to have an overview of all the work achieved in one session and create a memo reflecting on this
Category: Analysis – I would like to obtain statistics on my search results

This working process, research patterns and coding strategies develop in a tight-knit working modus between the Human Sciences and Computer Technologies teams. The feedback-mechanisms thus acquired have allowed an informed and efficient analysis for adapting human scientists' needs in combination with a technical feasibility analysis that enhances digital support of discourse analytical methodology. Centering Human-in-the-loop and approaching the tool suite development via user stories as a link between qualitative and quantitative research, between manual and digital research, can help gain a more nuanced understanding of relationships and connections – infrastructures between human and technological components (Koch 2018, p. 71).

Making the System Robust for Different Users. While the needs of discourse analytics in Human Sciences differ widely, the approach is extended to another level of putting Human-in-the-loop – via consultation of extended researchers from different disciplines. User stories after tool development[7] will be maintained through the realization of the fellow program, where user stories from different research areas will be developed, analyzed and implemented in the further software development.

While the ways of doing a discourse analytics in Human Sciences differ widely, the approach is extended to another level of putting the Human-in-the-loop – via consultation

---

[6] Schäffer refers here to Manovich 2013, p. 29.
[7] See paper by Binder et al. in this panel (preprint).

of extended researchers from different disciplines. Hence, the DWTS will enhance its feedback mechanisms by the implementation of a fellow program — Knowledge-related heterogenous user groups are involved in the software development.

The development of the D-WISE Tool Suite is a mixed method approach from top-down and bottom-up – collaborative efforts of the fellows shall lead to a work environment that works in different contexts, for different research questions and is built incrementally and focus on problem solution (Yimam et al. 2017, p. 6). The dialogue with the researchers from different disciplines will provide a system that enables a on a variety of tasks oriented tool suite and workflow that does not capture the worldview in ontologies based on the author but on the user (Schäffer et al. 2021, p. 3; Yimam et al. 2017). Additionally, a variety of user stories with different research questions may prevent the phenomenon of automated bias, where automated tools influence human decisions in significant, and often detrimental, ways (Green and Chen 2019, p. 2).

Guided questions shall be designed to ensure users attention and enhance the reflection process. The methodological approach can be enhanced by designing it as a digital tutorial, guiding the human user through a digital tutorial the user itself is advancing in process of working. At the end of the tutorial the user condensates the user experiences to the most important functionalities and oriented after the technical possibilities to realize the functions or to end the process of developing the tool because of technical limitations. This helps not only form a perspective of computer technology to understand what the human scientist need in discourse analytical processes, but also to detect missing and insufficient implementation and realization possibilities.

3.2   AI in D-WISE

Discourse analysis gets enriched by digital methods and features in Qualitative Data Analysis tools, such as topic modeling, co-occurrence analysis, sentiment analysis or by visualization of quantified discourses and patterns, which offer insights into trends and conjunctures, distribution of the usage of words over time. Digital methods also prove to be fruitful where they support the methodical guided reduction of large amounts of text as finding heuristics in the sense of filtering processes and serve the identification of potentially relevant data for manual processing. In this mode of human-computer interaction, the goal is also to constantly improve human analyses and the representations in the AI systems in the loop of our system, creating a win-win situation for both human understanding and training of the AI system. AI is in the loop of human analysis and supports human decision making instead of the human supporting the AI with intellectual monotonous tasks and reviews.

With D-WISE and the combined use of Human-in-the-loop and AI-in-the-loop, pointing to AI guided filter mechanisms and computer tools, efficiency or quality of hermeneutic analyses shall be improved. One main aspect to improve this hermeneutic work with AI is the AI guided process of material collection supporting the human in being able to process larger amounts of text by filtering processes.

Filtering. Potential for automatized processes and putting AI-in-the-loop to enhance manual research is relevant in several disciplines, as discourse analysis is a method used in different sectors of human and social sciences. Given the amount of data researchers can increasingly access via digitized archives, the need for technical solutions and digital tools for coping with these, in questions of collection, analysis, and interpretation, increases with this changing research process and access to born and made digital archival records.

For research processes on complex social realities require the methodologically guided reduction of research material to manageable excerpts by means of filters, filtering is therefore relevant (Koch and Franken 2020, p. 121). AI and algorithms in tools for qualitative discourse analyses offer automated functions for visualizations, coding, and the function of filtering (e.g. theoretical sampling, annotating, development of categories, simultaneous data expansion), supporting quantitative and qualitative analyses. Compared to the manual selection of a small case of resources for the close reading and deep analysis of qualitative data out of the big data, that can be used mainly for quantitative analyses, an automated system of filtering can mean a more efficient and possibly qualitatively enhanced process. Filtering as a method of epistemological reduction makes possible to condensate social reality into manageable excerpts by selecting discursive models representing a saturated cross-section of the most opposing/maximum different discursive statements (Koch and Franken 2020, pp. 124–126).

4 Language Technology: The D-WISE Tool Suite

4.1 Features

The D-WISE Tool Suite is developed since 2021 and designed on the basis of digital discourse analytical approach with focus on SKAD, where hermeneutic-circular methods, filtering and scalable reading are prevalent concepts. Further, AI-in-the-loop, multimodal and big data are core to the D-WISE project and, thus, are considered throughout the development of the tool's features.

There have been significant breakthroughs in various Computer Vision and Natural Language Processing tasks and AI models during the last few years. This progress in uni-modal models like BERT (Devlin et al. 2019) or GPT-3 (Brown et al. 2020) also led to a great leap forward in multimodal AI models, as scientists are starting to leverage these new insights to build models that work with two or more modalities simultaneously. State-of-the-art uni-modal and multimodal AI models like UNITER (Chen et al. 2020) or CLIP (Radford et al. 2021) enable the development of novel features enhancing the quality of (DH) research and allow the D-WISE Tool Suite to handle documents consisting of text, image, video, or audio data, or a mixture of all modalities.

4.2 Data Acquisition

To support the process of constantly building up the dossier of the discourse analysis, D-WISE Tool Suite offers an interface to upload local documents to a corpus or import online documents to the corpus by providing an URL. A more advanced technique is semantic crawling, which is an AI-powered, focused crawling process that — provided with thematic word lists, keywords, a topic, or even a document collection — retrieves relevant documents from the web. The process is developed in a way that users are able to reduce or extend the corpus in every stage of the work, following the hypothesis that corpus collection is never finished and an ongoing process changing parallel to the analysis process.

An interface is developed that allows to start and stop the semantic crawling process, to proofread the found documents, manually filter out bad results and add meta-information. Filtering out results (explicitly) and, later, working with the found documents (implicitly), creates valuable feedback for the semantic crawler in terms of which documents were considered relevant. This mechanism implements the AI-in-the-loop principle, benefitting both the AI to improve over time and the human researcher by reducing the time to find more relevant documents in a reasonable time.

Every uploaded document runs through a pipeline of multiple, AI-powered preprocessing steps, allowing the tool to extract desired (meta-) information and enrich the data. Examples include filling metadata like date, author, and origin, automatically finding keywords, detecting topics, extracting named entities, or filtering out noisy text passages like ads. In case of images, the D-WISE Tool Suite may automatically find and annotate objects, locations, or persons. For audio and video files, Automatic Speech Recognition (ASR) AI models allow it to automatically transcribe the material. This extracted information is useful in later stages of the research process and enables key features of D-WISE Tool Suite, which are described in the next sections.

4.3   Coding

An essential feature of the D-WISE Tool Suite and one of the main principles of GT within SKAD is the ability to annotate or code multimodal documents. With this effective method, researchers can find and analyze patterns and concepts in their data to discover and elaborate social phenomena.

The D-WISE Tool Suite supports the typical three consecutive coding stages of GT — i.e., open coding, axial coding, and selective coding — by offering functionalities like creating new codes on the fly (open coding), updating codes, building code hierarchies, or linking codes in a management view to refine codes and find potential relationships (axial and selective coding). The annotation module is accompanied by a code editor that allows to define hierarchical taxonomies. In addition to annotating spans in textual data, D-WISE Tool Suite supports annotating regions in images, sequences in audio streams as well as passages in videos. Further, the D-WISE Tool Suite supports document-level annotations denoting e.g., predominant categories or common topics. Hierarchical document-level classifications of multimodal data like that can help to organize and retrieve it.

Via functions like highlighting, commenting and annotating, documents of any modality can be edited in a collaborative setting making it possible to work together in teams. Collaboration is achieved through multiple functionalities, the most important one is displaying other users' annotations to compare and discuss contradictions.

The D-WISE Tool Suite plans to include means for fully automated, AI-powered annotation of German or English multimodal data. This feature is of very high importance to the D-WISE project as it allows scaling up and handling large corpora, which, in turn, should improve the quality of DH research. This feature is enabled by state-of-the-art AI models that learn from manually created codes to automatically annotate unseen data. Following the active learning paradigm, human coders can accept or discard the automatically annotated codes of previously unseen samples and thereby improve the models over time. This leads to a loop of AI predicting codes and humans correcting the predictions until the human researchers are satisfied with the results. This effectively allows researchers scaling up from a few annotated examples to the whole corpus.

In combination with the filtering component, D-WISE Tool Suite also enables semi-automatic annotations by first filtering for specific text passages and then applying certain codes to them.

4.4 Filtering

Another vital procedure in (digital) SKAD that includes the coding methodology is filtering. Here codes are used to find more documents so that the variety of arguments in the social discourse under investigation increases. Therefore, the D-WISE Tool Suite will offer filter functionality to find minimally, or maximally different documents based on used codes.

Besides standard search methods like full-text, keyword, or lexical similarity search, D-WISE Tool Suite will also be able to filter large corpora with AI-powered semantic search methods, like semantic-textual-similarity search or paraphrase mining. In those methods, AI models first compute a semantic representation of sentences or short paragraphs and then use this representation to find the most similar documents in the corpus. With modern clustering and indexing technologies, this can scale up to billion-scale corpora while still preserving real-time capable latencies. In addition, the D-WISE Tool Suite will provide multimodal and cross-modal search and filtering functionality. Therefore, state-of-the-art multimodal AI models are used to represent documents of different modalities in the same search space. This enables modality agnostic searching or filtering with multimodal queries. That is, a query can be either an image, a text, or even a short video or audio clip, and documents of all mentioned modalities will be retrieved.

In the search interface of D-WISE Tool Suite, users can create filters that represent different search methods described above. These filters can be combined with logical AND or logical OR operations. Adding new filters to a query will further reduce the large corpus until a human manageable document collection is retrieved. Furthermore, since it might be helpful to share the search result with other users or refine the filters later, the queries and the retrieved document collection can be saved.

4.5 Data Analysis and Visualization

The D-WISE Tool Suite will be equipped with several analysis functionalities and appropriate visualizations that we consider standard methods of DH researchers including word co-occurrence, concordance, collocation, and frequencies as well as sentiment analysis and topic modeling. These techniques allow for structural analysis as visualization from a distant reading perspective to get a first impression and a first structural qualitative analysis.

Transparency is central to D-WISE. All analysis and visualization functionalities are a product of an understandable, reproducible process so that a cognition process can be guaranteed, and insights can be traced back. Users will have to carefully select what goes into the visualizations — by manually selecting the data to analyze, formulating a query, and choosing from a range of visualization techniques — in order to maximize the findings and insights gained from them, but also to avoid confusion and incomprehension.

Considering the AI-in-the-loop paradigm, interactive visualizations are a promising direction where humans and AI benefit each other. While humans actively use AI-powered visualizations to leverage their research, AIs can learn from this interaction. Consider data clustering as an example: Data points are visualized on a 2D plane, where distance represents the similarity computed by an AI. Interacting with this visualization by rearranging the data points to create new clusters, adding data points to existing clusters or moving wrongly classified data points to a more fitting cluster creates valuable feedback for the AI, so that it can learn new similarities and dissimilarities. Another example are entity networks where named entities, extracted automatically by an AI, are linked by their interactions, enabling the analysis of cross-document relations. A visualization that supports merging, removing, renaming, and creation of new entities and edges creates a feedback loop where AI can learn about wrong entity identifications, different mentions for the same entity and new relations; also, common errors in the automatic processing — sometimes due to data-collection-specific artifacts — can be quickly fixed for the particular project at hand (Yimam et al. 2016).

The outlined examples are just a small excerpt of a vast, unexplored space of possible interactive visualizations for data analysis. There is considerable development and research potential in the area of interaction and analysis options with multimodal data, especially when aiming to create feedback loops that benefit both humans and AIs. Within the D-WISE project, we aim to further explore this research area. Considering collaboration, the D-WISE project may explore benefits of using interactive, explorative visualizations simultaneously.

4.6   Research Reflections

Writing down and newly gathered insights while researching according to the SKAD paradigm is vital to elaborate patterns and phenomena effectively. Hence, the D-WISE Tool Suite provides functionality to create memos and attach them to all kinds of virtual objects like codes, documents, document collections, saved queries, or visualizations. To keep an overview of memos, D-WISE Tool Suite will be equipped with an interface that allows to list memos created in a particular project, date, or date interval. Additionally, the interface will provide an overview of all actions, e.g., assigning a code to a document, creating a visualization, or creating a document collection. Finally, the interface offers a logbook to effectively describe summaries of a session or discovered phenomena in detail. With the research reflections feature, we claim that scientists can work much more efficiently because manually creating an overview in one application and then switching to another application to write down everything is distracting and takes more time.

4.7   General Features

The D-WISE Tool Suite also provides standard functionalities related to project management, user management, and the overall workflow. It is a project-centered, collaborative web-application, i.e., administrator users create a project and assign or invite other users to it. Furthermore, project administrators assign different roles to users and thereby allow or forbid certain actions like, e.g., uploading documents, viewing memos of other users, or only viewing a certain document collection. Additionally, the D-WISE Tool Suite is planned to support import and export functionality for projects, (annotated) documents, and codes in common data formats like CSV or JSON. This enables exchanging of data from different D-WISE Tool Suite instances and pre-processing or post-processing data with other tools.

4.8 Related Work

Many different annotation tools exist that offer similar functionality as the proposed D-WISE Tool Suite. Established tools in the DH include CATMA (Gius et al. 2021), MAXQDA and WebAnno (De Castilho et al. 2016).

Common to all tools is the annotation component. As in the D-WISE Tool Suite, these components allow defining hierarchical taxonomies and annotating text spans. However, the workflow and details differ among these tools. WebAnno is a multi-user tool for linguistic annotations and dataset creation and, consequently, offers additional chain annotations as well an annotation process optimized for achieving high inter-annotator agreements. In contrast, D-WISE Tool Suite, CATMA and MAXQDA are designed mainly for qualitative research offering — besides span annotations — additional functionalities like comments and memos to document thoughts. Automating the coding process is an important function of D-WISE Tool Suite to scale-up to big data. The goal is to develop an integration of iterative and active learning into the annotation process similar to WebAnno, but also offer semi-automatic methods like CATMA and MAXQDA.

Being tools for qualitative data analysis, CATMA and MAXQDA offer various analysis and visualization techniques. CATMA comes with its own query language allowing fine-grained analysis, an interactive query builder and multiple pre-defined visualization methods like word clouds or double trees. Similarly, MAXQDA offers search functionalities including keyword search, segment search lemma-lists, Boolean operators and wildcards as well as various visual tools that leverage qualitative analysis. Further, MAXQDA includes means for quantitative analysis and statistical data analysis. In the D-WISE project, we aim to offer selected pre-defined visualization tools which have proven to be useful for discourse analysis, like topic finder, word clouds or double trees. However, our main focus is on developing novel interaction techniques for interactive visual data analysis with AI-in-the-loop.

Handling multimodal data is a key feature of D-WISE Tool Suite. While MAXQDA already allows to annotate texts, images, audios and videos, the D-WISE Tool Suite will also offer functionalities to retrieve, search and analyze such material. Novelties of the Tool Suite also include the automatic retrieval of new sources (data acquisition) as well as the exploration and filtering of the found material (filtering). Equipped with state-of-the art multimodal AI models that enable the development of powerful automation, search and analysis functionalities, interactive visualizations that hone the AI-in-the-loop paradigm, novel data acquisition and exploration features as well as means to collaborate effectively, we believe that the D-WISE Tool Suite will be a noteworthy contribution to the DH community.

Acknowledgements. This research was supported by the German Federal Ministry of Education and Research, under grant no. 01UG2124, www.dwise.uni-hamburg.de.

References

Akata, Z., et al.: Research agenda for hybrid intelligence: augmenting human intellect with collaborative, adaptive, responsible, and explainable artificial intelligence. Computer **53**(8), 18–28 (2020). https://doi.org/10.1109/MC.2020.2996587

Brown, T., et al.: Language models are few-shot learners. In: Advances in Neural Information Processing Systems, vol. 33, pp. 1877–1901. Curran Associates Inc., Vancouver (2020)

Chen, Y.-C., et al.: UNITER: UNiversal image-TExt representation learning. In: Vedaldi, A., Bischof, H., Brox, T., Frahm, J.-M. (eds.) ECCV 2020. LNCS, vol. 12375, pp. 104–120. Springer, Cham (2020). https://doi.org/10.1007/978-3-030-58577-8_7

Carter, L., Liu, D., Cantrell, C.: Exploring the intersection of the digital divide and artifical intelligence: a hermeneutic literature review. AIS Trans. Hum.-Comput. Interact. **12**(4), 253–275 (2020). https://doi.org/10.17705/1thci.00138

Devlin, J., Chang, M.-W., Lee, K., Toutanova, K.: BERT: pre-training of deep bidirectional transformers for language understanding. In: Proceedings of the 2019 Conference of the North American Chapter of the Association for Computational Linguistics: Human Language Technologies, Minnesota, pp. 4171–4186. Association for Computational Linguistics (2019). https://doi.org/10.18653/v1/N19-1423

De Castilho, R.E., et al.: A web-based tool for the integrated annotation of semantic and syntactic structures. In: Proceedings of the Workshop on Language Technology Resources and Tools for Digital Humanities (LT4DH), pp. 76–84. The COLING 2016 Organizing Committee, Osaka (2016)

Fritz, A., Brandt, W., Gimpel, H., Bayer, S.: Moral agency without responsibility? Analysis of three ethical models of human-computer interaction in times of artificial intelligence (AI). De Ethica. A J. Philos. Theol. Appl. Ethics **6**(1), 3–22 (2020). https://doi.org/10.3384/de-ethica.2001-8819.20613

Gius, E., et al.: Catma 6 (Version 6.3). Zenodo, Online (2021)

Green, B., Chen, Y.: Disparate interactions: an algorithm-in-the-loop analysis of fairness in risk assessments. In: Proceedings of the 2019 Conference on Fairness, Accountability, and Transparency, FAT* 2019, Atlanta (2019). https://doi.org/10.1145/3287560.3287563

Holzinger, A.: Interactive machine learning for health informatics: when do we need the human-in-the-loop? Brain Inform. **3**(2), 119–131 (2016). https://doi.org/10.1007/s40708-016-0042-6

Keller, R., Hornidge, A.-K., Schünemann, W.J.: The Sociology of Knowledge Approach to Discourse. Routledge, London (2018)

Koch, G.: The ethnography of infrastructures. Digital humanities and cultural anthropology. In: Benardou, A., Champion, E., Dallas, C., Hughes, L.M. (eds.) Cultural Heritage Infrastructures in Digital Humanities, pp. 63–81. Routledge, New York (2018)

Koch, G., Franken, L.: Filtern als digitales Verfahren in der wissenssoziologischen Diskursanalyse. In: Klimczak, P., Petersen, C., Breidenbach, S. (eds.) Soziale Medien. ars digitalis, pp. 121–138. Springer, Wiesbaden (2020). https://doi.org/10.1007/978-3-658-30702-8_6

Krishna, R., Gordon, M., Fei-Fei, L., Bernstein, M.: Visual intelligence through human interaction. In: Li, Y., Hilliges, O. (eds.) Artificial Intelligence for Human Computer Interaction: A Modern Approach. HIS, pp. 257–314. Springer, Cham (2021). https://doi.org/10.1007/978-3-030-826 81-9_9

Li, Y., Hilliges, O. (eds.): Artificial Intelligence for Human Computer Interaction: A Modern Approach. HIS, Springer, Cham (2021). https://doi.org/10.1007/978-3-030-82681-9

Moretti, F.: Distant Reading. Verso, London (2013)

Oeste-Reiß, S., et al.: Hybride wissensarbeit. Informatik Spektrum **44**(3), 148–152 (2021). https://doi.org/10.1007/s00287-021-01352-0

Radford, A., et al.: Learning transferable visual models from natural language supervision. In: Proceedings of the International Conference on Machine Learning, pp. 8748–8763. PMLR (2021)

Schäffer, B., Klinge, D., Krämer, F.: DokuMet QDA: Softwarevermitteltes Forschen, Lehren und Lernen mit der Dokumentarischen Methode. Zeitschrift für Qualitative Sozialforschung, preprint. Budrich, Leverkusen (2021)

Wautelet, Y., Heng, S., Kolp, M., Mirbel, I.: Unifying and extending user story models. In: Jarke, M., et al. (eds.) CAiSE 2014. LNCS, vol. 8484, pp. 211–225. Springer, Cham (2014). https://doi.org/10.1007/978-3-319-07881-6_15

Yimam, S.M., et al.: New/s/leak – information extraction and visualization for investigative data journalists. In: Proceedings of ACL-2016 System Demonstrations, Berlin, pp. 163–168. Association for Computational Linguistics (2016). https://doi.org/10.18653/v1/P16-4028

Yimam, S.M., Remus, S., Pachenko, A., Holzinger, A., Biemann, C.: Entity-Centric Information Access with the Human-in-the-Loop for the Biomedical Domains. Incoma Ltd. Shoume, Varna (2017). https://doi.org/10.26615/978-954-452-044-1_006

KEEP Fit Worldwide: Cultural Adaptations of the User Interface of Mobile Fitness Apps in Different Language Versions

Yuwei Liu[1]([✉]) and Rüdiger Heimgärtner[2]

[1] Department of Economics, Business and Informatics, University of Zurich, 8006 Zurich, Switzerland
yw.liu97@gmail.com

[2] Intercultural User Interface Consulting (IUIC), Lehderstraße 71, 13086 Berlin, Germany
ruediger.heimgaertner@iuic.de

Abstract. KEEP, China's leading mobile fitness app, is expanding to the global market and is already available in multiple languages. However, successful localization not only means translating the app into other languages but also adapting the interface design according to the target culture. Meanwhile, little research has been done regarding user satisfaction of mobile fitness apps from a cross-cultural perspective. Our research applies quantitative and qualitative methods to examine the UX and UI differences between KEEP's English and the original Chinese interface design. We further validated our observations by usability tests and SUS questionnaires, which rejected our hypothesis that Chinese and English-speaking users prefer the interface design pattern of their own culture. In contrast, our results show strong preference for the English KEEP version by both Chinese and English-speaking users. Still, Chinese users tend to be more adaptive to English interfaces while English-speaking users experience more difficulty navigating through the Chinese KEEP version. Our study participants also provide detailed feedback for UX designers and digital health agencies on potential improvements and meaningful considerations in localizing user interfaces and developing multilingual fitness apps.

Keywords: Cross-cultural UX · Mobile fitness app · Intercultural user interface design · Usability test · SUS · KEEP

1 Introduction

Fitness apps keep our body in good shape by providing workout programs that can be performed at home. While following exercise videos on mobile devices has long been a popular alternative to gyms, it has become the only choice for fitness enthusiasts during the COVID-19 lockdown. When gyms were forced to close due to the pandemic, downloads of fitness apps increased by 46% worldwide [1]. Being the first country impacted by the COVID-19 pandemic, China has witnessed a 20% growth in monthly active users on its leading fitness app KEEP in February 2020 [8]. Firstly, established in

M. Rauterberg (Ed.): HCII 2022, LNCS 13324, pp. 84–104, 2022.
https://doi.org/10.1007/978-3-031-05434-1_6

early 2015 by Beijing Calories Technology, KEEP is now the industry leader with more than 1,200 exercise sessions satisfying different fitness goals. In 2019, the app is already available in 18 languages with 10 million users based outside China [29]. For successful internationalization, it is critical to adapt the user interface to different cultures rather than translate the language directly, given that user behaviors and preferences are often influenced by where they come from. This paper provides insights not only for KEEP developers to launch the app in new languages, but also for all related mobile fitness apps to localize their service to the Chinese users.

Past literature has shown common differences in Western and Chinese design patterns. Liu et al. [18] has mentioned visualization is more important for Chinese users, who particularly like cartoons and human depictions. When evaluating MOOC, a localized learning platform of Couseera in China, Liu et al. [18] also suggests "moderate high visual density, more icons and images and low to middle saturation colors" of MOOC lead to higher satisfaction of Chinese users. Specifically for fitness apps, Zheng and Hermawati [30] found that a friendly coaching style, use of animation and reward system are favored by users from Hong Kong, who are influenced both by mainland Chinese and Western cultures.

This article examines whether localized UX and UI design of fitness apps improves user satisfaction in the target region. Our hypothesis is that English-speaking users prefer the English KEEP interface over the Chinese one and the reverse also holds true, even if both interfaces are presented in the same language (English). To test our hypothesis, we conducted a GOMS task analysis on both app versions followed by usability tests and interviews on 5 English-speaking and 5 Chinese speaking college students. The evaluation is based on both qualitative interview feedback and quantitative analysis on System Usability Scale (SUS) score.

2   Methods

2.1   GOMS Task Analysis

The task analysis on both Chinese and English apps is under the CMN-GOMS framework (goal, operation, methods, and selection tools) on the following 3 most common tasks users perform on any mobile fitness apps:

1. Register a new account
2. Create a customized fat-loss workout program
3. Search for barbell squat instruction

CMN-GOMS provides an objective overview of the differences in Chinese and English UI's by illustrating how many operations and screens users need to navigate through to complete the same task under each selection alternative. Different approaches are taken on the 3rd task: "barbell squat" is searched via search bar on Chinese version while under exercise library on English one, due to the inconsistency between search results and exercise library we have noticed on the English app. The full GOMS analysis of each task is presented in pseudocode format and can be found in Appendix A.

2.2 Prototype

To further validate our findings, we applied usability tests to gather comparable insights and subjective comments from the users on each app version. To restore the interactivity, we re-engineered two prototypes from screenshots using design software Figma. Under the experiment scenario, users can navigate through the screenshots by clicking or dragging the icons just as they interact with a real mobile app. To avoid biases from language barriers, screenshots of the original Chinese version have been directly translated into English without any design modifications ("TC" (translated Chinese) version, see Fig. 1). Screenshots of the English version remained unchanged and related to interaction arrows ("OE" (original English) version, see Fig. 2). Due to regional app store limitations, we were only able to take the screenshots for the TC version from Android small (360 × 640 device dimension) taken by a non-experimenter in China while the OE version were based on screenshots from iPhone 11 (375 × 812 device dimension). To ensure blinding of the study, TC and OE versions are referred to the participants as Prototype 1 and Prototype 2 respectively. The app name "KEEP" has also been removed on both prototypes.

Fig. 1. Chinese app home screen, original version (left) and translated into English (TC version) (right)

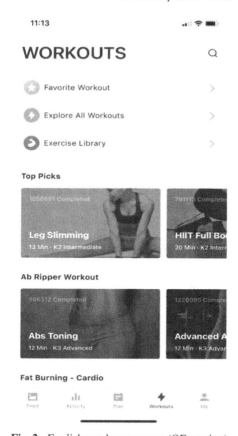

Fig. 2. English app home screen (OE version)

Each prototype consists of the 3 tasks as presented in the CMN-GOMS task analysis above. For simplicity, only one selection method is presented to the participants. Participants are informed of the testing protocols before performing the tasks on the experimenter's mobile phone (iPhone 11, 375×812 device dimension) with both TC and OE versions. We set up hypothetical testing scenarios for each version, which is independent from participants' own demographics, so that everyone follows the same interaction procedures.

2.3 Participants

10 students enrolled at University of Zurich and ETH Zurich participated in our usability testing. Recruited from social networks and referrals, 5 participants are native Chinese speakers (from mainland China) whereas other 5 are native English speakers (2 from USA, 1 from Canada, 1 from Australia and 1 from South Africa). The usability testing was conducted in person to observe the mobile screen interaction with the re-engineered app prototypes.

Participants were asked to imagine themselves as a hypothetical persona when testing each app to investigate how well the app content is tailored to the target group: In a 2019 report published on PMCAFF, a Chinese domestic product management website, KEEP users in China are predominantly female (72.4%) under 35 years old who aim to lose weight and get lean [16]. Meanwhile, the exercise experience of users ranges from absolute beginners to experts. We hereby set up the personas for each app as young females who aim to achieve the next-level fitness goal while performing exercise at correct volume and form.

2.4 Evaluation Criteria

Regarding the differences in UI design, home screens of Chinese and English versions are compared under 3 criteria: functionality, visualization, and conformity, with specific focus on the layout of pictures and text, information density as well as coloring. We also asked participants for verbal feedback on the following 3 interview questions at the end of the usability test: "What do you think is the biggest difference between the two versions from both UX and UI perspectives?" "Which app would you prefer and why?" "How do you think each interface can be improved?" We may ask for more specific details depending on individual response, which is later transcribed and summarized for the most frequently mentioned keywords. As manipulation checks, we asked participants which prototype they are evaluating as well as their first language. We preselected which prototype they were evaluating before participants started the questionnaire.

We also conducted empirical analysis based on SUS score questionnaires (replicated on Qualtrics) administered after finishing testing each prototype. The average SUS score of Chinese and English versions have been analyzed between-groups of Chinese and English speakers. The average SUS score of 68 is used as a benchmark to evaluate whether users are satisfied with each prototype. We conducted a t-test on our hypothesis with the significant level of 0.05 to determine whether the Chinese and English-speaking users give different SUS scores to the same prototype version.

3   Results

3.1 CMN-GOMS Task Analysis

Overall, significantly more steps were required to complete account registration (4 subgoals, 28 operations for the selection method presented in the usability test) as well as workout program customization on the Chinese KEEP app (3 subgoals, 18 operations for the selection methods in the usability test). In comparison, it only took 22 operations (2 subgoals) for account registration and 10 operations (3 subgoals) for workout program customization on the English version.

It is also noticeable that users needed to navigate through 13 screens for registering an account on the Chinese app, compared to 8 screens on the English one. The difference is even more obvious with workout plan customization: It took 14 screens on the Chinese KEEP completing the same task that could be illustrated with 8 screens on the English app. While typing "barbell squat" into the search bar did not display any movement instruction on the English version, participants could only access it through under "Exercise library → Glute", which led to slightly more operations (7) compared to the Chinese version (5). However, when searching for "barbell squat" in the Chinese app, a total of 17 search items containing the keyword "barbell" showed up in the search list. The required number of screens to find barbell squat instructions was identical for both KEEP versions.

The extra operations and screens on Chinese KEEP mainly comprise specific questionnaires about users' fitness level and how many repetitions of a particular workout they can perform. Designated to provide the individualized fitness solution, such questionnaires can however take up a greater cognitive load because users need to recall their past physical activities. In contrast, the questions asked in the English version are more generic, such as daily physical activity level during and after work. Yet despite the lengthy registration process on Chinese KEEP, users are given the option to skip the specific questionnaire at every stage and directly proceed to the home screen.

3.2 Home Screen Comparison

Chinese and English home screens also show distinctive UI characteristics. It is observed that the Chinese KEEP is more information-condensed with more images, live videos as well as icons for sub-navigation, which aligns with Liu et al.'s [18] findings about MOOC. Just like other major Chinese apps such as WeChat, KEEP has the "all-in-one" design pattern incorporated with more functionalities, even the not-so-relevant ones, to appeal to Chinese users. The icons and images are also clustered together without a particular order. In comparison, the English KEEP version contains less information in general with only 3 icons displayed vertically, which is consistent with Marcus & Baradit's description on US apps as "narrow-focused, minimalist and task driven" [19].

Although cross-cultural UI designers discover that Chinese apps are characterized with less white space [20, 31], it is quite the opposite on KEEP. While both versions use varied font sizes to represent different layers of information, the fonts on the Chinese KEEP appear to be smaller, leaving more white space than the English version. On the contrary, the home screen of the English KEEP is filled with fewer but larger images for workout programs. Nevertheless, both Chinese and English versions of KEEP have similar base colors (gray, pastel green, and pastel purple), which contradicts with Schaefer's observation that Chinese apps use brighter and higher-saturated colors [23].

Another noticeable difference is that the Chinese KEEP has the search bar "prefilled" with the most popular content, which is common in other Chinese social media apps but not the English ones. Besides, the original Chinese app include rankings for trending exercise videos with top-rated ones displayed on the home screen. We also find that users' comments, such as "a rare-find warmup targeting wrists and shoulder (难得一个注重于腕和肩周热身的练习)" are highlighted in green under some workout programs in the Chinese version.

3.3 User's Feedback

Most participants (8 out of 10), regardless of native language, prefer the OE version. The TC version has been criticized for "repetitive, overly-specific questions" (5 out of 10 participants), "too much information" (4 out of 10 participants) and "fonts too small" (3 out of 10 participants). 3 English speakers and 1 Chinese speaker also commented on the UI design of the TC version for having "too much white space" or "images too small". In comparison, 4 English-speaking and 2 Chinese-speaking participants find the OE version "easier to read and navigate" with "better flow and dynamics". One English speaker mentions that the OE version looks more "modern" while she does not need to "guess where to press (on the screen)". During the usability test, we have also observed that most English-speakers made more errors on the TC version than their Chinese counterparts interacting with the OE version, which is mainly due to confusion on finding the right navigation button.

Intriguingly, an English-speaking participant prefers the TC version because navigating the OE version is "slightly more complex". However, he also mentions that both versions look similar and "one could easily navigate either version if they get used to the other". While others favor the idea of gamification on the OE version, on which participants earn coins to unlock customized workout plans, he prefers the money-payment premium subscription because of the "microtransaction fatigue" caused by different app gamification currencies. On the contrary, another Chinese participant still gives a higher rating to the TC version despite living abroad since childhood. In her opinion, the greater amount of information is a positive attribute of the TC version because she can easily find everything on the home screen.

Two participants mentioned "user habits" during the interview. One Chinese-speaking participant notices that most functions that are displayed and "ready-for-click" on the TC version are hidden under the sub-navigation buttons on the OE version. However, he "personally prefers" the OE version because he gets familiar with the app interfaces in a similar structure. Another Chinese speaker has observed that the long list of search results reminds her of apps she has used back home. In the meantime, an English-speaking participant states that she is not used to "busy and crowded screens" of the TC version because she "grew up with less information around".

Participants also provide various suggestions on how either or both apps could be improved. A few are concerned about the navigation menu at the bottom of the home screens and comment that "it would be much easier to find where to click if choice buttons were bigger and the icons looked more intuitive". Still, two other participants believe a short guidance on the screen would be helpful for first-time users. Other feedback includes "allow navigation back to the home page at every screen instead of just the last one", "simplify questionnaires and refrain from asking too specific information", as well as "communicate the purpose of each stage in a clear manner, especially when it is payment-related".

3.4 US Score Analysis

For question 4 of SUS evaluation ("I think that I would need the support of a technical person to be able to use this system"), not all data has been collected. In this case, we took the average of the other even-numbered questions as the response to question 4 to calculate the overall SUS Score. Like in the usability tests, we coded the TC version as prototype 1 and OE version as prototype 2 in our data analysis.

The empirical analysis provides evidence to our user interview findings that the OE version is strongly favored by both English and Chinese-speaking participants. According to Fig. 3, the average SUS rating is 79.44 for the OE version while only 68.50 for the

TC version. The opinion towards the TC version is also slightly more varied: The minimum SUS score given to the TC version is 47.50, which is notably below the minimum OE rating of 63.75. In the meantime, 4 users (3 Chinese and 1 English speaker) give the TC version a SUS score lower than 68, indicating it is not user-friendly in their opinion. On the other hand, only one user (English-speaking) rates the OE version below 70.

SUS Score	N	Mean	Std. Deviation	Std. Error	95% CI Lower Bound	95% CI Upper Bound	Minimum	Maximum
TC	10	68,50	13,67	4,32	58,72	78,28	47,50	97,50
OE	10	79,43	10,46	3,31	71,95	86,92	63,75	97,50
Total	20	73,97	13,11	2,93	67,83	80,10	47,50	97,50

Fig. 3. Descriptive statistics of SUS score by prototype

Figure 4 and 5 illustrate that Chinese users' opinions vary at a greater range: Chinese-speaking participants give an average SUS score of 66.75 to the TC version and 81 to the OE version. In comparison, the average ratings by English-speakers are relatively alike between the TC (70.25) and the OE (77.875) version. 5 outliners are observed; however, we do not exclude them from analysis due to small sample size.

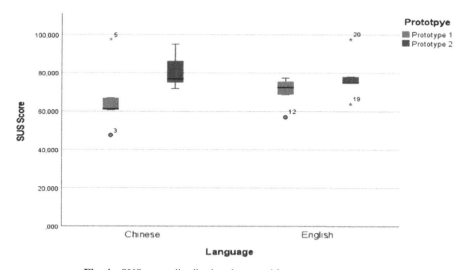

Fig. 4. SUS score distribution, by users' language per prototype

Our t-test results in Fig. 6 and Fig. 7 show that both one-sided and two-sided p-values are above the significant level of 0.05. This indicates that the difference between the SUS scores of each prototype and users' language is statistically insignificant. Therefore,

Language	Prototype		N	Mean	Std. Deviation	Std. Error Mean
Chinese	Prototype 1 (TC version)	SUS Score	5	66,75000	18,600445	8,318372
	Prototype 2 (OE version)	SUS Score	5	81,00000	9,484774	4,241720
English	Prototype 1 (TC version)	SUS Score	5	70,25000	8,180102	3,658253
	Prototype 2 (OE version)	SUS Score	5	77,87500	12,260200	5,482928

Fig. 5. Descriptive statistics of SUS score by language × prototype

the results do not significantly align with our research hypothesis that users prefer the app interface from their own linguistic and cultural context because both Chinese and English-speaking participants find the English KEEP app more user-friendly.

				Mean		Significance	
		t	df	One-Sided p	Two-Sided p	Mean Difference
SUS Score	Equal variances assumed	-1,526	8	,083	,165	-14,250000
	Equal variances not assumed	-1,526	5,948	,089	,178	-14,250000

Fig. 6. T-testing on 2 independent samples (prototype according to language group: Chinese participants)

				Mean		Significance	
		t	df	One-Sided p	Two-Sided p	Mean Difference
SUS Score	Equal variances assumed	-1,157	8	,140	,281	-7,625000
	Equal variances not assumed	-1,157	6,972	,143	,285	-7,625000

Fig. 7. T-testing on 2 independent samples (prototype according to language group: English participants)

Given that our sample size is relatively small (<20), we examined the magnitude of the observed between-group differences. We hereby conducted power analysis using Cohen's d and Hedge's g. We discovered that sample effect sizes are substantially large (>1), which implies that despite the difference in SUS score being statistically insignificant, our findings could be meaningful in the larger population (see Fig. 8). However, compared with Fig. 9, the sample effect size becomes insignificant (<0.2) when examining the effect of the language alone. Hence, it can be inferred that the prototype itself plays a more determinant role in the user experience.

Language	Prototype			Standardizer[a]	Point Estmate
Chinese	Prototype 1 (TC version)	SUS Score	Cohen's d	18,600445	3,589
			Hedges' correction	23,312201	2,863
	Prototype 2 (OE version)	SUS Score	Cohen's d	9,484774	8,540
			Hedges' correction	11,887401	6,814
English	Prototype 1 (TC version)	SUS Score	Cohen's d	8,180102	8,588
			Hedges' correction	10,252237	6,852
	Prototype 2 (OE version)	SUS Score	Cohen's d	12,260200	6,352
			Hedges' correction	15,365882	5,068

Fig. 8. Independent samples effect sizes, by language × prototype

		Standardizer[a]	Point Estimate	95% Confidence Interval	
				Lower	Upper
SUS Score	Cohen's d	13,469439	-,014	-,890	,863
	Hedges' correction	14,065148	-,013	-,853	,826

Fig. 9. Independent samples effect sizes, by language

4 Discussion

The design differences between Chinese and English KEEP app align with intercultural UI design literature when considering the feedback of the users. One notable adaptation is that information density is indeed significantly reduced on the English KEEP interface, which is consistent with Cheng & Nielsen's observation [4]. Instead, the English version is presented in a more linear layout without animation, live-videos, and clustered sub-navigation icons that users would find on the Chinese one. The rationale behind such change might be the higher uncertainty avoidance in English-speaking countries. Unlike in China, where users can process a larger amount of information and multi-tasking at the same time, English-speaking users tend to approach tasks in a monochronic order with only the most relevant information at hand [18, 24]. Low multimodality is also a preferred design attribute in individualistic cultures in which most native English speakers grow up [24]. Another reason for less content on the English version could be the icon-based Chinese language and that not all features on Chinese KEEP have been tested on the overseas market. Huang & Zhou have also observed that Chinese users particularly embrace "triathlon" mobile fitness apps including all the following objectives, namely modeling/observational learning, self-regulation, and social comparison/social support, which explains the extensive features in the Chinese app [14]. Qi argues from a business perspective that because all-in-one apps are favored in China, intense competition across all industries has forced Chinese app designers to display all possible features to users with the fear of being squeezed out of the market by competitors [23].

We also noticed that while the English version retains the community feature, the network effect does not seem to be as extensive as the Chinese one. In fact, community interactions on the English KEEP version are still predominantly contributed by overseas Chinese users, which could be related to collectivism. In contrast, the original Chinese app allows users to upload posts and comment on exercise programs, with top-liked content directly displayed on the home screen. The emphasis on testimony on Chinese apps is also shown as the search bar prefilled with trending content, which is not common in Western apps. In addition, [11] discovered from interviews that socialization is one of the top reasons for young Chinese women to trust KEEP and commit to its exercise program. Still, Moriuchi's study [22] on American and Japanese users implies that testimonies play an equally important role in decision-making in both collectivism and individual cultures. Yet unlike Chinese users, Spillers & Asimakopoulos [27] tested several jogging apps with American users and noticed that social features play little role in motivation towards fitness goals because some users regard workout as "personal" and would rather not to share.

Remarkably, an American user points out in Spillers & Asimakopoulos's study [27] that she prefers an app "giving clear suggestion of what exercise need to be done and for how long" in order to achieve target to achieve her target weight, which is exactly what KEEP offers and could explain why the app asks many detailed questions about personal information and fitness level: Instead of one-size-fits-all programs, KEEP aims to generate customized training plans as possible. Moreover, the Chinese KEEP asks users how fast they would like to see the results, which is defined by [11] as "perceived efficacy", one of 3 factors facilitating user relationships with mobile fitness apps. This question, however, is not presented on the English KEEP app version.

Nevertheless, the results from the usability test only partially agree with previous studies as well as our hypothesis. On the one hand, English-speaking participants do find the Chinese KEEP interface a bit "information overloaded" as [4] describe. On the other hand, most Chinese users do not show preference to the typical Chinese interface design either. Our study, however, supports Liljenberg et al.'s [17] as well as Miraz et al.'s findings [20] that both Chinese and English-speaking users can comfortably interact with Western interfaces and find Western design more visually appealing. Nevertheless, Chinese users demonstrate greater ease than English counterparts when navigating through Chinese-style interfaces.

It is further verified by our empirical analysis that SUS scores given by Chinese participants to the OE version are higher to scores given by English speakers to the TC version. One reason could be the higher uncertainty avoidance in English-speaking countries attributed to users' lower tolerance to unfamiliar design characteristics. Another important aspect is that all the Chinese participants have lived in Zurich for at least 6 months whereas only few English-speaking participants have ever traveled to China before. Since the UI design in Switzerland is largely like that of most Western countries, Chinese subscribers may already have become accustomed to the Western app structure in their daily lives. On the contrary, most English-speaking participants have never seen a Chinese user interface before.

5   Implication

Even though the overseas app has yet attracted many Western users, the overall higher satisfaction of the OE version implies that KEEP acknowledges the design differences between cultures and is well-adapted for Western context. Often, UI designers regardless of nationality easily fall into the trap of cultural assumptions, which not only affect the "look and feel" of a software interface but also evaluation criteria [3, 26]. Such assumptions can cause friction in UI design and misunderstanding of the users [9, 12]. Still, assumptions might also be biased if completely relying on users' culture of origin without recognizing individual differences and cross-culture mobility. According to Deasy's no-assumptive design approach [7], any opinions like "we know the users will do" are research questions that need to be constantly tested with a larger group of users [2].

We also learnt that users tend to focus more on universal UI attributes, such as "larger font for most important information", "easy navigation back to home page" and "concise questionnaires" before cultural-specific ones. [5] also suggest that implicitness, visibility, and customizability are the most important system characteristics across all languages.

Still, space should be saved to accommodate different characters when translating texts into other languages, especially when it involves pictographic and ideographic-based characters such as Chinese [20]. Another aspect worthwhile to examine is how individualism and collectivism drive the different incentives of Chinese and Western users on fitness apps: While Chinese users embrace the social value of gamification by competing with friends on leaderboards [10, 28] found out that American users appreciate gamification which enhances positive self-identification.

The study provides clues for UI designers and digital health agencies in developing multilingual fitness apps that target users from different cultures. While especially with the growing influence of Chinese software companies across the globe, Chinese UI designers and UX professionals may also benefit from our study when tailoring their products and services for the oversea audience. Reversely, little evidence has been found suggesting how Western apps can be localized for the Chinese market because our study is conducted in a Western country (Switzerland). Nonetheless, users from low uncertainty avoidance cultures such as China are adaptive to different interface design patterns, which might make localization less complicated in China than in Western countries.

6   Limitation

We acknowledge that several limitations exist in the study: First, not all app characteristics could be replicated on our reengineered, screenshot-based prototypes. Especially for the Chinese version consisting of some animations, now, we are unable to observe whether such animations affect user experience because our prototype screens are static. Usability testing also cannot fully simulate real-life scenarios when users need to update their fitness data regularly (e.g., weight). By asking participants to complete the tasks "registering a new account" and "create a customized workout plan" at the same time, some participants found it repetitive and lost interest in the TC version, because they were asked for height and weight information at least one time at every task.

In addition, direct translation of the Chinese app interface also alters the UI layout. Considering that Chinese characters convey more information per syllable than Roman letters [6, 15, 32], the content also becomes longer when translated into English. To ensure the translation fits on the interface as per original layout, the font sizes are adjusted smaller on the TC version. This makes it even more difficult for some participants to read, which results in lower ratings for the TC version. Meanwhile, due to the different original screen sizes, the TC version might look distorted on the testing device, from which screenshots for the OE version are taken. Both prototypes also lost some interaction sensitivity on the mobile screen after Figma re-engineering, requiring longer time for some users with thicker fingers to tap on certain smaller buttons, particularly on the TC version. It is also possible that the Chinese interface no longer looks natural to Chinese users after translation.

Furthermore, our sampling is also biased because several international students at Zurich universities cannot fully represent the preferences of Chinese and English-speaking users, even if college students are one of the major target groups of KEEP [16]. Most of our participants speak at least 2 languages and have lived abroad for at least 6 months. In this case, we cannot rule out the potential influence of multilingualism and international experience on user perception and therefore are unable to generalize our findings on the larger monolingual user population staying in their home countries. In addition, it is important to note that the sample size is very small. The 5 English-speaking participants come from 4 different countries, which are influenced by Chinese immigrants, while Chinese-speaking participants have more homogenous cultural demographics. Yet regional differences exist even within the same county: One participant points out in the interview that residents of urban metropolises are exposed to more information from the environment. As a result, she believes that urban citizens tend to have larger information capacity and are more tolerant to more crowded app screens. Our study, however, segments the participants by native language without taking geo-societal subcultures and global mobility into consideration.

Lastly, missing data regarding question 4 lead to a slightly higher SUS score. Such data collection errors could have been avoided by making responses to all survey questions mandatory. We need to examine if this aspect alters the SUS score results significantly. Other usability attributes, such as cognition load, learnability, and memorability, could also have been measured and evaluated quantitatively. Moreover, our results still should be verified using other theoretical approaches.

7 Conclusion

To conclude, the Chinese and English version of the mobile fitness app KEEP show obvious differences in the UI design. Generally, the Chinese version displays all functionalities on the home screen as past scholars have observed, which could be the result of cognition capacity, language script but also intense competition in the market. The typical display of icons as sub-navigation on major Chinese apps has also been observed on KEEP. However, its smaller font size leaves much white space on the screen. The English version, in contrast, looks more linear in structure with only the most task-relevant information. The Chinese version is more complex than the English one regarding the number of steps needed to complete the same task and asks users more specific questions. The gamification of each version also focuses on different aspects of user incentives: The Chinese KEEP has a stronger network effect, whereas the English one uses coins as reward for personal achievements, which can also be redeemed for future workout plans. Such differences can be explained by uncertainty avoidance and individualism under Hofstede's cultural dimension model. English-speaking countries score higher in uncertainty avoidance and individualism, in which people approach tasks in mono-chronical order and value personal achievement and fun. The Chinese, coming from a collectivistic country with lower uncertainty avoidance, are better in multitasking and embrace the sense of community.

Our quantitative and qualitative results demonstrate that the English KEEP is well-localized for Western countries and receives more positive feedback from both native English and Chinese speakers. On the one hand, it illustrates that universal UI design attributes, such as simplicity, is the predominant factor of system quality and should be prioritized before taking cultural-specific intercultural factors into consideration. The Chinese participants, on the other hand, might have already adapted to Western interface design patterns and formed interaction habits after living abroad for 6 months or longer.

On the contrary, high uncertainty avoidance could also explain that English speakers experience more confusion when interacting with the Chinese system, in addition to the fact that they have barely been to China.

Regarding research methods, the empirical analysis of SUS score questionnaires imply tendencies of user preference. However, the results are often not statistically significant due to small sample sizes. Qualitative feedback from user interviews, on the other hand, provides more detailed insight on why a system is considered superior to another, as well as suggestions on future improvement to the user interface and even decisive reasons for accepting or rejecting a particular system. Similar results were confirmed that quantitative results reveal tendencies for designing cross-cultural user interfaces, which shows that comparative studies can determine the causes of previously identified errors, identify policy violations, and statistically demonstrate cultural differences [13]. In this way, the problems of "culturally subjective" test results and resource-intensive on-site testing can be avoided. Based on a physical-objective measurement basis in the form of numbers, these culture-dependent procedures provide reliable results about cultural differences and thus generate cultural knowledge semi-automatically. Numbers do not need to be given additional meaning through interpretation, since they represent identically defined ordinal values mathematically worldwide (i.e., independent of culture). The use of such quantitative methods, which are methodologically less susceptible to interference or less culturally sensitive due to the lack of interpretation during data collection, is particularly advantageous for remote studies, which contribute significantly to cost savings in intercultural user interface design. However, for this study, recommendations for designing intercultural user interfaces could only be reliably identified, elaborated, and evaluated by qualitative feedback from user testing participants because of too few quantitative data sets. In short, at least for small samples, quantitative data cannot substitute the crucial role of qualitative data for meaningful conclusions in intercultural user interface design.

Appendix

Appendix A: CMN GOMS analysis
A1.1: Registering for a new account: TC Version

- GOAL: REGISTER A NEW ACCOUNT
    - o SUB GOAL: LOGIN AUTHENTICATION
        - ▪ [Select: LOGIN WITH MOBILE PHONE
            - • TYPE PHONE NUMBER
            - • CLICK "NEXT STEP"
            - • INPUT THE VERIFICATION CODE RECEIVED
            - • CLICK "CONFIRM"
              LOGIN WITH SOCIAL MEDIA
            - • CLICK SOCIAL MEDIA ICON OF CHOICE
            - • AUTHENTICATE TO LOGIN WITH SOCIAL MEDIA
            - • CLICK "CONFIRM"]
    - • SUB GOAL: ADD PERSONAL INFORMATION
        - o [Select: ADD MY INFORMATION
            - ▪ (Select: FILL OUT GENDER & BIRTHDAY
                - ▪ CLICK THE ANSWER OF "GENDER"
                - ▪ CLICK "PLEASE SELECT DATE OF BIRTH"
                - ▪ SCROLL TO SET DATE OF BIRTH
                - ▪ CLICK "CONTINUE"
                  "I WILL SKIP NOW AND MOVE ON"
                    - • DIRECTED TO HOME PAGE)
            - • (Select: FILL OUT HEIGHT & WEIGHT
                - o CLICK "PLEASE SELECT HEIGHT"
                - o SCROLL TO SET HEIGHT
                - o CLICK "PLEASE SELECT WEIGHT"
                - o SCROLL TO SET WEIGHT
                - o CLICK "CONTINUE"
                  "I WILL SKIP NOW AND MOVE ON"
                    - • DIRECTED TO HOME PAGE)
            - • (Select: SET UP WORKOUT PREFERENCE
                - o FIND THE TAB OF "YOUR FITNESS GOAL"
                - o CLICK THE TAB
                - o CLICK THE ANSWER CHOICE OF "YOUR FITNESS LEVEL"
                - o CLICK "CONTINUE"
                  "I WILL SKIP NOW AND MOVE ON"
                    - • DIRECTED TO HOME PAGE)
              "SKIP NOW"
                - • DIRECTED TO HOME PAGE]
    - • SUB-GOAL: SET WORKOUT NOTIFICATION
        - o [select: SET UP WORKOUT TIME
            - ▪ CLICK THE DAYS OF WORKOUT
            - ▪ SCROLL TO SET THE NOTIFICATION TIME
              "I WILL SKIP NOW AND MOVE ON"
                - • DIRECTED TO HOME PAGE]
    - • SUB-GOAL: CUSTOMIZE THE PLAN
        - o [Select: GET MY PLAN NOW
            - ▪ SCROLL TO SET HEIGHT
            - ▪ SCROLL TO SELECT WEIGHT
            - ▪ CLICK "CONFIRM"
            - ▪ CLICK THE ANSWER CHOICE OF "HOW LONG CAN YOU HOLD A PLAN"
            - ▪ CLICK THE ANSWER CHOICE OF "HOW FAR CAN YOU RUN"

- CLICK THE ANSWER CHOICE OF "HOW LONG CAN YOU HOLD A PLANK"
- CLICK THE ANSWER CHOICE OF "WHAT IS YOUR FITNESS GOAL"
- CLICK THE ANSWER CHOICE OF "HOW FAST WOULD YOU LIKE TO SEE THE RESULTS"
- CLICK "ACTIVATE YOUR PERSONALIZED PLAN"

"SKIP NOW"

- DIRECTED TO HOME PAGE]

A1.2: Registering for a new account: OE Version

- GOAL: REGISTER A NEW ACCOUNT
  - SUB GOAL: LOGIN AUTHENTICATION
    - [Select: LOGIN WITH MOBILE PHONE
      - TYPE PHONE NUMBER
      - CLICK "NEXT STEP"
      - INPUT THE VERIFICATION CODE RECEIVED
      - CLICK "CONFIRM"
      LOGIN WITH SOCIAL MEDIA
    - CLICK SOCIAL MEDIA ICON OF CHOICE
    - AUTHENTICATE TO LOGIN WITH SOCIAL MEDIA
    - CLICK "CONFIRM"]
  - COLLECT WELCOME COINS
  - CLICK "GO!"
- SUB GOAL: ADD PERSONAL INFORMATION
  - CLICK THE ANSWER CHOICE OF "WHAT'S YOUR GOAL"
  - CLICK "NEXT"
  - CLICK THE ANSWER CHOICE OF "DESCRIBE YOUR EXPERIENCE IN EXERCISE"
  - CLICK "NEXT"
  - CLICK THE ANSWER OF "GENDER"
  - CLICK "PLEASE SELECT DATE OF BIRTH"
  - SCROLL TO SET DATE OF BIRTH
  - CLICK "NEXT"
  - DROP DOWN TO SET HEIGHT
  - DROP DOWN TO SET WEIGHT
  - CLICK "NEXT"
  - DRAG TO SET COMMUTE TIME
  - DRAG TO SET HOUSEWORK TIME
  - CLICK "NEXT"
  - CLICK THE ANSWER CHOICE OF "DESCRIBE YOUR WORK NATURE"
  - CLICK "DONE"

A2.1: Create a fat-loss workout plan: TC Version

- GOAL: CREATE FAT-LOSS WORKOUT PLAN
  - SUB GOAL: ACCESS CUSTOMIZED WORKOUT PLANNING
    - FIND "PLAN" ICON ON THE SCREEN
    - CLICK "PLAN" ICON
  - SUB GOAL: FILL OUT FITNESS LEVEL EVALUATION
    - FIND SECTION "FITNESS LEVEL EVALUATION"
    - CLICK "GO TO QUESTIONNAIRE"
    - SCROLL TO SET HEIGHT
    - SCROLL TO SELECT WEIGHT
    - CLICK "CONFIRM'
    - CLICK ANSWER CHOICE TO ADD "GOAL"
    - CLICK ANSWER CHOICE TO ADD "RUNNING WORKOUT"
    - CLICK "NEXT STEP"

- CLICK ANSWER CHOICE OF "HOW FAST WOULD YOU LIKE TO SEE THE RESULTS"
- CLICK "NEXT STEP"
- CLICK ANSWER CHOICE OF "DO YOU FEEL SHORT OF BREATH AFTER CLIMBING 5 FLOORS"
- CLICK ANSWER CHOICE OF "HOW MANY KNEE PUSH UPS CAN YOU PREFORM"
- CLICK ANSWER CHOICE OF "HOW MANY SQUATS CAN YOU PREFORM"
- CLICK ANSWER CHOICE OF "CAN YOU REACH YOUR TOE IN A FORWARD BEND TEST"
- CLICK "GET MY PLAN NOW"
  - SUB GOAL: CONFIRM OR EXIT THE PLAN
    - [Select*: CLICK "BEGIN MEMBERSHIP AND"
      - DIRECTED TO PAYMENT PAGE
      CLICK LEFT ARROW
      - DIRECTED TO HOME PAGE]

* Selection rules for SUBGOAL: CONFIRM OR EXIT THE PLAN
If wish to confirm the plan, CLICK "UNLOCK PROGRAM"
      else CLICK LEFT ARROW

A2.2: Create a fat-loss workout plan: OE Version

- GOAL: CREATE FAT-LOSS WORKOUT PLAN
  - SUB GOAL: ACCESS CUSTOMIZED WORKOUT PLANNING
    - FIND "PLAN" ICON ON THE HOME SCREEN
    - CLICK "PLAN" ICON
  - SUB GOAL: FILL OUT PERSONAL INFORMATION
    - CLICK THE PROGRAM TYPE OF CHOICE
    - CLICK "NEXT"
    - CLICK THE FITNESS GOAL OF CHOICE
    - CLICK "NEXT"
    - CLICK THE FITNESS LEVEL
    - CLICK "NEXT"
  - SUB GOAL: CONFIRM OR EXIT THE PLAN
    - [Select*: CLICK "BEGIN MEMBERSHIP AND"
      - DIRECTED TO PLAN OVERVIEW
      CLICK LEFT ARROW
      - DIRECTED TO HOME PAGE]

* Selection rules for SUBGOAL: CONFIRM OR EXIT THE PLAN
If wish to confirm the plan, CLICK "BEGIN MEMBERSHIP AND UNLOCK PROGRAM"
      else CLICK LEFT ARROW

A3.1: Find barbell squat workout instruction, TC Version

- GOAL: FIND BARBELL SQUAT INSTRUCTION
  - SUB GOAL: SEARCH FOR THE EXERCISE
    - FIND SEARCH BAR ON THE HOME SCREEN
    - TYPE "BARBELL SQUAT"
    - CLICK "SEARCH FOR BARBELL SQUAT"
  - SUB GOAL: CHECK INSTRUCTION
    - CLICK "START TRAINING"
    - SCROLL TO CHECK FULL INSTRUCTIONS

A3.2: Find barbell squat workout instruction, OE Version

- GOAL: FIND BARBELL SQUAT INSTRUCTION IN GLUTE EXERCISE
  - SUB GOAL: FIND GLUTE EXERCISES
    - FIND "WORKOUT" ICON ON THE SCREEN
    - CLICK "WORKOUT" ICON

- FIND "EXERCISE LIBRARY"
- FIND "GLUTE EXERCISES"
- CLICK ON THE RIGHT ARROW NEXT TO "GLUTE EXERCISES"
- SUB GOAL: CHECK INSTRUCTION OF BARBELL SQUAT
  - SCROLL THE LIST TO FIND BARBELL (FRONT) SQUAT
  - CLICK ON THE RIGHT ARROW NEXT TO BARBELL "FRONT" SQUAT

References

1. Ang, C.: Fitness apps grew by nearly 50% during the first half of 2020, study finds. The World Economic Forum, 15 September 2020. https://www.weforum.org/agenda/2020/09/fitness-apps-gym-health-downloads/. Accessed 18 Nov 2021
2. Berk, G.G.: A framework for designing in cross-cultural contexts: culture-centered design process. University of Minnesota Digital Conservancy, June 2013. https://hdl.handle.net/11299/155725
3. Cardinal, A., Gonzales, L., Rose, E.J.: Language as participation: multilingual user experience design. In: Proceedings of the 38th ACM International Conference on Design of Communication (SIGDOC 2020), pp. 1–7, October 2020. https://doi.org/10.1145/3380851.3416763
4. Cheng, Y., Nielsen, J.: Are Chinese websites too complex? Nielsen Norman Group, 6 November 2016. https://www.nngroup.com/articles/china-website-complexity/. Accessed 31 Jan 2022
5. Chu, P., Komlodi, A.: TranSearch: a multilingual search user interface accommodating user interaction and preference. In: Proceedings of the 2017 CHI Conference Extended Abstracts on Human Factors in Computing Systems, pp. 2466–2472, May 2017. https://doi.org/10.1145/3027063.3053262
6. Cook, J.D.: Chinese character frequency and entropy. Applied Math & Data Privacy, 18 October 2019. https://www.johndcook.com/blog/2019/10/18/chinese-character-entropy/. Accessed 29 Jan 2022
7. Deasy, D.: Non-assumptive research. In: Laurel, B. (ed.) Design Research: Methods and Perspectives, pp. 234–240. Tit Press (2003)
8. Deloitte China: 2019–2020 China Health and Fitness Market White Paper, 27 January 2021. https://www2.deloitte.com/content/dam/Deloitte/cn/Documents/technology-media-telecommunications/deloitte-cn-tmt-2019-2020-china-gym-market-development-white-paper-en-210115.pdf. Accessed 12 Nov 2021
9. Domanitska, M.: The art of understanding: the danger of assumptions | by Myroslava Domanitska. UX Collective, 8 September 2020. https://uxdesign.cc/the-art-of-understanding-the-danger-of-assumptions-f8fd23d988af. Accessed 5 Feb 2022
10. Esmaeilzadeh, P.: The influence of gamification and information technology identity on postadoption behaviors of health and fitness app users: empirical study in the United States. JMIR Serious Games 9(3), e28282 (2021). https://doi.org/10.2196/28282
11. Fang, S., Aldoory, L.: Acquaintance, coach, or buddy?: perceived relationships between Chinese women and mobile fitness technology. Commun. Stud. 72(6), 1089–1111 (2021). https://doi.org/10.1080/10510974.2021.2011351
12. Gomes, S.: Why cross-cultural design really matters -. UX Magazine, 30 June 2021. https://uxmag.com/articles/why-cross-cultural-design-really-matters. Accessed 5 Feb 2022
13. Heimgärtner, R.: Cultural differences in human-computer interaction: towards culturally adaptive human-machine interaction. De Gruyter (2012). https://doi.org/10.1524/9783486719895

14. Huang, G., Zhou, E.: Time to work out! Examining the behavior change techniques and relevant theoretical mechanisms that predict the popularity of fitness mobile apps with chinese-language user interfaces. Health Commun. **72**(6), 1502–1512 (2018). https://doi.org/10.1080/10410236.2018.1500434

15. Ingraham, C.: Analysis | The languages that let you say more with less. The Washington Post, 28 September 2017. https://www.washingtonpost.com/news/wonk/wp/2017/09/28/the-languages-that-let-you-say-more-with-less/. Accessed 29 Jan 2022

16. lalalz: Keep产品分析报告[Keep product analysis report]. PMCAFF, 1 April 2020. https://coffee.pmcaff.com/article/2277524898754688/pmcaff?utm_source=forum. Accessed 14 Jan 2022

17. Liljenberg, M., Tian, K., Yao, M.: Cross-cultural user design: divergences in chinese and western human computer interface interaction. In: Stephanidis, C., Antona, M. (eds.) HCII 2019. CCIS, vol. 1088, pp. 39–45. Springer, Cham (2019). https://doi.org/10.1007/978-3-030-30712-7_6

18. Liu, S., Liang, T., Shao, S., Kong, J.: Evaluating localized MOOCs: the role of culture on interface design and user experience. IEEE Access **8**, 107927–107940 (2020). https://doi.org/10.1109/ACCESS.2020.2986036

19. Marcus, A., Baradit, S.: Chinese user-experience design: an initial analysis. In: Marcus, A. (ed.) DUXU 2015. LNCS, vol. 9187, pp. 107–117. Springer, Cham (2015). https://doi.org/10.1007/978-3-319-20898-5_11

20. Miraz, M.H., Excell, P.S., Ali, M.: User interface (UI) design issues for multilingual users: a case study. Univ. Access Inf. Soc. **15**(3), 431–444 (2014). https://doi.org/10.1007/s10209-014-0397-5

21. Monserrat, E.R.: China, the future of digital product design. | by Elias Ruiz Monserrat. Prototypr, 18 November 2018. https://blog.prototypr.io/china-the-future-of-digital-product-design-68fa7be383c0. Accessed 18 Jan 2022

22. Moriuchi, E.: Cultural aspect of informational and normative influences on purchasing intentions: an eye-tracking approach. J. Mark. Theory Pract. **29**(4), 498–517 (2021). https://doi.org/10.1080/10696679.2021.1877155

23. Qi, K.: Why do Chinese websites and apps look so busy? Thoughtworks, 10 June 2021. https://www.thoughtworks.com/insights/blog/why-do-chinese-websites-and-apps-look-so-busy. Accessed 4 Feb 2022

24. Romeo, P., Karreman, J., Li, Q.: Cross-cultural HCI and UX design: a comparison of chinese and western user interfaces, December2016. https://doi.org/10.13140/RG.2.2.18547.63525

25. Schaefer, K.: Proof of concept: are chinese app interface colors really brighter? 像素仓库 - The Pixellary, 2 April 2015. http://thepixellary.com/proof-of-concept-are-chinese-app-interface-colors-really-brighter/. Accessed 18 Jan 2022

26. Shannon, G.: Challenging assumptions and designing across cultures | by Gene Shannon. Shopify UX, 27 May 2020. https://ux.shopify.com/challenging-assumptions-and-designing-across-cultures-23a9fadd69f5. Accessed 5 Feb 2022

27. Spillers, F., Asimakopoulos, S.: Does social user experience improve motivation for runners? In: Marcus, A. (ed.) DUXU 2014. LNCS, vol. 8520, pp. 358–369. Springer, Cham (2014). https://doi.org/10.1007/978-3-319-07638-6_35

28. Tu, R., Hsieh, P., Feng, W.: Walking for fun or for "likes"? The impacts of different gamification orientations of fitness apps on consumers' physical activities. Sport Manag. Rev. **22**(5), 682–693 (2019). https://doi.org/10.1016/j.smr.2018.10.005

29. Zhang, Y., Cao, K., Lan, G.: Profile: Young tech-entrepreneur keeps the world moving. Xinhua Net, 11 May 2019. Accessed 18 Nov 2021

30. Zheng, F., Hermawati, S.: Cultural aspects for the user interface design of health and fitness apps. Ergonomics & Human Factors 2021, 8 Apr 2021. https://publications.ergonomics.org.uk/uploads/05_42.pdf

31. Zhong, Y.: Content or white space? Chinese vs. Western design aesthetics. UX Collective, 17 September 2018. https://uxdesign.cc/content-or-white-space-chinese-vs-western-design-aesthetics-2eef79e12844. Accessed 17 Jan 2022
32. Zhong, Y.: Key differences between designing for China and the West. UX Collective, 13 May 2021. https://uxdesign.cc/key-differences-between-designing-for-china-and-the-west-dad2c5132521. Accessed 31 Jan 2022

The Importance of Culturally-Situated Design on Children's Interaction with Speech-Enabled Features in an Online Spelling Tutor

Phaedra S. Mohammed[1]([✉]), André Coy[2], Paulson Skerrit[3], Yewande Lewis-Fokum[4], Asad Mohammed[5], and Aneeqah Hosein[6]

[1] Department of Computing and Information Technology, The University of the West Indies, St. Augustine Campus, St. Augustine, Trinidad and Tobago
Phaedra.Mohammed@sta.uwi.edu
[2] Department of Physics, The University of the West Indies, Mona Campus, Kingston, Jamaica
Andre.Coy02@uwimona.edu.jm
[3] School of Education, The University of the West Indies, St. Augustine Campus, St. Augustine, Trinidad and Tobago
Paulson.Skerrit@sta.uwi.edu
[4] School of Education, The University of the West Indies, Mona Campus, Kingston, Jamaica
Yewande.Lewis@uwimona.edu.jm
[5] Department of Mathematics and Statistics, The University of the West Indies, St. Augustine Campus, St. Augustine, Trinidad and Tobago
Asad.Mohammed2@sta.uwi.edu
[6] CARiLIT, The University of the West Indies, Mona Campus, Kingston, Jamaica

Abstract. Spelling is an essential anchor for literacy skills. In the Caribbean, there are limited resources to support struggling readers with their spelling practice. This paper describes an exploratory study of an online Spelling tutor, Ozzypi which was built in response to Covid-19 related school closures across the region and the subsequent need for novel approaches to facilitate spelling practice. It has since been transformed to feature an intelligent tutoring system core that supports children in spelling practice exercises using speech-enabled technologies. Twenty-eight users (14 learners and 14 parents/guardians) from Trinidad and Jamaica used a basic version of the tutor over several weeks. Analysis of interview responses and logged usage data revealed broad learner and parent engagement, positive shifts in on-task behaviour. Importantly, the need for a culturally-situated design emerged as students interacted with the speech-enabled features.

Keywords: Intelligent tutoring system · Spelling · Synthetic speech · Children

1 Introduction

Spelling is understood to be the skill with the most impact on the writing component of literacy [2, 8, 9, 18, 39]. Far beyond rote memorisation, learning to write is a process of language skill development, requiring vocabulary, phonological awareness, phonics

M. Rauterberg (Ed.): HCII 2022, LNCS 13324, pp. 105–119, 2022.
https://doi.org/10.1007/978-3-031-05434-1_7

knowledge, an understanding of text structure and, importantly, a firm grasp of the rules of spelling [17, 25]. Countries of the English-speaking Caribbean, such as Trinidad and Jamaica, teach spelling using a scaffolded approach. Firstly, children are taught to develop phonemic awareness, then building on this, phonetic spelling is introduced alongside learning special rules, spelling patterns, and the memorisation of sight words [23, 24, 30]. This approach lays the foundation for all spelling instruction throughout primary school (K-6) with the basic principles introduced up to grade 2 and reinforced in the upper grades - a broadly similar approach to that employed in phonics-based spelling pedagogy in other countries [14]. Once the groundwork has been laid, spelling instruction essentially consists of memorising lists of words for regurgitation in a test format [21]. While this has some benefits, it does not amount to spelling instruction, as it often precludes feedback, focused practice, modelling and self-correction [6, 13, 21, 27, 33, 35]. Importantly, the advantage gained by spelling out aloud in class is lost, and with it, the aural reinforcement that occurs when children sound words out as they spell, which has been shown to be highly effective in improving spelling skills, more so than traditional techniques [6, 21].

Ozzypie, an online spelling tutor, was developed in response to the lack of instruction in spelling; however, its utility extends beyond the current crisis, not least because of the widening of the existing learning gap that has arisen as a result of children missing school during this period [5, 7, 28, 34]. Despite the reported literacy rates of between 80 and 90%, there are reports of thousands of at-risk young people leaving the formal education system with limited literacy skills, subject to the attendant lack of opportunities, unemployment and crime [1]. This problem often arises because the young reader never grasped the basics of literacy, including the skill of spelling.

The rest of the paper is organised as follows: Sect. 2 describes related work, while Sect. 3 details the design of the Ozzypie spelling tutor. Section 4 outlines an exploratory study of the tutor, the results and analysis of which are presented in Sect. 5. Section 6 concludes the paper.

2   Related Work

The majority of advanced literacy tools that have been developed have been automated reading tutors. These tools have provided virtual environments in which learners can engage in independent, self-paced work. These tools employ a variety of approaches to engage readers and to provide reading instruction. Regardless of the theoretical approach, or the design philosophy, it has been shown that they all provide some level of improvement in literacy skills compared to no intervention, and for some, the level of improvement in some aspects of literacy was comparable to that achieved with human intervention [37].

The tools are broadly separated into those that employ a constructivist approach to learning and those that do not. In general, the non-constructivist tutors are first generation tools, such as Watch me Read!, Project Listen, the Colorado Literacy Tutor - COLIT and STAR [15, 26, 31, 38]. Tutors developed around a constructivist approach are the newer tutors, Alphie's Alley, conText, iStart-E, ITSS and Summary Street [4, 11, 19, 20, 22].

2.1 Intelligent Spelling Tutors

Leescircus is a reading and spelling tool that was developed for use by Dutch Children [36]. The tool contained a number of exercises aimed at teaching the basic skills, including spelling, that are required to become successful readers. Van Daal and Reitsma conducted experiments with kindergarten children, who used the tool at least three times a week, for 5 min each day, over a six month period [36]. Not only were the spelling gains significant, the children also learned positive behaviours related to on task focus, as a result of working with the Leescircus. A reading and spelling tutor, MultiFunk, was developed for Norwegian children [10] The tool was shown to increase the reading and spelling skills of young users, in particular boys, who improved more than the girls that used the tool. A Balanced Reading Approach for Canadians Designed to Achieve Best Results for All (ABRACADABRA) was developed to assist young Canadian learners to improve their reading and spelling skills [32]. The researchers reported increases in spelling and other skills, though they were not statistically significant. Importantly though, analyses of the intervention highlighted the need to involve teachers in the research stage of implementation, with extensive training sessions and support after the intervention ends, so as to ensure their buy-in and the long term use of the tutor [16].

The systems mentioned above combined spelling and reading tutors, using the spelling as a scaffold to reading and attempting to reinforce spelling skills by enhancing reading skills. One of the earliest dedicated spelling tutors, Spengels, was developed for Dutch learners to receive spelling instruction in English [3]. The tools utilised a morphological approach to spelling instruction in a dedicated intelligent tutoring system [3]. The tutor provided guided learning, exploited the errors of the user to build a dedicated student model, and tracked user progress to ensure that users were adaptively presented with increasingly challenging tasks.

3   Ozzypie Spelling Tutor

A modular component-based design was deliberately chosen for the Ozzypie Spelling Tutor. A layered architecture allows agile scaling of new features through incremental discovery, trial and error and testing with users and stakeholders. This was critical since an iterative design cycle was employed where early users tested Ozzypie, provided informal feedback and the development team then rolled out modifications and the cycle continued. The tutor's core however is based on the standard models (expert, domain, student and instructional) of a traditional intelligent tutoring system integrated within a web-based, microservices framework. Figure 1 shows the separation of the components into two distinct systems with interactions controlled via abstract application programming interfaces (APIs). The technology stack was based on React owing to the strong need for a flexible, component-based implementation with highly reusable modules.

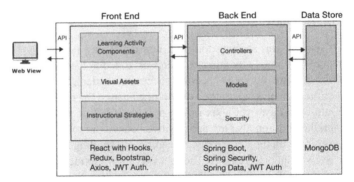

Fig. 1. The microservices architecture and technology stack of the Ozzpie spelling tutor

Several layers are central to the design: user modelling, interaction, instructional and content layers. The learning activity component in the front-end governed the different types of spelling-related activities available to users. Figure 2 shows how students are presented with options to view the words in a spelling list, try a spelling practice test or try a spelling quiz. Figure 3 shows how students can listen to word pronunciations and review word spellings before attempting a practice or quiz session.

Fig. 2. Speller dashboard three main activity paths: view spelling list, practice, quiz

The Practice and Quiz activities were developed to use different strategies such as a one-word-at-a-time attempt or a notebook style, multi-word attempt. The latter is similar to when children are tested in the classroom with written, paper-based assessments that allow a child to review an answer and modify it (by writing) before submitting for grading. The former mimics a mental test where children have to spell a word one letter at a time, with no option to review prior spelling words. Figures 3, 4 and 5 show the differences between the Practice and Quiz activities.

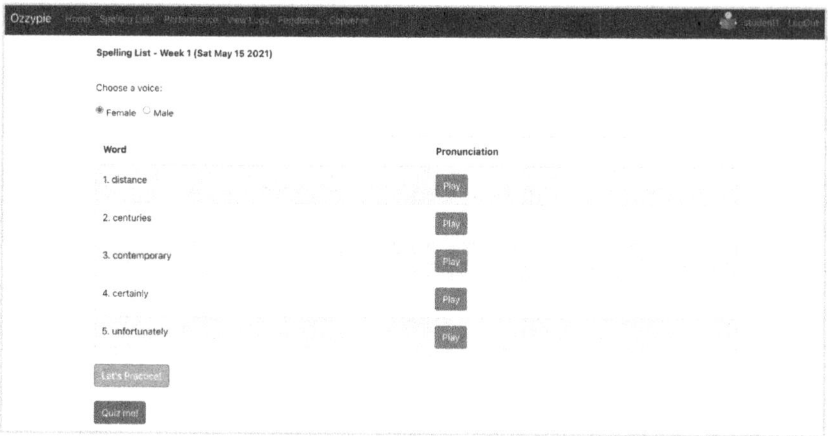

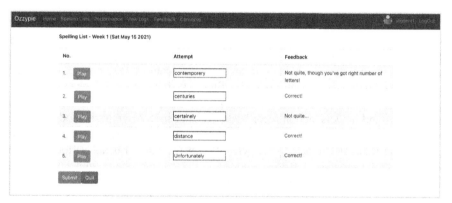

Fig. 3. Spelling list view showing word spellings and play buttons to hear pronunciations in a male or female voice

Fig. 4. Practice activity (notebook) view showing play buttons, sample text in the attempt area and basic corrective feedback

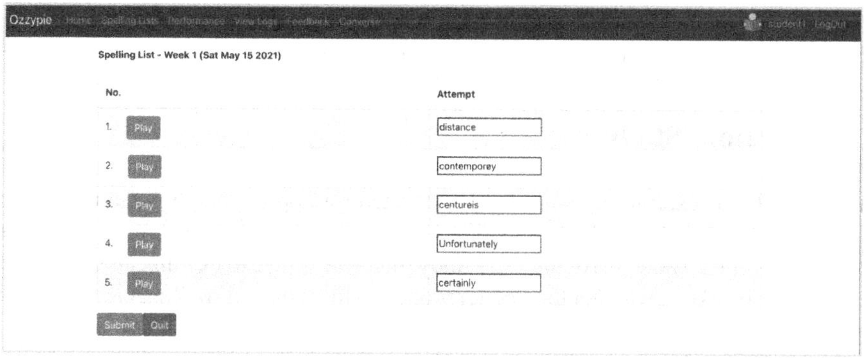

Fig. 5. Quiz activity (notebook) view showing play buttons, sample text in the attempt area and no feedback

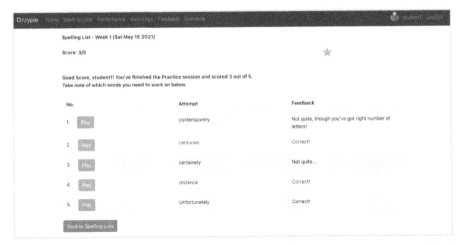

Fig. 6. Results view after a spelling practice session where attempts and feedback can be reviewed

The Instructional strategies component controlled the corrective feedback given to a learner in Practice tests where the aim is to strengthen fluency. This component also randomised the order of the spelling words and is capable of supplying word definitions and example sentences. However, the latter two features were not released in the speller for the study reported in this paper. Figure 6 shows a sample generated feedback for a notebook mode of practice. The Models component in the back-end stored the user roles and models, action record schemas and speech synthesis models. Three types of user roles and models were implemented: administrators, students and teachers. Synthetic male and female voice generation was achieved using various Google Speech API cloud services. A British voice was selected since the pronunciations were phonologically closer to accents in the Caribbean compared to an American voice. A text-to-speech (TTS) recognition feature was also included in the speller to accommodate voice-based interaction, dialogue and task-related question answering. However, the TTS feature currently relies on publicly-available speech models which do not fit the target user audience; it was therefore also excluded from this study. The Controllers and Security components were responsible for authentication of users, encryption of the various microservice end points, general error handling and session management.

4   Exploratory Study

A mixed-methods exploratory study was conducted for approximately three months in 2021 with several early users. As mentioned earlier, an iterative development process was adopted for the Ozzypie rollout. The study therefore aimed to examine how children used the Speller, assess whether the Speller promoted independent spelling practice work on a child's part, and gauge how the children responded to the Speller's synthetic voice. In addition, parents and guardians are critical stakeholders owing to their necessary involvement in supervising their children due to the remote instructional delivery of classes. Naturally, parents and guardians were included in the study for these reasons as they are also valid users.

4.1 Ethical Considerations

Children require special treatment in any research study owing to their ages and vulnerability. Informed consent from parents/guardians and informed assent from the children were therefore carefully sought. Participation was voluntary and withdrawal from the study was allowed and explained. Data logs were protected with administrator access restricted to principal investigators on the research team. Interviews were facilitated via video and/or audio, and text/written answers to respect the privacy of the parents/guardians who did not wish to have video or audio interviews. Ethical approval was received from the relevant review boards.

4.2 Participants

Twenty eight (28) participants were included in the study with the following distributions and characteristics:

- 14 Children: Trinidad (10); Jamaica (4); Male (5); Female (9); Average age (9.5);
- 14 Parents/Guardians: Trinidad (10); Jamaica (4); Male (2); Female (12)

The children attended different schools in their respective countries, and were in different classes ranging from Grades 1–4/Infants class to Standard 3.

4.3 Methodology

User accounts were first created for the children and their parents/guardians in Ozzypie. Instructions were shared with parents/guardians briefly describing how to add spelling lists to their profiles and how to share those lists with their child(ren). In several cases, 1–3 research team members filled the teacher role for some of the children by providing lists appropriate for their age or actual spelling lists from a school. The children and parents/guardians were allowed to use Ozzypie under their own direction for several months. No interventions or reminders to use Ozzypie were given since the intention was to observe how users chose to interact with it. Spelling lists for some children were regularly released by a research team member (especially for the cluster of children from a particular school) near to the end of term exams for schools. Small, new features were released also and/or critical bug fixes were done during the trial use as feedback was shared by parents/guardians. Student log data was then downloaded from Ozzypie for analysis near to the end of the trial, and interviews were conducted with both the children and their parents/guardians.

5   Results and Discussion

This section presents the statistics collected for general usage patterns, interview responses and interesting trends from the data log analyses.

5.1 General Usage Statistics

There was high variation in the general usage statistics for the student-initiated activities. Table 1 shows the large standard deviations for spelling exercise and individual word attempts indicating that some children used Ozzypie heavily while others did not.

Table 1. Summary of usage statistics for common student activities/actions in Ozzypie

Student activity/Action	Average number	Std. Dev	Max. number	Min. number
Spelling exercise attempts	9	10.6	41	1
Spelling word attempts	110	126.3	446	5
Repeat pronunciations	40	51.9	201	1
Quit spelling activity	3	4.8	18	0

5.2 Interviews with Parents and Children

Five closed-ended questions were designed to elicit feedback on the user experience and perceived utility; responses were scored on a 5-point Likert scale, with higher numbers indicating higher levels of acceptability. Slightly less than 85% of users found the tutor easy to use, 7.7% found it difficult to use, while the remainder were neutral about it. There was essentially no difference in how the male and female users perceive the ease of use. The majority of the users (69.3%) enjoyed using the tutor. Almost a quarter had no strong feelings about it, while 7.7% strongly disliked using it. There was a marked, though statistically insignificant, difference in how female and male users felt about using the tutor. All of the male users indicated that they enjoyed using the tutor while half of the female users were either neutral or strongly disliked using it. A similar pattern emerged when students were asked about their preference for spelling practice. Overall, 84.6% either preferred the tutor or had no preference, while the other 15.4% slightly preferred using a book during practice. Here again, male users were basically positive about using the tutor, while female users preferred using a book. Arguably, the most important finding is that 92.3% of all users felt that their spelling skills improved after using the tutor. There were none of the students that felt that using the tutor had a negative impact on their spelling.

As parents and guardians are likely to be involved with, at least, the initial setup of the tool for their ward, it was deemed important to understand their impressions of the ease of performing those tasks. Given the nature of the trial, most parents and guardians were already signed up and had their spelling lists populated. However, those that did interact with the signup and setup phases of the process found it to be straight-forward to input the spelling lists. The parents were all positive about the tool and many identified potential benefits for their child (useful drill and practice tool, aids preparation for in-school tests, encourages independent work, convenient to use, reduces supervision time needed to help children practice). More than 80% of parents/guardians thought the experience was positive, though many pointed to student's initial frustrations with the tool when they didn't score highly, or did not find the voice to be intelligible.

5.3 Data Logs

One hundred and twenty nine (129) interaction log records were produced by Ozzypie for the study. These logs can range from 200 to 500 records each in length depending on the actions taken by a student. The distribution of the logs for the different activity types are as follows: Practice (30), Quiz (10), Practice-Notebook (57), Quiz-Notebook (32). The Notebook activities produced further detailed interaction log data with the action codes shown in Table 2. The action codes correspond to particular actions taken by a student and provide a fine grained record of what a student did for a Practice or Quiz activity.

Table 2. List of action codes recorded by the speller for particular student actions on different speller activity tasks: View List (V), Practice Activity (P), Quiz Activity (Q)

Action code	Student action	Interpretation(s) of action code as student behaviour	Task
400	Press play button	Listening to word pronunciation	V; P; Q
401	Click in text field	Intention to start or continue typing answer for a spelling word	P; Q
402	Click of out text field	Intention to stop typing answer for a spelling word	P; Q
		Intention to get corrective feedback on answer typed	P
403	Key press (letter)	Typing a letter in an answer for a spelling word	P; Q
404	Key press (space)	Typing an impactless character in a spelling word	P; Q
405	Key press (backspace)	Deleting a letter in an answer for a spelling word	P; Q
406	Press quit button	Intention to end session without getting a score	P; Q
		Disinterest in activity task	
407	Press submit button	Finished entering all answers. Intention to get a score	P; Q

Figures 7 and 8 show graphs produced from the interaction logs collected for one student, Student A, who attempted a spelling list, Week 1, with the following words: business, beginning, accommodation, amateur, bizarre, aggression, basically, argument, achieve, believe, aggressive, accommodate, apparently, accidentally, acquire, appearance. A typical sequence went from pressing the play button (400), clicking in the text field to enter an answer (401), typing the characters of the word (403), clicking out the textfield (402) - getting immediate feedback of correct/incorrect, and then on to playing the pronunciation of the next word (400). Feedback was given in both conditions in the Practice activity (Fig. 7 and 8) thereby encouraging the repair of incorrect answers and accounting for many backspacing actions (405). It is clear in Fig. 7 that the student made many more error corrections (405) possibly due to confusion with the Female voice pronunciations. In comparison, Fig. 8 shows far less corrections. The voice is the only difference between the two events.

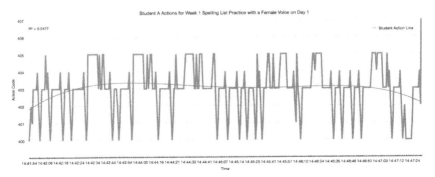

Fig. 7. Student A - actions for Week 1 spelling list practice with a female voice, Day 1

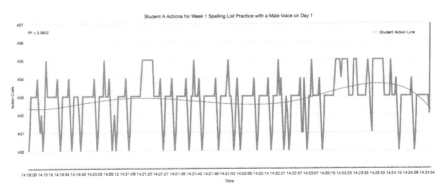

Fig. 8. Student A - actions for Week 1 spelling list practice with a male voice, Day 1

Another student, Student B, worked with the same Week 1 spelling list as Student A. This student maintained the female voice throughout. In Fig. 9 on Day 1, it is clear that Student B used the feedback feature, available in the Practice activity, more often as evidenced by the numerous oscillations from 403 to 401. Also, the student made many error corrections, shown by the oscillations from 403 to 405. Short bursts of typing as well as a longer time spent on the activity (numerous tick marks on the X-axis). The typing bursts however lengthened in Fig. 10, in the Quiz activity, possibly meaning that Student B spent more time typing answers. Notice as well that there is far less error correction occuring and a lower score (14/17) than the practice (17/17). The behaviour of longer typing bursts (403) and less error correction (405) continued on Day 2 for Student B as shown in Fig. 11. However, there was still considerable use of the feedback feature (oscillations from 401 to 402) since it was a Practice activity and feedback was available.

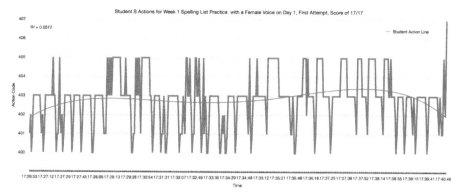

Fig. 9. Student B - actions for Week 1 spelling list practice with a female voice, Day 1, first attempt, score of 17/17

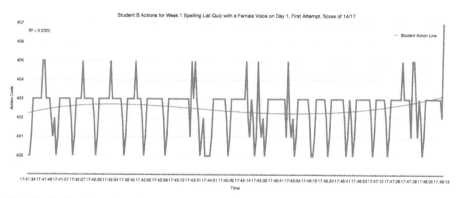

Fig. 10. Student B - actions for Week 1 spelling list quiz with a female voice, Day 1, first attempt, score of 14/17

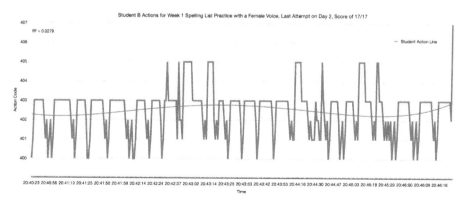

Fig. 11. Student B - actions for Week 1 spelling list practice with female voice, last attempt on Day 2, score of 17/17

Figure 12 shows that the student improved in the Quiz for the same words on Day 2. Fewer instances of error correction, smoother typing bursts and shorter time overall on the quiz were observed in Fig. 12 compared to Fig. 10 and a higher score (16/17). Figure 13 confirms the improvement where even fewer corrections are seen and the score is perfect at 17/17.

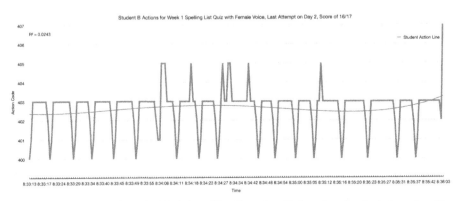

Fig. 12. Student B - actions for Week 1 spelling list quiz with female voice, last attempt on Day 2, score of 16/17

The students' performances may have been impacted by the speller's synthetic voice (more clarity with the male voice and less errors being made) despite the overall preference for the female voice. This observation could be a bias that children in the region may have for female voices owing to female teachers being more common at their class level in schools. Either way, the logs confirm that feedback had an impact on the learner's behaviour and led to improvements not only in the overall score but also in the consistency of the childrens' on-task behaviour during answer typing.

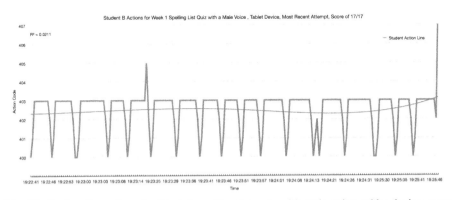

Fig. 13. Student B - actions for Week 1 spelling list quiz with male voice, tablet device, most recent attempt, score of 16/17

6 Conclusion

The Ozzypie Spelling Tool was motivated in response to the rapid school closures across regions in the Caribbean. Many parents and children were caught in situations that required quick adjustments to daily schedules for learning and doing school work. Most of the supervision fell on parents and presented a valuable opportunity to create a novel tool that would alleviate some of the burden. The combination of a data-driven and theory-grounded approach within Ozzypie's modular, microservice-based architecture was shown to be successful for flexible updates. The lightweight, simple interface design was mostly intuitive and easy to use by school-age children. By leveraging existing speech technologies and multi-modal interaction via text and voice, important requirements for a culturally-appropriate synthetic voice were clearly revealed. Analysis of interviews and log data learner behaviour and on-task activities revealed broad learner engagement, while parents/guardians report value in the learning support provided and anecdotal evidence of test score improvement. Importantly, the need for a culturally-situated design emerged as students interacted with the speech-enabled feature.

References

1. Bartlett, L., López, D., Mein, E., Valdiviezo, L.A.: Adolescent literacies in Latin America and the Caribbean. Rev. Res. Educ. **35**(1), 174–207 (2011)
2. Berninger, V.W., Nagy, W., Beers, S.: Child writers' construction and reconstruction of single sentences and construction of multi-sentence texts: contributions of syntax and transcription to translation. Read. Writ. **24**(2), 151–182 (2011)
3. Bos, E., van de Plassche, J.: A knowledge-based, English verb-form tutor. J. Artif. Intell. Educ. **5**(1), 107–129 (1994)
4. Chambers, B., et al.: Computer-assisted tutoring in success for all: reading outcomes for first graders. J. Res. Educ. Effect. **1**(2), 120–137 (2008)
5. De Lisle, J.: Insights on the marginalization of poor children in the education system of Trinidad and Tobago. In: Blackman, S., Conrad, D., Brown, L. (eds.) Achieving Inclusive Education in the Caribbean and Beyond, pp. 89–119. Springer, Cham (2019). https://doi.org/10.1007/978-3-030-15769-2_6
6. Drivas, M.K., Drevon, D.D.: The effect of a sounding-out step for cover-copy-compare on spelling word acquisition. Behav. Anal. Pract. **12**(3), 514–522 (2018). https://doi.org/10.1007/s40617-018-00322-5
7. Coe, R., Weidmann, B., Coleman, R., Kay, J.: Impact of school closures on the attainment gap: rapid evidence assessment. Education Endowment Foundation, Milbank, United Kingdom (2020)
8. Ehri, L.C.: Sources of difficulty in learning to spell and read. Adv. Dev. Behav. Pediatr. **7**, 121–195 (1986)
9. Farah, M.J., et al.: Childhood poverty: specific associations with neurocognitive development. Brain Res. **1110**(1), 166–174 (2006)
10. Fasting, R.B., Lyster, S.H.: The effects of computer technology in assisting the development of literacy in young struggling readers and spellers. Eur. J. Spec. Needs Educ. **20**(1), 21–40 (2005)
11. Franzke, M., Kintsch, E., Caccamise, D., Johnson, N., Dooley, S.: Summary Street®: computer support for comprehension and writing. J. Educ. Comput. Res. **33**(1), 53–80 (2005)

12. Galuschka, K., Ise, E., Krick, K., Schulte-Körne, G.: Effectiveness of treatment approaches for children and adolescents with reading disabilities: a meta-analysis of randomized controlled trials. PLoS One **9**(2), e89900 (2014)
13. Gough, P., Juel, C., Griffith, P.: Reading, spelling and the orthographic cipher. In: Reading Acquisition, pp. 35–48. Routledge, Abingdon (1992)
14. Graham, S., Santangelo, T.: Does spelling instruction make students better spellers, readers, and writers? A meta-analytic review. Read. Writ. **27**(9), 1703–1743 (2014)
15. Hagen, A., Pellom, B., Cole, R.: Children's speech recognition with application to interactive books and tutors. In: 2003 IEEE Workshop on Automatic Speech Recognition and Understanding (ASRU 2003), pp. 186–191. IEEE, St. Tomas Virgin Islands (2003)
16. Johnson, C.J., Beitchman, J.H., Brownlie, E.B.: Twenty-year follow-up of children with and without speech-language impairments: family, educational, occupational, and quality of life outcomes. Am. J. Speech Lang. Pathol. **19**(1), 51–65 (2010)
17. Joshi, R., Treiman, R., Carreker, S., Moats, L.: How words cast their spell: spelling is an integral part of learning the language, not a matter of memorization. Am. Educ. **32**(4), 6–16 (2008)
18. Juel, C.: Learning to read and write - a longitudinal-study of 54 children from 1st through 4th grades. J. Educ. Psychol. **80**(4), 437–447 (1998)
19. Lenhard, W., Baier, H., Endlich, D., Schneider, W., Hoffmann, J.: Rethinking strategy instruction: direct reading strategy instruction versus computer-based guided practice. J. Res. Read. **36**(2), 223–240 (2013)
20. McCarthy, K.S., Soto, C.M., de Blume, A.P.G., Palma, D., González, J.I., McNamara, D.S.: Improving reading comprehension in Spanish using iSTART-E: a pilot study. Int. J. Comput.-Assist. Lang. Learn. Teach. (IJCALLT) **10**(4), 66–82 (2020)
21. Mann, T.B., Bushell, D., Jr., Morris, E.K.: Use of sounding out to improve spelling in young children. J. Appl. Behav. Anal. **43**(1), 89–93 (2010)
22. Meyer, B.J., Wijekumar, K.: A web-based tutoring system for the structure strategy: theoretical background, design, and findings. In: McNamara, D.S. (ed.) Reading Comprehension Strategies: Theories, Interventions, and Technologies, pp. 347–375. Erlbaum, Mahwah (2007)
23. Ministry of Education, Youth and Information, Jamaica: National Standards Curriculum Guide Grade 1. Government of Jamaica, Jamaica (2018)
24. Ministry of Education, Youth and Information, Jamaica: National Standards Curriculum Guide Grade 2. Government of Jamaica, Jamaica (2008)
25. Moats, L.: How spelling supports reading. Am. Educat. Winter 12–43 (2006)
26. Mostow, J., Roth, S.F., Hauptmann, A.G., Kane, M.: A prototype reading coach that listens. In: The Twelfth National Conference on Artificial Intelligence (AAAI-94), pp. 785–792. Seattle, Washington (1994)
27. Murphy, J.F., Hern, C.L., Williams, R.L., McLaughlin, T.F.: The effects of the copy, cover, compare approach in increasing spelling accuracy with learning disabled students. Contemp. Educ. Psychol. **15**(4), 378–386 (1990)
28. Murray, J.: HUGE GAP TO BRIDGE - headmaster estimates it will take years to recover from COVID learning loss. Jamaica Gleaner. https://jamaica-gleaner.com. Accessed 11 Jan 2021
29. Rapp, B., Lipka, K.: The literate brain: the relationship between spelling and reading. J. Cogn. Neurosci. **23**(5), 1180–1197 (2011)
30. Ministry of Education, Republic of Trinidad and Tobago: Primary School Curriculum: Curriculum Guide English Language Arts, Infants 1 – Standard 5. Republic of Trinidad and Tobago (2013)
31. Russell, M., Series, R.W., Wallace, J.L., Brown, C., Skilling, A.: The STAR system: an interactive pronunciation tutor for young children. Comput. Speech Lang. **14**(2), 161–175 (2000)

32. Savage, R.S., Erten, O., Abrami, P.C., Hipps, G., Comaskey, E., van Lierop, D.: ABRA-CADABRA in the hands of teachers: the effectiveness of a web-based literacy intervention in Grade 1 language arts programs. Comput. Educ. **55**, 911–922 (2010)
33. Scott, C.M.: Principles and methods of spelling instruction: applications for poor spellers. Top. Lang. Disord. **20**(3), 66–82 (2000)
34. Seusan, L.A., Maradiegue, R.: Education on hold: a generation of children in Latin America and the Caribbean are missing out on schooling because of COVID-19. UNICEF, Republic of Panama (2020)
35. Treiman, R.: Learning to spell words: findings, theories, and issues. Sci. Stud. Read. **21**(4), 265–276 (2017)
36. Van Daal, V., Reitsma, P.: Computer-assisted learning to read and spell: results from two pilot studies. J. Res. Read. **23**, 181–193 (2000)
37. Westwood, P.: Learning to spell: enduring theories, recent research and current issues. Aust. J. Learn. Diffic. **18**(1), 1–16 (2018)
38. Williams, S., Nix, D., Fairweather, P.: Using speech recognition technology to enhance literacy instruction for emerging readers. In: Proceedings of ICLS2000, pp. 115–120. Erlbaum, Mahwah (2000)
39. Willson, V.L., Rupley, W.H., Rodriguez, M., Mergen, S.: The relationships among orthographic components of word identification and spelling for Grades 1–6. Lit. Res. Instruct. **39**(1), 89–102 (1999)

Bie—Modernism with Cultural Calculations in Multiple Dimensions

Zifeng Qi, Haiguang Chen$^{(\boxtimes)}$, Mingxing Liu, and JianJiang Wang

Shanghai Normal University, Shanghai 201418, China
598055818@qq.com

Abstract. Under the background of different Bie-modernism, starting from the "different from" way of thinking, seeking original words and thoughts, and establishing true modern thoughts, in which deep fake and deep identification can be compared with the cultural calculations in machine learning. The combination of computing technology and its technical support can realize the modernity of authenticity recognition. This paper mainly uses characters identification as an example. Because characters will have many characteristics, this paper adopts a multi-dimensional consideration, including the appearance, actions, language, and other aspects of the characters for cultural calculations, so as to show that computers can be effectively combined with other modern times with strong feasibility and high efficiency. The experiment uses the combination of Word2Vec algorithm and Transformer network to form a cultural calculation model for character identification tasks. Experiments on the Chinese dataset show that this model can obtain deep features in the text, and still has a good screening effect for data with similar surface features.

Keywords: Bie-modernism · Deep learning · Character identification

1 Introduction

1.1 Bie-Modernism

Bie-modernism is a concept in the field of aesthetics. Bie-modernism is encompasses the meaning of not wanting modernity, saying goodbye to modernity, being another kind of modernity, it is the negation of the negation of the post-modern, and it is the doctrinal idea with new thought structure and conceptual innovation [1]. Because of the rapid development of human civilization, pseudo-modernity is enveloping human civilization and hindering its further development. China is currently in the period of pre-modern, modern and post-modern convergence, and the collision of ideas in such period will become more and more intense, but Chinese aesthetics lacks original thought construction and the doctrinal leadership, which contrasts with the doctrinal theories of post-modern output in the West. Drawing on the innovative thinking of the post-modern era and fusing it with the philosophical thought of the Middle Way in the Chinese tradition, an all-modernism with a high degree of Chinese aesthetics and contemporary thought was refined. Therefore, Bie-modernism is now a contemporary feature of cultural studies.

M. Rauterberg (Ed.): HCII 2022, LNCS 13324, pp. 120–136, 2022.
https://doi.org/10.1007/978-3-031-05434-1_8

1.2 Machine Learning

Machine learning aims to use computers to solve complex problems in engineering applications and science. The study of machine learning allows computers to continuously identify existing knowledge, acquire new knowledge, discard invalid knowledge, and continuously improve their performance and learn from data. Computers build suitable mathematical models by employing mathematical methods; by simulating the human brain allowing computers to perform symbolic learning and neural network learning, all of which can serve to make machines solve engineering problems efficiently and accurately [2]. The development of machine learning can be roughly divided into four phases. The first stage was from 1950 to 1960, when people started to conduct a lot of iterative experiments on the system to improve its execution and operational efficiency, but it was far from meeting industrial needs; the second stage was from 1960 to 1970, when the first attempts to simulate the process of human learning using graphs and logical structures began, but the results achieved still lacked practicality; the third stage was from 1970 to 1980, more theories entered a more mature stage and began to be integrated with other fields; the fourth stage made the culmination of machine learning from 1986, when methods such as artificial network learning and symbolic learning began to emerge [3]. In the context of alibi modernism, the pseudo-deep techniques in machine learning can play a role in hindering the overall enhancement of human civilization, while alibi modernism, which aims to distinguish the true from the false, can be restored to the real world by using deep alibi techniques in machine learning. The use of cultural computing as one of the technical supports can better integrate computers with aesthetics for the purpose of identifying true and false modernity.

1.3 Cultural Computing

Cultural computing is a technical tool that uses social computing, big data, artificial intelligence, and other technologies to cross-fertilize with humanities and history to realize the excavation and dissemination of cultural contents, promote digital humanities research, and promote the development of cultural prosperity. The aim is to apply computing and related technologies to the cultural field, explore the laws of development, reveal their inner connections, and present and disseminate them visually. The purpose is to propose the basic path of cultural gene mining and characterization, and then to make full use of cultural genomics to quantitatively analyze the DNA of Chinese civilization, construct a cultural gene pool and civilization gene map, and combine the results of quantitative analysis with empirical investigation of folk culture, archaeological culture, and historical documents. The results of the quantitative analysis will be combined with the folk culture, archaeological culture and historical documents based on the empirical investigation, to realize the deep excavation of Chinese culture [4]. One of the important aspects of cultural computing is to reveal the evolutionary characteristics and laws of cultural change and development, and thus to provide historical reference for the development of present-day culture. The application of cultural computation in the context of other modernism can achieve a good effect of deconstruction. This paper elaborates on the application of cultural computation in alias modernism, taking the task of character identification as an example.

2 Related Work

This section will mainly discuss the deep-learning methods for character identification based on text information. The Doc2Vec model is used to digitally represent character information about its background, words and deeds, actions, and character descriptions. The current speech and deeds are judged by using a deep neural network learning method, so that it can determine the identity of the current character.

2.1 Text Classification Algorithm

Document classification is one of the most common applications in the field of natural language processing. It aims at solving the problem of accurately classifying a document or a piece of text given its context. Document classification often requires a combination of traditional text processing techniques and machine learning or deep learning algorithms to accomplish the task of "classifying" a document.

The main ideas of document classification algorithms are document annotation, document format conversion, lexicon generation, calculation of word weights, topic modeling, training of classification models, and prediction steps. In the process of training classification models, machine learning models such as support vector machines and logistic regression models can be applied, or deep learning, which is a popular method in recent years, can be used to build neural network classifiers for document classification tasks.

In this paper, we focus on the character identification task, which is also a text information-based classification task in essence. At the input level, both the document classification task and the person identification studied in this topic are textual information. At the output level, the document classification algorithm focuses on the problem of multiple classification, that is, the algorithm predicts the exact class of the document over a limited number of classes, while this paper aims to perform the target character identification, that is, to better character identification by transforming superficial features such as the character's speech, behavior, appearance, dress, and background into deeper features such as the character's personality traits and even the character's behavioral habits Characters, because character identification task is not a simple classification problem.

In addition to the algorithmic ideas, the character identification characters studied in this paper can be borrowed from the document classification algorithm; at the same time, the topic studied in this paper can also be borrowed from some of the implementation steps of the document classification algorithm. The textual information of the text input is used to generate the lexicon part of the information, and finally the deep character features are generated for character identification.

2.2 Word Separation Algorithm

For most natural language processing algorithmic models today, word separation is one of the most fundamental tasks. Word separation is the process of recombining consecutive word sequences into word sequences by certain specifications. Since the difference between Chinese and English is that there are spaces between words in English, it is easy to distinguish individual words, while Chinese only has punctuation marks between statements, and there is no way to divide between words, so the task of word separation for Chinese text is more complicated than that for English text.

At present, Chinese word separation algorithms are roughly divided into three categories. The first category is based on string matching, which mainly scans the string and matches if the substrings of the string are found to be the same as the words in the dictionary. The second category is based on statistical and machine learning word separation methods, which mainly model Chinese based on manually annotated lexical and statistical features, i.e., the model parameters are trained based on the annotated corpus information, and then the probability of occurrence of each subword is calculated by the model in the word separation stage, and the subword with the highest probability is taken as the final result. Currently, the common sequence annotation models are HMM [5] and CRF [6]. The core idea of the third class of Chinese word separation algorithms is to let the computer simulate the human understanding of the sentence and then produce the result of word separation, and this class of algorithms is the main research direction in the future, although there is no specific application yet.

For deep learning character identification based on textual information, the n-gram [7] model, a statistical as well as machine learning based word separation method, is used. The model is based on the assumption that the occurrence of the nth word is only associated with the first $N - 1$ words and not with any other words, and the probability of the whole sentence is the product of the occurrence probabilities of the individual words. In this paper, n is set to 3and the Trigram model is used because higher-order n-grams are more context sensitive but the data possess more sparsity, while lower-order n-grams consider very limited contextual information but have stronger robustness, and based on comprehensive considerations, the Trigram model is chosen to be used.

In this paper, we use the classical Jieba [8], which is the most commonly used Chinese word splitting tool, and comes with a dictionary called dict.txt, which contains more than 102,000 words, including the number of occurrences and lexical properties of the words. These2 more than ten thousand words are put into a trie tree for word graph scanning. trie tree is a kind of better known prefix tree, which means that the first few words of a word are the same, it means they have the same prefix, and it can be stored using trie tree, which has the advantage of fast finding speed.

2.3 Word2Vec Algorithm

Since the parameters of the Ngram model explode with N, the value of N is generally taken to be no more3 than. In addition, the Ngram model considers only the above of each predicted word and ignores the intrinsic connection between words and their similarity.

Since the Ngram model treats words as isolated atomic units, for each word it corresponds to a one-hot vector, in the Ngram model, the length of the vector corresponding to each word is the size of the lexicon, and if there are thousands of words in the corpus, then this faces the problem of word vector dimensionality explosion.

In order to solve the problem of Ngram model, Bengio et al. proposed the concept of word embedding in 20032007, which mainly solves the two major problems of calculating conditional probabilities in statistical language models and expressing word vectors in vector space models. However, there are still some limitations in this language model, and the main bottleneck is that the model is still difficult to handle variable-length sequences and the training speed is too slow. To solve this problem, Mikolov et al. proposed a Word2Vec method [9]. Word2Vec is divided into two main models: CBOW, which predicts central words based on their contexts, and Skip-gram, which, on the contrary, uses central words to predict contexts. Meanwhile, Word2Vec also has two optimization algorithms - Hierarchical Softmax and Negative Sampling, the former decomposes the complex normalized probability into a series of conditional probability scores and uses Huffman trees to improve the training efficiency, the latter is mainly to transform the likelihood function of the model to solve the parameter prediction problem for those probabilistic models that cannot be normalized.

The main purpose of Word2Vec is to vectorize the input text, specifically the "words" of the input text, to obtain a dense word vector that can characterize the semantics, thus preparing the foundation for the subsequent steps of the algorithm.

2.4 DOC2Vec Algorithm

After acquiring the individual word vectors of the text by the Word2Vec algorithm, it is how to associate the word vectors with the document vectors of the input text, i.e. how to use the acquired word vectors to generate the document vectors and maintain the semantic richness and high quality of the Word2Vec word vectors.

To solve this problem, the 2014 annual Doc2Vec algorithm [10] was proposed, which is an unsupervised learning algorithm to obtain vector representations of sentences, paragraphs, and documents, and belongs to the extension of Word2Vec. Doc2Vec is to add the document vector as an additional input to the input layer when the word vector is input, and map it to the projection layer with other word vectors for cascading or averaging.

For the content of the study, the Doc2Vec model is used to obtain the document topic vector representation directly, that is, for each segment of text of each character, the Doc2Vec algorithm can be used to obtain the set of text feature vectors of that character as the input vector set for training.

2.5 Transformer Network Model

Transformer is a model structure based entirely on the attention mechanism, consisting of an encoding component and a decoding component, both of which are stacked separately by the encoder and decoder layers [11]. This model can achieve very good results in natural language processing, being able to equalize the distance between any two words1, which is very effective in solving the intractable long-term dependency problem in the field of natural language processing; and has a powerful parallel computing performance, which can greatly reduce the computational complexity of the algorithm.

2.6 Character Identification Algorithm

This paper focuses on the task of character identification, so it needs to be based on the superficial characteristics of the given characters (including speech, behavior, dress and appearance), etc. The dataset used in this paper is the portrayal of each character in Journey to the West, lines from film and TV dramas and poems, mainly extracting the background, appearance dress, behavior and dialogues of the characters Sun Wukong, Pig Bajie, Tang Monk and Sha Monk.

The depiction of a character can be divided into direct and indirect depictions. In direct descriptions, there are three main dimensions that are analyzed. The first dimension is the physical dimension, which reflects the character's personality, family situation, and social relations by describing the character's appearance, dress, and objects in hand; the second dimension is the social dimension, which further explains the character's situation, the reasons for character formation, etc. by describing the character's interaction and social activities in the living environment, work, friends, family, etc.; the third dimension is the heart dimension, which directly or indirectly reflects the character's The third dimension is the heart dimension, i.e., the character's psychological state is further made more three-dimensional through direct or indirect reactions to what is in the character's mind, actions, looks, language, etc. In the side description, the character's characteristics are mainly set off by other people's comments on the character. This paper focuses on the identification of characters through direct descriptions of characters. It is mainly through collecting the characters' background, actions, appearance and language to obtain the characters' distinctive features and thus achieve differentiation from others.

3 Algorithm Introduction

3.1 Transformer Model Structure

Encoder Components. The encoder assembly is composed of a number of encoder stacks. For each encoder the structure is shown in the Fig. 1. Each layer of the encoder has two sub-layers, the first one is a self-attentive layer consisting of a multi-headed attention mechanism and a data normalization mechanism; the second sub-layer is a spatial transformation layer consisting of a fully connected feed-forward network and a data normalization mechanism. The residual connection is chosen to connect between the two sublayers, i.e., the output is expressed as a linear superposition of the input and a nonlinear transformation of the input.

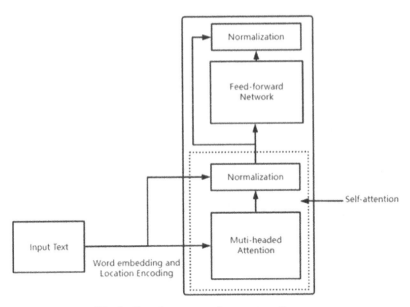

Fig. 1. Transformer encoder structure diagram

In the calculation of the self-attentive mechanism, the output of attention can be represented by Eq. (1):

$$attention\_ouput = Attention(Q, K, V) \tag{1}$$

where Q denotes query vectors (queries), K denotes keys vectors (Keys), and V denotes value vectors (Values). The query vector is the set of vectors formed by each vector of the sentence at the output; the key vector is the various weights corresponding to each vector of the sentence at the input; and the value vector is the set of vectors formed by each vector of the sentence at the input. In the self-attentive mechanism, by using the scaled dot product attention for computation, Eq. (1) can be transformed into Eq. (2) notational representation:

$$Attention(Q, K, V) = softmax\left(\frac{QK^T}{\sqrt{d_k}}\right)V \tag{2}$$

where d denotes the dimension of the key.

For the first encoder sublayer the multi-headed attention mechanism is computed and connected after projecting Q, K, V linearly h times to different dimensions such that d_k and d_v, the dimensions of keys and values, change. The attention function is performed in parallel on these projected versions to produce d_v dimensional output values, which are concatenated and then continue to project the final output. Multiheaded attention allows the model to jointly focus on information from different representation subspaces at different locations. This can be represented by Eq. (3), and Eq. (4):

$$Multihead(Q, K, V) = Concat(head_1, head_2, \ldots, head_h)W^o \tag{3}$$

$$head_i = Attention\left(QW_i^Q, KW_i^K, VW_i^V\right) \tag{4}$$

where q, k, v are mapped to the linear transformation matrices of Q, K, V, respectively, to obtain $W_i^Q (d_{model} \times d_k)$, $W_i^V (d_{model} \times d_v)$, $W_i^K (d_{model} \times d_k)$; mapping the output O to the linear transformation matrix of o to obtain $W_i^O (d_k \times d_{model})$.

The essence of multi-head attention is that the same query, value, and key are mapped to different subspaces of the original high-dimensional space for attention computation while the total number of parameters remains the same, and then the attention information in the different subspaces is merged in the last step. This reduces the dimensionality of each vector for computing the attention of each head and prevents overfitting in a sense; since the attention has different distributions in different subspaces, the multi-head attention mechanism actually looks for correlations between sequences from different perspectives and then combines the correlations captured in different subspaces in the final step of joining.

After passing through the self-attentive sublayer, it enters into the feedforward network, where ReLU is chosen as the activation function and is represented by Eq. (5):

$$FFN(x) = max(0, xW_1 + b_1)W_2 + b_2 \tag{5}$$

Decoder Components. The decoder component is similar to the encoder component in that it consists of several encoder stacks. In addition to the same two sub-layers as the encoder, a third sub-layer, the multi-head attention mechanism with mask, is added to the decoder. Since the Transformer is an autoregressive model, the role of mask is to ensure that the sequences generated in the generation phase are computationally generated in order according to the input order. In each time step it is guaranteed that the sequence in each time step can only be generated based on the sequence in the previous time step. So when entering the second self-attentive mechanism, the inputs are V and K generated from the Q and encoder components of the first self-attentive mechanism with mask. the structure of the decoder is shown in Fig. 2:

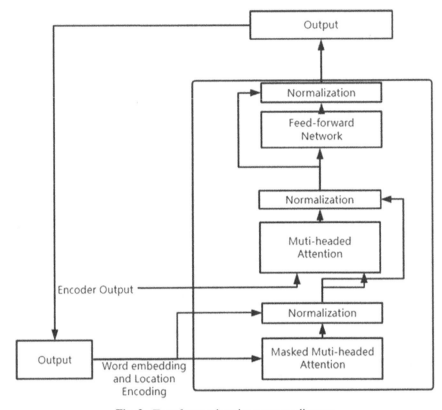

Fig. 2. Transformer decoder structure diagram

Location Coding. In the Transformer model, there are no operations of recursion and convolution. In order for the model to make use of the order of the input sequence, so it is necessary to tag the sequence with relative or absolute position information. The position encoding pattern formulas used in the transformer model are shown in Eq. (6) and Eq. (7):

$$PE_{(pos,2i)} = sin\left(pos/10000^{2i/d_{model}}\right) \tag{6}$$

$$PE_{(pos,2i+1)} = cos\left(pos/10000^{2i/d_{model}}\right) \tag{7}$$

where *pos* denotes position, *i* denotes dimension, and d_{model} denotes the dimension of position encoding and word embedding encoding. The model using the sine cosine function allows the wavelength to be longer in the case of smaller positions, and the encoding corresponding to each position is unique; it also allows the model to learn the relative position relationship between sequences.

3.2 Model Implementation Identification Task

For the character identification task studied in this paper, the Transformer model is mainly used to process the word vector matrix output by the Word2vec model and take advantage of the excellent performance of the Transformer in dealing with text-like sequence problems, reducing the computational complexity of each layer, making the computation parallelizable, with good effect of long-range sequence dependence. The iterative training of Transformer can be used to obtain text sequences that are dependent on the previous text, making the identification more accurate.

The flow chart of the entire algorithm for implementing the character identification task in the model is shown in Fig. 3:

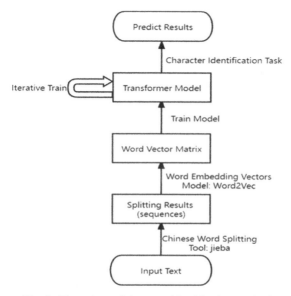

Fig. 3. Flow chart of character identification method

Pre-training stage: After the input text data is pre-processed by Jieba for word separation to remove redundant words, etc., the sequence data of word separation results are input into the Word2Vec model to make it vectorized. Because the Word2Vec model can capture the position of words and the direct connection of context well, it can generate dynamic word vectors with better results. This model can also be used to filter out high-frequency words, i.e., keywords, by calculating word frequencies and synthesizing the corpus under the same tags to obtain the keywords under the corresponding tags.

Training phase: The word vectors obtained in the pre-training phase are fed into the Transformer model. The input sequence is analyzed by the encoder component with attention mechanism, and then the generated sequence and the output of the encoder component at each time are simultaneously entered into the decoder component to further output the result probability to achieve the task identification task. The feature information is superimposed and discarded through each iteration of training, so that the most important features are retained to the maximum extent.

Prediction phase: The prediction phase is divided into two parts: the first part is tested using the test set and outputs the accuracy, F1 score and recall for each label. The average loss, average accuracy and confusion matrix are also output; the second part consists of the user inputting the utterance to be predicted and the label of the input utterance is determined by the model.

3.3 Confidence Judgment

In determining whether the generated data is accurate, the confidence index can be used to discriminate. The confidence score of the generated data reveals whether or how likely B will appear when A appears, which indicates the correlation between the real data and the generated data, and the higher the correlation, the more similar it is. The confidence level indicates the proportion of transactions containing A that also contain B, i.e., the proportion of transactions containing both A and B to those containing A. If the confidence level is too low, it means that the occurrence of A has little relationship with whether B occurs or not. The formula is shown as Eqs. (8):

$$confidence = \frac{P(A\&B)}{P(A)} \tag{8}$$

where $P(A\&B)$ denotes the probability of simultaneous appearance of A and B, and $P(A)$ denotes the probability of appearance of A.

In deep learning, correlation analysis can also be performed to determine the strength of correlation between data and individual measures. For example, the Pearson correlation coefficient method can find how closely the measures are correlated. Its formula is shown in Eq. (9):

$$\rho_{XY} = \frac{E((X - EX)(Y - EY))}{\sqrt{D(X)}\sqrt{D(Y)}} \tag{9}$$

where E denotes the expectation and D denotes the variance. The Pearson correlation coefficient takes values in the range of $[-1, 1]$. The larger the absolute value of the correlation coefficient, the higher the correlation between X and Y. Thus, it is possible to find the arrangement of indicators that have the greatest influence on their data.

As a result, it is possible to determine the degree of authenticity of the generated data in the character identification task, and thus to determine whether the generated data can be used as the result.

4   Experimental Argumentation and Analysis

4.1   Experimental Environment and Parameter Settings

The software environment of this experiment is Windows system, pycharm (version is 2021.1) is selected as the integrated development environment to carry out, python 3.6 is selected for program writing, and the deep learning framework is tensorflow1.10.0; the hardware environment uses the CPU of i7-10750H and the GPU of NVIDA RTX2070 max-Q, both parts are available for training.

In the process of vectorizing the result of word separation using the Word2Vec model, the parameters of Word2Vec are set to min_count = 1, size = 50, window = 5, workers = −1. min_count allows truncation of the dictionary, and words with a word frequency less than the number of min_count will be discarded, where workers indicates how many CPUs are currently used for training, depending on how many cores the CPU is, and workers = −1 means that all CPUs are currently used for training. for that task. After the word vectors are obtained using word2vec, all the word vectors are stitched into a document matrix for each description of the character.

4.2 Data Set Preparation

For the character identification task studied in this paper, the main purpose is to obtain deeper character traits based on "static text" data such as appearance description, action description and language description, and to accurately identify characters by combining other factors such as their background and history. At the same time, the algorithm used in this paper has certain universality.

In the process of establishing the dataset, the original text of "Journey to the West" (except the 86th episode), lines from film and TV dramas and descriptions related to the four teachers and disciples crawled from the web, starting from five aspects: background, character, appearance, action and language, the original dataset with the 20 total number of classification tags is established. The dataset will be tagged according to the description pointing to the described object and the described content. The amount of data for each tag is 100, and the total volume of the data set is a corpus of 2000 articles. For each tag in it, the data are randomly selected2 to form the validation set. The ratio of the training set to the validation set is 50:1. The test set mainly consists of 40 the 86th episode of Journey to the West and the descriptions of the characters. Examples of data sets are shown in Table 1:

Table 1. Example table of the data set of Journey to the West

Tags	Description
Sun Wukong (background)	One day the immortal stone burst, the birth of a stone egg, the wind blew, into a stone monkey, the stone monkey was born, the eyes of the two divine light, shot rushing the fighting House, alarmed the Jade Emperor in heaven
Sun Wukong (character)	Sun Wukong is a character with a very distinctive concept of right and wrong, he helps the poor and needy, compassionate to the widows and widowers, cynical as evil, to eliminate harm to the people
Sun Wukong (look-alike)	After leaving the Tang monk briefly and returning, wearing a tight band, the white cloth straightjacket on his body was also replaced with a brocade straightjacket
Piggybacking (background)	It bites and kills the sow, kills the swine, and recruits the second sister of Mao in the cloud stack cave of Fuling Mountain, but Mao dies a year later, leaving only a cave to him
Porky Pig (look-alike)	Black face and short hair, long beak and big ears, wearing a green not green, blue not blue woven cloth straightjacket, tied a flowered cloth handkerchief

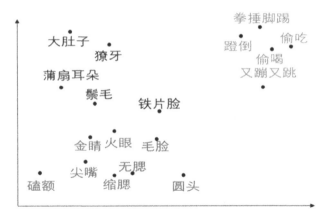

Fig. 4. Schematic diagram of word vector training

Taking the appearance of Sun Wukong as the input text, the word vectors after passing the trained model are shown in the Fig. 4. Black indicates the word vector of the appearance of InuYasha, blue indicates the word vector of Sun Wukong, yellow indicates the word vector of Sun Wukong's action, and red indicates the input text. When the input text is "with bright golden eyes, round head and hairy face without cheeks". When the input text is "kowtow and golden eyes, round head, hairy face and no cheeks", the word vectors are distributed in the area of the appearance of Sun Wukong after word separation, so it is known that this input text is probably the text describing the appearance of Sun Wukong.

For the selection of input texts, "Journey to the West" was chosen as the main text for analysis, combined with TV series, movie lines, poems and evaluations to form the data set. The Journey to the West is one of the Four Great Masterpieces of China, and although the length of the characters is not very long, each character in it appears to be very distinctive under the portrayal of the author Wu Chengen, so it has a certain research representative significance. At the same time, the use of "Journey to the West" as the character for analysis in this paper has certain authority, and has certain practical significance and reference significance in the issues related to natural language processing.

4.3 Analysis Results Display

At the end of the training phase, the accuracy curves obtained after the accuracy is verified by the validation set are shown in Fig. 5; the loss curve graph is shown in Fig. 6:

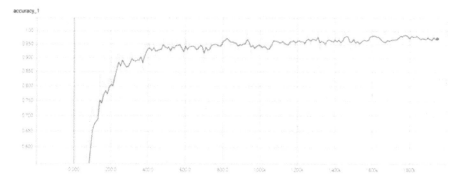

Fig. 5. Accuracy curve at the end of training

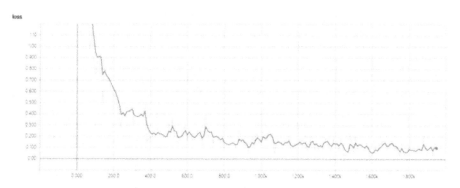

Fig. 6. Loss curve at the end of training

As can be seen from the above graph, there is a large change in accuracy and loss at the beginning of training, and a smooth optimization effect in the middle and second half of the training period, and the accuracy reaches 97.3% at the end of training.

In the text validation using the trained model with the user's own text input, it can be seen that the model can correctly recognize the category of the input text content. The validation results are shown in Table 2:

Table 2. Example table of user input text validation effect

Enter the statement to be tested	Results of model predictions
See a walker, sitting high on a stone platform, and the group of monkeys drinking wine for fun. He had yellow hair and golden hoops, golden eyes, and was wearing a straight jacket and a tiger skin skirt	Sun Wukong (external appearance)
You monkey, repeatedly hit the disaster! You stole his fruit, so suffer him some anger, let him scold a few words and so on	Tang Sanzang (Language)

In the test using the 58th episode of "Two Hearts Disturb the Great Heaven and Earth, One Body is Difficult to Cultivate True Silence", the first input text of the table, as Sect. 4.2 shown in the table, when the input text is "also has yellow hair and golden hoops, with golden eyes and fiery eyes; wears a straight jacket of brocade cloth and a tiger skin skirt at the waist", it will identify this input text as the appearance of the Monkey King, but it is actually used in the text to describe the appearance of the The fourth is a six-eared macaque monkey, good at listening to sounds, able to perceive reason, know the front and back, all things are clear. This text is used to describe the appearance of the six-eared macaque. This text is used to describe the background of the Six-Eared Macaque, so it is necessary to combine it with the text that follows: "The fourth is the Six-Eared Macaque, good at listening to sounds, able to perceive reason, know the front and back, and understand everything".

The predicted results reflect the maximum probability result that the input description is one of those corresponding to the combination of the four and five part descriptions of the master and disciple. It is also demonstrated that when the surface features are obtained, the deeper features of the characters can be obtained by the above-mentioned algorithmic model, and the character identification function is finally realized.

In this experiment, the confidence level and confidence interval were calculated (see Fig. 7). The smaller the confidence interval width, the more accurate the prediction model is. However, the smaller the confidence interval width, the smaller the confidence level. Therefore, in order to obtain a high confidence level, the confidence interval width must be expanded accordingly. From Fig. 7, we can see that if we want to keep the confidence level above 90%, the width of the confidence interval should be maintained at about 0.04, that is, [0.09, 0.13]. When mapping to the text, the mean value of the distance between word vectors needs to be controlled within this confidence interval to be a more credible result.

4.4 Experiment Summary

For the chapters of Journey to the West, the depictions of the four teachers and disciples with different aspects of their characteristics will be classified and predicted, and it is found that the different depictions can be distinguished based on textual information such as dialogue and appearance (i.e., surface-level features) in the dataset. This experiment shows that the model is able to distinguish not only between the four apprentices but also between the depictions of the input texts, which fully illustrates the feasibility and effectiveness of the algorithm. Thus, the character identification work under study is achieved.

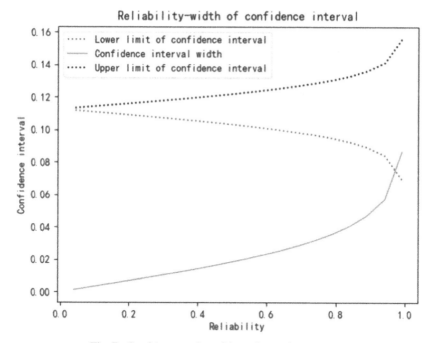

Fig. 7. Confidence and confidence interval correlation

5 Conclusion

In the context of Bie-modernism, it is important to remove fakes and keep the truth. In this paper, by combining cultural computing with Bie-modernism and taking character screening as an example, we demonstrate that machine learning still has efficient and accurate performance when combined with other fields, so it is a powerful help to identify the authenticity of Bie-modernism. The experiment uses a cultural computing model constructed by combining Word2Vec and Transformer network to achieve the screening function of its depicted characters through the depiction in Journey to the West, thus demonstrating that the model can obtain not only the surface features in the text, but also the deeper features in the text.

References

1. Wang, J.: Bie-modernism: Beyond aesthetics and after postmodern–a reaction to an international aesthetic trend. J. Shanghai Norm. Univ. (Philos. Soc. Sci. Edn.) **44**(01), 5–14 (2015)
2. Chen, K., Zhu, Y.: A review of machine learning and its related algorithms. Stat. Inf. Forum (05), 105–112 (2007)
3. Zhou, Y.: Introduction to machine learning and its related algorithms. Sci. Technol. Commun. **11**(06), 153–154+165 (2019)
4. Zhao, H., Peng, H., Chen, H.: Online service platform for Chinese cultural genes. Comput. Syst. Appl. **12**, 52–57 (2015)

5. Li, Y.: Research on Chinese automatic word separation based on HMM for single word valuation. Inner Mongolia Normal University (2010)
6. Deng, L., Luo, Z.Y.: Semi-supervised CRF-based cross-domain Chinese word separation. Chin. J. Inform. **31**(4), 9–19 (2017)
7. Laaroussi, S., Si, L.A., Yousfi, A.: Distant n-gram language model for contextual spelling correction applied to arabic language (2021)
8. https://pypi.org/project/jieba/
9. Mikolov, T., Chen, K., Corrado, G., Dean, J.: Efficient estimation of word representations in vector space. In: Proceedings of Workshop at ICLR (2013)
10. Le, Q., Mikolov, T.: Distributed representations of sentences and documents. In: International Conference on Machine Learning, pp. 1188–1196 (2014)
11. Vaswani, A., Shazeer, N., Parmar, N., et al.: Attention is all you need. arXiv (2017)

Artificial Speech is Culture:
Conversational UX Designers and the Work of Usable Conversational Voice Assistants

Elizabeth Rodwell[(⊠)] [iD]

University of Houston, Houston, TX 77077, USA
erodwell@uh.edu

Abstract. As conversational voice assistants (CVAs) like Alexa, Siri, and Google Home have become ubiquitous in some parts of the world, lab-based reception studies have captured perceived failures in their usability or accounted for ways that these devices reproduce problematic (often racialized and gendered) cultural conditions. But examining these devices solely as end products fails to account for the ways that UX design, like other expert labor, is a social practice born of daily workplace negotiations and inevitable compromises. This U.S. and Japan-based study argues that anthropological methods are critical to our understanding of conversation design and device training processes and explores why we must go beyond quantifying device usability to examine the work of the usability professionals themselves. For the conversational user experience (CUX) designers and researchers I interviewed and with whom I am conducting ongoing fieldwork, current technology frustrates their capacity to design for systems that go beyond being tools to also be enjoyable conversation partners. In some cases, the process of creating this category of AI turns the canonical literature on computers as social actors on its head, by identifying conscious intentions on the part of designers to replicate human personality and use it to drive the interactions we have with CVAs. It also suggests that the end users who most successfully adopt these tools are frequently those who best reproduce the culture of UX designers themselves.

Keywords: Conversational UX · Usability · UX · Conversation Assistants · Chatbots · Anthropology · Ethnography

1 Introduction

On an especially hot day in July, a Conversational UX Design Lead scratches his head thoughtfully as he walks down a street near his Manhattan office. "[Conversation Assistants] should deliver the best elements of human interaction". He smiles broadly. "Expression, emotion, and understanding. But [my team] gravitated away from designing personality recently" (*Interview*, 2021).

© The Author(s), under exclusive license to Springer Nature Switzerland AG 2022
M. Rauterberg (Ed.): HCII 2022, LNCS 13324, pp. 137–148, 2022.
https://doi.org/10.1007/978-3-031-05434-1_9

Mark[1] was one of several conversational user experience (CUX) designers I had interviewed by that point in the year, either in-person or remotely as I sought to understand the meaning of usability work in a context where the rules for the devices being worked on are routinely ambiguous to their users.

1.1 Methods and Argument

Rather than scrutinizing the logistics of building these (largely) commercial products, or assessing the experiences of end users, as has been done within a large body of earlier studies [1–3], I focus in this paper on the perspectives of those who must articulate, quantify, and measure usability in real time through their work on Conversational Voice Assistants (CVAs). I argue that this technology, which so often forces humans to adapt to its idiosyncrasies (training humans to work for and with AI rather than making AI work for humans), poses a significant challenge to the field of user experience. Academic assessment of conversational assistants has so far been limited by the absence of their designers' voices in theoretical work, but I argue that the most relevant and interesting data on usability and human-centered design, as applied to CVAs, is discoverable only through inquiry into the daily practices of UX professionals. In other words, the scholarship on CVAs cannot accurately represent these devices without accounting for the social conditions of scientific/design production and taking up earlier studies of expert labor. The work of those tasked with improving the usability of conversational assistants is characterized by an especially complex series of negotiations that often result in only marginal successes. Indeed, the most common feedback I have gotten when mentioning my study of these devices is negative impressions of their usability and anecdotes about moments of failure. Chris, a Conversational UX (CUX) designer working at a prominent international company acknowledged this struggle, and observed:

"Sometimes people are like 'wait, [the CVA] can't slice bread?' Well, it's not that she can't slice bread, it's that you already have a simple serrated knife in your kitchen" (*Interview,* July 2021).

What Can Anthropology Bring to the Study of Artificial Intelligence? By necessity, this project has taken a patchwork ethnographic approach [4], meaning that fieldwork (site n = 2) and interviews (n = 20) have been pieced together as all of our schedules and working conditions evolved over the past two years. But although this approach to ethnography (or labeling it as such) is relatively new, anthropological work on artificial intelligence is not– whether it is focused on creators of such tools [5] or the ways that these tools are received, engaged, and adapted by end users [6–9]. Anthropology in such contexts seeks to draw out and foreground that which is frequently taken-for-granted, or as Christine Hine writes about smart home devices: "the ethnographer must make special efforts to uncover their silences and to highlight the forms of visible and invisible work that bring them into being and sustain them in operation" [10]. If ethnography is "usually about breaching silences," as Hine writes, then this project seeks to breach the particular silence that occurs in the gap between the creation of CVAs and their reception. This

---

[1] All names used are pseudonyms, to allow my collaborators to speak freely about workplace challenges. Where possible, I have also tried to obscure their workplace.

creation space is as messy as any of expert innovation or corporate design and involves daily negotiations during routine practices like "table reads" of CVA scripts, and creative forms of usability testing in offices, homes, labs, and – in the COVID-19 era – on Zoom.

Anthropological theory is particularly well suited to unpacking the ethical concerns raised about conversational assistants and the ways that they can perpetuate societal biases [1], such as reproducing the ethnocentrism of their creators and of the field of artificial intelligence in general [11]. Directly engaging UX designers themselves is a means of answering a question posed by Ylipulli and Luusua: "What does it mean for design ethics if design is understood as an intervention that alters social relationships as well as material ones?" [12] A key to unpacking this question involves examining how culture informs what individual CUX designers consider to be a usable conversation partner.

A Transnational Study. This project spans both the U.S. and Japan, in response to suggestions that students of artificial intelligence refrain from taking Anglophone subjects as surrogates for a generic end user [13]. The decision to base my exploration of UX professionals in these two countries stemmed first from my prior work in Japan, but also arose in acknowledgement of the two countries as global leaders in the development of artificial intelligence. But despite frequent juxtaposition in studies of AI [14, 15], the U.S. and Japan have dramatically different adoption rates when it comes to CVAs; although smart speakers (*sumātosupīkā*) like Siri, Google Assistant, and Alexa are used in Japan, a recent survey showed that the overwhelming majority of people in Japan aged 10–60+ did not own, nor had any interest in acquiring or using one of these devices [16]. As robotics development continues to thrive there, the Japanese company that represents one of my field sites has felt compelled to create an anthropomorphic body for its CVA in hopes of marketing the device. This approach, i.e., the ways that CUXers think about *how* to engender anthropomorphism and what a conversation partner should sound like, is one of the topics most frequently raised by those I interviewed.

2   Background

"When we are testing, we just give the participant a set of adult coloring books and you have them pretend like nobody else is in the room. You want to do something hands-free and cannot glance up or look at something. You're busy either at work or you're cooking something in the kitchen, and you cannot look up from your coloring book and need to focus on that task while you get the assistant to do what you want it to do".
– *Interview,* CUX Lead, November 2020.

2.1   Defining the Field of UX

UX, also known as user experience or usability has its origins in the Human Computer Interaction (HCI) community of practice, but also in the areas of human factors and ergonomics. Usability practitioners and those in UX-adjacent fields frequently attribute its origins to either early forms of human centered design at Bell Labs in the 1950s

[17], or Don Norman's work at Apple Computers [18]. In its more contemporary form, user experience design focused on improving early user interfaces for home computing, software, and web design. While research incorporating UX as an approach or orientation is rapidly multiplying within venues like the Association for Computing Machinery's SIGCHI, UX still fundamentally lacks coherence as a discipline and pedagogy [19–22]. Further, teaching the tools used by the field is a moving target. There is neither a single academic path to one of the many new jobs in UX, nor wide-ranging adoption of the field by academic disciplines that commonly feed into the profession, like anthropology and psychology [21, 22]. Academic appropriation of UX methodologies is usually done at the level of individual courses or components of courses, or takes the form of new, lucrative certificate programs [21].

For the CUX researchers and designers I have interviewed, daily praxis was not as varied as the academic representation of its possibilities. Each person outlined similar processes of conversation design/mapping, script writing, internal testing, testing with participants (usability and user acceptance testing), interviewing, and occasional field-work. In my sample, there were several CUX designers with linguistics backgrounds, several cultural anthropologists and psychologists, and many interaction/graphic designers who had transitioned into this area. Only one person I interviewed had an academic background in computer science.

2.2 The Anthropology of Expert Practitioners

Within the field of anthropology, this project belongs to science and technology studies writ large, but more specifically to the anthropology of computing and robotics, pioneered by people like Diana Forsythe [5], and continued by studies of specialist-users [6, 23] and human-robot interaction (especially in Japan) [7–9, 14, 15, 24].

A related body of ethnographic projects examine the work of expert practitioners-ranging from nuclear scientists [25, 26] to stock traders [27], journalists [28], and particle physicists [29]. Prompted by such enquiries, ethnographers in the past half-century have reassessed their positioning relative to those they study, addressed the power imbalances that arise between researchers and subjects, and explored how studies of experts often cast the anthropologist in the role of "least power", i.e., less social and/or cultural capital. In this, and past projects I have generally felt a constant fluctuation between the position of studying "up" [30, 31] and studying "sideways" [32], or doing ethnography among those with access to comparable socioeconomic resources. As I write this sentence, I have just concluded an interview with one of many PhD-holding CUX researchers affiliated with a university. Therefore, I routinely feel as though my own positionality is under constant negotiation within the span of a single interview as we move through topics I understand, and ones about which I am there to learn.

Applied anthropologists have certainly studied the work of usability itself, as both practitioners and theorists–notably through organizations like EPIC (Ethnographic Praxis in Industry Community) and the SfAA (Society for Applied Anthropology). Studies that examine the roles of social scientists in business environments provide additional context for the work of UX professionals in general [33–35]. But owing to the rapidly evolving nature of this field, studies of these "UX-perts" are still missing.

2.3 Conversational Voice Assistants

I ask Bjørn why he chose to work on conversational agents (CAs), and he tells me: "There is recent interest in CAs because it's really fascinating. This is not to say there hasn't been any concern for user experience in CAs before, because there has been, since whenever, but there is a substantial increase in interest in the past five years. From an HCI perspective it means we're throwing away everything we knew about user interfaces and how to make good conversations possible. It's a new and very appealing challenge. Most research questions that have already been explored for GUI based systems have not yet been studied much [for CAs]" (*Interview*, December 2021).

So, what is a conversational assistant? The main voice-controlled assistants like Alexa, Google Assistant, Cortana, and Siri are now ubiquitous enough that most consumers in Japan and the U.S. have exposure to these tools, and the use of chatbots in customer service has rapidly become convention. Additionally, non-commercial, political (Resistbot) and even mainstream therapeutic text-based assistants have now existed for years. These CAs that seek our confidence follow the first acknowledged American chatbot, ELIZA, a Rogerian psychotherapist created by MIT Scientist Joseph Weizenbaum (1966). Its legacy surfaces in the recent smartphone-based Cognitive Behavioral Therapy tool "Woebot", or web-based chatbots Zeve and Replika, for example.

Studies of conversational assistants span several categories and kinds of technologies, ranging from chatbots with and without avatars to voice assistants housed in smart speakers. Further, the terminology used to classify relevant technologies has been inconsistent: conversational AI, conversational agents, virtual dialog systems, intelligent virtual assistants, intelligent voice/digital assistants, automatic speech recognition systems, etc. [36] Most studies of these tools are lab-based and assess user reception of CAs, in a manner resembling usability testing itself. Although growing overlap exists between studies of CAs and studies (at least mentioning) usability – including attempts to codify heuristics for "conversational user interfaces" [37–39] – this area of HCI research is currently emergent. To paraphrase Robinson et al., methodologies within the field of UX research are frequently applied belatedly to newer forms of technology in widespread use, like AR/VR [40]. There is still a lack of user-centered thinking about CAs, let alone that which incorporates the experiences of their creators.

3 Conversational UX Design

Understanding the role of human actors in producing AI systems is critically important, particularly as these systems are often appraised as technological end products. Specialists are needed to write the scripts, train, and review the output of conversational assistants, and these individuals bring with them accompanying cultural baggage and unique conversational sensibilities. Further, the negotiated process of conversation design remains easier when writing for a chatbot or other text-based CA than it is with voice systems:

ER: "What is Conversational UX?"

Bjørn: "I would start out by defining UX, which deals with people's cognitive and emotional responses to digital systems. And then conversational UX would be cognitive and emotional responses to CA systems."

ER: "Why does it need to be defined separately?"

Bjørn: "When designing other kinds of interactions, the design mainly concerns the system-how should the layout, info architecture be, etc. The experience of CUX has more to do with the content... if you read a really good article on a website, you wouldn't say that was part of the website UX, but if you had the content as part of a CA you would say it is part of the CA UX".

3.1 Ethics and Conversation Designers: Training the Humans

The work of CUX professionals frequently involves conversations about ethics that reflect their senses of what an ethical conversation partner should be. These are based on their own feelings about and experience with successful social transactions and refined in conversation with workplace teams. Concerns about ethical practice revolve around the appropriate amount of anthropomorphism a device should encourage, without misleading users as to the nature of a device. Asked about ethics, one CUX designer told me about the data her company has on how people abuse CVAs, which is driving an ongoing internal study of how a system can assert that "some abuse is not going to be tolerated" without unproductively changing the relationship individuals have with these devices (*Interview*, October 2020).

As has been suggested, the design of these tools often seems to reflect a relatively homogenous, male, and Western-centric body of creators [2]. Although the largest companies employ international teams, these still exclude languages spoken by fewer/less affluent people whose access to CVAs may be seen as a poor business investment [41]. Further, CVAs train their users to speak in unnatural ways even if they have an accent easily recognized by the system, and there is accordingly an entire genre of internet videos featuring people whose speech departs from default models trying to get CVAs to understand them. But: "We don't even release the American [CVA] in Ireland, even though we all speak English," a CUX researcher named Michelle asserted, defending the efforts of her team to localize its product (*Interview*, October 2020). Reflecting the difference between language as used with CAs, and applied to other contexts, a CUX principle named Fatima explained an internal study she'd recently come across:

"What I find really funny is people who don't speak English at all who are from different countries, but they weren't learning English, they were learning commands. So, they learned to say, like, "[Device], turn on the light" And they know how to say that in English and they know what it does but they're not learning how to speak English".

CUX professionals are aware that their systems struggle with variability in speech, misrepresent the words of Black speakers more often than White, men more than women, and the young (but not too young) over the elderly. They often fail to process the words of those with speech impediments, and non-native speakers of a language [1, 42]. Although one designer framed the problem as one of design's relationship to capitalism, most of the people with whom I spoke expressed resignation about time limitations and training data. Frowning, Fatima explained how difficult it was for her team to assemble sufficient training data for non-English speaking users and to ensure that data is free from errors. "We don't currently have any Mandarin speakers on our team," she lamented (*Interview*, November 2020).

Concerns about the linguistic competency of CVA devices were even more acute among Japan-based CUX designers, for whom this user quote was representative of a perceived disdain for the technology among native Japanese speakers: "[A CVA] can't hear what I'm saying and manages to type up random, weird sentences, so it's only going to be irritating" [43]. Inadequate training data in Japanese and a lack of native speakers represented on teams for the most prominent globally used devices was considered a significant impediment to adoption, and a motivation for prominent Japanese/Korean company LINE (Naver) to pursue development of its own "Clova" CVA.

Fatima's team often sourced training data from video and audio samples found online, and other teams licensed data from a handful of training data providers. Some of these services (e.g., shaip.com) promote their services through language about repositioning humans as part of "the loop", to curate and review conversational agent training data rather than (or in addition to) relying on automated systems. Despite the labor such data requires and the effort to "teach" CAs, they often fabricate a distinct and artificial human relationship with technology rather than responding to human needs. This is reflected in one of the main usability issues involved in this technology: absent a sense of what they can expect from a CA, most people scramble to uncover how they can use it to accomplish a goal.

If "user control" is a fundamental tenant of usability work [44], how can UX professionals integrate this possibility into conversational agents? Ylipulli and Luusua asked a similar question: "What would it mean to 'design for control'… to eventually give [people] control — over their technologies, buildings, everyday life objects?" [12] This must be part of the ethics of AI development, along with the related concepts of system transparency and discoverability. But these are elements of CA development with which usability researchers still struggle and are working to realize.

3.2   Gender and Conversational Voice Assistants

When asked about ethics and CVA development, most of the CUX professionals with whom I spoke focused immediately on gender. As has been mentioned in research on popular voice controlled devices [45], individuals working on the most popular consumer CVAs often point to their company's internal market data showing that, at least in the U.S., "low register" female voices are preferred when conservational assistants have a spoken component, even as their teams take steps to allow users to select from a range of possible voices.

But this raises a question common to user-centered design, and one that lends complexity to thinking about the ethics of these devices: should we design for problematic and already reified social trends such as conventional attitudes towards a particular demographic within a culture? Two CUX researchers voiced concern about the "conventional wisdom" in their profession that voice controls in vehicles are less well received when assigned a female voice; Gambino et al. similarly mentioned that autonomous vehicle AI was considered more trustworthy if communication styles corresponded with dominant male/female social expectations [46].

Ethnography has the potential to introduce nuance to our understanding of how gender comes to be represented within these tools, complicate our thinking about gender as a component of usability and the capture the decision-making around gendering AI at all. I mentioned earlier the self-reflexivity informing many CUXers' approaches to the relationship between gender and CAs, which challenges a conventional narrative about AI programmers blindly reproducing their own biases. Indeed, like the work of most expert practitioners, that of usability professionals is filled with extensive compromise. Although there are studies that support decisions to assign CAs a female gender by essentially proving that people like them (and why) [47], these neglect a large body of anthropological literature on affective labor and gendered work that could contextualize our relationship with tools designed to act as "assistants" [48, 49]. Other studies take as inevitable the gendering of systems as a consequence of anthropomorphism [2].

The use of female avatars with some CAs serves to further muddy the waters, particularly when these avatars so frequently default (in the U.S.) to an image of a white woman, or a Japanese woman (in Japan). Although tools like Replika (for example), allow you to select your CA's gender, race, and basic appearance, visitors to the site are immediately presented with a slim white female model before they create an account. And indeed, many CUX professionals themselves admitted during our interviews that they couldn't think of very many chatbots that weren't associated with a photograph of a woman – a practice some worried was associated with a user tendency to both abuse and complement these tools. However, when I asked Mark about his company's use of a female avatar to promote their CVA technology, he laughed:

"Initially, there kind of was an overestimating of the technology's ability to reflect personality. In what world do people need to make small talk with the AI?! We gravitated away from personality, and people don't really care what it looks like. People don't get as angry at avatars that are female, but the avatar has no utility. It doesn't need to have a face" (*Interview*, July 2021).

3.3 Anthropomorphism: "Fooling People is Not the Goal"

Mark's interpretation leaves out the role of desire (and a substantial body of Computers as Social Actors-related literature) in our interactions with AI. Whether it's possible for a CA to be perceived as not having a personality is also debatable, and the UX professionals with whom I collaborated were divided as to whether it was even productive to spend time trying to redirect users away from personification. This, despite a shared understanding within this community that system design can effectively mitigate our impulse to humanize these technologies; for example, introducing buttons and delayed responses into a system dampens perceptions of humanness [50].

Anthropomorphism as a concept has been broadly interpreted by anthropologists, as a means by which humans make inferences about the state of mind of other creatures and/or project familiar cognitive processes onto their behavior [24]. When robots are the target, the process can involve the transference of the human nature/culture of their creators onto the technology itself. As Richardson writes: "[robots] are in effect cultural beings… the robot was never imagined as pure machine" [24].

While roboticists dabble in the humanlike, and try to avoid triggering discomfort in humans in the "uncanny valley" [51], CA designers in my study universally described themselves as working within a "post-Turing" landscape [52]. Despite studies asserting that anthropomorphism correlates with user trust and perceptions of a device's competence [53], CUX researchers considered personality less important than efficient conversational transaction–i.e., driving the user towards accomplishing a goal.

This is in part an effect of the current state of CA development, particularly in voice-driven systems. In usability testing for these tools, people remain at a significant distance from conditions favorable to anthropomorphism, and, in effect, experience the opposite. Fatima described a typical encounter between human and CVA:

"When [a tester] is talking with their voice they're like: 'Well, I could say this, and I want to say this, but I don't know if [it's] going to understand that, so I'm going to say something simpler'. So, what we'll have to do is backtrack and be like: 'Okay, if you were talking to a human what would you say right now?' And they say, 'Well, I want to say this, but I figure that you hadn't built that so…' So, they're trying to compensate for what they know is not a person but a system." (Interview, October 2020).

Indeed, far from the territory of discomfiting techno-animism, CUX designers report testers approaching devices with hesitation and a sense that they must speak to them as they would someone who does not understand their language. "It's like, you have one chance to get this right and if you blow it then they're really not going to try again", Fatima reported of her users. Rather than pointing to its lack of appealing physical form or avatar, UX professionals identify CVA technology as its own impediment, despite all the table readings, script reviews, training data, paper prototyping, A/B testing, and developments in machine learning integrated by my interlocuters. People may ascribe gender to their devices, but many also experience significant difficulty eschewing self-policing when using them [54]. CVAs remain too much of a black box.

4 Conclusion

Work in collaboration with and the study of CUX professionals reveals the complexity of reproducing human communication. In many ways, it suggests that we have made much bigger strides in replicating the physical appearance of humans (particularly in Japan), than we have in creating artificially intelligence conversation partners.

CVAs especially represent a significant problem for UX because their lack of navigability and transparency create the conditions under which users find it difficult to solve their own problems. System responses can be uniquely frustrating–if a CA can't understand my command, how can I self-correct to accomplish my goal? A significant silence appears between the work of these devices' authors and its discovery by end users. Absent understanding of how CA technologies work and an ability to fill this silence, concerns about surveillance by major tech companies have become pervasive in both the U.S. and Japan.

The challenges are also why this area of UX excites its practitioners. "It brings HCI people much closer to the users", one noted (*Interview*, December 2021). UX professionals were inspired by how much of human psychology and how much social scientific thinking were integrated into their practice–thinking about what constitutes politeness, by a device, for example, and whether users will trust the same voice to tell them election results as well as fart jokes.

Because the user experience designers of CAs/CVAs are so steeped in anthropological and psychological theory themselves, this context becomes an important lens through which we can examine their design of socially interactive technologies. And while CVA user reception studies remain important, they provide less insight into how decisions about usable conversation agents are borne of the cultural conditions of their authors' workplaces.

References

1. Feng, S., Kudina, O., Halpern, B.M.S., Scharenborg, O.: Quantifying bias in automatic speech recognition (2021)
2. Abercrombie, G., Curry, A.C., Pandya, M., Rieser, V.: Alexa, Google, Siri: what are your pronouns? Gender and anthropomorphism in the design and perception of conversational assistants. arXiv preprint arXiv:2106.02578 (2021)
3. Schreuter, D., van der Putten, P., Lamers, M.H.: Trust me on this one: conforming to conversational assistants. Mind. Mach. **31**(4), 535–562 (2021). https://doi.org/10.1007/s11023-021-09581-8
4. Günel, G., Varma, S., Watanabe, C.: A manifesto for patchwork ethnography (2020). https://culanth.org/fieldsights/a-manifesto-for-patchwork-ethnography. Accessed 4 July 2020
5. Forsythe, D.E.: Studying Those Who Study Us: An Anthropologist in the World of Artificial Intelligence. Stanford University Press, Palo Alto (2002)
6. Kelty, C.: Geeks, social imaginaries, and recursive publics. Cult. Anthropol. **20**(2), 185–214 (2005)
7. White, D., Katsuno, H.: Toward an affective sense of life: artificial intelligence, animacy, and amusement at a robot pet memorial service in Japan. Cult. Anthropol. **36**(2), 222–251 (2021)
8. Robertson, J.: Gendering humanoid robots: robo-sexism in Japan. Body Soc. **16**(2), 1–36 (2010)
9. Otsuki, G.J.: Frame, game, and circuit: truth and the human in Japanese human-machine interface research. Ethnos. **86**(4), 712–729 (2021)
10. Hine, C.: Strategies for reflexive ethnography in the smart home: autoethnography of silence and emotion. Sociology **54**(1), 22–36 (2020). https://doi.org/10.1177/0038038519855325
11. Chan, J.K.: Design ethics: reflecting on the ethical dimensions of technology, sustainability, and responsibility in the anthropocene. Des. Stud. **54**, 184–200 (2018)
12. Ylipulli, J., Luusua, A.: Broadening horizons of design ethics? Importing concepts from applied anthropology. Nordes: Nord. Design Res. **8**, 1–5 (2019)
13. Katagiri, Y., Nass, C., Takeuchi, Y.: Cross-cultural studies of the computers are social actors paradigm: the case of reciprocity. Usabil. Eval. Interface Design: Cogn. Eng. Intell. Agents Virtual Reality 1558–1562 (2001)
14. Richardson, K.: An Anthropology of Robots and AI: Annihilation Anxiety and Machines. Routledge, New York (2015)
15. Robertson, J.: Robo sapiens japanicus: humanoid robots and the posthuman family. Crit. Asian Stud. **39**(3), 369–398 (2007)
16. Fuwa, R.: Searching for ownership and usage of smart speakers (Sumātosupīkā no shoyū riyō jōkyō o saguru) (2020). https://news.yahoo.co.jp/byline/fuwaraizo/20201024-00203730. Accessed 10 Jan 2021
17. Nielsen, J.: A 100-year view of user experience (2017). https://www.nngroup.com/articles/100-years-ux/. Accessed 25 Jan 2021
18. Norman, D., Miller, J., Henderson, A.: What you see, some of what's in the future, and how we go about doing it. In: CHI 1995. ACM Press (1995)
19. de Jong, M.D.T.: The quest for a usability theory. Tech. Commun. **61**(3), 145–146 (2014)

20. Getto, G., Beecher, F.: Toward a model of UX education: training UX designers within the academy. IEEE Trans. Prof. Commun. **59**(2), 153–164 (2016)
21. Rodwell, E.A.: A Pedagogy of its own: building a UX research program. Pract. Anthropol. **43**(2), 17–21 (2021)
22. Kou, Y., Gray, C.M.: A practice-led account of the conceptual evolution of UX knowledge. In: Proceedings of the 2019 CHI Conference on Human Factors in Computing Systems. Association for Computing Machinery, Paper 49 (2019)
23. Coleman, G.: Hacker, Hoaxer, Whistleblower, Spy: The Many Faces of Anonymous. Verso, New York (2014)
24. Richardson, K.: Technological animism: the uncanny personhood of humanoid machines. Soc. Anal.: Int. J. Soc. Cult. Pract. **60**(1), 110–128 (2016)
25. Masco, J.: The Nuclear Borderlands: The Manhattan Project in Post-Cold War New Mexico. Princeton University Press, Princeton (2006)
26. Gusterson, H.: Nuclear Rites: A Weapons Laboratory at the End of the Cold War. University of California Press, Berkeley and Los Angeles (1998)
27. Ho, K.: Liquidated: An Ethnography of Wall Street. Duke University Press, Durham (2009)
28. Boyer, D.: The Life Informatic: Newsmaking in the Digital Era. Cornell University Press, Ithaca (2013)
29. Traweek, S.: Beamtimes and Lifetimes: The World of High Energy Physicists. Harvard University Press, Cambridge (1988)
30. Nader, L.: Up the anthropologist: perspectives gained from studying up. In: Hymes, D. (ed.) Reinventing Anthropology, pp. 284–311. Vintage Books, New York (1972)
31. Gusterson, H.: Studying up revisited. PoLAR: Polit. Legal Anthropol. Rev. **20**(1), 114–119 (1997)
32. Ortner, S.B.: Studying sideways: ethnographic access in hollywood. In: Mayer, V., Banks, M.J., Caldwell, J.T. (eds.) Production Studies: Cultural Studies of Media Industries, pp. 183–197. Routledge, New York (2009)
33. Cefkin, M.: Ethnography and the Corporate Encounter: Reflections on Research in and of Corporations. Berghahn Books (2010)
34. Denny, R.M., Sunderland, P.L.: Doing Anthropology in Consumer Research. Routledge, New York and London (2016)
35. Ladner, S.: Practical Ethnography: A Guide to Doing Ethnography in the Private Sector. Left Coast Press, Walnut Creek (2014)
36. Feine, J., Gnewuch, U., Morana, S., Maedche, A.: A taxonomy of social cues for conversational agents. Int. J. Hum. Comput. Stud. **132**, 138–161 (2019)
37. Moore, R.J., Arar, R.: Conversational UX Design: A Practitioner's Guide to the Natural Conversation Framework, vol. #27. ACM Books (2019)
38. Moore, R.J., Liu, E.Y., Mishra, S., Ren, G.-J.: Design systems for conversational UX. In: CUI 2020: the 2nd Conference on Conversational User Interfaces. ACM (2020)
39. Kuligowska, K.: Commercial chatbot: performance evaluation, usability metrics and quality standards of embodied conversational agents (2015)
40. Robinson, J., Lanius, C., Weber, R.: The past, present, and future of UX empirical research. Commun. Design Q. **5**(3), 10–23 (2018)
41. Udupa, S., et al.: AI, extreme speech and the challenges of online content moderation. In: Project AD. LMU, Munich (2021)
42. Lima, L., Furtado, V., Furtado, E., Almeida, V.: Empirical analysis of bias in voice-based personal assistants. In: Companion Proceedings of the 2019 World Wide Web Conference. Association for Computing Machinery, San Francisco, pp. 533–538 (2019)

43. MyVoice: [Survey on smart speakers] About 8% of people use smart speakers by themselves, and more than 10% use them by themselves or their families. Intention to use is less than 20%, intention not to use is about 45% ([Sumātosupīkā ni kansuru chōsa] sumātosupīkā o jibun de riyōshiteiru hito wa yaku 8%, jibun matawa kazoku ga riyōshiteiru hito wa 1 warikyō. Riyō ikō wa 2 warijaku, hi riyō ikō wa yaku 45-pāsento) (2021). https://prtimes.jp/main/html/rd/p/000001038.000007815.html. Accessed November 2021

44. Nielsen, J.: 10 Usability Heuristics for User Interface Design (1994). https://www.nngroup.com/articles/ten-usability-heuristics/. Accessed 15 Jan 2021

45. Curry, A.C., Robertson, J., Rieser, V.: Conversational assistants and gender stereotypes: public perceptions and desiderata for voice personas. In: Workshop on Gender Bias in Natural Language Processing, pp. 72–78. Creative Commons, Barcelona (2020)

46. Gambino, A., Fox, J., Ratan, R.A.: Building a stronger CASA: extending the computers are social actors paradigm. Hum.-Mach. Commun. 1(1), 5 (2020)

47. Beldad, A., Hegner, S., Hoppen, J.: The effect of virtual sales agent (VSA) gender – product gender congruence on product advice credibility, trust in VSA and online vendor, and purchase intention. Comput. Hum. Behav. 60, 62–72 (2016)

48. Strengers, Y., Kennedy, J.: The Smart Wife: Why Siri, Alexa, and Other Smart Home Devices Need a Feminist Reboot. The MIT Press, Cambridge (2020)

49. Faber, L.W.: The Computer's Voice: From Star Trek to Siri. University of Minnesota Press, Minneapolis (2020)

50. Martinez, C., Morana, S.: Conversational UX Design #5 - social aspects of human-chatbot interaction. In: Martinez, C. Conversational UX Design (2021). https://www.meetup.com/conversational-ux-design/events/277488536/

51. Mori, M.: Bukimi no tani [The Uncanny Valley]. Energy. 74, 33–35 (1970)

52. Thompson, C.: May A.I. Help You? (2018). https://www.nytimes.com/interactive/2018/11/14/magazine/tech-design-ai-chatbot.html. Accessed 1 Dec 2020

53. Gong, L.: How social is social responses to computers? The function of the degree of anthropomorphism in computer representations. Comput. Hum. Behav. 24(4), 1494–1509 (2008). https://doi.org/10.1016/j.chb.2007.05.007

54. Manikonda, L., Deotale, A., Kambhampati, S.: What's up with privacy? User preferences and privacy concerns in intelligent personal assistants. In: Proceedings of the 2018 AAAI/ACM Conference on AI, Ethics, and Society, pp. 229–235 (2018)

An Audience Data-Driven Alternate Reality Storytelling Design

Xiaowen Sun[1,2(✉)], Daniel Gilman Calderón[2], Blair Subbaraman[2], and Jeffrey A. Burke[2]

[1] Neuroscience and Intelligent Media Institute, Communication University of China, Beijing, China
sunxiaowen312@163.com

[2] Center for Research in Engineering, Media and Performance (UCLA REMAP), School of Theater, Film and Television (UCLA TFT), UCLA, Los Angeles, CA, USA

Abstract. This case study, *@LAs*, made audiences the authors of exhibits as a way to unite audiences and artworks through a method of collecting their data and using artificial intelligence to process it. Three types of audience data were shared with this prototype exhibit system—identity data, real-time interaction data, and real-time location data. Tagged by folksonomy, audience data became a novel element for the AI system to process to yield media content. Thus, the system selected and generated real-time multimedia content with audiences' personal features and allowed real-time interaction between audiences and the system, which realized dynamic control in the alternate reality. Developed and built during the 2019 University of California, Los Angeles, School of Theater, Film and Television Future Storytelling Summer Institute program, *@LAs* contained three prototype exhibits for a multimedia alternate reality storytelling pavilion, created as a prototype for a hypothetical mixed reality pop-up installation run throughout Los Angeles during the 2028 Summer Olympic Games. The three exhibits—i.e., three different virtual interaction spaces—were thematically based on murals, foods, and public transportation development in Los Angeles. This paper 1) introduces the theoretical and practical bases of the case study for new forms of alternate reality, 2) describes the data processing method used and the audiences' experiences, and 3) shares the prototype's design lessons based on the questionnaire responses from designers.

Keywords: Audience data · Alternate reality · Artificial intelligence · Dynamic control · Personalized experience · Immersion

1 Introduction

This paper introduces a multimedia alternate reality case study that generated audience involvement in authorship with a shared data pool for artificial intelligence (AI) analysis. In the case study, audience members were invited to participate within alternate realities they co-created based on who they chose to be and what they chose to do within the boundaries of the artwork. They could share real data to create personalized media content and tell their stories. They could also share whatever they want to share (virtual data) to create unpredictable media content and tell other stories. Through this process, the data the audience chose to share served as a proxy for them within the experience. With the data, the project, which was co-created by the paper's authors, used AI to adapt the artwork to the audience.

To investigate how contemporary AI can be applied to balance narrative cohesion with possibilities for audience agency on emerging platforms, we (the research staff of REMAP and students from TFT) developed a multimedia alternative reality prototype installation during the 2019 University of California, Los Angeles (UCLA), School of Theater, Film and Television (TFT) Future Storytelling Summer Institute program. From September 9–21, 2019, in the Freud Playhouse at UCLA, we designed an audience data-driven location-adaptive alternate reality "pop-up" pavilion, @LAs (read as "at LAs" or "atlas"). The 2028 Los Angeles Summer Olympic Games served as the theme and spatiotemporal setting. The goal was to explore the diverse stories Los Angeles (LA) might want to tell within the context of the Olympic Games to audience members of LA residents and visitors from throughout the world. In taking the opportunity to explore the different layers of Los Angeles, people worldwide could communicate and interact within this alternate reality prototype and form social connections. We established five spaces. Three of them consisted of virtual scenes of Los Angeles. The other two were transitional and (audience accessible) behind-the-scenes spaces. To encourage the audiences to participate in authoring the exhibits to the greatest extent, we allowed them to share their data. We adopted the concept of three vectors—identity, emission, and exposure—to represent the audience data, multimedia content, and their intersections, respectively, within the exhibit system. With the help of vectors, contemporary machine learning was used to select media content and generate new media content. Thus, the system listened and responded to the audience in real time. Just as Los Angeles is created by its populations, the prototype was created by its audiences.

In the process of designing and establishing this audience member authored prototype, we also explored how human creation could cooperate with AI creation, whether personalized experiences could be harmonious with the collective experience, and how we could help audience members understand more about these abstract, AI-generated artworks.

We introduce this case study's related work in Sect. 2, and the third section provides a brief description of the audience experience. In Sect. 4, we present the data processing method. Next, in the fifth section, the alternate reality design's implementation and audience experience process are detailed. Section 6 provides a statement on the development of the prototype, and Sect. 7 discusses the design lessons based on the questionnaire responses from the designers of @LAs who also participated as audience members. Section 8 provides conclusions, and the last section cites acknowledgments. The lead author and second author of this paper are visiting graduate researchers who observed and participated in creating @LAs. The third author is one of the project's staff researchers and software developers. The fourth author is the professor who supervised the project in the context of an experimental summer institute.

2 Related Work

Italian novelist Umberto Eco concluded that artworks have the character of openness. Sometimes, the boundary between the audience and the author were blurry. Chiara Rossitto et al. summarized the audience's role as "a more active role" in the experience [1]. This activeness denotes intervention in the story, which makes the audience not only the recipient but also the author of the story. Some artworks are tangibly open to audiences and designed to be completed by audiences' bodies. Desert Rain serves as a canonical example. The audience members become the protagonists of the story and experience virtual warfare [1]. Rainbow Assembly is an artwork designed by Olafur Eliasson in 2016 [2]. Under multiple spotlights, rainbows appear over a circular curtain of fine mist. When audience members move, rainbows move with them. When audience members close their eyes, rainbows disappear. The eyes of the audience then become co-producers of the Rainbow Assembly. Eliasson said that when an audience experiences art, the art has already been prepared to listen to them [3]. Argentine conceptual artist Leandro Erlich created an illusory swimming pool that appears to be filled with water, and then audiences find that other spectators are walking under the water. When no one enters the space within the pool, the swimming pool looks no different from any other swimming pool [4]. Audience members could physically participate in the creation of these artworks.

Additionally, supported by computer science, many artworks are created with various kinds of audience data. In 1968, an exhibition called cybernetic serendipity was held in London. By collecting audiences' voice information through a microphone, Peter Zinovieff's artwork within the exhibition could generate music segments using the tan algorithm [5]. In 2003, media artist Lynn Hershman Leeson exhibited a chatbot called "Ruby" that could respond to audiences when they input words [6]. Tangible Air used Galvanic Skin Response (GSR) sensors measuring audience engagement level and used a sweater fitted with GSR, ECG and acceleration sensor to measure the presenter's engagement level. The data were used to control the helium- filled balloons' height in the auditorium and were visualized on the screen[7]. Multi Jumping Universe and Forest of Resonating Lamps, created by the TeamLab in 2020, tracks audience movements and location data to present a wonderful alternate reality around them [8].

Moreover, AI interaction designs have emerged with the development of machine learning and data processing technology, exposing audiences to alternate reality designs in new ways. As John Bowers and Jeffrey wrote in their articles, the physical computer disappears in the human-computer interactions experienced with mixed reality displays. All of the attempts of designers and engineers distill into various combinations of digital materials, physical manipulanda, algorithms, and display devices. The object is to blur the boundaries of the digital world and real world [9, 10]. Some database aestheticians have exhibited their artworks using AI. Media artist Refik Anadol created a series of immersive AI installations based on big data [11]. His installations, e.g., WDCH Dreams, Archive Dreaming and Melting Memories, are quite famous and esteemed but seldom interactive — he collects all data before installations are presented.

Artworks exploring audience engagement often begin with the simplest forms of audience participation and move towards a diversified collection of audience data. We observe two features from the above designs. First, audience members seldom create personalized real-time media content during their experiences. Strictly speaking, this makes audiences participants rather than the authors. Second, the designs are strong in eliciting personal (e.g., Desert Rain) or group experiences (e.g., WDCH Dreams) but not focused on valuing both personal and group experiences at the same time.

In 1995, Roger Dannenberg and Joseph concluded: "For art to become interactive, there must be input from the reader (who, in our terminology, becomes the player), and there must be some artistic intelligence that responds to the player" [12]. The "input from the reader" refers to audience data. However, some artists are concerned about AI's excessive involvement in art creation [13]. From the perspective of digital humanities, an open mind is more helpful. Edward A. Shanken noted that most of the art produced today serves as information about art [14]. Information provides data and involves intervening with technology. In the digital age, the combination of art and technology is unavoidable. David and Anders hold that the humanities need to adapt to digital technologies [15]. For artworks that work with audience data, audience data enter the media system, and media information gives feedback to the audience. Within this cycle, audience data can include all types of personalized information, including sound, image or text data from audiences; data on user-system interaction trajectories; the real-time location data of audiences obtained during audience experiences; data on audience gestures; and so on. Audience data is collected in real time, providing numerous possibilities in what can be captured. In digital systems that involve interaction, the collection of audience inputs (as data) is a fundamental direction towards involving the audience in creation. This practice grants media systems some "knowledge" of the audience, insofar as they choose to present themselves to the work. As a result, the system can generate a personalized experience based on data from the audience to support greater immersion and engagement.

As mentioned above, we reviewed how audiences have evolved from participating in experiences to authoring experiences. For designs in which the physical body participates, real-time personalized new media content is seldom generated by the audience, whereas for designs in which audience data participate, audience members are given opportunities to create real-time customized media content for themselves, rendering audience members the real authors of artwork. @LAs employs the latter by using audience data as a creative element and AI as a tool to "dynamically control" [16] media content and realize harmony between human and AI creativity through this prototype. In addition, the project values both personal and collective experiences. @LAs provides an alternate reality environment for audience members. It promotes audience members' social, emotional, and space immersion in the process of communicating and interacting with the design, with others, and with themselves.

3   Brief Description of the Audience Experience

Using Amazon Web Services and open source machine learning tools, the research staff of REMAP and students designed both a digital back-end and physical space for audience members to enjoy different layers of Los Angele. Figure 1 presents the physical layout of @LAs. Five functional areas can be observed in Fig. 1, namely, three interactive alternate reality exhibit spaces (m/UR/al, Sobremesa, and Activate LA), transition spaces (onboarding and offboarding spaces), and behind-the-scenes spaces. We projected the media content onto walls or screens and played sound media in every exhibit. As art, food, and traffic are three themes related to Los Angeles that can be communicated worldwide in addition to the theme of sports, the three connected interactive alternate reality exhibits were based on the three different virtual scenes of Los Angeles. The *m/UR/al* is a virtual mural gallery. Murals' colors and styles are affected by audience data. *Sobremesa* is a virtual restaurant in which audience members can create menus from their data and interact with each other with the help of a waiter played by an actor and a tablet that provides points of discussion. *Activate LA* is an audience location data-driven multimedia interaction area. We used OpenPTrack, a person tracking software, to help audience members control the rate of media changes with their bodies.

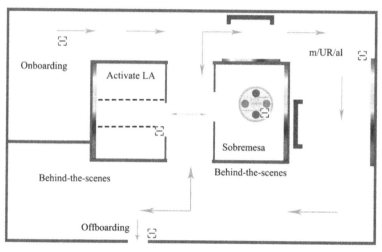

Fig. 1. The physical layout of @*LAs*. Gray solid lines represent walls. Color bars denote projection screens. Gray arrows denote the direction in which the audience walks. Brown lines denote benches. QR code signs denote the locations for scanning QR codes. (Color figure online)

With the exception of the transition spaces, the audience could move between the experiences freely. Similar to Desert Rain [1], our first goal was to enhance audience members' private experiences. However, the number of audience members involved in @*LAs* was more flexible. Only for *Sobremesa* did we recommend that more than two audience members enter the exhibit area simultaneously. One to thirty audience members were allowed to enter other exhibit areas at the same time. After scanning a QR code in the onboarding room and providing their identifying information, audience members entered the exhibit spaces. The QR codes represented the audience members' identifying information. and scanners were placed at the entrance of each exhibit. When an audience member scanned his QR code, location would be tracked, and his data would be triggered. Audience members scanned QR codes to enter the three interactive alternate reality exhibits, enjoyed the media content generated according to their data, communicated with other audience members, and could also visit behind-the-scenes areas after each experience. Finally, audience members scanned their QR codes in the offboarding space to end the experience.

In @*LAs*, on the one hand, audience members could choose to share their real data with the system. In this case, they could see the media content generated according to their data. This means that their own stories that were reflected in a multimedia art modality were presented back to them and they could tell their stories through the media content. On the other hand, they could also choose to participate as another person. In this case, they would experience another story by enjoying the media content that was generated according to whatever data they were willing to share. Designers were also waiting in each exhibit area to narrate and help audience members to understand the media content. We allowed thirty audience members to enter the prototype simultaneously to provide opportunities for them to share their experiences and feelings with each other in the alternate reality setting. For the virtual simulation of the 2028 Los Angeles Olympic Games and three virtual scenes belonging to this theme—by enjoying multimedia reflections of their identities, preferences, and relationships to Los Angeles—participants could choose an identity and determine how they related to the world around them.

4 Audience Data and Vectors

To ensure that each audience member could have an effect on the whole exhibit and that the cumulative output of the systems encountered by the audience could be taken into account, we investigated methods of collecting three kinds of data from alternate reality experiences. Additionally, we developed a way of using hashtags and tag vectors for processing and monitoring these audience data.

To connect social media with audience data and find ways of providing human inputs to AI, we made use of folksonomy hashtags selected both manually by the research staff of REMAP and automatically by machine learning. We also tagged the audience members' answers to certain questions as audience data. The folksonomy became popular in the early 2000s as an alternative to more top-down ontological structures and became more prevalent with the rise of social media. Hashtags of the social media application were generated according to folksonomy. Based on its powerful functions for labeling, sorting, and retrieving, which could be considered forms of metacommunication [17], we adopted folksonomy tags as our metadata. Machine learning was used to analyze the tags, and we then converted the tags into a collection of tag vectors—identity, emission, and exposure—to organize audience and media data in our prototype. An example of a vector is as follows: {transportation: {intensity: 0.5, sentiment: 0.0}}. Intensity was measured based on confidence values returned from machine learning processing (range of 0 to 1) and sentiment was measured for future usage (range of -1 to 1). As audience members experienced the installation, the system gathered audience identity data, location data, and interaction data.

The identity data collected was used to represent the audience members' personal information prior to engaging with the exhibits through a process of self-tagging. The audience members' identifying information related to the design, as shown in Fig. 2, was collected by posing questions on a webform in the onboarding area and was retrieved from the audience members' QR codes, which the audience members scanned from QR code cards while completing the webform. Then, the audience members carried their QR code cards throughout the exhibit. Four main identifying questions were presented on the webform: "Select a color", "Please pick an image from the following", "Please rank your top 3 favorite cuisine types" and "From not at all to very significantly, how much does LA traffic affect your life?" These were respectively the first, the last, the sixth and fifth questions listed on the webform (Fig. 2). The questions were designed to inform elements in each of the three exhibits. For example, the first and last questions were collected for *m/UR/al*, the fifth and sixth questions were collected for *Activate LA* and *Sobremesa*. By completing this webform within the onboarding area, audience members were granted a sense of agency and individuality before entering the group exhibits.

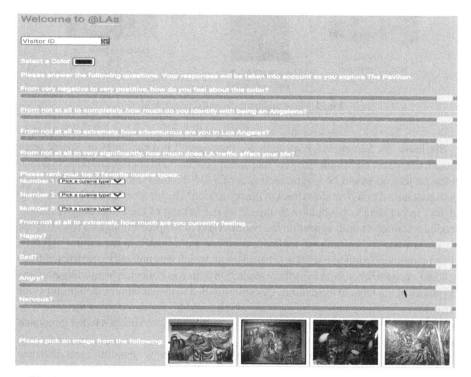

Fig. 2. The onboarding webform used for audience members to share their identity data.

We use *m/UR/al* as an example to explain how the audience identity data impacted the exhibit. For *m/UR/al*, as shown in Fig. 3, we used the style transfer method for the prototype instead of mural synthesis. The process involved selecting an image of a mural in Los Angeles, applying its style to another set of generated imagery related to our themes, and using the color chosen by the audience member. An audience member selecting blue for the first question and the first image for the last question on the webform would generate an image of the first image's style in blue. By choosing a particular color, the audience member could clearly see a visual representation of themselves in the mural. The content projected on the screen was cumulative and constantly updated. When one person scanned his QR code in front of the screen, the mural would be synthesized. When another person did so as well, both of their changes appeared on the mural together. Over time, these effects faded.

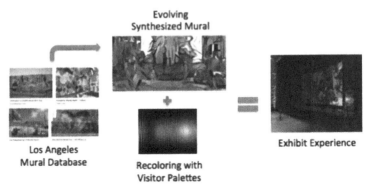

Fig. 3. How audience data affects *m/UR/al*

Similarly, for *Sobremesa*, if an audience member's 3 favorite types of cuisine were Korean, Chinese, and Middle Eastern, then the appetizer, main course, and dessert shown on the projection would be synthesized according to the three cuisine types separately when he scanned his QR code in front of the projection. The images tagged for these three cuisines in our database would then appear on the left top of the projection. A recommended restaurant would appear on the bottom right of the projection, also based on the chosen cuisines. When multiple audience members participated in the exhibit together, group recommendation was used to create a menu which was mutually constructed from each audience member's data. Further interaction data was collected from a tablet which was placed at the table in the exhibit. Questions issued to the tablet provided prompts for conversation between audience members, which could be discussed using the generated menu. Responses to the conversation prompt would propagate changes to the generated menu.

The system determined real-time location information by scanning each audience member's QR code at each exhibit entrance. The audience members' data were retrieved to compose media content. Additionally, within *Activate LA* exhibit, audience members' precise locations were tracked using a network of cameras as a creation element to manipulate the rate of media changes on the projection.

Vectors were written to the Amazon Web Services Dynamo database. Identity vectors carried audience members' identity data showing how a visitor self-identified during onboarding and carried the static folksonomy tags associated with each audience member. A simple identity vector mightbe [Angeleno: {intensity: 0.8, sentiment: 0.0}}, Traffic: {Intensity: 0.7, sentiment: −0.6}]. Emission vectors carried the tags of all media content displayed in each exhibit and reflected multimedia outputs of the exhibits at any given time. As mentioned above, QR scans provided information on which audience members were in which exhibit. By combining this information with the emission vector of an exhibit, each visitor was tagged with an exposure vector which represents the accumulation tags an individual has seen over the course of their experience. Exposure evolved in time as a function of the emission vector. Exposure vectors were published to Amazon Web Services notification services every second and represented the tags of media content being displayed to specific audience members, reflecting the intersection of identity and emission vectors. An exposure vector gathered by the system might include [1984_Olympics: {intensity: 0.25, sentiment: 0.1}, food_trucks: {intensity: 0.8, sentiment: 0.9}, displacement: {intensity: 0.4, sentiment: −0.2}], reflecting the "amount" and/or "sentiment" of media they have seen given where they were in the Pavilion. These vectors expressed what an audience member had been exposed to. Tags were generated on scraped databases of media using image recognition software.

Figure 4 shows the data flow of @*LAs*. Tags generated from answers to the onboarding questions were entered into the system as identity vectors. When an audience member scanned his QR code, identity vectors were sent to Amazon Web Services cloud object storage to match the identities with processed media by matching their tags. Then, authored content was generated. Emission vectors were sent to the system to monitor what media content was shown in each exhibit at the same time. Exposure vectors were sent every second to communicate to the system what content the audience was being exposed to. After the experience, the system had access to the accumulated content that each audience member was exposed to. Vectors were used to process and monitor the data.

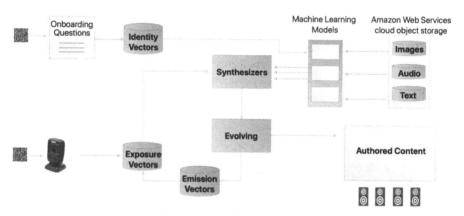

Fig. 4. The data flow of @*LAs*

5 Alternate Reality Design Implementation and Audience Experience

As shown in Fig. 1, when audience members entered the exhibit, students from the @*LAs* team welcomed them into the onboarding room. Audience members used their smartphones to open an online website, provide their identifying information and scan a QR code on the card. Then, the QR code was linked to their identity data. The audience members then started their experience holding their QR code cards.

The participants first walked through a hallway with five guiding colors on the ground, as shown in Fig. 5(a) and Fig. 5(b). Each audience member chose a preferred color to follow through the exhibit. For example, an audience member selecting the color orange experienced *m/UR/al* first. The *m/UR/al* was a corridor region generated by AI based on the Los Angeles mural conservancy dataset and identity data from the participants. The exhibit focused on the protection of tangible culture in Los Angeles. AI facilitated connections between individuals within the exhibit by creating a common meeting area and allowing the participants to see the media content authored by their data represented in space. This alternate reality exhibit first engaged audience members with history and then brought them back to the future. To reproduce historical events, we decided to create a tangible scene of a painter's studio through the use of props including a ladder, paint buckets, brushes, etc. Figure 6(a) shows scenes of the painter's studio used in *@LAs*. When entering *m/UR/al*, the audience entered areas enclosed by a few cones and a typical stationary "no stopping" street sign. On the other side of the space, we positioned a bench and a USA Magazine newsstand facing the wall that our painter was painting. Audience members could sit on the bench to watch movies about the history of Los Angeles residents who had created murals and street art. This process helped the audience better relate to murals painted in the past. Next, the audience explored murals to be created in the future. Upon turning the corner, murals projected behind a large dark screen became visible along with two benches, as shown in Fig. 6(b). In lieu of mural synthesis, for *m/UR/al*, we used the style transfer approach. An image of a Los Angeles mural was chosen by an audience member and its style was then applied to another set of generated imagery related to our themes. Then, the generated murals were recolored with other palettes. Therefore, when an audience member scanned his QR code, a new mural appeared on the large dark screen. Participants could also sit on the bench and watch other audience members' artworks and communicate with each other. While immersed in this large projection and experiencing the joys of their creation, audience members experienced historic murals and contemporary AI technologies at the same time.

(a)   **(b)**

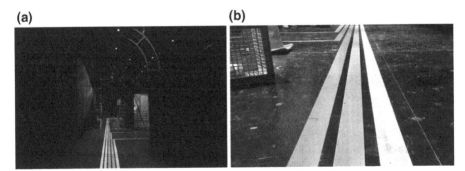

Fig. 5. (a) Upon leaving the onboarding room, participants were guided by colored paint on the ground. (b) The colored paint. (Color figure online)

(a)   (b)

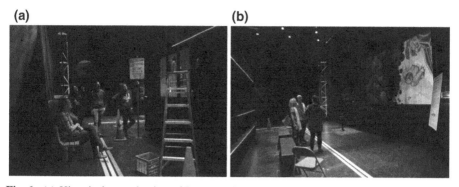

Fig. 6. (a) Historical reproduction of Los Angeles residents creating murals and street art. (b) New murals generated by combining Los Angeles murals with audience palettes.

As shown in Fig. 7, after walking through the mural area and turning the corner, audience members entered a behind-the-scenes area. Engineers and designers of each exhibit were working in this area, supporting the production of multimedia content. Audience members could clearly observe the work required to run the installation.

(a)   (b)

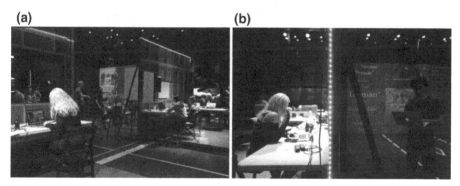

Fig. 7. (a) Engineers and designers supporting the exhibit in a behind-the-scenes area. (b) The behind-the-scenes area and exhibit were separated by a wall. The space was open to audience members.

From here, there was an exhibition on each side. The exhibit shown on the right was titled *Sobremesa* (Fig. 8). "Sobremesa" is a Spanish term for the conversation enjoyed after a meal. The space depicted an alternate reality of a virtual restaurant space created to focus on the experiences of the participants and to provide an interactive space for audience members to interact with the display. When audience members entered the exhibit, they were presented with a virtual restaurant in a square room. In it, there was a round table, four chairs, and a bar counter. To prompt conversation between the audience members and project the generated background imagery on the wall, surface-mapped projections were shown on the table and the wall. Energetic restaurant music was played. A live-action waiter gave experience guidance to the audience. He first had them sit around the table. At most, four audience members could sit at the table at the same time. Next, when the audience members scanned their QR codes, as shown in Fig. 8(a), dishes were generated based on both the audience members' culinary interest data and synthesized restaurant menus from Los Angeles that appeared on the wall. The audience members' favorite foods were re-contextualized, producing desirable and surreal dining options, as illustrated in Fig. 8(b). Then, the waiter reminded them to read a set of questions projected on the surface of the table. The questions were related to their experiences with food. They could use a tablet to select "Yes" to answer the questions or "No" to see another set of questions. After providing an answer, the audience members could share their views and memories relating to food based on the questions with one another. Food serves as a means of making interpersonal connections. By allowing AI to synthesize their food preference data, the audience members had opportunities to share their eating habits, showing that their interests extended beyond their own cultural identities.

(a)   **(b)**

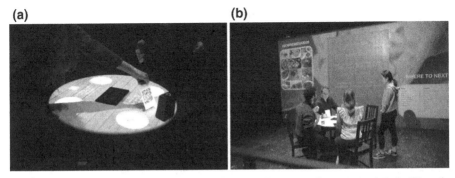

Fig. 8. (a) To notify the system of their identities, audience members scanned their QR codes when they sat at the table. (b) Audience members could share their experiences and histories related to food according to the multimedia content generated by both their data and the menus of LA restaurants. Questions were projected on the surface of the table as discussion topics.

When the audience members walked out of *Sobremesa, Activate LA* was shown to the left. This exhibit spoke to Los Angeles' development of public transportation and major highways in preparation for the 2028 Olympics. *Activate LA* used positional mapping to allow the audience to explore perceptions of Angeleno identities. On the wall, audience members could view a large projection that was divided into three columns, namely, with hashtags, images and text. Each column was coupled with a corresponding lane on the ground. The audience members could also hear words spoken via Amazon Polly, a text-to-speech service. Data from the exhibit was used to generate text using machine-learning, and this text was translated to various languages and broadcast within the exhibit. Before entering the exhibit area, the audience members scanned their QR codes beside the gate to *Activate LA*. The QR code then sent each participant's onboarding information to a machine learning processor. The processor then connected to online databases and imported relevant media on an ongoing basis. Then, on the projection, the audience members could see the hashtags, images and text related to public transportation. When an audience member moved to a particular area within each lane, the tracking system tracked this movement, and a small red circle appeared at the corresponding position on the projection, as illustrated in Fig. 9(a). As more audience members entered the exhibit, more red circles appeared in the corresponding columns. Audience members could work together in exploring this exhibit, as multiple audience members in the same lane manipulated provided new ways of manipulating media, as shown in Fig. 9(b). *Activate LA* encouraged audience members to explore Los Angeles in personal and collaborative ways, defamiliarizing common perceptions perpetuated within popular culture.

(a)   **(b)**

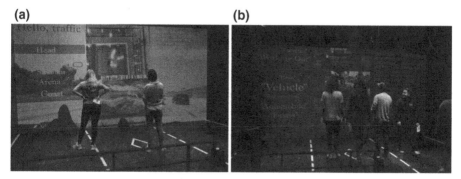

Fig. 9. (a) When an audience member stepped on a lane, a red circle appeared in the corresponding column on the projection. (b) As more audience members stepped in the same lane, media in the corresponding column moved faster. (Color figure online)

Upon leaving *Activate LA*, audience members could communicate with installation engineers, designers, and other staff. Alternatively, they could end their experience and go to the offboarding region. Here, they scanned their QR codes for the last time, bringing their adventure through Los Angeles in 2028 to an end.

6   The Innovation of @*LAs*

To allow audience members to control media content dynamically, @*LAs* explored a way of using audience data and AI to create variable and unpredictable media content as a design strategy. We developed a way for participants to explore the exhibit behind the scenes. We also explored the tension between personalized and group experiences.

6.1   Realizing Dynamic Control

Designers increasingly value the flexibility of delivery provided through live performances and cinema [16]. This flexibility of delivery is a necessary condition for dynamically controlling media content through design. For media content provided through alternate reality design, flexible delivery allows real-time variability and unpredictability in media content. Real-time variability allows designers or audience members to control media content in real time. With our prototype, although designers and engineers were monitoring and modulating the exhibits in real time, the central controller of content was the audience. By providing data in real time as creative elements when scanning their QR codes, participants guaranteed the variability of media content and thus provided personalized experiences. Media content is not known before it is presented on display materials. With our prototype, we provided raw media materials, audience data as creative elements, and rules for media generation through AI, but we could not precisely predict what media content would be generated.

There are many ways to realize media content variability and unpredictability. For example, real-time data generated by performers, audience members, or the environment are used as creative elements. We can also use machine learning, chemical reactions, or physical reactions to help create unpredictable media content. Through our prototype, we explored a way to use audience data as creative elements to achieve variability in media content while using AI to achieve media content unpredictability. Thus, we realized flexible delivery and dynamic control.

6.2   The Transparent Behind-the-Scenes Operations

Since AI-generated artworks are sometimes very abstract, we hypothesized that audience members' attitudes towards AI-generated artworks would be more forgiving than human-generated content. Our behind-the-scenes area was intended to provide audience members with an intuitive understanding of how AI was generating the artwork and how we controlled the prototype. Perhaps they did not understand the prototype's principle operations, but these behind-the-scenes operations may have helped audience members understand how they can interact with AI and broadened their experience [13]. Thus, they may have understood the creative process as a part of the experience rather than only viewing the media displayed.

Some designers explained to audience members the overall means through which their data were processed. The audience members were curious about how their data had evolved into artwork, but not all of them could understand the complexities of the process. One audience who visited the behind-the-scenes area communicated with almost every engineer and told us that he was studying algorithms. Other audience members may have viewed the behind-the-scenes area as performance art to some extent. Following from Umberto Eco's view of artworks as open works, the experiences of audience members who did not truly understand the prototype's principles may not have been affected because they may have viewed the behind-the-scenes area as simply a part of the exhibit.

6.3   Personalized Media Content with Collective Experiences

We collected nine questionnaires. The respondents to the survey were designers of the exhibit who also participated as audience members. From the feedback provided, 78% of the respondents thought the use of identity data worked well. This means that audience members noticed and enjoyed the personalized media content. Audience members were the spectators and the storytellers of the prototype. They enjoyed the media content created by their data and explained their media content to others because they viewed our prototype with others. According to our observations, the more personalized the content is, the more audience members were attracted to it. For example, a group of audience members created a colorful mural which prompted more audience members to enter the exhibit. They then scanned their QR codes to add more colors to the mural. A considerable volume of personalized media content thus supported the exhibit. The audience members could enjoy both their personalized media and the collective experience. The collective experience was enhanced when there was a great deal of media content on the screen, but it was difficult to identify the individual media content. We used two means to balance it. First, the audience members were separated by colored Paint. Second, designers explained to audience members how to identify their own personalized media.

7 Discussion of the @*LAs* Experience

In this case study, audiences shared data and made observations in authoring open works of art. Data, as a result, were central to an alternate reality that allowed them to explore experiences at the collective and individual levels. Folksonomy was used to capture and semi-structure the authors' evolving understanding of how to tag shared audience data and multimedia content. Tagged data and content were matched to generate new media content through contemporary machine learning techniques. Both technological efforts and design ideas were intended to increase audience member engagement. We would share some design lessons from questionnaires' responses.

Seven respondents viewed the concept of folksonomies as useful for organizing media and considered the identity, emission, and exposure vectors useful in their ability to author exhibits, showing that data processing was successful. Five of the respondents thought they were able to express their ideas using the datasets. They were able to experiment with group recommendations for media provided through the exhibits. We analyze these together with the quality of the @*LAs* experience in sharing lessons for similar work.

Quality of Alternate Reality Experience and QoE Influencing Factors from the International Workshop on Multimedia Alternate Realities present three factors for evaluating the quality of an alternate reality experience, namely, spatial immersion, emotion immersion, and social immersion [18]. The design of @*LAs* investigated a new relationship between authors and audience members. Through an alternate reality that embeds the audience into artwork in a new way through machine learning, the audience's sense of emotional and social immersion were enhanced according to the feedback provided. We also share lessons to improve levels of spatial immersion.

7.1 Collective Experiences in Augmenting Social Immersion

@*LAs* provided augmented social immersion through interpersonal cohesiveness, social interaction and a sense of belongingness. Interpersonal cohesiveness is the first quality metric of social immersion [18] and was a central focus of @*LAs*. All media content provided was cumulative and liquid. As an audience member's media content faded away, another audience member's media content appeared on the projection. The number of audience members present controlled the diversity of media content shown. As a result, the different audience members' identity data evolved into a fluid image with the help of AI. Taking *m/UR/al* as an example, if five audience members chose five different colors as identities, a mural composed of five colors moved from the left side of the screen to the right. New colors appeared from the left side as new audience members scanned their QR codes (Fig. 6). The audience members thus cooperated in enjoying this collective work and communicating freely, enhancing interpersonal cohesiveness.

Social interaction and a sense of belongingness were also encouraged through @*LAs*. The exhibit with the most apparent social immersion characteristics was *Sobremesa*. Three designers wrote in the questionnaires that only *Sobremesa* avoided providing too much media content because the exhibit was designed for group communication. We noticed that most audience members spent more time in *Sobremesa*, which differed from the other two exhibits because it encouraged audience members to communicate. We encouraged their social interactions and sense of belongingness by providing talking topics through this exhibit and keeping audience numbers to groups of two to four. An audience member needed to wait for at least one other person before entering *Sobremesa*, as coviewing enhances users' satisfaction when enjoying media content with others [19]. We gave the audience members opportunities to watch the content together and communicate.

7.2   Identity Data and Folksonomy for Enhancing Emotional Immersion

To achieve emotional immersion, Zhang et al. contend that audience members must abandon their own beliefs and thoughts to adopt virtual characters' identity and emotions [18]. In @*LAs*, "characters" were decided by the participants themselves. On the one hand, when audience members decided to share virtual data, they adapted to a virtual character's identity and emotions and experienced a virtual character's experiences. On the other hand, when audience members shared data on their real identities, they could experience their own stories and did not have to adapt to other characters' identities. They then had the opportunity to experience a dual alternate reality.

As emotional immersion was an outcome of participants' identity data creating stories in @*LAs*, efficient identity data processing needed to be guaranteed. Four designers wrote that the identity data worked well, showing that efficient data processing was achieved. Six respondents found the folksonomies to be extremely effective. As folksonomies played a crucial role in matching audience identity data with media content, the attractiveness of the media content shows that it was effectively generated by AI. The identity data and folksonomies worked well as storytelling elements, suggesting that audience members may have experienced emotional immersion through @LAs.

For @*LAs*, emotional immersion was also related to the length of aesthetic immersion. Chinese scholar Teng Shouyao said that the length of aesthetic immersion is determined by the audience's familiarity with the artwork [20]. When the audience is too familiar with the world of art, this will lead to boredom. However, being too unfamiliar with the world of art will lead to a loss of motivation to explore artwork. The best artwork gives its audience a sense of both the familiar and unfamiliar. This feeling can maximize the period of an aesthetic immersion. Although this feeling is difficult to measure, the commingling of the audience and the author can be used to explore it. With @*LAs*, we tried to achieve this balance by drawing on the participants' identities and the scenes that were highly similar to reality in every exhibit to create a sense of familiarity while using AI-generated content to provide a sense of unfamiliarity.

7.3 Intervening as a Means to Enhance Space Immersion

In @*LAs*, spatial immersion was triggered and maintained not only by the spatial qualities of the virtual environment [18] but also through personalized media content. First, we focused on the virtual environment's spatial design. The real world was simulated by enhancing recognition of familiar scenes, such as in *m/UR/al*, i.e., through the reproduction of historical scenes of mural creation. For *Sobremesa*, the layout was similar to that of a restaurant. Second, to provide experiences of cognitive identity to the audience members, all displays were based on their identity data. In this way, we accomplish spatial immersion by displaying personalized content layered over the real world.

From observation and questionnaire results, we note that spatial immersion is also affected by the number of audience members in the same area at the same time. Too many audience members in the same area would negatively impact the personalized experience as it is difficult to understand what content is contributed by whom. Although designers need to be careful with interventions in AI involved designs [21], face-to-face interventions are sometimes necessary. We used intervening as a means to enhance space immersion in two ways in @*LAs*. First, as narrated in Sect. 5, colored paint is used to guide and divide audience members to different exhibit areas without face-to-face communication. Second, in *Sobremesa*, a human is integrated into the exhibit as an actor who is able to provide explanation. These intervention options - lightweight visual communication and embedding human explainers as actors in exhibits - offer directions to enhance spatial immersion in future work.

8 Conclusion

This paper explored a new kind of alternate reality that embedded the audience into the artwork, thereby making the audience an author of other people's or their own stories. Through this process, we realized the real-time, dynamic control of design by using audience identity data, location data, and interaction data as creative elements with the help of machine learning and using identity, emission, and exposure vectors as process methods. Machine learning was used to select and sometimes generate multimedia content combined with audience data. We also demonstrate a way to make behind-the-scenes work visible and negotiate audience members' personalized experiences with a collective experience. Based on observation and designer feedback, the collective experience is helpful to augment social immersion. Identity data and folksonomy are useful techniques in enhancing emotional immersion. Using colored paint to separate audience numbers and narrating to them as modes of intervention can be means to enhance space immersion.

@*LAs* is an attempt to combine human creativity with AI creativity. Data makes it possible for designers, audience members and machines to communicate. Using QR codes to trigger audience data, and using folksonomy tags and vectors to classify and process data were proven to be effective from designers' feedback. These methods for collecting and processing data can be shared with other alternate reality designs. Our future work will modify the division of work between AI and participants, improve tag accuracy levels, and make media content more meaningful.

Acknowledgments. The Institute was supported by the UCLA TFT Skoll Center for Social Impact Entertainment.

References

1. Rostami, A., Rossitto, C., Waern, A.: Frictional realities: enabling immersion in mixed-reality performances. In: Proceedings of the 2018 ACM International Conference on Interactive Experiences for TV and Online Video, pp. 15–27, June 2018
2. Lens. http://www.lensmagazine.com.cn/video/Eliasson. Accessed 01 May 2020
3. Olafur Eliasson: The unspeakable openness of things (visitbeijing.com.cn). http://english.visitbeijing.com.cn/a1/a-XDIA6E3748D412F216808D. Accessed 01 May 2020
4. IGNANT. https://www.ignant.com/2016/01/07/an-illusory-swimming-pool-by-leandro-erlich/. Accessed 01 May 2020
5. MacGregor, B.: Cybernetic serendipity revisited. In: Proceedings of the 4th Conference on Creativity & Cognition, pp. 11–13, October 2002
6. Agent Ruby. https://wiki.ubc.ca/Agent_Ruby. Accessed 01 May 2020
7. Röggla, T., Wang, C., Perez Romero, L., Jansen, J., Cesar, P.: Tangible air: an interactive installation for visualising audience engagement. In: Proceedings of the 2017 ACM SIGCHI Conference on Creativity and Cognition, pp. 263–265, June 2017
8. Borderless. https://borderless.teamlab.art/zh-hans/. Accessed 01 May 2020
9. Bowers, J., SHAPE Consortium: TONETABLE: a multi-user, mixed-media, interactive installation. In Proceedings of COST G-6 Conference on Digital Audio Effects (DAFX-01), December 2001
10. Kim, J.Y., Allen, J.P., Lee, E.: Alternate reality gaming. Commun. ACM **51**(2), 36–42 (2008)
11. AIArtists.org. https://aiartists.org/refik-anadol. Accessed 01 Jan 2022
12. Dannenberg, R.B., Bates, J.: A model for interactive art (1995)
13. Elgammal, A.: AI Is blurring the definition of artist: advanced algorithms are using machine learning to create art autonomously. Am. Sci. **107**(1), 18–22 (2019)
14. Shanken, E.A.: Art in the information age: Technology and conceptual art. Leonardo **35**(4), 433–438 (2002)
15. Berry, D.M., Fagerjord, A.: Digital Humanities: Knowledge and Critique in a Digital Age. Polity Press, Cambridge (2017)
16. Burke, J., Stein, J.: Live performance and post-cinematic filmmaking. Perform. Matt. **6**(1), 28–47 (2020)
17. Daer, A.R., Hoffman, R., Goodman, S.: Rhetorical functions of hashtag forms across social media applications. In: Proceedings of the 32nd ACM International Conference on the Design of Communication CD-ROM, pp. 1–3, September 2014
18. Zhang, C., Hoel, A.S., Perkis, A.: Quality of alternate reality experience and its QoE influencing factors. In: Proceedings of the 2nd International Workshop on Multimedia Alternate Realities, pp. 3–8, October 2017
19. Morrison, M., Krugman, D.M.: A look at mass and computer mediated technologies: understanding the roles of television and computers in the home. J. Broadcast. Electron. Media **45**(1), 135–161 (2001)
20. Teng, S.Y.: The Description of Aesthetic Psychology. China Social Science Press (1985)
21. Koleva, B., et al.: Orchestrating a mixed reality performance. In: Proceedings of the SIGCHI Conference on Human Factors in Computing Systems, pp. 38–45, March 2001

Literature Bibliometrics Atlas Analysis of Experience Design

Yu Wang[1,2(✉)], Xiangyang Xin[1], Hao Yu[1], Haolun Cheng[2], and Beiting Jin[2]

[1] School of Design, Jiangnan University, Wuxi 214122, China
wangyu@bigc.edu.cn
[2] Beijing Institute of Graphic Communication, Beijing 102600, China

Abstract. To explore the research foundation of experience design through the traceability research of experience design and to clarify the context, boundaries, and connections between different research topics. The integrated advantages of both CiteSpace and VosViewer to draw a knowledge map of related literature on experience design, based on the retrieval results of academic literature related to experience design in the Web of Science academic engine. Data and visualization of the research results sort out the highly cited literature on experience design to illustrate bibliometric atlas. The induction method is used to track the four main related fields of experience design, based on quantitative data analysis, combined with our cognition of experience design. From the perspective of the development context and trend of experience design, the experience economy is the commodity experience scenario. The economy determines product form and then design content. The transformation of user experience design to experience design corresponds to changing people's material needs to spiritual needs. Experience management based on process optimization expands the commercialization field of experience design. From the perspective of knowledge cognition and exploration of experience design, macro-leveled experience design coordinates the system and the world, focusing on the long-term construction of macroecology and human cultural environment; meso-experience design tends to be a system centered on customer experience Management; micro-experience design focuses on a complete experience that has a specific meaning or impact on the individual.

Keywords: Experience design · Bibliometrics · Visual analysis · Development context · Research hotspots

1 Introduction

Experience design has become a hot research focus with economic development. However, experience design research is usually carried out in case studies on specific characters, behaviors, scenarios, etc., due to the differences in authors' knowledge, practical orientation, and cognitive level. It results in the diversity and ambiguity in the conceptual definition of experience design and the lack of a comprehensive and systematic combing on its development relationship and perspectives.

© The Author(s), under exclusive license to Springer Nature Switzerland AG 2022
M. Rauterberg (Ed.): HCII 2022, LNCS 13324, pp. 167–187, 2022.
https://doi.org/10.1007/978-3-031-05434-1_11

How to understand experience and experience design? Experience is neither the subjective cognition and feeling of the subject nor the objective existence in general. It results from dynamic and continuous interaction when people meet the environment. Each integrated experience (An Experience) is an individual worthy of attention because of the uniqueness of its process and results, a complete dynamic structure with "beginning, development, and end" guided by a specific purpose. All experiences are the result of the interaction between people and their surroundings. An experience is not just a simple behavioral interaction based on environmental perception. The behavioral process and behavioral effects must also be perceived and felt, thus forming the experience of being emotional, meaningful, and worth memorizing [1].

The interpretation of experience and experience design varies in specific industries. The experiencer is the customer or guest in the marketing stage, the user in the use stage, or the provider in the manufacturing stage. Views from the various stakeholders in the implementation phase are complicated. Experience is triggered when customers gain a certain sense of knowledge when interacting with multiple elements in the context created by the service provider (Gupta & Vajic, 1999). A successful experience means that a customer discovers a unique, memorable, and valuable experience, hopes to experience it again, and enthusiastically promotes it (Pine & Gilmore, 1998 & 1999). Experience design refers to the established method based on emotional connections with guests or customers through careful planning on tangible and intangible service elements. Service providers manage their customer experience through design and continuous innovation (Pullman & Gross, 2004). Good experience design can use all physical or contextual elements to support potential visions, metaphors, or themes (Alben, 1996; Carbone & Haeckel, 1994; Pine & Gilmore, 1998) [2].

Because the literature on experience design involves a wide range of fields, traditional literature analysis methods cannot fully understand all the relevant domains involved in experience design. The way to solve this problem is first to sort out the literature context map. Therefore, we applied the bibliometric visualization analysis software (VosViewer and CiteSpace) to conduct a macro-leveled and micro-leveled analysis on experience design, based on the WOS database core collection (Web of ScienceTM Core Collection). Further, this article provides an interpretation based on our research background on the perspective of humanities and social sciences.

2   Materials and Methods of Literature Atlas Analysis of Experience Design

At present, many literature search engines do not regard design as an independent first-level discipline. The research results of design are often scattered and included in multi-disciplines. These articles might create issues of narrow vision when they focus on the way of viewpoints or genre inheritance relations. However, the development of the quantitative analysis method of the literature context map has become mature. This method is particularly suitable for the comprehensive and interdisciplinary knowledge context combing represented by design science. This article takes the experience design-related literature collected in the database from 1991 to 2021 as samples, extracts effective keywords to construct a common-word matrix, analyses the literature and authors, research hotspots, and development context of experience design. This paper selects kernel research institutions, authors and teams, and high-frequency keywords in the scientific knowledge graph as arguments to systematically sort out the development context of experience design.

2.1   Why Use Bibliometrics Atlas for Literature Analysis

The theme of experience design is relatively new, which involves many fields such as economics, management, engineering, etc. Experience design has applied to multiple industries such as entertainment, education, medical care, etc., and scenarios such as management, marketing, service, use, etc. Suppose we use the early traditional literature analysis methods. In that case, we cannot fully carry out the research results in various fields related to experience design, nor can we guide the author to conduct in-depth research on cross-correlation and developing knowledge. That means our academic background will limit the breadth and depth. Therefore, we first use the scientific knowledge bibliometrics atlas to analyze the literature and then uses the atlas as an argument for subjective interpretation.

The so-called literature originally refers to written materials containing various information. Documents can divide into official, personal, and mass media documents. According to the propagation order, it can be divided into primary literature and secondary or second-hand literature. Literature research is a systematic review and analysis of various explorations related to the frontier understanding of multidisciplinary subjects. In addition to being close to select research topics, literature research will provide practical information for all parts of the research [3].

The knowledge graph is a chart or graph used to show the relationship between the knowledge development process and structure. It is a new field of scientometrics that has quietly emerged under the background of data science and visualization technology. Among them, bibliometric visualization is to visualize the knowledge units of documents and document contents to reflect the output of literature in a research field, the attention of scientific researchers to the scenarios, and the theoretical level and development speed of the discipline [4]. The citation analysis method is a biblio-metric research method [5, 6] that uses mathematical and statistical methods to analyze the citation and citation phenomenon of scientific journals, papers, authors, and other analytical objects to reveal their quantitative characteristics and internal laws. The mutual citations of documents reflect both the objective laws of scientific exploration and the accumulation, continuity, and inheritance of scientific knowledge, as well as the intersection and penetration between disciplines [7]. Based on the grounded theory, this paper conducts a visual analysis of the relevant elements of kernel documents and obtains the development context of experience design.

2.2   What Software Used for the Bibliometric Visualization Analysis

After obtaining the original literature data, we operate qualitative and quantitative analysis by two bibliometric visualization software (VosViewer and CiteSpace). VosViewer is a software tool for building and visualizing bibliometric networks, which provides text clustering used for constructing and visualizing co-occurrence networks of kernel terms

[8]. CiteSpace is a freely available Java application for visually analyzing trends and patterns in literature. CiteSpace provides various functions to promote the understanding of network and historical patterns, including identifying rapidly growing subject areas, finding citation hotspots, decomposing the network into clusters, automatically labeling clusters using the terminology of cited documents, and obtaining geospatial cooperation mode and field of international cooperation [9, 10].

The advantage of VosViewer is visualization, displaying the results from multiple views, can build a variety of matrices, and support text mining. But it is not good at showing the evolution path of a field through time evolution. Therefore, CiteSpace uses various bibliometric analysis methods to quantitatively analyze the visualization results, displaying the development of an area from multiple perspectives, supporting numerous databases, including Chinese databases, and building standard relational networks [11]. The article draws bibliometrics atlas by integrating the advantages of CiteSpace and VosViewer to explore kernel citations, topics, hotspots, frontiers, and evolution paths in the field of experience design.

2.3   Where the Data Sources Come and What Parameters Set

The literature comes from the WOS of the ISI Institute for Scientific Information. The database sources are Science Citation Index Expanded (SCI-EXPANDED), Social Sciences Citation Index (SSCI), Art & Humanities Citation Index (A&HCI), and Emerging Sources Citation Index (ESCI). All above covers humanities, humanity-related interdisciplinary, ergonomics, information engineering, art, applied psychology, and other disciplines, eliminating diagnosis, treatment, surgery, and other professional medical literature.

To accurately retrieve the literature in experience design and ensure credibility through the retrieval test of multiple retrieval algorithms after manually comparing analysis and removing the retrieval styles with irrelevant results. Finally, the title of the literature and the keywords from authors are decided to be the subject retrieval (TI = "experience design") OR (AK = "experience design"). The period is from 1991 to 2021, and the operation time was on November 17, 2021. The document type is Article, and the language is English. After a manual investigation of irrelevant documents, 680 valid document records were retrieved totally. Each item includes author, institution, abstract, keywords, publication year, issue (volume), references, etc. The raw data of the standardized document were operated after being downloaded from the WOS website. We set the time slice as 1 in the CiteSpace, divided into 31 periods, and set the threshold value to the top 50. By the minimum tree generation algorithm, we got the maps of research fields, research institutions, authors, countries, co-cited documents, keyword co-occurrence, etc. Then, by analyzing the keywords in the document metadata through calculations in VosViewer and setting the threshold to 7, 42 of 2515 words are detected to meet the threshold requirements, sorted according to the co-occurrence links.

3 Literature Bibliometric and Visual Analysis of Experience Design

3.1 The Trend from Annual Data

The experience design research can divide into four specific development periods based on the annual data results. Although the search for experience design literature began in 1991 (see Fig. 1), it was not until 2000 that an experience design literature appeared. From then to 2006, the number of articles published in those seven years was less than 5, and there was no significant increase. From 2007 to 2014, the literature grew slowly as the phenomenon of the alternate bearing of fruits; nevertheless, it burst during 2015–2018 with the development of the experience economy and the continuous expansion of the service market share. User experience and service experience represented by Internet platforms have become a new trend in research, and research literature has shown an explosive growth trend during this period. However, with the outbreak of the Covid-19 epidemic, the scale of academic papers has enormously reduced. The spread of the Covid-19 epidemic worldwide has caused a tremendous impact on all walks of life, and people have begun to re-examine the relationship between man and nature. On the one hand, designers strive to use service design and transformational design thinking to solve or optimize real problems. On the other, designers shift from concern about human subjective emotions to a balanced relationship between man and nature, so to consider environmental benefits and seek long-term benefits for the general development of the world based on the future design, green design, and the concept of sustainable design.

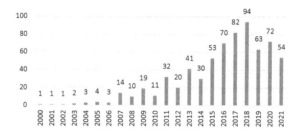

Fig. 1. Annual distribution of literatures of experience design.

3.2 Main Related Research Fields

In the past 30 years, in the research field of experience design, the first echelon is mainly distributed in computer science and engineering, emphasizing the fluency and execution efficiency of the systematic artificial and focusing on the measurement research of system-level efficiency. The second echelon is in social science, education, business economics, emphasizing the role of attitude, willingness, efficiency, and order driven by experience improvement in promoting the development of society, educational effects, and commerce. The third echelon includes art, telecommunications, information science, psychology, communication. The third echelon emphasizes the ethics, morality, and social vision of experience, which analyzes the importance, necessity, and causal relationship, as well as the interaction and user experience in the process of information communication, and emphasizes the cognition and improvement of emotion and behavioral logic (see Fig. 2). In human-computer interaction systems, experience has attracted much attention as a design principle and verification indicator to measure the pros and cons of products. The relevant scholars have conducted many quantitative analyses and case studies in the industry of business management, education, medical care, tourism, and telecommunications.

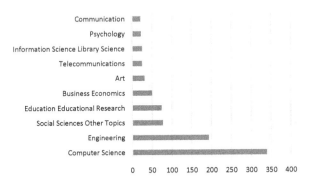

Fig. 2. Research field distribution of experience design.

3.3 Leading Countries or Regions of the Research

VosViewer analyzed the experience design literature in the past 30 years. The top ten countries (regions) in the number of documents (Documents) are the United States (166), mainland China (90), the United Kingdom (63), Italy (46), Germany (44), Finland (31), Australia (31), the Netherlands (30), South Korea (29), Canada (24). The average number of citations (Citations ÷ Documents) of American documents exceeds 10, followed by the United Kingdom (8.2), the Netherlands (7), and Finland. (6.5), Germany (4.8), Australia (4.7), Italy (4.4), Sweden (4.3), South Korea (4.1), Mainland China (1). Total link strength (Total link strength) - the number of co-occurrences, are ranked in order: The United States, the United Kingdom, the Netherlands, Italy, Finland, Germany, Australia, South Korea, Sweden, and Mainland China (see Table 1). A comprehensive comparison of the above three data shows that the United States is not only the country with the most significant number of publications but also the country with the most influence. Countries with a large number of publications may not necessarily have more contributions. Mainland China ranks second in the number of publications, but its current international influence is not high.

3.4 Key Research Institutions

The citations of the literature can reflect academic influence to a certain extent. The top ten highly influential research institutions reveal that the most experience design research institutions are located in European and American countries. Cornell Univ. and

Table 1. Countries (regions) with high-impact on experience design research.

Country (area)	Documents	Citations	Total link strength
USA	166	1719	5741
England	63	519	4750
Netherlands	30	211	2724
Italy	46	202	2194
Finland	31	201	2183
Germany	44	210	2065
Australia	31	145	1700
South Korea	29	119	1533
Sweden	15	65	1466
CHN	90	94	1449

Temple Univ. in the United States have higher citations and literature influence, followed by Folkwang Univ. of Arts in Germany, Tampere Univ. of Technology in Finland, and Polytechnic Univ. Milan in Italy, Univ. of Oxford in the United Kingdom, Delft Univ. of Technology and Breda Univ. of Applied Sciences in the Netherlands, Aalborg Univ. in Denmark, and James Cook Univ. in Australia. In general, the current experience design research institutions in the United States are the most influential in the world (see Table 2).

Table 2. Universities with high-impact on experience design research.

Organization	Country (area)	Documents	Citations
Cornell Univ.	USA	9	378
Temple Univ.	USA	6	210
Folkwang Univ. of Arts	German	6	132
Tampere Univ. of Tech.	Finland	8	100
Polytechnic Univ. Milan	Italy	16	97
Univ. of Oxford	England	8	97
Delft Univ. of Tech.	Netherlands	9	63
Breda Univ. of Applied Sciences	Netherlands	6	58
Aalborg Univ.	Denmark	7	35
James Cook Univ.	Australia	6	34

3.5 Highly Cited Authors

The following authors analyzed the literature from two aspects. On the one hand, it analyses the active authors (i.e., high-productive authors) and their cooperative teams in the research. On the other hand, it focuses on the highly cited authors of the literature. In this way, the situation of the primary research teams is estimated while influential researchers are focused [12]. Among the top ten authors of the highly cited literature in experience design, Marc Hassenzahl, professor of "Universal Design/Experience and Interaction" at the Institute of Business Informatics, University of Siegen, Germany, and his team members have published many influential articles and papers on experience design theory and practice. Cognitive psychologist Donald A. Norman has reinterpreted Affordance. His books, "The Design of Everyday Things", "Emotional Design", "Living with Complexity", and "Design of Future Things", are used as classic textbooks in design psychology. Charles Spence and his group's research focus on how a better understanding of the human mind will lead to the better design of multisensory foods, products, interfaces, and environments in the future. Strategic Vision Co-founder B. Joseph Pine II, the related papers and works of his "Experience Economy" are widely cited. The institutions and research fields of other authors are shown in Table 3.

Table 3. Authors of highly cited literature on experience design.

Author	Citations	Organization and position
Marc Hassenzahl	172	Marc Hassenzahl, PhD in Psychology, is Professor for "Ubiquitous Design/Experience and Interaction" at the Institute for Information Systems and Dean of the Faculty of Economics at the University of Siegen, whose focus is on the theory and practice of designing joyful, meaningful and transformative experiences [13]
Donald A. Norman	116	Donald A. Norman is currently Founder and Director of the Design Lab at the University of California, San Diego where he is also professor emeritus of psychology, cognitive science, and electrical and computer engineering [14, 15]
Charles Spence	112	Professor Charles Spence is the head of the Cross-modal Research Laboratory, whose research areas include applied cognitive psychology, consumer psychology, sensory marketing, multisensory perception [16]
B. Joseph Pine II	62	B. Joseph Pine II held a number of technical and managerial positions with IBM. Pine is an internationally acclaimed author, speaker, and management advisor to Fortune 500 companies and entrepreneurial start-ups alike, who is a co-founder of Strategic Horizons LLP [17]

(continued)

Table 3. (*continued*)

Author	Citations	Organization and position
Jakob Nielsen	55	Jakob Nielsen, PhD in human–computer interaction, is a User Advocate and principal of the Nielsen Norman Group, who established the "discount usability engineering" movement for fast and cheap improvements of user interfaces and invented several usability methods [18]
Kim J. Vicente	53	Kim J. Vicente is founding director of the Cognitive Engineering Laboratory at the University of Toronto where he is a professor in the departments of mechanical engineering, computer science and electrical and computer engineering [19]
Pieter Desmet	42	Pieter Desmet is professor of Design for Experience at the Faculty of Industrial Design Engineering. His main research interest is in understanding why and how design evokes emotion, and how design can contribute to the well-being and flourishing of individual users and communities [20]
Paulo Maldonado	38	Paulo Maldonado, Post-Doc and PhD in Design, is assistant professor of Department of Visual Arts and Design at University de Évora, visiting professor at post-graduation in Design at the Federal University of Rio Grande do Sul (Brazil) [21]
Mihaly Csikszentmihalyi	36	Mihaly Csikszentmihalyi, PhD in Psychology, and the head of the Department of Psychology at the University of Chicago and of the Department of Sociology and Anthropology at Lake Forest College, is Claremont Graduate University's Distinguished Professor of Psychology and Management [22]
Iis P. Tussyadiah	35	Iis P. Tussyadiah, PhD in Information Sciences, is Professor of Intelligent Systems in Service and Head of School of Hospitality and Tourism Management at University of Surrey. Iis conducts research on digital transformation in the travel and hospitality industry, focusing on human-computer interaction, consumer behavior, and mobility [23]

3.6 Highly Cited Literatures

Among the top 20 highly-cited documents in experience design, the iterative document of "Experience Economy" by B. Joseph Pine II and James H. Gilmore is the most highly cited. "User Experience" followed by Marc Hassenzahl, the other literature published by his team are also highly influential; the third place is "Emotional Design" by Donald A. Norman. Other highly-cited documents are shown in Table 4. In addition, ISO 9241–210:2010 provides requirements and recommendations for human-centered design principles and activities throughout the life cycle of computer-based interactive systems, which has been cited 16 times. It is intended to be used by those managing design processes and is concerned with ways in which both hardware and software components of interactive systems can enhance human-system interaction [24].

Table 4. Highly cited literatures on experience design.

Cited reference	Cited	Year	Author
Welcome to the Experience Economy	32	1998	B. Joseph Pine II, Joseph H. Gilmore
The Experience Economy: Work Is Theater & Every Business a Stage	19	1999	
Experience Economy	18	2011	
User Experience - a Research Agenda	35	2006	Marc Hassenzahl
Experience Design: Technology for All Right Reasons	18	2010	
Needs, Affect, and Interactive Products - Facets of User Experience	16	2010	
Designing Moments of Meaning and Pleasure, Experience Design and Happiness	16	2010	
Emotional design: why we love (Or Hate) Everyday Things	23	2004	Donald A. Norman
Framework of Product Experience	18	2007	Pieter Desmet
Technology as experience	18	2004	Peter Wright
Ability of Experience Design Elements to Elicit Emotions and Loyalty Behaviors	17	2004	Madeleine E. Pullman
Service Design for Experience-Centric Services	17	2010	Leonieke G. Zomerdijk
Toward a Theoretical Foundation for Experience Design in Tourism	17	2014	Iis P. Tussyadiah

(continued)

Table 4. (*continued*)

Cited reference	Cited	Year	Author
Self-concordance, goal attainment, and the pursuit of happiness: can there be an upward spiral?	16	2001	Kennon M. Sheldon
Sketching User Experiences	16	2007	Bill Buxton
Servicescapes: The Impact of Physical Surroundings on Customers and Employee	15	1992	Mary Jo Bitner
Using Thematic Analysis in Psychology	14	2006	Virginia Braun, Victoria Clarke
Designing Pleasurable Products an Introduction to the New Human Factors	13	2000	Patrick W. Jordan
Experience Prototyping	13	2000	Marion Buchenau, Jane Fulton Suri
River Magic: Extraordinary Experience and the Extended Service Encounter	12	1993	Eric J. Arnould

3.7 High Occurrence Keywords

Keywords are the author's essential summary of the research content of the literature., The hotspots and development trends of specific research fields are outlined through statistics and analysis of keywords [12]. High-frequency keywords are sorted to determine the hot issues of a research field. The following table presents the top 20 high-frequency keywords (Occurrences, the frequency of occurrence of keywords) and their link strength (Total Link Strength, the total number of co-occurrences of this keyword with other keywords) in the experience design literature. The keywords of experience design literature are listed in descending order as Experience Design, User Experience Design, Interaction Design, User-centered Design, Experience, Service Design, etc. (see Table 5). User Experience Design is not directly merged into Experience Design because the former has become a significant proprietary phrase, primarily referring to the experience design in the process of the user using the product, especially in the process of human-computer interaction. However, the former seems only to add a qualifier of affiliation to the latter.

The current hot research issues related to Experience Design include the following aspects: 1. Interaction design, product design, human factors engineering, usability research, and other ergonomic fields led by user experience design. 2. Design thinking, Evaluation elements, process methods, and other service management fields led by service design. 3. Design application fields of Extended Reality (including Virtual Reality, Augmented Reality, Mixed Reality) technology in entertainment, education, training, service, cultural heritage protection, etc. 4. Focus on the music, art, and the field of artistic or emotional experience, etc. 5. User-centered education design, game design, and other fields. These keywords are interrelated, overlap each other, and each has its emphasis. From the figure below, we can see the current focus from experts and scholars (see Fig. 3).

<header>Y. Wang et al.</header>

Table 5. High-frequency keywords in experience design literatures.

Keyword	Occurrences	Total link strength
Experience design	257	313
User experience design	227	227
Interaction design	42	73
User centered design	37	65
Experience	33	72
Service design	28	73
Emotion	28	72
Virtual reality	25	50
Usability	25	47
Human computer interaction	24	52
Behavior	20	44
Innovation	15	51
Quality	15	56
Augmented reality	15	41
Satisfaction	14	52
Tourism	14	38
Consumption	14	36
Technology	13	42
Model	13	35
Impact	12	35

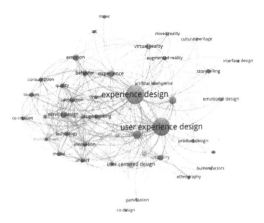

Fig. 3. Relationship network diagram of Keywords in experience design.

4 Tracing Experience Design from Four Main Development Contexts

The well-known American intelligence scientist SMALL H. proposed a method of co-citation analysis of literature [25]. The literature co-citation network analyzes the reference logic between kernel documents, the inheritance of viewpoints, the evolution direction, and other development laws and trends. High-frequency documents commonly cited by high-frequency cited documents represent kernel views or outstanding research results in specific fields. They are regarded as the core nodes of the research context. The research on co-cited documents can analyze the academic development of particular areas.

Although WOS does not separate the design literature from other subjects, as an interdisciplinary subject, design thinking and methodology are widely used in many fields. This paper tracked the four main related areas of experience design and then analyzed the relationship among experience economy in the field of economics, customer experience management in the field of management, ergonomics in the field of engineering, and experience design in the field of design.

4.1 Macroeconomic Development Promotes Experience Becoming a New Commodity Form and Design Object

From the British classical economist Adam Smith to John Maynard Keynes in the United States, whose mainstream western economic theories believe that the basis of economic activity is land-resource, capital, and labor. The economy is understood as the activities of production, distribution, exchange, and consumption of materials, ignoring the existence of a spiritual economy [26]. In the middle of the 19th century, Marx and Engels pointed out three forms of human production in "German Ideology": the production of one's own life (human survival and reproduction), the production of other people's life (material production), and the productivity of ideas, concepts, and consciousness (spiritual productivity) [27], thus breaking the predecessor's conceptual views of emphasizing material economy over the spiritual economy.

From material economy to spiritual economy, it has spent economic stages such as primitive economy, agricultural economy, industrial economy, service economy, and experience economy. Since service economy and experience economy, knowledge, wisdom, and emotion have become the primary labor resources of the spiritual economy.

The product form is the outcome of different economic stages and its representative Salient feature. The new high-value economy products will surely replace the old low-value economy products and become the main output form in the new economic development stage [28]. Primary products are materials extracted from the natural world. It is listed and traded with simple processing, refining, and storing in bulk. After the industrial revolution, manual work was gradually replaced by mechanization, and the economic structure developed to the stage of bulk commodities. Primary products are used as raw materials for production, inventory, wholesale, and retail in the commodity stage. Different pricing is formed by production costs, product differentiation, and the relationship between supply and demand. With technology changes and the advent of large-scale production, the industry is evolving toward electronics, informatization, and intellectualization. The labor required to produce a unit of product has been reduced. The accumulation of social wealth and material products has promoted the growth of people's demand for service. Many companies realize that services can be sold separately as a long-term profit model. As the difference in service quality and value gradually shrinks, products and services become increasingly primary. Facing the pressure of innovation value, Experience Economy has emerged.

The experience economy is a new economic form following the service economy. When companies consciously use services as a stage and products as props to attract consumers, experience occurs. As experience builders, businesses dealing with experience not only provide products and services but also generate a rich and comprehensive experience in the hearts of consumers.

The economy determines both the product form and the design content, principles, and methods. There is no decisive relationship between product forms in different economic stages, but during the development process of the former, the latter gradually occurs and participates in the evolution of the former; as the latter develops and grows, the continuous influence of the former will gradually weaken. That means the economic stage has a vertically decisive effect on the product form, and there is horizontal continuity and mutual influence among various product forms (see Fig. 4).

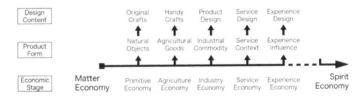

Fig. 4. Economy determines product form and then design content.

Product-manufacturing and service-providing companies have begun to establish experience management strategies. The traditional manufacturing industry's focus has changed from product to user. By focusing on the user's experience with the product, the company uses innovative design to make the product experience-oriented and develop the product's experience characteristics from multiple perspectives. Compared with product manufacturing companies, service providers have a more significant advantage. When customers buy goods and receive services, companies can turn the service into an unforgettable experience by creating an environment, creating surprises, and increasing sensory stimulation. In addition, companies begin to pay attention to improving internal efficiency, staff growth and cost savings through management optimization of processes, personnel, and funds to provide customers with a more satisfying, enjoyable, and meaningful experience.

4.2 Customer Experience is Rooted in the Enterprise, and Experience Management Runs Through the Development of the Enterprise

In 1998, the same year that "Welcome to the Experience Economy" was published, Harley Manning, who had 18 years of experience in "designing and building interactive services", came to Forrester and formed the Customer Experience Practice team as the research director [29]. He believed that customer experience is not a snapshot of the timeline of customer interaction with a company but the sum of the overall interaction with the company and brand. With the Gestalt principle, the whole is greater than the sum of its parts. Customer experience is the cognition and feeling generated from the interaction between the customer and the company. Customer experience is a key driving force of loyalty, satisfaction, and profit. From the perspective of customer perception, a good customer experience includes three aspects: usefulness (delivering value); usability (participation value); pleasure (emotion value) [30]. The customer experience at that time was a kernel indicator for evaluating the pros and cons of a company's service.

With the development of the definition of customer experience, customer experience management emerged, which means the company uses it to track, supervise and organize customers and each interaction process with the organization throughout the customer life cycle [31]. In addition, it aimed to design and respond to customer interactions, meet or exceed customer expectations, and improve customer satisfaction, loyalty, and support [32].

In 2017, Qulatrics, a platform provider of experience management, proposed deeper and broader experience management than customer experience and defined it as a discipline by using experience data (X-data) and operational data (O-data) to measure and optimize four core business experiences-customer experience (CX), employee experience (EX), product experience (PX), and brand experience (BX).

Nowadays, experience management uses machine learning and artificial intelligence to monitor and collect experience data, integrate with business systems, establish connections between customers, products, brands, and employees, and adjust organizational strategies promptly. In general, experience management is centered on customer experience, with in-depth insights and understanding of how people think, feel, and behave. Through strategies, management, and execution throughout the organization, it can improve organizational competitiveness and promote organizational change and development. It is defined as the meso-leveled experience design, which approaches system management centered on customer experience.

4.3 User Experience Design Sprouted from Human Factors Engineering

When it comes to micro-experience design for individual users, it has to start with early forms such as ergonomics and perceptual engineering. Henry Dreyfuss believed that industrial products should consider the functionality that makes people highly comfortable, and design must meet the basic requirements of the human body. He put forward five standards for industrial design from the stages of product design, manufacturing, sales, use, and maintenance: effectiveness and safety, maintainability, cost, sales attractiveness, and appearance [33, 34]. He published books such as "Design for People" and "Human Body Measurement", which laid the foundation for the development of ergonomics in industrial design. Ergonomics pays attention to people's physical scale, control ability, and psychological feelings in the interaction between people and products. Also, it pays attention to the role of the enterprise organization in the process of product design, production, and sales. Finally, it shows that ergonomics studies the interaction between humans and artificial objects and the environment, which is the early exploration stage of user experience based on the physical effects of the human body.

At the beginning of the 20th century, Bauhaus put forward the "form follows function" design concept, which profoundly influenced industrial product design. Under the guidance of this thought, the highly rational and functional standard of pragmatism has caused numerous design products to ignore the emotional appeal of users to the product. Kansei Engineering was born in Japan in the 1970s, which mainly studied human beings' dominant location and emotional expression as a creative activity, the evaluation of the relationship between product attributes and user behavior, and how product characteristics affect consumer purchase behavior by means of engineering, design, psychology, and brain science. At that time, a researcher at Hiroshima University, Mituo Nagamachi, first comprehensively considered the residents' emotions and needs in housing design and transformed it into engineering and technical innovation. Then he introduced Ergonomics concepts and technical standards into automobiles, home appliances, architecture, etc., which promotes the evolution of human physical parameters to environmental comprehensive parameter clusters. Scholars in this period tended to use the term "Kansei Engineering" to emphasize user experience research based on engineering metrological thinking. The change in the research method of Kansei Engineering reflects that user experience design no longer only pays attention to functional requirements but begins to pay attention to people's needs for the spiritual level of products to achieve a balance between technology and emotion.

In initial stage of the industrial revolution, consumers were passive in purchasing and accepting manufacturers' products. However, with the enormous abundance of material, the design pays more attention to the hidden needs of users, enhances the humanization of the product, and attaches importance to the interaction, dialogue, and user experience between the product and the user also encourages users to participate in the entire life cycle of the product's design phase, use phase, iteration phase, and sustainable development phase.

At the end of the twentieth century, the innovation of information technology has brought about the rapid development of the Internet industry. Compared with the tangible products of traditional industries, the information industry provides more intangible interactive products. Donald A. Norman (1993) proposed the term "user experience", which Norman hoped to use to cover many aspects of the human experience system: industrial design, graphics, interface, interaction, manuals, etc., including not only the user experience of the software interface but also the user experience of other products forms. However, things go contrary to his wishes, and many designers only take it as the design principle of digital products. Ergonomics has expanded from the study of the relationship between humans and things to the relationship among humans, machines, and the environment. Interaction design has gradually become independent from ergonomics, emphasizing cognitive psychology and behavior. Then user experience has become the core content of interaction design.

Information architecture designer Peter Morville (2004) designed the User Experience Honeycomb [35], which was used as the user experience design principle of website development and then expanded to various types of product design [36]. At this time, user experience is a term that tests product satisfaction and usability. Therefore, user experience design is a procedure centered on this concept, including target user definition, demand mining, function development, conceptual design, interaction design, system feedback, satisfaction evaluation, and final reports and results.

Jesse James Garrett (2008) defined user experience as follows: User experience does not refer to how a product itself works, but how the product connects and functions with the outside world, that is, how people contact and use it. To clearly explain the entire development process of user experience, he decomposed the construction of digital products into five levels: strategy, scope, structure, framework, and performance [37], which Garrett used to decompose user experience into specific design content at various levels of digital products, that is, design objects, rather than design principles, so that designers can implement design practices by user experience elements.

The views of outstanding scholars and pioneers of practice continue to develop and are comprehensively adopted and officially recommended by the design organization. The Swiss International Organization for Standardization defined the term "user experience" in Part 210: User-centered Interactive System Design of ISO 9241-210:2009 Human-Computer Interaction Engineering. User experience refers to how people feel and respond to products, systems, or services that they use or expect to use. User experience is naturally subjective because it is about personal feelings and thoughts. The user experience is dynamic because it changes when time and environment change. User experience design refers to the plan to improve the user's satisfaction, pleasure, and product accessibility and usability in the process of user interaction with the product in the field of product development.

4.4 Paradigm Shift from User Experience Design to Experience Design

Micro-leveled user experience refers to users' behaviors, thoughts, and feelings when operating or using a product or service, which involves the rational value and perceptual experience provided to users through products and services [38]. By analyzing the relationship between user experience design aimed at high task completion and experience design focusing on meaning and influence, a hierarchical model of the transformation from user experience design to experience design is established (see Fig. 5). Compared with user experience design, experience design is not just a reduction of an attribute used to restrict the subject but a change of concepts and models. User experience design pays more attention to the satisfaction with material and physical needs. In comparison, experience design focuses more on the satisfaction of spiritual and psychological needs. There is a "CHASM" between them that is difficult for experience providers to cross [39]. Task goals based on material needs are more practical and can be quantitatively evaluated; each person's background, experience, status, and needs are not the same, which requires higher professional and adaptable ability for experience providers. Experiential indicators based on spiritual needs are challenging to achieve standardization.

In 2001, Nathan Shedroff, an interface designer, wrote and published the book Experience Design, which provided digital industry practitioners with design inspiration for

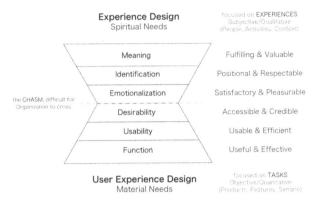

Fig. 5. From user experience design to experience design, human needs and design principles change.

online experiences and a method of designing products, services, environments, or events [40]. In 2008, Shedroff demonstrated the sustainable product development process and explaining how to apply user experience design to the business strategy level and then transform it into users Experience architecture [41]. Shedroff proposed a method model for studying customer emotions, values, and meanings and described its impact on business strategy and new product design [42], organically integrating experience design and customer experience management. In 2010, Norman's book "Living with Complexity" was published, with "Designing the Experience" as one of the subtitles, describing that the company must provide enough attention both to its employees and the needs of customers [43].

Many scholars represented by the above two experts began to integrate user experience design and customer experience management. They focused not only on the immediate experience of users using the product but also on the long-term and far-reaching impact, significance, and value brought to users. Unlike the user experience that focuses on the user's direct interaction and immediate emotions in the process of use, the meso-leveled experience design focuses more on the behavior, lifestyle, attitudes of people, and even the influence of trends in the entire process of interaction between people and products or services.

So, what is the relationship between a designer's experience design and personal experience shaping? In the experience design process, designers analyze the thoughts and emotions from the behavioral laws of individuals or groups based on phenomenology. The designer's design research process is: behavioral logic → thinking logic; The designer deduces the behavior logic from human thinking logic, and then the physical logic of the product/service/system, that is, the design planning process as thinking logic → behavior logic → physical logic. The experiencer initiates human behavior logic from the physical logic of the product/service/system, and then the impact on people, that is, the shaping process of human experience as physical logic → behavior logic → thinking logic. The designer makes design decisions on the product/service/system based on human instinctive emotion and experience. On the other hand, the experiencer has the intuitive response and feeling caused by the product/service/system (See Fig. 6).

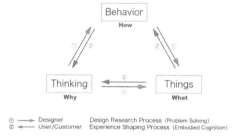

Fig. 6. The relationship between the designer's experience design and the individual's experience shaping.

In summary, the outputs of different economic stages are different. In the same period, new technologies or concepts will inevitably give rise to corresponding design content, design principles, and design methods [44]. The essence of experience is produced subjectively, and different people experience the same thing differently. User experience design pays more attention to the psychological needs of people in the process of interacting with products or services. At the stage of the experience economy, the experience itself appears as a product form, which has many particularities compared with previous product forms. In the paradigm shift from user experience design to experience design, experience has changed from the design principles of evaluating products and services to the object of the invention. The focus of innovation has shifted from the means of life to the meaning of life. Finally, designers have also completed the transition from creator to enabler.

5   Conclusion

We extracted four interrelated clusters of contextual themes from our academic background through the quantitative analysis of the kernel literature of experience design. We further interpret the development context of experience design and propose a macro, meso, and micro-leveled perspective to understand experience design: 1. The macro-leveled experience design coordinates the system and the world, focusing on the long-term construction of the macroecology and human cultural environment. 2. The meso-leveled experience design approaches customer experience-centric system management. 3. The micro-leveled experience design focuses on a complete experience having specific meaning or influence on individuals.

The experience economy is the soil where experience (as a commodity) occurs, while the economy determines product form and design content. Experience design based on process optimization expands the management and commercialization of experience. Finally, the transformation of user experience design to experience design corresponds to people's material needs to spiritual needs. The industry's focus on experience design reflects the people-oriented value proposition. However, from the perspective of sustainable development, experience as the demand and value of the economic exchange unit, and experience evaluation as the decision-making basis for management functionalization and standardization, experience design as the channel and medium of non-material value creation needs to be further explored.

References

1. Dewey, J.: Art as Experience, pp. 35–57. Capricorn Books, New York (1958)
2. Pullman, M.E., Gross, M.A.: Ability of experience design elements to elicit emotions and loyalty behaviors. Decis. Sci. **35**(3), 551–578 (2004)
3. Feng, X.: Social Research Methods, 5th edn., p. 219, 57. China Renmin University Press, Beijing (2018)
4. Yang, S.: A Comparative Study on the Knowledge Atlas of Library and Information Science at Home and Abroad. Science Press, Beijing (2015)
5. Li, J., Chen, C.: CiteSpace Scientific Text Mining and Visualization, 2nd edn. Capital University of Economics and Trade Press, Beijing (2017)
6. Li, J.: Scientific Literature Bibliometrics and Knowledge Network Analysis, 2nd edn. Capital University of Economics and Trade Press, Beijing (2018)
7. Yin, L., Liu, Z.: Research on the evolution of citation network of 'scientometrics', pp. 34–38. Information Technology, Library and Information and Digital Library (2006)
8. Leiden University. https://www.vosviewer.com. Accessed 20 Nov 2021
9. Chen, C.: CiteSpace II: detecting and visualizing emerging trends and transient pat-terns in scientific literature. J. Am. Soc. Inform. Sci. Technol. **57**(3), 359–377 (2006)
10. Chen, C.: Searching for intellectual turning points: progressive knowledge domain visualization. Proc. Natl. Acad. Sci. U.S.A. **101**, 5303–5310 (2004)
11. Li, Y., Zhang, Y., Zeng, K.: Comparison of literature information analysis tools. Chin. J. Med. Libr. Inf. **11**, 7 (2015)
12. Li, J., Li, H., Chen, W.: Analysis on the application of knowledge map in domestic social science research. Libr. Inf. Res. **12**(1), 74–81 (2019)
13. SIGCHI. https://www.sigchi.de/groups/human-computer-interaction-at-the-university-of-siegen. Accessed 20 Nov 2021
14. jnd.org. https://jnd.org/about. Accessed 20 Nov 2021
15. American Academy of Arts & Sciences. https://www.amacad.org/person/donald-norman. Accessed 20 Nov 2021
16. Somerville College. https://www.psy.ox.ac.uk/people/charles-spence. Accessed 20 Nov 2021
17. Columbia University. https://sps.columbia.edu/faculty/b-joseph-pine-ii. Accessed 20 Nov 2021
18. Nielsen Norman Group. https://www.nngroup.com/people/jakob-nielsen. Accessed 20 Nov 2021
19. Interaction Design Foundation. https://www.interaction-design.org/literature/author/kim-j-vicente. Accessed 20 Nov 2021
20. TUDelft. https://www.tudelft.nl/en/ide/about-ide/people/desmet-pma. Accessed 20 Nov 2021
21. Linkedin. https://pt.linkedin.com/in/paulo-maldonado-89970393. Accessed 20 Nov 2021
22. Claremont Graduate University. https://www.cgu.edu/people/mihaly-csikszentmihalyi. Accessed 20 Nov 2021
23. University of Surrey. https://www.surrey.ac.uk/people/iis-tussyadiah. Accessed 20 Nov 2021
24. ISO. https://www.iso.org/standard/52075.html. Accessed 20 Nov 2021
25. Small, H.: Co-citation in the scientific literature: a new measure of the relationship between two documents. J. Am. Soc. Inf. Sci. **24**(4), 265–269 (1973)
26. Lin, D.: From material economy to knowledge economy. J. Jiangnan Univ. **14**(1), 3–5 (1999)
27. Tu, T.: On marxist theory of "three kinds of production". Popul. Res. **27**(6), 48–51 (2003)
28. Pine II, B.J., Gilmore, J.H.: The Experience Economy, pp. 7–39. Harvard Business School Press, New York (2011)
29. SSRN. https://services.forrester.com/Harley-Manning. Accessed 9 Sept 2021

30. Harley Manning. https://go.forrester.com/blogs/definition-of-customer-experience. Accessed 1 Oct 2021
31. TechTarget.   https://searchcustomerexperience.techtarget.com/definition/customer-experi ence-management-CEM-or-CXM. Accessed 1 Oct 2021
32. Gartner. https://www.sas.com/en_us/insights/marketing/customer-experience-management. html. Accessed 1 Oct 2021
33. Luo, L.X., Hong, L.: Kansei Engineering Design. Tsinghua University Press, Beijing (2015)
34. Dreyfuss, H.: Design for People, pp. 178–185. Allworth Press, New York (2003)
35. Intertwingled. http://semanticstudios.com/user_experience_design. Accessed 1 Oct 2021
36. Intertwingled. https://intertwingled.org/user-experience-honeycomb. Accessed 1 Oct 2021
37. Garrett, J.J.: The Elements of User Experience: User-Centered Design for the Web and Beyond, 2nd edn., pp. 18–21. New Riders, California (2010)
38. Lucas, D.: Understanding User Experience. Web Techniques (2000)
39. Marcelosomers. https://marcelosomers.com/writing/shift-your-thinking-from-tasks-to-exp eriences. Accessed 1 Oct 2021
40. Shedroff, N.: Experience Design. Waite Group Press, Westlake Village (2001)
41. Phase.   https://www.phaseiidesign.com/posts/architecture-user-experience-part-3-sustai nable-process-design. Accessed 1 Oct 2021
42. CHIFOO.   http://chifoo.org/researching-meaning-to-identify-more-meaningful-customer-experiences-nathan-shedroff. Accessed 1 Oct 2021
43. Norman, D.A.: Living with Complexity, pp. 159–171. The MIT Press, Cambridge (2010)
44. Wang, Y., Xin, X., Yu, H.: The road to simplicity and the same goal: a study on the origin of experience design. Decoration **5**, 92–96 (2020)

Interactions with Tangible
and Intangible Cultural Heritage

CFFU Cycle Design Mode of Programmable Creases - An Example of Fibonacci Folding Sequence Pattern

Chiung-Hui Chen[✉] and Meng-Chih Lin

Asia University, 500, Lioufeng Rd., Wufeng, Taichung 41354, Taiwan
{930100839,mengchihlin}@asia.edu.tw

Abstract. Kirigami is a Japanese art of paper cutting. It is used to obtain three-dimensional shapes via cutting and folding the paper. Origami, however, is based on a series of precise geometric folding without any other changes to the paper. With the characteristics of dimensional change and form transformation as well as the advantages of being able to expand and zoom, both Kirigami and Origami have great potential in cross-domain applications. These include biomedical materials, deformable robots, adaptable building cortex, and aerospace science. These applications show different requirements for folding by Kirigami or Origami. This study considered that the knowledge of design must include the operational process used to solve design problems.

Keywords: Programmable creases · Kirigami · Folding

1 Research Background

The folding structure is an emerging research sector in engineering science. The advantage is to adjust the stiffness of the structure through the configuration of the folding unit, thereby achieving better structural load-bearing efficiency. Featured with the deformation structure, folding has the advantage of being able to expand and zoom. It has a great potential in cross-domain applications including biomedical materials, deformable robots, adaptable architectural cortex, and aerospace science. The folding structure of the large-scale artificial satellite Miura, the beech leaves, and even the small protein molecules are exerting their effects to enhance the mechanical and space use performance of the original system.

In the traditional Origami design method, Origami experts use their own experience and the texture of the paper to predict the shape of the finished product. The creased texture must first be planned in a two-dimensional plane in the traditional folding design program It is only suitable for experts with Origami experience or mathematical operations ability and who can predict three-dimensional folding patterns. However, folding design is a highly specialized subject and the existing technical software tends to solve specific types of design problems [8]. Due to the immature development of folding software, researchers in the computer field mostly develop folding technologies and

© The Author(s), under exclusive license to Springer Nature Switzerland AG 2022
M. Rauterberg (Ed.): HCII 2022, LNCS 13324, pp. 191–204, 2022.
https://doi.org/10.1007/978-3-031-05434-1_12

algorithms based on geometric principles. The designers without a good mathematical background cannot understand the application of design. Most of the researches based on advanced folding are focused on exploring new tuning methods and new physical phenomena. There is less consideration of the design methods of folding sequence patterns.

2   Origami and Kirigami Problems

2.1   Origami (Folding)/Kirigami (Cutting)

Most people regard Origami as a process of purely constructing a shape from a sheet of two-dimensional paper. It is found after the in-depth exploration that other non-folding methods are also included in the large category. The following is a clarification of the differences between Origami and Kirigami:

Origami. "Fold" can also be expressed with the term "Origami". Origami (折り紙) is the Japanese pronunciation of paper folding. In Japanese, "Oru" means "fold", and "kami" means "paper". From 1950 to 1960, a group of Origami-loving artists and scholars organized different Origami societies regionally and internationally published Origami creations in various places from time to time. Because the Japanese pronunciation of Origami is often used as the term of the art of paper folding in the English world, Origami has become an idiomatic word over time, generally referring to folding for the transformation of a two-dimensional state into a three-dimensional state [13].

Kirigami. The word Kirigami was coined by Florence Temko. In her book *Kirigami: The creative art of paper cutting* published in 1962. She had used the word Kirigami in the title [7]. The sales and educational influence of this book were very successful and the word Kirigami is accepted as the name of the art of paper cutting. In Japan, the term Kirigami has been used for a long time. It is the art of paper cutting in ancient Japan and a paper cutting technique to obtain three-dimensional shapes by cutting and folding paper. Kirigami (切り紙), in Japanese, "Kiri" means "cut" which is equivalent to the English "Cut" in meaning, and "kami" means "paper".

In summary, the similarity between Kirigami and Origami is that they both start with crease and involve folding. The difference is that Kirigami includes cutting and Origami does not. Origami is based on a series of precise geometric folds without any other changes to the paper while Kirigami is based on cutting with a blade or scissors to produce the desired final result.

The earliest description of the problem of Origami and Kirigami appeared in the Japanese book *Wakoku Chiyekurabe (Mathematics Competition)* published by Kan Chu Sen in 1721. The author proposed a series of solutions composed of simple folding with each folding done along a line [20]. This book contains various problem statements and solutions for testing mathematical intelligence. One of the problems is to fold a rectangular piece of paper into a flat sheet of paper and perform a completely straight cut to make a typical Japanese emblem called *sangaibisi*, which is translated as a three-fold rhombus.

A paper published by MIT professors Erik and Martin in 2004 proposed the Origami and Kirigami theorem. The corresponding problem solved by the theorem is called the Origami and Kirigami problem. A specific example is, for any shape with straight edges from being flat to folded, if we cut along the folded edge of the paper and make a single-sided straight cut we can obtain a complete piece of unit. Such shapes include polygons that may be concave, shapes with holes, and a collection of these shapes (without any need for connecting area). How to obtain a specific shape by folding and cutting is called an Origami and Kirigami problem.

2.2 Origami Structure

Miura folding is a folding technology invented by Kōryō Miura, professor emeritus of engineering at the University of Tokyo in Japan [11]. This technology works by pulling apart opposite corners and then pushing in the reverse direction when contracted. that is, to contract and expand respectively in the two-dimensional right-angle direction. This method saves space and avoids the loss caused by the folding and unfolding process. It can reduce the volume of the object by 25 times and increase the energy density by about 14 times. In Rigid Miura-Ori Tessellation, "rigid" means that the Origami paper itself cannot be flexed and is a completely flat paper, which is different from the general paper capacity. The term "tessellation" means that this Origami can be composed of multiple Origami units as if multiple Origami units are "inlaid" into a sheet of Origami. Rigid Miura-Ori Tessellation is currently used in artificial satellites.

Origami Applications. With the ability of dimensional and form transformation, Origami has become one of the design techniques favored by designers. Kostas Terzidis [18] mentioned in the *Expressive Form* that "folding is a complex process, and it can transform the dimensionality of the object". For example, turning a two-dimensional flat sheet into a three-dimensional object by folding. Because of the characteristics of folding, it is widely used in daily life. Many professional disciplines also use folding as the research theme. It can range from protein folding to space engineering. It changes the appearance of objects and the process of trans-dimensional changes and is fun exploring [6]. Folding techniques are not invented by humans and the most common phenomenon of folding in nature is the process of a flower blooming. There is a dynamic relationship between folding and unfolding and this dynamic relationship is achieved through symmetry, synchronization, and sequence [18].

Professor Tomohiro Tachi of the University of Tokyo showed the continuous process of folding a piece of paper into a folded shape with the new method. This new method uses the concept of folded molecules to fold the piece of paper into an arbitrary three-dimensional polyhedral surface, and the configuration of calculating the crease pattern via an interactive simulation system [14–17]. Folding is often referred to as a research object by fashion, science, machinery, and architecture. The concept of dynamic folding is widely used in the engineering and design circles including the stretchable solar panels for the international space station [21], telescopic operating table shields for sterile operating rooms [7], and the dynamic building exterior wall for the building to adjust the indoor physical environment [20].

To provide designers with a way to apply the folding concept to their designs, Jackson [9] developed a variety of folding textures. These folding textures include single-fold textures, parallel line textures, radial textures, V-shaped textures, X-shaped textures, and complex-shaped textures. Jackson mentioned that we should start with the most basic folding technique of folding in half, and then develop more complex folding textures while exploring various possibilities in the actual folding process. Continuous folding in half can develop parallel line folding units and radiation folding units. Translation, Reflection, Rotation, and Glide Reflection can be repeated by repeating the texture pattern of the small units.

In summary, all the above have focused on the technical application of Origami and an Origami operation mode has been constructed. It is based on the expandable and zoomable Origami map texture to perform rigid folding simulations. However, they have not yet involved discussion and development of Kirigami. The following is a comprehensive discussion on the development and application of the research on Kirigami in recent years.

2.3 Kirigami Structure

Scientists have discovered that the art of paper cutting can be used to transform two-dimensional sheet materials into complex three-dimensional geometric shapes with a wider range of options than traditional paper-cutting techniques. The shape of the mechanical metamaterials made with this Kirigami art can be seamlessly changed. Significant changes in their mechanical properties can happen under small geometric deformation conditions, and such materials can also adapt to shape changes through mainstream drive mechanisms. The most notable examples are the Kirigami Honeycomb digital crease and fold structure designed by K. Satio and T. Nojima [13].

Kirigami Application

Paper Electronic Products with Nanosilver Conductivity of Kirigami Method
In recent years, the display technology of printed electronic products has shifted from radio frequency identification and wearable devices to the printed circuit board with rigid substrates acting as the printed electronic device. Paper is used as a new medium for printed electronics because these printed electronic products can be bent, folded, or curled into a three-dimensional configuration with the function of soft and flexible forms. When researchers develop next-generation printed electronic products, they also consider such factors as material recyclability and toxicity in addition to enhancing the performance of electronic devices.

Due to paper's characteristics of recyclability, degradability, low cost, and easy production, it is an ideal material for sustainable printed electronic products. Printing conductive inks made on paper, such as nano silver ink on the electrode pattern of the paper is a commonly used method. However, although the paper is flexible the electrode printed on it is not, and when the substrate is folded cracks start to form in the electrode which eventually leads to cracking. This limitation seriously hinders the research and development of various forms of paper-based electronic devices.

Yang and Shintake [19], research teams from Japan and Taiwan proposed novel solutions with the ancient Japanese paper cutting art Kirigami. According to their article "Foldable Kirigami Paper Electronics", published in *Physical Status Solidi(A)Applications and Materials Science-*, Kirigami method can be used to cut along the folded edge of the paper, so that the area near the folded edge could be twisted when the paper substrate was folded. The Kirigami method could maintain the structural integrity of the nanosilver conductive electrode and the conductivity of paper electronic products. When the paper substrate was completely folded, the resistance of the Kirigami electrode increased by 30%, and the conductivity was still maintained after the full folding. The article also mentioned that the electrode without the Kirigami structure would be disconnected under normal folding. The team further proved that the Kirigami method could be used to give paper electronic products higher-order functions and possibilities. It was important research for the future (see Fig. 1).

Fig. 1. Paper electronic products with nanosilver conductivity of Kirigami method

Honeycomb Structure with Rigid-foldability of Kirigami Design
Callens and Zadpoor [3] pointed out in 2018 that rigid-foldability is important for engineering applications. Rigid-foldability is widely used in various engineering fields, many units completed by the same folding method are assembled into groups. No piece will deform during the folding movement and the folding line can be replaced with a hinge. The dynamic process of folding has a certain degree of rigidity. Therefore, deformation will not occur in the process of changing from the initial form to the final form and the material itself will maintain its toughness. The architectural design with a dynamic mechanism, rigid-foldability is considered to be very advantageous. This is because the analysis of rigid dynamic mechanism is relatively simple. The panel can be replaced with any strong material and no panel will be warped during the deformation process. If Kirigami's technical cutting and folding are used to design and manufacture deformed honeycomb structures, and the creases are folded into many repeating small unit modules through similar geometries, 2D sheet materials can be converted into 3D honeycomb structures. These are different from the traditional honeycomb structures with reduced density and variable rigidity that depend on the loading direction and loading type. It is also possible to embed actuators and geometric features into the honeycomb to control deformation (see Fig. 2).

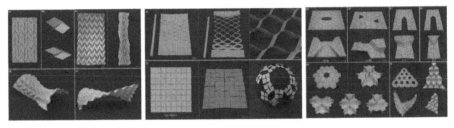

Fig. 2. Honeycomb structure with rigid-foldability of Kirigami design

Kirigami Strategy Has a Pop-Up 3D Structure with Adjustable Mechanical Characteristics

To create flat materials, scientists and engineers have recently used the art of Origami combined with complex calculator algorithms to cut planes into three-dimensional structures. This technology can produce stretchable and deformable structures that can be used in electronic products, mechanical parts, and robots. Most Origami designs so far have relied on simple parallel cutting. Researchers at Harvard University have used simple parallel cutting to perforate thin plastic sheets in orthogonal patterns and stretch them in different directions. They have been able to make them pop out to form a unique three-dimensional shape composed of regular peaks and valleys. This technology has been used for researches in making deformable materials, stretchable batteries, and solar cells that track the sun.

Harvard University professor, Katia Bertoldi, and her postdoctoral researcher Ahmad Rafsanjani have reported on the use of flat paper technology to make Origami structures with different cubic patterns in an article [12] published in *Physical Review Letters* in 2017. Some structures could be folded into a flat shape while others could be bent into a saddle shape. These flat materials could be programmed to deform and reconfigure complex shapes. A laser cutting machine was used to punch holes in the plastic sheet. The square cuts were at right angles to each other forming a square network connected by small ligaments. The article also mentioned that this famous pattern has been studied for 10 years but they wanted to figure out what would happen when the sheet is very thin. When the thickness was reduced, there would be instability and bending. The direction in which the paper was pulled would lead to different final 3D shapes depending on the angle between the cut and the pulling direction. The Kirigami technology was employed to develop materials that could provide adjustable friction properties. Stretching will cause buckling which depends on the buckling of the flat plate. This will cause the drawing to pop out into a three-dimensional shape determined by the cut. After the stretching is loosened, the flexible plastic sheet will spring back to its original flat shape (see Fig. 3).

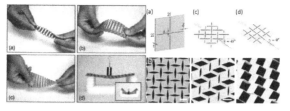

Fig. 3. Kirigami strategy has a pop-up 3D structure with adjustable mechanical characteristics

3   CFFU (Cut-Fold-Form-Unfold) Cycle Design Mode of Programmable Creases

Through literature review, this study considered that the folding process of converting from the two-dimensional form into the three-dimensional form can be regarded as a systematic cyclic method, which is explained below:

A piece of paper that has not been folded and cut is assumed as Form 1, which represents the original two-dimensional state. When it is cut, we will get Form 2. If the Form 2 state is subjected to a series of folding, the folded and completed three-dimensional state of Form 3 will be generated, and then reverse engineering is carried out for Form 3 to unfold it to produce a piece of paper with a rich crease pattern. If these four forms are simply viewed as separate objects, they are completely different. Through the combination of Kirigami and Origami technology, it can be understood that every crease and cut is composing the appearance of the final form.

This study indicated that the knowledge of design must include the operation process of solving the design problems. On the strength of the design process of cutting (Kirigami) and folding (Origami) for transforming from a two-dimensional state to a three-dimensional state, a design method based on open source model was proposed:

The CFFU cyclic design mode (Cut-Fold-Form-Unfold) of programmable creases, as shown in Fig. 4, aims to expose the calculation mode of folding development to the Internet for sharing. The designers can carry out the three-dimensional simulation with the existing folding modes on the co-creation platform and present digital folds as a paper model. The mode uses a folding programming language (*.FOLD) that is easy to edit and modify, allowing the designers to compare the Origami model in the computer for real-time simulation feedback. Finally, it is also possible for researchers and developers to discuss the correctness of the calculation model to inherit and deduce more folding design patterns.

Fig. 4. CFFU cyclic design mode (Cut-Fold-Form-Unfold) of programmable creases.

4   Programming Language Describing Programmable Creases *.FOLD

The FOLD format was created by MIT professors Erik Demaine [2, 4, 5] and Robert Lang [10, 11]. FOLD has the following three characteristics:

1. Universality: FOLD can represent a variety of folding structures of different sizes, including universal polyhedral complexes and multiple folding in the same file, and it is easy to add new model examples.
2. Simplicity: FOLD can simply represent common folding structures and the pattern library provides the function of automatically filling in optional fields. If you only store a frame in the file, you can completely ignore the concept of a frame.
3. Adhesion: Lightweight data exchange format makes it easy for people to read and write, machines to parse and generate, and it is easy to glue the existing platform software.

Definition of FOLD format: FOLD is a file format (*.fold). It is used to describe Origami models and crease patterns (valleys). The folded state is mainly a FOLD file that can store a grid and vertices, edges, faces, and the links between them. 2D or 3D geometric shapes that can be specified with the topological stacking order of geometric overlapping surfaces. The grid can also store other user-defined data. A FOLD file can even store multiple grids in frames. FOLD is essentially like the *.OBJ format is used to store 3D grids. Its main distinguishing features are the easiness to parse and expand, the ability to eliminate overlapping surfaces in the stacking order and to define edges so that the attributes of edges (such as the assignment of peaks and valleys) and arbitrary polyhedral complexes can be defined. In addition, FOLD can also support links. For example, to import the FOLD file format and fill in the following fields:

1. edges_assignment: Specify edge attributes, such as B: boundary, M: mountain fold, V: valley fold, F: unfolding and folding.
2. foldedForm: Specify the folding form, such as unfolding or 3D folding.

3. vertices_coords: For each vertex, it is an array of coordinates such as [x, y, z] or [x, y] (where z is implicitly zero). In higher dimensions, all unspecified coordinates are also implicitly zero.

4. edges_foldAngle: The edges_foldAngle field is used to specify the target fold angle of each fold. The degrees of fold angles are within the range of [−180, 180]. For valley folds the fold angle is positive; for mountain folds the fold angle is negative; for flat unallocated, and boundary folds the fold angle is zero. If unsure whether the FOLD file is valid, the FOLD Viewer can be used for inspection as shown in Fig. 5.

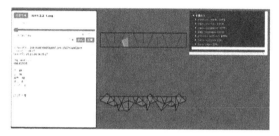

Fig. 5. Viewer interface.

5   Method of Constructing Programmable Crease Pattern

A Pattern Language was written by Christopher Alexander [1]. The key to the idea behind Pattern Language is to assume that in the process of creating a man-made environment, certain structural traits will not change over time. These traits will govern human behavior and the way the environment is generated. Behind these structural traits are hidden internal mechanisms that can be systematically thought by humans and generally operable modes. Similar design issues can be solved similarly and a pattern is used to record the general solution corresponding to a problem. Its content includes the description of the problems and the answers, and the related contexts or contextual information.

This study considered that knowledge must be effectively constructed to facilitate its reuse. Design-based knowledge must include the operation process which is used to solve design problems. Christopher Alexander's Design Pattern concept was cited as the method of knowledge recording, and a different approach was taken as the pattern construction methodology. The operation of the CFFU cyclic design mode (Cut-Fold-Form-Unfold) for programmable creases proposed according to the research.

It is divided into seven parts: (1) mode designation (2) calculation logic (3) geometry definition: mathematical principle conversion construction (4) calculation formatting (5) FOLD file import platform simulator: 3D-Form digital model generation (6) digital crease pattern and cut secant and finally (7) output model production. The Fibonacci Sequence Pattern developed by this study was taken as an example to illustrate the systematic steps of the mode operation (see Fig. 6).

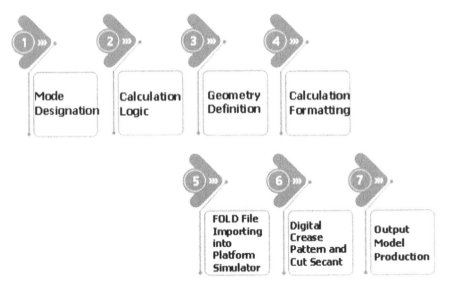

Fig. 6. Fibonacci fold sequence pattern

(1) **Mode Designation**

   Fibonacci Sequence is characterized by pulling one end to expand and then pushing in reverse recursively for contracting. That is, contracting and expanding simultaneously in the two-dimensional horizontal direction. This method can save space and avoid loss caused by the process of folding and unfolding.

(2) **Calculation Logic**

   The unique ratio of the recursive operation of the golden section is similar to the nature of a series of numbers called the Fibonacci Sequence. This series was named after the introducer as Fibonacci Sequence. It is generally referred to as the Fibonacci Numbers and was introduced to Europe together with the decimal math system about 800 years ago. In this sequence of 1, 1, 2, 3, 5, 8, 13, 21, 34…, the recursive deduction of numbers is the addition of the previous two numbers to get the following number, that is $Fn = Fn - 1 + Fn - 2$.

   For example, $1 + 1 = 2$, $1 + 2 = 3$, $2 + 3 = 5$…and so on, and the ratio between the numbers of this series is very close to the golden ratio. In this series, the ratio between the numbers will gradually approach the golden ratio. The ratio of any number after the fifteenth number divided by the next number after it is 0.618 (by taking the three digits after the decimal point), and such a number divided by its previous number will get a ratio of 1.618 (by taking the three digits after the decimal point).

(3) **Geometry Definition**

   For the golden section dynamic rectangle, using the method of cutting triangles to establish the golden section ratio can define the side length of the golden section rectangle. In addition, a series of circles and squares generated based on the golden section ratio can be drawn this way. All Rectangles can be divided into two categories: static rectangles formed by the ratio of rational numbers such as 1/2,

2/3, 3/3, 3/4, etc., and dynamic rectangles formed by the ratio of irrational numbers such as $\sqrt{2}$, $\sqrt{3}$, and $\sqrt{5}$.

Static rectangles cannot be subdivided into the appearance of the visually pleasing proportions and their subdivision state follows predictable rules and lacks changes, but dynamic rectangles can be infinitely divided into the harmonic subdivision and appearance proportions because their proportions are composed of irrational numbers (see Fig. 7).

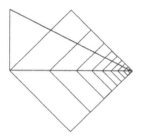

Fig. 7. Golden section dynamic rectangle

(4) **Calculation Formatting**

The geometric calculation logic formatted was written into the file (*.fold) to determine the Kirigami crease line as the skeleton and the Origami length, width, angle, coordinate, period, and other attribute data (see Fig. 8).

```
 3  +  "file_creator": "Crease Pattern Editor",      22  +  ],                                                42  +  "faces_edges": [
 4  +  "file_classes": [                             23  +  "edges_assignment": [                             43  +    [0,4,3],
 5  +    "singleModel"                               24  +    "B",                                            44  +    [1,2,4]
 6  +  ],                                            25  +    "B",                                            45  +  ],
 7  +  "frame_classes": [                           26  +    "B",                                            46  +  "edges_faces": [
 8  +    "creasePattern"                            27  +    "B",                                            47  +    [0,null],
 9  +  ],                                            28  +    "V"                                             48  +    [1,null],
10  +  "vertices_coords": [                         29  +  ],                                               49  +    [1,null],
11  +    [0,0],                                     30  +  "cpedit:page": {"xMin":0,"yMin":0,"xMax":1,"yMax":1},  50  +    [0,null],
12  +    [1,0],                                     31  +  "file_title": "diagonal",                         51  +    [1,0]
13  +    [1,1],                                     32  +  "vertices_edges": [                               52  +  ],
14  +    [0,1]                                      33  +    [0,3],                                          53  +  "faces_flatFoldTransform": [
15  +  ],                                           34  +    [1,4,0],                                        54  +    [[1,0,0],[0,1,0]],
16  +  "edges_vertices": [                          36  +    [1,2],                                          55  +    [[0,-1,1],[-1,0,1]]
17  +    [0,1],                                     36  +    [3,4,2]                                         56  +  ],
18  +    [1,2],                                     37  +  ],                                               57  +  "vertices_flatUnfoldCoords": [
19  +    [2,3],                                     38  +  "faces_vertices": [                               58  +    [0,0],
20  +    [3,0],                                     39  +    [0,1,3],                                         59  +    [1,0],
21  +    [3,1]                                      40  +    [1,2,3]                                          60  +    [1,1],
                                                                                                        61  +    [0,1]
```

Fig. 8. Writing into FOLD program.

(5) **FOLD File Importing into Platform Simulator: 3D Form Digital Model Generation**

In terms of Fibonacci crease pattern digitization, the Fibonacci folding mode has the characteristic of rigid folding. This means, that all quadrilateral grids can be transformed from two-dimensional to the folded state, and then to the completely folded two-dimensional state. There is no three-dimensional deformation of the quadrilateral in the process and the four vertices of each piece are maintained in a coplanar state. The parallel line texture is composed of several parallel and alternating mountain and valley lines. They enable the two-dimensional state to pop up the three-dimensional shape brought out by the Kirigami. When Origami is observed from the side view, the whole presents several mountain-shaped interlocking unidirectional linear translations and the arrangement shows the sequence of peaks and valleys (see Fig. 9).

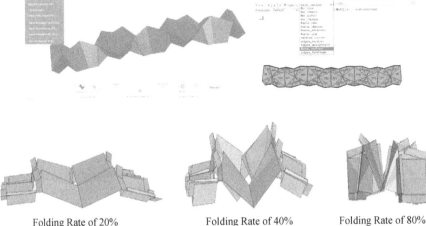

Folding Rate of 20%   Folding Rate of 40%   Folding Rate of 80%

Fig. 9. 3D form

(6) **Digital Crease Pattern and Cut Secant**

The folded three-dimensional shape has the flexibility to develop into a two-dimensional crease pattern. The red line represents the mountain fold line, the blue line represents the valley fold line, and the green line represents the cut secant line (Kirigami) (see Fig. 10).

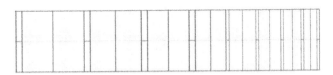

Fig. 10. Digital crease pattern and cut secant (Kirigami)

(7) **Output Model Production**

To create a three-dimensional, stretchable, and deformable structure, the calculation results were cut in a paper model. It can be simultaneously contracted, expanded, and folded in the horizontal direction to present a pop-up 3D structure (see Fig. 11). It formed into a unique three-dimensional shape consisting of mountains and valleys.

Fig. 11. Fibonacci mode folded entity

6 Conclusions and Follow-Up Research

With the maturity of digital tools, designers can simulate the dynamic appearance of the folding process. They can choose the form of folding and determine the free angle of movement after the work is completed by setting different parameters. The simulation objects can even be realized in the real world with the combination of digital manufacturing tools. Also, there are many different challenges in the process.

Open Source, in a narrow sense, refers to a mechanism that allows all users to freely edit and modify the source code of open programs. In a broad sense, the value behind it lies in the belief that knowledge belongs to all mankind, and knowledge should be made public so that everyone has the opportunity to learn it. This kind of thinking has flourished in recent years and the thinking of software development has gradually become open source, moving from efficiency to customization and self-made. Professional designers also use program control and simulation and communicate through online tools for information. These digital tools have become indispensable for the design development process.

In summary, because of the recognition of knowledge sharing, cross-domain cooperation and exchanges are increasingly valued in the digital era of knowledge sharing. The thinking of software development has also begun to target the general public as the designers or non-designer have lowered the threshold of program design, encouraged knowledge and convenience brought by the technology, and use digital skills to solve immediate problems. The CFFU cycle design mode of programmable creases will continue to develop and summarize the folding mode, and then establish more calculation rules of the Kirigami mode. Open the developed mode for sharing on the network platform, pass on knowledge and obtain feedback from real-time simulation, and extend the content of more libraries of shared example modes.

References

1. Alexander, C., Sara, I., Murray, S.: A Pattern Language. Oxford University Press, New York (1977)
2. Callens, S.J.P., Zadpoor, A.A.: From flat sheets to curved geometries: origami and kirigami approaches. Mater. Today **21**(3), 241–264 (2018)
3. Demaine, E.D., Demaine, M.L.: Fold-and-Cut Magic, Tribute to a Mathemagician, pp. 23–30. A K Peters (2004)

4. Demaine, E.D., O'Rourke, O.P.C.S.J.: Geometric Folding Algorithms: Linkages, Origami. Cambridge University Press, Polyhedra (2014)
5. Dureisseix, D.: An overview of mechanisms and patterns with origami (2012)
6. Temko, F.: Kirigami: the creative art of paper cutting (1962)
7. Francis, K.C., Rupert, L.T., Lang, R.J., Morgan, D.C., Magleby, S.P., Howell, L.L.: From crease pattern to product: considerations to engineering origami-adapted designs Paper Presented at the 38th Mechanisms and Robotics Conference, Buffalo, New York, USA (2014)
8. Gardiner, M., Aigner, R., Ogawa, H., Hanlon, R.: Fold mapping: parametric design of origami surfaces with periodic tessellations. Origami 7, 105–118 (2018)
9. Jackson, P.: Folding Techniques for Designers: From Sheet to Form. Laurence King Publishing, London (2011)
10. Lang, R.J.: Origami Design Secrets: Mathematical Methods for an Ancient Art. AK Peters, Natick (2003)
11. Miura, K.: Method of packaging and deployment of large membranes in space. Inst. Space Astronaut. Sci. Rep. **618**, 1–9 (1985)
12. Rafsanjani, A., Bertoldi, K.: Buckling-induced Kirigami. Phys. Rev. Lett. **118**(8) (2017). https://doi.org/10.1103/physrevlett.118.084301
13. Saito, K., Pellegrino, S., Nojima, T.: Manufacture of arbitrary cross-section composite honeycomb cores based on origami techniques. J. Mech. Des. **136**, 051011 (2014)
14. Sloman, P.: Paper: Tear, Fold, Rip, Crease, Cut: Black Dog (2009)
15. Tachi, T.: Generalization of rigid-foldable quadrilateral-mesh origami. J. Int. Assoc. Shell Spat. Struct. (IASS) **50**(3), 173–179 (2009)
16. Tachi, T.: Freeform variations of origami. J. Geom. Graph. **14**(2), 203–215 (2010)
17. Tachi, T.: Freeform rigid-foldable structure using bidirectionally flat-foldable planar quadrilateral mesh. Adv. Archit. Geom. **2010**, 87–102 (2010)
18. Tachi, T.: Designing freeform origami tessellations by generalizing Resch's patterns. J. Mech. Design **135**(11), 111006-111006-111010 (2013). https://doi.org/10.1115/14025389
19. Terzidis, K.: Expressive form: A Conceptual Approach to Computational Design. Spon Press, London, New York (2003)
20. Tibbits, S.: 4D printing: multi-material shape change. Archit. Design **84**(1), 116–121 (2014)
21. Zirbel, S.A., Trease, B.P., Thomson, M.W., Lang, R.J., Magleby, S.P., Howell, L.H.: HanaFlex: a large solar array for space applications. Paper Presented at the Micro-and Nanotechnology Sensors, Systems and Applications VII, Baltimore, Maryland, USA, 20–24 April 2015

Retouching System to Ease Difficulty of Craft Design for Paper-Cutting

Takafumi Higashi[✉]

Tokyo Denki University, Senjuasahimachi 5, Adachi-ku, Tokyo, Japan
htakafumi@acm.org

Abstract. We present our system for quantifying artistic production difficulty and adjusting retouching difficulty to improve production. A paper-cutting artwork is created by controlling a knife and cutting designed paper. Paper-cutting craft designs have two parts: a white area for cutting out and a black area for painting. We have measured the difficulty of the picture based on the thickness of the cutting borderlines. In this paper, we have developed the retouching system that eases the difficulty of craft design by adjusting the line thickness. We have experimented with the effect of this system on the novice's production. As a result, we found that the system improved the accuracy and psychological state (flow state) by retouching craft design.

Keywords: Cutting · Pressure · Steering law · Flow theory · Human motor performance

1 Introduction

In artistic creation, preparing a craft design plays an essential role in realizing the creator's image. A craft design appropriate for the artist's skill level enhances the work. Novices should practice based on the recommended difficulty level appropriate for their skills. However, although some textbooks for novices indicate the task's difficulty level as "for novices" or "Level 3," the criteria are vague. Thus, we have difficulty selecting a difficulty level that is appropriate for our skills. Each craft design has a difficulty level, and it suggests practicing at a level that is appropriate to one's skills. The novices attempt to challenge themselves with difficulty levels disproportionate to their skills. Consequently, they start with failure or frustration because the difficulty level they tackle is too high. Hence, controlling the difficulty of the production is an essential factor in practice aimed at improving skills.

We focus on paper-cutting one of the artwork. Paper-cutting is an art performed by cutting paper printed craft designs with a knife. We assume that cutting with a knife is like writing with a pen. This suggests a model based on human-computer interaction (HCI). A craft design for paper-cutting is a picture with a white area and a black area for painting. Thus, novices often use image-editing software to binarize an arbitrary image before beginning a craft design

M. Rauterberg (Ed.): HCII 2022, LNCS 13324, pp. 205–216, 2022.
https://doi.org/10.1007/978-3-031-05434-1_13

Unfortunately, the software ignores the difficulty of retouching, so the result is difficult for novices to achieve. In artistic creation, creating an image with a difficulty level that is too difficult and inappropriate for the artist's skills will affect the artist's production.

We are studying the skills and difficulty of producing paper-cutting, one artwork. The paper analyzes the relationship between production skills and craft design difficulty. We have evaluated "skills" by measuring the cutting pressure, time, and accuracy of pictures cut by creators with a wide range of skills, from novice to expert, and comparing them with those of artists [17,18]. We have also decomposed the picture into lines and evaluated the "difficulty" of the image using the length of the distance and width of the cutting lines, based on the steering law [16,19]. Paper-cutting and many other artworks connect the artist's skill and the difficulty of production. Based on the previous studies, we analyze the relationship between the skill and difficulty of paper-cutting creation. We assume that the level of difficulty perceived by the creators is closely related to their skills. We analyze the effect of the combination of skill and difficulty on the change in the psychological state during production [15]. Our goal is to make it possible for everyone to work at a level of difficulty appropriate to their skills for artistic creation based on the HCI field. In this study, we evaluate the difficulty of the craft design in the textbook and retouch the design to ease level. Our system improves the user experience by allowing novices to work with the retouched design.

In Sect. 1, we describe the background and purpose of our study. In Sect. 2, we describe the related works. In Sect. 3, we describe our previous studies. In Sect. 4, we analyze the support of workshop instructors in ease of craft design for students. In Sect. 5, we describe our retouching system, which automatically eases the difficulty of craft design. In Sect. 6, we analyze the changes in the creator's performance with our system. In Sect. 7, we summarize and discuss this paper.

2   Related Works

2.1   Production Support for Artistic Creation Activities

In this paper, we describe support for the paper-cutting production of pictures using a knife. Many researchers are working on supporting the production of various artworks as well as paper-cutting. In the production support of sketches, drawings, and oil paintings, the system often provides feedback to the user by comparing the product and sample. The observation and imitation of an expert is one method for novices to improve their creative skills [27]. The use of technology as a means of assisting users in the drawing has been explored in modeling applications. Studies [10] have proposed methods of assisting users in drawing faces and eyes. These methods rely on a face and set of sketch recognition algorithms to generate domain-specific instructions and textual or on-canvas feedback. In a study [23], a projector displayed images onto paper and drew lines using the projected guide to prevent distortion and misalignment, providing production support using augmented reality. In another study [13], the projector appeared to support the expression technique of overlapping colors in oil paintings. In these studies, a picture is projected layer-by-layer on the canvas, and the user draws a picture with a brush based on the image to reproduce the expression of color layering typical of an oil painting. Further, the behavior of the user is compared with that of experts. Similarly, our system improves users' cutting pressure control by comparing the users' cutting pressures with those of experts in real-time. This is to enable users to cut paper with the same pressure used by experts. These systems enable novices to imitate the behaviors of experts.

2.2 Difficulty Level Based on the Steering Law

The steering law uses an index of difficulty (ID) and moving time (MT) to determine the difficulty level and the time required for cutting patterns [1,32]. Modeling human movement is a core theme in the field of HCI. Fitts law [12] predicts the time to complete a one-dimensional pointing task, and Accot and Zhai [3] refined the model for two-dimensional tasks. Further, the standard model predicts the time needed to navigate a long, narrow path, known as the steering law [1]. The difficulty of a manipulation task depends on the target's path and shape. In the steering law, the difficulty level of a straight tunnel is calculated as follow.

$$ID = \frac{D}{W}$$

Here, D is the length of the tunnel and W is the tunnel width. The steering law is calculated as

$$MT = a + b \times ID$$

for both straight and curved tunnels. Several studies have measured the performance of various devices and multiple shapes. For example, researchers have investigated the operations for various types of input devices (such as mice, styluses, touch panels, and trackballs) [2]. Research has examined the usage of pen stroke gestures for letter writing [4] and the drawing of simple figures using the steering law [25]. Zabramski analyzed drawing tasks as pointing and steering tasks [31]. In this paper, we evaluate the difficulty level during the production of paper-cuttings based on the distance and width of each cutting line with a knife.

2.3 Flow State with Based on Skill and Challenge

Csikszentmihalyi proposed a "flow state" in his analysis of immersion [6,7]. Further, he mentioned "balance between challenge (difficulty) and skill" as an element that attracts attention and constitutes concentration [8]. Performers tend to reach flow states when immersed in high-level efforts within their skill level. However, the assessment of flow status was not a method for judging flow other than a direct declaration. Thus, Jackson created a 36-item questionnaire, the Flow State Scale (FSS), to measure flow state in sports situations [21]. According to the Flow Manual, flow scales are available for universal life, such as age differences [29] and daily living [22]. Researchers have also studied the adaptation of FSS in several languages [28].

Researchers have studied the relationship between flow states and the HCI field. [20] analyzes flow state when creating artwork in a virtual reality (VR) environment. [26] also discusses the potential for education by analyzing how learning experiences and flow states are involved. In this paper, we evaluated the flow during the production of paper cuttings by combining the "skill to control cutting pressure" and "difficulty level of the cutting line."

3   Our Previous Studies

3.1   Skill Instruction and Production Difficulty for Novices

We interviewed five paper-cutting instructors. The purpose is to clarify what the instructor needs to teach in the student's actions. They (4 males, 1 females, average age: 36.2 years, SD: 6.00) were artists and instructors of paper-cutting class. They were active artists, and four instructors had five years of experience, and one had six years of experience.

As a result, we have found that the novices had a tendency to cut paper slowly and with intense pressure. The workshop teaches the students to cut smoothly by controlling the pressure to a suitable level. Too high pressure affects steering performance and decreases the accuracy of cutting. Therefore, the controlling pressure is important in production paper-cutting. In [19], we have confirmed the novices had stronger cutting pressure and lower accuracy than the experts.

They have described low difficulty as a tendency for the cutting lines with straight lines and simple shapes. For novices to improve their skills more effectively, it is necessary for them to practice at a difficulty level that is correct for their current skills. However, definitions for levels of skill and difficulty are ambiguous, and it is hence challenging to evaluate them quantitatively. In [18], we have analyzed the effect of production difficulty. As a result, we have shown that the width and length of the cutting line have an effect on the difficulty level, and we have confirmed that the cutting time and difficulty level are adapted to the steering law.

3.2   Cutting Device

We have developed the stylus to collect data by attaching a blade (NT BDC-200P) to the tip of the stylus (Wacom PenPro2) (Fig. 1). We can determine the cutting coordinates of the blade by using our device. It recognizes the cutting distance from 0.1 mm at a response speed of 250 ms. The drawing display (Wacom Cintiq Pro16, 3860 × 2140 pixels, 275 dpi) shows pictures. The system only responds when the stylus is in contact with the screen. The user cut paper on the drawing display using our system.

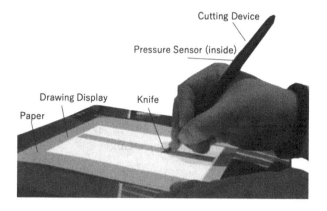

Fig. 1. Participants cut paper placed on the drawing display.

3.3 Difficulty Level

We have confirmed that the relationship between cutting time and difficulty during production adapted to the steering law. We have developed a system to measure the ID and determine the target distance (D) and width (W) of each target based on the boundary coordinates.

The distance (D), width (W), and index of difficulty (ID) of each cutting line are defined as follows.

$$ID = \frac{D}{W} \tag{1}$$

In our system, we measure the distance (D) that a single cut line has by obtaining the coordinates of the black and white boundaries of the craft design, as well as the distance (d) between them. The distance (D) is the sum of the distances (d) between the coordinates.

$$d_n = \sqrt{(x_s - x_{s+1})^2 + (y_s - y_{s+1})^2} \tag{2}$$

$$D = \sum_{k=1}^{n} d_{k-1} \tag{3}$$

Our system measures the width(w) to the nearest coordinate across the truncated region (black area) and the distance to the closest position across the truncated region (white space) of the target. As w is the width of one side of the target, the width of the cutting line (W) is the average of twice the value of width (w).

$$W = 2 \times \frac{1}{n} \sum_{k=1}^{n} w_k \tag{4}$$

3.4 Combining Skills and Difficulty Based on Flow Theory

In [15], we have analyzed the flow state by the combination of skills and difficulty. Flow theory states that a balance between skill and difficulty is essential to immersion (Csikszentmilhalyi, 1982). In the Flow State Scale (FSS), Csikszent-mihalyi measures the user's experience flow. We also developed a quantitative questionnaire based on Csikszentmilhalyi's flow-statistical theory to assess the flow conditions during the production of paper-cutting. The questionnaire items served as expressions that made it easier to recall paper-cutting creation. The questionnaire items were our FSS for paper-cutting in the Japanese language. The participants answered a questionnaire consisting of 36 items on a 5-point scale. We evaluate the constitutive factors of flow state in the production stage of the paper-cutting by the FSS for paper-cutting.

4   Ease Support in Workshops

We interviewed five instructors for paper-cutting workshop. The purpose of the interview was to ascertain the issues for which the instructors provided support to novices. It was revealed that the novices tended to cut paper slowly and with intense pressure when using a knife.

We have developed a system to quantify the difficulty of production based on the steering performance of the cutting trajectory [19]. Our system extracts the contour coordinates of the boundary of a rough sketch and measures the width and distance of the target cutting path. It evaluates the Index of Difficulty (ID) from a distance and the length of the width.

We focus on immersion during production as one of the values for experience. Positive psychology have investigate flow theory, which states that the balance between skill and difficulty is an essential condition for immersion. We have evaluated the constitutive factors of flow state in the production stage of the paper-cutting by creating the FSS for paper-cutting. We have confirmed the highest skill-improvement effects and flow states when the novices who practiced using our practice system with high-difficulty designs.

5   Retouching System to Ease Craft Design

We developed a retouching system that eases parts of a craft design with a high difficulty level. We selected 4 craft designs (Fig. 2(A)–(D)) of level 2 and level 3 difficulty from the 5 levels in the textbook for novices. Our system eased these pictures (Fig. 2(A*)–(D*)). Table 1 shows the changes in the difficulty level caused by retouching.

The average difficulty was reduced from 14.90 (Fig. 2(A)) and 13.76 (Fig. 2(B)) to 9.38 (Fig. 2(A*)) and 9.87 (Fig. 2(B*)) by retouching all the thin areas. The system also corrected the average difficulty to less than 10 (Level 1). The original average difficulty of 26.28 (Fig. 2(C)) and 26.95 (Fig. 2(D)) became 16.54 (Fig. 2(C*)) and 19.01 (Fig. 2(D*)). Our retouched sketch thickens the whole line for the lower part of the detail.

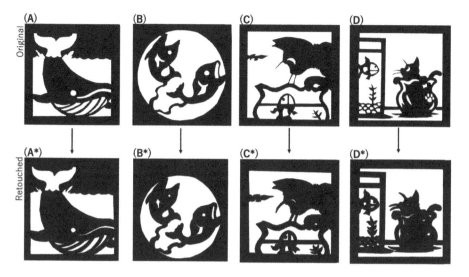

Fig. 2. 4 original drafts are shown in the textbooks; (A) and (B) are Level 2, (C) and (D) are Level 3. Our system reduces the difficulty by retouching the image; (A*) and (B*) are Level 1, (C*) and (D*) are Level 2.

6   Experiment: Evaluating the User Experience with Retouching Systems

6.1   Participants and Procedure

The participants were 10 novices (average age: 24.0 years, SD: 1.55, 7 males, 3 females) who had never created a paper cutting. They all exhibited a visual acuity that did not interfere with creating paper cuttings, and everyone was right-handed.

We evaluate the accuracy and flow of the participants' productions. Participants had to perform the task as quickly and accurately as possible during the experiment. They performed the following four tasks:

Table 1. The frequency distribution of cutting line difficulty.

	1–5	6–10	11–15	16–20	21–25	26–30	31–35	36–40	41–45	46–50	Average ID
Figure 2(A)	0.10	0.15	0.24	0.32	0.14	0.06					14.90
Figure 2(A*)	0.17	0.33	0.24	0.17	0.10						9.38
Figure 2(B)	0.18	0.20	0.23	0.18	0.13	0.07					13.76
Figure 2(B*)	0.13	0.22	0.30	0.25	0.10						9.87
Figure 2(C)	0.05	0.09	0.10	0.11	0.14	0.14	0.12	0.11	0.07	0.07	26.28
Figure 2(C*)	0.10	0.13	0.20	0.21	0.19	0.11	0.05	0.03			16.54
Figure 2(D)	0.05	0.08	0.10	0.10	0.11	0.13	0.16	0.14	0.10	0.04	26.95
Figure 2(D*)	0.09	0.11	0.14	0.21	0.20	0.13	0.09	0.04			19.01

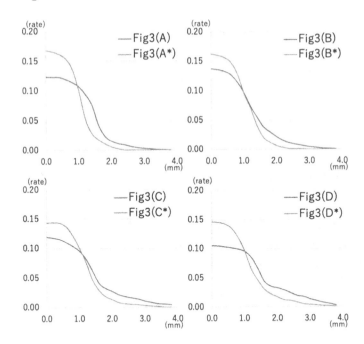

Fig. 3. Error of difference between the original line and cut trajectory in Fig. 2

Step 1: They cut the original pictures (Fig. 2(A)–(D)) in random order.
Step 2: They answered the questionnaire on the paper-cutting FSS about the production in Step 1.
Step 3: They cut the retouched pictures (Fig. 2(A*)–(D*)) in random order.
Step 4: They answered the questionnaire about the Step 3 production.

6.2 Results

Cutting Accuracy. We compared the distance between the original line and the cut trajectory in Steps 1 and 3. The original line is the black and white border of the picture. The cut trajectory is the line the participants cut with a knife device. If they cut the same way along the original line, the difference is infinitely closer to zero because the bar and the trajectory are identical. We evaluated the accuracy of the cut line by measuring this difference.

The relative degree of the distance between the original line and truncated coordinates is shown in Fig. 3. The horizontal axis shows the difference between the original and truncated lines. The left side of the vertical axis shows the relative frequency, and the right side shows the cumulative rate of the difference. The accumulation in Level 2 (Fig. 2(A*), 2(B*)), and Level 3 (Fig. 2(C*), 2(D*)) decreased in Step 3.

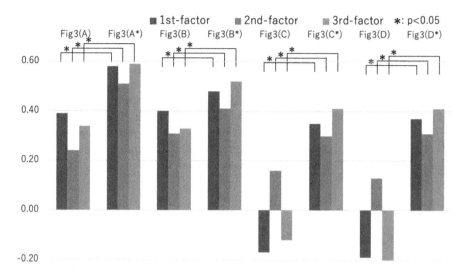

Fig. 4. Difference in factor scores on Flow State Scale.

Questionnaire Based on Analysis of Flow. We followed the same procedure as several studies on flow states in the field of psychology [21,29]. We compared the difference between the responses of the questionnaire for the efforts in Step 2 and Step 4 using factor analysis. We conducted an exploratory factor analysis to evaluate the flow in the production process using our FSS for paper-cutting in Japanese.

We interpreted the first-factor as a "balance between skill and challenge", "concentration on efforts" and the third-factor "change in the sense of time". The results of the factor scores of each group that responded to the paper-cutting FSS are shown in Fig. 2. We analyzed the factor scores for each group using the Steel-Dwass test. The results confirmed that the effect size was more significant for the first-factor at $p < 0.05$. We did not see any significant differences in Level 1 (Fig. 2(A) and 2(B)). Based on the above results, we have confirmed that our system has improved the accuracy and flow of the participants' production by modifying the difficulty of the Level 2 and Level 3 drafts (Fig. 4).

7   Conclusion and Discussion

This study aims to quantify the difficulty of artistic production and provide a design to adjust the difficulty of retouching to enhance the user experience. This paper has developed the retouching system and confirmed its impact. Our system eases the difficulty of craft design by adjusting the line thickness. We have quantified the difficulty of the picture based on the thickness of the lines based on the steering law. The system can retouch a picture from Level 2 (difficulty between 10 and 20) to Level 1 (difficulty below 10) and from Level 3 (difficulty above 20) to Level 2. We have experimented with the effect of this system on the novice's production. As a result, we found that the system improved the accuracy and flow of the production by retouching the craft design.

In general, workshop instructors help prevent errors by correcting difficult areas of the craft design. The teacher retouches according to the skill of the student. On the other hand, our system retouches based on novices' textbooks and does not refer to users' skills. We aim to evaluate the user's skill to a unique value in our future work. The system in this paper makes it easier by making the cutting lines thicker. The new retouching system makes it possible to make it difficult and easy by making the lines thinner. We will support users in creating images with a level of difficulty that matches their skills.

References

1. Accot, J., Zhai, S.: Beyond fitts' law: models for trajectory-based HCI tasks. In: Proceedings of the ACM SIGCHI Conference on Human Factors in Computing Systems, pp. 295–302. CHI 1997, ACM, New York, NY, USA (1997). https://doi.org/10.1145/258549.258760, http://doi.acm.org/10.1145/258549.258760
2. Accot, J., Zhai, S.: Performance evaluation of input devices in trajectory-based tasks: an application of the steering law. In: Proceedings of the SIGCHI Conference on Human Factors in Computing Systems, pp. 466–472. CHI 1999, ACM, New York, NY, USA (1999). https://doi.org/10.1145/302979.303133, http://doi.acm.org/10.1145/302979.303133
3. Accot, J., Zhai, S.: Refining fitts' law models for bivariate pointing. In: Proceedings of the SIGCHI Conference on Human Factors in Computing Systems, pp. 193–200. CHI 2003, ACM, New York, NY, USA (2003). https://doi.org/10.1145/642611.642646, http://doi.acm.org/10.1145/642611.642646
4. Cao, X., Zhai, S.: Modeling human performance of pen stroke gestures. In: Proceedings of the SIGCHI Conference on Human Factors in Computing Systems, pp. 1495–1504. CHI 2007, ACM, New York, NY, USA (2007). https://doi.org/10.1145/1240624.1240850, http://doi.acm.org/10.1145/1240624.1240850
5. Csikszentmihalyi, M., Csikszentmihalyi, I.S.: Optimal Experience: Psychological Studies of Flow in Consciousness. Cambridge University Press, Cambridge (1988)
6. Csikszentmihalyi, M., Csikszentmihalyi, I.: Optimal Experience: Psychological Studies of Flow in Consciousness. Donald F. Koch American Philosophy Collection, Cambridge University Press, Cambridge (1992)
7. Csikszentmihalyi, M.: Flow: The Psychology of Optimal Experience. Harper Perennial Modern Classics, New York City (1990)
8. Csikszentmihalyi, M., Nakamura, J.: The Concept of Flow. In: Flow and the Foundations of Positive Psychology, pp. 89–902. Springer International Publishing, Heidelberg (2002). https://doi.org/10.1007/978-94-017-9088-8
9. Csikszentmilhalyi, M., Csikszentmilhalyi, I., Graef, R., Holcomb, J., Hendin: Beyond boredom and anxiety. The Experience of Play in Work and Games (2012)
10. Cummmings, D., Vides, F., Hammond, T.: I don't believe my eyes!: geometric sketch recognition for a computer art tutorial. In: Proceedings of the International Symposium on Sketch-Based Interfaces and Modeling, pp. 97–106. SBIM 2012, Eurographics Association, Goslar Germany, Germany (2012). http://dl.acm.org/citation.cfm?id=2331067.2331082

11. Dixon, D., Prasad, M., Hammond, T.: Icandraw: using sketch recognition and corrective feedback to assist a user in drawing human faces. In: Proceedings of the SIGCHI 2010, pp. 897–906 (January 2010)

12. Fitts, P.M.: The information capacity of the human motor system in controlling the amplitude of movement. J. Exp. Psychol. **47**(6), 381–391 (1954). https://doi.org/10.1037/h0055392

13. Flagg, M., Rehg, J.M.: Projector-guided painting. In: Proceedings of the 19th Annual ACM Symposium on User Interface Software and Technology, pp. 235–244. UIST 2006, ACM, New York, NY, USA (2006). https://doi.org/10.1145/1166253.1166290, http://doi.acm.org/10.1145/1166253.1166290

14. Hammond, T., et al.: It's not just about accuracy: metrics that matter when modeling expert sketching ability. ACM Trans. Interact. Intell. Syst. **8**(3) (2018). https://doi.org/10.1145/3181673

15. Higashi, T.: Evaluation of skill improvement by combining skill and difficulty levels during paper-cutting production. Proc. ACM Hum.-Comput. Interact. **4**(ISS) (2020). https://doi.org/10.1145/3427319

16. Higashi, T., Kanai, H.: Improve cutting skill according to skill and difficulty level. In: Kurosu, M. (ed.) HCII 2019. LNCS, vol. 11567, pp. 247–258. Springer, Cham (2019). https://doi.org/10.1007/978-3-030-22643-5_20

17. Higashi, T., Kanai, H.: Stylus knife: improving cutting skill in paper-cutting by implementing pressure control. In: Proceedings of the 34th ACM/SIGAPP Symposium on Applied Computing, pp. 714–721. SAC 2019, ACM, New York, NY, USA (2019). https://doi.org/10.1145/3297280.3297348, http://doi.acm.org/10.1145/3297280.3297348

18. Higashi, T., Kanai, H.: Improvement in the effectiveness of cutting skill practice for paper-cutting creations based on the steering law. IEICE Trans. Inf. Syst. **E103-D**(4), 730–738 (2020)

19. Higashi, T., Kanai, H.: Improvement of pressure control skill with knife device for paper-cutting. IEICE Trans. Inf. Syst. **E103-D** (2020)

20. Huang, M.H., Tsau, S.Y.: A flow experience analysis on the virtual reality artwork: la camera insabbiata. In: Proceedings of the International Conference on Machine Vision and Applications, pp. 51–55. ICMVA 2018, Association for Computing Machinery, New York, NY, USA (2018). https://doi.org/10.1145/3220511.3220514

21. Jackson, S., Eklund, R.: The flow scales manual. fitness information technology (2004)

22. Jackson, S., Eklund, R.: Assessing flow in physical activity: the flow state scale-2 and dispositional flow scale-2. J. Sport Exerc. Psychol. **24**, 133–150 (2002). https://doi.org/10.1123/jsep.24.2.133

23. Kim, H.J., Kim, H., Chae, S., Seo, J., Han, T.D.: Ar pen and hand gestures: a new tool for pen drawings. In: CHI 2013 Extended Abstracts on Human Factors in Computing Systems, pp. 943–948. CHI EA 2013, ACM, New York, NY, USA (2013). https://doi.org/10.1145/2468356.2468525, http://doi.acm.org/10.1145/2468356.2468525

24. Lee, Y.J., Zitnick, C.L., Cohen, M.F.: Shadowdraw: real-time user guidance for freehand drawing. ACM Trans. Graph. **30**(4), 27:1–27:10 (2011). https://doi.org/10.1145/2010324.1964922, http://doi.acm.org/10.1145/2010324.1964922

25. Long, Jr., A.C., Landay, J.A., Rowe, L.A., Michiels, J.: Visual similarity of pen gestures. In: Proceedings of the SIGCHI Conference on Human Factors in Computing Systems, pp. 360–367. CHI 2000, ACM, New York, NY, USA (2000). https://doi.org/10.1145/332040.332458, http://doi.acm.org/10.1145/332040.332458

26. Oliveira, W., Toda, A., Palomino, P., Rodrigues, L., Isotani, S., Shi, L.: Towards automatic flow experience identification in educational systems: a theory-driven approach. In: Extended Abstracts of the Annual Symposium on Computer-Human Interaction in Play Companion Extended Abstracts, pp. 581–588. CHI PLAY 2019 Extended Abstracts, Association for Computing Machinery, New York, NY, USA (2019). https://doi.org/10.1145/3341215.3356311
27. Polanyi, M.: Personal Knowledge-Towards a Post-critical Philosophy. University Of Chicago Press, Chicago (1973)
28. Sako, T.: Flow experience in traditional Japanese body techniques. J. Japan Soc. Sport Soc. **10**, 36–48,134 (2002). in Japanese, https://doi.org/10.5987/jjsss.10.36
29. Tenenbaum, G., Fogarty, G.J., Jackson, S.A.: The flow experience: a rasch analysis of jackson's flow state scale. J. Outcome Meas. **33**, 278–94 (1999)
30. Williford, B., Doke, A., Pahud, M., Hinckley, K., Hammond, T.: Drawmyphoto: assisting novices in drawing from photographs. In: Proceedings of the 2019 on Creativity and Cognition, pp. 198–209. CC 2019, Association for Computing Machinery, New York, NY, USA (2019). https://doi.org/10.1145/3325480.3325507
31. Zabramski, S., Stuerzlinger, W.: Activity or product? Drawing and HCI. In: Proceedings of the International Conference on Multimedia, Interaction, Design and Innovation, pp. 4:1–4:9. MIDI 2013, ACM, New York, NY, USA (2013). https://doi.org/10.1145/2500342.2500346, http://doi.acm.org/10.1145/2500342.2500346
32. Zhai, S., Kong, J., Ren, X.: Speed-accuracy tradeoff in fitts' law tasks: on the equivalence of actual and nominal pointing precision. Int. J. Hum.-Comput. Stud. **61**(6), 823–856 (2004)

Research on the Influence of Weak-Ties Social Interaction on the Gamification Experience of Science and Technology Museums

Hongli Jia and Linong Dai[✉]

School of Design, Shanghai Jiao Tong University, Shanghai, China
jiahongli@sjtu.edu.cn, Lndai@126.com

Abstract. With the advent of the era of experience economy, museums in our country have ushered in a new development trend - gamification experience, attracting more and more young people to visit and explore museums. At the same time, under the dual stimulation of Internet technology and experience economic innovation, Science and Technology Museums are shifting from the traditional functional space emphasizing popular science knowledge and education to a diversified experience space [1]. Among them, social experience has attracted attention as an indispensable factor in gamification experience and museum experience. However, in Science and Technology Museums, there is very little interaction between a large number of strangers, making it difficult to arouse the positive emotions of science and technology science popularization learning. This paper concludes that weak ties social interaction has a positive impact on the gamification experience of Science and Technology Museums through the comparative experiment method, and uses the correlation analysis method to obtain the correlation between gamification interaction and user experience factors in Science and Technology Museums.

Keywords: Science and Technology Museum · Weak-ties social interaction · Gamification · User experience · Correlation analysis

1 Background

Under the influence of the epidemic and the rapid development of interactive technology, people's social needs and social interaction scenarios and methods have changed. The scale of social network users in China reaches 1.017 billion. The proportion of young users aged 18–24 increased to 21.7%, and the proportion of users aged 24–30 reached 25%. Users of almost every age group have social needs. The overall growth of the social market for basic applications in China has slowed down [2], and vertical segmentation scenarios have certain vitality and prospects for development. With changes in experience demands and technological innovations, people not only socially interact online, but also look forward to offline immersive social interaction.

In recent years, Science and Technology Museums in China are developing rapidly, and participatory experience has become an inevitable trend. According to the report, the number of museum visitors nationwide in 2019 was nearly 1.227 billion, maintaining a high growth rate from 2010 to 2019 [3]. More and more young users experience Science and Technology Museums and become an important user group for museums. With the development of Internet technology, artificial intelligence, big data, etc., the display methods of Science and Technology Museums and their interactions with visitors have changed. People visit Science and Technology Museums no longer just for an intellectual experience, but also for leisure, entertainment and emotional and social experiences. In China, the functional characteristics of Science and Technology Museums are obvious, and it is difficult to meet the multi-dimensional experience needs of visitors, especially social interaction experience.

At present, in China, the social experience design of Science and Technology Museums is mainly aimed at parent-child families and acquaintance groups. There are few studies on social experience for the characteristics of young people, and the design is not yet mature. Therefore, exploring new social modes of Science and Technology Museums is of great significance for improving the visiting experience.

Gamification interaction is a new social mode favored by young groups, and gamification is a bridge connecting museums and young users. Studies have shown that gamification helps to enhance the learning and entertainment experience of museums, while less research has been done on weak-ties interaction in museums.

2 Literature Review

2.1 Weak-Ties Social Interaction

Weak-Ties Theory
Weak-ties theory was first proposed by American sociologist Mark Granovetter in the 1970s. Weak tie connection is a kind of flexible and extensive weakly dependent social relationship [4]. Weak ties have three distinct characteristics [5]: (1) Extensive, weak ties have a large number of individuals, and weak ties can be formed except for intimate relationships. British anthropologist Robin Dunbay has speculated that 80% of all human contacts are weak ties. (2) Heterogeneity. Individuals who are in weak ties are very different in many aspects. (3) Intermediary, which can establish ties between groups and maintain connections.

In the study of social interpersonal relationship, stranger relationship is a typical weak relationship. Researchers such as Deya Xu pay attention to the social networking of mobile apps for strangers in contemporary China. Through qualitative research, they find that social networking with strangers has functions that cannot be brought about by strong ties, and can help users meet certain emotional needs and bring positive emotions [6].

Definition of Weak-Ties Theory
Weak-ties Interaction is a kind of socialization based on weak ties. Stranger Interaction is a type of weak-tie socialization, which also has the characteristics of weak connection. Professor Zhenhua Lei mentioned in his article that strangers in social networks have two

characteristics: (1) a sense of distance in space and society; (2) a sense of psychological and emotional closeness [4].

The Application of Weak-Ties Theory
In China, in recent years, due to changes in social ways and in social needs, there have been many products with weak ties, such as Momo, Tantan, Weibo, soul, etc. These products are aimed at different user groups and have different relationship operation modes. Xumin Wu and Dongdong Liu researched and summarized the experience design elements of public welfare social platforms under weak ties, and obtained the experience elements related to weak ties, such as emotional connection, social interaction participation cost, etc. [7]. During visiting the museum, it is found that young user groups are bringing this habit of weak-ties social interaction in cyberspace to offline exhibitions.

2.2 Gamification Experience Theory

Research on Gamification Experience in Museums
Gamification learning is a new trend in museum education. Di Wu and Ying Xie compiled a review of gamified learning research in Chinese museums. Many domestic scholars have done related research on the theory and design of gamified learning. A large number of empirical studies have proved that gamified learning can improve learners' interest in learning and stimulate learners, develop learners' creativity, problem-solving ability, decision-making ability and other higher-order thinking skills [8]. Gamified learning has become a new way for museums to spread knowledge and engage users. According to research by foreign scholars, gamified learning is widely used in various museums. Studies by Sanchez, Eric and others have shown that the application of gamification in museums can enhance the learning experience of young users in museums. In the context of informal learning in museums, gamification provides young visitors with a collaborative and fun learning experience [9]. Gamified learning is a development trend in museum experience, and gamification can enhance the collaborative learning experience of young users in informal learning scenarios in museums.

2.3 Museum Experience Research

The Significance of Museum Experience Research
Many scholars at home and abroad have shown that the museum experience should include multiple dimensions, including physical, cognitive, emotional and social. Through the study of museum audiences, the Smithsonian Institution summarizes the audience's experience into 14 types and 4 dimensions. The four dimensions are: (1) physical experience; (2) cognitive experience; (3) introspective experience; (4) social experience. Physical experience refers to items other than the museum users themselves and is related to the objects in the exhibition itself; Cognitive experience refers to the understanding and absorption of museum items or exhibition contents, acquiring knowledge or enriching understanding; Introspective experience refers to some introspective and introspective responses triggered by the visit, including a sense of connection at the

spiritual level; Social experience refers to the experience of communicating with others during the visit. The museum experience is multi-dimensional, and the dimension of social experience attracts attention. Studies by Vassiliki Kamariotou and others show that museums have a trend of digitization, and user experience of visiting has changed [10]. Research by Neta Shaby et al. proposed that most interactions in exhibits have sociability in nature, and for learning groups, exhibits support social experience that help to enhance emotion and cognition [11]. Research from Ran Meng and Ying Chen shows that the introduction of social attributes will connect more young user groups, broaden the dimension of gamification experience and make Science and Technology Museums a "topic" connecting people to people. It can be seen that optimizing the multi-dimensional experience of the museum and paying attention to the social and social experience can improve users' emotions, cognitive understanding, and social connection, which is of great significance.

Museum Experience Measurement
To measure museum experience, the Smithsonian Institution's 4-dimension questionnaire has the strongest credibility and practicality. In 1999, the Smithsonian Institution conducted research on museum user experience, and its team emphasized that museum experience research is a topic that needs continuous research [13]. Combining the characteristics of modern museums, researchers such as Gong Huaping divided the museum experience into several dimensions such as aesthetic experience, cognitive experience, interactive experience and emotional experience in the evaluation of mobile museum experience research [14]. Combined with literature research and the characteristics of modern museums, the museum experience measurement is summarized into 5 dimensions of physical experience, emotional experience, cognitive experience, social experience and interactive experience, and 22 influencing factors.

In terms of measuring the degree of social interaction, Nicholls (2008), Jiang Ting and Zhengming Hu (2011), Ting Jiang (2012) and others divided the degree of interaction into three dimensions, namely basic etiquette, advice and help, and social interaction. The scale questionnaire based on 3 dimensions used by Huang Jian (2017) has high reliability. The basic etiquette is divided into the scope of indirect interaction. Advice and help belong to the most basic direct interaction. Social interaction mainly includes joint participation and mutual cooperation, which is a deep direct interaction [15].

When it comes to measuring cognitive experience, emotion can be used as a yardstick. Researchers such as Yusi Han showed that positive emotions can positively predict learning perception, while negative emotions can negatively predict learning perception [16]. Positive emotions can mobilize users to actively explore and understand museum-related knowledge, while negative emotions can easily make users feel uncomfortable in the museum and lose interest in further visiting and understanding. Therefore, it is of great significance to enhance the positive emotions of users during the museum visit.

To measure positive and negative emotions, the most widely used internationally is the PANAS Positive and Negative Emotion Scale [16]. The mood scale has 20 items, including Interested, Distressed, Excited, Upset, Strong, Guilty, Scared, Hostile, Enthusiastic, Proud, Irritable, Alert, Ashamed, Inspired, Nervous, Determined, Attentive, Jittery, Active, Afraid.

2.4 Research Significance

Theoretical Significance

For museums, studying the dimension of social interaction experience will help to broaden and enhance the user's visiting experience and enhance the viscosity of users visiting museums. The introduction of weak ties social mode can enhance the museum social experience and emotional experience of young users. The research on the correlation between interaction degree and gamification mode and museum experience factor is helpful to guide the experience design of weak ties social mode in Science and Technology Museums.

Practical Significance

Weak ties social interaction can mobilize positive emotions in users' visits, helping users to gain more emotional experience and cognitive expansion while having fun and relaxing.

3 Research Methods and Processes

3.1 Research Purposes

By simulating the visiting experience scene of a science and technology museum, using a comparative experiment method to measure the user's cognitive perception and emotional perception, to explore the influence of weak-ties social interaction on young people's gamification experience when visiting a science and technology museum.

Through the questionnaire method, this paper further studies the degree of correlation between the degree of weak-ties social interaction and each factor of the experience of Science and Technology Museums, and the degree of correlation between gamification interaction and each factor of the experience of Science and Technology Museums. Finally, based on the research conclusions, suggestions are put forward for the optimization of the experience of Science and Technology Museums.

3.2 Research Process

The research process is shown in Fig. 1, which is divided into two stages. In the first stage, comparative experiments were used to verify that weak-ties social interaction is conducive to enhance the positive emotions of the gamification experience of Science and Technology Museums. In the second stage, the questionnaire method is used to further analyze the correlation between gamification participation and collaborative interaction based on weak-ties and the experience factor of Science and Technology Museums by distributing questionnaires.

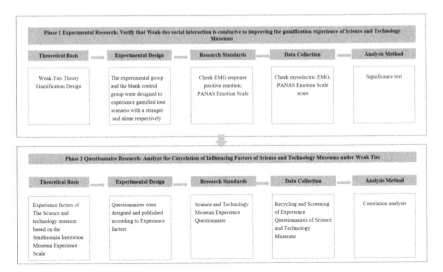

Fig. 1. Research process

3.3 Research Hypotheses

H1: Gamification interaction based on weak-ties is conducive to enhancing positive emotions in visiting Science and Technology Museums

H2: Gamification interaction based on weak-ties social interaction is conducive to improving the experience of Science and Technology Museums

H3: Gamification participation method which is based on weak-ties are significantly correlated with the emotional, social, interactive, physical, and cognitive experiences in Science and Technology Museums

H4: Collaborative interaction with others which is based on weak-ties is significantly correlated with social experience, interactive experience, emotional experience, and cognitive experience in Science and Technology Museums

4   Experimental Research

4.1   Experimental Design

Set up a comparative experiment, including an experimental group and a blank control group. In order to exclude the influence of the knowledge possessed by the subjects themselves, astronomy-related content was selected as the content of the experiment. At the same time, it is necessary to ensure that the subjects are non-astronomy expert enthusiasts, so as to avoid the influence of the subjects' factors on the experimental variables during the experiment. When setting up the experiment, based on the social characteristics of weak ties and gamification design elements, the variable is whether to "participate in the gamification experience with a stranger". The experimental examples are shown in Table 1.

Table 1. Experimental example.

Groups	Experience form	Interactive way
Experimental group	Complete a mission with a stranger	Exchange information, Operate the screen together
Blank group	Complete a mission alone	Operate the screen alone

4.2   Experimental Tools and Procedures

Experiment Equipment
One Psytech-10 multi-channel physiological instrument, EMG sensor, BioTrace+ software, MR3 software.

Measurement Standard
Positive/negative emotion measurement: The positive/negative emotion measurement is calculated using the PANAS scale. Positive emotion and negative emotion in the PANAS scale are two relatively independent systems. In the scale design, the 1st, 3rd, 5th, 9th, 10th, 12th, 14th, 16th, 17th, 19th items are positive emotion system, and the rest are negative emotion system.

Cheek EMG index: Qiyong Zhang and other researchers have shown that EMG index changes are related to emotions, and are usually used to measure positive emotions. When positive emotions increase, the EMG index will also increase [17].

Paired sample t-test: An analytical method used to test whether two groups of sample data are significantly different. In this experiment, the experimental group and the blank group are set up, and the experimental data are obtained by the same subject. The paired sample T test can be used to analyze whether there is a significant difference between the two groups of data, and the P value is used to measure the significance. When $P < 0.05$ means that there is a significant difference between the experimental group and the blank group.

One-way ANOVA: Also known as the F test, it is a method used to analyze whether a single factor has a significant difference in experimental data. This experiment is a univariate comparison experiment, which can be used to measure the influence of a single variable on the data of different experimental groups.

Experiment Process
The experimental process is shown in Fig. 2:

Fig. 2. Experiment process

4.3 Experiment Overview

Experiment Equipment

In the experimental part, a total of 18 pairs of candidate participated validly in the experiment and completed the entire experimental process. The test group includes 9 male groups and 9 female groups, aged between 18–30 years old, in line with the user positioning of this study. The Cronbach α value of the reliability coefficient of PANAS scale filling is $0.876 > 0.8$, so the reliability and high efficiency of PANAS emotional scale filling are suitable for extracting information and can be used for further analysis.

4.4 Experimental Results

Weak-ties social interaction helps to enhance young people's positive emotions towards gamification experience in Science and Technology Museums, and has a significant impact

In the experimental part, compared with the blank group, the EMG representing positive emotions in the experimental group showed a more stable upward fluctuation trend with the experience time. Figure 3 shows the EMG changes in the experimental group, and Fig. 4 shows the EMG changes in the blank group.

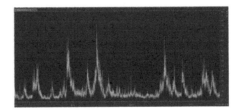

Fig. 3. The EMG changes in the experimental group

In this experiment, the experimental group and the blank group were set up, and the one-way analysis of variance was used to test the significance of the initial values of the two groups of data. As shown in Table 2, it can be seen from the table that the EMG baseline significance test $P = 0.913 > 0.05$ of the two groups can prove that there is no difference in the baseline between the experimental group and the blank group, that is, the initial conditions of the two groups are the same.

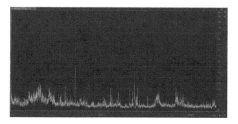

Fig. 4. The EMG changes in the blank group

Table 2. One-way ANOVA test of EMG cardinality.

Name	Average value ± Standard deviation		F	P
	B-EMG cardinality (n = 18)	E-EMG cardinality (n = 18)		
EMG Cardinality one-way ANOVA test	3.69 ± 7.36	3.97 ± 8.24	0.012	0.913

$*p < 0.05$ $**p < 0.01$

Take the first 10 sample data as an example, calculate and analyze the increase of myoelectric. The increase in myoelectric was calculated as the increase in the mean value of myoelectric during the experiment compared to the baseline value of myoelectric at the beginning of the experiment. Table 3 for data details. It can be seen from the table that during the gamification experience, both the EMG of the experimental group and the blank group increased, but the increase of the cheek EMG of the experimental group is greater than that of the blank group. It can be seen that weak-ties social interaction is conducive to enhancing the positive emotions in the gamification experience process of Science and Technology Museums, and is conducive to improving the visiting experience.

Paired sample T test was further performed on the data of cheek EMG increase in the experimental group and the blank group to analyze whether there was a significant difference. The test results are shown in Table 4. In the EMG paired T test of the experimental group and the blank group, the EMG mean $P = 0.000 < 0.01$, and the EMG increase $P = 0.030 < 0.05$. It can be concluded that the gamification experience process in the science and technology museum. There are significant differences in the mean and increase of EMG between the experimental group and the blank group. Therefore, it is concluded that weak-ties social interaction has a significant impact on improving positive emotions in the process of gamification experience in Science and Technology Museums.

Table 3. Experimental data of EMG.

Number	E-EMG Cardinality	E-EMG growth	B-EMG cardinality	B-EMG growth
1	0.78	278.11%	1.04	121.69%
2	0.79	336.76%	0.45	207.24%
3	1.11	369.28%	0.76	113.71%
4	1.03	590.43%	1.50	67.01%
5	1.06	2105.92%	1.60	116.72%
6	1.73	364.94%	4.50	109.14%
7	1.20	60.71%	0.57	54.29%
8	1.52	236.99%	0.77	180.33%
9	2.00	696.68%	0.97	315.45%
10	1.42	490.14%	1.61	131.09%
Average of all samples	1.26	553.00%	1.38	141.67%

E = experimental group B = Blank group

Table 4. Paired-samples T-test results of EMG.

Paired-samples t-test results			
Project	Pairing (mean ± standard deviation)		p
	Pair 1	Pair 2	
E-EMG average pair B-EMG average	12.54 ± 10.98	4.79 ± 5.90	0.000**
E-EMG growth pair B-EMG growth	6.36 ± 9.33	1.38 ± 1.27	0.030*

*p < 0.05 **p < 0.01 E = experimental group B = Blank group

Statistical analysis and paired sample T test were further performed on the PANAS scales filled in by the two groups of users to verify the above conclusions. Take the previous 10 sample data as an example, as shown in Table 5. It can be seen from the table that the positive emotion score of the experimental group after the gamification experience is higher than that of the blank control group, and the negative emotion scores of the experimental group and the blank control group are not significantly different. Paired T-test was performed on the positive and negative emotions of PANAS users, and the test results are shown in Table 6. The positive emotion index of users in the two groups of experiments is $P = 0.034 < 0.05$. It can be seen that there is a significant difference in the positive emotion index after the end of the experiment between the two groups of experiments. To sum up, the conclusions drawn from the experimental data can be verified, and weak ties social interaction has a significant impact on improving the positive emotions in the process of gamification experience in Science and Technology Museums. Negative emotion index $P = 0.164 > 0.05$, there is no significant difference in reducing negative emotion.

Table 5. PANAS scale score.

Number	B-Positive emotion score	E-Positive emotion score	B-Negative emotion score	E-Negative emotion score
1	32	36	27	20
2	22	31	11	11
3	16	23	12	14
4	27	30	19	19
5	31	40	23	13
6	29	28	12	17
7	32	38	13	16
8	23	34	22	32
9	22	26	15	11
10	28	25	21	27
Average of all samples	26.2	31.1	17.5	18

E = experimental group B = Blank group

Table 6. Paired-Samples T-test results of PANAS scale score.

Paired-samples T-test results			
Project	Pairing (mean ± standard deviation)		p
	Pair 1	Pair 2	
E-Positive emotion score pair B-Positive emotion score	29.72 ± 6.72	26.56 ± 5.60	0.034*
E-Negative emotion score pair B-Negative emotion score	18.06 ± 5.92	16.17 ± 4.66	0.164

*p < 0.05 E = experimental group B = Blank group

5 Questionnaire Research

5.1 Questionnaire Design

Questionnaire Design

Through questionnaire survey and correlation analysis, this paper explores the degree of correlation between gamification participation based on weak ties, collaborative interaction based on weak ties and the experience factor of Science and Technology Museums. According to the Museum Experience Scale of the Smithsonian Institution and the Interaction Scale of other researchers, we designed a questionnaire to evaluate the museum experience related weak ties. The questionnaire survey is divided into two parts: pre-test and formal distribution and recovery. The question setting of the questionnaire subdivides and simplifies the definition and characteristics of weak-ties social interaction to ensure that users can easily substitute different experience situations when filling in, which is consistent with the stage one. The questions of experience factor scale are shown in Table 7 (taking social experience as an example). The questions of Interaction level scale are shown in Table 8 (taking social interaction as an example).

Table 7. Questionnaire scale example of museum experience.

Factor	Question	Scale						
Social Experience	Find potential friends who like the Science and Technology Museums	1	2	3	4	5	6	7
	Have a pleasant interaction with other visitors	1	2	3	4	5	6	7
	During the visit, have a sense of identification with other visitors	1	2	3	4	5	6	7
	Spend visiting time with others	1	2	3	4	5	6	7

Analysis Method

Reliability Analysis: Reliability analysis is an analytical method for judging whether the quality of research data is credible. This experiment uses Cronbach's alpha reliability coefficient; if the value is higher than 0.8, the reliability is high; if the value is between 0.7 and 0.8, the reliability is good; if the value is between 0.6 and 0.7; The reliability is acceptable; if the value is less than 0.6, the reliability is poor.

Validity Analysis: Validity analysis is a design rationale analysis method used to study quantitative data. In this experiment, KMO value was used as the analysis index. If the value is higher than 0.8, the validity is high; if the value is between 0.7 and 0.8, the validity is good; if the value is between 0.6 and 0.7, the validity is acceptable. The data can be used for further research analysis. If this value is less than 0.6, the validity is poor and the data cannot be extracted for research analysis.

Table 8. Questionnaire scale example of interaction.

Factor	Question	Scale						
Social Interaction	Greet with other visitors	1	2	3	4	5	6	7
	Other visitors are happy to share service facilities with me; vice versa	1	2	3	4	5	6	7
	Share experience with other visitors	1	2	3	4	5	6	7
	In some exhibition activities, collaborate with other visitors to complete	1	2	3	4	5	6	7

Correlation analysis: An analytical method used to analyze the correlation between two or more variables. It is used to study the relationship between quantitative data, whether there is a relationship, and the degree of closeness of the relationship. In this study, cross-correlation analysis of different factors can be carried out to obtain the correlation between gamification participation based on weak ties, collaborative interaction based on weak ties and experience factors.

5.2 Overview of Questionnaire Recovery

A total of 118 questionnaires are recovered, of which 91 are valid questionnaires. The Cronbach's alpha reliability coefficient of the questionnaire was 0.937, and the Cronbach's alpha value is greater than 0.9, indicating high reliability and quality of the data, which could be used for further analysis. The KMO value is 0.844, and the KMO value is greater than 0.8, the research data is very suitable for extracting information.

5.3 Data Analysis and Conclusion

When interacting with the non-acquaintance, young people in Science and Technology Museums feel that emotional experience, interactive experience, cognitive experience and physical experience are more important than social experience, and social experience is not satisfied

After collecting the questionnaire, the correlation between gamification participation and collaborative interaction and museum experience factors related to weak ties is further analyzed, and the research content is supplemented and expanded.

The importance of different experience factors to young users is obtained through the experience factor scale questions. As shown in Table 9, the weight ranking of different experience factors is calculated. It can be seen that the current young users pay more attention to the emotional experience, interactive experience, physical experience and cognitive experience in Science and Technology Museums. In contrast, the social experience score is low, and their needs are not well met.

Table 9. Experience factor weight ranking.

Experience factor weight ranking

Factor	Mean	Contribution rate%
Emotional Experience	6.14	33.47
Interactive Experience	5.93	26.24
Physical Experience	5.87	18.80
Cognitive Experience	5.86	18.18
Social Experience	5.14	3.31

Gamification participation and certain factors of interactive experience and social experience have significant positive correlations

Further, the correlation analysis of the gamification participation and experience factors of Science and Technology Museums is carried out. The correlation analysis results are shown in Table 10. It can be seen from the table that under weak-ties social interaction, gamification participation and interactive experience have a significant positive correlation with the factor:simple and easy-to-use operations, and have a significant positive correlation with the factor:finding common friends and communicating happily with others in social experience.

Collaborative interaction based on weak ties and the social experience, interactive experience, emotional experience and cognitive experience of Science and Technology Museums have significant positive correlations

Further correlation analysis was carried out on the interaction and experience factors in the process of visiting Science and Technology Museums. The correlation analysis results are shown in Table 10. It can be seen from the table that when interacting with the non-acquaintance, users pay more attention to social experience, interactive experience, emotional experience and cognitive experience when they collaborate and interact with others in Science and Technology Museums, which have a significant positive correlation.

Table 10. Correlation analysis.

The Correlation Analysis of Experience Factor and Gamification Interaction			
Factor (Experience)	Description	Gamification Participation (Visiting Method)	Collaboration with other visitors (interactive level)
Interactive	The exhibition is simple to operate, and easy for new users to get started	0.281**	0.438**
Social	Find potential friends who like the Science and Technology Museums	0.240*	0.398**
Social	Have a pleasant interaction with other visitors	0.220*	0.554**
Cognitive	Meeting new people and things, and broadening horizons	0.2	0.395**
Physical	Clear and rich layout of exhibition items	0.199	0.348**
Social	Spend visiting time with others	0.192	0.549**
Interactive	Supports multiple interaction methods	0.188	0.441**
Emotional	Happy to recommend to others to visit the museum	0.182	0.442**
Interactive	Safe and reliable, my personal privacy will not be revealed during playing	0.179	0.301**
Interactive	Support multiple people to interact and operate at the same time	0.169	0.471**
Emotional	Feel happy	0.157	0.324**
Emotional	Find the exhibition interesting	0.157	0.311**
Interactive	Convenient to re-request an operation or modify information	0.144	0.477**
Social	During the visit, have a sense of identification with other visitors	0.113	0.494**
Emotional	Enjoy/immerse yourself in visiting the museum	0.107	0.213*
Cognitive	Enriched my understanding during the visit	0.071	0.251*
Cognitive	Increase my understanding of people and things	0.07	0.276**
Emotional	Feel soothed and relaxed	0.054	0.337**
Cognitive	Obtain exhibition information or knowledge	0.048	0.222*
Physical	Exhibits are beautiful in design and reasonable in color	0.015	0.270**
Physical	See "Actual/Prototype"	−0.087	0.148
Physical	See rare/extraordinary/valuable exhibits	−0.114	0.07

*$p < 0.05$ **$p < 0.01$

6 Discussion

6.1 Questionnaire Design

This research combines the experimental method and the questionnaire method, collects data from the simulated visit experience scene and the actual visit experience, validated the positive impact of weak-ties social interaction on experience, and further analyzed the correlation between factors affecting experience. In the experimental stage, the user's EMG data was mainly measured and collected to evaluate the user's positive emotions. Combined with the analysis of PANAS emotional scale and experimental EMG data, it is concluded that weak-ties social interaction has a significant impact on improving the positive emotions of the gamification experience of Science and Technology Museums. However, due to experiment conditions, the content discussed in this article is limited in the case of laboratory simulations. Further experiments beyond laboratory simulation can be conducted to verify whether same results show in the real museum condition or not. But, combined with the survey results of the questionnaire method, it is Verified that weak-ties social interaction has a positive impact on improving the experience of Science and Technology Museums.

In the questionnaire survey part, the recovered questionnaires have high reliability and validity, and the data can be used for research analysis. However, in the question setting of some experience factors, there are still problems of unclear expression and low degree of differentiation. The physical experience factor and the interactive experience factor can be optimized in combination with the current state of the experience of Science and Technology Museums.

7 Conclusion

Through the experimental method, this research concludes that weak-ties social interaction has a significant impact on improving the positive emotions of the gamification experience of Science and Technology Museums, which is conducive to improving the museum experience.

Through the research of questionnaire method, it is analyzed that when experiencing gamification interaction with the non-acquaintance in Science and Technology Museums, users pay attention to three aspects: simple operation of exhibition equipment, being able to meet people with common hobbies, and pleasant communication with others. When cooperating and interacting with others, optimizing the social experience, cognitive experience, interactive experience and emotional experience will help to improve the visiting experience of Science and Technology Museums.

References

1. Ying, C., Chen, W., Wei, S., Lin, F., Ran, M.: Constructing the multi-dimensional experience of popular science museums in the future—strategic design of visitor experience in shanghai planetarium. Industrial Design Industry Research Center. Industrial Design Research (Sixth Series). Industrial Design Industry Research Center (2018)

2. Lean Growth Breaking Out: China Mobile Social Marketing Development White Paper (2021). https://trendinsight.oceanengine.com/arithmetic-report/detail/325. Accessed 28 May 2021
3. Statistical charts of national museums. https://www.sohu.com/a/399414417_819453?qq-pf-to=pcqq.c2c. Accessed 03 June 2020
4. Wu, K.: Research on User Experience Design of Weak Ties Social App. Beijing Jiaotong University (2020)
5. Wei, C., Sheng, X.: A review of weak ties and strong ties and their applications in information sharing. Library (04), 18–21+27 (2014)
6. Xu, D., Liu, T.: Strong and weak ties and acquaintance with strangers: a social research based on mobile applications. News Univ. (03):49–61+119 (2021)
7. Wu, X., Liu, D.: Research on the design elements of the structural model of internet public welfare social platforms under weak relationships. Des. Art Res. **10**(01), 20–25 (2020)
8. Wu, D., Xie, Y.: A review of gamification learning in museums in my country. Sci. Educ. Museums **6**(03), 160–166 (2020)
9. Eslam, N., Georgia, P., Rabee, M.R., Hendrik, H., Vanessa, B., Andrew Vande, M.: Situated tangible gamification of heritage for supporting collaborative learning of young museum visitors. J. Comput. Cult. Herit. **13**(1), Article 3 (2020)
10. Vassiliki, K., Maria, K., Fotis, K.: Strategic planning for virtual exhibitions and visitors' experience: a multidisciplinary approach for museums in the digital age. Digit. Appl. Archaeol. Cult. Heritage **21**, e00183 (2021)
11. Neta, S., Orit, B., Tali, T.: Engagement in a science museum – the role of social interactions. Visitor Stud. **22**(1), 1–20 (2019)
12. Ran, M., Ge, X., Chen, Y., Chen, W., Shi, W., Lin, F.: Museum visiting experience design from the perspective of gamification—taking the experience design of shanghai planetarium as an example. Technol. Commun. **11**(07), 185–187 (2019)
13. Quan, W.: Research on Museum Audience Experience. Central Academy of Fine Arts (2019)
14. Gong, H., Zhou, J.Y., Zhang, X.B., Zhang, J.: Research on user experience evaluation of mobile museum based on APEC model framework. Shanxi Arch. (04), 132–146+153 (2020)
15. Gong, S.Y., Han, Y.S., Wang, L.X., Gao, L., Xiong, J.M.: Relationship between task value, academic emotion and online learning satisfaction. Electr. Educ. Res. **37**(03), 72–77 (2016)
16. Huang, J.: Research on the relationship among tourists' interaction, experience value and post-tour behavior intention in entertainment theme parks. Zhejiang University of Technology (2017)
17. Zhang, Q.Y., Yan, Z.Y.: The regulation of negative pre-emotions to positive emotional contagion: Reverse and lowering thresholds—taking teaching situations as an example. Acta Psychologica Sinica **50**(10), 1131–1141 (2018)

Innovative Design of Chinese Traditional Textile Patterns Based on Conditional Generative Adversarial Network

Miao Liu$^{(\boxtimes)}$ ⓘ and Binbin Zhou$^{(\boxtimes)}$

East China University of Science and Technology, Shanghai 200237, People's Republic of China
183797875@qq.com, binbinadv@foxmail.com

Abstract. With the continuous development of society and economy, Chinese traditional patterns with regional and ethnic characteristics have received more and more attention in international cultural exchanges, and the long history of Chinese traditional patterns has become a valuable resource for design creation. As a valuable cultural heritage, traditional patterns are at a critical point of inheritance and development in today's information society where artificial intelligence, Internet, VR and other technologies are developing rapidly.

This study takes Chinese traditional textile patterns as the research object, and uses conditional generative adversarial network model and computer-aided technology to carry out research on the classification and generation of Chinese traditional textile patterns to solve the problems of old styles, lack of innovation and high cost of manual design of Chinese traditional textile patterns. We introduced deep learning conditional generative adversarial network model for pattern classification of Chinese traditional patterns; at the same time, we conducted theoretical research and innovative practice of conditional generative adversarial network model in the design of Chinese traditional patterns for cultural and creative purposes.

After several training iterations, the conditional generative adversarial network model was able to follow the instructions to generate brand new patterns with traditional pattern features, generating brand new patterns with clear contours but pattern quality to be improved, with traditional textile pattern style features and clear pattern types, while generating brand new visual features that the patterns in the existing dataset do not have. The results of the design application of some patterns show that the designer can better realize the artificial intelligence collaborative design development of traditional textile patterns through the model, and the final design application works also present the artistic characteristics and cultural connotation of Chinese traditional textile patterns to a certain extent.

Keywords: Chinese traditional textile pattern · Conditional generative adversarial networks · Deep learning · Image classification generation

1 Introduction

Early human clothing developed along the line from scratch, from simple to complex, and China, known as the "Kingdom of Clothes", had an exceptionally prosperous clothing culture. Since the feudal society had extremely strict regulations on clothing, the

M. Rauterberg (Ed.): HCII 2022, LNCS 13324, pp. 234–245, 2022.
https://doi.org/10.1007/978-3-031-05434-1_15

traditional clothing in China did not change much in terms of style and structure, therefore, the pattern elements were important in the design of traditional clothing. With the continuous development of social economy, Chinese traditional patterns with regional ethnic characteristics have received more and more attention in international cultural exchanges, and the long history of Chinese traditional patterns has become a valuable resource for design creation. As a valuable cultural heritage, traditional patterns are at a critical point of inheritance and development in today's information society where artificial intelligence, Internet, VR and other technologies are developing rapidly.

With the increasing demand for traditional pattern design development, more and more scholars are joining the research of AI-aided design. Yu Minggang [1] realized pattern simulation by Photoshop and Ultra Fractal with the help of fractal principle, including extraction, fractal and planar design to form a variety of tie-dye patterns; Qin Zhen et al. [2] took the key semantics of design requirements as the driver, and used technical means such as TextRCNN, Extension semantic scale and deep learning, respectively, to establish a design model including semantic input and Liu et al. [3] developed an intelligent integrated environment for computerized embroidery, which realized the automatic processing of embroidery patterns and stitch generation by using artificial intelligence technology, computer-aided design, and image processing technology; Chu Miao et al. [4] combined artificial intelligence network learning technology and proposed SOFM-based image segmentation method for clustering natural background images, which better preserves the detailed texture of images and optimizes the automatic design method of camouflage patterns; Lin et al. [5] introduced the design and implementation of an intelligent embroidery sketch-assisted creation system. Combined with the drawing generation technology in the drawing-assisted creation subsystem, the methods of general rule-based pattern generation and instance inference-based pattern assembly of drawing were elaborated, which greatly improved the production efficiency and pattern variety of embroidery drawing; In the field of artificial intelligence, Ian Goodfellow proposed generative adversarial network (GAN) in 2014, which greatly improved the learning ability of the model due to GAN's groundbreaking network structure. improved the learning ability of the model and had a great impact on unsupervised learning, especially a seminal contribution to the field of image generation [6].

In recent years, with the continuous development of artificial intelligence algorithms and the dramatic increase in computer computing power, the learning ability of neural network models has also increased dramatically. The speed and effectiveness of processing information such as text, images, and sound have reached a high level. Generative adversarial networks, as the biggest innovation in the field of deep learning in recent years, have great advantages in the field of image generation. Using generative adversarial networks for traditional pattern innovation design can give full play to the advantages of artificial intelligence algorithms to provide new ideas for traditional pattern design. The use of computer-aided technology to study traditional patterns is in line with the trend of inheriting and developing traditional culture and the digitalization of design.

This study takes Chinese traditional textile patterns as the research object, and uses conditional generative adversarial network model and computer-aided technology to carry out research on the design of Chinese traditional textile pattern classification generation to solve the problems of old styles of Chinese traditional textile patterns, lack of innovation in design, and high cost of manual design. The experiments on pattern classification of Chinese traditional textile patterns are conducted by introducing the conditional generative adversarial network model in deep learning; at the same time, the theoretical research and innovative practice of the conditional generative adversarial network model in the design of Chinese traditional patterns.

This study takes Chinese traditional textile patterns as the research object, and uses the conditional generative adversarial network model and computer-aided technology to carry out the research of Chinese traditional textile pattern classification generation design, so as to solve the problems of old styles of Chinese traditional textile patterns, lack of innovation in design, and high cost of manual design. The experiments on pattern classification of Chinese traditional textile patterns are conducted by introducing the conditional generative adversarial network model in deep learning; at the same time, the theoretical research and innovative practice of the conditional generative adversarial network model in the design of Chinese traditional patterns.

2 Analysis Study of Chinese Traditional Patterns

2.1 Overview of Chinese Traditional Patterns

Chinese traditional patterns are all kinds of patterns with the characteristics of Chinese national art style handed down from different periods of Chinese history. China has a long history, and each era has produced many distinctive patterns and motifs, each of which reflects the style and characteristics of the era to which it belongs and has a rich ideological connotation, and is an important and indispensable part of traditional Chinese culture [7]. In different historical stages, the style characteristics shown by the traditional pattern also have great differences, for example: the pattern of primitive society is simple, abstract, with barbaric, primitive charm; the pattern of the Shang and Zhou period is solemn and mysterious, reflecting the sacredness and majesty of the ruling class; the pattern of the Warring States period is more lively and vivid, favoring realistic style; the pattern of the Han and Tang periods is grand and thick; the pattern of the Song and Yuan periods is gorgeous and rich; the pattern style of the Ming and Qing periods becomes more realistic, carving image, delicate and lifelike. Chinese traditional patterns are always in the process of development and change, and in today's era of information and intelligence, traditional patterns have great potential for development. It is worthwhile to conduct in-depth research and combine with emerging technologies to explore more possibilities.

2.2 Analysis of Traditional Chinese Pattern Design Applications

Pattern is a visual language that expresses the creator's thoughts and visions through the arrangement and combination of various graphics such as dots, lines and surfaces, and derives new connotations and meanings with the passage of time. The application of patterns can bring visual enjoyment to the viewer on the one hand, and convey unique national culture and ideas to the viewer on the other. At present, the design and application of traditional patterns are more in the field of cultural and creative product design, and the design development ideas are divided into element extraction, form abstraction, imagery reproduction and re-enrichment of connotation. In the future, with the continuous development of information technology, the application methods and ideas of traditional patterns are bound to produce new changes.

Directly extracting graphic elements from traditional patterns can simplify the design development process, reduce redesign costs, and highly restore the original stylistic features of the patterns. On the surface of the torch designed for the 2008 Beijing Olympic Games (see Fig. 1), the designer directly extracted the cloud pattern from the traditional Chinese pattern for redesign, reflecting a peaceful and harmonious image and expressing the confident and positive spiritual state of the Chinese nation.

Fig. 1. The 2008 Olympic Torch.

To abstract and simplify the overall form of the pattern, it is necessary to deeply understand the meaning and connotation expressed by the pattern itself, so that the pattern can be refined appropriately. The logo design of Bank of China is a typical case of abstract simplification of traditional patterns. The logo of Bank of China starts from the main business of the company, using the square-hole copper coin pattern to symbolize the banking business, and cleverly combines the square-hole copper coin pattern and the Chinese character pattern to symbolize the connection between Bank of China and the world, and the combination of square and circle symbolizes the ancient Chinese world view of heaven and earth (Fig. 2).

The use of computer-aided technology to assist traditional pattern design development is a new trend in traditional pattern design development. There are already a large number of algorithms and software to assist designers in pattern design, which can greatly improve the efficiency of design development and maintain high design quality. For example, Alibaba's Ali Intelligent Design Lab has developed the Lu Ban AI algorithm, which can design 8,000 posters in one second on average. In the 2016 Double 11, Lu Ban produced 170 million ad images, doubling the click-through rate. The designer's role has changed from designing a large number of posters repeatedly to being a machine

Fig. 2. Bank of China logo.

trainer, responsible for teaching the machine design style and controlling the machine's aesthetics (Fig. 3).

Fig. 3. Lu Ban press conference.

3   Generating Adversarial Network Model Building and Optimization

3.1   Generate Adversarial Network Model Building

Based on the deep learning generative adversarial network, a neural network model framework consisting of a generative network and a discriminative network is built. The generative network undertakes the task of image data generation in the whole framework, and finally achieves Nash equilibrium by continuously outputting random data and adjusting the learning parameters based on the feedback from the discriminative network, so as to finally output the image data as expected.

The discriminant network, on the other hand, takes on the task of training the generative network in the model by feeding the generated images into the discriminant network, getting the error between the data distribution of the current generated image and the expected data distribution to train the generator to extract the data distribution features of the traditional textile pattern and to determine whether the input pattern is of the real image or re-generated by the generative network.

Whether it is a true image or a geometric pattern, GAN can generate realistic pseudo-samples by continuous learning. Although the type of data generated by GAN can be controlled by selecting the dataset, it is not possible to specify any features of the samples generated by GAN. For example, in the 5-category generation task of geometric, plant, animal character, and text, it is not possible to control GAN to generate geometric patterns instead of plant patterns at a given time. Traditional generative adversarial networks cannot generate images of a specified type and can only output image types at random. If the network is to generate images with specified features, the type label of the image needs to be input to the network as one of the image features as well.

CGAN (conditional generative adversarial network) is a generative adversarial network introduced in 2014 by Mehi Mirza, a PhD student at the University of Montreal, Canada, and Simon Osindero, an AI architect at Flicker. The generator and discriminator of such a network are constrained by labeling information during training. First, random labels are fed into the generator along with random seeds to generate random sample-label pairs; second, images and the type labels corresponding to the images are fed into the discriminator, which learns to discriminate between true sample-label pairs and false sample-label pairs. In CGAN, the discriminator does not learn which classification the samples belong to, but only learns true samples and correct sample-label pairs as true and false sample-label pairs or false samples as false. The main change in conditional generative adversarial networks compared to traditional generative adversarial networks is that type labels are added to the input data of both generators and discriminators, instead of a single image data. After sufficient training of the generator, it is possible to specify the type of samples generated by passing specific labels (Fig. 4).

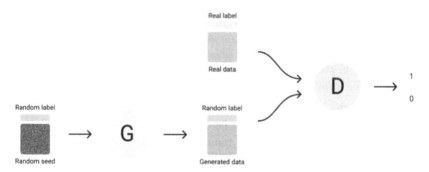

Fig. 4. CGAN Architecture diagram.

3.2 Optimizing Conditional Generative Adversarial Network Models

The biggest difference between traditional pattern generation research and most computer vision research is that traditional patterns are artificially created images, while the research objects of many research topics in deep learning computer vision are mostly physical images, and deep learning with artificially created images as the object There are uncertainties and certain difficulties in the research, and the model needs to be optimized and adjusted according to the characteristics of the image. Based on the model torso architecture, this paper adds a training sample normalization preprocessing module, and uses batch normalization mechanism, Leaky ReLU, tanh, sigmoid, Adam optimizer, BCELoss function and other optimization designs. The performance of the model is optimized and improved, making it more suitable for learning the image data distribution law of traditional textile patterns.

Leaky ReLU (Linear Unit with Leakage Correction). The Linear Unit with Leakage Correction (Leaky ReLU) function is a variant of the classic, and widely used, ReLU activation function. Leaky ReLU has the advantages of the ReLU function in solving the gradient disappearance problem and accelerating convergence, while the output of the function has a small slope to negative inputs. As the derivative is always non-zero, the presence of silent neurons is reduced, allowing gradient-based learning and solving the problem of the ReLU function entering negative intervals, which leads to neuron failure. Therefore, Leaky ReLU is used as the activation function in the hidden layer of the discriminator neural network.

Adam (Adaptive Moment Estimation) Optimizer. Kingma and Lei Ba, two scholars, proposed the Adam optimizer in 2014, which combines the advantages of both the AdaGrad and RMSProp optimization algorithms. The First Moment Estimation, which is the mean of the gradient, and the Second Moment Estimation, which is the uncentered variance of the gradient, are combined to calculate the update step. the Adam optimizer has many advantages such as simplicity and efficiency, adaptive learning rate, and adaptability. Therefore, the Adam optimizer was chosen to perform back-propagation calculations on the generator and discriminator.

BCELoss (Binary Cross-Entropy Loss Function). Since the discriminator only needs to determine whether the input is true or false, which is a binary classification task, the binary cross-entropy loss function is chosen to calculate the loss values of the discriminator and generator. In addition, since the binary classification task requires the output value is in the range of 0 to1, the output layer of the discriminator uses a sigmoid activation function to ensure that the output value is in the range of 0 to1.

BN (Batch Normalization). Batch Normalization is an algorithm that was created to overcome the difficulty of training neural networks due to the deepening of the number of layers. When the sample data in the training set and the target sample set are not distributed in the same way, the trained model cannot be generalized well. In a neural network, the input data of each layer will inevitably be distributed differently from the corresponding input data after the intra-layer operation, and the changes in the previous layer will be accumulated and amplified by the later neural network. One solution to this problem is to correct the training samples according to the ratio of the training samples to the target samples. The BN algorithm can be used to normalize the inputs of some or all layers, thus fixing the mean and variance of the input signals of each layer. Thus, the data distribution of the model is optimized by BN.

4   Results and Analysis

4.1   Experimental Environment and Data Preparation

The experimental platform used for model training is Windows system, CPU AMD 3700X, GPU NVIDIA GTX1660 SUPER X. Software and IDE configuration: The model construction is based on the deep learning framework Pytorch, implemented using the programming language Python3.7, and the IDE is Pycharm. The training sample set contains about 3000 traditional textile patterns of different sizes, and the patterns are divided into 5 types: geometric, plant, animal, character, and text. The initial learning rate of the model is set to 0.0002, and the pattern automatic preprocessing module is set in the network model, so the training sample pattern does not need manual preprocessing.

4.2   Training Process

After about 2,000 unsupervised learning training cycles, the output of the network model gradually evolves from noisy images to calligraphic textile patterns developed by the machine simulation design. Figure 5 shows the output patterns corresponding to the selected time points in the 2,000 training cycles, and it can be seen that the pattern generated by the generation module is getting closer and closer to the real one through continuous learning training and confrontation with the discriminator module. Finally, at around 24 h, the training basically reaches a plateau, the loss function stops updating (Fig. 6).

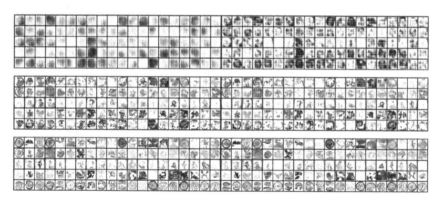

Fig. 5. The output of generator in the training process.

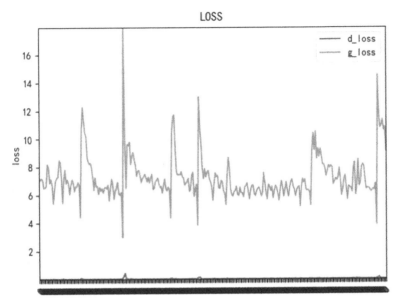

Fig. 6. The loss curve of generator in the training process.

4.3 Analysis of Results

After 2,000 rounds of training iterations, the model training process is stopped. The generator is run to generate a total of 100 new images with the characteristics of the traditional pattern style, 20 images of each pattern type. The image resolution is 64 × 64, and the image quality and resolution need to be improved. The generated images have the general features of the pattern type they belong to, but generate new features that the original patterns do not have. Compared with the traditional pattern development methods, the method proposed in this paper has the advantages of efficiency, low cost and sustainability. Also, compared with other non-deep learning computer-aided development methods such as Photoshop, Ultra Fractal, and fractal art, and non-generative adversarial network deep learning models such as TextRCNN and SOFM, the model built in this study has a great improvement in quality and efficiency, and compared with ordinary generative adversarial network models, conditional generative The conditional adversarial networks show better synergy and design efficiency in designer-model co-design compared with ordinary generative adversarial network models, which is related to the network characteristics of conditional generative adversarial networks themselves (Fig. 7).

Fig. 7. The output of generator after training.

4.4 Design Practice

Based on the analysis of the application of traditional Chinese pattern design, we develop the design of Chinese traditional textile pattern cultural and creative products based on the conditional generative adversarial network model. With the maturity of the domestic textile industry, the flexibility of the pillow product in shape, fabric, pattern and color also makes it occupy a place in the textile products, just as the handbag has a strong attraction for today's fashionable women, the pillow product also has a strong attraction for the soft decoration package in the home [8]; nowadays, consumers' emotional needs and experience needs are diversified, and the spiritual level of the product Nowadays, consumers' emotional needs and experience needs are diversified, and the demand for products at the spiritual level is increasing, so integrating Chinese traditional patterns into the design of pillow products can enrich the cultural connotation of pillow patterns and meet consumers' aesthetic needs on the one hand, and increase people's cultural confidence and cultural identity on the other.

Based on the above analysis, it was decided to start from the pillow product and use the model in the design of the pillow product based on the Chinese traditional pattern. The result shows that the designer can better realize the collaborative design development of Chinese traditional textile patterns based on conditional generative adversarial network through the model, and the final design works also present the artistic characteristics and cultural connotation of Chinese traditional textile patterns to a certain extent (Fig. 8).

Fig. 8. Design application of some patterns generated by the model.

5 Conclusion

Based on the conditional generative adversarial network, this paper builds a conditional generative adversarial network model with Chinese traditional textile patterns as the research object, learns the data distribution characteristics of Chinese traditional textile patterns, generates new, clear pattern types and new style patterns with Chinese traditional textile pattern style characteristics, and assists designers in innovative design, completing the transformation from computer software-aided design to artificial intelligence algorithm The transformation from computer software-aided design to artificial intelligence algorithm-aided design is completed. The use of conditional generative adversarial network to assist in the innovative design of traditional Chinese textile patterns greatly improves the efficiency of the innovative design of traditional textile patterns, ensures the uniformity of pattern styles and the diversity of pattern types, reduces the cost of pattern redesign, and provides new design ideas and methods for the innovative design of traditional textile patterns. The model performance is optimized through hyperparameter adjustment and module optimization of the generative adversarial network. The theoretical and practical values of the model are verified in design practice. The method provides a new solution idea to address the high demand of contemporary Chinese traditional textile pattern design and the inability of traditional design methods to meet the current design needs, and will play a positive role in the digital inheritance and innovation of Chinese traditional textile patterns. However, due to the high computer hardware requirements for model training, the training effect of the model is limited under the existing equipment conditions, and we will look for collaborators to fund and continue to optimize the model training effect in the subsequent research.

References

1. Yu, M.G.: Application of computer aided technology in the design of dye patterns. Text. Aux. **35**(7), 45–48 (2018)

2. Qin, Z., Liu, Y.H., Zheng, D.Y.: Aided design path of dong brocade pattern driven by semantics. Packag. Eng. **42**(14), 65–73 (2021)
3. Liu, H.T., Guo, L., Chen, S.F.: Design and implementation of intelligent environment for computer embroidery programming. J. Softw. **12**(9), 1399–1406 (2001)
4. Chu, M., Tian, S.H., Yu, J., Chen, H.S., Hu, Z.Y.: Sofm based background image clustering in camouflage pattern design. Comput. Appl. Softw. **26**(10), 218–221 (2009)
5. Lin, H., Xie, Q., Chen, Z.Q.: On the design and realization of the aided creating system for intelligence embroidery drawings (2001)
6. Goodfellow, I.J., Pouget-Abadie, J., Mirza, M.: Generative adversarial nets. Adv. Neural. Inf. Process. Syst. **3**, 2672–2680 (2014)
7. Pang, B., Zhang, T.T., Zhan, Z.M., Jiang, C., Cui, X.: Applying Chinese traditional pictures in the design of textile picture. Shandong Text. Econ. **1**, 61–62 (2010)
8. Zhuang, J.R., Liu, X., Luo, Y.R., Qian, Y., Hong, W.J.: Pillow design and new trends. Shandong Text. Econ. **6**, 89–90 (2013)

Lucky Hero's Legacy: An Interactive Game that Explores the Potential of 3D Scenarios to Engage Teenagers in Cultural Heritage

Louis Michael Sousa Rodrigues[1,2]([✉]), João Freitas[1], Mara Dionísio[1,2][iD], and Sergi Bermudez i Badia[1,3]

[1] University of Madeira, Funchal, Portugal
{2038415,2051816}@student.uma.pt,
{mara.dionisio,sergi.bermudez}@staff.uma.pt
[2] ITI-LARSyS, Funchal, Portugal
[3] Madeira N-LINCS, Universidade da Madeira, Funchal, Portugal

Abstract. In this paper, we explore the potential of using 3D scenarios to visually reconstruct part of the rich cultural heritage of Madeira Island. Through an adventure game called: Lucky Hero's Legacy, we aim to engage teenagers in embracing and getting to know their cultural heritage. The game was designed to provide freedom for teenagers to explore the 3D scenarios of Madeira Island, thus dynamically and engagingly discovering its legends, folktales, and heritage. The work describes the entire process, techniques used in the process of recreating the heritage in the digital world, the creation of cinematics for the transmission of educational content and a preliminary evaluation with 15 teenagers showing the games potential in engaging the target audience with cultural heritage.

Keywords: Cultural heritage · 3D modeling · Cinematics · Video game · Blender · Photogrammetry · Madeira Island · Videogame · Education

1 Introduction

Within the United Nations Agenda 2030, the Sustainable Development Goal (SDG) 11 is dedicated to cities and human settlements. In target 11.4, it is specifically called upon to "strengthen efforts to protect and safeguard the world's cultural and natural heritage" [23]. Ethnographic museums are the infrastructures responsible for conserving, displaying, and contextualizing items relevant to the field of ethnography, the systematic study of people and cultures, but a recent report regarding the current state of museums in Portugal revealed that these sorts of museums are the least attended [7]. Furthermore, there seems to be a general lack of interest from Portuguese citizens in their cultural heritage when compared to other countries in the EU [7]. Looking at the context where this research develops, Madeira Island, the local Ethnographic Museum has revealed that they are facing many challenges to capture the attention of the general population. However, a specific target group is even harder to engage with cultural and natural heritage: the teenagers. Cultural heritage is a legacy left to us by previous generations, and those of us living in present times have the responsibility to cherish and transmit it to the generations to come. Teenager plays an essential role in this process, and it is crucial to empower them to increase their awareness and involvement in protecting their heritage [22].

Video games are enormously popular; if, in the past, video games were considered a supplement to such media mainstays as television and the movies, this is no longer the case [20]. Not only are games popular, but they are often deeply engaging and, as a result, may well influence a wide range of attitudes and behaviors [18]. Hence, we want to take advantage of the significance of this medium in young people's lives [13] so that we can understand how to leverage games to promote cultural heritage engagement among a young audience.

Hence, the main objective of this research is to design a video game, with accurate 3D representations of Madeiran Cultural Heritage, from structures, legends, and folklore, with the intention of not only preserving Madeiran Culture in a virtual world but also to engage teenagers in getting to know more about their heritage.

2 Related Work

The preservation of cultural heritage for the digital world brings benefits in many ways; thanks to this digitization, it is possible to share the heritage for studies and the public offering. Not only this approach allows for the preservation of artifacts without being affected by corrosion or degradation with time, but it also allows for better disclosure of the culture among the society and future generations [9]. This section delves into the different approaches to represent cultural heritage in 3D format, and then it highlights current efforts and the potential of digital games to raise awareness towards cultural heritage and its preservation.

2.1 3D Techniques for Cultural Heritage Representation

For this type of process, there are two ways of gathering data by photogrammetry, which is the science and technology of making measurements through photographs. The process involves taking overlapping photographs of an object or structure and converting it into a 3D digital model [5]. The second method is the technology of using lasers to measure the object. This process results in using a beam of light to calculate the depth or measures of the object converting it to a 3D digital model [21]. In the case of photogrammetry, we can find several challenges; the most relevant is to select only what is intended. In this scenario, it is common to have a group of images and merge them to achieve a 3D object.

The second method collects depth data using a tracking device like a Kinect with infrared lights. This data is processed in a program called KinectFusion [12] that allows the 3D reconstruction of the object. This method is the most accurate in data gathering, although it is the most expensive [1]. When using one method or the other the final presentation of the 3D object is dependent on the textures used to achieve the desired result.

The Digital Michelangelo, [15] is one of the most important models and the oldest in the digitization field related to heritage. Thus, this method utilizes various tools to achieve the final result. The reconstruction of the Great Buddha of Bamiyan, in Afghanistan, used only one tool. The model ended up being reconstructed in 3D as a statue for a local museum by using static images to reconstruct this 53 m Buddha [10] (Fig. 1).

Despite photogrammetry being used for other purposes, not only for 3D reconstruction [6,24]. Some studies, present an incredible evolution of this method. For example, in the work of Covas [6], this method was used images to reconstruct two castles in Portugal that were of difficult access. The principal limitations of this method are how much it relies on the ambient involving the structure or object being photographed and the intensive process of generating precise replicas of this reconstruction. For example, it is difficult to split the background from the main object; this can be overcome by resourcing to a scanner which allows tweaking on the information gathering of the process, resulting in a more clean final product.

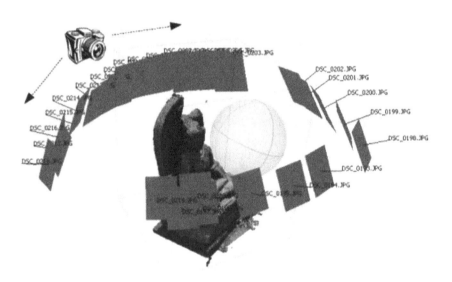

Fig. 1. Image acquisition process [24]

2.2   Cultural Heritage Representation in Video Games

Cultural Heritage (CH) dissemination and preservation have been the focus of several research projects, and initiatives [9]. The body of works spam from Games, Augmented Reality, and Virtual Reality applications [3]. One popular example where we can see CH dissemination and preservation is the game series created by Ubisoft "Assassin's Creed" [8]. The storyline is purely fictional, but the surrounding world is filled with real monuments, characters and it recreates historical events in detail from the war between the Crusaders and Saracens in the year 1191. In these types of games created for pure entertainment, the cultural heritage is used to give realism and shape the world around the game, but these games have the potential to be used for educational purposes [16].

Research shows that playing Serious Games (SG) [2] has proven benefits to acquiring greater problem-solving skills; this, combined with their strong visual components and their interactive nature, indicate that games are a powerful tool for the dissemination and preservation of cultural heritage [3] (Fig. 2). One of the challenges that some SG faced was the lack of freedom in the player's decisions, actions, and creativity. This issue can be tackled by introducing a Sandbox aspect in the educational matter of the game. In this way, all the knowledge delivered in the game is spatially organized and should be simple activities for the user to embody the knowledge that can be discovered. Thus, this type of approach opened a new world on how we could immortalize the cultural heritage of a given area and a new way to induce knowledge to every user of this type of game [11]. Moreover, the knowledge distributed in the game is as important as the environment design surrounding that game. A virtual representation of Cultural Heritage can create adventures and reconstruct places where the player can have a contextualized experience through gaming. Another thing to consider regarding serious games is to specify the video game genre. An SG can be specifically focused on, for example: Cultural Awareness, Historical Reconstruction, Artistic/Archaeological Heritage Awareness, Architectural/Natural Heritage Awareness [17]. However, entertainment-focused video games can bring improvements on enhancing SG experience. For example, adventure-type games combined with quizzes and puzzles can improve the learning process because their 3D realistic environment allows users to interact with the world. Furthermore, video games can be suited to deliver knowledge by creating a game character and a plot, in which we can create empathy between the player and character, also in which the plot can help a better understanding of historical events and different cultures.

Despite all this potential, we can not overlook the fact that the usage of new technologies for educational purposes is often depreciated, as there is still the idea of video games being a bad influence on teenagers. This is due to the fact that the majority of games known to the general audience are focused on pure entertainment [11]. In summary, as we see the serious games industry is growing, the development of a serious game for CH needs to be well planned. Balancing the visuals (3D style) with accurate data for the educational purpose and the entertainment levels is essential to ensure that teenagers embrace the game, allowing it to spread among the younger community and eventually lead to the intended outcome: the dissemination and preservation of CH.

Fig. 2. Serious games for cultural awareness [17]

3   Lucky Hero's Legacy

The general concept was to create an adventure game on Madeira Island at the time of the discoveries. The game portrays the adventures of Lucky an endemic Lizard, in the search for the wisdom pearl that was scattered into fragments spread around Madeira Island. To collect them, the player has to learn about Madeira's cultural heritage to gain leverage and overcome all the enemies and the challenges posed by Madeira Island terrain. To deliver knowledge about Madeira's cultural heritage, the information present in the video game is mostly based on legends and their respective locations or buildings, which are still preserved today.

3.1   Narrative

The Lucky hero Legacy fictional story was designed according to Campbell's Hero Journey [4], where the protagonist undergoes a series of adventures and challenges culminating in a significant event and transformation of the character. The events are set in the XV century, presenting the players with information regarding the history and legends of the island. After an extensive research phase, three popular legends were selected to be featured in the game narrative. As

Fig. 3. Gameplay of Lucky Hero's Legacy

the narrative was developed, several characters and maps were introduced to complement the story, thus giving meaning and fluidity (Fig. 3).

The narrative invites the audience to enter a virtual quest to follow the hero, Lucky. A Lizard that was stranded on the coast of Madeira Island, aided by an old man who saw in this lizard a potential hero. The old man tells a tale to Lucky about what is tormenting the island calling for his help to recover the pearl fragments spread across the island. Both go on an adventure through some historical locations in Madeira, presenting the audience with some information regarding the legends and history of Madeira. As the hero grows stronger in power and knowledge, facing many challenges from the evil forces of Wilson II that come across his path to replenish peace on the island.

The main narrative plot points that guides the game are:

- Lucky starts his adventure in search of the Pearl of knowledge fragments guided by the help of Sebastião. This plot point is linked with the "Legend of Machim", which is one of the first legends since it dates back t to the island's discovery(which happened by accident).[1]
- Lucky grows in power after finding a mythical sword. Thus, it is related to the "Legend of Arguim" in which the sword reassembles the one that D. Sebastião speared on the cape of Garajau.[2]

---

[1] This legend remounts to the first village of Madeira, Machico named after Machim, which is the protagonist in this legend. https://www.visitmadeira.pt/en-gb/madeira/legends/legend-of-machim.

[2] Legends say that D. Sebastião did not perish in battle but fled to an island called Arguim, on his way to the island speared his sword on Cape Garajau Madeira Island. https://www.visitmadeira.pt/en-gb/madeira/legends/legend-of-arguim.

– Wilson II captures the Old Man leaving Lucky hopeless. The fortress of Pico is used as a cultural reference and is one of the villain's lair.
– A crow helps Lucky to complete his adventure and become much stronger by defeating Ladislau in Câmara de Lobos.[3]
– Lucky defeats Wilson II and unshackles the Old Man. Allowing Lucky to place all the pearl fragments on the Chapel of São Vicente near the sea.[4]

3.2   Game Development

In this section, we delve into the aspects of the game development, focusing on describing the details behind the creation of the 3D environments and assets that portray the CH of the island. The game was developed in the Unity game engine and compiled for Windows.

Cultural Heritage 3D Creation

The recreation of immovable cultural heritage in the game is one of the main focus of this game, hence we recreate some of the heritage sites in the digital world, in this way preserving them for posterity. The first step was to select the cultural heritage sites according to the locations mentioned in the game's narrative. After the selection, a mood board is made based on paintings and photographs for each of the heritage sites. This process is vital for the creation of 3D models, serving as a method of comparison between the real and the virtual. Then based on the research carried out at the beginning of this process, we decided to focus on two types of recreation techniques: through photography observation and analysis, as well as through photogrammetry [24].

Photogrammetry

This method was applied only to represent the chapel of São Vicente because it has a very natural and organic shape. The first step of this process is to capture the images, and it is crucial to have a clear image without any noise or blur. To have as little noise as possible in the image it is necessary to reduce the aperture (f) and the sensitivity to light (ISO) of the camera to minimum values. For the reconstruction of the chapel, 45 photos were taken to obtain 360° information about the object. The photo taken was loaded in the MeshRoom software[5] and with the help of the nodes defining the parameters desired. Parameters should be adjusted until the desired mesh is achieved. Then a filter is applied to smooth it out, reducing the number of vertices and increasing the simplification factor, turning it into a simplified model. In the nodes panel, the texture output is defined for this new mesh. After this phase is completed, the textured model with a good topology is ready to be imported in Blender[6] (Fig. 4).

---

[3] Ladislau was king of Poland and Hungary, he was defeated in battle, but he was never found. Legends say that he was the mysterious knight named Henrique Alemão that appeared in Madeira ten years after the battle. https://www.visitmadeira.pt/en-gb/madeira/legends/legend-of-ladislaus.

[4] http://www.somosmadeira.com/2015/05/capela-de-sao-vicente.html.

[5] https://alicevision.org/#meshroom.

[6] https://www.blender.org/.

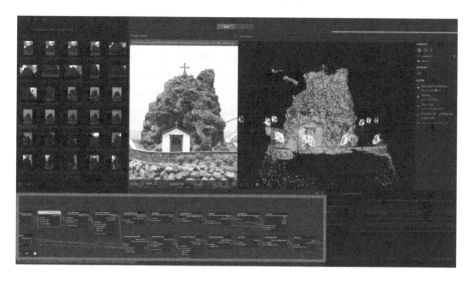

Fig. 4. Creation of the 3D model of the Capela de São Vicente in MeshRoom

3D Modeling

The chapel was placed on a plane so that its base was flat, and through the sculpting method, unnecessary mesh points were removed. At the end of this process, the mesh is more realistic, and its original texture can be removed for a better view of the base mesh itself. After reconstructing the mesh, the "Unwrap" is performed in order to be able to apply custom textures to it. The process is done using Quixel Mixer[7], applying rock textures as the base color of the mesh, made with the help of Photoshop[8], to achieve the same graphic style as the rest of the game. With the help of masks, by selecting only the deepest areas and applying a darker color to convey the notion of depth. Regarding the chapel, a painted wall texture was applied. The same process was applied to the rock.

Observation of Images

Modeling through the observation of images was the most used method because of two factors. First, due to the pandemic, it was not possible to visit the selected heritages, which interfered with the photo gathering. Thus, it was decided to

---

[7] https://quixel.com/mixer.
[8] https://www.adobe.com/pt/products/photoshop.html.

create a mood board with various photos and paintings related to each heritage to create an exact digital representation from that era (Fig. 5). The second factor was related to the need to reduce the level of detail in these buildings, allowing for a simplified version. The following patrimony: Traditional Madeiran Housing, Chapel of "Nossa Senhora dos Milagres", Fort of "São João Batista do Pico", and Typical Madeiran fishing boat "Xavelha" was modelled using this method. In this example, it all started by modeling the base structure of the fort by addressing image references of the structure, adding a cube and manipulating it, moving vertices, and extruding faces until the desired base shape is achieved. After having the shape of the walls, a Boolean modifier was added to remove the excess points of the structure, thus forming the grooves. This stage was completed by adding the floor and some details. In the second phase of this reconstruction, all possible details are added, such as: doors; gates; windows; roofs; stairs and rocks at the ends of the wall. All these objects are modeled following the same process, previously described. With the modeling phase concluded, the Texture phase begins. By Unwrapping the model to apply textures with ease.

CH Cinematics

The game was enriched with cinematics in key points of the gameplay. They exhibit the created 3D models in detail and add crucial information about legends or cultural facts. Five heritage cinematics were created to capture the CH value of several of the game locations. For example, in the first cinematic: Traditional Madeiran Housing, we can learn about the construction of one of the oldest shelters in Madeira Island. In the second cinematic: Chapel of Senhor dos Milagres, we can learn about the Legend of Machim and the origin of the chapel's construction. In the third cinematic: Fort of São João Batista do Pico, we learn in which era it was built and what purpose it served. In the fourth cinematic: we learn why the boat "Xavelha", is painted in different colors and the purpose of each color. In the fifth cinematic: Chapel of São Vicente, we learn a local legend about its patron saint and why this chapel was built on a rock by the sea. The Fig. 6 showcases screenshots of each of the cinematics. For each cinematic, it was necessary to develop a storyboard of where it aided to visualize where to place cameras and what information they would contain. With the help of Photoshop[9], the video interface was created, as well as the title of each and a background. Within Unity[10], a canvas was built for displaying the information adjusting the canvas to the desired positions and sizes. In this phase, the Unity Cinemachine plugin was used, which allows to control cameras by defining a focus point in which, regardless of the movement performed by the camera, it will always keep the focus in the same place, giving thus the freedom and ease of animating the scenario. It was necessary to create an animation and define the keyframes that store the coordinates at that exact moment. This process was carried out for the various desired positions and at different times. After this phase was completed, a timeline was developed in order to link all the intended elements from information, camera movement, and the narrator's voice.

---

[9] https://www.adobe.com/pt/products/photoshop.html.
[10] https://unity.com/.

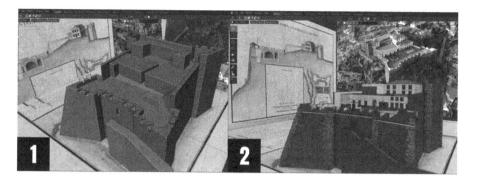

Fig. 5. 1 - 3D modeling using reference images; 2 - 3D model with textures implemented;

Fig. 6. 1 - Traditional Madeiran Housing; 2 - Chapel of "Senhor dos Milagres"; 3 - Fort of São João Batista do Pico; 4 - Typical Madeiran fishing boat "Xavelha"; 5 - Chapel of São Vicente;

4   Evaluation

4.1   Protocol

Participants were recruited for this study using a convenience sample; they needed a computer, mouse, keyboard, audio output, and internet connection. Each participant was given a link to a Discord server created for this evaluation and had access to a link to download the game. The evaluation protocol was the following:

- (1) Consent form: where the user accepts to volunteer to be part of this study evaluation.
- (2) A pre-questionnaire probing: Age, Gender, Video games experience, and a set of four questions to measure cultural knowledge about Madeira Island, about legends and some cultural heritage.
- (3) Gameplay: each user was asked to share their screen to allow the observation of their behavior during gameplay. At the end of the game, each user was put through an in-game test of five questions about cultural facts and legends present in the game that needed to be answered to be able to complete the experience. Each response was collected by the observers and placed in a private questionnaire.
- (4) A post-questionnaire consisting: of four questions to measure cultural knowledge about Madeira Island (same as in the pre-questionnaire), a reduced version of Game User Experience Satisfaction Scale (GUESS scale) [14], and an open section for general feedback of the game experience.

4.2   Measures

To evaluate the overall game experience, we used a reduced version of the GUESS scale [19] called: GUESS-18 [14]. It consists of eighteen questions with a total of eight parameters related to experience satisfaction: Usability, Narrative, Play Engrossment, Satisfaction, Creativity, Sound, Visuals and Self Gratification, Communication. This last parameter was not used in our questionnaire as our game does not support multiplayer or co-op features. GUESS-18 uses an evaluation from one to seven points, being one point equal to "completely disagree" and seven "completely agree". Once the data is all collected, the mean is calculated of each parameter, giving a result for each criterion. In the end, each result would be added, forming a composite score that is later measured on a scale from nine to sixty-three points.

To evaluate if the game had produced any awareness and knowledge regarding CH, we applied one questionnaire with items designed by us about the local CH. Applying this before and after the gameplay experience allowed us to compare the influence of the game on the participants' knowledge.

4.3   Results

Demography

Testing was done with fifteen male users with an average age of fifteen years old. The majority played video games frequently, with a high count of hours in game.

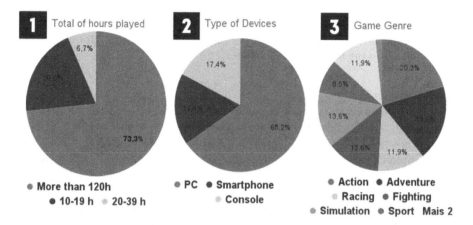

Fig. 7. 1 - Total of hours played of users tested; 2 - Type of devices most used by the users; 3 - Game Genre played by the users;

Hence, most of the users resource the use of the computer as the main source of entertainment. Leading to an increase of capabilities and knowledge of different video game genres (Fig. 7).

In-Game Questionnaire

As we mentioned, five multiple-choice questions about the cultural heritage and legends were included within the game-play. These appeared at the end of the video game. Once the results from the in-game questionnaire were evaluated, it was possible to realize that the majority of our users had chosen the right answer (85.3%) and only (14.7%) were incorrect answers, see Fig. 8.

Madeira's Cultural Heritage Knowledge

When comparing the results obtained in the pre-questionnaire versus the results obtained in the post-questionnaire, we can see a clear positive outcome. Thus, it shows that the experience successfully delivered knowledge to our participants about Madeira's Cultural Heritage. Since more users got the correct answers after the game experience.

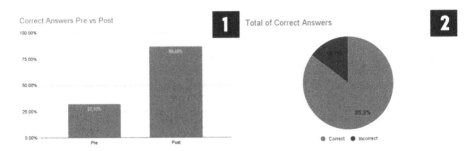

Fig. 8. 1 - Comparison of correct answers pre vs post questionnaire; 2 - Total of correct answers related to the in-game questionnaire;

Game Experience

In the last parameter of evaluation, we used the GUESS-18 scale to evaluate our game in general. The graphic demonstrates the mean scores for the GUESS-18 parameters were between 5.4 and 6.5 (on a scale from 1 (completely disagree) to 7 (completely agree). The parameters with higher scores were: Enjoyment, Personal Gratification, and Visual Aesthetics. This indicates that the 3D visuals and the representation of Madeiran Culture in the game were successfully portrayed, which allowed for enjoyment of the game and enabled some degree of learning (Fig. 9).

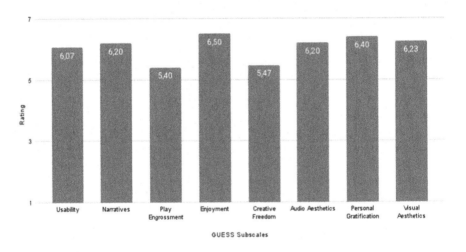

Fig. 9. Results of the Guess 18 sub-scales, related to the overall aspects of the game.

5   Discussion

An adventure game enriched with the cultural heritage of Madeira Island was created. The game incorporates in its narrative several legends of Madeira Island

and part of its cultural heritage is portrayed in a total of five heritage cinematics. The information described in these cinematics was conceived in order to convey the cultural value in the best possible way. Since our target audience is teenagers, we tried to describe this information in a more intuitive way for those ages. The use of a narrator was successful in bring out some of the most relevant details and information but the camera animations used gave more details and dynamism to the showcasing of the heritage sites. Results show that these cinematics were a successful approach to deliver the information that we intend to pass on to the teenagers. In the pre-questionnaire it was possible to verify that 32.1% of the users answered correctly, and after viewing the cinematics this percentage increased to 86.6%, thus demonstrating that there was an increase in cultural knowledge. In the game Lucky Hero's Legacy, we faced the same situation, where we highlight the comment of a user: "I enjoyed seeing the chapel of São Vicente that looks just like the real one and I also learned new things like the legends of Wilson II and also about the island I live on", thus demonstrating that the learning factor was present in this experience.

It is important to highlight that during the development of the game we had some unexpected situations related the pandemic situation. The vast majority of the 3D models had to be build based on reference images since we were not able to visit some of the heritage sites in question. Thanks to this game, we developed a more detailed and accurate workflow with regard to 3D modeling. Defining the steps in a more practical and faster way. We also developed skills in photogrammetry, achieving a good final result. To improve this process, it would be an idea to visit the heritage sites themselves as well as talk to historians, to be able to add more important details regarding certain periods. This information could influence the way in which the cinematics are carried out, thus portraying these details in animations that help the user to retain more information about a particular heritage and its time.

6 Future Work

The CH content present in the game is limited, as we only approach three legends and five heritage sites. Hence, the game could be expanded by adding more legends and heritage throughout Madeira Island, increasing the CH content present in the game. Looking at the results, it is possible to say that this game has the potential to be a learning tool for young people. In the future, it would be interesting to present the game to schools in partnership with the Local Department of Education to evaluate it on a larger scale and verify whether an expansion of the game would be viable. Furthermore, a partnership could be established with several museums island to showcase artifacts belonging to their collections in the game. By including these artifacts in game-play we could increase the awareness about them eventually creating a curiosity to visit the museums and see the artifacts live. Regarding the game design, it would be valuable to increase player interaction, and new Non-Playable Characters could be introduced with different traditional costumes from each of the local villages, where the daily life of the villagers in the time of the discoveries could be presented, thus creating secondary missions. It could be interesting to increase the gamification by allowing players to collect, buy and sell heritage items.

7 Conclusion

This research effort showcases the potential that an adventure game enhanced with cultural characteristics can have as an effective method in raising awareness towards CH among young people. Part of Lucky Hero's Legacy game process was presented, highlighting the critical role of 3D models, visuals and cinematics in portraying cultural heritage scenarios and stories. The 3D models, together with the scenery, played an essential role in motivating and creating enthusiasm among the participants to know a little about our past and our culture.

To summarize, our main contribution is the design of this artifact: Lucky Hero's Legacy game. The game incorporates different methods: creating scenarios through heights maps, creating 3D models using the photogrammetry method, and by observation. This work also shows that it is possible to learn about culture by portraying cultural heritage in a game and that 3D artifacts play an essential role. Furthermore, thanks to this game, it was possible to transfer part of our heritage to a digital world, thus preserving it for future generations and maintaining proximity between the past and the future.

References

1. Banerjee, S., Dutta, S., Biswas, P.K., Bhowmick, P.: A low-cost portable 3D laser scanning system with aptness from acquisition to visualization. In: 2013 Digital Heritage International Congress (DigitalHeritage), vol. 1, pp. 185–188. IEEE (2013)
2. Bellotti, F., Berta, R., De Gloria, A., D'ursi, A., Fiore, V.: A serious game model for cultural heritage. J. Comput. Cult. Herit. (JOCCH) 5(4), 1–27 (2013)
3. Bontchev, B., et al.: Serious games for and as cultural heritage. In: Digital Presentation and Preservation of Cultural and Scientific Heritage (V), pp. 43–58 (2015)
4. Campbell, J.: The Hero's Journey: Joseph Campbell on His Life and Work, vol. 7. New World Library, Novato (2003)
5. Collier, P.: Photogrammetry and aerial photography (2020). https://doi.org/10.1016/b978-0-08-102295-5.10583-9
6. Covas, J., Ferreira, V., Mateus, L.: 3D reconstruction with fisheye images strategies to survey complex heritage buildings. In: 2015 Digital Heritage, vol. 1, pp. 123–126. IEEE (2015)
7. Juventude Desporto e Cultura Comissão Europeia, Direção-Geral da Educação: Eurobarómetro especial 466 - outubro 2017 - património cultural, p. 125 (2017)
8. El Nasr, M.S., Al-Saati, M., Niedenthal, S., Milam, D.: Assassin's creed: a multicultural read. In: Loading..., vol. 2, no. 3 (2008)
9. Gomes, L., Bellon, O.R.P., Silva, L.: 3D reconstruction methods for digital preservation of cultural heritage: a survey. Pattern Recogn. Lett. 50, 3–14 (2014)
10. Grün, A., Remondino, F., Zhang, L.: Photogrammetric reconstruction of the great Buddha of Bamiyan, Afghanistan. Photogram. Rec. 19(107), 177–199 (2004)

11. Haddad, N.A.: Multimedia and cultural heritage: a discussion for the community involved in children's heritage edutainment and serious games in the 21st century. Virtual Archaeol. Rev. **7**(14), 61–73 (2016)
12. Izadi, S., et al.: KinectFusion: real-time 3D reconstruction and interaction using a moving depth camera. In: Proceedings of the 24th Annual ACM Symposium on User Interface Software and Technology, pp. 559–568 (2011)
13. Kahne, J., Middaugh, E., Evans, C.: The Civic Potential of Video Games. The MIT Press, Cambridge (2009)
14. Keebler, J.R., Shelstad, W.J., Smith, D.C., Chaparro, B.S., Phan, M.H.: Validation of the GUESS-18: a short version of the Game User Experience Satisfaction Scale (GUESS). J. Usability Stud. **16**(1), 49 (2020)
15. Levoy, M., et al.: The digital Michelangelo project: 3D scanning of large statues. In: Proceedings of the 27th Annual Conference on Computer Graphics and Interactive Techniques, pp. 131–144 (2000)
16. Majewski, J.: Cultural heritage in role-playing video games: a map of approaches. Furnace **2**, 24–36 (2015)
17. Mortara, M., Catalano, C.E., Bellotti, F., Fiucci, G., Houry-Panchetti, M., Petridis, P.: Learning cultural heritage by serious games. J. Cult. Herit. **15**(3), 318–325 (2014)
18. Ouariachi, T., Olvera-Lobo, M.D., Gutiérrez-Pérez, J., Maibach, E.: A framework for climate change engagement through video games. Environ. Educ. Res. **25**(5), 701–716 (2019)
19. Phan, M.H., Keebler, J.R., Chaparro, B.S.: The development and validation of the game user experience satisfaction scale (GUESS). Hum. Factors **58**(8), 1217–1247 (2016)
20. Picard, M., Fandango, G.: Video games and their relationship with other media. The video game explosion: a history from Pong to Playstation and beyond, pp. 293–300 (2008)
21. Raimundo, P.O., Apaza-Agüero, K., Apolinário, A.L., Jr.: Low-cost 3D reconstruction of cultural heritage artifacts. Revista Brasileira de Computação Aplicada **10**(1), 66–75 (2018)
22. Röll, V., Meyer, C.: Young people's perceptions of world cultural heritage: suggestions for a critical and reflexive world heritage education. Sustainability **12**(20), 8640 (2020)
23. United Nations: Transforming our world: the 2030 Agenda for Sustainable Development. shorturl.at/uO468
24. Utomo, A.P., Wibowo, C.P.: 3D reconstruction of temples in the special region of yogyakarta by using close-range photogrammetry. arXiv preprint arXiv:1702.06722 (2017)

3D Digital Heritage and Historical Storytelling: Outcomes from the Interreg EMR Terra Mosana Project

Muriel van Ruymbeke[1]([⊠]) [iD], Eslam Nofal[2] [iD], and Roland Billen[1] [iD]

[1] Geomatics Unit, Liège University, Allée du 6 Août, 19, 4000 Liège, Belgium
{mvanruymbeke,rbillen}@uliege.be
[2] Faculty of Engineering, Department of Architecture, Assiut University, Assiut 71511, Egypt
eslam.nofal@aun.edu.eg

Abstract. This paper will explain how the activities undertaken in the Terra Mosana project have combined the writing of new heritage narratives with the creation of digital 3D virtual experiences. The main objective of the project was to strengthen the sense of belonging to the same community for the citizens of the Euregio Meuse-Rhine by recreating their common history and heritage in 3D. This was achieved through virtual and augmented reality experiences based on cross-border and renewed historical storylines.

Keywords: 3D digital experiences · Digital heritage · Digital narratives

1 Introduction

Most often understood as "the use of 3D data of heritage sites or monuments" [1], the domain of 3D digital heritage remains, until today, mainly a scientific topic for archaeologists, architects, geomaticians and computer scientists. Indeed, some scientific papers have pointed out that the current use of 3D digital heritage is reserved for a scientific elite and does not really benefit the general public. Moreover, a recent study demonstrated that these data were not sustainable [2]. For this reason, these researchers recommend that 3D digital heritage data should also be thought of in terms of sustainable educational resources.

Historical storytelling plays "a fundamental role both as a discipline in itself and as a connective tissue of other disciplines, a way of anchoring cultural experiences in their own time and at the same time of considering them in a diachronic dimension, to understand the past and our complicated present" [3]. But, as two recent studies have shown, the historical narrative, whether urban, regional, national or international, is never neutral. It carries political, cultural or even cognitive biases [4, 5]. The emergence of the use of 3D for cultural heritage has an undeniable impact on the way historical facts are presented and therefore, and it is not surprising, the concept of historical storytelling is sometimes understood as the power to model several phases of the evolution of an object in the form of sequences [6, 7]. The reflection about the historical narratives developed around digital data also focuses on the audience interested in this type of new media. The public often appreciates being involved, such as by being consulted in advance and having their opinions considered [8–10].

Based on the implementation and exploitation of 3D Digital Heritage experiments, the main objective of the Interreg Euregio Meuse-Rhine (EMR) Terra Mosana project was to strengthen the sense of belonging to the same region by the citizens of the Euregio. In order to strengthen this sense of belonging, several authors had shown that it was necessary to radically transform the way history and heritage are usually transmitted [11]. History taught in schools is presented in a predominantly national framework. Events do not cross borders, neither does heritage. However, "the constitution of the transnational as a central object of analysis shifts things significantly. It shifts the focus from simply 'international' issues to the flows themselves, to the circulations, the intermediaries, the interconnected and crossed histories" [12].

The different partners of the Terra Mosana project were therefore given a triple mission. Firstly, they had to work on the cross-border presentation of historical facts and heritage data. Secondly, they had to exploit the new stories with digital 3D products and finally, they had to involve the public in order to find out their preferences and, if possible, take their recommendations into account. At first sight, these three constraints seemed heavy and difficult to combine. However, it appeared that each aspect could represent a potential enrichment for the other two as the following paper will show.

2 Background on the Terra Mosana Project

The expression "Terra Mosana" refers to a territory, bathed by the river Meuse, which crosses it from south to north. This area is currently shared between three countries, the Netherlands, Germany and Belgium, and covers four provinces: the province of Liège, the province of Belgian Limburg, the Land of North Rhine-Westphalia, and the province of Dutch Limburg (see Fig. 1). This area is completely included in the slightly larger EMR area. It should be pointed out that all the activities undertaken within the funded project, also titled Terra Mosana, were aimed at the public of the EMR territory and even, in general, at tourists and cultural public.

Launched on 1 June 2018 and closed on 30 November 2021, Terra Mosana brought together twelve funded partners as well as some non-funded institutions. The funded partners consisted of five cities (Maastricht, Aachen-Liège, Tongeren and Leopoldsburg), four universities (ULiège, Maastricht University, RWTH and the KULeuven) and three museum institutions (the citadel of Jülich, the Archéoforum of Liège (AWAP) and the Be-Mine project of Beringen. The project partners had different backgrounds varying from historians, archaeologists, and heritage professionals to developers, computer scientists, economists, and communication specialists. Each partner joined the project with different skills and the activities they carried out were related to their resources and the means at their disposal.

Fig. 1. Terra Mosana Map: Medium grey on the Est corresponds to North Rhine-Westphalia, light grey is Dutch Limburg, medium grey on the West is Belgian Limburg and dark grey is the province of Liège. The hatched areas indicate the German-speaking parts of the Province of Liège.

3   Methodology

To provide a brief overview, multiple methodologies were used in the Terra Mosana project activities, which were organised into five work packages. The activities and results presented below took place within the three work packages titled "project sustainability strategy", "EMR digital storytelling" and "On-site digital experiences."

The work package "project sustainability strategy" covered the issues of intellectual property rights, sustainability of project outputs, but also participatory surveys and workshops to sound out the potential audience for their experiences and stories to be included. The work package "EMR digital storyline" consisted of selecting and telling historical facts and phenomena in a connected and cross-border way. At that point, it should be noted that before the beginning of the 19th century, the notion of border, as we understand it today, did not exist and the inhabitants of the Euregio interacted in a less compartmentalised way than today. The Terra Mosana partners wanted to highlight these interactions [13]. The narratives developed then served as the backbone of the activities undertaken in the work package "On-site digital experiences". These experiences used 3D technologies to reconstruct virtual settings but also to provide access to existing monuments and sites, where access to certain areas is difficult. The augmented reality and VR reconstructions offered to the public allowed people to immerse themselves in the past, in various forms depending on the site visited.

3.1 The Narrative Themes

Before surveying the public about scenarios that might be of interest to them, the partners chose to work on defining important themes to be addressed. By meeting several times for brainstorming, the different participants in the EMR digital storyline working group selected 13 themes to be presented to the different citizen panels. The criteria for choosing these themes were their temporal recurrence, their cross-border aspect and their relevance for the Terra Mosana territory.

The 13 themes examined were as follows: Mobility, Fortifications, Central Places, Religious Infrastructures, Political Infrastructures, Crafts, Urbanism, Natural Resources, War and Peace, Languages, Migration, Innovation and Intangible Heritage.

These themes were researched and interacted with by the partners in order to highlight the different aspects of each topic and how it impacted the multiple areas of the Terra Mosana territory. Then, in order to be easily understood by the workshop participants, the 13 themes were presented in an identical format, in the form of A3 posters.

3.2 Public Participation in the Terra Mosana Project

The involvement of local communities in heritage-related projects commonly generates a larger sense of shared ownership and leads to a greater chance of outcome acceptance and satisfaction among the community, resulting in a larger support base [14]. Thus, the pro-active management of project stakeholders decreases the chances of the failure of a project. Moreover, early involvement of local communities in heritage projects speeds up the process and decreases the chances that costly project revisions having to be made later [15].

The valuable experiences people have with heritage objects or sites is personal and subjective, and cannot only be shaped by relying on the expertise of museum curators and heritage professionals [16]. Therefore, to engage with new and existing audiences, more participative models of interpretation and governance are needed that involve civil society and the private sector.

One of the core qualities of the Terra Mosana project is the aspect of public participation. Throughout the project, several methods were followed in order to achieve meaningful public participation, and to involve and engage the public in the design activities of the project. Our methods included an online survey at the early phase of the project (early 2019) and interviews with stakeholders (i.e. narrative providers and technical developers) that took place in early 2020.

These were followed by a series of six participatory design workshops in late 2020 for involving and engaging the residents of Euregio Meuse-Rhine (EMR) in design activities about the investigation and communication of the shared history of the EMR through digital storytelling. During the COVID-19 crisis, we moved our participatory design workshops online and developed a scenario facilitating both synchronous and asynchronous activities. After the completion of the workshops, a focus group was organized with project partners to evaluate the participatory process of Terra Mosana. In addition, the project followed a community-engagement strategy through social media channels, official website, temporary exhibitions and on-site experiences.

Online Survey. As a preparation for the participatory design workshops, an online survey was developed in the early phase of the project and disseminated with the residents of the EMR to enable them to sort the different themes of the project, such as fortifications, languages, migration, religious infrastructure, immaterial heritage, etc. Participants were also allowed to suggest more themes or a combination of themes. The last part of the survey asked how the themes should be communicated to the public in interactive scenarios. We received a total of 400 completed surveys (190 male; 210 female) from the local community of the EMR in different languages. Our results show enough variation in the background demographics in terms of age ranges, education, place of residence, and frequency of travel. A general tendency was obtained about what themes are the most preferred, and what are the preferred ways of interaction.

Interviews with Stakeholders. The second phase of public participation focused on developing an approach to collect data through semi-structured interviews from two groups of stakeholders. First group are content providers, who are involved in writing the narratives of the project storylines (e.g. archaeologists, historians, archive managers of historical sites, etc.). The second group were related to development the outputs and technical development of media technology (e.g. communication team, technicians, technical advisors, policy makers of a cultural service, etc.). The interview questions with content providers revolved around topics such as cultural learning and public participation, while with the development team, the focus was shifted to topics such as visitor engagement and public participation. The results of the interviews were insightful for crafting the guidelines for public participation in digital heritage projects, such as how the public could co-create the content, and how the content should be presented to the public based on their interests.

Participatory Design Workshops. Participatory design is an approach of active user involvement within the field of user-centered design, enabling users to share their insights and feedback in design decisions that influence their lives [17]. Therefore, the Terra Mosana project adopted the approach of participatory design through a series of workshops that were held in different cities of the EMR. With these workshops, we wanted to involve and engage citizens in design activities about the investigation and communication of the shared history of the EMR through digital storytelling. Our main aim was to elicit local knowledge rooted in local residents' lived experiences and concerns, as well as to collect feedback on the proposed storylines and interaction designs.

The workshop dynamics were based on virtual co-creation methods that encouraged participants to tell stories collaboratively and reflect on the shared history of EMR. The insights gained from the workshops inform the writing of the storylines, and the communication of EMR shared history to the public. An average of 15 participants were recruited for each participatory design workshop, which consisted of several activities that were completed in sub-groups. The first group activity was card sorting in order to prioritize the themes of the shared history and to discover what provokes participants in their preferred theme, such as fortifications, languages, migration, religious infrastructure, immaterial heritage, etc.

The second was storyboarding to build a sequential narrative about how the chosen theme could be communicated to the public in an interactive way. This involved developing a persona as a representation of the real target audience, and then visualizing a scenario by drawing a sequential narrative of the experience and writing captions about some of the persona's actions. To this end, four online participatory design workshops were organized for the cities of Maastricht, Tongeren, Liège and Aachen.

Focus Group with Project Partners. At the end of the project, a focus group with relevant project partners was organized in order to investigate how useful and meaningful the workshops had been for the project, and to what extent the results of the workshops will be considered in developing the different outputs of Terra Mosana (e.g. exhibitions, mobile apps, and onsite experiences). The questions of the focus group revolved around three main themes: (a) the design of participatory design workshops, (b) the move of workshops to online environments, and (c) the impact of workshops on the objectives of Terra Mosana.

3.3 The Storylines Writing

Within the 13 themes, and considering the preferences and recommendations given by the workshops' participants, 23 storylines were written [18]. The main principle behind the writing of each storyline was that it should tell a fragment of the common history of the Euregio in an innovative way. It was also necessary to go beyond geographical boundaries and the limits of our usual modes of representation. To this end, the storyline writers used the "Historical 3D Matrix - model" method developed in 2016 by Eric Wetzels who was also a Terra Mosana partner in the name of Maastricht municipality [19].

Elaborating these storylines, as with the themes, required a lot of research beforehand. One very important aspect was to ask for a lot of information exchange between the different partners. Since the format of the storylines was deliberately cross-border, each storyline author asked his or her partner(s) to provide any "local" elements of interest for the subject being dealt with. For example, for the storyline "1673" about the siege of Maastricht by the French armies (during which the musketeer d'Artagnan was killed), the Dutch partners asked all the other participants to provide them with a list of archival documents or museum objects (such as weapons) for example [20].

4 The Example of Moving Central Places Theme

The moving Central Places theme explains the fact that the territory covered by the Terra Mosana project has known several central places, which can be viewed as "ephemeral capitals" [21, 22]. Contrary to neighboring regions, in the Terra Mosana territory, the seeds of temporal, spiritual or judicial power moved several times.

Initially, the territory was a Roman city - state (*civitas*) before being a diocese in the modern sense. This territory has known various forms of unity (political, religious, cultural, economic, …) for about 15 centuries, from 10 BC (approximate date of the creation of the city of Tongeren) until 1559 AD, the date of the reform of the dioceses of Philip II of Spain, which considerably reduced the size of the medieval diocese. Like other city states and regions of the Gallo-Roman provinces, the *Civitas Tungrorum* was likely the basis for the constitution of the diocese of the Christian Church, which took the name of its new capital Liège around the 8th century. From then on, the medieval texts refer to *Civitas Leodium*, which is translated as the bishopric or diocese of Liège, whose borders remained until 1559. During the Middle Ages and besides Tongres, Maastricht and Liège, the important cities of this diocese were notably Louvain, Looz, Aachen, Limburg, Namur, Bouillon [23, 24].

Before the achievement of the roman conquest during the 1st century BC, the Eburons were occupying the territory corresponding to the current provinces of Liège, Belgian and Dutch Limburg and the region of Aachen. Although several hypotheses exist on this subject, the location of their capital, *Atuatuca*, is still unknown today. When the Romans had completed their conquest, they created a new municipality, capital of the city – state: *civitas Tungrorum*. They founded and named its capital "*Atuatuca Tungrorum*" (today Tongeren) [21, 25]. In addition to an administrative and economic centre, Tongeren became, at the latest from the 4th century, the see of a bishopric which took its name. From that time also, the bishops exercised judicial power. In the 6th century, the bishop's see was transferred to Maastricht probably by St Monulphe. Since the middle of the 5th century Tongeren has been almost deserted. Maastricht on the contrary was a living and fortified city [22].

At the end of the 7th century, or at the beginning of the 8th century, the Bishop of Tongeren-Maastricht Lambert was killed in Liège. He was first buried in Maastricht but, following the emotion caused by his death, the site of his assassination became a place of pilgrimage. In 718 at the latest, his body was brought back to Liège for a secondary burial. The bishopric see (the bishop's religious jurisdiction that crosses, at that time, political borders) followed and was also transferred to Liège, probably at the end of the 8th century. In 985, the Bishop of Liège also became a temporal lord who ruled over an area directly under the authority of the Emperor of the Holy German Empire [24]. He died in Aachen and was buried in the Palatine Chapel in 814. It was here that, from 936 and for the 600 following years, the Emperors of the Holy Roman Empire were crowned [26, 27].

4.1   The Storyline

The written storyline focuses on how the transfer of the episcopal see from Maastricht to Liège is an indirect consequence of the assassination of Saint Lambert in Liège, both a criminal case and a historical fact that has conditioned the whole regional history. Liège's first settlement in historic times was a Roman villa. Lambertus is said to have been killed in "the roman *villa*", but he was probably murdered in part of the *villa*, which was re-used, probably using the existing stone walls and covering it with a new roof. Unlike the sites of Namur, Huy or Maastricht in particular, Liège does not seem to have developed artisanal zones during antiquity or the very early Middle Ages. At that period, Liège was a little off-centre in relation to the main traffic axes: upstream of the ford between Herstal and Jupille, two roman *vici* located along the road that linked Tongeren to Trier. These two *vici* provided housing structures equipped with thermal baths and decorated with mosaic pavements, necropolises for incineration, storage areas and craft areas. A small temple dedicated to Apollo was also discovered in Jupille.

Bishop Lambert. Lambert was an aristocrat, born in Maastricht in the middle of the 7th century in a noble family. Maastricht was already at that time the episcopal see of Tongeren-Maastricht. Lambert gained importance under the Merovingian king Childeric II, who in 675, was assassinated and then a very unstable period ensued. In 679 or 680 Pépin de Herstal seized power in Austrasia as mayor of the Palace. In the meantime, bishop Lambert had been deposed in favour of Pharamond who ran the church of Tongeren-Maastricht for seven years. In 682 Pharamond was deposed in his turn and Pépin de Herstal restored Lambert on the episcopal throne. One can think from all these events that there was, at that time, a clan hostile to Lambert's clan and that the death of Childeric II strengthened this clan, then that the coming to power of Pépin de Herstal weakened it. At that time, the struggle of family groups for local territorial power was common. It is also likely that this clan and power feud was the cause of the assassination of Saint Lambert. Lambert's murder is thus one episode among others of a clan war, a *vendetta* [28, 29].

Assassination of Lambert. During the night of 17 September of an unknown year between 696 and 705, Lambert was murdered in the village of Liège. According to the *Vita vetustissima*, an anonymous document written between 727 and 743, two members of Lambert's clan, perhaps even his nephews, Petrus and Autlaecus, would have killed Gallus and Rivaldus, two brothers, relatives or in any case members of Dodon's clan. It would therefore be the one who, in retaliation, would be at the instigation of the bishop's murder. According to the *Vita vetustissima* still, the attackers would have entered the place where Lambert was gathering; one of them would have climbed on the roof, removed the vegetal covering and killed the bishop with a spear.

At first, Lambert had an aristocratic reflex, that of taking up a weapon. Then he renounced it and behaved like a man of God. Given the exemplary nature of his life (and death), Lambert was immediately considered as a martyr and a saint. Dodon and his clan were powerful and even the mayor of the Palace, Pepin de Herstal, was relatively powerless. Perhaps it is to erase this relative impotence, another explanation for the assassination was that the second wife (or concubine) of Pepin de Herstal, Alpaïde, would have asked Dodon (presented in this version as her brother) to eliminate Saint Lambert. The reason given by later authors of this version is that Lambert would have reproached Pepin for his relationship with Alpaïde. Contemporary historians have broken this legend in order to re-establish a narrative closer to the actual course of events [28, 29].

After the Murder. Just after Lambert's murder his successor, Bishop Hubert, brought his body by boat to the Saint Peter's church of Maastricht, probably the current Saint Servatius church. In Liège, however, emotions quickly grew up around the place of the murder, where then miracles began to happen. The cult of Saint Lambert developed to the point that a first building (a basilica), placed under the patronage of Notre-Dame, was built.

Several years after the assassination, Bishop Hubert had Lambert's relics returned to Liège to be buried in the newly constructed building. From then on, the site became a place of pilgrimage. The war of the clans that had killed Saint Lambert continued, since in 714 Grimoald II (son and designated successor of the mayor of the palace of Pepin de Herstal, who died the same year) was assassinated while he was praying at the tomb of Saint Lambert in Liège. It can therefore be assumed that Lambert's body had already been brought back from Maastricht at that time and that therefore the assassination of Saint Lambert is in fact prior to 705 and, it could have been 17 September 705 [30–33].

It is difficult to know exactly when the see of the bishopric was transferred from Maastricht to Liège. It must certainly have been between the middle of the 8th century and the beginning of the following century. All the successors of Pepin II: Charles Martel, then Pepin III and then Charlemagne regularly resided in their palaces in the Liège region, notably Charlemagne who celebrated Easter in Liège in 770 and in Herstal in 784. We also know, thanks to archaeology, that the first building built after Lambert's death was replaced by a larger Carolingian edifice. The latter probably coincides with the double cathedral dedicated to Saint-Lambert and Notre-Dame erected when the seat of the bishopric was transferred. From then on, Liège became the centre of a bishopric, and then of an episcopal principality. For almost a thousand years, the city's physiognomy was marked by the juxtaposed presence of a cathedral and an episcopal palace. This functional duality of the place was broken shortly after the French and Liège revolutions when, in 1794, the revolutionaries began the demolition of the cathedral, which they considered to be the symbol of the power of the prince bishop [34, 35].

Impact of the Transfer of the Bishopric See. The murder of Saint Lambert and its indirect consequence, the transfer of the episcopal see, had a considerable influence on the history of the city of Liège but also on regional history. Let us note however that three elements contributed to increase the consequences of this various fact: Hubert's choice to bring the body back to Liège, the devotion of the Pippinides family (who later became Carolingian) and finally the setting up, just before the year 1000, of the system of the Imperial Church which made the chief town of the diocese the capital of a territorial state. Once this configuration was in place, Liège acquired a religious, political and economic position of primary importance at the regional (and even international at certain times) level. Its architecture and town planning benefited from this, as did the territory of the former *civitas tungrorum*, which became the Principality of Liège and was therefore entirely reorganised around this new centre.

4.2   From Storytelling to 3D Experiences

The places chosen to set up the two 3D virtual immersion experiments resulting from the Central Place storyline are located under the current Place Saint Lambert in Liège. They are both situated inside the Archéoforum of the Walloon Agency for Archaeology and Heritage (AWAP). The Archéoforum of Liège is both a museum and an archaeological site. It is located underneath the current Place Saint-Lambert and covers more than 3,725 m². Excavations in the Place Saint Lambert have brought to light remains dating back almost 9,000 years. Mesolithic, Gallo-Roman, Merovingian, Carolingian, Romanesque and Gothic traces are still visible today. With them, the roots of Liège have been carefully preserved. Indeed, it was here in an annex of the Gallo-Roman villa, that Bishop Lambert was murdered at the beginning of the 8th century.

The Archéoforum offers visitors a museum trail through the still preserved remains: from the Gallo-Roman villa to the foundations of the Gothic cathedral, each period is physically represented by fragments of walls, architectural elements or objects from daily life. The scenography is structured around a timeline, evoking the urban landscape over the centuries. A series of showcases containing numerous previously unseen pieces from the collections and reserves of the Grand Curtius and the Walloon Region's Provincial Archaeology Service punctuate the tour and explore the various themes addressed. The Archéoforum also provides its visitors with interactive digital tablets. Quadrilingual, they offer, with flexibility and simplicity, an exceptional set of documents. They cover topics as varied as excavation techniques, conservation measures, daily life in a Gallo-Roman villa and the construction of cathedrals. Therefore, the two 3D experiments had to fit into a pre-existing museographic project that had to be complemented in a relevant way. They also had to fit into a symbolically charged environment.

Archéoforum 3D Experience 1: The first crypt was built by Prince Bishop Notger as a shrine to house the relics of St. Lambert and to allow pilgrims to worship. The crypt was likely built on the site of the martyrium, i.e., the place where Lambert was murdered around the year 700. At the moment, it is difficult for the visitor to imagine that this sort of cellar was originally a wooden hut, which stood against the Roman villa. It is also difficult to imagine the interior of the Notgerian crypt, which was so popular in the 11th century.

The virtual reality (VR) experience manages to re-implant a 3D digital Merovingian hut in the place where it was originally located. The assassination of Lambert is evoked through a filmed scene embedded in the virtual hut. In a second step, this hut is then transformed into the 3D modelled interior of the 11th century crypt. The shrine containing the relics of St. Lambert is shown and pilgrims walk around the shrine.

Fig. 2. Positioning of two screens – doors to the past into the current crypt remains

The reproduction of these two scenes is carried out through two immersive devices positioned in the ruins of the Crypt. The exact positioning of these devices is described in Fig. 2. These devices are made up of a vertical television, a computer and a camera sensitive to the movements of the viewer. The camera is placed on the top edge of the television. It follows the movement of the head of the viewer watching the television, and when the viewer moves his or her head, the image is adapted to give the effect that the viewer is looking through a window and not a television.

Archéoforum 3D Experience 2: The hemi-dome allows visitors to observe the current tangle of western walls of the various buildings that succeeded the Gallo-Roman villa following Lambert's assassination. These buildings are: the Merovingian church, the Carolingian cathedral, the Notgerian - Romanesque cathedral, and the Gothic cathedral.

The position of the visitor's area is outside these ancient buildings. In the current state of the room, it is rather difficult to make non-specialists aware of two important things, such as where they are in relation to St. Lambert's Square or the actual elevation of the ancient buildings. The VR experience helps to answer these two questions. Visitors can witness the successive reconstruction of each of these walls, from the most recent to the oldest, using virtual glasses. The viewer - manipulator of the virtual helmet - can explore these old gables by deciding where to point his binoculars. Then the walls disappear to make way for the Gallo-Roman villa. The visitor steps back and gradually rises into the air. They discover the Roman landscape and begin a slow aerial rotation around the site and witness its evolution over time.

Softwares and Other Technical Questions: The two experiences of the Archéoforum were designed following the same creative protocol. First of all, the computer graphics designers used the point clouds of the archaeological sites obtained by laser scan. To reconstruct the buildings in elevation, they used the excavation plans and established a dialogue with the archaeologists for the details of the elevations (superstructures, textures etc....). The 3D models were designed using Unity software.

5   Discussion

Archéoforum onsite experiences 1 and 2 are intended to complement the existing museographic arsenal. It aims to offer visitors an experience that enriches their understanding of the site and the remains that are still visible. It helps them, in an interactive and stimulating way, to understand several elements such as where they are, or how the ruins are located comparing with the current urban infrastructures.

In comparison with other scientific teams working on similar projects [36], we also used a laser scan and a point cloud for our two experiments. However, we used this field data to set the virtual scene. We then detached ourselves from modelling reality in favour of a modelled historical reconstruction. An important choice was made here to let storytelling drive development and technical decisions, not the other way around.

For these models and reconstructions, we also adopted a resolutely didactic and non-spectacular position. Our aim was not to make visitors feel like they were in a cinema, but to make them exercise their critical thinking and curiosity, because they were in a museum. From a more general point of view, the three missions that Terra Mosana's partners had to fulfil influenced each other to the point of increasing their respective benefits. Since the projects have been recently launched, we cannot yet present feedback from visitors. These opinions will obviously be taken into account in the near future.

Public participation influenced the storylines by showing a greater interest in topics related to contemporary issues. It also influenced the choice of the implementation of the onsite experiences by favouring experiences delivered in a mixed form (mixing virtual and real). The writing of storylines has had an obvious impact on 3D experiences since it has provided them with a subject and the framework for the scenarios implemented. The storytelling, resolutely turned towards a cross-border point of view, had an impact on the audience because they were presented with an international perspective, which is not common in these types of digitally reconstructed historical experiences to date (Fig. 3).

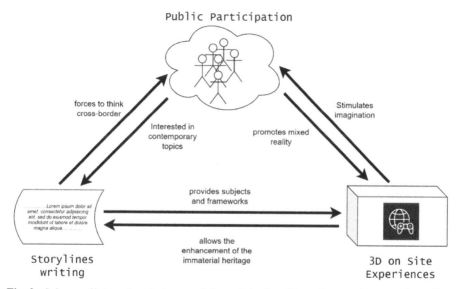

Fig. 3. Schema of interactions between public participation, 3D on site experiences and storylines writing

Finally, the onsite 3D experiments influenced the user panels involved in participatory workshops by stimulating their imagination, but we can speak here of an impact 'in absentia'. At the time of the participatory workshops, the experiments did not yet exist, so the participants were therefore free to imagine any type of digital restitution such as an augmented reality application following the visitors of an exhibition to provide them with the explanations of the documents exposed in real time. Finally, these experiments also influenced storytelling by allowing authors to tackle historical or heritage issues that were detached from the "only possible" (that is the tangible locations visible today) to tackle intangible events or places.

Besides these undeniable gains however, one limitation was that we did not manage to express the transregional aspect of the subject matter to the level we desired to implement within the experiences. Moreover, the deadlines for the realization of the 3D models and the pre-established choice of their locations placed some constraints on the participatory workshops and the writing. Therefore, some recommendations from the participatory workshops, which came after the choice of the storyline, could not be included. This led to a learning for future project planning that we should organize the order of the methodology differently for the story construction process.

6 Conclusion

In conclusion, it can be recalled that the actors of the Terra Mosana project had to overcome several challenges. These included, establishing an efficient collaboration between 12 partners coming from different disciplines, using different modes of operation, and they had several tasks to fulfil. They needed to obtain public participation, write cross-border storylines and base the onsite 3D experiments on the pre-established 13 story themes. We demonstrated that the Terra Mosana project largely overcame the difficulties along the way and succeeded in producing 3D onsite experiences based on original scenarios that were themselves partly inspired by suggestions from the public. However, there is still work to be done to connect all these achievements across the project partners' outputs into a global framework and to further increase the visibility and marketing efforts. Here too, public and citizen participation will prove to be a very important asset.

Acknowledgements. The Terra Mosana project was made possible thanks to the financial support of Interreg Euregio Meuse Rhine, the Walloon Region, the Land of North Rhine-Westphalia, the Province of Limburg in the Netherlands and the Province of Limburg in Belgium.

References

1. Grilli, E., Remondino, F.: Classification of 3D digital heritage. Remote Sens. (Basel, Switz.) **11**, 847 (2019). https://doi.org/10.3390/rs11070847
2. Champion, E., Rahaman, H.: 3D digital heritage models as sustainable scholarly resources. Sustainability (Basel, Switz.) **11**, 2425 (2019). https://doi.org/10.3390/su11082425
3. Frontani, N.: Historic storytelling: living the past, looking at the present with different eyes. Italiano a scuola **2**, 201–210 (2020). https://doi.org/10.6092/issn.2704-8128/10894
4. Braun, S.: L'après chute du Mur et la construction d'un narratif historique commun franco-allemand: l'interprétation des trente ans de la chute du Mur dans la presse allemande et française. Allemagne d'aujourd'hui **233**, 123–139 (2020). https://doi.org/10.3917/all.233.0123
5. Pappalardo, M.: Narrations et appropriations dans le centre historique de Naples : des constructions identitaires situées. Les Cahiers d'EMAM. Études sur le Monde Arabe et la Méditerranée (2019). https://doi.org/10.4000/emam.2064
6. Brusaporci, S., Ruggieri, G., Sicuranza, F., Maiezza, P.: Augmented reality for historical storytelling. The INCIPICT project for the reconstruction of tangible and intangible image of L'Aquila historical centre. In: Proceedings, vol. 1, p. 1083 (2017). https://doi.org/10.3390/proceedings1091083

7. Brusaporci, S., Graziosi, F., Franchi, F., Maiezza, P., Tata, A.: Mixed reality experiences for the historical storytelling of cultural heritage. In: Bolognesi, C., Villa, D. (eds.) From Building Information Modelling to Mixed Reality, pp. 33–46. Springer, Cham (2021). https://doi.org/10.1007/978-3-030-49278-6_3

8. Wonneberger, A., Kim, S.J.: TV news exposure of young people in changing viewing environments: a longitudinal, cross-national comparison using people-meter data. Int. J. Commun. (19328036) **11**, 72–93 (2017)

9. Rosas, O.: Public engagement with, and trust in, online news media in French-speaking Belgium. Recherches en Commun. **40**, 169–187 (2013)

10. Mascheroni, G.: A practice-based approach to online participation: young people's participatory habitus as a source of diverse online engagement. Int. J. Commun. (19328036) **11**, 4630–4651 (2017)

11. Tchernia-Blanchard, M.: De Paris à New York. Charles Sterling et l'écriture d'une histoire de l'art transnationale au musée. Revue germanique internationale (Evry) **21**, 207–218 (2015). https://doi.org/10.4000/rgi.1533

12. Pestre, D.: Épistémologie et politique des science and transnational studies. Revue d'anthropologie des connaissances **6**, 469–492 (2012). https://doi.org/10.3917/rac.017.0001

13. European Association of Archaeologists: Terra Mosana: a crossborder identity newly explained. https://www.youtube.com/watch?v=XsyCt8vQuqU. Accessed 31 Jan 2022

14. Hajialikhani, M.: A systematic stakeholders management approach for protecting the spirit of cultural heritage sites. In: Presented at the 16th ICOMOS General Assembly and International Symposium: "Finding the Spirit of Place – Between the Tangible and the Intangible", Quebec (2008)

15. James, O.: Public Participation in Heritage Redevelopment Projects: An Improvement of Public Participation in the Planning Phase of Heritage Redevelopment Projects in the Netherlands (2016). https://research.tue.nl/en/studentTheses/public-participation-in-heritage-redevelopment-projects

16. Nofal, E., van Saaze, V., Wyatt, S.: Online Participatory Design of Heritage Projects. In: Participatory Practices in Art and Cultural Heritage: Learning Through and from Collaboration (2022, in Press)

17. Muller, M.J., Druin, J.: Participatory design: the third space in HCI. In: The Human-Computer Interaction Handbook: Fundamentals, Evolving Technologies and Emerging Applications, pp. 1051–1068. CRC Press (2008). https://doi.org/10.1201/9781410615862

18. Wetzels, E.: Digital storylines in Terra Mosana. In: Terra Mosana Closing Conference 2021 (2021)

19. Wetzels, E.: The Historical 3D Matrix-model 2016 (H3DM©CHAM)

20. Wetzels, E.: Terra Mosana Storyline Craftsmanship The killing of d'Artagnan in Maastricht in 1673 (2021)

21. Vanderhoeven, A.: Tongres/Atuatuca (Belgique). In: Ferdière, A. (ed.) Capitales éphémères. Des capitales de cités perdent leur statut dans l'antiquité tardive. 25è Supplément à la Revue Archéologique du centre de la France, pp. 481–485, Tours (2004)

22. Raepsaet-Charlier, M.-T., Vanderhoeven, A.: Tongres au Bas-Empire romain. In: Ferdière, A. (ed.) Capitales éphémères. Des capitales de cités perdent leur statut dans l'antiquité tardive. 25è Supplément à la Revue Archéologique du centre de la France, pp. 51–73, Tours (2004)

23. Rolland, J.-N.: L'évêché de Liège sous le règne de Charlemagne: Fulchaire, Agilfrid, Gerbaud, Walcaud (2014)

24. Demoulin, B., et al.: Histoire de Liège: une cité, une capitale, une métropole. Editions Marot, Bruxelles (2017)

25. Grisart, A.: L'Atuatuca césarienne au Fort de Chaudfontaine? L'Antiquité Classique **50**, 367–381 (1981). https://doi.org/10.3406/antiq.1981.2017

26. Werner, M.: Der Lütticher Raum in frühkarolingischer Zeit: Untersuchungen zur Geschichte einer karolingischen Stammlandschaft. Vandenhoeck & Ruprecht, Göttingen (1980)

27. Dierkens, A.: Im Zentrum der karolingischen Macht im 8. Jahrhundert: Herstal, Jupille und Chèvremont. In: Pohle, F. (ed.) Karl der Grosse/Charlemagne. Orte der Macht. Essays, pp. 210–217. Sandstein Verlag, Dresden (2014)

28. Kupper, J.-L.: Saint Lambert: de l'histoire à la légende. Revue d'Histoire Ecclésiastique **79**, 5–49 (1984)

29. Kupper, J.-L.: Saint Lambert: de l'histoire à la légende. Fondation Saint-Lambert, Liège (1993)

30. Kupper, J.-L.: Du VIIè siècle à 1468. La cité médiévale. In: Demoulin, B. (ed.) Histoire de Liège: une cité, une capitale, une métropole, pp. 47–78. Editions Marot, Bruxelles (2017)

31. Henrard, D., van Der Sloot, P., Léotard, J.-M.: La villa de la place Saint-Lambert à Liège (Belgique): nouvel état des connaissances. Revue du Nord **378**, 157–174 (2008)

32. Henrard, D., Léotard, J.-M.: Liège au Haut Moyen Âge: un état de la question. In: Proceedings of the 60th Sachsensymposion, pp. 47–54, Maastricht (2011)

33. de la Haye, R. (ed.): Lambertus, laatste bisschop van Maastricht. Hubertus, eerste bisschop van Luik. Hun eigentijdse evensbeschrijvingen. Publications de la Société Historique et Archéologique dans le Limbourg, pp. 9–66 (2007)

34. Kupper, J.-L.: Archéologie et histoire: aux origines de la cité de Liège (VIIIe–XIe siècle). In: The La genèse et les premiers siècles des villes médiévales dans les Pays-Bas méridionaux: un problème archéologique et historique: 14e colloque international de Spa, 6–8 Septembre 1988, Bruxelles (1990)

35. Kupper, J.-L.: Liège au VIIIe siècle: naissance d'une ville sanctuaire, Luxembourg (2000)

36. Van Nguyen, S., Le, S.T., Tran, M.K., Tran, H.M.: Reconstruction of 3D digital heritage objects for VR and AR applications. J. Inf. Telecommun. 1–16 (2021). (Print). Ahead-of-print. https://doi.org/10.1080/24751839.2021.2008133

Culture and Computing in Arts
and Music

Investigation of Art Abstraction Using AI and Psychological Experiment

Cong Hung Mai[1]([✉]), Naoko Tosa[2], Takashi Kusumi[2], and Ryohei Nakatsu[2]([✉])

[1] Osaka University, Toyonaka 560-0043, Japan
mai.cong.hung.t3f@osaka-u.ac.jp
[2] Kyoto University, Kyoto 606-8501, Japan
{tosa.naoko.5c,kusumi.takashi.7u}@kyoto-u.ac.jp,
ryohei.nakatsu@design.kyoto-u.ac.jp

Abstract. The history of painting began as drawing natural objects, and modern painting has entered the era of abstract painting. Although the relationship between the real things and the figurative paintings that depict them is clear, real things and abstract paintings have not yet been clarified. On the other hand, AI has made rapid progress in recent years, and new technologies such as converting photographs into art-like images have emerged. This study examines the relationship between abstract paintings and natural objects by combining the AI style transfer function and psychological experiment.

Keywords: Abstract art · Abstraction · GANS · Style transfer · Psychological experiment

1 Introduction

The history of painting began as drawing the landscapes and other natural things around us as accurately as possible and gradually began to express them abstractly. Moreover, modern painting has entered the era of abstract painting. What and how does painting abstract and express? This question has been discussed in various ways, but it has not been clarified yet. Traditional discussions are primarily by art experts, and there are few examples of science and technology approaching this issue.

On the other hand, AI based on deep learning has made rapid progress in recent years [1]. New technologies emerge to generate fake images of exact human faces [2] and convert photos into art-like images of a particular genre [3]. Can these new AI technologies approach painting evaluation and abstraction issues in art?

In this research, we will approach the issue of what paintings are trying to abstract by examining the relationship between paintings and real things using the style transfer function of AI. We use the AI style transfer function to convert a natural object into an image with a specific art style and evaluate whether the conversion is successful or not. If the evaluation result is good, there is a strong relationship between the real thing and the art style. In other words, the art style is an abstraction of reality. We adopted the methodology of the psychological evaluation experiment to evaluate the image obtained by the style transfer. By combining AI's style transfer function and psychological evaluation experiments, we approach what painting is trying to abstract.

M. Rauterberg (Ed.): HCII 2022, LNCS 13324, pp. 279–290, 2022.
https://doi.org/10.1007/978-3-031-05434-1_18

2   Related Works

2.1   Art Style Transfer Using CycleGAN

Recent advances in AI have created new technologies called GANs [1]. GANs consist of generation networks that try to generate images as close to the real thing as possible and identification networks that try to distinguish between real and fake images as accurately as possible, as shown in Fig. 1. It has the characteristic that training converges with fewer training samples.

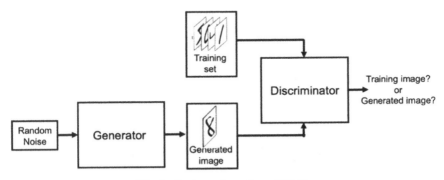

Fig. 1. Basic configuration of GANs

Among various GANs, we focused on CycleGAN [3]. CycleGAN aims to generate an image similar to the original image by reconverting the converted image, as shown in Fig. 2. CycleGAN allows mutual conversion between two image sets. For example, using this capability, a photo can be converted into a Monet-like image, as shown in Fig. 3, called the style transfer function.

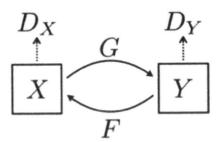

Fig. 2. Basic concept of CycleGAN

Fig. 3. Conversion between landscape photos and Monet painting using CycleGAN [2]

2.2 Research on Art Style and Art Abstraction

Research on how people evaluate the art, especially painting, began in the late 19th century when Fechner began experimental aesthetics to measure people's emotions, such as comfort and discomfort, quantitatively. Since then, various studies in psychology have been conducted to investigate the beauty of art and the emotions that derive from it. Various studies have also been conducted on art style research.

For example, Okada and Inoue [4] conducted a psychological experiment on whether figurative painting or abstract painting was preferred and showed that figurative painting was preferred. Farkas [5] investigated people's favorite works of art using Surrealist paintings and found that famous artworks were preferred. As a study investigating the differences in the evaluation of paintings between art professionals and amateurs, Winston and Cupchik [6] experimented on whether professionals and amateurs prefer fine art paintings or mundane paintings. As a result, it was found that experts prefer fine arts, and amateurs prefer secular paintings. Elina Pihko et al. [7] also studied how professionals and amateurs change their assessments as the abstraction of paintings progresses. They found that, while experts do not change much in their assessments as the abstraction progresses, the evaluation value by amateurs decreases as the abstraction progresses.

Much research has been done on what and how art is abstracted [8, 9], but all are qualitative based on the subjective opinions of art experts. Few types of research from the science and technology side have approached this issue.

3   Relationship Between Real Things and Art

In this paper, we try to approach the issue of what the painting is trying to abstract by combining the style transfer function of CycleGAN and the psychological evaluation experiment. The basic idea is as follows.

By using the style transfer function of CycleGAN, it is possible to model the relationship between a real thing and a painting. Figure 4 illustrates the relationship between landscape and landscape painting, showing that the landscape painting is a transformation of the landscape. Figure 5 shows this more abstractly. Figure 5 shows that art is an expression of the essence of a real thing. If this transformation works, there is a strong relationship between the painting and the real thing. In other words, it shows that the painting takes out and expresses the essence of the real thing or abstracts the real thing.

The framework of psychological experiments by the subjects can be used to evaluate whether or not the conversion was successful. Using such a methodology makes it possible to know what the painting is trying to abstract and express.

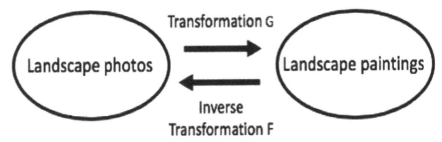

Fig. 4. Relationship between landscape photos and landscape paintings.

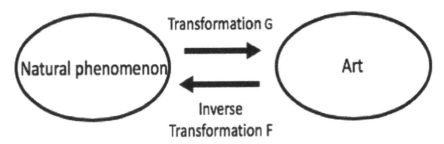

Fig. 5. Relationship between natural phenomenon and art.

4   Style Transfer of Real Things Using Cycle GAN

We will carry out experiments to investigate the relationship between real things and art using CycleGAN. To do this, we use the style transfer function of CycleGAN to convert multiple types of natural things into images with multiple art styles.

We used the following three types of paintings as abstract art of the West and the East.

(1) Ikebana (Japanese Flower Arrangement)

Ikebana expresses nature using actual flowers and plants. However, it does not represent nature as a miniature but tries to express nature with as few flowers and vegetation. Ikebana is trying to express nature in a minimalistic way. So we can think of Ikebana as art that abstractly expresses nature.

Here, we used about 500 images selected from Flicker for training CycleGAN.

(2) Shan-Shui

Shan-Shui is a painting born in China in the 5th century. At first glance, it looks like a figurative painting that expresses the natural landscape in black and white, and many people understand it as such. However, it is not a drawing of the actual natural landscape but the painter's imagination. In that sense, it can be said that the Shan-Shui is an abstract painting. Furthermore, in contrast to the perspective method that follows the laws of physics in the West, the perspective method called "San-en," which incorporates landscapes seen from multiple directions into one painting, is adopted. Therefore, Shan-Shui is an oriental abstract painting.

We used about 300 images selected by Google Image search for training CycleGAN.

(3) Kandinsky Painting

Kandinsky is considered to be the founder of Western abstract painting. Compared to recent abstract paintings, they have some relationship with real things. Therefore, we decided to use Kandinsky's painting to represent Western abstract painting.

Here, we used about 300 images selected from WikiArt for training CycleGAN.

On the other hand, we used the following two types as natural objects.

(4) Landscape Photo

Many realist paintings are realistic representations of landscapes. At first glance, Ikebana and Shan-Shui paintings look like figurative representations of natural landscapes, but as mentioned earlier, they are considered abstract representations of natural landscapes. Therefore, it is an interesting question whether or not the landscape photos can be converted into an Ikebana style or a Shan-Shui painting style by style transfer. On the other hand, the relationship between Kandinsky's abstract paintings and landscape photography is unknown, so it is interesting to find out what the relationship is.

Here, we used about 1000 images selected from https://www.pexels.com/search/landscape/ for training CycleGAN. About 500 of them are distant views of natural scenery, and the remaining about 500 are near views.

(5) Cityscape photo

We used a city landscape photograph as another real thing. Artificial urban landscapes are modern landscapes instead of natural landscapes and are expected to be compatible with Western abstract paintings. It is also interesting to see how this relates to Ikebana and Shan-Shui paintings.

Here, we used about 1000 images selected from https://www.pexels.com/search/city%20landscape/ for training CycleGAN. About 500 are distant views of cityscapes, and the remaining about 500 are near views.

5 Psychological Evaluation Experiment of Obtained Image

5.1 Data Used in Psychological Evaluation Experiments

The above style conversion experiment obtained the following 12 types of image sets.

1. Image set that converts landscape photos (distant views) into Ikebana style
2. Image set that converts landscape photos (distant views) into Kandinsky style
3. Image set that converts landscape photos (distant views) into Shan-Shui style
4. Image set that converts landscape photos (near views) into Ikebana style
5. Image set that converts landscape photos (near views) into Kandinsky style
6. Image set that converts landscape photos (near views) into Shan-Shui style
7. Image set that converts cityscape photos (distant views) into Ikebana style
8. Image set that converts cityscape photos (distant views) into Kandinsky style
9. Image set that converts cityscape photographs (distant views) into Shan-Shui style
10. Image set that converts cityscape photos (near views) into Ikebana style
11. Image set that converts cityscape photos (near views) into Kandinsky style
12. Image set that converts a cityscape photograph (near views) into Shan-Shui style.

Fifteen images were selected from each of these image sets and used in psychological experiments. Figure 6 shows several examples of the image used in the experiment.

5.2 Subject

Forty-eight students from Kyoto University were used as subjects. The age is from late teens to 20s.

5.3 Experimental Method

A total of 180 images, consisting of three types of art styles (Ikebana style, Kandinsky style, Shan-Shui painting style) × 4 types of original photos (natural landscape distant view, natural landscape near view, cityscape distant view, cityscape near view) × 15 images mentioned above, were evaluated by the subjects.

The evaluation was based on a psychological method in which the subjects answered the following four types of questions in seven stages (1 to 7).

Question 1: How similar is it to (Ikebana, Kandinsky art, Shan-Shui painting)?
Question 2: Please evaluate the newness as (Ikebana, Kandinsky art, Shan-Shui painting).
Question 3: Please evaluate when viewed as figurative art.
Question 4: Please evaluate when viewed as abstract art.
The experiment was conducted online using Google Form.

(Top: Landscape photos of distant views, Bottom: Images converted from landscape photos into Ikebana, Kandinsky, and Shan-Shui styles.)

(Top: Cityscape photos of distant views, Bottom: Images converted from cityscape photos into Ikebana, Kandinsky, and Shan-Shui styles.)

Fig. 6. Examples of images used in the psychological experiment.

6 Experiment Results and Discussion

6.1 Experiment Results

Figures 7, 8, 9 and 10 show graphs of the obtained results for each of the above four questions.

6.2 Discussion

(1) Similarity with the Original

In this evaluation item, we asked the subjects to evaluate how similar the presented image is to the original art (Ikebana, Kandinsky art, or Shan-Shui painting). In other words, the question is how much the characteristics of the original art are retained.

It should be noted here that the evaluation value of the natural landscape is generally higher than that of the cityscape. This seems to support the assumption that art

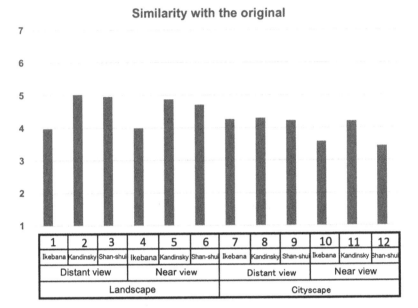

Fig. 7. Similarity to the original

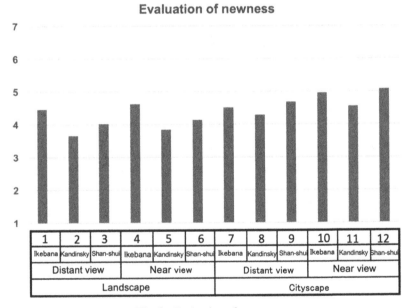

Fig. 8. Evaluation of newness

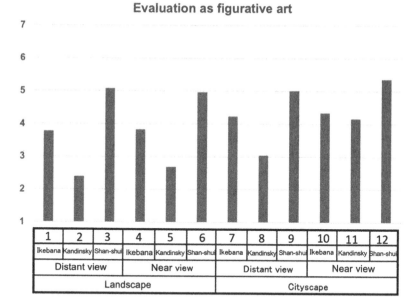

Fig. 9. Evaluation as a figurative painting

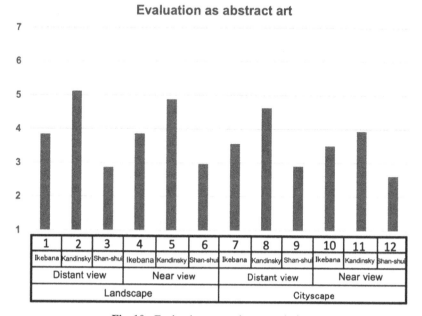

Fig. 10. Evaluation as an abstract painting

is essentially an abstraction of the natural landscape. In particular, it is noteworthy that Kandinsky's evaluation value is high. This, when combined with the fact that Kandinsky has been said to be the founder of abstract painting, may indicate that abstract painting is the continuation of the flow of realists and impressionists who express real things.

On the other hand, it is also noteworthy that the evaluation value of Ikebana is near the median value of four and not very high. Initially, we expected that Ikebana would be highly evaluated because it is thought that the affinity between Ikebana and the natural landscape is good, but the results were contrary to expectations. This may be because the subjects are almost all Japanese, and Japanese people have many opportunities to watch various types of high-ranked Ikebana. Therefore, they have a strict appreciation eye for the ideal appearance of Ikebana, and it is not easy to recognize a landscape image that has been style-converted as a real Ikebana.

(2) Evaluation of Newness

In this evaluation item, we asked the subjects to evaluate whether the presented image is recognized as a new form for the original art (Ikebana, Kandinsky art, or Shan-Shui painting).

What is noteworthy here is that cityscapes generally have higher evaluation values than natural landscapes. It can be understood that the image obtained by style transfer of the cityscape, which is an artifact, is evaluated higher for its newness as art than the image obtained by style transfer of the natural landscape. In particular, the Shan-Shui painting has a higher evaluation value than the Ikebana and Kandinsky art. This means that the subjects evaluated that a new landscape painting was obtained by converting the cityscape into a Shan-Shui-like image. We sometimes see artworks by Chinese artists in which the cityscape looks like a Shan-Shui painting. Probably there is something similar to this.

(3) Evaluation as Figurative Art

We asked the subjects to evaluate how much the presented image looked like figurative art in this evaluation item.

The evaluation value of Kandinsky art, an abstract painting, especially the evaluation of natural scenery converted into Kandinsky style, is low when evaluated as figurative art. On the other hand, Shan-Shui paintings have a high rating of 5 or higher for natural and urban landscapes. Understandably, a Shan-Shui-style natural landscape is highly evaluated as a figurative painting. However, it is interesting that an image of a city landscape in a Shan-Shui painting style also has a high evaluation value. This may correspond to what we mentioned earlier that the Shan-Shui painting looks like a figurative painting at first glance but has the aspect of an abstract painting that expresses a mental landscape.

It is also noteworthy that the evaluation value of the natural landscape image made into an Ikebana style is low. As mentioned earlier, the subjects, mostly Japanese, are usually in contact with high-quality Ikebana and have a high aesthetic eye for Ikebana, which may lead to strict evaluation results.

(4) **Evaluation as Abstract Art**

We asked the subjects to evaluate how much the presented image looks like an abstract image in this evaluation item.

It may be natural, but the evaluation of Ikebana and Shan-Shui paintings is low. This corresponds to Ikebana and Shan-Shui paintings are generally understood as figurative expressions rather than abstract expressions. As mentioned earlier, Ikebana and Shan-Shui paintings are high-dimensional abstract expressions while seemingly figurative. Such high-dimensional expressions may be difficult to reflect in the evaluation values at this stage.

7 Conclusion

In this study, we investigated the relationship between real things and art. Art is an abstract expression of a real thing or an expression of the essence of a real thing. However, it seems that research to prove it has not been done. Here, we focused on a technology called style transfer, which is achieved by a recent AI technology called GANs, especially a technology called CycleGAN, which can generate images with art styles of a specific art genre on photographs.

Using this technology makes it possible to make photographs, etc., into images with a specific art style. Of course, everything cannot be well converted into an image with an art style. It has the characteristic that it can be converted well when there is some similarity between the original photo and the art. This means that successful conversion shows a close relationship between the original image and the art. For example, successfully converting a natural landscape into a landscape painting style means that the landscape painting is an abstract expression of the natural landscape.

We decided to investigate the relationship between Ikebana, Kandinsky art, and Shan-Shui paintings and natural things from this way of thinking. As the actual objects, we decided to use natural landscapes and urban landscapes and also decided to use two types of landscape photographs, distant and near landscapes, for each. First, these landscape photographs were converted into Ikebana style, Kandinsky art style, and Shan-Shui painting style using the style transfer function of CycleGAN. Then, the obtained images were evaluated based on psychological experiments. The evaluation criteria were the following. How similar the converted images are to the original art genre. Whether or not they can offer new possibilities for the original art genre. How high they are evaluated when viewed as figurative art, and how high they are evaluated as abstract art. Since AI itself does not have a function to evaluate the generated images, the evaluation used the framework of the psychological evaluation experiment by the subjects.

As a result, some new findings were obtained as described in the discussion. Since sufficient analysis has not been performed yet, we would like to perform detailed analysis such as analysis of variance (ANOVA) in the future. Based on this, we plan to proceed with future studies.

References

1. Creswell, A., et al.: Generative adversarial networks: an overview. IEEE Signal Process. Mag. **35**(1), 53–65 (2018)
2. Karras, T., Laine, S., Aila, T.: A style-based generator architecture for generative adversarial networks. arXiv:1812.04948 (2019)
3. Zhu, J., Park, T., Isola, P., Efros, A.A.: Unpaired image-to-image translation using cycle-consistent adversarial networks. In: 2017 IEEE International Conference on Computer Vision (ICCV), pp. 2242–2251 (2017)
4. Okada, M., Inoue, J.: A psychological analysis about the elements of artistic evaluation on viewing paintings. Educ. Sci. J. Yokohama Natl. Univ. **31**, 45–66 (1991)
5. Farkas, A.: Prototypicality-effect in surrealist paintings. Empirical Stud. Arts **20**(2), 127–136 (2002)
6. Winston, A.S., Cupchik, G.C.: The evaluation of high art and popular art by Naïve and experienced viewers. Vis. Arts Res. **18**, 1–14 (1992)
7. Pihko, E., et al.: Experiencing art: the influence of expertise and painting abstraction. Front. Hum. Neurosci. **5**, Article no. 94, 1–10 (2011)
8. Gortais, B.: Abstraction and art. Philos. Trans. R. Soc. B **358**, 1241–1249 (2003)
9. Zimmer, R.: Abstraction in art with implications for perception. Philos. Trans. R. Soc. B **358**, 1285–1291 (2003)

Using *k*-Means Clustering to Classify Protest Songs Based on Conceptual and Descriptive Audio Features

Yanru Jiang[1(✉)] and Xin Jin[2,3]

[1] Department of Communication, University of California Los Angeles, Los Angeles, CA 90095, USA
`yanrujiang@g.ucla.edu`
[2] Department of Media and Communication, City University of Hong Kong, Kowloon 999077, Hong Kong SAR
`xin.jin@my.cityu.edu.hk`
[3] Center for Intelligent Media and Communication Research, College of Literature and Journalism, Central South University, Changsha 410017, Hunan, China

Abstract. Protest music is a phenomenal and widely circulated form of protest art in social movements. Previous protest music research has extensively focused on lyrics while ignoring other musical features that also contribute to the role of protest music in social movements. This study fills a gap in previous research by converting 397 unstructured musical pieces into structured music features and proposing a *k*-means clustering analysis to categorize protest songs based on both high-level conceptual features collected from Spotify and low-level descriptive audio features extracted via Librosa. The Davies–Bouldin index, inertia curve, Silhouette curve, and Silhouette diagram were the main measurements used to compare model performance. An innovative threshold filtering approach (optimizer area) was used to label 128 protest songs. Through a bottom-up folksonomy approach to music classification, this study overcomes the limitations of traditional genre classification by introducing other high-level features (e.g., energy, danceability, instrumentalness) and their roles in determining protest music categories.

Keywords: Cultural computing · Music classification · Protest art

1 Introduction

2020 has been "the year of the social movement," from the Hong Kong Anti-Extradition Bill (Anti-ELAB) movement to Black Lives Matter (BLM). In all of these social movements, music has become a phenomenal and widely circulated form of protest art [1]. Unlike most political songs, which serve the propagandistic function of promoting and solidifying an official state perspective, protest songs challenge dominant ideologies and powerful groups [2]. Previous protest music research has extensively focused on lyrics, discussing their rhetorical effects, while ignoring other musical features—such as melody, harmony, timbre, rhythm, and tempo—that also contribute to the role of protest music in social movements [3].

M. Rauterberg (Ed.): HCII 2022, LNCS 13324, pp. 291–304, 2022.
https://doi.org/10.1007/978-3-031-05434-1_19

This study bridges the gap in existing protest music research by converting unstructured musical pieces to structured musical features and proposing a k-means clustering analysis to categorize protest songs based on both high-level conceptual and low-level descriptive audio features extracted using the Spotify API and the Librosa music analysis tool. The Davies–Bouldin (DB) index, inertia curve, Silhouette curve, and Silhouette diagram were the main measurements used to compare model performance of the k-means algorithms. An innovative threshold filtering approach called optimizer area was also employed to generate labels for 128 protest songs based on the clustering analysis.

2 Literature Review

2.1 Protest Music

Mondak [4] defines protest music as a form of political persuasion, as one of its functions is "the attempt to generate outside support for the critical views it expresses" (p. 25). Emphasizing lyrics, Denisoff [5] identified two functions of protest songs—the magnetic and the rhetorical—viewing the music as secondary to the lyrics in realizing these functions. Magnetic songs encourage and recruit non-participants to join the social movement and reinforce existing participants' commitment through the messages of group solidarity and identity. Rhetorical songs, rather than appealing to group identity and promoting a large movement, describe the dissent, repression, and struggles faced by individuals in a group. In his research on the lyrics of protest music after the 2000s, Cort [6] reflects on the progression of music's roles in social movements and extends Denisoff's [5] twofold classification. After advocacy for issues like climate change began to emerge after the millennium, group solidarity and individual adversity were no longer the sole messages delivered by protest songs. Rather, as identified by Cort [6], protest music in the modern world progressively came to include the roles of "challenging a power structure, empowering the listener to overcome adversity, communicating a message to solidify members of a social movement, and encouraging societal change" (p. 5).

As research on the lyrics of protest music began to reach a consistent and comprehensive conclusion regarding the role of protest songs in social movements, Eyerman and Jamison [7] challenged this unilateral emphasis on lyrics for studying protest songs. Responding to Denisoff's [5] study, which overemphasized lyrics, the authors argued that the music itself also contributes to protest songs' magnetic and rhetorical functions. Specifically, the structure of protest songs, which are "buil[t] around known and catchy melodies, repeating verses, [and] simple chords" (p. 43), conveys an explicit persuasive effect. Additionally, Eyerman and Jamison [7] focus on a cultural perspective: since protest music's contextual messages and status as a bearer of musical traditions could be reflected in its familiar tunes and genres, which appeal to certain groups and cultures, the cultural elements of protest music link the past, present, and future of the revolutionary groups. Preexisting African American songs provided new kinds of emancipatory and visionary messages for the U.S. civil rights movement in the late 1950s and early 1960s. White power music—including country, folk, Viking, black metal, and hard rock, which developed in the Western world—is commonly found in neo-fascist movements [8].

At the same time, numerous cognition and psychology studies have investigated the impact of audio features on audiences' perceptions. Bainbridge et al. [9] found that both infants and adults demonstrated psychological responses to unfamiliar foreign songs, indicating that audio features alone could affect perception without any additional context. Given that most previous protest music studies have been conducted from lyrics-focused, cultural, generic, and qualitative perspectives, this study selects audio-level music features, such as arousal, melody, rhythm, and timbre, to empirically analyze the following research questions [10, 11]:

RQ1: How should protest songs be classified based on high-level features and low-level descriptors?
RQ2: Which combination of features produces the optimal results for classifying protest songs?

2.2 Music Categorization

Though most previous studies on music classification have focused on genre classification, Scaringella and Zoia [3] claim that most generic approaches remain fuzzy and use loosely defined generic concepts. Possible issues arising from genre classification include the simplification of artists' discourse, unstandardized merging of multiple genres, the need to split one genre into various subgenres, and the overall difficulty in agreeing on a universal taxonomy for music classification. This study challenges the traditional generic approach by incorporating high-level musical features to identify how different sets of features could stimulate different emotional reactions from audiences.

Scaringella and Zoia [3] proposed an innovative solution for classifying music termed "folksonomy," a bottom-up approach wherein users generate classifiers through an interactive mutual agreement. This study recruited two content coders and adopted a folksonomy-based method for labeling clusters of protest songs.

3 Conceptual Framework

Early research on music classification used static clustering methods and has since continually advanced, especially after the introduction of deep learning and neural networks [12]. The primary focuses in this area have two components: (i) feature selection and extraction, and (ii) classifier designs [13]. The majority of music classification research explores genre classification using the GTZAN dataset created by Tzanetakis and Cook [14] which contains 10 genre labels: blues, classical, country, disco, hip hop, jazz, metal, pop, reggae, and rock [15]. Audio feature extraction and music clustering have also shown promise in music tagging, recommendation, and classification with regard to previously undifferentiable music categories, such as traditional music and song emotion recognition [16, 17].

3.1 Audio Feature Extraction

Feature extraction allows researchers to convert unstructured musical pieces into structured data input by using high- and low-level features to capture the differences between pieces of music.

High-Level Features. High-level statistical acoustic features are generally found to have better classifying performance than low-level features [18]. Lidy and Rauber [19] conducted research on psychoacoustic transformation in the context of music genre classification by measuring audiences' psychological responses and connecting those responses to certain high-level audio features of the music. Additionally, high-level features demonstrate better performance in emotion recognition compared with low-level features [19].

Rodà et al. [20] identified valence and arousal as the most frequently researched dimensions among high-level music features. According to Dillman Carpentier and Potter [10], arousal, level of hedonic intensity, and energetic value are commonly studied along with valence (i.e., the negative or positive value of the hedonic level). While the valence–arousal plane has been dominant in studies of musical features, Rodà et al. [20] recommend including other features, such as loudness, roughness, and spectral features, to measure the emotional power of the music.

Low-Level Features. Most of the research on genre classification is conducted on low-level descriptors, mainly focusing on features in music signal processing that simulate human auditory perception, including rhythmic, temporal, cepstral, spectral, and perceptual audio descriptors [21]. Scaringella and Zoia [3] found that low-level descriptors in audio signals could capture melodic and harmonic elements of music more robustly than high-level features.

3.2 Music Classifier Design

With the development of greater computing power and advanced deep learning algorithms, the research focus of music classifier design has shifted from more static, classic models—such as logistic regression, *k*-nearest neighbors, and support vector machines (SVMs)—to more novel, dynamic approaches, including convolutional neural networks (CNNs) and recurrent neural networks (RNNs). Tzanetakis and Cook [14] pioneered the genre classification field with their use of a mixed-methods design consisting of *k*-nearest neighbors and Gaussian mixture models to introduce a comprehensive clustering pipeline. The two authors further standardized the feature categories for music clustering (rhythm, pitch, and temporal structure) for future studies. Li et al. [22] proposed content-based genre clustering, emphasizing the multiclass attributes enabled by the histogram classification approach. Xu et al. [23] applied an SVM for music classification tasks, while Fu et al. [24] challenged the SVM design by combining a naïve Bayes classifier with an SVM to produce an NBSVM algorithm.

Regarding dynamic music classifiers, neural networks have shown success in reflecting the temporal features in a sequence of music timesteps. Vishnupriya and Meenakshi [25] proposed a CNN architecture and implemented it on Mel spectrum and MFCC feature vectors for each song. Grzegorz [26] trained a CNN model for image recognition and conducted transfer learning by reusing the bottom levels of that trained model for genre recognition. Considering music as a sequence of sounds with embedded temporal features, Ghosal and Sarkar [12] designed a model consisting of four layers of CNNs with a final long short-term memory (LSTM) RNN layer to construct a new clustering augmented learning method for genre classification. With the convolutional layer and LSTM autoencoders in the last layer, the authors were able to capture both spatial and temporal features from the music signal.

Among all classifier designs, *k*-means clustering is one of the most commonly used and most straightforward algorithms for clustering analysis. Jondya and Iswanto [27] extracted the most relevant audio features through principal components analysis and used *k*-means clustering to categorize Indonesian traditional music based on 36 low-level descriptors. Kim et al. [17] innovatively applied *k*-means clustering to a music recommendation system and introduced a dynamic clustering algorithm capable of reflecting changes in users' playlists.

4 Methods

4.1 Data Collection

Several steps were involved in the data collection process. First, I used the Wikipedia protest songs category to generate a list of protest songs from the 19th through 21st centuries. Second, I matched Wikipedia songs with the Spotify music database to collect Spotify music features and 30-s MP3 music demos to be used for Librosa feature extraction in the next step.

Wikipedia List. As there lacked an existing list comprehensively covering global protest songs, I ensured the representativeness and authority of the data by confirming our list synthetically based on qualitative literature on typical protest songs (e.g., *Dear Mr. President*), lists published by authoritative music brands (e.g., RadioX), and the Protest Songs Wikipedia Typology page, which is under the authority of the Library of Congress. I ultimately produced a list of 457 songs with music production information, such as language, release date, genre, and composer.

Spotify. I next used the Spotify API to match songs in the Wikipedia list with the Spotify database according to title, artists, album, and release year. Because the official Spotify Web API is based on the REST (Representational State Transfer) principle, which is not directly compatible with the Python language, Spotipy—a lightweight Python library for the Spotify Web API—was used instead to query music features from the Spotify database. Realizing that the search results in Spotify may not automatically refer to the same songs in the Wikipedia list, I filtered out irrelevant songs when the number of songs in the search results was greater than 50.

Content Coding. Two coders specializing in social movement studies conducted content coding on 457 protest songs by manually verifying whether the search result in the Spotify database matched the music indicated on the Wikipedia list. The MP3 music demos provided by Spotify were used to confirm and select the corresponding song version, while the two coders also used the YouTube video search results to cross-check the accuracy of the Spotify music selection. After a systematic data cleaning procedure, 397 songs that could be matched with the Spotify API were retained for feature extraction.

4.2   Feature Extraction

Feature extraction and selection were performed for both the high-level conceptual features provided by the Spotify API and the low-level descriptive features extracted from the Librosa Python library. The study conducted k-means clustering on high-level and low-level features, respectively, to compare the performance of both sets of features. Considering that differences in feature values may substantially distort the mapping and clustering process, I normalized both high-level and low-level features from 0 to 1.

High-Level Features: Spotify. To operationalize the conceptual-level audio features, the Spotify API was used to extract the technological-level audio features of each protest song. The Echo Nest, a music intelligence and data platform, first introduced audio feature extraction algorithms to the music world; its algorithm has been integrated with the Spotify Audio Feature API since Spotify acquired The Echo Nest in 2014 [28] According to the Object Index in the Spotify API documentation, 10 audio features (acousticness, danceability, energy, instrumentalness, key, liveness, loudness, speechiness, tempo, and valence) are provided by the Spotify API. A detailed description of each audio feature is provided in the Appendix.

For each piece of music, I selected eight features—danceability, energy, speechiness, acousticness, instrumentalness, liveness, valence, and tempo—from the Spotify API for clustering analysis based on their relevance to the music being categorized. Loudness was excluded because its presence would not substantially affect audiences' emotional perceptions of the protest music. Loudness can fluctuate based on the user's volume setting, while liveness can also easily vary based on the recording environment during the music production. Therefore, liveness has only a moderate effect on the clustering results (Fig. 1).

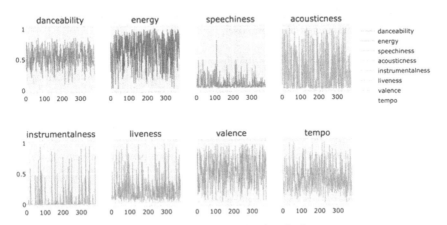

Fig. 1. Distribution of high-level audio features

Low-Level Descriptors: Librosa. Librosa, first introduced by McFee et al. [29], is a commonly used Python package for music and audio signal processing. Unlike the Spotify API, which extracts high-level audio features, Librosa extracts low-level descriptive features from audio clips, some of which are not readily perceptible to audiences, such as spectral features. Librosa is usually considered comprehensive for music studies because it provides all relevant parameters for audio analysis [29].

In total, 320 music files downloaded using the Spotify API were used for Librosa feature extraction. This number is smaller than the number of songs selected for Spotify feature extraction because 77 songs were excluded due to their lack of MP3 demos. To enable Librosa to process the music files, I converted the 320 MP3 files to WAV format using an online converter tool on a pay-as-you-go basis. Librosa reads WAV files into a one-dimensional NumPy array (denoted as *y*) and calculates the song duration in seconds based on the sampling rate:

$$Duration\ Seconds = \frac{float(len(y))}{sampling\ rate} \tag{1}$$

Spectral features, defined as "the distribution of energy over a set of frequencies" [29], are the dominant features in Librosa feature extraction and in digital signal processing. Among all spectral features, the Mel spectrogram frequency scale (*melspectrogram*) and its derivatives (*mfcc, rms, poly_features*) are frequently used to capture the timbral element of music. Specifically, the spectrogram represents the music's time and frequency information and has been widely used in recently developed music classification models [12].

Besides capturing timbral elements, "pitch class representations (chroma_stft, chroma_cqt, chroma_cens, tonnetz) are often used to encode harmony while suppressing variations in octave height, loudness, or timbre" [29]. Additionally, Librosa provides spectral statistic representations for music, including spectral centroid, bandwidth, roll-off, and contrast. Zero-crossing rate, a temporal feature measuring "signal changes from positive to zero to negative or from negative to zero to positive" was also added to the feature selection [3, 30]. One rhythm feature, Fourier tempogram, was also included for the purpose of clustering Librosa audio features.

4.3 Clustering

I used *k*-means clustering to categorize music computationally, ultimately arriving at 10 clusters for high-level features and seven clusters for low-level descriptors based on the DB index. The clustering results of the perceptual high-level feature set were further verified and adjusted by human coders through a folksonomy classification approach. Six subcategories and three parent categories were ultimately identified for this feature set.

Several metrics, including the inertia curve, Silhouette curve, Silhouette diagram, and DB index, were used to compare and measure model performance. After realizing that the inertia curve, Silhouette curve, and Silhouette diagram could not easily identify the optimal number of music clusters for both datasets in the study, I selected models based on which had the lowest DB index.

4.4 Music Category Optimization

Once I determined the number of clusters using the DB index, I defined an optimizer area to select protest songs that were more likely to be aligned with the corresponding clusters and filter out the less relevant ones.

In the optimization step, I calculated the mean value of eight features in each cluster and selected them as baselines by adding or subtracting the standard deviation with various multipliers to obtain the optimizer area. Songs with feature values outside this area were excluded. Based on the optimized clusters, whose category attributes are more aggregate and salient, I ultimately identified six categories of protest music by dropping noise clusters and merging similar ones (Table 2; dataset: https://bit.ly/3vg6n6c).

$$Optimizer\ Area = Mean_{feature} \pm Multiplier \times Standard\ Deviation_{feature} \qquad (2)$$

Table 1. Comparison of four measurements used to evaluate clustering model performance

	High-level (Spotify)	Low-level (Librosa)
Davies-Bouldin	The DB index was smallest *(DB =* 1.25) when the number of clusters was set to 10	The DB index was smallest (*DB =* 1.48) when the number of clusters was set to 7
Inertia curve		
Silhouette curve		
Silhouette diagram		

5   Results

5.1   Performance Measurement

For both high-level and low-level features, the inertia curve, Silhouette curve, and Silhouette diagram were not able to produce a distinct pattern in the clustering analysis (see Table 1). The DB index was thus selected for comparing model performance. As the DB index was used to measure similarity across clusters, a lower DB index indicates a better clustering result.

High-Level Features. The DB index was smallest when the number of clusters was set to 10 ($k = 10$) for the high-level feature set. According to the inertia curve and Silhouette curve above, none of these graphs shows a distinct elbow (i.e., turning point) for identifying the best number of clusters for the high-level feature set. The Silhouette diagram indicates the same result as the DB index: protest songs are less likely to be misclassified to the wrong clusters when k equals 10 for high-level features.

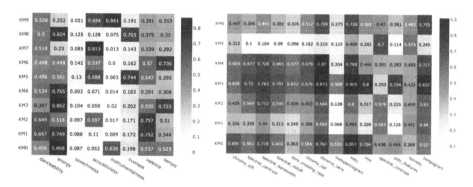

Fig. 2. Heat map of cluster results of high-level (left) and low-level feature set (right)

The heat map (see Fig. 2) reveals the similarities and differences in feature values across the 10 clusters. Specifically, KM4 and KM8 share a similar distribution of music features, and clusters tend to have distinctive values in the energy and valence features.

Using the optimizer area approach, I identified 128 protest songs that were more likely to be aligned with the feature pattern in their corresponding clusters (Fig. 3).

Low-Level Descriptors. Neither the inertia curve nor the Silhouette curve graph below shows a distinct elbow for identifying the best number of clusters for the low-level feature dataset. The Silhouette diagram indicates the same result as the DB index: for low-level features, protest songs are less likely to be misclassified to the wrong clusters when k equals 7.

The heat map for the cluster results of the low-level feature set reveals that KM3 and KM4 have similar distributions of music features, and clusters tend to have distinctive values in the tempogram and MFCC features.

The distribution of the low-level features across the seven clusters reveals that KM0 and KM6 have similar distributions of music features, while most clusters are substantially different from the remaining clusters (Fig. 4).

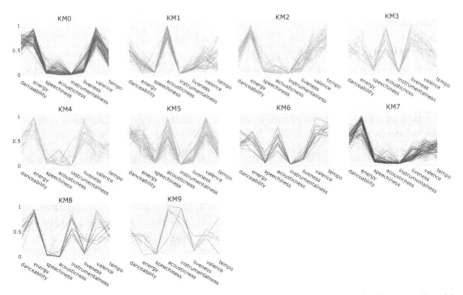

Fig. 3. Distribution of high-level music features by cluster. Gray curves indicate music with feature values outside the optimizer area.

5.2 Clustering and Annotating Results

Through an unsupervised clustering analysis, this study makes a pioneering classification of protest songs into six subcategories within three overarching categories by emphasizing audio feature variation. Category A shows that the salient attributes of rock music are its typically high energy and low acousticness. Category B is associated with a high volume of vocal sounds (high acousticness). Category C, representing the attributes of folk and country music, maintains relatively balanced values of energy and acousticness. Moreover, for each subcategory, some other features were also significant in categorizing the music. For example, high danceability provides songs in subcategory KM0 with strong beats; thereby, our study challenges the traditional generic categorization of protest songs (Table 2).

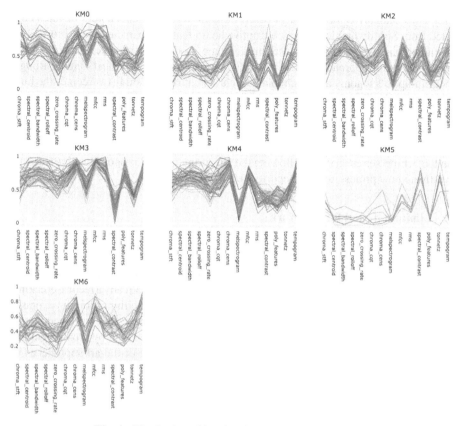

Fig. 4. Distribution of low-level music features by cluster

Table 2. Final music categories with quantities, descriptions, and Spotify links.

Category	N	Description	Representative music
A-km0	21	Dance rock, post-punk, dance music	https://spoti.fi/3pRZUdH
B-km1	21	Highly vocal songs	https://spoti.fi/3bBpgaQ
A-km2	21	Hard rock with high tempo	https://spoti.fi/3dIOWF7
C-km3/5	32	Folk and country music with low tempo	https://spoti.fi/3aRFrl6
C-km6	13	Folk and country music with high tempo	https://spoti.fi/3sqPTWt
A-km7	20	Soft rock	https://bit.ly/3uzmVWk

6 Conclusion

This study fills a gap in previous protest music research, which has historically ignored audio features when classifying music. Specifically, this research converted 397 unstructured musical pieces into structured music features and proposed a *k*-means clustering analysis to categorize protest songs based on both high-level conceptual features collected from Spotify and low-level descriptive audio features extracted via Librosa. The DB index was the main metric used to compare model performance. An innovative threshold filtering approach (optimizer area) was used to label 128 protest songs. Through a bottom-up folksonomy approach to music classification, this study overcomes the limitations of traditional genre classification by introducing other high-level features (e.g., energy, danceability, instrumentalness) and their roles in determining music clusters.

Due to the lack of perceivability of Librosa features, this study did not manually label the final categorical results for the low-level feature set. Future research could conduct a time-series analysis following the clustering method proposed in this study to investigate how protest music categories shift across centuries.

6.1 Limitations and Future Work

The research has several limitations. First, the Wikipedia typology might not present a comprehensive list of protest songs. Several songs also were dropped due to a lack of matching results in the Spotify database. However, covering almost 400 protest songs from the 19th through 21st centuries for music categorization is already a record-breaking feat in protest music studies [6]. Second, due to the imperceptibility of low-level music descriptors, this study could not manually verify the clustering results produced by the Librosa feature set. In future research, this issue could be overcome by cross-checking with the categorizing results of Spotify features or other state-of-the-art approaches in the music classification field. Lastly, the Librosa feature set contains several audio features that share similar attributes and are highly correlated, such as Mel spectrogram and MFCC, which might lead to collinearity in the feature selection process. It is recommended to verify multicollinearity within spectral and rhythm features before clustering music based on low-level descriptors.

7 Data and Code Availability

Data and code: https://github.com/JoyceJiang73/Protest_Music_Clustering.

References

1. Green Jr., D.F.: Views from the bricks: notes on reading and protest. CLA J. **63**, 169–173 (2020). https://doi.org/10.34042/claj.63.2.0169
2. Philpott, S.: Of country and country: twang and trauma in Australian Indigenous popular music. Politik **23**, 94–98 (2020). https://doi.org/10.7146/politik.v23i1.120312
3. Scaringella, N., Zoia, G., Mlynek, D.: Automatic genre classification of music content. IEEE Signal Process. Mag. **23**, 133–141 (2006). https://doi.org/10.1109/MSP.2006.1598089
4. Mondak, J.J.: Protest music as political persuasion (1988). https://doi.org/10.1080/030077 68808591322
5. Denisoff, R.S.: Songs of persuasion: a sociological analysis of urban propaganda songs. J. Am. Folk. **79**, 581–589 (1966). https://doi.org/10.2307/538223
6. Quirk Cort, M.E.: The Power of Lyrical Protest: Examining the Rhetorical Function of Protest Songs in the 2000s (2013)

7. Eyerman, R., Jamison, A.: Taking traditions seriously. In: Music and Social Movements: Mobilizing Traditions in the Twentieth Century, pp. 26–47. Cambridge University Press (1998). https://doi.org/10.2307/767983
8. Eyerman, R.: Music in movement: cultural politics and old and new social movements. Qual. Sociol. **25**, 443–458 (2002). https://doi.org/10.1023/A:1016042215533
9. Bainbridge, C.M., et al.: Infants relax in response to unfamiliar foreign lullabies. Nat. Hum. Behav. **5**, 256–264 (2021). https://doi.org/10.1038/s41562-020-00963-z
10. Dillman Carpentier, F.R., Potter, R.F.: Effects of music on physiological arousal: explorations into tempo and genre (2007). https://doi.org/10.1080/15213260701533045
11. Rosenthal, R.: Serving the movement: the role(s) of music. Pop. Music Soc. **25**, 11–24 (2001)
12. Ghosal, S.S., Sarkar, I.: Novel approach to music genre classification using clustering augmented learning method (CALM). In: CEUR Workshop Proceedings, vol. 2600 (2020)
13. Tsai, W.H., Bao, D.F.: Clustering music recordings based on genres. J. Inf. Sci. Eng. **26**, 2059–2074 (2010)
14. Tzanetakis, G., Cook, P.: Musical genre classification of audio signals. In: IEEE Transactions on Speech and Audio Processing, pp. 293–302. IEEE (2002)
15. Cheng, Y.H., Chang, P.C., Kuo, C.N.: Convolutional neural networks approach for music genre classification. In: Proceedings of 2020 International Symposium on Computer, Consumer and Control, IS3C 2020, pp. 399–403 (2020). https://doi.org/10.1109/IS3C50286.2020.00109
16. Choi, K., Fazekas, G., Sandler, M., Cho, K.: Convolutional recurrent neural networks for music classification. In: ICASSP, IEEE International Conference on Acoustics, Speech and Signal Processing Proceedings, pp. 2392–2396 (2017). https://doi.org/10.1109/ICASSP.2017.7952585
17. Kim, D.M., Kim, K.S., Park, K.H., Lee, J.H., Lee, K.M.: A music recommendation system with a dynamic K-means clustering algorithm. In: Proceedings of the 6th International Conference on Machine Learning and Applications, ICMLA 2007, pp. 399–403 (2007). https://doi.org/10.1109/ICMLA.2007.97
18. Atmaja, B.T., Akagi, M.: On the differences between song and speech emotion recognition: effect of feature sets, feature types, and classifiers. In: IEEE Region 10 Annual International Conference Proceedings/TENCON, November 2020, pp. 968–972 (2020). https://doi.org/10.1109/TENCON50793.2020.9293852
19. Lidy, T., Rauber, A.: Evaluation of feature extractors and psycho-acoustic transformations for music genre classification. In: ISMIR 2005, 6th International Conference on Music Information Retrieval, pp. 34–41 (2005)
20. Rodà, A., Canazza, S., De Poli, G.: Clustering affective qualities of classical music: beyond the valence-arousal plane. IEEE Trans. Affect. Comput. **5**, 364–376 (2014). https://doi.org/10.1109/TAFFC.2014.2343222
21. Blaszke, M., Koszewski, D.: Determination of low-level audio descriptors of a musical instrument sound using neural network. In: Signal Processing: Algorithms, Architectures, Arrangements, and Applications Proceedings, SPA, September 2020, pp. 138–141 (2020). https://doi.org/10.23919/spa50552.2020.9241264
22. Li, T., Ogihara, M., Li, Q.: A comparative study on content-based music genre classification. In: Proceedings of the 26th Annual International ACM SIGIR Conference on Research and Development in Informaion Retrieval, pp. 282–289, Toronto, Canada (2003). https://doi.org/10.1109/ISSPA.2003.1224828
23. Xu, C., Maddage, N.C., Shao, X., Cao, F., Tian, Q.: Musical genre classification using support vector machines. In: 2003 IEEE International Conference on Acoustics, Speech, and Signal Processing, pp. 429–432 (2003)
24. Fu, Z., Lu, G., Ting, K.M., Zhang, D.: Learning Naive Bayes classifiers for music classification and retrieval. In: Proceedings of the International Conference on Pattern Recognition, pp. 4589–4592 (2010). https://doi.org/10.1109/ICPR.2010.1121

25. Vishnupriya, S., Meenakshi, K.: Automatic music genre classification using convolution neural network. In: 2018 International Conference on Computer Communication and Informatics, ICCCI 2018, pp. 4–7 (2018). https://doi.org/10.1109/ICCCI.2018.8441340

26. Gwardys, G., Grzywczak, D.: Deep image features in music information retrieval. Int. J. Electron. Telecommun. **60**, 321–326 (2014). https://doi.org/10.2478/eletel-2014-0042

27. Jondya, A.G., Iswanto, B.H.: Indonesian's traditional music clustering based on audio features. Procedia Comput. Sci. **116**, 174–181 (2017). https://doi.org/10.1016/j.procs.2017.10.019

28. Skidén, P.: New Endpoints: Audio Features, Recommendations and User Taste. https://developer.spotify.com/community/news/2016/03/29/audio-features-recommendations-user-taste/

29. McFee, B., et al.: librosa: audio and music signal analysis in Python. In: Proceedings of the 14th Python in Science Conference, pp. 18–24 (2015). https://doi.org/10.25080/majora-7b98e3ed-003

30. Stürmer, S., Simon, B.: The role of collective identification in social movement participation: a panel study in the context of the German gay movement. Personal. Soc. Psychol. Bull. **30**, 263–277 (2004). https://doi.org/10.1177/0146167203256690

ESTENDERE: A Design Concept to Enhance Audience Experience in Theatre

Yifan Kang[1] , Bingjian Liu[2,3](✉), and Xu Sun[2,3]

[1] University of Nottingham Ningbo China, Ningbo, China
[2] Faculty of Science and Engineering, University of Nottingham Ningbo China, Ningbo, China
bingjian.liu@nottingam.edu.cn
[3] Nottingham Ningbo China Beacons of Excellence Research and Innovation Institute, Ningbo, China

Abstract. Theatre performance is forming a trend in countries like China. However, the study of enhancing audience experience in theatre is not conducted enough. The research shows that the major requirements of the audiences on theatre performance include immersion, self-resonance and self-identification. To fulfill their needs, a product design called *ESTENDERE* is proposed. It is a redesign of the traditional ticket but integrated with linear motor and an optical heart rate sensor and can be reassembled into a bracelet. By generating different vibration patterns which are enabled by the haptics brought from the linear motor, the sense of engagement and immersion could be partly improved. However, the choice of proper pattern which can suit the scene relates to the faith in simulation of the story. In addition, a symbolic memorial in the design can foster a sense of self-identification among the audience. By recognizing a shared experience, it is easier to form a conversation about the performance so that self-resonance could be enhanced during the process. Furthermore, the infographic on the ticket provides a preview for the audiences to get familiar with the performances, which helps them understand the plot more easily. Finally, heart rate data is used to monitor emotional feedback so that the performance could be improved later. The user evaluation results showed that, by applying the parameters above to *ESTENDERE*, users can gain an improved experience in theatre.

Keywords: Theatre performance · Audience experience · Haptics · Emotion detection

1 Introduction

Theatre performance, as a complex art form of human beings [1], is becoming more and more popular in countries like China. It was described as a phenomenon with the properties of society and experience rather than a rigid product [1] and the number of grand theatre venues built has rapidly increased [2]. However, the investigation into the reasons people go to the theatre and their satisfaction towards experience is not conducted enough [3]. Thus, this study is undertaken to focus on enhancing audience experience in theatre and fulfilling their needs through product design.

M. Rauterberg (Ed.): HCII 2022, LNCS 13324, pp. 305–315, 2022.
https://doi.org/10.1007/978-3-031-05434-1_20

Audiences in live performances can be divided into two groups: ordinary audiences and enthusiasts [4] and the audience experience can be measured from five aspects: Engagement and concentration, Learning and challenges, Energy and tension, Shared experience and atmosphere, Personal resonance and emotional connection [5]. In addition, Bergadaa and Nyeck [6] divide these values into four groups: hedonism, social conformism, personal development and communal pleasure. They also state that the common motivation for theatre audiences and producers is their shared culture [6]. Among these factors, different group of audiences has different focal points, for instance, according to Pitts's study [4], the enthusiasts tend to engage and understand the performance better, while the casual audiences respond more passively. Based on the above findings, it is believed that the aspects of shared experience, self-reflection and self-identification are more concerned for theatre lovers, while the immersion, the understanding of the plot and the entertainment aspects are more focused for casual audiences.

In addition, previous research has defined that the process of categorizing oneself into a group [7] is called identification [8] and cultural symbols can be used to accelerate classifying this process [9]. For self-identification and self-reflection, Nicholson and Pearce [10] state that the experience of enhancing socialization was one motivation behind audience decision. Additionally, Arai and Pedlar [11] indicate that the focus on social identification could provide a shared feeling between audiences. Furthermore, according to Edmund [12], receiving the reaction of others improved the awareness of self-emotions reacting to the performance. Thus, it is important to create an opportunity for the audience to communicate.

As for the immersion and entertainment aspects, it is stated that the resonance between audience and actor on stage can be affected by physical presence, including the scenic design [13]. On this basis, helping audiences acquire the ability to understand the environment and plot could improve the sense of immersion. The study conducted by Biggin [14] provides evidence of the similarity between interaction in immersive theatre and in video games which include both real elements and virtual elements. These two types of immersion both relate to the activity of human brains [14]. Previous research indicates that engagement and immersion in video games could be enhanced by applying haptics [15]. It can provide another dimension of sensing and expand the user experience towards not only the scenery but also the motions of characters. Moreover, a previous study [16] finds that the application of haptics in immersive theatre could improve the enthusiasm of the audience to explore and interact with the environment. Thus, the methodology in video game area is used for reference here for the design development.

Another dimension to improve audience experience is to provide a scientific method for the performance to improve round by round. Owing to the reaction of the audiences not only indicates that they are positively engaged in the performance [17], but also serves as a means to communicate with the actors [18], the recognition of audience emotion during the performance is the entry point for this study. Shu [19] indicates that the change in mood could result in the change of heart activities. For example, the emotions of anger or fear lead to an increase in heart rate and disgust results in a decreased rate [20] and an emotional happy state maintains a lower heart rate than that of during neutral mood [21]. Furthermore, heart rate differed significantly between fear and relaxation moods [22]. Meanwhile, previous test confirmed that the result of recognition for individual emotion performed more accurately than the baseline [23]. In addition, the interest of using wearable devices has increased significantly in affective computing due to its multiple practices [24]. Ultimately, it was achievable to detect and monitor real-time emotion using wearable devices [19]. Wearable devices which could collect physiological data illustrate a great potential in the application of detecting emotion [25].

Based on the analysis above, several aspects including audience social identification, immersion and engagement, and the improvement of further performances are the major focuses of this study and an interaction system called *ESTENDERE* was designed to fulfill the needs of audience in those areas.

2 Designed Concept

2.1 Concept Introduction

To fill the gap in traditional theatre market and improve the audience experience, the design concept *ESTENDERE*, an interaction system to enhance audience's understanding for theatre performance and immersion is proposed (see Fig. 1). The name ESTENDERE comes from Italian word meaning "extension", showing that this product can extend audience's feelings in the theatre. It is a redesign of the traditional theatre ticket and can be reassembled from a ticket to a bracelet. The audience is provided a continuous experience from the moment they receive it. The design contains a linear motor to provide extra haptics to improve the immersion in the theatre as suggested by Gomes [15] and, by generating the vibration through the motor, the product can provide an extra dimension to understand and feel the plot that can help the audiences experience the story with the characters on the stage. For example, an instant and strong type of vibration could represent a gunshot. Meanwhile, the optical heart rate sensor inside would work to collect data during the performance, so that the crews and director can receive the computed data of audience's reacted emotions, by recognizing five essential elements in heart rate data [19], to accomplish further improvement of the performance, and then achieve the expected audience reaction. The electronic elements, such as PCB, sensor, battery, etc. are located within the core part of the bracelet (see Fig. 2).

The surface of the ticket, which could be personalized according to various plays, demonstrates the key information and style of the performance for the audience to preview. In this case, it would be easier for the audience to know what to expect as a preview could help people to understand the narrative context [26]. In addition, by using the same illustration for one performance, self-identification among the audiences could be enhanced with this symbolic recognition memorial. They would simply recognize the audience group that shared the same performance, then construct their identification within the group.

Fig. 1. Overall view of *ESTENDERE*.

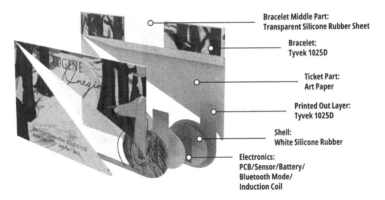

Fig. 2. Details of *ESTENDERE*.

2.2 Modeling and Evaluation

In the beginning the concept development, to explore the potential application of wearable concepts, several sketches were generated to find the best solution (see Fig. 3).

The concept of combining the ticket and bracelet into one product was chosen as the final concept to carry on, as it was the most senseless form among the first round of concepts according to the product design expert feedback through an interview.

A sketch model was then produced to test the usability and size of the design concept (see Fig. 4). The disassembling method and the ergonomics of the bracelet were examined by a female tester from a university. The tester successfully tore the two parts from the ticket and assembled them into a bracelet. In addition, the size of the bracelet was adjustable to suit her wrist. The result of the testing confirmed that the process of forming the ticket into a bracelet was simple and that it was easy to wear.

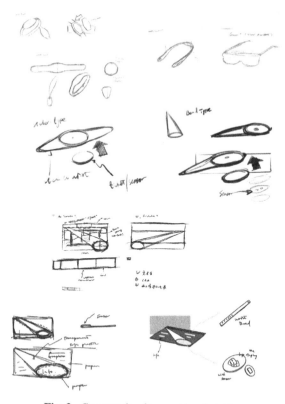

Fig. 3. Concept development by sketching

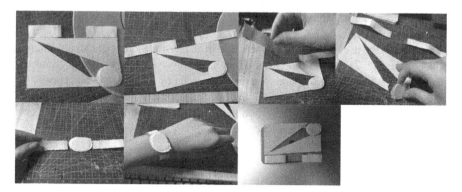

Fig. 4. First sketch model.

Finally, a final sketch model was produced to test the real appearance of the concept with the graphic design printed (see Fig. 5).

Fig. 5. Final sketch model.

2.3   Working Process

A storyboard (see Fig. 6) is produced to help people better understand the process. Before entering the theatre, the ticket can be torn off and transformed into a bracelet. This bracelet can be scanned and verifies the authority of entrance by a machine. During the performance, it would vibrate following the story to stimulate realness within scenes. Directors can design the types and point-in-time of vibration as needed. The heart rate data of all audiences would be collected to indicate to the crews how the audiences react at certain points by recognizing specific reflective features, so that the performance can be improved later. This function also allows the interaction between actors and audiences, which makes the audience more engaged and becomes a more important part of the performance. After the play, the inner electronic part can be recycled and reused for the next event. The bracelet can be kept as a memorial and a symbol by the audiences to improve self-identity among the audience group that shared the same performance.

The emotion recognition method proposed by Lin Shu, Yang Yu et al. [19] is used to compute the result. They use five standard heart rate parameters including up amplitude, up time, down amplitude, slope and T continue to extract features of different emotions. The result after training shows 70.4% and 52% accuracy in recognizing two and five emotional types [19].

In addition, the user flow of user experience in analyzing audience feedback phase is produced (see Fig. 7) and the sample of UI interface illustrates the major functions and appearance (see Fig. 8). These parameters are only seen by the directors and crews after each performance. The major sections of the interfaces include date of the performance, name of the performance, audience emotion, keywords of comments on the platform, audience body temperature and audience heart rate.

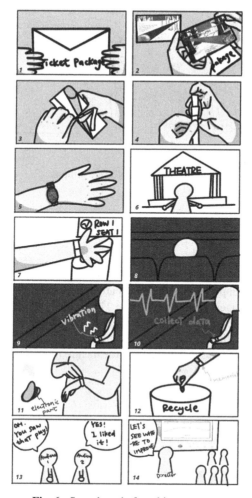

Fig. 6. Story board of working process.

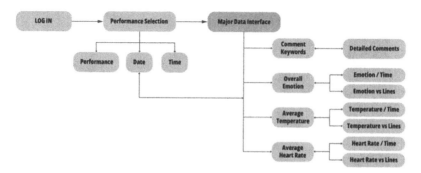

Fig. 7. User flow.

Fig. 8. Major UI interface sample.

3 Primary User Test

3.1 Participants

A primary user test was conducted to test the efficiency of strengthening the understanding of performance by applying haptics. Five participants were gathered in this study (2 females, 3 males, with ages ranging from 19 to 24 years old, M = 21.6, SD = 1.85). All participants were university students. Two male participants were ordinary audiences who went to theatre less than 2 times a year, while the other three participants (2 female, 1 male) were theatre enthusiasts who went to the theatre more than once a month.

3.2 Method of Evaluation

Firstly, the 1:1 scale model was used to test the usability and ergonomics (see Fig. 9). After a 3-min observation period, the participants were told to disassemble the ticket

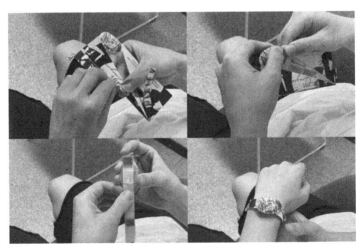

Fig. 9. Usability test.

and reassemble them into a bracelet. Moreover, the comfort of length and width of the ticket was also tested.

Secondly, a 10-min fragment extracted from the drama *Onegin* produced by Vakhtangov State Academic Theatre of Russia was played to the participants. The characters were full of emotional engagement represented by the narrator [27]. Moreover, the chosen fragment was an emotional peak in the story which described the decisive battle scene of two main characters and ended up in one's death. A smart watch was used to simulate the vibration during the performance. The type of haptics and the time period applied was designed according to the story (see Table 1). In the end, the bracelet was kept by the participants and then they were allowed to discuss the performance.

Table 1. Haptics types and time applied

Point-in-time	Type of Haptics	Storyline
05:22	Short, strong and instant vibration (●)	Gunshot sound (Lensky Died)
06:33-08:10	Long lasting and fine vibration (- - - - - -)	Blizzard after Lensky's death
07:47-08:01	Constant but stronger vibration (———)	People dragged Lensky over a sledge

3.3 Result

The result of the test (see Table 2) proved that applying haptics can partly increase the sense of engagement, however, only when applying the appropriate types of haptics that suit the storyline. For example, all participants agreed that during the gunshot scene, the clean instant haptic improved their engagement into the performance, however, for the blizzard vibration pattern, 40% of the participants didn't understand the connection between the haptics and the scene.

In addition, the test confirmed that the memorial bracelet could provide a participant with cordial feelings towards another person holding the same thing. Furthermore, the confirmation of attending the same venue could give participates a chance to discuss their feeling and form the sense of self-identity among the group. As mentioned by 3 participants:

"It is easier to start the conversation when you confirmed that the other person would know what you are talking about." (P1)

"The bracelet certainly provided me the feeling that me and others belonged to the same gang." (P3)

"After recognition of the bracelet, it is easy to know that we shared the same experience and somehow you just wanted to know the other people." (P4)

For the ease of using, all participants reported that the method of disassembling and reshaping was interesting to do. There was no report of confusion during assembling.

Table 2. Comments and feedbacks.

	Comments	Mentioned by (No.)
1	Vibration represented gunshot well	5
2	Vibration was confused for blizzard	2
3	Haptics improved watching experience	3
4	Memorial bracelet enhanced self-identification	4
5	The infographics on ticket was useful	3
6	Overall experience was interesting	4

4 Conclusion and Limitations

In conclusion, the primary test confirmed that haptics allowed the audiences to experience the plot as first-person perspective so that the sense of immersion could be improved. It shows a great potential in improving theatre experience. Meanwhile, symbolic icon could construct self-identity among groups, so that the sense of belonging could be formed.

The concept of *ESTENDERE* can provide an extended experience for audiences in theatre. It satisfies the needs of audiences in immersion and engagement, understanding and personal resonance, and social identification part. Firstly, with the correct pattern of the haptics, the immersion of the performance can be strengthened. As a result, producers must choose and design haptics patterns wisely. Secondly, the illustration of the play printed on the ticket provides the chance for the audience to preview the performance so that they would be familiar with the story and understand the story better. Finally, the recognition of the memorial bracelet increases the chance of conversation among the audiences so that a sense of self-recognition can be formed.

However, with the regard of limitations, the age group and occupation of the participants could not fully represent the real audience group. A larger scale of user testing could be conducted later to improve. The part of using emotion feedback to improve the performance is not tested. The efficiency of the method remains unknown. Moreover, the ethics of collecting data from audience should be set to avoid privacy leakage and misuse. A pre-notice should be published and ticked before gathering personal information.

References

1. Hume, M., Mort, G.S., Winzar, H.: Exploring repurchase intention in a performing arts context: who comes? And why do they come back? Int. J. Nonprofit Voluntary Sect. Mark. **12**, 135–148 (2007)
2. Sun, W.H.: The theatre of purgation and the theatre of cultivation: a comparative study of theatre and culture from a Chinese perspective. TDR **65**, 8–28 (2021)
3. Walmsley, B.: Why people go to the theatre: a qualitative study of audience motivation. J. Customer Behav. **10**, 335–351 (2011)
4. Pitts, S.E.: What makes an audience? Investigating the roles and experiences of listeners at a chamber music festival. Music Lett. **86**, 257–269 (2005)

5. New Economics Foundation: Capturing the Audience Experience: A Handbook for the Theatre. New Economics Foundation London, England (2008)
6. Bergadaà, M., Nyeck, S.: Quel marketing pour les activités artistiques: une analyse qualitative comparée des motivations des consommateurs et producteurs de théâtre. Recherche et Appl. en Mark. (French Edn.) **10**, 27–45 (1995)
7. Turner, J.C., Hogg, M.A., Oakes, P.J., Reicher, S.D., Wetherell, M.S.: Rediscovering the Social Group: A Self-categorization Theory. Basil Blackwell, Oxford (1987)
8. McCall, G.J., Simmons, J.L.: Identities and interactions (1966)
9. Stets, J.E., Burke, P.J.: Identity theory and social identity theory. Soc. Psychol. Q. **63**, 224–237 (2000)
10. Nicholson, R.E., Pearce, D.G.: Why do people attend events: a comparative analysis of visitor motivations at four South Island events. J. Travel Res. **39**, 449–460 (2001)
11. Arai, S., Pedlar, A.: Moving beyond individualism in leisure theory: a critical analysis of concepts of community and social engagement (2003)
12. Feldman, E.B.: Varieties of Visual Experience. Harry N. Abrams. Inc. Publishers, New York (1992)
13. Lindelof, A.M., Hansen, L.E.: Talking about theatre: audience development through dialogue. Participations **12**, 234–253 (2015)
14. Biggin, R.: Immersive Theatre and Audience Experience. Springer, Cham (2017). https://doi.org/10.1007/978-3-319-62039-8
15. Gomes, H.M., Savionek, D.: Measurement and evaluation of human exposure to vibration transmitted to hand-arm system during leisure cyclist activity. Revista Brasileira de Engenharia Biomédica **30**, 291–300 (2014)
16. van der Linden, J., et al.: Haptic reassurance in the pitch black for an immersive theatre experience. In: Proceedings of the 13th International Conference on Ubiquitous Computing, pp. 143–152 (2011)
17. Martin, J., Sauter, W., Fischer-Lichte, E., Ström, O.: Understanding Theatre: Performance Analysis in Theory and Practice. Almqvist & Wiksell International, Stockholm (1995)
18. McConachie, B.: Engaging Audiences: A Cognitive Approach to Spectating in the Theatre. Springer, New York (2008). https://doi.org/10.1057/9780230617025
19. Shu, L., et al.: Wearable emotion recognition using heart rate data from a smart bracelet. Sensors **20**, 718 (2020)
20. Ekman, P.: An argument for basic emotions. Cogn. Emot. **6**, 169–200 (1992)
21. Britton, A., Shipley, M., Malik, M., Hnatkova, K., Hemingway, H., Marmot, M.: Changes in heart rate and heart rate variability over time in middle-aged men and women in the general population (from the Whitehall II Cohort Study). Am. J. Cardiol. **100**, 524–527 (2007)
22. Valderas, M.T., Bolea, J., Laguna, P., Vallverdú, M., Bailón, R.: Human emotion recognition using heart rate variability analysis with spectral bands based on respiration. In: 2015 37th Annual International Conference of the IEEE Engineering in Medicine and Biology Society (EMBC), pp. 6134–6137. IEEE (2015)
23. Quiroz, J.C., Yong, M.H., Geangu, E.: Emotion-recognition using smart watch accelerometer data: preliminary findings. In: Proceedings of the 2017 ACM International Joint Conference on Pervasive and Ubiquitous Computing and Proceedings of the 2017 ACM International Symposium on Wearable Computers, pp. 805–812 (2017)
24. Nalepa, G.J., Kutt, K., Giżycka, B., Jemioło, P., Bobek, S.: Analysis and use of the emotional context with wearable devices for games and intelligent assistants. Sensors **19**, 2509 (2019)
25. Li, S., Cui, L., Zhu, C., Li, B., Zhao, N., Zhu, T.: Emotion recognition using Kinect motion capture data of human gaits. PeerJ **4**, e2364 (2016)
26. Denner, P.R., Rickards, J.P., Albanese, A.J.: The effect of story impressions preview on learning from narrative text. J. Exp. Educ. **71**, 313–332 (2003)
27. Cravens, C.: Lyric and narrative consciousness in Eugene Onegin. Slavic East Eur. J. **46**, 683–709 (2002)

Electroencephalography and Self-assessment Evaluation of Engagement with Online Exhibitions: Case Study of Google Arts and Culture

Jingjing Li[1]([✉])[ID], Chengbo Sun[2], Vargas Meza Xanat[1], and Yoichi Ochiai[1]

[1] Library and Information Media, University of Tsukuba, Tsukuba, Japan
li@digitalnature.slis.tsukuba.ac.jp
[2] Zhejiang University, Hangzhou, Zhejiang, China

Abstract. The COVID-19 pandemic has and will continue to have an unprecedented impact on museums and exhibition galleries worldwide, with online visitors to museums and exhibitions increasing significantly. The most common method used by web user experience researchers to study user engagement is questionnaires, usually conducted after the user has completed the website experience and relying on the user's memory and lingering feelings. Therefore, the purpose of this paper is to propose a new method of assessment based on a combination of user electroencephalography (EEG) signals and a self-assessment questionnaire (UES-SF). Since EEG signal measurement is a practical method to detect sequential changes in brain activity without significant time delays, it can comprehend visitors' unconscious and sensory responses to online exhibitions. This paper employed the Google Arts & Culture (GA&C) website as an example to study 4 different exhibition formats and their impact on user engagement. The questionnaire results showed that the "game interaction" was significantly higher ($p < 0.05$) in terms of participation than the "2D information Kiosks" and "3D virtual exhibitions" and was the marginally significant ($0.05 < p < 0.10$) than "video explanation". However, when we combined the EEG data, we could determine that "game interaction" had the highest user engagement, followed by "video explanation", "3D virtual exhibition", and the "2D information kiosk". Therefore, our new evaluation approach can assist online exhibition user experience researchers in understanding the impact of different forms of interaction on engagement more comprehensively.

Keywords: Online exhibition · Museum · COVID-19 · User Engagement (UE) · User Experience (UX) · Electroencephalography (EEG) · Self-assessment

1 Introduction

Museums assume the critical functions of historical and cultural transmission, cultural heritage preservation, education support, information exchange, etc. However, visiting museums in the physical world during the COVID-19 pandemic is difficult, so online museum visitors increased significantly [1]. With the development of 5G technology, the formats of cultural and artistic exhibitions have become more diverse. In response to the "digitization" of museums and galleries, this study will focus on the user engagement of online exhibitions. The purpose is to help UX researchers understand the impact of different forms of online exhibition interaction on user engagement.

1.1 Museums and Galleries Under the COVID-19 Pandemic

The cultural sector has been severely and persistently affected by the COVID-19 pandemic, with museums particularly hard hit: UNESCO reported that nearly 90% (an estimated 85,000 institutions) had been closed for varying lengths of time [1]. Museums in the majority of states were able to remain open in 2021. Based on their responses, less than half (43%) of the institutions have experienced a period of closure in early 2021[2]. ICOM reported the results of three surveys on the state of museums under the COVID-19 pandemic (1st survey Apr-May 2020/2nd survey Sep-Oct 2020/3rd survey Apr-May 2021), and the results of the third survey show a breakdown of the data by region [3]. It is well known that different regions of the world are affected by the virus to different degrees, especially due to its mutations.

In summary, cultural tourism and transportation worldwide have experienced a considerable slowdown, having a practical impact on museums and galleries, even those that have reopened their doors. Addressing these issues requires rapid planning for what was quickly termed the 'new normal' [4], which exacerbates the uncertain future for museums and galleries. A response to this is to turn to digital formats.

1.2 Background of Online Exhibition Under the COVID-19 Pandemic

Online Exhibitions in the Online Activities of Museums and Galleries. ICOM reported that online activities will continue to increase, in particular through the creation of new digital communication channels in the wake of lockdown. Besides, more museums and galleries are planning to add online exhibitions to their online activities after lockdowns (increasing 5.6%), and more are planning to start doing online exhibitions (increasing 6.5%) [3]. Digital communication activities increased for at least 15% of museums, whilst NEMO (2020) reported that 58% of museums held digital activities, (increasing 37%), and 23% started new ones [6]. Within the growing trend of online activities, exhibitions also show an increasing trend. Also, online exhibitions are more inclusive, allowing access to groups that would not normally have access to these spaces (physical museums and galleries).

2 User Engagement Evaluation Methods

Engagement is an essential aspect of measuring the quality of user experience, which emphasizes the positive aspects of interacting with an online application, especially the desire to use the application longer and repeatedly [7]. Web UX researchers want to develop more engaging interactive interfaces that help users actively participate in online exhibitions [35]. Figure 1 provides a roadmap of User engagement and User experience features applicable to online contexts. The roadmap shows that the interaction factor (the manners in which users interact with the interface) is the basis of user experience, which influences the immersion and emotion of the user throughout the interaction, and ultimately affects the user's engagement (see Fig. 1). In other words, the user, far from being passive, is an active actor that manipulates objects in a 3D environment, affecting their mood and, in turn, their engagement.

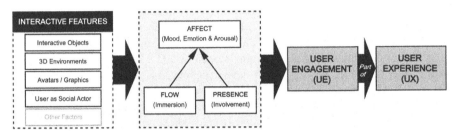

Fig. 1. This diagram represents the relationship between interaction features and UE and UX.

The evaluation methods of user engagement in user experience research are mainly divided into subjective and objective measurement methods. Regarding personal measurement methods, some researchers have developed self-report questionnaires based on UE attributes [8–10]. Jacques' Survey of Evaluated Engagement (SEE) consists of 14 questions related to attention, motivation, control, need satisfaction, time perception, and attitude, suggesting that the SEE could derive either an overall user engagement score or a score for each attribute [8]. Webster and Ho's questionnaire was made up of two questions for each of the Engagement and Influences on Engagement measures, as well as an overall item, "The presentation medium was engaging," for a total of fifteen questions [10]. O'Brien built on the work of Jacques and Webster and Ho with the User Engagement Scale (UES) [9, 11].

The UES proposed by O'Brien was constructed through an iterative scale development and assessment process. There is overlap with the SEE, Webster and Ho questionnaires (e.g., attention is a core component), but there are also differences. In addition to the supervisor measure, another aspect of the engagement assessment methodology is an objective measure [25]. This paper will conduct a subjective study based on a short-form version of the questionnaire proposed by O'Brien for the UES (UES-SF) [15], summarizing the objective measures of the six attributes of involvement as presented in Table 1.

Table 1. Summary of six attributes of user engagement. Potential objective methods of measurement (beyond subjective research methods, such as questionnaires, if any) are included.

Attribute	Description	Measure methods	Ref
Focused Attention (FA)	Feeling absorbed in the interaction and losing track of time	Apparent fast pacing of time, follow on task performance, eye tracking	[7, 11–15]
Perceived Usability (PU)	The perceived high degree of control and low effort spent in the interaction	Evaluation Scale for Perceived Usability (e.g., SUS, UMUX, CSUQ)	[16]
Aesthetic Appeal (AE)	The attractiveness and visual appeal of the interface	Online activity (Curiosity-driven Behaviour), Physiological sensors (e.g., Eye Tracking)	[15, 17, 18]
Endurability (EN)	The overall success of the interaction and users' willingness to recommend an application to others or engage with it in the future	Website access data (e.g., Number of mouse clicks, number of visits), Online activity (e.g., bookmarking)	[19–22]
Novelty (NO)	Variety of sudden and unexpected changes (visual or auditory) that cause excitement and joy or alarm	Physiological sensors (e.g., Blood Pressure)	[10, 23, 24, 37]
Felt Involvement (FI)	The sense of being "drawn in" and having fun	Physiological sensors (e.g., Heart Beat)	[7, 11]

Regarding online exhibitions, it is unclear which types of interaction scenarios or interfaces are more appealing to exhibition users. There are no sufficiently systematic or comprehensive strategies to assess how users engage with different interaction formats. Moreover, the current evaluation methods of user engagement are mainly questionnaires and interviews, which rely on users' recollections of their online interaction experiences and have some drawbacks. For example, users usually forget detailed information about the experience process, leading to incomplete judgments about their experience feelings. Conventional assessment methods are not sensitive to how an interaction changes over time [7]. Furthermore, there have not been enough studies on engagement in online exhibitions in conjunction with users' EEG signal data. This study hopes to fill this gap with a case study of the Google Arts & Culture (GA&C) website.

3   Methodology

This study is based on the questionnaire research method and explores a new approach to evaluate user engagement by combining the user's real-time EEG signal. Current research employing users' EEG signals is extensive and applied to many fields [26, 39]. However, there is little research on the relationship between interface interaction and user engagement in online exhibitions based on EEG signals, which is the focus of this work.

Users' interaction with interfaces is a complex cognitive activity with three dimensions: affective, cognitive, and behavioural [27]. The most immediate measure of user involvement is human brain activity signals, which can highlight the degree of involvement and affective states during interactions with an artefact through a digital interface. The contribution of this study is to combine EEG signals with the self-assessment report UES-SF [28] to develop a more comprehensive user engagement evaluation method in the context of 4 different types of exhibition interactions.

3.1   Case Study: 4 Forms of Interaction in Google Culture & Arts

The GA&C project was launched in 2011 in partnership with 17 of the world's most renowned museums. The collaboration has since grown to include over 1500 museums and cultural institutions. With the aim of making culture more accessible, the project has digitized millions of artefacts and made them available online for anyone to access [29].

The available features in the GA&C platform are [30]: Virtual Museum Tour, Explore and Discover, Zoom Views, Create Your Own Collections, and Educational Content. Moreover, the platform has search features that help users find artworks easily and intuitively, such as filtering searches by artist, museum, medium, date, country, art movement, historical event, and colour. It can also suggest relevant artworks based on any of these criteria. Since the GA&C online exhibition platform includes most of the functions of currently popular online exhibitions, it was selected as a case study in this paper.

Four Forms of Interaction in GA&C. In this paper, we classify online exhibitions websites into four types based on the differences in the interaction methods between exhibits and users in the GA&C online exhibitions website.

These four types are as follows (also see Fig. 2):

1. 2D Information Kiosk: it communicates information about the exhibits to the visitors in a graphic format, including pictures/text/diagrams, etc.
2. 3D Virtual Exhibition: virtual recreation of physical three-dimensional (3D) exhibitions or museums that allow a visitor to navigate in a way that is closer to reality [31].
3. Interactive Game: puzzles/colouring games/photography games that the visitors can manipulate, etc.
4. Video Instruction: videos that teach the background of the exhibits, the author's story/content of the exhibition analysis, etc.

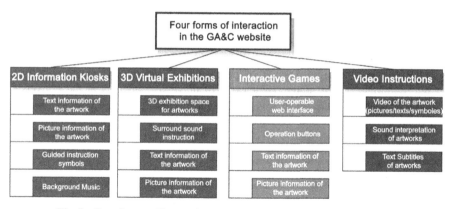

Fig. 2. Four forms of interaction in the GA&C online exhibition website

3.2 User Data Collection: EEG and Self-assessment Questionnaire (UES-SF)

Electroencephalography (EEG) Signal Data. The human brain contains neurons that communicate through electrical impulses [32]. EEG signal measurements are a practical method for detecting sequential changes in brain activity without significant time delays, which can aid our understanding of visitors' unconscious and sensory responses to online exhibitions. In addition, with the development of EEG detection devices, non-invasive headset-based detectors are now dramatically more accurate and have been used in a broader range of applications [5].

User Engagement Scale - Short Form (UES-SF). The User Engagement Scale (UES) is a tool developed to measure user engagement and has been used in a variety of digital domains [38]. It is designed to measure six attributes of user engagement: aesthetic appeal, focused attention, novelty, perceived usability, felt involvement, and endurability. The UES-SF is a short form (SF) of the UES, shortened from 31 items to 12 items, reducing user response time [28]. It is composed by:

- FA: Focused attention, definitions are described in Table 1 (3 items).
- PU: Perceived usability, definitions are described in Table 1 (3 items)
- AE: Aesthetic appeal, definitions are described in Table 1 (3 items).
- RW: Reward Factor, which is a single set of items made up of the EN (Endurability), NO (Novelty) and FI (Felt involvement) components in the original UES (3 items).

3.3 User Data Analysis: Evaluation of User Engagement

The data from the self-assessment questionnaire for self-engagement (UES-SF) were subjected to repeated ANOVA to derive differences in engagement across interaction modalities. Then, the two-dimensional brain function network maps corresponding to the different interaction modalities were analyzed based on the EEG data of the users. Results of the analysis of the corresponding users' questionnaire data were combined with the users' two-dimensional brain functional network maps, thus further describing the differences in the users' engagement under different interaction modalities of online exhibitions.

4   Experiment Design

4.1   Experiment Participants

We conducted tests (in English) on 20 participants (N = 20), ten self-identified as male and ten as female in this study. They were all university students at the University of Tsukuba, and their age range was 23–27. Furthermore, they are all right-handed individuals.

4.2   Experiment Scene and Equipment

Online Exhibition Website Experience Scene. The study cases were selected from the GA&C website, and we divided them into four tasks corresponding to the four forms of exchange on the website (refer to chapter 3.1 for more detailed information), each with an experience time of 5 min. The four tasks were Task 1 (2D information kiosk), Task 2 (3D virtual exhibition), Task 3 (interactive game), and Task 4 (video instruction). Each task had a total duration of 5 min:

1. Task 1: Selected from the "1. 2D Information Kiosk" interaction format, two web pages.
2. Task 2: From the "2. 3D Virtual Exhibitions" interactive format, one virtual scene.
3. Task 3: Selected from the "3. Interactive Games" interactive format, two interactive games.
4. Task 4: Selected from the "4. Video Instructions" interactive format, one video.

Indoor Experiment Space. We recreated a scenario of users experiencing the online exhibition website at home during the experiment. Being in a scenario similar to daily life can help participants relax quickly and get into the state they usually do when using the website in their own homes. A relaxed state also helps to collect stable user EEG data. The experimental indoor space was identical for the 20 participants and was kept well ventilated to mitigate the possibility of COVID-19 transmission (see Fig. 3).

Fig. 3. Front and back view of indoor experimental space.

Experimental Equipment. The experimental equipment was of two main types:

- Participants visited the online exhibition website using a PC, a mouse, and earphones.
- The experiment performer collected data from participants' feedback with a PC, an EPOCX headset [33], a tablet, and a phone.

4.3 Experiment Steps

At the beginning of the experiment, the researcher explained the experiment's purpose, procedure, and helped the participants wear the device to ensure their comfort. Participants learned how to operate Task 1 to 4 in online exhibitions to familiarize themselves with the specific interaction processes; the whole process lasted 5 min. We collected EEG signal data from participants during each task experience with EPOCX [34]. At the end of each experience, participants were asked to complete a UES-SF questionnaire. They then moved on to the next task until all four tasks and questionnaires were completed within one hour (see Fig. 4). The questionnaires during the experiment were created in Microsoft Forms, while the collected results were organized in Microsoft Excel and analyzed statistically in SPSS. Data collected throughout the experiment was entered anonymously to protect the participants' privacy.

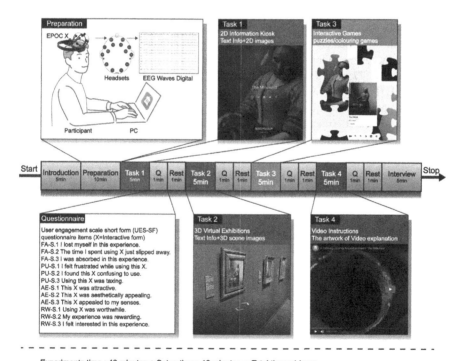

Experiments time : 48 minutes + Setup time : 12 minutes = Total time : 1 hour

Fig. 4. Flow diagram of experimental tasks

5 Results

5.1 USE-SF Self-assessment

Results of the USE-SF questionnaire yielded the mean values of the four tasks in four aspects (FA: Focused Attention/PU: Perceived Usability/AE: Aesthetic Appeal/RW: Reward Factor) and the mean values of the overall engagement (refer to chapter 3.2). The bar chart below represents the above results (see Fig. 5), revealing that Task 3 had the highest overall engagement.

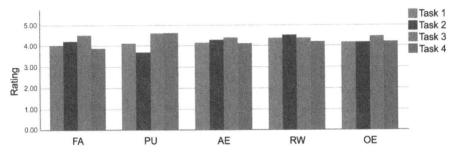

Fig. 5. Bar chart based on the average value of the four tasks in different aspects of the questionnaire results and the average value of the overall engagement.

Table 2 shows repeated-measures ANOVA on all subjects' scores to compare the differences between the four tasks. The four tasks differed significantly on two indicators, FA ($F(3,57) = 4.377$, $p = .008$) and PU ($F(3,57) = 10.797$, $p = .000$), but not on two indicators, AE ($F(3,57) = 1.005$, $p = .367$) and RW ($F(3,57) = 1.157$, $p = .334$). Paired comparisons showed that subjects' overall engagement was significantly higher in Task 3 than in the other tasks (mean score 4.475 of a total score of 5). Table 3 presents paired comparisons of the overall engagement values for the four tasks.

Table 2. Within-subjects effect test for different indicators under four tasks

UES-SF	SS	df	MS	F	p
Focused Attention (FA)	4.415	3	1.472	4.377**	.008
Perceived Usability (PU)	12.300	3	4.100	10.797**	.000
Aesthetic Appeal (AE)	1.078	3	.359	1.005	.397
Reward Factor (RW)	1.015	3	.338	1.157	.334
Overall Engagement (OE)	1.268	3	.423	2.082	.113

5.2 Participant's EEG Signal Data Analysis

We can analyse users' EEG activity at different periods based on the real-time EEG signals. A screenshot of the interface from 1 to 5 min at each minute (see Fig. 6), and

Table 3. Paired Comparisons for the four tasks

(I) OE	(J) OE	Average deviation (I-J)	Standard deviation	P-value[b]
Task1	Task 2	.000	.173	.999
Task1	Task 3	−.300	.167	.088
Task1	Task 4	−.033	.125	.793
Task2	Task 3	−.300*	.120	.021
Task2	Task 4	−.033	.144	.818
Task3	Task 4	.267*	.116	.033

*. Significance at the .05 level.
[b]. Multiple comparisons without adjustment.

the corresponding users' aggregated EEG activity state in 2D brain functional network diagrams while experiencing the four tasks (see Fig. 7) are shown below.

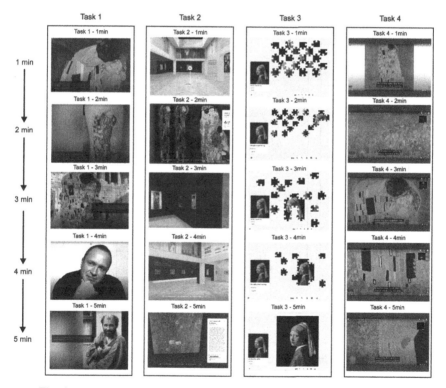

Fig. 6. Screen display status of five times for four tasks at 1, 2, 3, 4 and 5 min.

In Tables 2 and 3, the highest overall engagement was observed for Task 3, coinciding with the corresponding more active EEG signal in Fig. 7, engaging several parts of the brain corresponding to it. The EEG signal activity was less signal active in Task 1.

The functional brain network plot in Fig. 7 is an average of the sum of data from 20 participants. The red dots in the figure represent the 14 channels of the detected brain (7 channels each on the left and right), which match the 14 detection points of the detection device (EPOCX) we used. The line between the red dots represents the active EEG signal between the two points. The figure shows that the EEG activity during the participants' experience of task 1 was mainly concentrated in the left brain, with relatively little activity in the right brain. In comparison, EEG activity was active throughout the brain in Task 2, Task 3, and Task 4 and was particularly obvious in Task 3. The differences between the four tasks illustrate that different interaction experiences stimulate EEG signal activity between different regions.

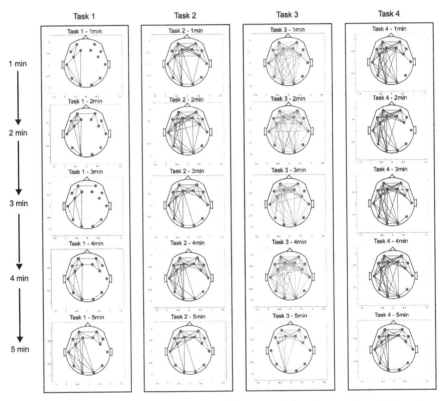

Fig. 7. 2D Functional brain network diagram of the users during the experiment. The columns indicate each interaction task at 1, 2, 3, 4, and 5 min.

Therefore, the authors used 2D functional brain network maps to distinguish the interaction forms that did not differ significantly in USE-SF. Our study summarized a bar chart based on the number of EEG signal activities in the 2D brain functional network map and divided the bar chart into six sections (see Fig. 8). These six sections are the number of times participants had EEG signal activity at 1, 2, 3, 4, and 5 min of each task and the average number of EEG signal activities from 1–5 min.

Regarding the number of EEG signal activities for the four tasks in the two-dimensional brain functional network map, we performed repeated ANOVAs, including within-subject comparisons and paired comparisons. In the within-subject comparison, the significance was 0.000001, indicating a significant within-subject difference. In Table 4, we performed in paired comparisons, and it can be seen that there were significant differences between Task 1 and the other three tasks ($p < 0.05$), respectively. Moreover, it can be seen that there is a significant difference between task 3 and task 1 and task 2 ($p < 0.05$), and a borderline significant difference with task 4 ($p = 0.059$). However, there was no significant difference between task 2 and task 4 ($p = 0.313$).

Therefore, combining the results of subject and paired comparisons, this study classified the four forms of interaction into three levels of engagement (high/medium/low). The number of EEG signal activities per minute was divided into three levels: the high level was 45–60 times/min, the medium level was 25–35 times/min, and the low level was 10–20 times/min. Based on the division of this level, the highest level of engagement was Task1, the medium was Task2 and Task4, and the lowest was Task1.

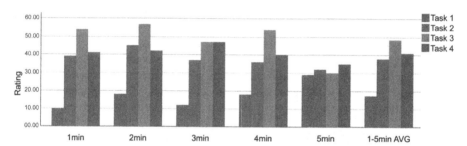

Fig. 8. Bar graphs based on the number of EEG signals averaged over 1, 2, 3, 4, 5 min and 1–5 min overall time for each interactive task in a 2D functional brain network map of activity.

Table 4. Paired Comparisons for the four tasks

(I) OA	(J) OA	Average deviation (I-J)	Standard deviation	P-value[b]
Task 1	Task 2	−24.750*	2.394	.002
Task 1	Task 3	−38.500*	2.021	.000
Task 1	Task 4	−28.000*	3.028	.003
Task 2	Task 3	−13.750*	1.750	.004
Task 2	Task 4	−3.250	2.689	.313
Task 3	Task 4	10.500	3.524	.059

*. Significance at the .05 level.
[b]. Multiple comparisons without adjustment.

6 Conclusion and Discussion

Our study collected data on users' EEG signals and self-assessment questionnaires, evaluating four forms of interaction with the online exhibition based on EEG and self-assessment questionnaires.

Task 3, a puzzle game, engaged most areas of the brain, showing high activation that faded gradually as the task was completed. The frontal part of the brain, where working memory and selective attention are located, was continuously active. Further, the nearly continuous anterior activation suggests that areas of the brain associated with problem-solving were functioning at different moments of completing the task. The result of playing a game can be viewed as a beneficial exercise for the brain, particularly if there is a training phase [36]. Therefore, it is not surprising that Task 3 received the highest score in the survey.

Task 2 consisted of visiting an online gallery, while Task 4 was a video. Both tasks activated nearly the same brain regions, with slightly more intense activity likely related to visual perception in Task 4, while Task 2 was more focused on motor/spatial navigation. However, based on our survey results, we can conclude that attention levels were not as high as in Task 3. Finally, in Task 1, participants encountered various artefacts. Based on the network diagram, their brains were likely assessing similarities and differences of each item, as shown in the left frontal and left parietal lobes. Further, they were paying little attention, based on the low activity of the frontal lobe. This last result is clearer based on the EEG signals than in the survey responses.

Our study concludes that the four tasks can be understood in a basic way by the results of the self-assessment questionnaire, which showed the highest involvement in task 3. Then, combined with the brain function network map of the participants' EEG signal activity during the completion of each task, it was clarified that the engagement of task 2 and task 4 was second only to task 3, and task 1 had the lowest engagement. Furthermore, based on the average of this bar chart for minutes 1–5, compared to the overall engagement average of the questionnaire, we can see a more significant variation between the four tasks (see Fig. 9).

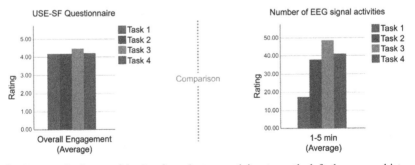

Fig. 9. Comparative image of the data from the two participants: on the left, the average histogram of the overall participation of the USE-SF questionnaire; on the right, the average histogram of the number of EEG signal activities per minute in 1–5 min.

This paper offers proof that relevant information will be lost in the study of user engagement if only questionnaires or interviews are used. Therefore, by increasing the collection of user EEG data, this paper can help UX researchers to understand information about the state of users during experiencing online exhibitions in a more comprehensive way.

Regarding limitations of our study, there were no controls for differences in the level of interest in art among participants. It was conducted only among young people with higher levels of education located in the same country. Moreover, there was no detailed comparison of differences in the activity of different brain regions (e.g., left and right brain) across the four tasks for the 20 participants [39]. If there were significant differences between different brain regions, that could indicate that different interaction styles affect users' creativity or logical thinking skills.

7 Future Work

Future research should consider more carefully the potential impact of external factors on EEG signal users, e.g., the potential impact on EEG signals of the way users manipulate web pages when visiting online exhibitions. Furthermore, future research could develop a global user database using EEG combined with other methods. In this way, user engagement across online exhibitions and other digital interactions could be evaluated faster and more accurately.

Acknowledgements. This work was supported by JST SPRING (grant number JPMJSP2124), and CREST (grant number JPMJCR19F2).

References

1. United Nations Educational, Scientific and Cultural Organisation: UNESCO Report: Museums around the world in the face of COVID-19. UNESCO (2020). https://unesdoc.unesco.org/ark:/48223/pf0000373530/PDF/373530eng.pdf.multi
2. United Nations Educational, Scientific and Cultural Organisation: UNESCO Report: Museums around the world in the face of COVID-19. UNESCO (2021). https://unesdoc.unesco.org/ark:/48223/pf0000376729_eng/PDF/376729eng.pdf.multi
3. International Council of Museums: ICOM Report: Museums, museum professionals and Covid-19: third survey. ICOM (2021). https://icom.museum/wp-content/uploads/2021/07/Museums-and-Covid-19_third-ICOM-report.pdf
4. Johnson, H.: Arts and culture in a 'new normal.' Psychologist **33**, 98–99 (2020)
5. LaRocco, J., Le, M.D., Paeng, D.-G.: A systemic review of available low-cost EEG headsets used for drowsiness detection. Front. Neuroinform. **42** (2020)
6. King, E., et al.: Digital responses of UK museum exhibitions to the COVID-19 crisis, March–June 2020. Curator: Museum J. **64**, 487–504 (2021)
7. O'Brien, H.L., Toms, E.G.: What is user engagement? A conceptual framework for defining user engagement with technology. J. Am. Soc. Inform. Sci. Technol. **59**(6), 938–955 (2008)
8. Jacques, R.D.: The nature of engagement and its role in hypermedia evaluation and design. Diss. South Bank University (1996)

9. O'Brien, H.: Defining and measuring engagement in user experiences with technology. ProQuest (2009)
10. Webster, J., Ho, H.: Audience engagement in multimedia presentations. ACM SIGMIS Database: Database Adv. Inf. Syst. **28**(2), 63–77 (1997)
11. O'Brien, H.L., Toms, E.G.: The development and evaluation of a survey to measure user engagement. J. Am. Soc. Inform. Sci. Technol. **61**(1), 50–69 (2010)
12. Baldauf, D., Burgard, E., Wittmann, M.: Time perception as a workload measure in simulated car driving. Appl. Ergon. **40**(5), 929–935 (2009)
13. Jennett, C., et al.: Measuring and defining the experience of immersion in games. Int. J. Hum.-Comput. Stud. **66**(9), 641–661 (2008)
14. Csikszentmihalyi, M., Csikzentmihaly, M.: Flow: The Psychology of Optimal Experience, vol. 1990. Harper & Row, New York (1990)
15. Ikehara, C.S., Crosby, M.E.: Assessing cognitive load with physiological sensors. In: Proceedings of the 38th Annual Hawaii International Conference on System Sciences. IEEE (2005)
16. Lewis, J.R.: Measuring perceived usability: SUS, UMUX, and CSUQ ratings for four everyday products. Int. J. Hum.-Comput. Interact. **35**(15), 1404–1419 (2019)
17. Jennings, M.: Theory and models for creating engaging and immersive ecommerce websites. In: Proceedings of the 2000 ACM SIGCPR Conference on Computer Personnel Research (2000)
18. Tractinsky, N., Katz, A.S., Ikar, D.: What is beautiful is usable. Interact. Comput. **13**(2), 127–145 (2000)
19. Read, J.C., MacFarlane, S., Casey, C.: Endurability, engagement and expectations: measuring children's fun. In: Interaction Design and Children, vol. 2, no. 2002. Shaker Publishing, Eindhoven (2002)
20. Peterson, E.T.: How do you calculate engagement? Part I. Web Analytics Demystified (blog) (2006). http://blog.webanalyticsdemystified.com/weblog/2006/12/how-do-you-calcul ate-engagement-part-i.html. Accessed Oct 2009
21. Piwowarski, B., Dupret, G., Jones, R.: Mining user web search activity with layered Bayesian networks or how to capture a click in its context. In: Proceedings of the Second ACM International Conference on Web Search and Data Mining (2009)
22. White, R.W., Dumais, S.T.: Characterizing and predicting search engine switching behavior. In: Proceedings of the 18th ACM Conference on Information and Knowledge Management (2009)
23. Huang, M.-H.: Designing website attributes to induce experiential encounters. Comput. Hum. Behav. **19**(4), 425–442 (2003)
24. Said, N.S.: An engaging multimedia design model. In: Proceedings of the 2004 Conference on Interaction Design and Children: Building a Community (2004)
25. Attfield, S., et al.: Towards a science of user engagement (position paper). In: WSDM Workshop on User Modelling for Web Applications (2011)
26. Jap, B.T., et al.: Using EEG spectral components to assess algorithms for detecting fatigue. Expert Syst. Appl. **36**(2), 2352–2359 (2009)
27. Lalmas, M., O'Brien, H., Yom-Tov, E.: Measuring user engagement. Synth. Lect. Inf. Concepts Retrieval Serv. **6**(4), 1–132 (2014)
28. O'Brien, H.L., Cairns, P., Hall, M.: A practical approach to measuring user engagement with the refined user engagement scale (UES) and new UES short form. Int. J. Hum. Comput. Stud. **112**, 28–39 (2018)
29. WIKIPEDIA, Google Arts & Culture Page. https://en.wikipedia.org/wiki/Google_Arts_% 26_Culture#cite_note-15
30. St. Francis College Library, Google Arts & Culture Page. https://library.sfc.edu/Google/art sandculture

31. Carmo, M.B., Cláudio, A.P.: 3D virtual exhibitions. DESIDOC J. Libr. Inf. Technol. **33**(3), 1–14 (2013)
32. Khurana, V., et al.: EEG based word familiarity using features and frequency bands combination. Cogn. Syst. Res. **49**, 33–48 (2018)
33. EMOTIV. EPOC X. Product information page. https://www.emotiv.com/epoc-x/
34. Andujar, M., Gilbert, J.E.: Let's learn! Enhancing user's engagement levels through passive brain-computer interfaces. In: CHI 2013 Extended Abstracts on Human Factors in Computing Systems, pp. 703–708 (2013)
35. Hart, J., Sutcliffe, A., di Angeli, A.: Evaluating user engagement theory (2012)
36. Denilson, B.T., Nouchi, R., Kawashima, R.: Does video gaming have impacts on the brain: evidence from a systematic review. Brain Sci. **9**(10), 251 (2019)
37. Aboulafia, A., Bannon, L.J.: Understanding affect in design: an outline conceptual framework. Theor. Issues Ergon. Sci. **5**(1), 4–15 (2004)
38. O'Brien, H.L., Toms, E.G.: Examining the generalizability of the User Engagement Scale (UES) in exploratory search. Inf. Process. Manag. **49**(5), 1092–1107 (2013)
39. Kowatari, Y., et al.: Neural networks involved in artistic creativity. Hum. Brain Mapp. **30**(5), 1678–1690 (2009)

Artwork Reproduction Through Display Based on Hyperspectral Imaging

Kyudong Sim[1] , Jong-Il Park[1]([✉]) , Masaki Hayashi[2] , and Meeko Kuwahara[3]

[1] Hanyang University, Seongdong-gu, Seoul, Republic of Korea
{kdsim,jipark}@hanyang.ac.kr
[2] Uppsala University, Gotland, Sweden
masaki.hayashi@speldesign.uu.se
[3] Meisei University, Hodokubo, Tokyo, Japan
meeko.kuwahara@meisei-u.ac.kr

Abstract. If an actual artwork is photographed with a camera and rendered through a display for observation, the color expression changes three times when photographed with a camera, displayed, and observed again. This paper introduces a color correction method that makes the actual artwork and the displayed artwork look the same. This correction method performs color correction by understanding the lighting environment where the artwork is located and the color sensitivity of the observer. The proposed color correction method is a two-step process, using hyperspectral imaging and color mapping of display device. Hyperspectral imaging is a method that can acquire each pixel of an artwork as a reflection spectrum, and can be used for re-illumination on a spectral level. Color mapping performs mapping between the digital values of 343 color samples and the captured values of the displayed color samples. These two steps of color correction provide an experience in which the actual artwork and the displayed artwork look the same. The method proposed in this paper is expected to contribute to a more realistic virtual experience.

Keywords: Hyperspectral Imaging · Reproduction · Color correction · Display

1 Introduction

With the development of digital technology, opportunities to access artworks in virtual environments are increasing. However, the virtual experience of the artwork through the display will look different from the actual artwork. The reason is the illumination environment of the place where the artwork is placed, and there are various causes such as the camera that took the artwork, color expression of display, and the eyes of the observer. To solve this problem, cameras and displays have been enhanced to render and photograph based on standard colors, respectively. However, this process has a limitation in that lighting is premised and the characteristics of the camera and the display are measured separately.

© The Author(s), under exclusive license to Springer Nature Switzerland AG 2022
M. Rauterberg (Ed.): HCII 2022, LNCS 13324, pp. 332–342, 2022.
https://doi.org/10.1007/978-3-031-05434-1_22

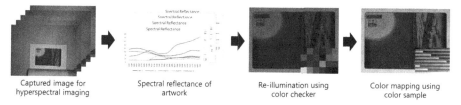

| Captured image for hyperspectral imaging | Spectral reflectance of artwork | Re-illumination using color checker | Color mapping using color sample |

Fig. 1. Pipeline of proposed method.

In this paper, we propose a method of displaying artworks looking the same as real artworks using hyperspectral imaging. The pipeline is shown in Fig. 1. First, the artwork is photographed using hyperspectral imaging. The artworks acquired in this way have information in the spectral reflectance. The spectral reflectance can be re-illuminated as RGB images based on the lighting and camera of the place where the artwork is present. The re-illuminated image is color-converted through color mapping created from the display's color samples. The final image generated in this way is displayed through a display that looks like an actual artwork through color conversion.

2 Related Works

This paper consists of hyperspectral imaging and color correction. The hyperspectral imaging is a method that can acquire spectral reflectance, and related studies include methods using multiple lights or multiple cameras [1–3]. We obtain the spectral reflectance with sufficient number of lights to acquire the spectral reflectance and use it as a means for re-illumination.

On the other hand, it is difficult to find research directly related to the color correction we are propose. However, studies related to calibration and color errors for cameras and monitors are being studied so that existing art works can be seen identically on the display.

A typical camera detects three colors red, blue, and green from visible light with a light sensor. By using a representative color such as a color checker, the color of the camera can be calibrated by comparing it to the color detected by the camera sensor. In general, since it is difficult to obtain an ideal color from a color checker, there are studies such as a method of correcting the color with the minimum error [4] and a method of overcoming the non-uniform illumination field [5].

A general monitor combines colors by emitting light of three colors: red, blue, and green. Various studies are being conducted to check whether the colors combined with the monitor light are the intended colors. There are methods such as calibrating the monitor to check whether the light intensity is properly controlled [6], and adjusting the color by calculating the color difference [7].

The above correction is affected by the method of calculating the color difference. The difference in color can vary depending on where the standard is placed, and since they are equipment for human vision, research has been conducted in the direction of measuring the color error close to the color difference perceived by humans [f1-3].

3 Hyperspectral Imaging and Re-illumination

Hyperspectral imaging can be obtained from a linear camera model as in Eq. 1.

$$I = \int s(\lambda)c(\lambda)p(\lambda)d\lambda \tag{1}$$

where I is the RGB value, $p(\lambda)$ is the power spectrum of the light, $c(\lambda)$ is the spectral response of the camera, and $s(\lambda)$ is the spectral reflectance of the object, and λ is the wavelength. Here, the spectral reflectance of the object can be expressed with fewer variables through the Parkkinen basis function, which is the result of PCA of the spectral reflectance [11]. If we summarize the equations expressed in wavelength including the basis function into one, the following Eq. 2, 3 can be obtained.

$$I = \sum_{k=1}^{K_s} \sigma_k \int b_k(\lambda)c(\lambda)p(\lambda)d\lambda \tag{2}$$

$$I = \sigma F \tag{3}$$

Here, if an object with a known spectral reflectance, such as a color checker, is used, the F matrix can be obtained because the RGB values and σ values are determined. This F matrix expresses the characteristics of lighting and camera as shown in Eq. 2. And by using this F matrix, it can be arranged as in Eq. 4, and the spectral reflectance R can be obtained using this.

$$BF^{-1}I = B\sigma = R \tag{4}$$

Here, B and σ are the basis functions and coefficients, and Eq. 2 is expressed as a matrix. Re-illumination is obtained using the F matrix containing the camera and illumination information, and the spectral reflectance. Using the characteristic of the basis function, the coefficient σ can be obtained from the spectral reflectance, and the RGB values can be obtained using the F matrix, which is shown in Eq. 5.

$$I = \sigma F = B^T R F \tag{5}$$

4 Color Mapping for Display

Display color mapping uses a color sample generated by sampling RGB values at regular intervals. The color sample was made to have a total of 343 colors by dividing 3 RGB channels into 7 sections each. A color value with a fixed digital value is displayed like a color sample, and if we capture by a camera, we can check which camera's RGB value is mapped to the displayed digital value. Through the mapping values obtained in this way, we can check how the camera receives the displayed RGB digital values, and vice versa. With the mapping in the opposite direction, we get color corrections that look like real artwork (Fig. 2).

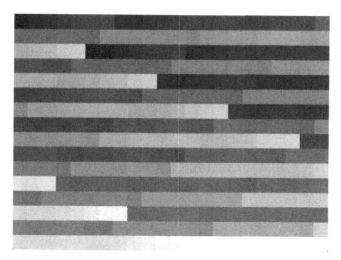

Fig. 2. Color samples used for display color mapping.

Finding the digital color of the display from the colors acquired by the camera proceeds as shown in Fig. 3. The digital value of the color sample that appears on the display will be referred to as digital data, and the color of the color sample acquired with the camera will be referred to as captured data. And two color data exist in each color space. 343 color samples are mapped to each other in two spaces. Digital data is positioned regularly, such as how color samples were created, while captured data is irregular. Using internal division in each color space, we can find which captured data maps digital data that does not correspond to a color sample. As the digital data changes, it is mapped to other captured data, and as the digital data continues to change, the captured color we are looking for will be found. After all, the color captured by the camera can be found on the display what digital value it is.

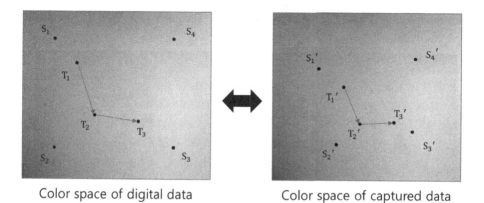

Color space of digital data   Color space of captured data

Fig. 3. Color mapping in color space. SS stands for color sample and SS shows the change to find SS in the captured data space.

5   Experimental Results

The proposed method in this paper uses re-illumination from the spectral reflectance and color correction. Each of the two processes uses a color checker and a color sample, and when both information is acquired at once, it appears as shown in Fig. 4. In the actual experiment, the display is captured after the light is turned off to avoid the reflection of the monitor.

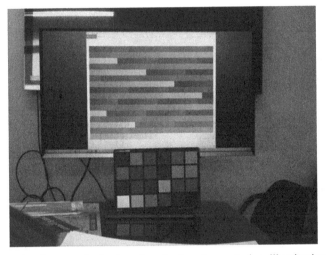

Fig. 4. Displayed color sample (top), color checker for capturing illumination and camera characteristics (bottom).

    For capturing color sample on monitor, the brightness of the monitor varies depending on the position of the camera. The position facing the camera is brighter and the edges are darker. To reduce this difference, a white screen is displayed and the screen is captured. This information is used to correct the brightness. The color samples thus obtained is

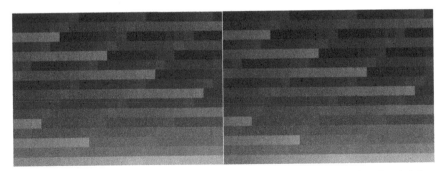

Fig. 5. Color sample before brightness correction (left), and color sample after brightness correction (right)

shown in Fig. 5. The picture on the left is before brightness correction, and the picture on the right is after brightness correction.

Spectral reflectance can be acquired using multiple lights and color checkers by hyperspectral imaging. In this experiment, 5 types of lights were used and 5 type of images were acquired as shown in Fig. 6.

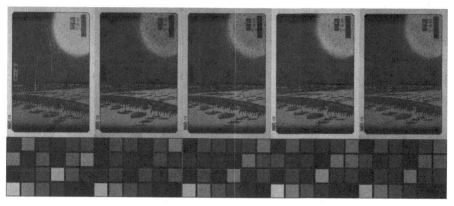

Fig. 6. Artwork and color checker images obtained using 5 different lights.

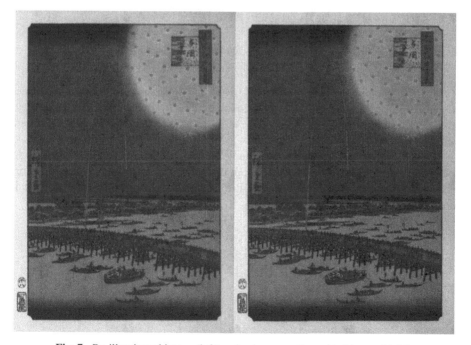

Fig. 7. Re-illuminated image (left) and color correction added image (right).

The re-illuminated image from the spectral reflectance and the image with color mapping added are shown in Fig. 7, 8. It can be seen that the color mapping of the display affects the color change.

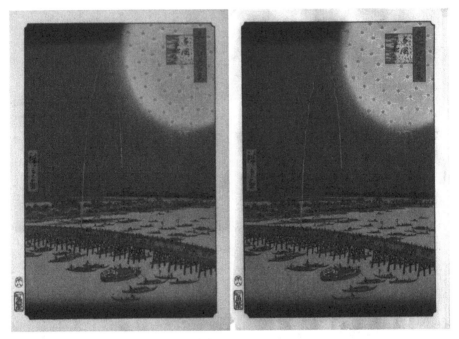

Fig. 8. Displayed artwork (left) and real artwork (right).

Figure 9 is a picture taken of the real artwork and the displayed image at the same time. By capturing at the same time, the location of the artwork changed, and the display was also affected by the fluorescent light, but it can be seen that almost similar images were obtained.

Macbeth color checker was used to evaluate the performance of the proposed method. The RGB image obtained by re-illuminating the spectral reflectance of Macbeth color checker with current illumination, the RGB image with color mapping, and the actual color checker were used.

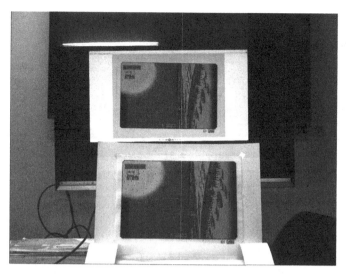

Fig. 9. Virtual artwork by display (top) and real artwork (bottom).

Figure 10 shows color checkers with only re-illumination applied and no color mapping applied. It can be seen that the color characteristics of the monitor is not considered, and the color difference between the two color checkers is very large. Figure 11 shows color checkers applied up to color mapping. It can be seen that the colors of the two color checkers have been greatly reduced.

The color difference between the actual color checker and the re-illuminated image and the color difference between the actual color checker and the color mapped image were obtained as shown in Table 1. The average color difference of 24 colors is shown.

Table 1. Color difference between created color checker image and actual color checker

Created image	R	G	B	ΔE^*_{00}
Re-illuminated image	28.2	42.6	30.8	19.2
Color mapped image	4.5	5.1	5.3	4.4

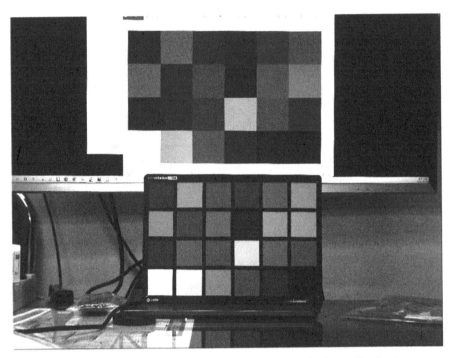

Fig. 10. Actual color checkers (bottom), and color checker by re-illuminating

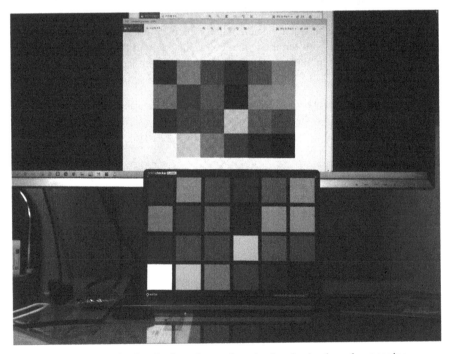

Fig. 11. Actual color checkers (bottom), and color checker by color mapping

6   Conclusion

In this paper, we proposed a method of displaying an image like an actual artwork using hyperspectral re-illumination and color mapping using display. Through this method, it was confirmed that the artwork was displayed similarly regardless of the illumination of the place where the artwork was located. In addition, the performance was confirmed through the actual color checker and the displayed color checker. In this way, it is expected that experience in the virtual environment through the display will be further improved (Figs. 12, 13 and 14).

Fig. 12. Virtual artwork (top) and real artwork (bottom) output to the display.

Fig. 13. Re-illuminated image (left) and color correction added image (right).

Fig. 14. Displayed artwork (left) and real artwork (right).

Acknowledgement. This work was supported by the National Research Foundation of Korea (NRF) grant funded by the Korea government (MSIT) (No. 2019R1A4A1029800).

References

1. Park, J.-I., et al.: Multispectral imaging using multiplexed illumination. In: 2007 IEEE 11th International Conference on Computer Vision, pp. 1–8 (2007)
2. Oh, S.W., et al.: Do it yourself hyperspectral imaging with everyday digital cameras. In: Proceedings of the IEEE Conference on Computer Vision and Pattern Recognition, pp. 2461–2469 (2016)
3. Jiang, J., Gu, J.: Recovering spectral reflectance under commonly available lighting conditions. In: 2012 IEEE Computer Society Conference on Computer Vision and Pattern Recognition Workshops, pp. 1–8 (2012)
4. Barnard, K., Funt, B.V.: Camera calibration for color research. In: Human Vision and Electronic Imaging IV, vol. 3644, pp. 576–585 (1999)
5. Funt, B., Bastani, P.: Irradiance-independent camera color calibration. Color Res. Appl. **39**(6), 540–548 (2014)
6. Liu, L., Wang, X., Li, J.: The establishment of uniform color space based on LCD monitor. Optik **139**, 338–346 (2017)
7. Brainard, D.H.: Calibration of a computer controlled color monitor. Color. Res. Appl. **14**(1), 23–34 (1989)
8. Robertson, A.R.: The CIE 1976 color-difference formulae. Color. Res. Appl. **2**(1), 7–11 (1977)
9. Sharma, G., Wu, W., Dalal, E.N.: The CIEDE2000 color-difference formula: implementation notes, supplementary test data, and mathematical observations. Color Res. Appl. **30**(1), 21–30 (2005)
10. Gómez-Polo, C., et al.: Comparison of the CIELab and CIEDE2000 color difference formulas. J. Prosthet. Dent. **115**(1), 65–70 (2016)
11. Parkkinen, J.P.S., Hallikainen, J., Jaaskelainen, T.: Characteristic spectra of Munsell colors. JOSA A **6**(2), 318–322 (1989)

Creation of Fluid Art Under Microgravity Using Free-Fall

Naoko Tosa[1], Yunian Pang[1], Shigetaka Toba[1], Akihiro Yamada[2], Takashi Suzuki[2], and Ryohei Nakatsu[1(✉)]

[1] Kyoto University, Kyoto 606-8501, Japan
{tosa.naoko.5c,pang.yunian.2c}@kyoto-u.ac.jp,
toba.shigetaka.57z@st.kyoto-u.ac.jp,
ryohei.nakatsu@design.kyoto-u.ac.jp
[2] Toppan Inc, Tokyo 110-8560, Japan
{akihiro_1.yamada,takashi.suzuki}@toppan.co.jp

Abstract. The time is approaching when space travel will become a reality. What new art will emerge in the space age is an important issue. We have been creating art called "fluid art" using fluid dynamics. Since what kind of new fluid art could emerge under zero-gravity is one example of how art should be in the space era, we plan to create fluid art under zero-gravity or microgravity. To create microgravity on the ground, we designed and constructed a system that creates microgravity using free-fall. This system can create microgravity for about 0.5 s by free-falling a device that generates fluid art from a height of 1.5 m. "Sound of Ikebana," one of the fluid art we have been creating using the vibration of sound, uses a phenomenon that occurs in about 0.5 s and matches well with the constructed microgravity generation system. We confirmed that a new type of fluid art emerged using this system, where the height the fluid jumped up was significantly larger than under normal gravity.

Keywords: Microgravity · Fluid art · Free-fall · High-speed camera · Sound of Ikebana

1 Introduction

Recently, there have been many topics related to space. NASA succeeded in launching the spacecraft on Mars [1]. The SpaceX Crew Dragon plans to carry civilians into orbit around the earth and even around the moon [2], making us realize that space travel will become a reality.

Although the day when ordinary people can go out into space is still a long way off, we need to think seriously about our space travel in the future. Given that space travel will become familiar to the public, it is necessary to think about how the culture that we have built up in our society will change in the space age.

Art has been deeply linked to human spirituality since ancient times, and what art will become in the space age is an essential and exciting issue [3].

M. Rauterberg (Ed.): HCII 2022, LNCS 13324, pp. 343–353, 2022.
https://doi.org/10.1007/978-3-031-05434-1_23

We are interested in what art will look like in zero-gravity or microgravity, which is an environment peculiar to space travel. We have been producing "fluid art" [4, 5], which is an art utilizing fluid dynamics. However, since the fluid behavior would be significantly different under zero-gravity, it is necessary to research fluid art under a zero-gravity environment. However, it is quite challenging to achieve zero-gravity on the earth.

In this paper, firstly, we describe the concept of fluid art production under zero-gravity. Then, we propose a method to realize microgravity with a relatively simple system and describe its development process. Finally, we will describe the system's fluid art production experiment results.

2 Related Research

2.1 Scientific Experiments Under Zero-Gravity

Our bodies have adapted to the environment of gravity, which significantly influences human mental aspects such as thinking. It is an exciting topic how these change in the new environment of zero-gravity.

(1) Physical Science
Many physics experiments have been conducted in the particular environment of zero-gravity. For example, experiments have been conducted on how a specific object behaves in a microgravity space. For example, in zero-gravity, convection does not occur. So high-quality crystals can be obtained [6]. This makes it possible to create new substances that cannot occur on the ground.

(2) Biology and Biotechnology
Various experiments have been conducted on how organisms and plants are born and grow in the unique environment of zero-gravity. Previous studies have revealed that roots and stems change the direction in which it grows in response to a slight difference in humidity [7].

(3) Human Research
Many experiments have been conducted on how weightlessness affects the human body in outer space. Studies have been conducted on the relationship between weightlessness and bone. It was found that when exposed to weightlessness for an extended period, the bone under load under gravity becomes brittle because the load is removed in zero-gravity [8].

2.2 Creation of Art Under Zero-Gravity

JAXA (Japan Aerospace Exploration Agency) has a Japanese laboratory called "Kibo" on the ISS and uses it to carry out various experiments in the scientific field and art areas. From 2008 to 2011, the first theme was solicited and implemented, and nine experiments related to art were conducted in "Kibo" [9]. From 2011 to 2013, eight themes were implemented in the second phase [10].

For example, the "Hiten Project" is an experiment to verify what kind of dance a person can perform under zero-gravity [11].

3   Fluid Art

3.1   Fluid Art "Sound of Ikebana"

Fluid behavior is a large part of natural phenomena. Water flow, wave behavior, ocean currents, etc., are typical examples, and the weather is also a fluid phenomenon due to the atmosphere. Many natural phenomena occur as the behavior of fluids.

We have developed a method to visualize fluid phenomenon and make it into artwork. Specifically, as one of the basic techniques for creating fluid art, we have developed a method for photographing the formation of a liquid made from sound vibration with a high-speed camera. We found that creating a flower-like shape with fluid is possible by giving sound vibration to a fluid such as paint. Figure 1 shows the experimental environment. When a speaker is placed face up, a thin rubber film is put on it, a fluid such as paint is placed on the rubber film, and the speaker is vibrated by sound, then the paint jumps up and makes various shapes. Furthermore, the created form is captured by a high-speed camera of 2000 frames/second [4].

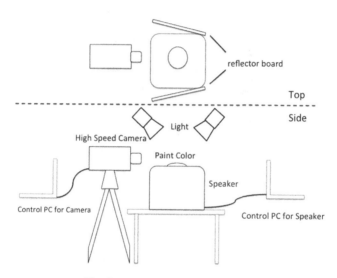

Fig. 1. Fluid art generation system.

3.2   Fluid Art "Sound of Ikebana"

Using this environment, we systematically changed the shape of sound (sine wave, sawtooth wave, etc.), frequency of sound, type of fluid, fluid viscosity, etc., and shot various fluids with a high-speed camera. One of the authors, Naoko Tosa, confirmed that Ikebana (Japanese flower arrangement) like shape emerges. Moreover, she created a video art called "Sound of Ikebana [5]" by editing the obtained video images. Figure 2 shows scenes of the work. In April 2017, as part of Tosa's Japan Cultural Envoy activities, an exhibition was held at Times Square in New York using more than 60 digital billboards. Figure 3 shows a scene of the exhibition.

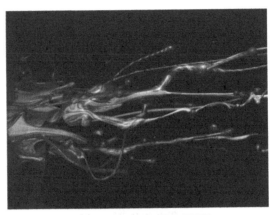

Fig. 2. Scenes of "Sound of Ikebana."

Fig. 3. Exhibition of "Sound of Ikebana" at Times Square, New York.

3.3 Meaning of Fluid Art Generation Under Zero-Gravity

We are currently researching to generate various fluid art represented by the Sound of Ikebana under zero-gravity. Now that space travel is not just a dream story, we believe producing the Sound of Ikebana under zero-gravity has the following meanings.

Art is an essential element of society for us. In the future, where people's lives in space will become commonplace, it is necessary to think about what art will become in the space age. New art suitable for the space age may arise in the space age. Therefore, it is necessary to search for a new form of such art. Also, as mentioned earlier, the behavior of fluids under zero-gravity is an important research topic. Similarly, an important issue is what kind of fluid art shape would emerge under zero-gravity.

4   Microgravity Generation Method

Zero-gravity is a normal state in outer space. However, gravity is always working on the ground. There are two typical methods to realize zero-gravity or microgravity.

4.1   Free-Fall Generator

Gravity G is always working downwards and pulling things downwards on the ground. However, when an object falls downward, it is in a weightless state (actually, it is not complete weightlessness due to the air resistance). In other words, zero-gravity is possible by creating a free-fall state by dropping things from a high place.

Fig. 4. The ZARM drop tower

The Micro-Gravity Laboratory of Japan (MGLAB) in Toki City, Gifu Prefecture, has a free-fall distance of 100 m and a free-fall time of 4.5 s. This drop tower evacuated the inside of the tower to eliminate air resistance and allow the fall capsule to fall freely [13]. Unfortunately, this facility has already stopped working.

Overseas, the ZARM microgravity experimental facility at the University of Bremen in Bremen, Germany, is famous. The height is 147 m (actual fall distance is 110 m), and if the falling capsule drops in a tower that has been evacuated, weightlessness for almost 4.7 s can be achieved [14]. Figure 4 shows the ZARM drop tower.

4.2 Parabolic Flight

Parabolic flight means flying along a parabolic flight path [15]. After gaining sufficient speed by a rapid descent, the aircraft is raised, and parabolic motion is performed by narrowing the thrust to the extent that it compensates for air resistance. A microgravity environment of about 10^{-2}G to 10^{-3}G can occur in the aircraft for 10 to 20 s during the parabolic flight. So it is used for microgravity experiments and training of astronauts. Figure 5 shows the flight curve in parabolic flight and the gravity in each phase.

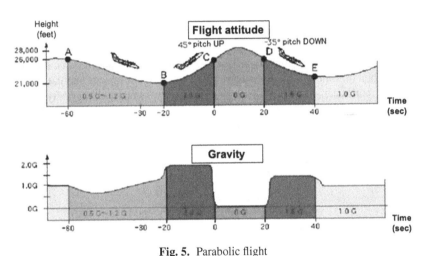

Fig. 5. Parabolic flight

5   Creation of Fluid Art Under Microgravity

5.1   Prototype of Free-Fall System

As mentioned earlier, we are at the beginning of the space age, and we think it is time to consider how art should be in the space age. Art has been produced under normal gravity, such as the Sound of Ikebana as we are doing. Therefore, the behavior of fluid in zero-gravity greatly influences art production. Moreover, attempts to create art using fluid dynamics in zero-gravity are of great significance.

Under such circumstances, we are very interested in how the art Sound of Ikebana created using fluid dynamics will be shaped under zero-gravity. We are planning to try this art creation in a zero-gravity environment using parabolic flight among the methods for realizing zero-gravity mentioned above.

However, at the same time, the parabolic flight is a large-scale experiment, as it is necessary to work in collaboration with a company that can achieve parabolic flight using their airplane, which is costly. Based on an estimate by a company providing parabolic flight service, one experiment costs US$50K or more. Therefore, it is risky to carry out the parabolic flight experiment without knowing what shape will emerge. Also, even in experiments using free-fall devices described in Sect. 4.1, only a limited number of free-fall devices can carry out experiments that include equipment such as speakers and high-speed cameras, which also require lots of preparation and budget.

When we wondered what to do, a researcher who worked at JAXA advised us to develop a small-scale free-fall experimental system indoors. After studying according to this advice, we found that a small-scale free-fall in our laboratory environment very well matches the fluid art creation we have been doing.

Experiments under regular zero-gravity experiments require at least tens of seconds, or even minutes or more. On the other hand, the fluid art that we have been doing is to create art by shooting a fluid dynamics-based phenomenon that occurs in a short time of 1 s or less, with a high-speed camera. This means that free-fall for a short time within 1 s can occur without the need for such a large-scale device.

As is well known, the relationship between the fall distance h and the time t when a free-fall starts from a stationary state is expressed by the following equation, where g is the gravitational acceleration.

$$t = \sqrt{\frac{2h}{g}} \tag{1}$$

If there is air resistance, it becomes a little complicated and is expressed by the following formula. Here, m is the mass of the falling object, and k is the air resistance coefficient.

$$t = \sqrt{\frac{m}{gk}} \operatorname{acosh}\left(e^{\frac{hk}{m}}\right) \tag{2}$$

Table 1 shows the time when free-fall occurs from the height of 1 m, 1.5 m, and 2 m, where $g = 9.80665$, $m = 20$ kg, and $k = 0.24$.

Table 1. Free-fall distance and time

Free-fall distance	Time without air resistance (sec)	Time with air resistance (sec)
1 m	0.452	0.453
1.5 m	0.553	0.555
2 m	0.639	0.641

From Table 1, a microgravity time of 0.553 s can occur when falling from a height of 1.5 m, and 0.452 s can occur from a height of 1 m. It is clear that even when the air resistance is taken into consideration, the fall time is only increased by about 0.001 to 0.002 s compared with the case where the air resistance is not taken into consideration. This is because the velocity is low at the beginning of the transition from the stationary state to the free-fall, so it is not easily affected by air resistance. This is also a condition suitable for creating a microgravity environment by utilizing a free-fall state for a short time.

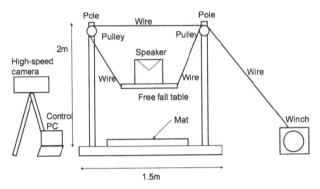

Fig. 6. Conceptual diagram of free-fall system (High-speed camera is installed outside)

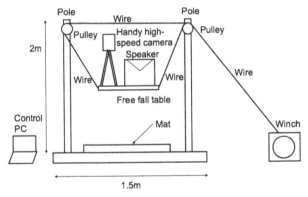

Fig. 7. Conceptual diagram of free-fall system (High-speed camera is installed on the table)

Figure 6 shows a conceptual diagram of the free-fall system. The free-fall table, made of lightweight iron frames with the speaker, is prepared and set in a cubic frame made of sturdy iron pipes. The steel wires are attached to the four corners of the free-fall table, and the four steel wires are gathered and connected to the winch through the pulleys attached to the tops of the four steel poles. By winding up the winch, the free-fall table raises to a height of about 1.5 m. Then the free-fall table freely drops in synchronization with the drive of the speaker on which the paint is placed and the start of shooting with the high-speed camera.

Although it is desirable to mount the high-speed camera on a drop table, Fig. 6 shows a diagram in which it is installed outside in consideration that it leads to an increase in weight. In addition, a high-speed camera is a delicate device and may break by the impact of a drop. If the fall distance is 1 m to 1.5 m, the fall speed is not high. So, if we need a still image, we can shoot with this setting. Of course, if we want to obtain video images, it is better to install the high-speed camera on the drop table. Figure 7 shows the diagram in which the high-speed camera is on the free-fall table.

Fig. 8. Full view of the free-fall system.

Fig. 9. The scene when the free-fall table and speaker are pulled up.

Figure 8 shows a complete view of the free-fall system. In addition, Fig. 9 shows the state in which the free-fall table and the speaker placed on it are pulled up. In this state, the drop table freely drops in synchronization with the start of driving the speaker on which the paint is placed and shooting with the high-speed camera. The free-fall of the drop table can occur by removing the winch stopper. However, to avoid the influence of the winch friction, it was found that it is more suitable to generate microgravity by cutting the wire every time.

5.2 Fluid Art Under Microgravity

We are currently conducting experiments to generate the "Sound of Ikebana" under microgravity using the free-fall system above. Figure 10 shows several shapes of the "Sound of Ikebana" created under microgravity using the system.

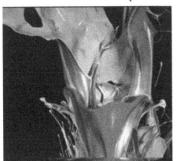  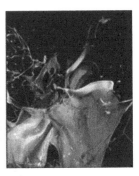

Fig. 10. The shape of "Sound of Ikebana" created under microgravity.

Full-scale experiments are yet to be completed. However, compared to the "Sound of Ikebana" made under normal gravity, the liquid jumps up highly and spreads laterally. More dynamic and beautiful liquid forms can be obtained.

6 Conclusion

As the space age arrives, it is essential to consider the future form of art in the space age. Based on such an awareness, we are interested in new forms of our video artwork, "Sound of Ikebana," produced by giving sound vibration to liquids such as color paints under zero-gravity and microgravity.

In this research, we investigated the method for creating zero-gravity and described the concept, design, and development of a free-fall system for creating microgravity in our laboratory. We also described examples of creating the "Sound of Ikebana" by creating a microgravity environment using the free-fall system.

In parallel with this, we are preparing to produce "Sound of Ikebana" under complete zero-gravity by using parabolic flight. By comparing the production of artworks using the free-fall system in the laboratory described in this paper with the artworks in parabolic flight, we can improve the free-fall system to create fluid art under more complete zero-gravity conditions. As our free-fall system installed in our laboratory is simple to use and capable of adding more functions, the system could be used to create a new type of fluid art.

References

1. Williford, K.H., et al.: The NASA Mars 2020 rover mission and the search for extraterrestrial life (chap. 11). In: From Habitability to Life on Mars, pp. 275–308. Elsevier (2020)

2. Seedhouse, E.: Space X's Dragon: America's Next Generation Spacecraft. Springer, Cham (2016). https://doi.org/10.1007/978-3-319-21515-0

3. Murnik, M.: Art in the environment of zero-gravity: a sketch. Virtual Creat. **6**(1–2), 67–74 (2016)

4. Pang, Y., Zhao, L., Nakatsu, R., Tosa, N.: A study of variable control of sound vibration form (SVF) for media art creation. In: 2017 International Conference on Culture and Computing (2017)

5. Pan, Y., Tamai, H., Tosa, N., Nakatsu, R.: Sound of Ikebana: creation of media art based on fluid dynamics. Int. J. Humanit. Soc. Sci. Educ. **8**(3), 90–102 (2021)

6. Lind, M.D.: Crystal growth from solutions in low gravity. AIAA J. **16**, 458–462 (1978)

7. Morohashi, K., et al.: Gravitropism interferes with hydrotropism via counteracting auxin dynamics in cucumber roots: clinorotation and spaceflight experiments. New Phytol. **215**(4), 1476–1489 (2017)

8. Leblanc, A., Ohshima, H., et al.: Bisphosphonates as a supplement to exercise to protect bone during long duration space flight. Osteoporosis Int. **24**, 2105–2114 (2013)

9. https://iss.jaxa.jp/kiboexp/field/epo/pilot/first/

10. https://iss.jaxa.jp/kiboexp/field/epo/pilot/second/

11. https://iss.jaxa.jp/kiboexp/news/epo_090430.html

12. Bernard, P.S.: Fluid Dynamics. Cambridge University Press, Cambridge (2015)

13. Tagawa, Y., et al.: Present state of microgravity laboratory of Japan. J. Jpn. Soc. Microgravity Appl. **6**(2) (1989)

14. Dreyer, M.: The drop tower Bremen. Microgravity Sci. Technol. **22**(4), 461 (2010)

15. Shelhamer, M.: Parabolic flight as a spaceflight analog. J. Appl. Physiol. **120**, 1442–1448 (2015)

New Media Art and Post-human Masks

Hantian Xu, Lin Zhang$^{(\boxtimes)}$, and Ziruo Xue

Communication University of China, Beijing, China
zhlin197412@126.com

Abstract. In this paper, from the perspective of posthumanism and by centering on the dialectical relationship of binary unity of opposites between mask and body, the new style presented by mask art under the intervention of new media art was studied. The characteristics of remote presence, face structure and sensory augmentation of post-human mask were summarized from the perspective of detachment, embodiment, and augmentation presented by the new media art presents the characteristics, which sets up the theoretical interpretation premise and thinking paradigm for the creative practice of body and mask art of new media art.

Keywords: Posthumanism · Mask art · New media art

1 Mask Culture and Function

Mask, as one of the oldest human art forms, plays an indispensable role in all kinds of human cultural activities, which is "not as something nice to look at, but as something powerful to use" [1]. Masks are used for not only decoration but also for conveying emotions. From the Neolithic age to today, masks and their related art forms have been the object and subject of artistic practice and research conducted by artists and scholars of various nationalities, and the cultural connotation and application of masks are no longer limited to religious rituals and dramas. Costume, sculpture, makeup, painting, photography and even digital art are all within the mapping range of mask forms in different art fields. Although the mask art of different nationalities varies in material selection and modeling techniques, as a form of expression rooted in the collective unconsciousness of the whole human race, masks born in different cultural contexts also show some common characteristics, namely, symbolism, sensory extension, and memorable presence.

From the perspective of material use, the mask is an ornament. In the Paleolithic age, primitive people had learned to make ornaments by processing animal bones, beadstone, and other materials. However, mask wearing wasn't limited to the non-pure aesthetic dimension, and the application of masks involves a lot of temporary situations such as prayer, sacrifice, celebration, and exorcism. In life practice, the symbolic nature of masks sometimes even surpasses its materiality. Masks are not necessarily worn on people's faces in a physical form, and their birth has the same origin as makeup. Makeup and mask are used to disguise to a certain extent by covering and transforming the face, which is actually an imitation and presentation of the face. Therefore, no matter they are used as handicrafts or facial makeup, the face is solidified into a certain expression, while society has control over this expression.

According to the etymology, "mask/Macka" can be explained in two ways in the Detailed *Dictionary of Russian* compiled by Shay Y Auregov et al.: one refers to the veneer covering the face, which is used for covering the eye area; or it refers to a person wrapped in a cover-up, or a cast of plaster or other materials taken from the face of a deceased person. The other refers to the make-up or typical dress used for the ball, or the mask worn by the revelers; People wearing masks during Christmas. [2] Based on the basic functions of masks, Zhou Xianbao and Yu Xiaoyin divided masks into artistic masks and practical masks from the psychological perspective [3].

The characteristic of artistic masks is that masks give full play to their symbolic and camouflage properties, making masks become a "phantom face", which imitates the objects such as deities, monsters, and alien races [4]. The "phantom face" is the result that people project their image onto another world and impose it on the supernatural strength, which elevates those who are born in the flesh, especially the ancestors and leaders of the community, to the highest rank of ghosts and gods. By wearing masks, users can impersonate others, break away from their daily identities, and even get super humanity and nature close to the essence of divinity. Such masks include festival masks, decorative masks, deities masks, and so on, such as Nuo Opera masks with extremely strong "avatar" colors that are still popular in the Yangtze River Basin of China. In the ceremony, the wizard wears a mask and hide, presents a fierce appearance waving arms and dancing, shows its strength and searching every part of the city or village, lets evils have no hiding place, and finally drives away evil things (maybe one person, a sheep, and a chicken, as a symbol that evil has been expelled) [5].

In addition to providing identification codes, the human face behind the mask itself is also a gathering area of vital human organs for the protection or function extension of organs. In production and life, practical masks designed from the perspective of utilitarian functions such as "defense", "acoustic irradiation", and "gas defense", such as the war mask worn by Di Qing army in the Song Dynasty (when facing the enemy, they wear a copper mask to fight enemies [6]. It also has the dual function of helmet protection and deterring enemies. The mask worn by ancient Roman actors was called "persona", which explains the characteristic of per-sonare that the actors used the megaphone of the mask to amplify their voice [7]. In the middle ages when the plague spread widely, the beak masks (see Fig. 1) (there is transparent glass in the eye region, and it can isolate from patients with body tissues, blood, or droplets, and there is a bump like a bird's beak in the front, which is filled with sweet material) worn by doctors on the European Continent is the source of inspiration for the design of current gas masks.

Fig. 1. Paul Fürst Doctor Schnabel von Rom © Steve Heikkila [8]

Finally, when existing as the image of the face, the mask itself can exist as the symbol of the face. The mask can get rid of the attachment to the body, and its symbolic nature will not be damaged by the absence of the body. As described by Ernst Hans Gombrich in Mask and Face, humans "first see a mask before they recognize a face" [9]. The mask here is not a simple set of the five sense organs, but exists as a face image field. For example, there is a tradition of "skull worship" in numerous primitive cultures. Primitive people believed that the soul could still exist on earth by attaching to the skull after the body's death. In the religious sacrifice system of ancient China, there was a tradition of offering sacrifices by the human head (head-hunting blood sacrifice) [10]. (Refer to Zeng Qi's *Tombs in Prehistoric China* and *Archaeological Discovery and Research in New China*.) In some minority cultural traditions, when a person died, he or she was smeared with cinnabar or chicken blood to exorcise evil spirits. In the western world, people have a tradition of making death masks, which reproduce the appearance of the dead by means of Abbild (see Fig. 2). More importantly, the masks replicate the social characteristics of the face so that the dead can continue to exist among the living in the form of masks. Hans Berting believes that this allusion between mask and face developed into portraiture and photography in modern Europe. Whether it's a painting or a photograph, by objectifying the face, the image is formed, and the person with the absence of the physical body gains the presence of memory [7].

Fig. 2. Shakespeare's Death Mask © Gordon Jack/Scotimage.com, Getty Images [11]

2 Posthumanism and Post-human Masks

In *The History of The Face*, Hans Berting described the scene that European adventurers displayed masks looted from Africa in art museums, and the masks from the colonies became the idol of the "other" civilizations. However, due to the loss of the context and usage of the original culture, the original meaning of masks was completely deprived. Its dual separation from the wearer and the character makes it become a magic work of art. Today, with the decline of pantheistic primitive religion and witchcraft culture, the function of masks as a prayer ritual prop has been completely lost. Bruce Mazlish summarized the development of the idea of humans into the transition of people's epistemology to the world: The first transition is that people began to understand the universe through Copernicus' heliocentric theory; The second is that people can understand nature through the theory of evolution; The third is that people can know themselves through Freud's psychoanalysis; The last is that people began to face the alienation and erosion brought by machines and information with the three industrial revolutions [12]. As a matter of fact, when the first transition of thought appeared and humans questioned God for the first time, the mask, as a symbol of God, appeared the hint of the collapse of meaning. In the fourth transition, namely, when entering the Post-Human Age, human beings finally destroyed the rule of the old god, broke down the idols of God, and replaced them with the enthronization of a new god, that is, human beings themselves. The mask of human worship became the simulacrum of the human face, and the tradition of skull worship gained a new interpretation in the Post-Human Age.

With the development of information technology and the spread of the concept of science fiction, the concept of "posthumanism" is gradually entering the realm of everyday language. In the literal sense, posthumanism is a rebellion against anthropocentrism, but as the definition of "post-modern" is full of debates, the definition of "posthumanism" is still in a suspended state. Relevant topics deduced by science fiction films, novels, and new media art, such as politics, ethics, and interpersonal relationships, are called speculative posthuman, and some higher-concept features can be summarized, for example, the essence of life is information, while the operation essence of biological organisms is no different from the operation of machines, aiming to emphasize that the essence of human identity is a mode of information, and posthumanism is a human media existence [13]. Thus, the meaning of the physical body is greatly diminished, the body can be replaced by machinery, and the mind can be displayed by computer programs. The separation of identity and physical body leads to the separation of face and body. A series of media such as celebrity magazine covers, film close-ups, posters of political leaders, and social media profile pictures are creating an "absolute mask" [14]. When faced with dream symbols, people generally hide from their eyes and become an "anonymous face", and the two stare at each other to create a face-to-face illusion. As in the famous American recruitment poster of 1917, Uncle Sam pointed his index finger at the viewers and addressed the crowd directly, "I WANT YOU" (see Fig. 3). The Post-human mask becomes the code of identity, the face as the information of the body is inherited and replaced by the mask function, and the mask becomes the extension, criticism and mirror of face, and the mask even becomes the object of human beings' self-gazing and a post-identity reference of posthumanism.

Fig. 3. 1917 American recruitment poster © James Montgomery Flagg [15]

Another Post-human knowledge also focuses on the dramatic changes of media and body, but it is more rooted in science, technology and practical implementation, for example, big data, artificial intelligence, and virtual survival investigate the changes experienced by the human body in the current context as well as the existence coordinates of human beings themselves. As described by Tai Daixing in *Post-human Social Orientation of Technological Existence*, "The so-called post-human refers to anti-body, anti-fertility, anti-environment, anti-nature, and anti-divine human beings. Or they can be called technically existed human beings [16]…" The post-human proposition inherits the research contents such as "post-body", "enhanced human", and "abnormal body", involving plastic surgery, genetic engineering, electronic organs, cyborg, and so on, and these technical practices involve the field related to "face-mask". From the perspective of transformation, the most basic transformation and the most extensive field are the plastic prosthetics in the medical field. If the original mask art was born out of makeup, with very strong colors of witchcraft culture, then today's plastic surgery technology is constantly disciplined by the media, and the face has become a symbolic landscape and a mask metaphor. It's not uncommon to hear stories that some fans spend a lot of money on plastic surgery to become a celebrity. Some plastic surgery receivers are even commissioned to appear at commercial events as copycat celebrities, acting like "a replacer". The mask replaces the original face, and the new identity replaces the old one. Just as Merleau-Ponty said, "The body is the place where the reality and the reality itself of phenomena are expressed [17]." Furthermore, the widely used Post-human masks in the technical field of vision mainly include electronic organs and enhanced mask applications. On the one hand, the progress of scientific and technological means has expanded the material connotation of masks, and their effectiveness in sensory augmentation has been greatly increased, including VR helmets, glasses, and other wearable devices. On the other hand, taking advantage of the virtual reality function of masks, human beings can realize their disembodied existence in the virtual world. In the medical and health care field, wearable devices can help disabled people with congenital diseases overcome some sensory obstacles. Neil Harbisson, an avant-garde artist, cooperated with experts from the University of Plymouth to develop a head-wearing device, called Eyeborg (see Fig. 4), which converts colour signals into sound to compensate for his colour blindness. After a long period of time, mask art itself is constantly experiencing technological changes, and new materials, new forms, and new meanings are constantly emerging, so it has become an important theme of digital media art in the Post-Human Age.

Fig. 4. Eyeborg © Cmfdesigner [18]

3 The Media Mask of Remote Presence

In *How Can We Become Post-Human?* N. Katherine Hayles describes the concept of Post-Human through four hypotheses, and its core point is that the core of the construction of life is the information path, so the human body is just a kind of primitive prosthesis that can be replaced by simulation technology and technological devices [19]. In the definition given by Hyles, the discussion and proposition of the duality of body and mind throughout the history of western philosophy should end with the fact that the soul overtakes the body, because depending on the development of science and technology, human beings can get rid of the bondage of the human body sooner or later to realize dematerialization. However, after dematerialization, Post-human still has the requirements for information communication and image recognition. Post-human information is not only stored in the binary code of 0 and 1, but also needs to be presented by various forms of sensory symbols. Therefore, the visualized post-human mask becomes the remote presence of dematerialized human beings, and the eliminated post-human body is resurrected remotely through virtual technology.

First of all, through choosing remote media masks, people can completely get rid of the influence of the human body, select the presence or concealing of their real identity, and carry out idealized construction of self-image to obtain a highly saturated "mirror experience" (Lacan language). The most common media phenomenon is that in social networking services, in addition to data information, the virtual account corresponding to each person often requires a visualized head portrait as the core recognition symbol.

Meanwhile, users' head portraits are not necessarily their real photos, but they can usually be the stars they admire, the virtual characters and animals they like, and even some non-biological images. By wearing ideal image masks, users themselves present self-satisfied self-images to people in social networks. These media masks constructed by images all present their aesthetic preferences or value tastes and construct their ideal "selves" without exception. MATTHEW MOHR STUDIOS launched "As We Are" (2017), which can be called celebrity installation art. It is placed at the Columbus Convention Center, with a height of 4.3 m (see Fig. 5). It contains 3,000 customized LED panels and more than 850,000 LED lights to create a virtual face of the audience. There is also a camera area behind the device, where 29 cameras will record the information of the audiences' faces and generate a 3D model of the head for simulation. The device attracted a large number of onlookers and participants during the exhibition. In 2019, domestic artists invited by Xi'an Municipal Government reproduced this face device and placed it in Beilin District, Xi'an, which also attracted a lot of attention. When developing this project, Matthew Moore team studied more than 5,000 3D faces to obtain the most ideal head model that can match the image information of most faces. So what the device finally presents is actually the face of a person with facial feature information. The nose is neither high nor short, the forehead is neither big nor small, and it is a facial proportion after data correction. Then a face under the guidance of average significance is obtained. Remote masks give idealized images to faces and then provide media masks with democratic color for the public through imaging technology.

Fig. 5. "As We Are" © Matthew Mohr [20]

Secondly, the remote media mask realizes the virtual presence of the absent body, which is different from the landscape presence constructed by film features and propaganda posters. The virtual field formed through the media mask is a synchronic presence, which is not only the presence of image and identity but also the presence of consciousness. This is one of the manifestations that posthumanism realizes the disembodied existence through digital technology. As long as people sit in front of the computer, everything in the world is shown to them. During the COVID-19, teleconferencing and remote classes have become an important way for people to continue their work and study.

By relying on modern information technology, people from all over the world can gather together and communicate. The National Basketball Association (NBA) used Microsoft Teams to transplant the busts of more than 300 online fans to 17-foot-high screens at US basketball games during the COVID-19 (see Fig. 6). Jared Spataro, Microsoft Vice President said, "It makes fans be able to not only enjoy the safety and comfort at their own home but also experience the feeling of sitting side by side with other fans in live competitions, and the athletes and fans are inspired and enthusiastic by each other [22]." (In addition to the technological upgrade of communication tools and the construction of more efficient information transmission scenes, media masks are also transforming the social landscape. Paul Virilio believes that when physical presence is replaced by the remote presence and the human face is replaced by remote mask, the expansion of space and the continuation of time are actually eliminated, and the whole world becomes a remote present society, which is a "deomocratic revolution". In *Speed and Politics, Paulo Villio*, Villio asserts that there is no industrial revolution, but only a speed-master revolution; There is no democracy, but only speed [23]. Political propaganda and historical interpretation no longer rely on the unilateral interpretation made by social elites. Through the media mask, the public face can be separated from the public mask. By relying on short video platforms such as Tik Tok and Snack Video, everyone can be a narrator of history.

Fig. 6. NBA Brings Basketball Fans to the Court with Microsoft Teams © Joe Murphy/The New York Times [21]

4   Flesh Mask of Face Construction

In Bodies in Technology, Don Ihde puts forward the conception of Bodies in three dimensions: first, the body in phenomenology, that is, Material Body; Second, the body under the construction of ideological discourse, that is, Cultural Body; Third, the human body under science and technology is Technological Body. Under the context of posthumanism, the body is not only "an idealized form pointing to Platonic reality", but transformed into "a specific example generated from the noise of difference", that is, embodiedness [24]. The meaning of face liberated from the abstract symbolic meaning of "aggregation of five senses" or "existence of soul", and the transcendence of face is gradually replaced by experience. Throughout history, the transformation of human faces through masks has never ceased to be. On the one hand, human beings are dissatisfied with their own faces and transform and hide their face images through various means. On the other hand, through masks, human beings worship and adore a more exaggerated and strange the other based on human images. In this process, self-worship and the other worship continue to cycle and superimpose, and obtain the ontological unity in the posthuman era. By applying Information Technology and Bioscience, the means of "false shape", "painting face", "coating" and "covering" have been inherited and become an important manifestation of the embodiedness of posthumanism masks [25].

"False shape" is a form of imitation and play of animals, plants and even gods and ghosts through masks. Julian Robinson, a British cultural historian, found that people have a common aesthetic pursuit, that is, to dress up their biological organs with various materials and connect them with the divine world. [26] In the posthuman era, false shape means not only for human beings to obtain the protection of natural or supernatural forces by alienating themselves and playing others' role, but also that human beings have become a part of supernature. "Cyborg" itself is a non-human and non-mechanical super species. Haraway defined Cyborg as cybernetic organism in his famous *A Cyborg Manifesto*, which refers to the mixture of machine and organism. It is not only a fictional organism, but also a social reality organism [27]. With the advent of medical cosmetic surgery and biotechnology, mask materials have extended from natural materials to man-made materials to the body itself. Compared with ritual masks and religious masks, the human body masks are no longer temporal decorations - masks used to entertain gods or ward off evil spirits in ceremonies and celebrations, but an inseparable part of divine. Rebecca Horn created three sets of mask-themed devices from 1972 to 1973, namely, *Pencil Mask* (1972) (see Fig. 7), *Cockfeather Mask* (1973) (see Fig. 7) and *Cockatoo* (1973) (see Fig.7). Rebecca Horn combines industrial ready-made products (*Pencil Mask*), animal morphological characteristics (*Cockfeather Mask*) and animal habit characteristics (*Cockatoo*). In the creation of *Pencil Mask* and *Cockatoo*, Rebecca Horne applies the false shape to expand the use function of the mask and participate in the embodied practice. In *Pencil Mask*, the pencil on the mask can be used to draw with the head moving, to paint complex patterns and have a dynamic record of the face. *Cockatoo* uses feather as a material to build a centripetal dialogue space. The wings of feathers on the mask can completely wrap the heads of two interlocutors. The mask shape participates in the practice of physical communication. The radial pencil shape in the *Pencil Mask* constructs a hard to touch shell and a symbol of horror movies or sexuality props. *Cockfeather Mask* blocks the observation of binocular vision through decorative feathers, and grafts the visual characteristics of herbivores onto the human face as omnivores, which helps the discussion of multiple species become real. In addition, both pencils and feathers have been used as writing tools in the Western history. Rebecca Horn's mask hides the "speaking" of the mouth, but it finishes the translation from oral language to visual writing by the metaphor of "writing".

Fig. 7. Pencil Mask(Left), Cockfeather Mask(Middle), Cockatoo(Right) © DACS [28]

"Painted face" is a kind of "picture" behavior that uses drawing or painting the face, to temporarily change their social role or hide their true identity. The masked makeup formed by painted face is also known as "plastic makeup" (Qiang Li. A *Research on Ancient Chinese Totem Decoration and Nuo Play*. P60). Compared with physical masks, painted face is easier to disguise. What's more, it will not affect the expression of the face itself, and in many cases, can better highlight the actor's vocal performance. The painting materials include colored pigments mixed from minerals, plant fibers and egg white, or artificial materials such as inks, as well as natural materials such as animal blood and ash bran. The former is more decorative and highlights the painting nature of the painting ceremony, while the latter directly comes from animals and plants, leaving traces of sympathetic witchcraft. In 2016, Nobumichi Asai's team projected computer images onto the face through real-time facial tracking plus projection mapping, and realized digital makeup through accurate facial tracking and image correction. This technology was applied in the singing of Lady Gaga at the opening ceremony of the Grammy party that year. And Lady Gaga sang a classic song by singer David Bowie, which paid tribute to him. In the opening concert, Nobumichi Asai introduced lightning and sun into the face, paying tribute to David Bowie's classic dress. And a spider came out of Lady Gaga's forehead, crawled around her face and then disappeared (see Fig. 8). During this process, all images fit perfectly with Lady Gaga's facial muscles. Nobumichi Asai called the technology "omote", which was invented by his team, signifying the masks in Japanese Noh. Prior to this, Nobumichi Asai has conducted a large number of experiments and creations through omote. In 2014, in the work of *FACE HACKING*, Nobumichi Asai tried to overlap different makeup and masks on the face, including digital changes, abstract colors and metal masks.On top of that, the faces of robot and Cheetah are overlapped on the human face while people and images will automatically adjust the distorted pictures with people turning their heads. Nobumichi Asai believes that in the future, with the development of imaging technology, people can turn the of transformation anytime and anywhere a real thing. Not only can face achieve remote presence through scanning technology and the Internet; but also in the area of human body, digital technology is invading the real body.

Finally, "coating" and "covering" are both a kind of mask, which protect and cover the face, and they are also the explicit embodiment of the mask's function. In *A humble Opinion on the Origin of Masks,* the author puts forward that masks were likely to

Fig. 8. Lady Gaga Grammys 2016 [29]

originate from war. The "bronze head and iron forehead" of Chiyou troops can be explained as defensive masks. Meanwhile, using masks in war also involves intimidating the enemy and hoping the blessing of ancestors [30]. War is cruel and human life withers. Therefore, soldiers wear masks to increase their senses of estrangement, temporarily ignoring their own existence and reduce their fear of death. Besides, masks not only provide protection and shelter for the living, but also cover the dead in many nationalities. For example, the Oroqen people in northern China are used to covering the dead's face with a piece of cloth or paper to stabilize his soul [31]. Most of these customs have the function of warding off evil spirits. It is hoped that the dead can get rid of the memory and fetters of the world as soon as possible. Face acts as the most social organ of human body and the core symbol of human identity. Therefore, the living people deprive the identity of the deceased in the form of coating and covering, in order to achieve the identity inheritance and power transition between the new and old people. American artist Leo Selvaggio has launched a campaign called "URME Surveillance" since 2014. The name is homonymous with *"YOU ARE ME"* (see Fig. 9). In the "URME Surveillance", Leo Selvaggio produced and promoted a 3D printed mask based on his face to resist the surveillance of cameras everywhere in American society. Leo Selvaggio spared no expense to make highly simulated face masks, because the masks are made of pigment hardened resin material, have scalability, and 100% duplicate Leo Selvaggio's facial features. The cost of each mask is nearly $200. Then, relying on the "URME Surveillance", Leo Selvaggio continued to focus on identity and monitoring, and to create through masks and other forms. In order to promote the project, Leo Selvaggio launched a paper mask with lower cost. Supporters can even print Selvaggio's paper mask at their own home, which greatly enhances the scalability of the project. In the virtual world, Selvaggio developed a software called Facial Video Encyrptor. Once being instantiated, it can recognize all videos in personal electronic devices, and automatically replace the face with Selvaggio's, so as to prevent privacy leakage.

5   Sense Mask of Sensory Augmentation

In 2018, the science fiction film *Ready Player One* (see Fig. 10) directed by Spielberg was released in China. In the movie, VR technology is developed by The OASIS, a company

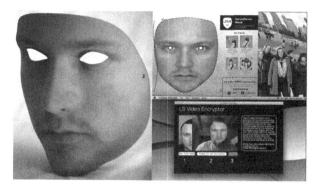

Fig. 9. "You Are Me" © Urme Surveillance [32]

that can bring players into the virtual game. Information about the player's five sense is projected into the game with the help of VR helmet, and then generates feedback with the virtual game world in real time. With this set of sensory augmentation imitation equipment, the game has become a more realistic place than the real world. It exists scenes that make adrenalin and dopamine soar everywhere. In contrast, the real world is increasingly deserted and has become a marginal space that few people pay attention to. In the movie *Matrix* (see Fig. 11), helmet equipment is replaced by brain computer interface. The virtual world replaces the human body, and the immortality of the soul is realized through the continuous updating of neural information and data. Ranging from paintings, photos, movies to wearable devices represented by VR helmets, human depiction art continues to approach the reality understood by the senses, and even surpass the reality brought by the senses. In this process, human beings surpass themselves and become a "transitional human" or "transhuman". Nick Bostrom believes that human being itself is a dynamic concept, a "half - baked" or "a work in - progress" [35]. If the media mask of pure informatization is the final form of human existence, the illusion mask used to enhance sensory energy efficiency, and build a digital virtual world can be the transitional stage of human development from physical model to information model.

Fig. 10. Ready Player One © Sohu [33].

Fig. 11. The Matrix © Neuralink [34]

The Objectuals (1995), a series of transparent helmet sculptures by a Korean artist Hyungkoo Lee, presents the human face after organ magnification (see Fig. 12). His transparent helmet is inlaid with convex lens and concave lens, which can optically deform his five senses. Some helmets decide the wearer's appearance, and some look exaggerated and humorous, and some are deformed and terrible. However, from the perspective of sensory augmentation, Hyungkoo Lee's object series only exaggerates the appearance of five senses, and does not exert an influence on the enhancement of functional function. A Polish artist Krzysztof Wodiczko designed the enhancement and guidance of auditory senses in the wearable head device *Personal Instrument* (1969) (see Fig. 13). The device consists of a headset microphone, noise reduction headphones, a sound filter and gloves equipped with an image receiver. Artists can edit the noise received by the microphone through gloves and gestures. Noise reduction headphones isolate all ambient sounds. Artists and other participants will only hear the sound created by the artist. Under this device, Wodiczko realized the simple control and enhancement of hearing and senses, and created a purely virtual sound world. With the development of science and technology, today's sensory mask can process and simulate a variety of sensory information. After Neil harbisson tried to wear EyeBorg's headgear and achieved great success, he set about setting up a "cross species association". The team members tried to implant machine senses into their bodies. Some people can sense earthquake motion, others can sense temperature and weather changes. Neil's next project is to install a biological clock system under his head to sense time through the movement of heat sensing points around his head every 24 h. In addition, other sensory masks for sensory augmentation are not uncommon, especially for visual enhancement, and have been commercialized: for example, oculus rift launched by oculus VR in 2013, hololens launched by Microsoft in 2015, and Apple plans to launch Apple glass's augmented reality device in 2022, which further promotes the combination of sensory virtual technology and daily life. In other sensory fields, such as the sensory mask of taste and smell level, there are also some functional and artistic works: the Choi team develops a *Sound Perfume* (2013) headwear system, which provides users with additional auditory and olfactory sensory input functions (as shown in Fig. 2.9), and in the course of interpersonal communication, when meeting an acquaintance, the system will retrieve the relevant fragrance and prompt sound from the database to help users recollect their impression of the person [35]. In 2018, ranasinghe team developed the multi-sensory VR tour system of *Season Traveller*. Different from traditional VR equipment, season traveler system combines audio-visual system with smell, heat and wind system to realize multi-dimensional immersion. With the support of virtual technology and bioscience research, sensory masks will be more and more widely used in daily life, and the form of intervention will change from temporary intervention to permanent intervention. Opponents also questioned that man cannot play God. "The greatest danger of mankind comes from this arrogant and unbridled impulse to play with fire" [38]. In Zhigang Wang's VR work *Shooting Game* (2017), the virtual game is divided into two time and space (see Fig. 14). Participants wear VR glasses to aim at human targets in the game for design. What can be shot on the external screen is the child's image. On the one hand, the virtual world constructed by sensory mask expands the dimension of human activities, on the other hand, it also creates an "The Information Cocoon", confining people to the barriers of sensory perception.

Fig. 12. The Objectuals © Hyungkoo Lee [36]

Fig. 13. Personal Instrument © Krzysztof Wodiczko [37]

Fig. 14. Shooting Game © Zhigang Wang [39]

6   Conclusion

In *Media Archaeology,* Siegfried Zielinski believed, that the enrichment of experience and knowledge production brought by human cultural collection and storage, far exceeds the development limitation of human body under the genetic mechanism. Therefore, although the overall development of scientific and technological level of mankind belongs to the development of tools from low to high, the development of media is not an all-round process from primitive to complex. Because the human body has not undergone revolutionary changes since tens of thousands of years, which leads to "the existence of something in the past" [40].

Following the posthuman era, the concept of mask art has been expanded, and new materials and new forms of masks are emerging every day. Even with the intervention of media, the entity mask can be completely cancelled, and then the mask almost equals to visual illusion or analog signals. However, under the changing of technical tools, the mask and face still maintain an ambiguous imitation relationship. Sometimes masks imitate faces, and vice versa. The former is that human beings objectify themselves to resist the vulnerability of the flesh; The latter is that human beings play the other and become the other by wearing masks. New media artists further present and enlarge the interactive mode between man and mask: mask is the face, self is the other. Whether this is an art or a prophecy? Only time can tell.

References

1. Gombrich, E.H.: The Course of Art. Shaanxi People's Art Publishing House, Shaanxi (1987)
2. Zhao, X.: A glimpse into the emergence and development of mask theory in Western literature. Foreign Lit. Stud. (1), 153–165 (2019). https://doi.org/10.19915/j.cnki.fls.2019.01.015
3. Zhou, X., Yu, X.: Disguise and reveal: the dramatic transformation and projection behind the mask--on the practical method and symbolic symbolism of mask use in drama therapy. J. Nanjing Arts Inst. (Music & Perform.) (2), 139–144 (2014). https://doi.org/10.3969/j.issn.1008-9667.2014.02.029
4. Zhang, L., Wang, T.: Functional change of ancient masks. Art Panor. (7), 74 (2007)

5. Wang, S., Shi, Y.: Interpretation of the aesthetic connotation of the art of masks of Nuo Opera in Chizhou. J. Shayang Teach. Coll. **7**(6), 55–58 (2006). https://doi.org/10.3969/j.issn.1672-0768.2006.06.017
6. Zhang, B.: The History of Song, Liao, Jin and Yuan Novels. Fudan University Press, Shanghai (2001)
7. Bertin, H.: The History of the Face. Peking University Press, Beijing (2017)
8. Heikkila, S.: Paul Fürst Doctor Schnabel von Rom – In Dark Times. https://www.indark times.com/freedom-and-life-in-an-age-of-contagion/paul-furst-doctor-schnabel-von-rom-in-dark-times/. Accessed 16 Jan 2022
9. Gombrich, E.H., Hochberg, J., Black, M.: Art, Perception, Reality. Suhrkamp Verlag, Frankfurt (1977)
10. Wang, S.: Yunnan Ethnic Drama. Yunnan University Press, Kunming (2011)
11. "Death mask" vs "living mask" -- K.O. https://www.sohu.com/a/411199568_120640560?_trans_=000014_bdss_dkhkzj. Accessed 16 Jan 2022
12. Graham, E.: Representations of the Post/Human. Manchester University Press, Manchester (2002)
13. Wang, K.: On the three dimensions of post-human aesthetics. Acad. Res. (3), 160–166 (2021)
14. Barthes, R.: Mythologies. Seuil, Paris (1970)
15. Why is America jokingly called "Uncle Sam"? http://www.xixik.com/content/1843974f0e36 e2cb. Accessed 16 Jan 2022
16. Tang, D.: The posthuman social orientation of technologized existence. Jianghai Acad. J. (1), 47–54 (2019)
17. Merleau-Ponty, M.: Phenomenology of Perception. The Commercial Press, Beijing (2001)
18. EyeBorg: color blind artists hear color. https://www.ifanr.com/408167. Accessed 16 Jan 2022
19. Heller, K.N.: How We Became Post-human. Peking University Press, Beijing (2017)
20. Mohr, M.: Multimedia public installation art: from self portrait to giant 3D sculpture. https://www.sohu.com/a/201571517_100005635. Accessed 16 Jan 2022
21. Murphy, J.: What It's Like to Be a Virtual NBA Fan. http://news.hexun.com/2020-08-12/201 859600.html?_t=t. Accessed 16 Jan 2022
22. Spataro, J.: Reimagining how NBA fans and teams experience the game of basketball with together mode in Microsoft teams. https://www.microsoft.com/en-us/microsoft-365/blog/2020/07/24/reimagining-teams-experience-basketball-microsoft-teams. Accessed 24 July 2020
23. Virilio, P., Bratton, B.H.: Speed and Politics. Semiotext(E), New York (2006)
24. Ran, D., Cai, Z.: Cyber and posthumanism. Stud. Dialect. Nat. **28**(10), 72–76 (2012). https://doi.org/10.19484/j.cnki.1000-8934.2012.10.015
25. Guo, J.: Chinese Mask Culture. Shanghai People's Publishing House, Shanghai (1992)
26. Li, Q.: Research on ancient Chinese totem decoration and Nuo play. Res. Lit. Cult. Minor. Resid. Guizhou Gener. (0), 40–61 (2014)
27. Haraway, D.: A cyborg manifesto: science, technology, and socialist-feminism in the late twentieth century in simians, cyborgs and women. In: The Reinvention of Nature, p. 154. Routledge, New York (1991). https://doi.org/10.1007/978-1-4020-3803-7_4
28. Horn, R.: 'Pencil Mask', Rebecca Horn, 1972|Tate. https://www.tate.org.uk/art/artworks/horn-pencil-mask-t07847. Accessed 16 Jan 2022
29. At the Grammy, Lady Gaga presented her idol David Bowie with black technology. https://www.sohu.com/a/59648372_119510. Accessed 16 Jan 2022
30. Gu, P.: A humble opinion on the origin of masks. Lit. Art Stud. (6), 136–147 (1992)
31. Song, E.: Chinese Minority Religions. Yunnan People's Publishing House, Kunming (1985)
32. Urme Surveillance: "You Are Me" http://www.urmesurveillance.com/. Accessed 16 Jan 2022
33. We don't have to wait until 2045 to become a "number one player" https://www.sohu.com/a/227097385_160923. Accessed 16 Jan 2022

34. After the popularization of brain computer interface, how to wash your hair? https://new.qq.com/rain/a/20201227a0hd2d00. Accessed 16 Jan 2022

35. Wang, R.: An analysis of the signs from "human" to "transhuman" from the perspective of human enhancement. Stud. Philos. Sci. Technol. (1), 78–83 (2021)

36. 'The Objectuals' By Hyungkoo Lee. https://www.ignant.com/2017/08/17/the-objectuals-by-hyungkoo-lee/. Accessed 16 Jan 2022

37. Wodiczko, K.: The Instrument (1971). https://artmuseum.pl/en/performans/archiwum/2519/127282. Accessed 16 Jan 2022

38. Lu, F.: Human empowerment and human rights. J. Guangxi Univ. (Philos. Soc. Sci.) **38**(2), 8–15 (2016). https://doi.org/10.13624/j.cnki.jgupss.2016.02.002

39. Spotlight on ICEVE 2017 Wang Zhigang: reflections on the ontology of virtual reality art: d-arts. https://www.d-arts.cn/article/article_info/key/MTE5MTE0NzY0NDaE34Vw.html. Accessed 16 Jan 2022

40. Zielinski, S.: Media Archaeology. Commercial Press, Beijing (2006)

Design and Research of Huangmei Opera Lightweight H5 Game Based on Media Convergence

Yiran Zhang[1], Shangshi Pan[2], and Rongrong Fu[1(✉)]

[1] College of Art Design and Media, East China University of Science and Technology, Shanghai, China
2651963146@qq.com
[2] Shanghai Art and Design Academy, Shanghai, China

Abstract. Huangmei Opera is an important art form of traditional Chinese opera. At present, Huangmei Opera, which mainly focuses on oral communication and stage communication, cannot cater to the media usage habits of current audiences, and cannot be effectively spread in the context of media convergence. In this paper, users' preference for lightweight game samples was obtained based on EEG experiment; Secondly, the factors influencing user experience of Huangmei Opera lightweight H5 game were acquired through the focus group; Then, supported by the questionnaire design of the focus group, user experience hierarchy was constructed according to the results of questionnaire data analysis, based on which the design practice of Huangmei Opera lightweight H5 game was completed; Finally, the design effect of the game was evaluated. The results show that lightweight H5 games can realize the effective communication of cultural connotation of Huangmei Opera as an important carrier, which provides new ideas for the contemporary dissemination of traditional Chinese opera.

Keywords: Huangmei Opera · Intangible cultural heritage · Lightweight H5 game

1 Introduction

Huangmei Opera, one of the five major operas in China, has a certain influence in Asia. Its music for voices, performance characteristics and artistic style have high aesthetic value, and play an important role in the development of film art in Hong Kong, Taiwan and other regions. It is a main art form that supports the development of Chinese art film and the epitome of Chinese national culture. During the research process, the author found that 79.8% of people knew about Huangmei Opera, but they would not watch Huangmei Opera performances, exhibitions or purchase related products offline, 16.08% had some knowledge of classic plays and representative artists, and only 4.12% were very familiar with Huangmei Opera. This indicates that the audience has a certain cognitive foundation for Huangmei Opera, but they do not understand this traditional art form.

How to effectively communicate cultural connotation via new media techniques is a crucial issue for traditional operas today.

HTML5 was selected as the carrier of Huangmei Opera cultural propaganda in this research. On the one hand, H5 games are easy to communicate and form topics against the dilemma of Huangmei Opera, which accord with the community communication habits of contemporary young people, and can effectively expand the user group of Huangmei Opera. On the other hand, lightweight H5 games are highly easy to learn and play by inserting knowledge points in the process of game experience, which can effectively bridge the problem between the lengthy content of Huangmei Opera and fast-food reading. In order to design a lightweight H5 game that meets the cultural needs of contemporary people, the design practice of Huangmei Opera lightweight game was completed by the EEG experiment, focus group and questionnaires.

2 Research on Influencing Factors of Communication Effect of Huangmei Opera Lightweight H5 Game

2.1 Identification of Target Users of Huangmei Opera Lightweight H5 Game

In this paper, young people aged 18–30 were selected as the target users of H5 games. This generation has been greatly influenced by information technology products such as the Internet, intelligent communication and tablet computer, and has its own media usage habits; also deeply influenced by China chic culture, they have a certain understanding and appreciation of traditional culture.

2.2 Extraction of User Experience Hierarchy of Huangmei Opera Lightweight H5 Game

Garrett ranked the user experience hierarchy from high to low as: presentation layer, framework layer, structure layer, scope layer and strategy layer. Based on the five elements of user experience proposed by Garrett, combined with the characteristics of Huangmei Opera and the media preferences of contemporary youth groups, the hierarchy of experience elements of Huangmei Opera lightweight H5 games was further extracted, that is, the presentation layer corresponds to audio-visual design; The framework layer corresponds to story frame design; The structure layer corresponds to interaction design; The scope layer corresponds to content design; The strategy layer corresponds to H5's audience expectation.

2.3 Acquisition of User Preference Samples by EEG Experiment

Experimental Design. In order to obtain the games with higher user preference among the existing lightweight games on the market for further research, in this experiment, based on the principle of EEG technology, user preference degree for different types of lightweight games was mined from EEG data. The higher the Active value is, the higher the preference degree of subjects to the sample is. Each user experienced six H5 games, and the top three popular H5 games were finally selected for the subsequent study of the focus group.

Experimental Samples. A comparative study was performed by selecting six lightweight games with cultural propaganda function launched by China authoritative institute of culture, authoritative media, head game company, well-known museums, etc., which are: "Riverside Scene at Qingming Festival 3.0," "Dunhuang Frescoes Exhibition," "Join Me to Repair the Qin Tomb Terra Cotta Warriors," "Dunhuang Poetry Scarf," "Heritage Watch Program," "The Vast Land."

Experimental Subjects. 20 target users aged 20–30 were invited, including 8 mature users who use lightweight H5 games frequently, 5 users engaged in cultural communication research, and 7 ordinary users who initially experience lightweight H5 games. All subjects participated in the experiment independently, and they were in good mental state before the experiment and had no prior knowledge of experimental materials.

Experimental Equipment. The EEG device used in the experiment was Muse2, which collects EEG data with several dry electrodes and outputs real-time EEG information.

Experimental Indicators. As shown in Fig. 1, Muse consists of seven sensors, of which FP1 and FP2 are forehead sensors corresponding to the frontal lobe of the brain. In this paper, the feedback from the frontal lobe was selected as the main reference data, and Muse App used Active, Neutral and Calm as evaluation indicators of the frontal lobe activity of the tested subjects.

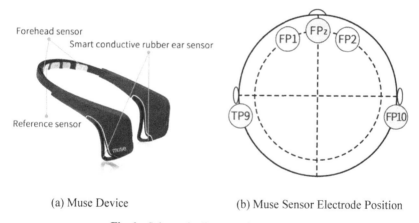

(a) Muse Device   (b) Muse Sensor Electrode Position

Fig. 1. Schematic diagram of muse device

Experimental Process. The subjects were told to have an overall perception of the game to be displayed, and were guided to gaze at the cross in the center of mobile phone screen for 10s. They were then displayed the first game and told they had two minutes to play the game on their own. At the end of the experience, the screen went blank for 30s, then the second game was displayed, and so on until all 6 games were experienced.

Analysis of Experimental Results. The Active values of the 6 samples are shown in Table 1. The three samples with the highest Active values were Sample 3, Sample 4, and Sample 5, corresponding to "Join Me to Repair the Qin Tomb Terra Cotta Warriors," "Dunhuang Poetry Scarf," "Heritage Watch Program." The three games were more arousing to the users' brain, and can be used for further research.

Table 1. Summary of muse data statistics

	Sample 1	Sample 2	Sample 3	Sample 4	Sample 5	Sample 6
Subject 1	1	8	1	0	19	2
Subject 2	0	1	15	2	5	0
Subject 3	0	0	0	0	17	3
Subject 4	6	6	5	58	6	0
Subject 5	0	0	4	11	9	3
Subject 6	0	0	0	0	0	13
Subject 7	7	6	2	6	19	0
Subject 8	0	8	0	1	2	0
Subject 9	0	2	0	3	3	0
Subject 10	1	1	6	12	0	3
Subject 11	0	0	7	7	3	3
Subject 12	0	0	0	7	2	0
Subject 13	0	0	9	0	0	0
Subject 14	0	0	1	9	0	0
Subject 15	3	0	5	0	0	0
Subject 16	0	0	11	16	0	1
Subject 17	0	2	0	7	0	5
Subject 18	2	0	0	5	1	6
Subject 19	0	3	0	0	0	10
Subject 20	0	1	0	0	6	0
Total	20	38	66	144	92	49

2.4 Selection of Influencing Factors of Communication Effect of Huangmei Opera Lightweight H5 Game

Design and Implementation by the Focus Group. The focus group is to make a perceptual analysis on the causes for the high brain arousal of the first three games, and to put forward the secondary factors influencing the communication effect of Huangmei Opera lightweight H5 game based on the cultural characteristics of Huangmei Opera. The specific interview outline is shown as follows (Table 2):

Table 2. Interview outline

Interview dimensions	Interview questions
Audio-visual design	1. What is your impression of the style and composition of the three H5 games?
	2. Do you think this H5 needs to be improved in terms of audio-visual design?
Framework design	1. Please describe which part of the three H5 games impresses you the most and explain why
	2. Which of the three H5 games do you prefer? Why?
	3. What are the differences between the three H5 games and other H5 games you were exposed to earlier?
	4. Are you satisfied with the ending of H5?
Interaction design	1. How is the experience of the whole operation process? Which part do you think is good and which part is bad?
	2. Is the story scene switching smoothly?
Content design	1. Do you have any understanding of the cultural knowledge described in H5 after the experience?
	2. Which of the three H5 storylines appeals to you the most? What do you dislike?
Audience expectation	1. Please talk about your first impression of the three H5 games
	2. What do you think it looks like before touching this kind of H5? Does it meet your expectations now?

After the interview, the author summarized the interview results and sorted out the influencing factors of the dimensions of audio-visual design, framework design, interaction design, content design and market target according to the evaluation dimensions affecting user experience, as shown in Table 3.

Table 3. Factors influencing user experience of lightweight H5 games

Dimensions	Extraction of key elements	Notes
Audio-visual design	Background music	An immersive atmosphere is created by combining with images
	Color	Color matching should conform to cultural characteristics and create cultural association
	Overall style	Words, music and images are coordinated to create the proper cultural atmosphere
Framework design	Guidance mechanism	Users are given relevant prompts in necessary links to ensure that users complete all links
	Effect presentation	After the game, there can be some reward mechanisms or the work of art designed by user can be derived
Interaction design	Operating method	Easy to operate
	Way of presentation	The way of presentation accords with cultural characteristics
Content design	Storyline	The storyline should objectively show cultural knowledge
Market target	Emotion goal	Able to achieve emotional resonance and promote a complete user experience
	Cultural goal	Able to spread cultural knowledge

Extraction of Influencing Factors of Huangmei Opera Lightweight H5 Game.
According to the factors influencing user experience of lightweight H5 game summarized above and the cultural characteristics of Huangmei Opera, the factors influencing the experience of Huangmei Opera lightweight H5 game were proposed (Table 4).

Table 4. Factors influencing user experience of Huangmei Opera lightweight H5 game

Dimensions	Primary influencing factors	Secondary influencing factors
Audio-visual design	Background music	Light music
		Words
	Color	High saturation
		Low saturation
	Overall style	Flat illustration style
		Ink painting style
		Line drawing style
Framework design	Guidance mechanism	Text description
		Voice prompt
	Effect presentation	End directly
		Reward exchange
		My DIY art work
Interaction design	Operating method	Single story advancement
		Independent exploration
	Way of presentation	Picture + text
		Animation + voice explanation
Content design	Story selection	Artist story
		Opera story
		History of Huangmei Opera
Market target	Emotion goal	Immersion
		Sense of achievement
		Sense of gain
	Cultural goal	Learnability
		Interestingness

3 Attribute Analysis of Influencing Factors Based on KANO Questionnaire

3.1 Questionnaire Design of Huangmei Opera Lightweight H5 Game

The KANO questionnaire was designed with 24 secondary demands summarized in Table 3 as main contents, and users' attitudes towards relevant demands were obtained through forward and reverse questions, as shown in Table 5.

Table 5. Questionnaire example

1. Background music: light music					
Attitude	I like it	Deserved	I do not care	Acceptable	I do not like it
Satisfied					
Dissatisfied					

3.2 Analysis of Questionnaire Data

Reliability and Validity Analysis. The rationality of questionnaire was tested with Cronbach's alpha reliability coefficient, KMO value and Bartlett. With reliability coefficient value as 0.927, KMO value as 0.889, and Barlett test of sphericity value as sig = 0.000, the questionnaire had good reliability and validity, and can be used for further research.

Attribute Analysis of Influencing Factors. According to the recovered data, the Better-Worse coefficient values were introduced to rank the influencing factors numerically. The calculation results are shown in Table 6.

Table 6. The better-worse coefficients

功能	Better	Reorder	Worse	Reorder
Q1. Light music	50.77%	3	-8.21%	14
Q2. Words	17.89%	22	-5.79%	5
Q3. High saturation	16.48%	23	-6.04%	6
Q4. Low saturation	30.20%	12	-6.44%	7
Q5. Flat illustration style	39.22%	9	-8.33%	15
Q6. Ink painting style	27.09%	15	-6.90%	9
Q7. Line drawing style	30.00%	13	-5.50%	4
Q8. Text description	25.00%	17	-7.21%	10
Q9. Voice prompt	15.38%	24	-5.29%	3
Q10. End directly	21.11%	21	-5.03%	2
Q11. Reward exchange	44.44%	6	-8.08%	12
Q12. My DIY art work	41.92%	7	-8.08%	12
Q13. Single story advancement	24.51%	18	-4.90%	1
Q14. Independent exploration	45.00%	5	-8.50%	17
Q15. Picture+text	34.48%	11	-8.87%	19
Q16. Animation + voice explanation	25.77%	16	-6.70%	8
Q17. Artist story	21.29%	20	-7.43%	11
Q18. Opera story	28.00%	14	-8.50%	17
Q19. History of Huangmei Opera	24.38%	19	-8.46%	16
Q20. Immersion	37.50%	10	-10.50%	23
Q21. Sense of achievement	55.61%	2	-16.84%	22
Q22. Sense of gain	46.73%	4	-14.57%	20
Q23. Learnability	40.70%	8	-14.57%	20
Q24. Interestingness	61.54%	1	-22.56%	24

According to Table 6, the scatter diagram was drawn to divide the influencing factor attributes. One-dimensional Quality includes: Q20 sense of achievement, Q22 sense of gain, Q23 easy to learn, Q21 immersive experience, Q24 interestingness. The Worse value in this quadrant was the highest, so when the corresponding demands are not met, users will be dissatisfied with the H5.

Attractive Quality includes Q1 light music, Q14 independent exploration and advancement, Q11 DIY ending, Q12 social reward, Q5 ink painting style, Q15 image-text display, among which Q1 light music, as the demand with the highest Better value in this quadrant, has a great impact on user satisfaction. Q15 image-text display is the demand with the highest Worse value in this quadrant, indicating that when this demand is not met, users are most dissatisfied with H5. The rest are Indifferent Quality (Fig. 2).

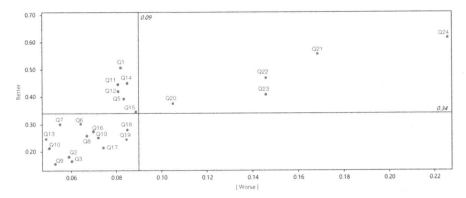

Fig. 2. Scatter diagram

4   Design Practice of Huangmei Opera Lightweight H5 Game

4.1   Design Strategies and Principles

The design of Huangmei Opera lightweight H5 game should first follow the principle of precise communication, that is, H5 games need to convey the cultural characteristics of Huangmei Opera through audio-visual design, so the selection of the overall visual style and background music should be consistent with the artistic style of Huangmei Opera; Secondly, the principle of real-time feedback should be followed. H5 has strong real-time interaction, so continuous operational feedback is required to inform the user of the current state, progress, operation results, etc., so that users can get a better sense of experience during the game; Finally, the principle of empathy needs to be observed. According to user research feedback, sense of experience, immersion and sense of achievement are One-dimensional Quality. H5 needs to arouse emotional resonance, so that users can better perceive the cultural connotation of Huangmei Opera in the experience process.

According to the design principles of Huangmei Opera lightweight H5 game and the results of previous questionnaire analysis, the following design strategies were made in this paper: In the audio-visual design, light music was used as the overall background music of the game, and Chinese traditional art forms such as ink painting and line drawing with low saturation color matching were adopted as the overall style; Text description was used as the guiding mechanism in the framework design, and social rewards were set at the end of the game; The game was advanced by a single story and users were given certain independent exploration space; As a whole, the game focused on guiding users to understand the development process of Huangmei Opera art through the artist's life and art characteristics of Huangmei Opera at each stage.

4.2 Design Scheme

There are a number of famous artists and classic repertoires in the development of Huangmei Opera. The author hopes that users can understand performance genres, typical characters and classic works of Huangmei Opera in the process of using and experiencing the Huangmei Opera lightweight H5 game. At the same time, H5 can guide the offline stage performance and exhibition as a port, and help the audience to obtain relevant information for in-depth understanding after initial experience of Huangmei Opera culture.

Storyline Design. In content design, "classic repertoire" and "development history of Huangmei Opera" had relatively high Better values, but the three influencing factors showed the same attribute. Therefore, the storyline was constructed from a comprehensive narrative perspective by connecting the life track of representative artists and representative works to reflect the development vein of Huangmei Opera.

To this end, important historical events of Huangmei Opera from 1879 to 1981 were sorted out, based on which the development history of Huangmei Opera was divided into four important stages, and the artists and works of each stage were mainly displayed to users. The specific content design is shown in Table 7.

The game is called "A Huangmei Opera," and the specific story script is described as below: The player is a student majoring in History, who is studying the development process of Huangmei Opera. When being confused, he found that he could travel to different stages in history and study the representative artists and art works at each time node as well as the artistic characteristics of Huangmei Opera at that stage, thus completing the task of sorting out the historical context of Huangmei Opera. In the game, typical artists such as Ding Yongquan, Ju Guanghua and Hu Puya, as well as classic repertoires such as The Story of Silk Kerchief, Goddess Marriage, Emperor's Female Son-in-law, were introduced alternately and the characteristics of Huangmei Opera's costumes and makeup were displayed through stage design.

Game Mechanism Design. The "independent exploration" and "pictures + text display," which were highly preferred by users in the previous research, were included in the design of game mechanism. The specific gameplay is shown in the figure. After entering the scene, players can explore the scene by themselves by sliding left and right and NPC prompt, find the information trigger point, click the person or object with prompt label to complete the historical information collection task, and proceed to the next scene after collecting (Fig. 3).

Table 7. Content design of of Huangmei Opera lightweight H5 game

Important symbols	Historical events, knowledge content
Origin of Huangmei Opera	About Hu Puya
	Artistic features of early Huangmei Opera
From country to city	About Ding Yongquan
	How did Ding Yongquan sing Huangmei Opera in Anqing City with the help of fans?
	New Stage and Airen Theater competed with each other
	The first performance of Shuangxi Troupe in Shanghai
Further development of expression	About Wang Shaofang
	Peking Opera and Huangmei Opera performed on the same stage
	Jinghu was introduced as accompaniment for Huangmei Opera
	Yan Fengying was popular all over China
National development of Huangmei Opera films	The first story film *Goddess Marriage* was made
	The first black-and-white documentary film of Huangmei Opera, *Couple View of Lights*, was shot
	Huangmei Opera film *Emperor's Female Son-in-law* was shot
	Huangmei Opera film *Liang Shanbo and Zhu Yingtai* was shot in Hong Kong
	The color version of *Goddess Marriage*, renamed *Shadow of a Scholar-Tree*, was preliminarily planned to shoot

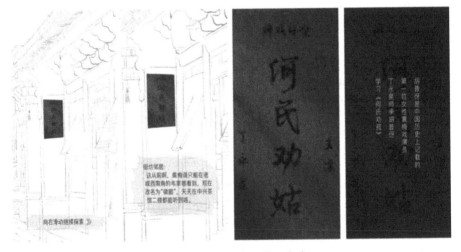

Fig. 3. Main scene interface design

In order to solve the problems of audience's unwillingness to download and low viscosity after downloading, and to meet the users' demand for the attribute of "reward exchange," a certain reward mechanism was set at the end of the game. Players can get relevant points after collecting relevant information in each scene. After the game is over, it jumps to the online shopping mall of Huangmei Opera. In the mall, players can buy peripheral products, books and tickets for offline performances of Huangmei Opera. Part of the amount can be deducted by points in the game (Fig. 4).

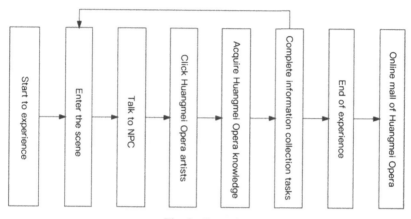

Fig. 4. Gameplay

Audio-Visual Design. The "ink painting style" with higher user preference was employed as the initial interface of the game, and low saturation color matching was the overall tone. The overall color matching is shown in Fig. 5. The classical repertoire accompaniment of the scene artist was applied as the background music of the scene in the game, to meet the user's preference for "light music" attribute.

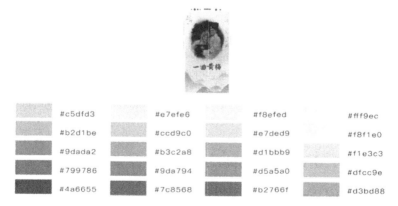

Fig. 5. Color use paradigm

Application Scenarios. The main application scenario of the game is the exit of Huangmei Opera related history museum, which means "bringing Huangmei Opera home". Audiences can learn relevant knowledge in the process of experiencing lightweight mini-games, and can also connect historical stories with offline cultural relics, to better spread relevant cultural knowledge, which has demonstrative value for digital exhibition of oral skills museums (Fig. 6).

Fig. 6. "A Huangmei Opera" interface display

4.3 Result

In China Huangmei Opera Museum are mainly static cultural relics + text introduction boards and voice explanation by scanning QR codes. The introduction of lightweight H5 games can change the original written and unidirectional introduction in the museum, so as to enhance the effect of cultural communication of Huangmei Opera. In addition, H5 has strong cross-terminal and cross-regional characteristics and can disseminate culture relying on online community.

5 Design Effectiveness Evaluation

5.1 Experimental Design

In order to verify the effective communication of "A Huangmei Opera" among young people, the EEG data of different types of users in the game experience was recorded by the Muse experiment, and a questionnaire was added on this basis for subjective evaluation. The secondary influencing factors of user experience of Huangmei Opera lightweight H5 game obtained above were combined with the experimental samples, and relevant questionnaires were made according to Likert scale method.

5.2 Experimental Subjects

A total of 20 subjects were invited and divided into two groups, with 10 people in each group. Group A consisted of experienced players with frequent exposure to lightweight H5 games, but did not know Huangmei Opera; Group B was composed of Huangmei Opera fans, but had not been exposed to lightweight H5 games.

5.3 Experimental Process

The subjects were told to have an overall perception of Huangmei Opera lightweight H5 game to be displayed. The game "A Huangmei Opera" was presented for users to experience independently for one minute, and a questionnaire was distributed after the experiment (Table 8).

Table 8. Summary of muse data statistics

	Active	Neutral	Calm
Subject 1	0	64	36
Subject 2	9	71	40
Subject 3	14	93	13
Subject 4	3	66	51
Subject 5	17	60	43
Subject 6	7	93	20
Subject 7	0	47	73
Subject 8	1	74	45
Subject 9	29	62	29
Subject 10	30	67	23
Subject 11	11	59	50
Subject 12	37	68	15
Subject 13	24	62	24
Subject 14	20	79	21
Subject 15	18	64	38
Subject 16	15	63	42
Subject 17	7	57	56
Subject 18	17	90	13
Subject 19	21	74	25
Subject 20	28	79	13
Total	308	1392	670

Table 9. Questionnaire data statistics after experiment

	Mean
Visual design	4.4
Guidance mechanism	4.25
Immersion	4.3
Sense of achievement	4.2
Readability	4.5
Easy to play	4.55
Interestingness	4.4

Muse EEG experiment results show the Active value of "A Huangmei Opera" was higher than that of six experimental samples described above, that is, users have a higher degree of preference for this game, compared to several other existing cultural promotion lightweight games on the market. At the same time, important influencing factors such as immersion, readability and interestingness, which were highly preferred by users in the early research of the game, were asked in the form of a questionnaire. The results of the questionnaire show that users generally hold a high evaluation of "A Huangmei Opera." (Table 9)

6   Conclusion

With Huangmei Opera as the research object, the design practice was carried out based on EEG experiment, focus group and questionnaire analysis, and the specific research results were summarized as below: First, the research model of cultural propaganda lightweight game was constructed from the angle of physiology and psychology; Second, by discussing the attributes of different influencing factors that affect the experience of Huangmei Opera lightweight H5 games, a research method on how to increase the viscosity of young users to cultural propaganda games through quantitative analysis was proposed; Third, the idea of taking lightweight H5 as the carrier of traditional culture communication provides a new idea for the contemporary communication of Huangmei Opera and other Chinese opera intangible cultural heritage.

Research and Exploration on Light Environment Interactive Art Promoting Development of Night Economy in China

Mu Zhang[1(✉)] and Xiao Sun[2]

[1] Shandong University of Art and Design, No. 02, Nineteen floor, Unit 1, Building 5, Huaiyin, Jinan, China
153962234@qq.com
[2] National Academy of Chinese Theatre Arts, No. 187, Jingliu Road, Huaiyin, Jinan, China

Abstract. Light environment interactive art is based on optical media and electronic media, which is a new art form. With the certainty of "keeping pace with the times", the light environment interactive art mainly creates interactive art based on the research of light environment. Through the latest scientific and technological achievements, it is also the artwork with the light as the creative medium. Artists create extraordinary visual effects and immersion experience with various high-tech materials and technologies. As the most important medium of information dissemination, light has become an indispensable creative material of artists, which plays a crucial role in many artistic works. Through the research on the interactive art of urban environmental lighting and light environment, this paper summarizes the relevant theories of urban light environment interactive design, which can be integrated with China's urban night economy culture, so as to increase China's night economy.

Keywords: Light environment · Interactive art · Installation · Public space

1 Research Background

The study of light originated in ancient Greece. Plato and Pythagoras believed that our eyes would emit weak light for detection, which would collect information about the objects around us and bring it back in some way. About a thousand years later, an Arab mathematician, Alhazen, proved that these philosophers were wrong. He thought that why we could not see anything in the dark if our eyes could shine? Thus, he believed that our eyes captured light rather than generating. According to what he said, the image we see comes from the sunlight reflected from the object into our eyes. Light transmits most of the information we can perceive.

Night economy is also called moonlight economy and night market economy, which is not only the extension of urban economy with service industry as the main body in the relative spacetime, but also an important part of modern urban economy. Moonlight economy shows a city's economic development level, consumption level and agglomeration radiation ability, reflecting urban activities as well as the development, openness and attraction of a city. As a public economy and livelihood economy, it directly marks the economic prosperity of a city, which is conducive to improving residents' consumption and economic growth. Based on the light environment design, light environment interactive art integrates new media interactive elements to connect people with light, making it a dynamic interactive device rather than static lighting. While interacting with games, users can convey emotion with enriched space, inherited culture and enhanced communication. Besides, it can also attract consumers to know the goods well, increasing their stopping time, so as to improve the night economic consumption to make lighting a new medium for information transmission (Fig. 1).

Fig. 1. Night economy

1.1   Research Status in China

China has carried out the research and practice of light environment for nearly 20 years, especially in the theoretical research of light environment interactive art. Through the analysis of many new media interactive design cases, Extraordinary Application of Interactive Thinking in Contemporary Architecture, written by Xing Zhaohe, summarizes the specific methods and thinking of interactive design, combining with the relevant practice of light environment design to find out the features and laws between them. From the perspective of design, Dai Zhizhong, Jiang Ke and Lu Xin discuss the role of light in architectural construction, architectural space and architectural functions in their book, Light and Architecture. At the same time, it also tells how to introduce light into specific architectural design and how to create richer modeling and spatial effects with light. In terms of papers, based on the indoor space design, Li Weiying's Application of Light Environment Design in Indoor Space mainly tells what kinds of new methods that designers use to create a different light environment with the development status of light environment, so as to meet the new needs of the new era. In the Value of Light in the Night Economy in Hangzhou Scenic Spot of the Beijing-Hangzhou Canal, the author takes the Hangzhou scenic spot of the Beijing-Hangzhou Canal as an example to analyze how to skillfully show the brilliant history of the Canal with light, so that it can create the canal night economy to promote the transformation and development of urban industries, which can be the reference for other cities to develop the night economy. In 2018, the Urban Night Image Planning and Design Talent Training Project of China National Arts Fund was carried out by the Communication University of China, cooperating with the Arts Department of the Communication University of China and the joint research center of light environment design and application.

1.2 Research Status Abroad

Like the research status in China, there are also two aspects of the foreign research on the interaction mode and interface of building light environment. In terms of theory, Chris van Uffelen tells in Light in Architecture that light has become an organic part of architecture in the past few years, because it is a prerequisite condition of spatial perception. Then the design of light environment becomes more and more vivid and colorful. Mary Guzowski, a famous American architectural thinker and natural light expert, shows the practical design strategy of light environment design to architects and people who care about the impact of built environment with her hardworking. Architect W and artist Daan Roosegaarde record their exploring result of the interaction between architecture and natural environment under the condition of high-tech touch in Interactive Landscapes. Foxlin analyzes in Interactive Architecture that the interaction between architecture and environment must have certain requirements for the dynamics and flexibility of architecture through rethinking the traditional and static architecture with single function.

2 Definition, Classification, Characteristics and Functions of Light

2.1 Definition and Classification of Light

For science, light or visible light is electromagnetic radiation that can be perceived by human eyes. Light is an electromagnetic wave, which is also a beam of particles, so, it is called wave-particle duality. Light can propagate in many media, such as water, transparent crystals, etc., which also carries the information of these media at the same time, such as the shape and color of the media. Light has different wavelengths as it is an electromagnetic wave, and human eyes have different sensitivities of light to different wavelengths. Normal human eyes are most sensitive to yellow and green light sources with a wavelength of 555 nm, while the visibility of emission beyond 555 nm will gradually decrease. The wavelength of visible light is 390 nm to 780 nm, while the wavelength that the human eye can perceive is between 312 nm and 1050 nm [1] (Fig. 2).

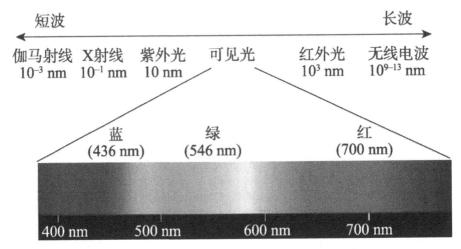

Fig. 2. Wavelength

Physically, there are two types of light: natural light and artificial light. Natural light refers to the light we can feel in nature, such as sunlight, light generated by natural phenomena, etc. While, artificial light means the light generated by human beings through artificial light sources like electric bulbs, lasers, etc. From the perspective of perception, light can also be divided into warm light and cold light. Light has energy and people can perceive the temperature of light. Thus, heat source light is called warm light, on the contrary, it is called cold light. On the other hand, from the perspective of psychology, the warmth and coldness of the light source can make people feel different vision and emotion. Warm light makes people feel warm, comfortable and enthusiastic, which represents sensibility. While, cold light makes people feel cold and calm, showing rationality.

2.2 Characteristics and Functions of Light

The penetration, mixing and plasticity are the main characteristics of light. Penetration mainly refers to that light can penetrate transparent or translucent objects in the process of propagation, which can even cut objects in visual perception. Intensity of light will be decreased when passing through objects, which is often used by artists for artistic expression. Light mixing means that light with different wave bands, or different colors can be superimposed, which will gradually become white for many times. The plasticity of light makes it leave traces through the diffuse reflection of micro media in the process of propagation, which will usually form a cylinder. For example, the spotlight on the facade of a building can form a light column at starry night. In addition, when a laser enters a space with smoke, the propagation trace will become a straight line. The plasticity of light can be used by artists to create different shapes of light in the void space, so as to change people's inherent concept that light is "invisible", giving light " personality".

Most of the purposes of human beings to create light sources are to serve human's basic life. However, with the continuous development of science and technology, especially the human civilization, light begin to enter the field of art. The lighting function is mainly to ensure the basic needs of human life to prolong the human activities without natural light. At present, the lighting function is widely applied in urban lighting and human life with virous application methods based on different scenes and fields. For example, objects under the spotlight will be emphasized to attract the audience; Street lights can improve visibility at night to ensure safety; The light beside the product emphasizes the characteristics, so as to promote consumption.

With what is found in the research on cognition and psychology, the color and intensity of light will affect human psychological and visual perception, which makes the function change from simplification to diversification. The psychological function of light mainly brings different psychological effects on people through the illumination and color temperature. The visual acuity increases with the illuminance, so, the intensity of illumination has different effects on people's visual response and psychological feeling. Relevant research indicates that the satisfaction of people's visual and psychological feelings can decrease when the illumination is reduced. While the color temperature can affect people's central nervous system, making the excitement of people's mood and brain different. For instance, the coffee shop is a place for people to relax, so, the color temperature of the internal light source needs to be lower than that of the outdoor. Because the light source with low color temperature can relax people's nerves to make the brain calm down. On the other hand, the color temperature must be increased in playgrounds and examination rooms to stimulate brain vitality and mobilize physical enthusiasm. Moreover, the environment with different illuminance can make people feel different size of space, such as the illusion of object position caused by different illumination of light in different directions and modes. The white light source can widen the space, while the dark light source is opposite (Fig. 3).

The visual function of light mainly shows in the change and transformation of space. Human visual imaging mainly relies on the optic nerve to capture two-dimensional information pictures, which can form three-dimensional images in consciousness through brain processing. The human eye can distinguish the three-dimensional and two-dimensional space through different intensity of light. Therefore, the light intensity of the object\surface can be changed to achieve visual unity, so that the three-dimensional space seems to become two-dimensional. The two-dimensional or three-dimensional properties of objects can be changed to aim to realize artistic expression through black-and-white and intensity, so that the space can pay more attention to shaping light rather than the dimension. This is the main expression method of light in the light environment interactive art.

Fig. 3. Color temperature

3 Application of Light Environment Interactive Art in Modern City

3.1 Application of Light in Interactive Art

Through the research on functions and characteristics of light, light can be applied in art for auxiliary design, or can be created as the main body. In traditional painting, light is indispensable. The artist expresses light in the picture, shaping the realistic effects such as volume and perspective of the object by depicting the characteristics of light. In terms of classical painting, painters often express light realistically. Light and shadow make the picture vital, with the space, volume, temperature and diurnal change of things, conveying the spiritual theme of the work while expressing their emotions. Monet is an outstanding representative of impressionism, who has his own unique artistic expression of light [2]. His masterpiece, Impression Sunrise, integrates the sky, water and rising sun, which cleverly unifies the early sun, sky and sea surface through highlight, diffuse reflection and specular reflection even without specific light drawing. Artists can express their feelings for nature through the artistic expression of light in traditional painting, which makes the temperature and color of light are indispensable. Therefore, without a doubt, light plays a crucial role in traditional painting (Fig. 4).

As the modern art rising, especially post-modern art, physical materials begin to become a part of painting, and traditional painting is no longer the only form for art

Fig. 4. Impression Sunrise

expression. Kiefer's comprehensive material painting brings material entities into the picture with a new visual impact on the audience through the combination of two-dimensional canvas and three-dimensional entities. At that time, the physical properties of light and shadow became a part of artistic creation for the first time. Therefore, when color on the picture is combined with the light and shadow of the entity, the three-dimensional object seems to fall into the two-dimensional space, bringing a new expression to painting arts [3]. New media art begins to show on the historical stage with the development of science and technology. So, the light plays the most important role in new media art. Artists use the characteristics of light to analyze and reconstruct the light media which can be a unique artistic language for artists, so, the artists can integrate their own spiritual ideas into it. James Turrell, American contemporary artist, once transformed three-dimensional space into two-dimensional plane with the diffuse reflection characteristics of light.

3.2 Theoretical Support for the Implementation of Light Environment Interactive Art in Cities

The characteristics of light environment interactive art can be integrated with China's urban night economy culture, so as to find measures to promote the China's urban night economy with relevant strategies in the research process. In the interactive design of light environment, the propagation distance is closely related to vision. Within 500 m, the interactive experience effect is focused. From 500 m to 1000 m, the visual aesthetic effect is more important. More than 1500 m, it is more suitable for the information dissemination. Following this law, interactive installations with different carriers and methods at different distances can make different social, cultural and economic benefits.

From the perspective of cognitive experience theory, there are three aspects that need us to care about. First of all, people's attention determines whether the audience can quickly enter the experience process. People can only care about one point at any time, so the audience has no time to experience "interaction" when "appreciating" and vice versa. Therefore, there needs to be a point that can immediately attract the audience at the beginning of the experience, and it can also make the audience try to explore. It needs always grasp the curiosity of the audiences to keep them in the device experience. Besides, it should comply with Miller's Law: 7–2 Principle, which means that the number of tourist concerns shall not exceed 5 at any time. This is the limit of human perception. With more choices, audiences can take more time to make decisions, which will affect the experience. Secondly, in the process of device experience, it is necessary to make the audience quickly reach the mental flow. When we want something, we want to get with difficulties. We like challenges and rewards. Interactive design can be carried out through game or dynamic thinking to make the installation "alive". Intervention design, directional design and active design can give audiences the "independent space" (it can be physical space like telephone booth, semi-open space like work partition and symbolic space like the circular area projected on the ground), so as to provide personal security and privacy for the audiences to experience more deeply. It can also guide the audience to know the specific process at a specific time, such as "light arrow" (which is very suitable for games or the dynamic interaction design of hierarchy). Things that the audience likes or pursues can be provided to immerse them in their own choices (refer to Maslow's hierarchy of needs). Finally, artists need to focus on the user's memory and desire. The interaction process follows the Pareto principle, which means that 20% of the things in the installation can bring 80% of the effect. The quality of design is often determined by a few of the most "exciting" highlights that people can remember. Therefore, some designers deliberately make some parts of the installation mediocre, so as to highlight 20% to realize deep and directional memory. The device experience needs to follow the serial position effect, which refers to the beginning and end of the experience should be designed with no effort spared, while the middle part can just avoid defects as much as possible. The principle of Zeigarnik effect shows that unfinished task is easier to stay in people's mind than the completed one (suspense creation or exploration experience). Therefore, we can create suspense when arousing the audience's curiosity to a high level, and this suspense may be answered in the next issue of the installation, in the purchased commodity or in our offline APP.

When studying the relationship between light environment interactive art and China's night economy culture, we need to master the relevant theories of light environment design, new media art and interactive design. Moreover, it is also necessary to gradually create our own conceptual system, realization means and innovation sources through the intersection with economics, culture, communication, psychology, engineering and other disciplines. Combined with multimedia artificial intelligence technology, the final achievements will be gradually reached.

3.3 Necessity of Implementing Light Environment Interactive Art in Cities

Recently, there have been many problems in the process of developing night economy and culture in China, such as single market format, strong seasonality of operation as well as lack of cultural characteristics, supporting facilities and overall planning of the government. Besides, the solutions to these problems and academic research are quite scarce. Under this circumference, the application of light environment interactive art for solving some problems in domestic urban night economy makes up for the blank of relevant academic research to a certain extent, which is innovative and practical (Fig. 5).

Fig. 5. Application of light environment interactive art

Developing the "night economy" culture in China's cities is an inevitable requirement to boost China's economy. For example, in order to solve the problems, such as Jinan's "inactive night economy, insufficient lighting at night and single business forms of night economy", pointed out by Liu Jiayi, secretary of Shandong Provincial Party Committee, Jinan took the development of night economy as the "number one" project in 2019. Driven by a series of measures, Jinan won the titles of "China's Top Ten Night Economy Cities" and "China's Top Ten Night Economy Influential Cities". For the current popular cultural tourism lighting, urban night economy has become a new economic growth point, which is emerging. So, how to explore and shape the night image of cities and cultural places is the key factor to attract people, keep people and promote consumption. Therefore, the light environment design and light interaction design with information transmission and cultural construction as the main tasks have attracted more and more attention, which plays an significance role in guiding the further improvement of the night economy in China's cities.

3.4   Case Analysis of Light Environment Interactive Art in Cities

Artist dancorson once again turned the public space channel under two overpasses in downtown San Jose, California, into a bright, dynamic and interactive art experience installation as urban lighting show. The light show installation contains more than 1000 color rings and 81 independently controlled LED rings which are equipped with motion sensors to sense the fluctuation of sidewalks and bicycle lanes under the overpass. The light show device contains two lighting art works: "sensing YOU" and "sensing WATER", which use plants, lights and interactive technology to add a beautiful dynamic landscape to the downtown. From the perspective of safe driving, when the vehicle passes by, the lighting change will be very slow, so the passing vehicles will not be affected by the lighting change. But when the pedestrian passes by, the lighting change will become very active (Fig. 6).

Fig. 6. LED

Wavelet is an interactive light installation created by GeeksArt, a new media art group. They mimic the flowing water with the changing light, adding some romance. The main body of this installation is composed of 1,300 light-responsive light bulbs, arranged to undulating surface. When participants approach one of the "teardrops" with a luminous object, it will be lit immediately, and this light will be transmitted to the surrounding "teardrops". A visible "light wave" then extends all the way to the edge of the installation, like the ripple on the water caused a stone. Each of the teardrop-shaped light bulb is embedded with custom-made electronics analyzing the light and color at the same time. In the process of light transmission, it may "mutate" due to the influence of ambient light, which also adds more unpredictable mystery to the installation. When multiple participants use light sources with different colors to trigger the installation from virous positions, the colorful light waves spread out like a series of dominoes to shine enduringly and brightly (Fig. 7).

Fig. 7. Wavelet

Echo of Heart is a large imaging device, which is composed of a large circular lamp band on the ground and an array with 20 circular fans around the audience. In each separate screen, the image generated by sine and cosine calculation evokes a cognitive breakthrough of the ancient circle: "cyclotomic method" to a certain extent, the rotation change of which is the appearance of the circle under the generative algorithm. The continuous rotation of the screen itself and the large circle surrounding the screen array on the ground emphasize the presence of the circular circle as the external structure, and audiences are also regarded as a part of the installation. Audiences in the center of the installation, together with the Echo of Heart, make the original world illustration of "Round Sky and Square Earth" perceptually come into effect in an aesthetic way (Fig. 8).

AMYGDALA listens to shared thoughts, interprets states of mind and translates the data gathered into an audiovisual installation capable of representing the collective emotional state of the net and its changes on the basis of events that take place around the world. The aim is to make visible the flow of data and information that are constantly being created by users, and that may be heard and interpreted by anyone, in the attempt to stimulate a reflection on the opportunities and dangers of the digital revolution that we are currently going through. Big Data may in fact be used to monitor the spread of an epidemic in real time, or to prevent a crime and improve the safety of a city; likewise, they may also be exploited by companies and institutions to store – often unknown to

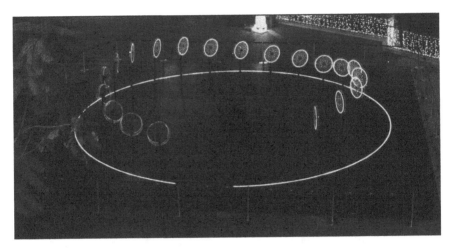

Fig. 8. Echo of heart

us – infinite quantities of information on our own private lives. We believe that gaining awareness of these mechanisms may be of help in the protection of individual and collective free speech (Fig. 9).

Fig. 9. AMYGDALA

4 Conclusion

With the study on functions and characteristics of light, this paper summarizes the experience of light environment interactive art in promoting the night economy with deep analysis of the light environment interactive art cases in cities, discussing the development direction of China's urban night economy. The theoretical application value of this paper is to design a series of new media interactive installations through the design theory of light interactive art in urban night economic areas like nightlife areas, parks, squares, etc. In the interactive process of the installation, the stopping time and communication scope of consumers and the publicity of different commercial brands can be improved to promote the benefits of night economy. The research theory of this paper can solve some problems in the development of China's urban night economy to improve the popularity of China's urban night economy culture, which can better inherit and promote excellent traditional culture. Furthermore, it can also enrich the lifestyle at night to bring more economic benefits, making corresponding contributions to China's nighttime GDP growth.

References

1. Wang, W.F.: Impact of light on human physiology and psychology and light strategy in claustrophobic environment. Manned Spaceflight 418–426 (2018)
2. Yu, L.: On Space Shaping with Light and Shadow as the Medium in Contemporary Art. Dalian University of Technology, Liaoning Province (2021)
3. Zhang, C.: Application of Digital Media Technology in Urban Public Space -- Based on Optical Media. Jiangnan University, Jiangsu Province (2014)

Reflections on ICT and Culture

Bie-Modernist Culture Computing is on the Road of Deep Distinguishing

Jun Chang[✉]

Shanghai Normal University, Shanghai, People's Republic of China
215244990@qq.com

Abstract. The combination of Bie-modernism and culture computing to the field of artificial intelligence is an exploration under the background of the intersection of literature and science. It has changed the concept of Bie-modernism distinguishing between true and false modernity into culture computing, and realized a leap in Bie-modernist theory. In the field of artificial intelligence writing, Bie-modernist culture computing can complement the artificial emotion computing in artificial intelligence writing, so that artificial intelligence writing may complete complex spiritual and emotional activities related to emotion, memory, aesthetics and thinking like human brain, and has a broader prospect in the future virtual space.

Keywords: Bie-modernism · Culture computing · Artificial intelligence writing · Artificial emotion calculation · The future space of writing

1 The Birth of Bie-Modernist Culture Computing in Deep Distinguishing

Bie-modernism is a social form theory put forward by Professor Wang Jianjiang in 2014 based on China's current social reality of a mixture of pre-modern, modern and post-modern. Since the Bie-modernism was put forward, it has attracted extensive attention from academic circles at home and abroad. Southwest State University of Georgia established China modern research center independently in 2017 (CCBMS), The University of primosca in Slovenia established its own modern research center in 2019 (CBMS), Italy has established a modernist website (www.biemodernism.org). Wikipedia has a special introduction. Baidu's search for the word "Bie-modernism" has an online click through rate of more than 100 million. Bie-Modernism has gained international academic status in the comparative study between Western philosophers and famous western philosophical theories, [1] and gradually into other research areas. The 23rd World Conference on Human-Computer Interaction (HCII2021), which was scheduled to be held in Washington, D.C., USA from July 24–29, 2021, was rescheduled to be held online due to the epidemic. Wang Jianjiang, founder of Bie-modernism, professor and doctoral supervisor of the College of Humanities of Shanghai Normal University, was invited to attend the conference as a member of the organizing committee, and submitted a proposal to conference on "*establish a Global Bie-modernist Culture Computing System for establishing a real modern world*" [2]. He then gave a talk on "Bie-modernism & Culture Computing" together with Chen Haiguang, a professor of computer science at Shanghai Normal University [3]. This paper organically combines Bie-modernism with culture computing, aesthetics and computers, and tries to implement Bie-modernism into human-computer interaction and culture computing. The new model of "philosophy+technology+art" formed by culture computing in recent years is combined with Bie-modernism of creative space to form Bie-modernist culture computing, which combines Bie-modernism and culture computing. This marks the entry of Bie-modernism into the field of technology and the convergence with international artificial intelligence technology.

Wang Jianjiang believes that civilization is the host of barbarism. Barbarism parasitizes civilization through camouflage but eats civilization back. With the development of modern human society, barbarism obtains unprecedented opportunities with the help of pseudo modernity, which has a huge potential threat to society and individuals. Pseudo modernity is not only reflected in social form, but also in artificial intelligence and culture computing. The most typical pseudo modernity in culture computing is the pseudo world brought by the wide application of deep pseudo technology [4]. At the conference, the host, Matthias Rauterberg, director of the Institute of artificial intelligence of Eindhoven University of technology in the Netherlands, compared the speeches of several other well-known scholars with those of Professor Wang Jianjiang, and guided the speakers to have an in-depth discussion around the high-frequency words used by Wang Jianjiang, such as "distinguishing" and "fake", Objectively, it enlarges the key words of Bie-modernism, such as "distinguishing" and "fake".

According to Wang Jianjiang, deep distinguishing comes from the opposition of deep fake, and deep fake is not only the face changing technique of artificial intelligence, on the contrary, it permeates all aspects of society. Therefore, deep distinguishing is used in English to show the difference from the deep identity [5] of other scholars. The theory of Bie-modernism in deep distinguishing is the latest theory of Bie-modernism. It is the value tendency of Bie-modernism to the global social phenomenon composed of pseudo modernity, pseudo democracy, pseudo civilization and pseudo technology in the whole field of society, science, technology and culture, as well as the application of this value tendency in the field of culture computing.

"Deep fake" technology is the product of modern high-tech development. It means that the ability of technocrats and technicians who master artificial intelligence technology to deliberately distort the truth has been further improved. With this technology, people can create deep-seated illusion, which has far exceeded the forgery level of fake cigarettes, fake wine and fake drugs, and is even difficult to be seen through by artificial intelligence anti-counterfeiting technology. This does not exist in pre-modern society. Deep fake technology uses high-tech means to create false news, false video and other false information on the network to confuse the modern public, which poses a huge potential threat to individuals and society. In 2017, the case of deep pseudo technology appeared for the first time in the United States. The faces of young Hollywood actresses, such as Scarlett Johansson, were superimposed into pornographic films, which had a great impact on their careers [6]. In May 2018, a fake video of Donald Trump's speech to the Belgian public urging his government to withdraw from the Paris climate agreement appeared on the Internet. This fake video with realistic effects synthesized by artificial intelligence immediately aroused people's anger [6]. It can be seen that the abuse of deep fake technology not only infringes on personal reputation and privacy, but also causes the panic and anxiety of the modern public. It is a systematic phenomenon, involves all aspects of society and poses a great threat to individuals and society.

In essence, deep fake technology is a means for pseudo-modernists to use high technology for pseudo-faces, pseudo-democracy and pseudo-civilization. In today's network era, virtual space and daily life have become inseparable, and deep fake technology can invade daily life and work on everyone, forming a pseudo-modern social phenomenon of misinformation caused by the misuse of technology, thus becoming a problem that needs urgent attention and solution in today's society.

Bie-Modernism, whose mission is to distinguish between true and false modernity, puts forward the theory of deep distinguishing, which not only reveals that deep pseudo technology is hindering the overall improvement of human civilization, but also advocates restoring a real world through deep distinguishing technology. Bie-Modernist culture computing advocates a technical and theoretical confrontation against "deep fake" technology starting from "deep distinguishing, which has attracted the attention of scholars in the computer field and the Organizing Committee of the conference.

The first international demonstration of Bie-modernist culture computing is to use culture computing to distinguishing the character features of the text of *Journey to the West*, using Word2vec model+CNN algorithm model to analyze the personality scores of the main characters to achieve a multi-dimensional analysis of character features, and then to distinguishing the real and fake Sun Wukong based on the feedback data. Finally, with reference to the primitive and derivative meanings of "Bie", the culture computation is used to arrange, compare and calculate the various vectors of true and false modernity one by one, so as to highlight the true and false modernity respectively and finally complete the task of screening. The key to Bie-modernist culture computing is to establish a system of authenticity recognition, such as a visual recognition system and a digital recognition system, which will eventually extend from the identification of authenticity in texts to the screening of authenticity in virtual space and the real world [3].

The presentation on Bie-modernist culture computing generated a lively discussion at the World HCI Conference. Co-moderator Prof. Vaslis spoke highly of Prof. Wang Jianjiang's presentation and followed up with questions about Prof. Wang's presentation.

1) Where is Bie-modernist culture computing going? What direction has been chosen? What will be the result?

   Wang Jianjiang replied that the Bie-modernist culture computing comes from the need of social reality and goes into social reality to solve social problems, and its result will help avoid or reduce the threat of pseudo-modernity to modern civilization and contribute to the establishment of modernity and the realization of modernization in third world countries.

2) What is the theoretical source of the idea of using culture computing to distinguishing true and false modernity?

Wang Jianjiang responds that the culture computing of Bie-modernism, which distinguishes true from false, is based on the consideration of the current global social formations, rather than on the application of Western modernity theories.Bie-modernism is an original theory that does not necessarily follow the existing Western theories, but as some Western philosophers say, it is closer to the reality of the country and better able to solve its problems.

Another issue that made the participants more interested was the concluding remark made by Professor Wang Jianjiang after his demonstration of the culture computing of the real and fake Monkey King: "The new car is walking on the old road", indicating that the art of algorithm should be in line with the main road, with a philosophical meaning that starts from the algorithm but goes beyond it, thus triggering a discussion.

After this international conference, several smaller conferences were held in China to discuss the specific issues of Bie-modernism and culture computing, as well as product development, which attracted the interest of many scholars in the intersection of literature and science.

It is clear from the above that Bie-modernist culture computing is the product of an organic combination of original ideas and advanced technological tools.

2   The Combination of Bie-Modernist Culture Computing and Artificial Intelligence Writing

2.1   The Possibility of Combining Bie-Modernist Culture Computing with Artificial Intelligence Writing

First of all, the requirement for AI writing is to converge or reach the real level of human writing, and for this reason, the culture computing of Bie-modernism, which advocates the distinction between true and false modernity, communicates with AI writing in spirit. Artificial intelligence writing is an intervention of modern technology into the traditional literary field, drawing on and activating classical aesthetic factors to produce a unique aesthetic. Compared with traditional writing, AI writing is a deep simulation and learning of previously created human literary works, which improves the ability to analyze and summarize data, reorganize and transform texts, and then complete literary works that resemble human creations. For example, the artificial intelligence writing software "Xiao Bing" studied the creation of 519 modern Chinese poets since 1920, and after tens of thousands of iterations of training, it basically acquired the ability to write modern poetry, and published the first artificial intelligence poetry book Sunshine Lost the Glass Window in May 2017. Compared with "Xiao Bing", which writes modern poems, "Jiu Ge", an automatic Chinese poetry generation system developed by the AI research team of Tsinghua University in 2017, focuses on the writing of ancient poems, which is based on 800,000 classical poems for training and creates a rich It is based on 800,000 classical poems and creates a rich database of ancient poems, and interacts with human-machine assistance. At present, it can write poems in various formats, such as verse, rhyme, stanza, hidden-head poem, five-words, seven-words and words, etc. Since its launch, it has created more than 4 million poems for users. As a new type of creative media, artificial intelligence, supported by powerful data analysis and reorganization, highlights its writing advantages as massive inventory, ultra-fast writing speed and amazing writing quantity. Since the launch of the AI writing system "Xiao Bing", it can create countless poems by keywords within ten seconds, and its writing speed is unmatched by human writers. However, because literary creation is not a simple synthesis process, but a cohesive writer's vivid emotional experience and life experience, the composition of the work layout, language organization, chapter arrangement, etc. can not be separated from the writer's unique creativity and aesthetic emotions. Therefore, AI writing needs to further improve the ability of culture computing in order to achieve the purpose of the real level of human writing, including the purpose of seeking truth in terms of sincerity of emotion, truth of feeling, and truth of writing level. In this case, the Bie-modernist culture computing for the purpose of truth-seeking will coincide with AI writing with emotional sincerity, feeling truth, and level of truth, and has the possibility of two-way interconnection.

Secondly, both Bie-modernist culture computing and artificial intelligence writing are based on data analysis and emotional sincerity. Bie-modernist culture computing emphasizes deep distinguishing under the guidance of the concept of "eliminating the false and preserving the true". Its recognition is based on data analysis, including the data analysis of emotional elements. Artificial intelligence writing deeply studies and simulates the data of human writers' creative way, emotion, image, language and other aspects, also in order to obtain an expression closer to human real emotion. The training of artificial intelligence writing is embodied in the selection of image, the simulation of emotion, the organization of language, the arrangement of logic, the setting of plot and the construction of structure. It is this common pursuit of truth that builds a bridge between the theory of Bie-modernitm in deep distinguishing and AI creation, thus forming Bie-modernist AI literary creation.

Artificial intelligence literary creation will tend to emotional sincerity in the simulation and learning of image selection. AI writing first analyzes the images with high frequency in poetry through technical calculation, and then collects the images with similar usage and emotional color in the same symbol cluster to facilitate the replacement of words. For example, when the author inputs an image "well" into the artificial intelligence writing system "jiuge", nine jiuge creates a small word with unique charm:

Beside the open wells, the leaves of Wutong fall down/the curtain falls low./alone by the pingshan, the banana is accompanied by the wind/tears/tears/infinite desolation.
（露井梧桐叶坠/帘幕低垂 不起/独自倚屏山/窗外芭蕉风细/清泪/清泪/无限凄凉意味。）

In the poem, the images of open well, wutong leaves, curtain, "pingshan", banana, tears, embody the writer's bleak and bitter emotions in traditional Chinese poetry.These imagery coalesce with the writer's emotions to create the poignant and lonely aesthetic mood of the whole piece. In the process of artificial intelligence writing, we use emotional computing as a breakthrough, and through culture computing and data analysis, we classify the related images that form an intertext with "well" through culture computing and data analysis to create a bleak meaning around the central image of "well", and then re-categorize them according to human The poems are then rearranged and combined according to human language habits and thought patterns, resulting in poems that are emotionally compatible and similar in style.

Thirdly, the calculation and analysis of the frequency of using imagery in human writing as an algorithmic strategy for AI writing to approach real human writing provides an opportunity to combine AI writing with Bie-modernist culture computing in terms of method. In Xiao Bing's poetry collection *Sunlight Lost the Glass Window*, commonly used imagery recurs in the poetry collection, taking *I took my eyes* as an example: "No lights/this strong fresh/and his eyes/I am a lonely dream/lonely lights my clay man/can save the fresh wine/my fate's can gift to my good man/I took my eyes ". Among them, eyes, dream and lamp are the imagery appearing in this poem. By reading the whole collection, we find that besides the above imagery, several other imagery such as sun, eyes, ocean and night also appear in the collection in large numbers repeatedly. These frequently recurring images are the same ones that are often used in the poems of 519 modern poets since 1920, whom Xiao Bing studied. The key to the rhythm of the poems lies in the true feelings in the poems of previous poets learned through deep learning and expressing such true feelings in a culture computing way, so that the AI writing will coincide with the Bie-modernist culture computing.

Finally, in terms of language organization, the most important manifestation of AI writing is to borrow the rhetorical techniques of ancient poetry, such as allusion and intertextuality, but behind this technique is the expression of sincerity for emotions. Huang Tingjian wrote in his *Reply to Hong Jufu*: "Self-composed language is the most difficult, DuFu's poetry, HanYu's composition, there is no word without a source". Artificial intelligence writing is based on the imitation of the ancient poems of the predecessors, so it forms intertext with the poems of the predecessors to a certain extent. For example, in the artificial intelligence writing system "Nine Songs", the author entered "peach blossom" and formed the following poems.

The front of peach and plum flowers is new, and one branch is relatively dust-free. Now it's not like many people, only Dongfeng willow in spring.

This poem is in accordance with Cui Hu's "last year, today, in this gate, the peach blossom is red. People don't know where to go, the peach blossom is still smiling in the spring breeze". They all borrow the image of peach blossom to express similar emotions and form a isomorphic relationship in language organization, ideological connotation and structural arrangement. Through the comparison between "people face new" and "people don't know where to go" and the peach blossom in spring, echoing with the original poem, it expresses a kind of emotion that things are right and people are wrong. However, it is worth noting that although artificial intelligence imitates the same structure, what can arouse people's interest, emotion and freshness is still the sincere, mellow and deep emotion deeply hidden in classical poetry. This sense of true feelings, like the old cellar, ferments in new media and emits fragrance, forming the true feelings and beauty in intertextuality.

In short, artificial intelligence writing tends to human creation and is more and more loved by the public through the training of image, plot, language and structure. But the most fundamental reason is that the artificial emotion technology that simulates human emotion tends to be synchronously coupled and resonant with the reality in its imitation object. It is in the above many aspects that there are many possibilities for the combination between modernist culture computing and artificial intelligence writing.

2.2 "Seeking the Truth": The Fit Between Artificial Emotional Technology and Bie-Modernist Culture Computing

The main task of the Bie-modernist culture computing is to distinguish between true and false modernity, and the core of its spirit is "seeking truth". The key to the fit between artificial intelligence writing and Bie-modernist culture computing lies in the projection and simulation of real human emotions, so as to complete works similar to those created by human writers, thus the deep analysis of human emotions becomes the focus of artificial intelligence creation. Emotion is the main component of literary writing. Writers condense emotions into literary language and imagery, linking internal and external texts such as text worlds and readers, forming an emotion-centered literary network. Writing is the writer's processing and creation based on vivid life experiences and life experiences. The conceptual layout, language organization and chapter arrangement of literature cannot be separated from the unique creativity and aesthetic emotions brought by the writer's aesthetic experience. The breakthrough of artificial intelligence writing, which is becoming more and more realistic and close to human creation, lies in the deciphering of human emotion codes and the introduction of artificial emotion computing technology to simulate human writers' emotions and psychological mechanisms so as to achieve realistic effects.

The connection between the Bie-modernist culture computing and artificial emotional computing lies in the search for truth. Artificial affective computing is a concept introduced by Professor Picard at MIT in 1995, and is defined as a computation that relates to, derives from, or may affect emotions. After more than 20 years of continuous application and improvement, artificial affective computing has made great development and realized human-computer emotional interaction. Artificial affective computing plays a key role in promoting AI writing, and the most important reason why AI writing is so popular among a wide range of readers is that AI scholars have introduced artificial computing into comprehensive disciplines such as philosophy and psychology. By adding sensory and psychological recognition to the computer, it directly identifies the state of the user's feelings so that it can work more efficiently and run programs that converge on human emotions based on this. This engineering approach to emotion generation is often taken from the field of psychology. As per Paul Ekman, a leading psychologist professor in the field of emotion and nonverbal communication, "by placing six basic feelings namely fear, surprise, anger, hate, sadness and happiness occurring on specific triggers (Ekman, 2007). Each emotion has a facial expression and a patterned biological symptom. During the evocation of pattern-generated facial expressions, specific sensations behind the impulses generate specific reflexes in facial expressions or body postures that trigger specific automatic neurological responses and activity of sensory experiences [7]." Ekman brings artificial emotion computing into the scope of psychology and neurophysiology to study, so that the machine has the function of emotion expression, which is understood by some people, The emotion computing technology of artificial intelligence "analyzes the memory and external events by creating and updating the memory, using deep learning, establishing emotion transfer model and other technologies, so as to synthesize and express the machine emotion" [8], Thus, the artificial affective computing and the Bie-modernist culture computing are in harmony with each other in terms of algorithms and concepts of "truth-seeking". The main task of the Bie-modernist culture computing is to distinguishing the true and false modernity, especially those who use modern technology and culture computing to conceal the truth, falsify products, and conceal the truth, and to transform the achievements of modern technology into anti-civilizational pseudo-modern means, while in the field of emotion, art, and aesthetics, it is to keep sincerity and express sincerity. Therefore, the essence of Bie-modernist culture computing is the pursuit of truth and true modernity. Similarly, the key to AI writing is the truth-seeking of human emotions by artificial affective computing, so that machine creation is as close as possible to human emotional expression. By simulating multiple human emotion patterns, recording and restoring real scenarios, artificial intelligence is given to human emotions and psychological mechanisms, thus gaining the ability to seek truth and simulate truth, and realizing the purpose of artificial intelligence emotional computing.

In AI writing, the database summarizes, classifies and concludes words or symbols indicating different emotions through culture computing. As long as the corresponding key words are input, the intelligent database will automatically analyze its degree and color of emotion and replace them with words of similar emotional color to create poems of the same emotional tone. Artificial emotion computing adds human emotional thinking to the AI writing system, making it not only a writing system, but also an avatar with human emotional empathy and emotional communication ability. For example, the team that designed the AI writing system "Xiao Bing" set the subject of AI creation (Xiao Bing) as a combination of IQ and EQ, that is, both intelligence and emotional intelligence, during the process, and believed that "the process of AI creation must correspond to some kind of creative human behavior The process of AI creation must correspond to some creative human behavior, not to a simple replacement of human labor [9]." This AI creation "must correspond to some creative human behavior", and is likely to create what Professor Wang Jianjiang calls "Bie-humans" [10]. Bie-humans will follow and potentially walk with humans in all aspects of intelligence, emotion, and feeling. Undoubtedly, the further exploration of real human emotions by AI writing will help realize human interaction with virtual agents. When AI gets closer to human intelligence and emotional intelligence, that is, when the AI singularity is reached, the interaction between Bie-humans and AI humans will also become more emotional and diverse.

2.3 Bie-Modernist Culture Computing Word2vec Model + CNN Algorithm Model to Analyze Character Image

The shaping of character image is very important in literary works. Artificial intelligence writing system introduces different modern culture computing word2vec model+CNN algorithm model to analyze the character image and its characteristics in literary works, which can complement artificial emotion computing technology and make artificial intelligence writing super intelligent.

Human emotions and character images are multi-level, multifaceted and complex. Chinese characters also have surface meaning and deep meaning. They are very suitable for expressing human emotions. Through Chinese characters, they express the beauty of implication and the artistic conception of "endless words and infinite meaning". Artificial emotion calculation can infer the trend of human emotion through data analysis and reorganization, understand the shallow emotion and the shallow meaning of language, and form a human like writing mode or output program, which has almost human emotion, but it is difficult to fully reflect the complexity of human emotion and the deep connotation of words at once. The designer of "Xiaobing" said that Xiaobing has emotional intelligence and intelligence quotient. After learning a lot of human emotional data, she has emotional ability and even swear. However, "brain science has not fully studied the hippocampus, amygdala and other regions of human brain memory, so there are some unsolved problems in artificial emotion simulation. The existing artificial emotion simulation is rarely analyzed in combination with memory, but adjusts emotions according to current experience, which is inconsistent with human actual performance" [8]. Xiaobing's emotional judgment is mainly based on the accumulation and logical deduction of roughly the same emotional response to common scenes, but she can't make accurate judgment in the face of complex scenes and new emotions. Taking the "tears" in poetry as an example, tears in poetry can express either joy and tears, or sadness and pain. In literary works, the same image contains different meanings in different poems. For example, Du Fu's sad tears of "flowers splashing tears when feeling, hate other birds startling" and the happy tears of "Jibei suddenly spread outside the sword, and tears filled his clothes at the first smell" have different connotations. At present, artificial emotion computing technology can not accurately grasp the multiplicity and complexity of literary language and images. Take *I took my eyes* in Xiaobing's poetry collection *the sun lost the glass window* as an example:

No lights/this strong fresh/and his eyes/I am a lonely dream/lonely lights my clay man/can save the fresh wine/my fate's can gift to my good man/I took my eyes.

This artificial intelligence writing lacks overall image characteristics and deep emotional connotation in emotion and image, making the whole poem seem confusing and incoherent. In response to the deficiency of artificial emotion technology, Bie-modernist culture computing can analyze character traits and deep emotions of characters through Word2vec model+CNN algorithm model and technical algorithm to form a deep alias for characters. This model includes various computer algorithms such as character personality calculation, convolutional neural network calculation, Word2vec algorithm, etc. From multiple dimensions such as physical dimension (e.g. character's appearance, behavior, clothing, etc.), social dimension (interpersonal interaction and social activities in real life) and psychological dimension, the character characteristics, growth background, character's behavior and habits and deep emotions of the target character image can be systematic and data-based quantitative analysis, and finally generate deep emotions and character traits of characters through document classification algorithms to complement artificial emotion technology, thus preparing AI writing to further approach human true feelings and express rich human true emotions.

In conclusion, artificial emotion computing makes AI writing closer to human creation, although this technology is still developing and there are still some problems, such as insufficient mining of deep emotions or character features, etc. However, with the combination of artificial emotion computing and culture computing, its shortcomings will be compensated.

3   The Future Direction of Don't Modernist Artificial Intelligence Writing

With the development of Bie-modernist culture computing and artificial emotional computing, AI writing has a broader future prospect in the virtual space, and it may accomplish complex mental and emotional activities related to emotion, memory, aesthetics, thinking, etc., just like the human brain. The future directions of Bie-modernist AI writing can be broadly divided into the following three categories.

First of all, to construct a new relationship of "human-computer multiple emotional interactions" to enrich and improve AI writing. Human-computer interaction (HCI) is the main cultural mode of human entering the information age, which has decisive influence on design, production, control, feedback and communication. In the virtual space, AI has the same emotional speculation and emotional reflection as humans, and can better communicate, interact and even cooperate with humans. Artificial intelligence has incomparable inherent advantages in terms of speed and accuracy in literary information processing, capacity and durability in literary data storage, and timeliness and quantification in literary literature collection and arrangement. In order to build a huge database of contemporary Chinese literature, the Chinese Story Database, the AI software developed in 2018 collates, analyzes and refines the data of literary works published by many literary journals and literary publishers. This database can provide authors with rich creative resources and experience in character setting, plot development, aesthetic style and thematic refinement. With the help of Bie-modernist culture computing and artificial emotional computing, artificial intelligence can analyze the deep emotions and character traits of characters through big data and algorithms to filter out the types of texts that readers like and meet their personalized reading needs. In life, AI can also use this technology to interact with humans at a deeper level of emotion and exchange of ideas, a technology known abroad as infant computer nerve babies (Tosa and Nakatsu 1996) [7]. It has its own sensory model and facial expression. It can recognize the user's feeling from the input sound and facial expression, so as to interact with human emotion. The computer character "nerve baby" was born by combining these elements. It can communicate with people through feeling [7]. Furthermore, cultural emotion computing may help us to establish a higher-level communication system, and a global cross-cultural communication is expected to be realized. "Each individual's culture reflects the differences of emotion, consciousness and memory. If these systems are realized, the expression of social, practical and cultural information can be enabled in various fields through various language, sound and film systems [7]." In the future space, the boundary between human and artificial intelligence will become more and more blurred, human and Bie-human will be more difficult to distinguish, and the interaction between human and computer will become more diverse and complex. Therefore, it is more necessary to construct a new relationship of "multi emotional interaction between human and computer", coordinate in difference and distinguish in coordination, so as to enrich and improve artificial intelligence writing.

Secondly, AI writing stimulates the vitality of the literature and art market and realizes the truth-seeking purpose of Bie-modernism. The writing principle of artificial intelligence is technical production, including information reorganization, deformation, mass production, etc. Therefore, artificial intelligence can replace mediocre authors and perform well in patterned and typed literature. According to the images provided by readers, the artificial intelligence software "Nine Songs" can produce regular poems, quatrains, five character poems, seven character poems, hidden head poems, collection poems and poems in various formats. The author inputs two images of "dusk and breeze" into the "Nine Songs" software, and artificial intelligence produces a poem in just a few seconds:

The breeze outside the curtain blows away/the drizzle drizzles in the courtyard at dusk/sleeping lazily combing your hair/idle chair painting bar human face/who sees/who sees/thousands of lovesickness after farewell.

Through the images of dusk, drizzle and breeze, this poem expresses the deep thoughts and sadness of the woman in the boudoir towards her sweetheart. Together with human works, it is also difficult to distinguish. When AI writing is more and more like human writing, it is undoubtedly a wake-up call to modern literature. Some shoddy and patterned network literature and randomly pieced together poems will be eliminated when the era of artificial intelligence writing comes. At the same time, writers with insufficient originality will undoubtedly feel at risk under the impact of artificial intelligence writing, so as to stimulate and tap their creativity and originality.

Thirdly, in the future development of literature, AI writing will involve all aspects of life and play a greater role. In January 2020, the legal recognition of the creative copyright of AI writing software has proved that AI writing has certain feasibility and creativity in applied texts, press releases, public cases and other typed texts. In the press, now widely used "robot journalists", they can monitor all kinds of information, fully present the five elements of the news, and convey the information to people with faster writing speed, more timely updating and sending speed. AI writing can also be involved in online novel creation. With the support of cloud services and big data, it can capture the content of the whole network, analyze the opening, structure, words and types welcomed by readers, and carry out efficient and batch commercial production. The goal of online novel is the same as that of news writing. It does not try to create top novels, but to seize the reader market through "rapid" writing and a large number of imitation. In non-literary texts that do not need too much creativity and emotion, artificial intelligence writing is expected to replace human writing. At the same time, not only in the field of literature and art, artificial intelligence writing also plays a great role in daily life. It can not only be used as an excellent learning partner of human beings to cultivate creative interests and hobbies, but also replace human beings to become an emotional intimate partner to a certain extent, so as to realize the real world in human-computer interaction.

It is a leap of Bie-modernist theory for Bie-modernism to enter the field of artificial intelligence with culture computing, and the accuracy and powerful data analysis of Bie-modernism will be more powerful in the distinguishing of true and false modernity. The two complement each other to promote the realization of genuine modernity in Third World countries. As the Bie-modernist culture computing enters and influences artificial intelligence writing, artificial intelligence opens up unlimited virtual space for emotion, language, and style, which will further liberate the creativity of literature and art. The new interaction between human and machine has a more open prospect in the future virtual space.

References

1. Lu, Y.: Bie-modernism on the way to explain and transform the world, by. In: The Collection of the 7th Bie-modern International Conference, November 2021
2. Wang, J., et al.: Proposal to the 23rd world HCI conference in January 2021: a proposal to establish a global Bie-modernist culture computing system for establishing a real modern world. In: Wang, J. (ed.) PPT Bie- Modernist Public's Workshop on the Integration of Automated Writing and Modern Culture, 7 August 2021
3. Wang, J., Chen, H.: Bie-modernism and cultural computing. In: Rauterberg, M. (ed.) HCII 2021. LNCS, vol. 12795, pp. 474–489. Springer, Cham (2021). https://doi.org/10.1007/978-3-030-77431-8_30
4. Wang, J.: New developments in the creation and research of the theory of bie-modernism since 2019. In: The Collection of the 7th Bie-modern International Conference, November 2021
5. Mu, L., Zuo, W., Zhang, D.: Deep identity-aware transfer of facial attributes (2016). https://www.researchgate.net/publication/309283897
6. Faragó, T.: Deep fakes–an emerging risk to individuals and societies alike (2019). http://creativecommons.org/licenses/by-nd/4.0/
7. Tosa, N.: Cross-Cultural Computing: An Artist's Journey, p. 23. Springer, London (2016). https://doi.org/10.1007/978-1-4471-6512-5. www.allitebooks.co
8. Chen, J., Jiang, D.: A study on a machine-oriented artificial emotion simulation framework. J. Shantou Univ. (Nat. Sci. Ed.) 35(2) (2020)
9. Xiao, B.: The Sun Lost its Glass Window, p. 21. Beijing Union Publishing Company, 1 May 2017
10. Wang, J.: Reconsideration of the stock of life in Bie-modernism. Bie-Modernism Public, 26 August 2018

Placing Blame in Multi-agent Systems

Jaana Hallamaa[ID] and Taina Kalliokoski[(✉)] [ID]

University of Helsinki, Helsinki, Finland
{jaana.hallamaa,taina.kalliokoski}@helsinki.fi

Abstract. The article discusses the concept of blame, the acts of placing blame, and blaming in the context of multi-agent systems (MAS). The conceptual resources used for analyzing MASs and their functioning mainly concentrate on successful action while attempts to understand the phenomena concerning erring, making mistakes, and wrongdoing have received less attention. Legal accountability and moral responsibility have a central role in discussions concerning the detrimental and harmful effects of MASs. However, encounters with failing systems give rise to blame and placing blame. The article analyzes the psychological, social, and moral connotations of blame and blaming and their links to responsibility and accountability. It also explores whether the ideals of responsibility and accountability should be complemented with blame-analysis to cover various failure modes and cases of non-ideal occurrence of human-machine cooperation.

Keywords: Blame · Responsibility · Multi-agent system · Failure · Ethics

1 Introduction

Computerized activities and expectations from it form an inseparable combination as digitalization incorporates the promise to make life easier and all kinds of functions more effective. AI systems help overcome the restrictions of temporality and locality as they make services accessible via the internet. In real life, the AI enhanced products do not work and the services do not run as smoothly as their manufacturers promise in the instruction videos and marketing brochures.

Failing functions give rise to frustration in those who have no other option but to rely on a system. If using a device, product, or service is claimed to be effortless, failing to perform the intended task increases the level of user's frustration. One's inability to locate the fault or understand the cause of failure may turn the emotion into anger, and even despair. In addition to the need to find a solution to the problem, an urge to identify the object of blame arises.

Although there are promising suggestions to conceptualize different failure modes of multi-agent systems (MAS) [Manheim 2019], it is more common to theorize their functioning in ideal terms; the intended cooperation between agents—whether human or artificial—runs smoothly and the operations are successfully completed [Rocha, Boavida-Portugal and Gomes 2017]. In practice, nothing is perfect. Human agents err, make mistakes, and may even willfully act against the designated common goals. Devices fail in their functions, and the programs that form and direct the systems contain programming errors, bugs, and deficiencies causing malfunction. In the following discussion, we define failure as any outcome of actions that do not meet the intended goals, the planned operations fall through for some reason, or the target groups do not appreciate the achieved results.

Failures in an MAS raise questions concerning accountability and responsibility of artificial agents and the MAS in its totality. An MAS may be a pure MAS consisting of only one kind of agent, natural or artificial, or a hybrid MAS with both natural and artificial agents [Misselhorn 2015]. Hereafter, we use the term MAS to refer to pure artificial and hybrid MASs.

In the context of AI ethics, it is more common to discuss responsibility and accountability [see e.g., Dignum 2020; Floridi 2015] than to reflect blame. Accountability and responsibility are morally central concepts. However, concentrating the analysis only on them downplays a feature that is relevant for human agents as they encounter systemic failure or detect mismanagement—the need to place blame on someone or something. For example, the on-going discussion on the responsibility of self-driving cars seems to focus on identifying who is to blame and who may be sued if the car is involved in causing harm [Dignum 2020, 220; Noorman 2021]. Such situations reveal the need to analyze the concept of blame in hybrid MAS settings more closely.

The word blame can be used both as a verb and a noun. The verb is used to express what one feels or declares when someone or something is responsible for a fault or wrongdoing. The verb can also be used to assign responsibility for a bad or unfortunate situation or phenomenon to someone or something. As a mass noun, blame means responsibility for a fault or wrong [MOT Oxford Dictionary]. The definitions make visible the use of the word in relation to moral responsibility and assessing the morality of someone's actions; doing something morally wrong makes a morally responsible agent blameworthy. Blame is related to responsibility; however, it has connotations that do not accord with the concept of responsibility.

To understand the aspects of blame and its relation with other central concepts concerning human action, we will first discuss moral agency and responsibility, and examine how AI technology changes the conditions that define these notions. We will analyze the concept of blame and the role it plays in psychological, social, and moral contexts. Blame is a concept related to nonideal action and harmful outcomes of action. Hence, we will discern components that explain the usability of the notion of blaming as a relational action in the context of failures in hybrid MASs.

2   Moral Agency, Responsibility, and Accountability

Conceptually, human agency is linked with intentionality; people do things to realize their goals, thereby narrowing the gap between the prevailing state of affairs and their wishes. Actions are instances of goal-oriented activity with the purpose of bringing forth something the agent values or deems as—in some sense and in the time being—desirable. Intention binds together aims and deeds, as actions are the means to achieve or to further the wished-for goals. Even daily routines and automatized sequences of acts are intentional actions since the agent could—if someone asked—justify their activity by referring to its purpose. The link between an action and a wished-for goal implies that actions display what agents regard as worth realizing [Moya 1990, 9–10, 46–48: Davidson 2001, 22, 45, 83–84].

Intentionality entails a commitment; by acting towards a goal, the agent makes a commitment to their goal and their action as a means of realizing it. Successful actions have effects that concern not only the agent but others as well. From their perspective, what an agent does can be favorable, harmful, or neutral. The effects of actions on others' good and wellbeing open a moral point of view to agency and acting. Actions that are good, beneficial, or favorable in terms of their consequences to others are morally good, acts that do not affect the well-being of others are morally neutral, and acts that harm other sentient beings are morally bad or evil. Actions often have different outcomes for different parties depending on their position in the situation. An action can thus be both favorable and unfavorable [von Wright 1968, 110–119].

The intention of the agent binds their goal and action together and makes the agent morally responsible for the deed and the effects of their actions. Recognizing one's own responsibility and holding others responsible for their respective actions, and what they causally bring forth, form a fundamental part of moral practices and interpersonal relations [Talbert 2019, Noorman 2021].

Praising and blaming (competent) agents for what they have done and what their actions have caused is an essential moral practice connected to moral responsibility. Morally praiseworthy actions are favorable for others and deserve positive acknowledgment, whereas moral blame is the price of inconsideration of or causing harm to other sentient beings. There is a discrepancy between blame and praise, and we pay more attention to the blameworthiness than the praiseworthiness of actions. The asymmetry between blame and praise displays our implicit expectations concerning each other's behavior. Acting in accordance with the requirements of morality is the expected standard and meeting it does not justify praise. In contrast, even a slight deviation from normative expectations may give rise to reproach [Talbert 2019].

Moral responsibility connected to moral agency involves a general obligation to acknowledge that moral norms are binding and apply to everyone as a member of the moral community. A more common use of the word binds responsibility to particular people and their circumstances. The duties and obligations of a person stem from their roles and positions in their various social settings. Taking one's role seriously involves carrying out the tasks that constitute the role. A responsible agent acknowledges the accountability for their actions, and what they bring forth or cause [Talbert 2019].

There is also a social perspective embedded in the concept of moral responsibility, as other members of the community are entitled to critically comment on each other's behavior and actions. Moral responsibility entails accountability as we are justified in requiring certain conduct from one another and have a reason to react negatively when someone does not meet the standard. Accountability is the basis for placing blame and it justifies the requirement to repair the harm one has caused [Talbert 2019].

The social aspect of responsibility helps understand the ways in which placing blame and accountability contribute to fairness and retributive justice. Since antiquity, philosophers have regarded social justice as the key feature of a good human community. Retributive practices are an important part of the system that supports moral balance in the community. Their function is to ensure that those who violate common norms or who have secured themselves unjustified benefits must pay back what is not rightfully theirs, repair the ills and harms they have caused, and that they will be punished for violating the common norms [Talbert 2019].

2.1 Moral Responsibility in Digitalized Systems: Reformulating Moral Agency

Technological development and complex structures of the modern society have made assigning responsibility more difficult, resulting in a problem of "many hands"; to figure out who handled what, when so many different actors contributed to the outcome of the event [Noorman 2021].

As responsibility is tied to what an agent does and the consequences of their action, holding someone morally responsible for a particular event presupposes that the person has been able to influence its occurrence. MASs enhanced with AI technologies weaken the link between individual agents' actions and the outcomes of systemic action even more than action mediated through traditional technological systems. Completing tasks successfully depends on multi-faceted cooperation and coaction between various parts of the whole. Similarly, systemic failures and accidents are seldom a result of a single faulty action, instead they are the outcome of several codependent factors [Noorman 2021].

Currently, human beings have become parts of various MASs and their agency enmeshes into systems of interacting agents, both human and machine enhanced. Such environments change the preconditions of human action and moral considerations. MASs are new types of social communities that affect the ways in which human agents deliberate, make decisions, and take responsibility. The traditional social norms supporting structures that safeguard responsibility, accountability, and liability do not cover the conditions that prevail in such environments. We need conceptual rethinking to develop tools to tackle the ethical concerns arising in the new settings [Noorman 2021].

There are several suggestions on how to conceptualize and deliver responsibility within hybrid MASs that consist of human agents and AI systems, or AI enhanced machines. Some of these reformulate the concept of moral agency while others concentrate on changing the concept of moral responsibility [Noorman 2021]. While we concisely present both alternatives, we focus on the latter, justifying our decision along the way.

Dennet [1997] and Sullins [2022] argue that computerized systems can be—at least in the future—counted as moral agents. The observation that an external observer would interpret a system that carries out tasks assigned to it in an expected manner as doing what it ought to do based on its beliefs and desires serves as a basis for the view. For Dennet, intentionality consists of any system acting in a predictable and explainable way based on the assumption that it has beliefs and desires and that its functions are a result of rational decision-making processes. Although the present AI systems cannot carry out higher-order reflections concerning their own mental states, future machines will have this capability.

Sullins [2022] bases his solution on a narrowed understanding of autonomous action, a precondition for responsibility. For him, autonomy consists of the ability to carry out tasks assigned to them without human control and in a way that meets the external criteria of intentionality. AI agents assigned with such characteristics could be given tasks that consist of a set of responsibilities they would fulfil. When performing its role, the AI agent would appear to act, relying on beliefs about its duties. It could also be said to understand its tasks based on it carrying out its given duties [Sullins 2022, 28].

Views that assign moral agency to AI systems based on external criteria of intentionality have been strongly criticized. Instead of solving the problem of moral responsibility in an MAS, they make the concept incomprehensible. AI enhanced systems cannot suffer or feel moral feelings and it would be senseless to blame or punish them. AI systems are simply incapable of moral reasoning as they do not understand the meaning of the data they process [Noorman 2021].

Allen and Wallach [2012] have suggested that AI systems could be integrated into the realm of moral agents by programming moral features into the algorithms that govern their functions. Programming would allow developing agents with varying levels of moral agency resulting in implicit ethical agents, explicit ethical agents, and full ethical agents [Moor 2006]. Implicit ethical agents replicate the ethical decisions their designers have inscribed into the code directing their behavior. Explicit ethical agents regulate their actions according to the ethical models the programmers have embedded into their algorithms. They act as proxies of their human users and designers as they realize the kinds of decisions that correspond with the ethical norms of their programmers. Full ethical agents act as competent human actors; they can make justifiable ethical judgements [Moor 2006].

Programming ethics into machines does not, however, solve the problem of moral responsibility. The ethical solutions that stem from the algorithms are a human construction and can therefore be ascribed to those who selected the normative principles programmed into the algorithms. The focus of the approach is not right, either, as concentrating on AI sets aside the sociotechnical nature of MASs. Acting as a part of a sociotechnical system changes the ways in which human agents see themselves and their agency. Although technologies are not moral agents, they play a part in moral action by reshaping human action [Noorman 2021; Hallamaa and Kalliokoski 2020].

Verbeek [2006] stresses that in a technological world, artifacts have a mediating role in shaping human behavior and the conditions of moral agency. What humans do and produce by using artifacts form a systemic whole encompassing three types of agencies. The human agent performing the action, the designer of the artifact, and the artifact, all represent aspects of agency that come together in a technological system. The divided nature of agency motivates Verbeek to call the combination of human and technological components, a subject that acts and makes moral decisions [Verbeek 2006].

Suggestions based on reformulating the concept of moral agency have not been successful in terms of solving the problems concerning moral responsibility in human-machine cooperation. They tend to devalue the moral content of the concept and narrow the moral perspective. Researchers who have emphasized the sociotechnical nature of MASs, stress a crucial point. They pave the way to solve our problem by redefining the concept of moral responsibility.

2.2   Moral Responsibility in Digitalized Systems: Reformulating Moral Responsibility

The simplest way to assign responsibility in a human-machine MAS is to narrow the scope of the concept. We could exempt the technological parts of the system from considerations concerning responsibility and concentrate on the contribution of human agents. However, according to Gotterbarn [2001], such attempts are simply a tactic for avoiding responsibility.

Holding only humans responsible, would solve the problem of how to administer moral reproach and blame in MASs, but narrowing the concept would cause other problems. Separating human and artificial agents from each other would disregard the effects that acting as part of a sociotechnical system has on human behavior. Likewise, focusing on the role of only human agents is based on a conception of technology as something neutral. Artifacts mediate the values and choices that their designers and users have made during the processes of human-machine interaction. This is not possible without a rich conception of responsibility that covers the agents' commitments to their roles and duties—as positive responsibility—and the institution of holding agents accountable and placing blame on them—in the form of negative responsibility [Gotterbarn 2001, 27; Noorman 2021].

Including both positive and negative aspects in responsibility is possible only if we integrate various social functions in the concept. To do so without having to assign moral agency to computerized agents, Stahl [2006] introduces the concept of quasi-responsibility. It is a social construction that serves several useful functions in the technologized world. Instead of focusing our discussion of responsibility on single agents or the complexities of globalized socio-technical networks, it would be more useful to concentrate on mid-level technical systems. By holding them responsible, it would be easier to deal with the actual problems of accountability and liability as problems arise without sinking into the depths of philosophical discussions on the conditions of moral agency [Stahl 2006].

Stahl's solution resembles Sullins' suggestion (see Sect. 2.1). Sullins redefines the concept of moral agency whereas Stahl gives a new interpretation to moral responsibility. Both rely on external criteria as they define the concepts they discuss. Since artificial agents seem to act as morally responsible agents, we may treat them as such. Stahl takes the social dimensions of action more seriously than Sullins, and agrees that adopting the concept of quasi-responsibility as such would not help solve the practical problems concerning identifying those responsible and adequately placing blame [Stahl 2006].

For Stahl, the criterion for the usefulness of the concept of quasi-responsibility depends on whether relying on it would serve the social functions of making and holding people responsible for what they do and cause. Following the argumentation of Hakli and Mäkelä [2019] we could, however, claim that Stahl's concept of quasi-responsibility does not take the social nature of moral notions and practices seriously. Being part of the moral community does not depend on meeting a set of external criteria but on a process of growing up and developing as a part of a historical community and adopting its conceptions and practices [Hakli and Mäkelä 2019].

An important part of the social significance of moral responsibility is that the concept has both forward and backward-looking features. Prospectively, the expectations of others maintain the will and motivation of an agent to carry out their duties, in other words, act responsibly. In its forward-looking meaning, responsibility can be conceptualized as a social relation [A, x, B], where A stands for a responsible agent, x is the scope of A's responsibilities, and B an agent or a collective to whose expectations A must account and to whom A must respond. Retrospectively, the degree to which an agent has met the expectations will serve as a basis for praise or blame, which in turn may invoke different emotional responses in the object of praise or blame, such as pride, shame, joy, or anger. One's fear of a negative reaction may encourage commitment to do one's best—act responsibly. The backward-looking features of responsibility highlight a possibility of failure, an inherent part of both responsibility and—even to a greater degree—blame.

The social functions embedded in the concept of responsibility become real through reciprocal social practices. To understand what is at issue in moral responsibility in hybrid MASs, we must therefore consider the organizational and cultural contexts in which AI enhanced MASs exist and function [Nissenbaum 1997].

The complexities of sociotechnical systems tend to erode the structures that support social practices of responsibility. People carry out their tasks by using faceless and nameless applications as coagents. If things do not run smoothy—which is often the case—there is no one to answer for what went wrong, and why. Organizations waste time and resources trying to tackle recurring problems in systems, the functions of which are inscrutable to them. As there is no one who is accountable for what is taking place, fixing the malfunctions becomes difficult [Nissenbaum 1997].

Nissenbaum [1997] identified features that deteriorate practices of responsibility. It is a common practice that digitalized systems and AI applications are published long before they function properly. The lowered expectations concerning usability have resulted in a general acceptance of malfunctioning devices due to programming errors and bugs. Most people do not understand what lies behind a digitalized system. Blaming the faceless AI then becomes an easy exit for those whose task it is to design and provide systems for others to use. The problems become worse as the companies that develop and publish products restrict their ownership to the software but disclaim any accountability for the actual performance of the system and thereby also dismiss having any liability for the harmful effects of the use of the product they have sold their customers [Nissenbaum 1997, 47].

The discussion concerning responsibility in a hybrid MAS shows that the concept plays an important role if we wish to strengthen mechanisms and practices that support the development of morally sustainable AI enhanced systems. Expanding the realm of moral agents to include AI agents is not a viable solution. Human agents are morally responsible even in computerized milieus and part of it is taking seriously the effects of technology on human agency. Placing blame and blaming remain important parts of social practices that support responsibility and accountability, although their role may need redefining. Next, we will analyze blame and placing blame more closely.

3   Varieties of Blame

There are degrees in the severity of moral blame. Willfully harming others is most blameworthy; negligence, defecting, carelessness, and thoughtlessness are less grave moral offences—the measure being the agent's intention to harm or assent to the detrimental consequences. Often harm to others can be traced to a mistake or an error the agent made or their inability to carry out the intended action in an appropriate manner, thereby causing harm or damage [Talbert 2019; Tognazzini and Coates 2021].

After harmful actions, mistakes, or errors, agents usually have the need to defend themselves by presenting excuses and compiling explanations for their behavior as they try to reduce their responsibility or eschew blame. Psychologically, the phenomenon finds its explanation in the human need to maintain a positive view of oneself. Failing to meet moral standards poses a serious threat to one's integrity and self-esteem [Hogg and Vaughan 2008, 132–135].

The agent's point of view to a harmful or detrimental action is different from the perspective of those who have been harmed by it or have suffered damage. Human beings have a need to find points of orientation and adversities increase the urgency of the need [Staub 1989, 41]. There is also a discrepancy between explanations for making sense of the harm a person has caused to others and the harm they have suffered themselves. We are prone to explain our own failings by referring to situational factors—that things went badly was not our fault but traceable to circumstantial facts. Things are quite different when we are the ones to have suffered harm. Psychologically, the most satisfactory explanation is that there is someone who has—quite intentionally and due to ill will—caused harm, is morally responsible for the consequences, and must therefore be blamed for what has happened. They should be exposed and made to pay for their deeds [Hogg and Vaughan 2008, 91–97; Zimbardo 2007, 212].

What does the human need to find the guilty party and make them an object of blame imply? In what sense does placing blame and blaming have moral significance? What happens when the harming agents consist of a MAS in which human and AI based agents' actions cannot be separated from each other?

Several theorists have tackled the problem of blame by defining the key emotions, cognitive attitudes, and conative belief-desire pairs, which the blamer has towards the blamed. In the context of a MAS, scrutinizing the agents' internal processes would make little sense. Instead, it is crucial to focus on the functional and social roles of blame. Blame is a part of a social communicative process in which the blamer imposes a negative reaction—in the form of disapproval, condemnation, or protest—towards the blamed, wishing to evoke a morally significant response in them. [Tognazzini and Coates 2021]. The assumed purpose or reasons behind communicating blame may vary.

For Fricker [2016] the purpose of mediating blame is to bridge the gap between the moral reasoning of the blamer and the blamed. Blame serves as a tool for stating and enhancing one's moral philosophical understanding and can also be used to transfer emotional reactions. In the act of victim blaming [see Ryan 1971, a classic presentation of the phenomenon], the blamer manipulates the victim and transfers their own negative psychological effects of moral wrongdoing to the victim. Another social psychological technique where misplacing blame serves the interests of at least some of the cooperating agents or the members of a community attempting to shun their responsibility, is the phenomenon of blame shifting. Here placing blame and blaming serve as a psychological projection mechanism with the purpose to save the one who blames others from being held accountable for their harmful decision or act [Snyder 1987].

In organizations, blame practices can be a sign of a detrimental organizational culture that prevents the employees and the management to detect and correct conditions and practices that contribute to errors and failure. The search for the guilty and the blameworthy becomes a barrier to honesty and humbleness, and erodes trust between the staff [Hinterleitner 2016; Hood 2007].

The psychological connotations of blame open a view that is wider than the traditional discussion concerning moral responsibility and accountability. The social mechanisms that contribute to blame placing have for some time been an object of lively discussions in safety research, which offers a resource for widening the discussion concerning morally responsible action in AI systems [see, e.g., Hollnagel and Braithwaite 2019; Hallamaa 2021].

The different uses of the word blame explicate the nuances of its meaning and display how placing blame can be analyzed both from a moral and a socio-psychological perspective. We can place blame on or blame other moral agents, technology, systems, and circumstances. Situating blame on someone or something satisfies the wish to maintain moral order. Despite soothing the feelings of the blamer, it does not necessarily improve the situation in terms of reasonable and responsible action. If there is no attempt from anyone to repair the ills or cover the losses, placing blame simply equals an emotional reaction. Blame and placing blame have socially favorable effects only if they are connected to mechanisms that enhance taking and bearing responsibility. Blame and blaming must be connected to careful examination of how to explain what happened, and why and what should be done to remedy the situation and help the affected parties thereafter.

Morally, placing blame is linked to accountability and responsibility, but the scope of its concept is much wider. Having a cause to blame someone is not a sufficient condition for holding the one being blamed accountable or responsible. Though blame can be placed on inanimate actors, systems, and circumstances, responsibility and accountability only apply to moral agents. To be able to react meaningfully to an act of blaming, one must be able to accept moral reproof, possible legal consequences, and do one's part to mitigate the ills and harms. This is something that only human agents—but not all human agents—can and are in position to do.

Placing blame is effective to improve the situation only if there is someone who is ready to take the responsibility of the blame. Assigning oneself as accountable for some harm is not a position people willingly adopt, however, if one does step forward and declares responsibility, others may not feel the urge to place blame on them [Zimbardo 2007, 452–453].

As the short analysis shows, blame may provide a perspective to hybrid MASs, that discussion concerning accountability and responsibility cannot cover. Could the human need to place blame on inanimate agents, systems, and circumstances help in revealing morally relevant features that remain invisible in the discussions focusing on responsibility and accountability? How should we deal with harms and ills that the use of AI in MASs cause, when locating responsibility and accountability is difficult?

4   Placing Blame in Failing Hybrid Multi-agent Systems

Hybrid MASs are ecosystems of human agents and computing entities programmed to realize certain functions in the system. The single entities can be treated as agents, assigned to solve their individual subtasks that contribute to the complex objective, the system is designed to manage. They interact and cooperate with each other by exchanging and sharing information within a network of agents [see, e.g., Balaji and D. Srinivasan 2010; Rocha, Boavida-Portugal and Gomes 2017]. The system can manage tasks and solve problems that none of the individual agents could manage on their own.

In failing functions of a MAS, the *locus* of the blame and the intensity of blaming differ depending on the reason behind the miscarriage. We call any cooperative enterprise a failure if it does not reach its assigned goals. Why action falls short of the aim depends on variety of factors. Safety scientists have categorized them into two main groups: errors arise from problems related to information processing, whereas violations stem from motivational causes [Reason 2016, 14].

Part of the errors can be characterized as slips or lapses. People are absent-minded, and their inattention leads them to doing something wrong or missing something during a routinized sequence of actions. The agent intends to actualize the planned process but fails to carry it through in the correct way. Mistakes stem from a planning error as the agent does not have enough knowledge that would help them design a plan that could provide the basis for realizing the wanted goal [Reason 2016, 14–16].

Agents who err, do it unwillingly, whereas violations are intentional deviations from the normative standards. The motivation leading to such acts may be the will to simplify the task by skipping the parts of the process that seem irrelevant, cumbersome, or time-consuming. Sometimes the working conditions make it impossible to follow the standards as there are not enough resources to follow the normative practices. The motivation behind such violations is the will to carry out one's tasks and contribute to the common goal, despite breaking the rules [Reason 2016, 14, 35].

Moral violations are different in nature as the motivation behind them is to utilize the cooperative processes to further the agent's self-interest instead of working for the common goal. The processes designed as means to advance the given goals become ineffective, inappropriate, or start to fail if there are agents in the system that intentionally violate the norms directing the processes, or act against the values that support the socio-technical structures of the MAS. The system can also become internally corrupt if there are subgroups that do not value the outcomes of the common enterprises [Kalliokoski 2020, 161–164; Sheer 2018, 169–170, 179–181].

MASs are complicated networks of agents in which various reasons for malfunctioning coexist. Single agents and groups may fail to coordinate their action, there may be dishonest persons who use the organization for their private purposes, or rivalry, envy, and competitiveness may lead to concealing necessary information from other members of the MAS, thereby preventing them from contributing fully to the common goals. Inability to coordinate action and appreciate one another may foster a culture where subsystems concentrate on realizing their own goals that are irreconcilable with the aims of other subgroups. Most of the failures in MASs can be traced to systemic operations based on preconceptions that fail to incorporate the behavior of other agents and its effects in the plan [Manheim 2019].

As MASs usually take care of important and wide-ranging tasks, their failing functions are a cause of irritation. The users tend to locate the cause of minor inconveniences to the technical system, whereas major failings give rise to the need to find those responsible for the design and implementation of the system and place blame on them. There seems to be no way for the human agents to hide themselves behind the computerized systems to avoid blame.

Blame is a useful concept even in a world where human beings act as part of hybrid MASs. However, the socio-technical environment has changed the social meaning of blame. We suggest that instead of focusing on blame as a moral notion, we could explore *blame as a relation*. Blaming establishes a relation between 1) the blamer and 2) the blamed, which is determined by 3) the reason for blaming, and 4) the content of blame. The reason for blaming consists of the negative moral evaluation of the blamer towards the blamed, and the content of blame is the emotional reaction of the blamer towards the blamed.

Within the community of human agents, each person may blame themselves—a first person relation of blame—or blame another person—thereby establishing a second-person relation of blame [Fricker 2016]. In a second-person blame-relation the blamer and the blamed may even form a two-way relation which depends on the response of the one being blamed to the blamer in the form of accepting or rejecting the reason for blame as a morally relevant answer, not just reacting to the content of blame.

In failing hybrid MASs, the number of objects of potential blame is far greater than in human cooperative systems. In such contexts, blaming establishes a third-person relation, where the blamer is a human agent and the blamed is a distant subject or object; either an artificial entity or a human party responsible for programming, designing, providing, maintaining, or operating the system.

When the one being blamed is inanimate, it cannot give a meaningful response even when a blamer tries to place it in a blame relation. Should we then abstain from blaming hybrid MASs? We noticed (see Sect. 2.2) that blame and blaming have important social functions as they make visible the need to repair a failing system, mitigate ills, recompensate losses, and improve processes. Placing blame on an inanimate system may serve as an excuse for the human agents to askew their responsibility, leaving the users in a fight against a faceless, impersonal mechanized system they cannot understand or affect.

However, placing blame on a hybrid MAS may open a more constructive prospect by offering a cover for human agents against the psychological and emotional burden connected to the role of the blamed. Blaming the machine could help human agents act in their roles and carry out their duties to find adequate solutions to the ills that initiated the expressions of dissatisfaction. Non-personal blame does not generate emotional, defensive responses. This could help the human agents act appropriately and concentrate on their tasks instead of reacting to alleged accusations and investing resources in getting over the painful situation and regaining the approval from their moral community.

Erring is a basic human experience and failing to reach one's goal may be a more common outcome of one's actions than reaching the wished-for target. Use of tools and developing technology has multiplied the effects of human action; success takes place in a larger scale than ever before, but so does failure. In the continuing search for measures to manage failures and mitigate risks of hybrid MASs, the social institutions of placing and expressing blame have a meaningful role to play in safeguarding the conditions of responsible action and moral agency.

References

Allen, C., Wallach, W.: Moral machines. contradiction in terms of abdication of human responsibility? In: Lin, P., Abney, K., Bekey, G. (eds.) Robot ethics. The ethics and social implications of robotics, pp. 55–68. MIT Press, Cambridge, Mass (2012)

Balaji, P.G., Srinivasan, D.: An introduction to multi-agent systems. In: Srinivasan, D., Jain, L.C. (eds.) Innovations in Multi-Agent Systems and Applications - 1. Studies in Computational Intelligence, vol. 310, p. 27. Springer, Berlin, Heidelberg (2010). https://doi.org/10.1007/978-3-642-14435-6_1

Dennett, D.C.: When hal kills, who's to blame? computer ethics. In: Stork, D. (ed.) Hal's Legacy: 2001's Computer as Dream and Reality, pp. 351–365. MIT Press, Cambridge, MA (1997)

Dignum, V.: Responsibility and artificial intelligence. In: Dubber, P., Das (eds). The Oxford Handbook of Ethics of AI, pp. 215–233. Oxford University Press, New York (2020)

Davidson, D.: Essays on Actions and Events. Oxford University Press, Oxford (2001)

Floridi, L.: The Ethics of Information. Oxford University Press, Oxford (2015)

Fricker, M.: What is the point of blame? paradigm-based explanation. Noûs **50**(1), 165–183 (2016). https://doi.org/10.1111/nous.12067

Gotterbarn, D.: Informatics and professional responsibility. Sci. Eng. Ethics **7**(2), 221–230 (2001)

Hakli, R., Mäkelä, P.: Moral responsibility in robots and hybrid agents. Monist **102**(2), 259–275 (2019)

Hallamaa, J.: What could safety research contribute to technology design? In: Rauterberg, M. (ed.) HCII 2021. LNCS, vol. 12795, pp. 56–79. Springer, Cham (2021). https://doi.org/10.1007/978-3-030-77431-8_4

Hallamaa, J., Kalliokoski, T.: How AI systems challenge the conditions of moral agency? In: Rauterberg, M. (ed.) HCII 2020. LNCS, vol. 12215, pp. 54–64. Springer, Cham (2020). https://doi.org/10.1007/978-3-030-50267-6_5

Hinterleitner, M., Sager, F.: Anticipatory and reactive forms of blame avoidance: of foxes and lions. Eur. Polit. Sci. Rev. **9**(4), 587–606 (2016). https://doi.org/10.1017/S1755773916000126

Hogg, M.A., Vaughan, G.M.: Social Psychology. 5th (edn.). Pearson, Harlow (2008)

Hollnagel, E., Braithwaite J.: Resilient Health Care. CRC Press (2019). ISBN 9781317065166

Hood, C.: What happens when transparency meets blame-avoidance? Public Manage. Rev. **9**(2), 191–210 (2007). https://doi.org/10.1080/14719030701340275

Kalliokoski, T.: Yhteisöllisyyden rajat yhteistoiminnan jaihmisen perushyvien näkökulmasta. Diss. University of Helsinki, Helsinki (2020). http://urn.fi/URN:ISBN:978-951-51-6077-5

Manheim, D.: Multiparty dynamics and failure modes for machine learning and artificial intelligence. Big Data Cogn. Comput. **3**(2), 21 (2019). https://doi.org/10.3390/bdcc3020021

Misselhorn, C.: Collective agency and cooperation in natural and artificial systems. In: Misselhorn, C. (ed.) Collective Agency and Cooperation in Natural and Artificial Systems. PSS, vol. 122, pp. 3–24. Springer, Cham (2015). https://doi.org/10.1007/978-3-319-15515-9_1

Moor, J.H.: The nature, importance, and difficulty of machine ethics. Intell. Syst. (IEEEI) **21**(4), 18–21 (2006)

Moya, C.J.: The Philosophy of Action. Polity Press, Cambridge (1990)

MOT Oxford Dictionary of English. https://mot.it.helsinki.fi/

Nissenbaum, H.: Accountability in a Computerized Society. In B. Friedman (ed.) Human Values and the Design of Computer Technology. Cambridge University Press, Cambridge, pp. 41–64. https://nissenbaum.tech.cornell.edu/papers/accountability.pdf

Noorman, M.: Computing and moral responsibility. In: Zalta, E.N. (ed.) The Stanford Encyclopedia of Philosophy (Spring 2020 Edition) (2020). https://plato.stanford.edu/archives/spr2020/entries/computing-responsibility/. Accessed 31 Jan 2022

Reason, J.: Organizational Accidents Revisited. Ashgate, Farnham (2016)

Rocha, J., Boavida-Portugal, I., Gomes, E: Introductory Chapter: Multi-Agent Systems. In: Multi-agent Systems, pp. 3–13. IntechOpen, Rijeka (2017)

Ryan, W.: Blaming the Victim. Pantheon Books, New York (1971)

Sheer, M.: The Dynamics of Change. Tavistock approaches to Improving Social Systems. Routledge, London, New York (2018)

Snyder, M.: Public Appearances/Public Realities: The Psychology of Self-Monitoring. Freeman, New York (1987)

Stahl, B.C.: responsible computers? a case for ascribing quasi-responsibility to computer independent of personhood or agency. Ethics Inf. Technol. 8(4), 205–213 (2006)

Staub, E.: The Roots of Evil The Origins of Genocide and Other Group Violence. Cambridge University Press, Cambridge (1989)

Sullins, J.P.: When is a robot a moral agent? Int. Rev. Inf. Ethics 6(2), 23–29. https://philpapers.org/rec/SULWIA-2. Accessed 03 Feb 2022

Talbert, M.: Moral responsibility. In: Zalta, E.N. (ed.) The Stanford Encyclopedia of Philosophy. Winter 2019 Edition (2019). https://plato.stanford.edu/archives/win2019/entries/moral-responsibility/. Accessed 31 Jan 2022

Tognazzini, N., Coates, D.: Blame. In: Zalta, E.N. (ed.) The Stanford Encyclopedia of Philosophy (Summer 2021 Edition) (2021). https://plato.stanford.edu/archives/sum2021/entries/blame/. Accessed 25 Jan 2022

Verbeek, P.P.: Materializing morality: design ethics and technological mediation author(s): Peter-Paul Verbeek source: science, technology, and human values. Ethics Eng. Des. 31(3), 361–380 (2006)

von Wright, G.H.: The Varieties of Goodness. Routledge & Kegan Paul, New York (1968)

Zimbardo, P.: The Lucifer Effect. How Good People Turn Evil. Rider, London (2007)

Psychological and Cognitive Challenges in Sustainable AI Design

Mari Myllylä$^{(\boxtimes)}$ (iD)

Faculty of Information Technology, University of Jyväskylä, P.O.Box 35, 40014 Agora, FI, Finland
mari.t.myllyla@jyu.fi

Abstract. To design sustainable AI designers must be able to understand and think about complex technical, ecological, social, and economic systems and their interactions. Their reasoning and decisions need to be based on ethics and scientific facts. They must acknowledge different stakeholders' social and cultural norms, practices and current and future needs. Unfortunately, designers' thinking is prone to err, biases, and other psychological phenomena, which can negatively affect how they understand, reason, and make decision, and which can lead to unsustainable and unethical AI solutions. Thus, it is important to investigate errors in designers' thinking. This study presents a cognitive scientific overview about some common errors when making arguments, inferring, and reasoning, when drawing analogies, or in situations where problems are complex, uncertain, challenging the status quo, or framed differently. Also, processing information, emotions and social and cultural aspects can be source of errors in thinking. Designers must become aware of the risk of errors in their own perceptions, thinking, and reasoning and to explain why, what, and how they design sustainable AI. This can lead to more ethical and sustainable solutions in AI design.

Keywords: Sustainable design · AI design · Thinking errors · Cognitive bias

1 Introduction

The digitalizing world and the growing use of artificial intelligence (AI) and intelligent technologies will in many ways revolutionize the lives of individuals and societies. Societies are now entering the era of the fourth industrial revolution, which underlies the development of information and communications technologies (ICTs) and their many different digital applications, such as AI [1]. The term AI can be defined as "computerized abilities to solve problems and achieve goals" [2, p. 2] where there is a "non-human intelligence programmed to perform specific tasks" [3, p. 2].

Industrialization in its preceding forms has been accompanied by scientific and technological innovations, which have enabled humans to significantly alter earth's natural environments, systems, and cycles [4]. Unfortunately, these actions are now threatening global environmental conditions and have contributed to worldwide human-induced phenomena, such as climate change [4, 5]. Further negative impacts of industrialization on environmental, societal, and economic issues at the systemic, interconnected, and planetary levels must be urgently reduced to ensure that the needs of current and future generations are met. It is essential that designers understand and implement these core concepts of sustainability when designing new technologies, such as AI [2, 6–9].

The ongoing transformation regarding what and how ICTs are produced and used has direct and indirect effects on sustainability. For instance, AI applications can be used to decrease the carbon footprint of other products and systems by increasing resource efficiency and by automating and optimizing processes regarding, for example, manufacturing, production, logistics, and land, marine, and air traffic [1, 10, 11]. AI can help to identify and compare important signals and patterns and make mathematical predictions from large and complex data. This can aid people in areas such as food production, waste reduction, energy consumption, the conservation of biodiversity and the forecasting of social opinions, natural disasters, water systems, and climate change [1, 2, 11]. AI can also help in terms of design work. It can be used to research and explore issues that are relevant to designers' work and to assist their design thinking. It can even be used to inform about designers' own physiological, emotional, and cognitive states and how these can affect their design performance [12].

While AI can be used to help designers, consumers, organizations, governments, and societies to make better decisions regarding the impact of digital technologies, it cannot solve all sustainability problems. AI can both enable and inhibit sustainable development [1]. AI technologies themselves are based on energy intensive physical electronic devices and systems for processing, storing, and transporting information, which produce carbon dioxide emissions and have negative impacts on the environment [2, 10]. A huge amount of energy is required for AI training and using AI software for complex data modeling, as well as for maintaining data centers [2]. Intelligent technology products can consume a lot of raw materials, such as rare metals, glass, plastic, and energy. Presumably, in the future, these resources will be even more in demand as the use of data intensive technology, such as AI, is likely to increase in ways that are currently impossible to predict [10]. The abundant production, availability, and consumption of digital technologies, despite their aim of increasing eco-efficiency, can create "an illusion of boundless material and digital opportunities" [13, p. 345] and usher development in an unsustainable direction [2]. Unintended local consequences and rebound effects can negatively affect people's behavior and the sustainability of AI technology [2].

Several problematic issues are also related to, for instance, the production of rare metals that are needed for electronics and batteries used in AI devices. These range from carbon emissions and pollution and environmental damage to the use of child labor [10]. Increases in the international demand for minerals creates a pressure to expand the mining industry, which in turn, can threaten, for example, local indigenous populations' lives and delicate natural environments [14]. In addition to the need for energy, water, and other natural resources, AI technology that is based on electronics requires the use of plants, facilities, processes, and human workforces throughout the different phases of its lifecycle, from the refining of raw materials to the postprocessing of redundant technology [15]. To design AI ethically, current and future challenges that are related to environmental and social sustainability in manufacturing, producing, transporting, storing, using, terminating, and recycling technology must also be considered, although manufacturing sustainability issues are often more related to the supply chain than design decisions [9].

Several solutions that can be utilized by technology designers already exist for climate and environmental challenges, and new solutions are also being developed [10]. New raw materials, such as bioplastics or natrium-based battery materials, have been developed from renewable natural sources [10]. By designing longer-lasting, repairable, and efficiently recyclable electronic devices with minimum material waste, designers can decrease technological devices' burden on the climate and the environment [15]. Source codes that are used in AI can be designed to be as usable, riskless, long-lasting, and resource efficient as possible [10]. Designers can adopt participatory design processes and methods to gain multilevel and holistic views from stakeholders who are directly and indirectly affected by the production and usage of such technology [1, 2, 4]. Those stakeholders can bring totally new or unexpected aspects to AI designers' attention and help to create more sustainable solutions.

AI designers' knowledge about sustainable technology and AI design can be increased with training or personal experience [7]. However, there seems to be a gap between being taught something, learning it, and putting that knowledge to use in everyday practices, as people constantly keep acting in unsustainable ways [5].

To implement sustainability in AI design requires transformative learning regarding sustainability and "experiencing a deep, structural shift in the basic premises of thought, feelings, and actions" [5, p. 168]. To avoid superficial greenwashing, designers need to become aware of and embed in their designs ways to minimize the negative impact on ecosystems and the use of materials and energy, to optimize their products for eco-efficiency and the circular economy, and to increase the long-term positive benefits and quality of lives for humans and environments, at the individual, group, local, and global levels [6–9, 13]. Designers must be able to understand and think about complex technical, ecological, social, and economic systems and their interactions; their reasoning and decisions need to be based on ethics and scientific facts; and different stakeholders' social and cultural norms and practices must be identified and updated to correspond to current and future needs [2, 4, 7, 16]. Thus, many of the challenges present in sustainable AI design are, in their essence, psychological ones that include cognitive, emotional, and social aspects [2, 17].

Unfortunately, human thinking is prone to err, biases, and a multitude of other different psychological phenomena, which can negatively affect reasoning and decision-making and even lead to risky behavior [18–21]. People's receptivity to fallacious reasoning was pointed out by Plato over 2,000 years ago [22]. However, this topic has scarcely been discussed from the point of view of AI designers' thinking. Thus, it is important to investigate errors in thinking that can affect designers' understanding and decisions regarding sustainable AI design. Risky, erroneous, or biased thinking can lead to poor decisions, which can further result in the creation of unsustainable and unethical AI solutions.

A good amount of literature exists with regard to different biases [18, 19] and argumentation fallacies [e.g., 23] and how these thinking errors are present, for example, in working life [19, 20]. It is not possible to cover all of them in this paper. Instead, this study presents a cognitive scientific contemplation where examples and explanations are based on literature from, for example, sustainability science, design science, and cognitive psychology.

1.1 Thinking as a Mental Phenomenon

It can be argued that all humans' psychological and cognitive functioning is built on a similar, species-typical biological basis. At the same time, everyone possesses unique characteristics, such as age, personality, past life experiences, and cultural and factual knowledge, which can alter individuals' mental information, thinking, reasoning, and behavior. These can affect what and how information is processed and experienced and how problems are solved by different people with different domains of expertise, for example [4, 24]. These differences in conceptual level knowledge, perspectives, and specialist language that different groups are accustomed to can also hinder the mutual understanding and definition of problems, communication, and the co-creation of insights between people [4].

Thinking itself can be understood as a skill, which within humans is based on certain evolutionary developed, species-specific cognitive properties [21]. Evolution has provided humans with rationality and thinking, which are imperfect, but, nevertheless, good enough in terms of survival and reproduction [28]. Even though cognitive processes, such as thinking, that evolved to serve the lives of early humans have remained somewhat the same in the biological sense, the world and contexts that people interact in are very different. Situations requiring fast, physical reactions to immediate and local threats have changed into the need for long-term planning, consideration at the complex, global level, and thoughts about ambiguous and abstract concepts, their connections, and their effects [21].

According to mental model theory, when people think about things, they rely on their own mental models [25]. These can be described as knowledge representations that imitate the world and what is possible and true and that have a similar structure to that which they represent. Mental models can refer to information, such as that related to space and time, "entities and persons, events and processes, and the operations of complex systems" [25, p. 136]. Alternative theories state that thinking and reasoning are based on dual processes, often termed the fast, unconscious, and automatic "system 1" and slow, conscious, and deliberate "system 2" [19].

Some cognitive functions, such as language processing or visual processing, are localized in certain areas of the brain, and the activation, association, or dissociation of the different areas can affect thinking and reasoning [30]. The functioning of working memory, "the cognitive construct responsible for the maintenance and manipulation of information" [26, p. 457], is especially important for considering and inventing new solutions. Working memory activates, inhibits, and preserves information as momentary dynamic representations, operates based on that information, and binds information from the long-term memory and perceptions together in different ways during conscious thinking [26]. This makes working memory important for the apperception process, where emotional and perceptual information and knowledge from one's memory are constructed in mental representations, and for thinking, where these representations are reconstructed into new ones [28]. When an individual perceives new information in interaction with their social and physical environments, it is matched with pre-existing information in the individual's memory, such as conceptual knowledge and mental schemas, to create a sensemaking, semantically meaningful, and coherent, conceptual mental representation of the world [4, 17, 27–29]. Much of this information processing is unconscious or intuitive, as opposed to conscious reasoning, although both these faculties are in constant interaction with each other [19, 28, 29].

When children grow older, they become better at applying thinking strategies and more capable of inferring the meanings of more complex things [30]. The development of thinking is linked to neural maturation and growth in synapses and dendrites and connections between different brain areas, as well as to cortical development in the prefrontal cortex, which is responsible for processing cognitive executive functions, such as directing attention, making plans and controlling goal-directed and emotional behavior [30]. In later life, acquiring new knowledge and skills in a particular domain through deliberate practice can lead to expertise in that area [31]. While gaining expertise, individuals acquire mental representations with context-dependent and meaningful patterns and large and highly nuanced knowledge structures, which are stored in their long-term memory and effectively retrieved during the performance of reasoning and certain behaviors [29, 31].

1.2   Design Thinking and Sustainable AI Design

Design can be described as anything that is created by humans to solve problems, and design thinking is an intentional, evolving, and unique way of thinking or a mindset or strategy that focuses on finding, defining, reframing, and solving those problems with a fitting solution [32, 33]. Design thinking is a creative, empathic, human-centered, and iterative cognitive process that combines convergent and divergent thinking [6, 7, 34].

Convergent and divergent thinking can be understood as forms of creative cognition—cyclic, creative, and exploratory thinking processes for incubating, transforming, and maturing design ideas and concepts [35], where both types of reasoning draw from the designer's existing knowledge [36]. Convergent thinking is a type of reasoning where "cognitive operations are intended to converge upon the single correct answer to a problem" [36, p. 465]. Divergent thinking is a free-flowing thought process that is "used to generate creative ideas through the exploration of many possible solutions" [33, p. 13] from one's memory or imagination and to answer ill-defined or open problems, without narrowing down one's thinking too early on [33, 36].

Design thinking depends on the social situation, available tools, and the designer's characteristics, such as those related to previous experiences and learning [6, 7, 33]. For instance, experts in design can switch between different cognitive styles and use both conscious reasoning and intuition in problem framing and sketching. This helps them to understand the general problem description and recognize relevant pragmatic cues to enable the generation of alternative, less stereotyped ideas [29, 37].

Design thinking is well suited to developing AI for sustainability [2]. Design thinking for sustainability can be understood as "the systematic consideration of design performance with respect to environmental, health, safety, and sustainability objectives over the full product and process life cycle" [6, p. 19]. Sustainability challenges are often considered to be wicked problems [13, 33]. Wicked problems are "unique, interconnected, and poorly defined problems that cannot be definitively described" [33, p. 12]. According to Raami [29], wicked problems are also the most challenging types of problems to solve. Solving wicked sustainability problems requires a flexible and creative mindset, shared mental models, and an ability to view ambiguous, complex, and often urgent problems from multiple angles, using different strategies, methodologies, and methods or their components [6, 13, 29, 32, 33].

2 Erroneous Thinking in Sustainable AI Design

When it comes to thinking, behavior, and decision-making regarding sustainability, humans are not very rational creatures [21]. The reasons behind this vary from the limitations of human cognitive processes and capacities to emotional, social, and contextual factors. Sustainable design, engineering design, and design in general are mentally challenging and stressful. They require different cognitive processes and skills for exploring and reasoning, problem structuring and constraining, solution space searching, and idea generating to solve complex, ill-structured, ill-defined, or wicked problems that contain unknown variables and unique contexts [7, 12, 34, 38]. However, having to work with ambiguous information and concepts is not necessarily a negative thing as it can also stimulate a designer's thinking [35].

2.1 Argumentation, Reasoning, and Inferencing

Mental activities in design include making deductive, inductive, and abductive inferences, concept evaluations, and analogies that are based on a designer's prior, existing knowledge and previous design cases [34]. Deductions, inductions, abductions, and the use of analogies are different types of arguments, symbolic structures, or complex speech acts, such as dialogues, which provide the reasons behind claims and where conclusions are supported by and follow on from some premises [39]. Argumentation and reasoning are different but closely related phenomena and can be investigated with research on thinking and reasoning [39].

The first theory of deductive reasoning was presented by Aristotle as early as 350 BC [40]. Aristotle introduced the concept of a premise as "a sentence affirming or denying one thing of another" [40, p. 1]. In deductive reasoning, "the truth of the premises is supposed to guarantee the truth of the conclusion" [39, Types of Arguments section], and people can use strategies where reasoning is based on relations and quantities and make suppositions by constructing chains of interlinked conclusions or lists of various possibilities that can be drawn from the premises [25]. These can improve the speed and accuracy of reasoning and result in valid and sound arguments but can also lead to the tendency to always use a particular strategy, when certain premises are met [25, 39].

Inductive reasoning is part of "a range of cognitive activities such as categorization, probability judgment, analogical reasoning, scientific inference, and decision making" [41, p. 278]. In inductive reasoning, people make probabilistic inferences about new situations, where a particular occurrence is explained using a general reason, principle, or some particular information based on the reasoner's existing knowledge and past experiences [25, 39, 41]. Inductive reasoning is often based on perceived causality between a particular occurrence and a conclusion [41] and on statistical frequencies, which are then generalized [39]. Thus, it can be defined as "a process that increases semantic information" [25, p. 146]. Inductions can be affected, for instance, by unconsciously ruling out probabilities and alternatives that are in fact possible or consistent [25]. Humans also tend to generalize based on perceived similarity, on how typically a premise represents some general, simpler category [41]. However, prior experiences and domain expertise can reduce many inductive fallacies because, presumably, "domain experts often generalize properties on the basis of relations" [41, p. 281] that are different and within a broader range than non-experts do, presuming experts have enough time for this kind of complex reasoning.

Abduction is a form of reasoning where "from the observation of a few relevant facts, a conclusion is drawn as to what could possibly explain the occurrence of these facts" [39, Abduction section]. Abduction can be understood as a type of inference that is based on knowledge and perceived possible causalities and which can produce general theories, descriptions, and explanations that, however, do not necessarily preserve the truth [25, 39, 42].

How humans draw conclusions is typically based on the tendency to make their judgements based on existing semantic information that they already possess and to deduce only a limited number of new conclusions [25]. Conclusions can err in terms of either being inconsistent and conflicting with their premises or not following on from their otherwise consistent premises [25]. When an individual is faced with an inconsistency or mismatching evidence, they are more prone to construct sensemaking causal claims that, for example, something happened because of some probable reason, than to check their existing beliefs [25]. People, regardless of their level of expertise, can also make inferences that something is possible or impossible when, in reality, only the opposite can be true [25]. This illusion is related to how people interpret certain wordings that give them hints as to whether an assertion might be true or not, not on how people use their logic [25]. People focus on events that can be directly observed to draw quick conclusions about what was perceived and what happened. Not taking into consideration other possible, hidden factors and jumping to conclusions can lead to erroneous judgements and wrong solutions [5].

In reasoning that is based on mental models, it is easier, more accurate, and faster to assume that situations are possible rather than impossible and that situations are unnecessary rather than necessary [25]. Reasoning and making inferences from premises often cause errors because people easily base their explanations on simplicity and a minimal number of mental models, which is easier in terms of memory and cognitive processing [25, 39, 42]. Explanations can err because, for instance, why something is like something is accepted as proof that it is the case [42]. It is also difficult to notice circularity in explanations, they can be affected by irrelevant information, and people can also "overestimate the accuracy and depth of their own explanations" [42, p. 270]. Reasoning can be affected by at least two types of belief biases. People tend to mostly accept the kind of information and conclusions that support their already existing mental models and beliefs [17, 19, 37]. When people are presented with information or conclusions that are in conflict with or unbelievable when compared to their pre-existing models, beliefs, and values, they tend to disregard them or selectively search for contrasting examples [17, 19, 37]. However, finding counterexamples can sometimes help people to detect and correct faulty and inconsistent conclusions and reasoning [25].

Analogies. A central part of inductive reasoning that is used, for example, in problem solving, creative thinking, rational argumentation, and causal inferences, is creating analogies [43]. As Dutihl Novaes [39, Analogy section] summarizes: "Arguments by analogy are based on the idea that, if two things are similar, what is true of one of them is likely to be true of the other as well." Analogies are important mental processes that people unconsciously use to make sense and understand the world as they perceive, learn, and interact with things [27]. Designers draw analogies between different representations and similar problems, structures, and solutions when they are solving design tasks [24].

In analogies, mental representations of the domain-specific source and target and the relevant similar relational roles of their elements, attributes, characteristics, causes, and effects are compared in a structured way to achieve some goals [43, 44]. These goals can be used to understand concepts, come up with new conclusions, and make discoveries [43, 44]. Analogies are usually based on some prior, base knowledge in one's long-term memory, which includes beliefs about causalities and connections within a concept or object [43, 45]. They can also be about, for example, emotions [46] or stereotypes [44]. Analogies can also include special kinds of comparisons, such as *metaphors*, which can be described as "forms of symbolic expression" [43, p. 236] that compare semantically distant situations, and *metonyms*, where a concept is associated with another symbolic figure (such as using the word "sword" as an analog to weaponry) [43]. Humans often use metaphors to describe and understand their experiences in common language [43].

As Holyoak emphasized, because analogy is a form of inductive reasoning, "analogical inferences are inevitably uncertain" [43, p. 235]. For example, drawing analogies between semantically distant entities can provide more creative but less plausible inferences than analogies that compare things with more similar relational resemblances in their structural features and functions [43]. The quality of analogical inference is affected by learning and development, which increases the number and details of categories in terms of analogy-making [45]. Also, more pressure on working memory and attention can impair symbol-level, relational role mapping, which requires more cognitive effort and instead increases the number of analogies based on similarities [43]. Thus, individuals can "fail to notice superficially dissimilar source analogs that they could readily use" [43, p. 244]. In addition, the retrieval of an analog can be more successful when performed by experts rather than novices, if analogs are presented in a spoken instead of a written format, and when individuals need to generate examples rather than remember earlier cases. Analogical reasoning can also unconsciously and unintendedly be activated because of an individual's previous learning and priming. Analogical mapping can also be strongly affected by the goals of the reasoning individual [43].

Fallacies and Fallacious Arguments. Fallacies can be understood as "false but popular beliefs" or as "deceptively bad arguments" [23, Fallacies section]. Fallacious arguments are arguments that seem to be true but are not [39]. Several well-known or core fallacies exist [22, 23, 40]. For example, in *circular arguments* that are based on the fallacy of *begging the question*, a conclusion (for instance, "God exists") is justified with a premise ("because the Bible says so"), which is based on the same proposition as the conclusion ("the Bible is the word of God") [23, 39]. In the *ad hominem fallacy*, some negative characteristics or the situation of the arguer are used to contest their statements [23, 39]. Examples of this kind of fallacy in rhetoric are based on an individual's personal characteristics or on more general stereotypes when making decisions when, in reality, these have nothing to do with solving the actual problem [20]. On the other hand, the arguer can appeal to authority, expertise, or popular knowledge or opinion instead of argument reasoning [23, 39]. For example, in Plato's [22] work *Gorgias*, it was noted how persuasive rhetoric is often used in politics, where speakers use flattery without any possession of expert knowledge in that domain, which in turn, can lead to fallacious beliefs and judgements among the public.

Arguments for ignorance are types of fallacies where something is assumed to be true because it has not been proven otherwise [23]. In the fallacy of the *slippery slope*, "from a given starting point one can by a series of incremental inferences arrive at an undesirable conclusion, and because of this unwanted result, the initial starting point should be rejected" [23, The core fallacies section]. Other common fallacies include, for instance, when the ambiguity and changes in the meanings of used terms are exploited, when a response to a question is already implied in the question itself, when two temporally succeeding events are mistaken as having a causal relationship, or when arguments are based on imagined threats, harm, or sympathy [23, 39].

2.2   Knowledge and Managing Information

Designers tackling sustainability need to possess the necessary knowledge as well as explicit and tactical cognitive skills in terms of what and how information about different dimensions of sustainability is managed [7]. While exploring new solutions, designers cognitively and simultaneously operate between solution and problem spaces that interact and co-evolve with each other [34]. However, problem solving is limited by the human information processing capacity and affected by other constraints, such as a lack of information [29], mental shortcuts, or the possession of fallacious information [20, 21]. This can result in errors with regard to problem structuring and setting its requirements, constraints, and goals; wrong conclusions; and the fidelity and correctness of both the created mathematical design models and designers' own mental models [9, 20, 21]. While mathematical models can be beneficial to test the feasibility and tradeoffs of potential new solutions and to make risks and tradeoffs more visible, creating and analyzing models that include sustainability measures is difficult [9]. For instance, it can be difficult to transform social impacts, such as the consequences of an accident on people and their lives, into clearly defined, manageable, and measurable units without reducing the multiple dimensions of different social phenomena down into too narrow a format [9]. It can be difficult to estimate probabilities and accept randomness in events because humans are inclined to perceive or expect to observe patterns even where there are none [19].

Designers must be able to view things holistically and avoid getting hindered by confining details, especially at the beginning of their design process when they are trying out ideas using high-level concepts and prototypes that can provoke thinking and new questions [33–35]. Prototypes are examples of tools that can be used to assist design thinking. Technology and tools can be used to sense and measure sustainability parameters and their data, such as carbon foot- or handprints or product life cycles, which can also be used to help sustainable design [8]. However, risks exist in relation to using data-driven design. Accurate and adequate amounts of information from, for example, operationally, locally, and temporally scattered sources can be difficult and expensive to acquire. A lot of uncertainty can exist with regard to the quality and details of such data and how to understand and analyze them. Data need to be analyzed against the correct context, and this often requires specialized knowledge about processes and systems and about both sustainability dimensions and human behavior [8].

For example, Faludi et al. [32] noted that experts in sustainable design can conduct theoretical analyses of, for instance, environmental or social issues or product life cycles, but these analyses are not necessary always founded on facts. Many different methods exist for sustainable design, which creators use opportunistically; which methods or their parts are used together often depends on the designer's level of expertise [32]. Motivation, too, can affect the way information is searched for and analyses are conducted [47]. For example, individuals can be either more motivated to find accurate information and conduct complex analyses or to complete the task at hand quickly by using less information and performing fewer considerations [47]. Also, correct information can be processed in an erroneous manner. Designers can overemphasize visual information, interpret correlations as causation, imagine that they can manage variables outside of their influence, and have "the preference to look for evidence that supports the preconceived model instead of disproving it" [21, p. 89] (belief bias).

Detailed information given too early on can lead to design fixation [7]. Design fixation can be defined as "a blind adherence to a set of ideas or concepts limiting the output of conceptual design" [48, p. 3], where designers get mentally stuck and focus on only one aspect, problem, or solution relating to a design [38]. Humans can be fixated by certain mental models, often the ones that first come to their minds and that they have an unconscious preference for, even if they are offered new information [20]. Fixation on a certain idea can also be caused by emotional factors, such as impulsiveness, and the avoidance of experiencing certain themes or explanatory models that are too emotionally distressing [20]. Functional fixedness is a phenomenon related to problem solving as a mental activity [24]. In functional fixedness, an individual is accustomed to perceiving an object and its uses and purpose in a habitual way and has difficulty finding any other meanings or uses for it in other contexts [24]. Design fixation has been found in both novice and skilled designers, such as engineering design students and educators [49]. Fixated designers can become emotionally stressed and incapable of processing more or alternative information because generating new concepts while one is fixated requires substantial cognitive effort [38].

Ideas that are generated in the early phases of design and development often form the basis for the following phases, where solutions are created [7]. If these ideas are based on misinformation or insufficient or wrongly generated or reasoned information, it can have devastating effects on the development of the rest of the design project.

2.3 Heuristics, Intuition, and Unconscious Thinking

In reasoning as a mental process, humans often use mental shortcuts and quick heuristic judgements to minimize their cognitive load, despite the risk of biased thinking [19, 37]. Heuristics are based on a minimal number of cues, little reflection, and the mental models the reasoning individual uses, and such reasoning can also lead to illusory conclusions [25, 37].

Using heuristics or "rules of thumb" as shortcut strategies is also one form of fast, intuitive thinking [24], although according to Evans [37], intuitive inferences are based on more information than heuristic judgements. Sometimes, design ideation can also activate the unconscious incubation of mental content [29]. Designers can unconsciously restructure information into new representations, which might be consciously experienced as ranging from "small hunches" [29, p. 214] to moments of insight or even a eureka experience or what Raami described as "re-centring—an experience of new permutations of relations between ideas and a novel and unconventional combination of thoughts" [29, p. 213].

Unconscious cognitive intuition processes information and selects the relevant parts for further conscious processing [29]. Although unconscious processes are prone to bias, according to Raami [29], intuitive information processing can also be developed to provide more accurate and reliable results. It can even be argued that, at least within scientific intuition, "intuition is the primary thinking mode used for discoveries and inventions while conscious reasoning is used for argumentation" [29, p. 209]. Even though an individual can either have a sense of being correct or have doubts, these feelings do not reveal anything about how accurate the intuition actually is. Analyzing the accuracy of intuitions is important, but it can also become problematic as it can lead to, for example, the overanalysis or reduced accuracy and reliability of the unconscious intuition [29]. As opposed to unconscious intuition, conscious, explicit reasoning and reflective thinking are typically understood as slower processes, which have more limited processing capacity than unconscious processes [19, 29, 37].

2.4 Framing Effects

Different contexts can be framed and reframed to affect reasoning and behavior. Even the exact same scenario, context, or issue can be presented and reformulated in different ways to influence how that event is interpreted and what kind of judgements are made [21, 27, 44]. This phenomenon, called the framing effect, can be found in certain cases, such as when forming opinions about climate engineering techniques or in political environmental discourses, where framing effects can even shape public and political opinions and guide discussions in a certain direction [21]. Problem solving, such as designing, also depends on and is affected by specific physical and psychological contexts, which "provide frames of orientation and they trigger norms and expectations" [27, p. 7].

A framing effect can be illustrated with the following imaginary example of climate change thinking. For instance, it has been argued that climate change is a natural phenomenon, which causes the average temperature to fluctuate between -0.1 degrees Celsius and + 0.1 degrees Celsius [50]. This is based on scientific data and is true. However, this fact can be framed without the context in question and the temporal and physical scale of the phenomenon, creating a dangerous illusion that nothing needs to be done. The same information can be presented together with the fact that natural fluctuations occur over tens of thousands of years and that the earth's temperature has increased by approximately 1.07 degrees Celsius during the last 140 years because of human activity [50]. With different framing, the same information and how it is interpreted can lead to a totally different conclusion.

In addition, humans can respond to AI in psychologically and socially different ways, depending on an individual's position and how the future goals and losses are framed. For instance, as Nishant et al. [2] noted, AI applications that can be used to automatically manage work that has previously been done by people can be seen as acceptable or not, depending on whether AI is understood as increasing or reducing individuals' employment opportunities.

2.5 Complexity, Maintaining the Status Quo, and Uncertainty

The ability to ponder complex new ideas and realize new solutions for difficult design problems, such as sustainability in AI design, requires resources, such as time, and cognitive skills to construe new mental representations [19–21]. Implementing sustainability dimensions into the problem-solving equation creates even more cognitive challenges for designers in their already complex work in terms of, for example, engineering [7]. Often, when sustainability influences a design, the creators need to choose their design philosophy, include sustainability issues, such as eco-efficiency or eco-effectiveness, in their design checklists, and create models where different relationships between sustainability issues, design parameters, and their tradeoffs are presented [9]. When considering sustainable AI design, there is the risk that designers focus on certain, one-sided parameters in their models, especially if some design parameters are found to be difficult or uncertain [9].

It is very cognitively demanding for humans to think about abstract phenomena related to sustainability, such as climate change, when their temporal and physical properties, proportions, and complexity exceed measures that are familiar to everyday life [21], especially if the individual is not given enough time to reason [41]. These difficulties can lead to the problem being pushed to one side to be dealt with in the future or to reductionist thinking and "game-theoretical forms of interactions where self-interest is in play" [2, p. 2], although people can also engage in different, value-based behavior [51].

Thus, it is easy for people to err with regard to their thinking when they need to make plans and decisions about the future [20]. Instead of making rationally argued decisions that would benefit sustainability in the long term, many people tend to reason and behave based on short-term goals and selfish motives [2, 21]. The inability to act persists [21], even though scenarios about what will happen if nothing is done give alarming future projections about environmental conditions, diseases, poverty, and injustice [52].

Maintaining the Status Quo. According to *prospect theory*, people can unconsciously focus on possible gains or losses, not only regarding monetary values but also involving reasoning that affects life quality [19]. People often find it more important to try to prevent losses than gain new wins—a phenomenon called *loss aversion* [19]. This can lead to a bias toward maintaining the current situation and avoiding change. This *status quo bias* can be found in many decision-making situations ranging from economic to health-related phenomena [53]. For example, Samuelson and Zeckhauser [53] found status quo bias in experiments with students of economics and in field studies where people were making choices about health plans and retirement funds. Status quo bias can also be found in decisions made by professionals within their domains [21].

In the phenomenon of *design resistance*, a designer can erroneously think and insist that because something has worked successfully before, the same solution will also work for new problems; thus they argue that it is not necessary to change the strategy or actions [16, 20, 54]. Even though using existing design solutions can sometimes be the right decision for safety, economic, or logistic reasons or to avoid resistance from end users, for example, other times, alternative reasons, such as the designer's nostalgia, pride, or knowledge, can underlie such judgements [54]. Designers can also find it problematic to evaluate the quality of new and innovative design ideas [27]. Evaluations of new designs are often conservative and biased toward some familiar and pre-existing concepts and experiences, at least at first [27]. Avoiding making conservative estimations of novel ideas and design innovations requires that the evaluating individual has "the opportunity and time for familiarization and elaboration" [27, p. 6]. To detach their thinking from fixations and to challenge the status quo, designers need to have mental flexibility and be "comfortable with failure" [33, p. 15]. Unfortunately, in many situations, individuals are not able do this and instead become cognitively inflexible [16]. Breaking away from the existing, habitual thinking models and strategies is difficult but necessary, especially when new concepts and solutions are desperately needed to develop sustainable AI.

Effects of Uncertainty. Another factor that makes sustainable design difficult is that making "predictions for the future become even more uncertain" [21, p. 87] when the environment is perceived as or imagined to be harsh. Alarming messages about the climate and environmental issues might "trigger cognitive systems that are sensitive to such threats and urge people to think about their own advantage first" [21, p. 87], leading to erroneous thinking and unsustainable actions.

Uncertainty is common in life in general [55]. Uncertainty can be perceived as especially high in work domains involving sustainable design [4, 8, 13, 21, 29] and AI design [55]. Uncertainty and negative emotions and pressures can affect thinking and emotions and lead to irrational, hurried, and over- or undersized behavior, such as making hasty decisions or not doing anything at all [20, 21]. For example, climate anxiety can cause the emotional state of paralyzing apathy [13]. Strong emotional reactions can also be caused by, for instance, individuals' personal difficulties in terms of emotional control [20] or learned, cultural conventions to either react strongly or feel indifference about phenomena such as climate change [13].

2.6   Emotions and Values

Emotions affect whether people are concerned about and how they deal with different issues [20]. Emotions are important for self-regulating, controlling, and motivating behavior, and they also act as signals of internal values and their conflicts, making the individual aware of these [13, 20, 56]. Design work can cause different positive or negative emotions in designers. They can feel pressure and stress with regard to inventing the best concepts and solutions to complex design problems [21, 38]. Stress may even be caused by cognitive dissonance, which is experienced when a designer is faced with either too challenging or too easy a task [38]. On some occasions stress can be experienced as a positive factor that improves cognition, motivation, creativity, and concentration [38]. However, long-lasting stress, in particular, can lead to negative problems and affect both physical and mental health and well-being, as well as mental performance, by limiting cognitive processing and slowing down attentional processes [20, 38]. Thus, stress can negatively affect designers' design cognition and concept generation [38].

Topics such as climate change or AI are often emotionally charged issues [2, 13]. To manage and respond appropriately to emotional challenges, it is important that an individual has enough "time and space for expression and critical reflection either individually or collectively" [13, p. 351]. In their work, designers need to create radical new ideas, which can be faced with resistance from others [29]. Fears and hopes can affect how people think and reason by "biasing, narrowing or restricting the free flow of intuition" [29, p. 222]. Emotional biases, such as having conflicting emotional values between sustainability and political goals, can cause irrational judgements about issues such as global warming [17]. Also, different people can pay attention in different ways and experience different positive or negative emotions even when considering the same situation [20], which can make it difficult to form a common understanding.

Many philosophers have suggested that "emotions provide us with our most basic cognitive access to values" [56, p. 488]. Thus, values and emotions are closely connected [56]. For instance, if something is valued as dangerous, it can be felt with the emotion of fear; something valued as sublime can be felt with awe or astonishment [56]. Many basic values and moral concepts are learned in early childhood from family and through other close relationships [51]. These values can affect one's thinking and behavior in later life and are hard to change, even when they lead to conflicts in lives of individuals and communities [51]. In technology design, there is a risk that designers unconsciously invoke their personal values and biased preconceptions [3] through their products. Such products can display and enhance negative stereotypes, indiscriminate different users mentally, physically, or socially, or allow unethical behavior [3, 11]. Thus, in sustainable AI design, it is important that designers can understand different values from different perspectives and make design decisions that are based on shared economically, socially, and ecologically sustainable values.

2.7 Social and Cultural Aspects

Design thinking is a human-centered design approach, where all design activities are fundamentally social [33]. To discover the different aspects of people's lives that are affected by the design problem, designers need to explore and investigate their users and stakeholders, use empathy to understand what it is like to be them, and address the problems they encounter in their real contexts of interaction [7, 16, 33, 57].

To identify the diversity of the possible positive and negative sustainability issues and design constraints and to generate new ideas and concepts, designers can use brainstorming sessions together with other stakeholders [9, 38]. However, techniques such as brainstorming have been found to require high cognitive effort and cause frustration within groups of designers [38]. In group brainstorming sessions, designers' creativity can also be affected both positively and negatively by social and procedural factors, such as feeling stimulated and influenced and elaborating on other team members' ideas, and by group dynamics, such as the existence of controlling personalities in brainstorming groups [35]. A critical thinker can be silenced by social or emotional pressures set by the group or due to the individual's inability to explicitly explain their own reasoning with proper, fact-based arguments [20]. These kinds of social thinking models can lead to group-level neglect of important information and faulty decisions [20].

Empathy can enable an understanding of the local circumstances and experiences of the most vulnerable people affected by sustainability problems. It can urge designers to take moral responsibility to act and invent solutions to decrease their losses and increase their well-being and their sense of hope [13]. However, it is very difficult, or even impossible, for an individual to fully observe and understand the experiences, lives, goals, and values of other individuals. Understanding the mind and behaviors of others becomes even harder the more "different" that other one is observed or imagined to be [28]. Empathic understanding also can be built on both inferential and embodied processes based on, for example, stories and imagined body movements [28]. Embodied understanding is important in design and also when designing sustainable AI [11]. An AI engineering designer who spends most of their time in front of a computer may miss out on a lot of important embodied knowledge through not really experiencing the physical world of their stakeholders [11].

Different people feel empathy in distinct ways and to different degrees. It can require intuitive thinking [29] or be hindered by education focusing on technical issues instead of human welfare [57]. However, according to Chang-Arana et al., there is no adequate proof that empathy in fact helps designers to better understand other people or to generate better ideas and solutions [57].

It is an illusion to think that all people understand, value, and forecast about sustainable AI technology in similar ways. For example, Marquardt and Nasiritousi [58] researched what kind of different future imaginaries existed within different stakeholder groups regarding fossil-free Sweden. The authors categorized the identified imaginaries into four groups: Techno-optimistics saw the climate crisis as something that can bring opportunities and competitive perks, and ecological modernists both welcomed technological innovations and called for political actions with regard to creating a greener economy. In contrast, the other groups expressed "the need for disruptive changes in business models, institutional settings, and individual lifestyles" [58, p. 13]. In another study, Gherhes and Obrad [59] investigated views about AI in terms of its development and sustainability among Romanian undergraduate students of humanities and technical studies. These researchers found that there were notable differences in the knowledge and perceptions of AI between the two groups and that "the students following technical studies show a higher level of confidence for the AI sustainable development in the future," whereas the students of humanities were "more interested in the human value, which they protect, and seem more willing to perceive the disadvantages of the AI development" [59, p. 15].

3 Conclusion

Sustainable AI design requires thinking, reasoning, and performing actions based on often difficult and cognitively, emotionally, and socially multidimensional and interacting issues. It requires the ability to solve ill-defined and wicked problems, to make correct and fact-based inferences, and to come up with new and sometimes radical solutions in design. It requires that designers possess the mental skills and resources to think about highly complex, interrelated, abstract, and cognitively challenging concepts and systems and to critically review their learned knowledge, cultural concepts, beliefs, attitudes, and values [4, 20]. These mental processes are involved in arguing and reasoning, inferring, possessing and processing knowledge and information, and when using heuristics and intuition, unconscious thinking. They are involved in framing things, thinking about complex matters, challenging the status quo, and coping with uncertainty, emotions, and values in social interactions and when managing cultural aspects. More research that focuses especially on thinking errors among sustainable AI designers is needed.

Arguably, sustainable AI design is not an easy task. Designers must process different types of information and be aware of their own positions and perceptions. They must be able to reason why, what, and how they design when implementing sustainable AI. Designers must be prepared to become aware of and tackle the risk of errors, biases, and fallacies in their own thinking, reasoning, arguments, problem solutions, and decision-making, which can lead to errors and risks. They must be open to new ideas, be mentally flexible, and extend their thinking to consider the direct and indirect impacts of their designs on the environment and people in all phases of the product life cycle. This will, hopefully, lead to ethically, economically, ecologically, and socially better solutions in sustainable AI design.

Acknowledgements. . This work was supported by Etairos & SEED STN-project of the Academy of Finland [decision number 327355].

References

1. Goh, H.-H., Vinuesa, R.: Regulating artificial-intelligence applications to achieve the sustainable development goals. Discov. Sustain. **2**(1), 1–6 (2021). https://doi.org/10.1007/s43621-021-00064-5
2. Nishant, R., Kennedy, M., Corbett, J.: Artificial intelligence for sustainability: challenges, opportunities, and a research agenda. Int. J. Inf. Manage. **53**, 102104 (2020). https://doi.org/10.1016/j.ijinfomgt.2020.102104
3. Dwivedi, Y.K., et al.: Artificial Intelligence (AI): multidisciplinary perspectives on emerging challenges, opportunities, and agenda for research, practice and policy. Int. J. Inf. Manage. **57**, 101994 (2021). https://doi.org/10.1016/j.ijinfomgt.2019.08.002
4. König, A.: Sustainability science as a transformative social learning process. In: König, A., Ravetz, J. (eds.) Sustainability science: key issues, pp. 3–28. Routledge (2018)
5. Laininen, E.: Transforming our worldview towards a sustainable future. In: Cook, J.W. (ed.) Sustainability, Human Well-Being, and the Future of Education, pp. 161–200. Springer, Cham (2019). https://doi.org/10.1007/978-3-319-78580-6_5

442   M. Myllylä

6. Garcia, R., Dacko, S.: Design thinking for sustainability. In: Swan, S., et al. (eds.) Design Thinking: New Product Development Essentials from the PDMA, Wiley. University of Warwick (2015)
7. Hu, M., Shealy, T., Milovanovic, J.: Cognitive differences among first-year and senior engineering students when generating design solutions with and without additional dimensions of sustainability. Des. Sci. 7, E1 (2021). https://doi.org/10.1017/dsj.2021.3
8. Kim, H., Cluzel, F., Leroy, Y., Yannou, B., Yannou-Le Bris, G.: Research perspectives in ecodesign. Des. Sci. 6, E7 (2020). https://doi.org/10.1017/dsj.2020.5
9. Mattson, C., Pack, A., Lofthouse, V., Bhamra, T.: Using a product's sustainability space as a design exploration tool. Des. Sci. 5, E1 (2019). https://doi.org/10.1017/dsj.2018.6
10. Ojala, T., Mettälä, M., Heinonen, M., Oksanen, P. (eds.) Ekologisesti kestävällä digitalisaatiolla ilmasto- ja ympäristötavoitteisiin. ICT-alan ilmasto- ja ympäristöstrategiaa valmistelevan työryhmän loppuraportti. Liikenne- ja viestintäministeriön julkaisuja 2020:19. Liikenne- ja viestintäministeriö (2020). http://urn.fi/URN:ISBN:978-952-243-606-1
11. Wahlström, M.: Koneet, joilla pelastamme planeetan: älyteknologialla ilmastonmuutosta vastaan. Gaudeamus (2021)
12. Hay, L., Cash, P., McKilligan, S.: The future of design cognition analysis. Des. Sci. 6, E20 (2020). https://doi.org/10.1017/dsj.2020.20
13. Lehtonen, A., Salonen, A.O., Cantell, H.: Climate change education: a new approach for a world of wicked problems. In: Cook, J.W. (ed.) Sustainability, Human Well-Being, and the Future of Education, pp. 339–374. Springer, Cham (2019). https://doi.org/10.1007/978-3-319-78580-6_11
14. Wessman, H., Salmi, O., Kohl, J., Kinnunen, P., Saarivuori, E., Mroueh, U.: Water and society: mutual challenges for eco-efficient and socially acceptable mining in Finland. J. Clean. Prod. 84, 289–298 (2014). https://doi.org/10.1016/j.jclepro.2014.04.026
15. Balkenende, A.R., Bakker, C.A.: Developments and challenges in design for sustainability of electronics. In: Curran, R., et al. (ed.) Transdisciplinary Lifecycle Analysis of Systems, pp. 3–13. IOS Press (2015)
16. Cañas, J.J.: The human mind and engineering models. In: Rauterberg, M. (ed.) HCII 2021. LNCS, vol. 12795, pp. 197–208. Springer, Cham (2021). https://doi.org/10.1007/978-3-030-77431-8_12
17. Thagard, P. Findlay, S.: Changing minds about climate change: belief revision, coherence, and emotion. In: Thagard, P. (ed.) The Cognitive Science of Science: Explanation, Discovery, and Conceptual Change, pp. 61–80. MIT Press (2012)
18. Evans, J.S.B.T.: Bias in human reasoning: causes and consequences. (Essays in cognitive psychology). Lawrence Erlbaum Associates Ltd., Publishers (1989)
19. Kahneman, D.: Thinking, Fast and Slow. Penguin Books (2011)
20. Saariluoma, P.: Ajattelu työelämässä. Erehdyksistä mahdollisuuksiin. Werner Södeström Osakeyhtiö (2003)
21. Sonnleitner, P.: Cognitive pitfalls in dealing with sustainability. In: König, A., Ravetz, J. (eds.) Sustainability Science: Key Issues, pp. 82–95. Routledge (2018)
22. Plato: Gorgias [B. Jewett, Trans.]. Virginia Tech. (Original work published 380 BC) (2001)
23. Hansen, H.: Fallacies. In: Zalta, E.N. (ed.) The Stanford Encyclopedia of Philosophy (Summer 2020 Edition) (2020). https://plato.stanford.edu/archives/sum2020/entries/fallacies/
24. Bassok, M., Novick, L.: Problem solving. In: Holyoak, K.J., Morrison, R.G. (eds.) The Oxford Handbook of Thinking and Reasoning. Oxford University Press, Oxford (2012). https://doi.org/10.1093/oxfordhb/9780199734689.013.0021
25. Johnson-Laird, P.N.: Inference with mental models. In: Holyoak, K.J., Morrison, R.G. (eds.) The Oxford Handbook of Thinking and Reasoning. Oxford University Press, Oxford (2012). https://doi.org/10.1093/oxfordhb/9780199734689.013.0009

26. Morrison, R.G.: Thinking in working memory. In: Holyoak, K.J., Morrison, R.G. (eds.) The Cambridge handbook of Thinking and Reasoning, pp. 457–474. Cambridge University Press, Cambridge (2005)
27. Carbon, C.: Psychology of design. Des. Sci. **5**, E26 (2019). https://doi.org/10.1017/dsj.2019.25
28. Myllylä, M.: Embodied mind and mental contents in graffiti art experience. (Publication No. 2922) [Doctoral dissertation, the University of Jyväskylä]. JYX Digital Repository (2022). http://urn.fi/URN:ISBN:978-951-39-8991-0
29. Raami, A.: Towards solving the impossible problems. In: Cook, J.W. (ed.) Sustainability, Human Well-Being, and the Future of Education, pp. 201–233. Springer, Cham (2019). https://doi.org/10.1007/978-3-319-78580-6_6
30. Baars B.J., Gage, N.M.: Cognition, Brain, and Consciousness: Introduction to Cognitive Neuroscience, 2nd (edn.). Elsevier (2010)
31. Ericsson, K.A.: An introduction to the second edition of the Cambridge handbook of expertise and expert performance: its development, organization, and content. In: Ericsson, K.A., Hoffman, R.R., Kozbelt, A., Williams, A.M. (eds.) The Cambridge Handbook of Expertise and Expert Performance, 2nd (edn.), pp. 3–20. Cambridge University Press, Cambridge (2018)
32. Faludi, J., Yiu, F., Agogino, A.: Where do professionals find sustainability and innovation value? empirical tests of three sustainable design methods. Des. Sci. **6**, E22 (2020). https://doi.org/10.1017/dsj.2020.17
33. Clarke, R.I.: Design Thinking. ALA Neal-Schuman (2020)
34. Hay, L., Duffy, A., McTeague, C., Pidgeon, L., Vuletic, T., Grealy, M.: Towards a shared ontology: a generic classification of cognitive processes in conceptual design. Des. Sci. **3**, E7 (2017). https://doi.org/10.1017/dsj.2017.6
35. Sauder, J., Jin, Y.: A qualitative study of collaborative stimulation in group design thinking. Des. Sci. **2**, E4 (2016). https://doi.org/10.1017/dsj.2016.1
36. Smith, S.M., Ward, T.B.: Cognition and the creation of ideas. In: Holyoak, K.J., Morrison, R.G. (eds.) The Cambridge Handbook of Thinking and Reasoning, pp. 456–474. Oxford University Press, Oxford (2012). https://doi.org/10.1093/oxfordhb/9780199734689.013.0023
37. Evans, J.S.B.T.: Dual-process theories of deductive reasoning: facts and fallacies. In: Holyoak, K.J., Morrison, R.G. (eds.) The Cambridge handbook of Thinking and Reasoning, pp. 115–133. Oxford University Press, Oxford (2012). https://doi.org/10.1093/oxfordhb/9780199734689.013.0008
38. Nolte, H., McComb, C.: The cognitive experience of engineering design: an examination of first-year student stress across principal activities of the engineering design process. Des. Sci. **7**, E3 (2021). https://doi.org/10.1017/dsj.2020.32
39. Dutilh, N.C.: Argument and argumentation. In: Zalta, E.N. (ed.) The Stanford Encyclopedia of Philosophy (Fall 2021 Edition) (2021). https://plato.stanford.edu/archives/fall2021/entries/argument/
40. Aristotle: Prior analytics. (A. J. Jenkinson, Trans.). Infomotions, Inc. (Original work published 350 BC) (2000)
41. Hayes, B.K., Heit, E., Swendsen, H. Inductive reasoning. WIREs Cogn. Sci. **1**(March/April), 278–292 (2010). https://doi.org/10.1002/wcs.44
42. Lombrozo, T.: Explanation and abductive inference. In: Holyoak, K.J., Morrison, R.G. (eds.) The Cambridge Handbook of Thinking and Reasoning, pp. 260–276. Oxford University Press (2012). https://doi.org/10.1093/oxfordhb/9780199734689.013.0014
43. Holyoak, K.J.: Analogy and relational reasoning. In: Holyoak, K.J., Morrison, R.G. (eds.) The Cambridge handbook of Thinking and Reasoning, pp. 234–260. Oxford University Press (2012). https://doi.org/10.1093/oxfordhb/9780199734689.013.0013
44. Bar, M.: The proactive brain: using analogies and associations to generate predictions. Trends Cogn. Sci. **11**(7), 280–289 (2007)

45. Hofstadter, D.R.: Analogy as the core of cognition. In: Gentner, D., Holyoak, K.J., Koki-nov, B.N. (eds.) The Analogical Mind: Perspectives from Cognitive Science, pp. 499–538. Massachusetts Institute of Technology (2001)
46. Thagard, P., Shelley, C.: Emotional analogies and analogical inference. In: Gentner, D., Holyoak, K.J., Kokinov, B.N. (eds.) The Analogical Mind: Perspectives from Cognitive Science, pp. 335–362. Massachusetts Institute of Technology (2001)
47. Molden, D.C. Higgins, E.T.: Motivated thinking. In: Holyoak, K.J., Morrison, R.G. (eds.) The Cambridge handbook of Thinking and Reasoning, pp. 390–410. Oxford University Press (2012). https://doi.org/10.1093/oxfordhb/9780199734689.013.0020
48. Jansson, D.G., Smith, S.M.: Design fixation. Des. Stud. **12**(1), 3–11 (1991)
49. Linsey, J.S., Tseng, I., Fu, K., Cagan, J., Wood, K.L., Schunn, C.: A study of design fixation, its mitigation and perception in engineering design faculty. J. Mech. Des. **132**, 041003-1–041003-12 (2010)
50. Masson-Delmotte, V., et al. (eds.): IPCC: climate change 2021: the physical science basis. Contribution of Working Group I to the Sixth Assessment Report of the Intergovernmental Panel on Climate Change. Cambridge University Press (2021). (in Press)
51. Narvaez, D.: Moral development and moral values. Evolutionary and neurobiological influences. In: McAdams, D.P., Shiner, R.L., Tackett, J.L. (eds.) Handbook of Personality Development, pp. 345–363. Guilford Press (2019)
52. Leal Filho, W., et al.: Heading towards an unsustainable world: some of the implications of not achieving the SDGs. Discov. Sustain. **1**(1), 1–11 (2020). https://doi.org/10.1007/s43621-020-00002-x
53. Samuelson, W., Zeckhauser, R.: Status quo bias in decision making. J. Risk Uncertain. **1**, 7–59 (1988)
54. Youmans, R., Arciszewski, T.: Design fixation: Classifications and modern methods of prevention. Artif. Intell. Eng. Des. Anal. Manuf. **28**(2), 129–137 (2014). https://doi.org/10.1017/S0890060414000043
55. Li, D., Du, Y.: Artificial intelligence with uncertainty, 2nd (ed.). CRC Press (2017). https://doi.org/10.1201/9781315366951
56. Mulligan, K.: Emotions and values. In: Goldie, P. (ed.) The Oxford Handbook of Philosophy of Emotion, pp. 475–500. Oxford University Press (2009). https://doi.org/10.1093/oxfordhb/9780199235018.003.0022
57. Chang-Arana, Á., et al.: Empathic accuracy in design: exploring design outcomes through empathic performance and physiology. Des. Sci. **6**, E16 (2020). https://doi.org/10.1017/dsj.2020.14
58. Marquardt, J. Nasiritousi, N.: Imaginary lock-ins in climate change politics: the challenge to envision a fossil-free future. Environ. Polit. (2021). https://doi.org/10.1080/09644016.2021.1951479
59. Gherheş, V., Obrad, C.: Technical and humanities students' perspectives on the development and sustainability of Artificial Intelligence (AI). Sustain. **10**(9), 3066 (2018). https://doi.org/10.3390/su10093066

About Non-living Things and Living Systems as Cultural Determinants

Matthias Rauterberg[(⊠)] [iD]

Eindhoven University of Technology, Eindhoven, The Netherlands
g.w.m.rauterberg@tue.nl

Abstract. For the future development of cultural technology, access to the cultural foundations of these culture carriers is necessary. One relevant aspect of this cultural foundation is the distinction between non-living things and living systems. Culture can be preserved, transported, and adapted by non-living things and living systems. Cultural development is only possible through living systems (e.g., humans). Non-living things (e.g., books, fossils, paintings, sculptures) are for preserving, archiving, and displaying the past. First, I present and discuss the theoretical and practical implications of the mechanistic worldview. Second, I give an overview of the ways to define non-living things and life forms. Third, I argue that our mechanistic worldview and the way we grasp the truth is limited by our way of thinking to deal with non-living things only. To resolve the main challenges, we must change our thinking and our acting in the world. Finally, I provide two primary sources of inspiration for this new way of thinking: the Asian way and the way of Indigenous people.

Keywords: Context · Culture · Development · Environment · Indigenous knowledge · Life · Mechanistic world view · Non-living things · Ontology · Sustainability · Traditional ecological knowledge · Transformative power

1 Prolog

Now, close to the end of my academic life, I started to reflect on how I was trained in scientific research and design. Several books and discussions with colleagues helped me to sort out some relevant aspects. In this paper, I will address how we as Western academics think and act, in contrast to how we *should* think and act. Our cultural embedding enables us to achieve astonishing things but also constrains us from seeing and thinking beyond. The following books (among many others) helped me better understand why we as humanity run into problems like climate crisis, pandemics, etc.: "The mechanization of the world picture" from Dijksterhuis [1], "Steps to an ecology of mind" from Bateson [2], and "The science delusion" from Sheldrake [3]. In particular, Sheldrake is a very courageous colleague, traveling along the edges of our worldview to make us aware of our limits. In a nutshell, I am trained to think and rationalize in a mechanistic manner (in particular the 'mechanization of qualities' [1, p. 431f]), although this way of reasoning is probably only applicable for non-living things consisting of 'dead' matter. This way of reasoning is what I mean when saying: "Quality and quantity are different qualities." So, how can we overcome this to be fair and correct in addressing living systems adequately to harmonize with nature? (see [4]).

2   Introduction

We can distinguish our environment in many ways; however, the following distinction appears to be fundamental: (1) non-living things (NLT) versus (2) living systems (LS). The prime discipline to investigate this distinction is biology [5]. We had different worldviews over the last centuries (see Table 1). Our most recent one is the materialistic one which treats nature as a complex 'machine'; Freudenthal [6] carefully worked out how the mechanistic world view has emerged over the last centuries.

Table 1. Worldviews over the last centuries; time goes from top to bottom (from [3, p. 39]).

Worldview	God	Nature
Traditional christian	Interactive	Living organism
Early mechanistic	Interactive	Machine
Enlightenment deism	Creator only	Machine
Romantic deism	Creator only	Living organism
Romantic atheism	No god	Living organism
Materialism	No god	Machine

Today academia (but not only academia) is operating mainly under the worldview of *materialism* where we don't need a God anymore [7] and can think of "nature as a complex machinery" [8]. Sheldrake [3] argues to strive for an *organic* worldview to capture and nurture nature as a living organism. Why is this relevant or even important to overcome materialism? As Merchant [9, p. xvii] describes it: "The machine image that has dominated Western culture for the past three hundred years seems to be giving way to something new. Some call the transformation a 'new paradigm'; others call it 'deep ecology'; still others call for a postmodern ecological world view." It seems to be obvious that the way we think and act today (at least in Western cultures) has lead us into severe problems (e.g., climate crisis [10] and many others). Most people see the solution to such problems in *more* science and technology. But listing to the warning of Einstein, "we cannot solve our problems with the same thinking we used when we created them," let me doubt that this is the right way. Taking Einstein's warning seriously, we must change our way of thinking and acting. How should we do this cultural transformation?

First, I will explain what the mechanistic worldview is all about. Second, I will elaborate on what we know already about life in contrast to 'dead' machines. Finally, I will sketch how we should think and act.

3   The Mechanistic Worldview

By far, the most important single factor in world history has been the process of a technological revolution whereby small-scale agricultural societies have been transformed into massive industrialized and urbanized communities. This development has occurred over a long period of time, but its most significant thrust has been concentrated over the last two centuries, beginning in the West, in Europe, and North America, and then spreading through the rest of the world. Buchanan [11] systematically analyzed this process, showing how increasing mastery over sources of power provided increased industrial and agricultural productivity, and created radically new methods of transport and communication. He then examines the impact of these technical achievements on society, paying particular attention to the political and ecological consequences of a vastly increased world population, the facilities for rapid transport and instantaneous communication, and the possession of weapons of immense destructive force.

Hornborg [12, p. 2] argues that three possible meanings of 'machine power' exist and can be distinguished as follows: (1) power to conduct work (i.e., automation), (2) power over other people (i.e., weapons), and (3) power over our minds. These three meanings are aspects of a single cultural phenomenon and historical development [13]. Today, the third meaning can be described as the 'mechanization of our mind' and summarized as the *mechanistic worldview* (MWV). MWV is dominant today, not only in academia [14] but also in public and political debates [13]. Hence it is essential to understand its nature and characteristics. According to Merchant [9, p. 228], "the following assumptions about the structure of being, knowledge, and method make possible the human manipulation and control of nature:

1. Matter is composed of particles (the ontological assumption).
2. The universe is a natural order (the principle of identity).
3. Knowledge and information can be abstracted from the natural world (the assumption of context independence).
4. Problems can be analyzed into parts that can be manipulated by mathematics (the methodological assumption).
5. Sense data are discrete (the epistemological assumption)."

Based on these five assumptions about the nature of reality, science has been widely considered to provide objective, value-free, and context-free knowledge of the external world. Following Sheldrake [3, pp. 7–8], "here are the ten core beliefs that most scientists take for granted:

1. *Everything is essentially mechanical*[1]. Dogs, for example, are complex mechanisms rather than living organisms with goals of their own. Even people are machines, 'lumbering robots,' in Richard Dawkins's vivid phrase, with brains that are like genetically programmed computers.
2. *All matter is unconscious.* It has no inner life or subjectivity, or point of view. Even human consciousness is an illusion produced by the material activities of brains.

---

[1] *Italic* formatting added by author.

3. *The total amount of matter and energy is always the same* (with the exception of the Big Bang, when all the matter and energy of the universe suddenly appeared).
4. *The laws of nature are fixed.* They are the same today as they were at the beginning, and they will stay the same forever.
5. *Nature is purposeless*, and evolution has no goal or direction.
6. *All biological inheritance is material*, carried in the genetic material, DNA, and in other material structures.
7. *Minds are inside heads* and are nothing but the activities of brains. When you look at a tree, the image of the tree you are seeing is not 'out there,' where it seems to be, but inside your brain.
8. *Memories are stored as material traces in brains* and are wiped out at death.
9. *Unexplained phenomena like telepathy are illusory.*
10. *Mechanistic medicine is the only kind that really works."*

In this paper, I will concentrate on points (1), (2), and (6). Like Sheldrake, is Radin convinced that there is more 'out there' than what he calls the "materialistic monism." Radin's quest to search for limitations and anomalies in our state of the art knowledge describes eight scientific doctrines that constrain our way of thinking as follows [15, chap. 16]:

1. "1. **Realism**[2]: The physical world consists of objects that are completely independent of observation. This means, with a little exaggeration for the sake of illustration, that the moon is still there when you're not looking at it. …
2. **Localism**: Objects are completely separate. There is no such thing as 'action at a distance.' …
3. **Causality**: The arrow of time points exclusively from past to future, with no exceptions. …
4. **Mechanism**: Everything can be understood in the form of causal networks, like the gears of a clock that operate in a strictly local, causal fashion. …
5. **Physicalism**: Everything can be described with real properties that exist in space and time, and all meaningful statements are either analytically provable, as in logic and mathematics or can be reduced to experimentally verifiable facts. …
6. **Materialism**: Everything, including the mind, is made of matter or energy; anything else thought to be "immaterial" doesn't exist. …
7. **Determinism**: There is no free will, and all events are fully caused by preceding states. …
8. **Reductionism**: Objects are made up of a hierarchy of ever-smaller objects, with subatomic particles at the bottom. All causation is strictly 'upward,' from the microscopic to the macroscopic world. …"

Radin consequently provides very strong arguments against each of those doctrines (i.e., the consequences of quantum physics regarding space-time, locality, etc. [16]) to create space for scientific investigations beyond the materialistic monism into the realm of supernormality [15]. "That is, we know that every single one of the eightfold doctrines

---

[2] **Bold** formatting added by author.

has been falsified by advancements in physics. For example, the doctrine of *realism*[3] is falsified by quantum mechanics. That is, we know through theory and experiments that quantum objects do not have fully determined properties before they are observed. *Causality* is falsified by general relativity, where a fixed arrow of time is known to be an illusion. *Locality* is falsified by quantum mechanics, in which quantum-entangled objects display 'spooky action' at a distance and display instant correlations that are not located 'inside' ordinary space-time. *Physicalism*, like realism, is falsified by quantum mechanics, partially because quantum events are not fully localized with real properties until they are observed, but more speculatively because of the possibility that 'observation' may require consciousness, which in turn may or may not be a purely physical phenomenon. Experiments on mind-matter interaction, as discussed in earlier chapters, support this speculation. *Materialism*, at least a simple physicalist form of materialism, looks like it may be headed for falsification if it turns out that psi phenomena cannot be accommodated by any known form of matter or energy. This is by no means certain yet, but the possibility remains. It may also fail because of quantum-inspired theories proposing that the physical world is better described in terms of mindlike *information* instead of material 'stuff'. … Finally, *determinism* fails because of the collapse of causality, and *reductionism* breaks down because mind-body effects demonstrate 'downward' causation from mind to body, and because psychokinesis demonstrates a more far-reaching form of downward causation, directly from mind to matter." [15, chap. 16].

In physics,[4] all irreversible processes based on energy transformation will - in the long term - end in a state of minimal order, called 'heat death' [17, 18]. So, how is it then possible that we experience an ordered nature? In the context of the second law of thermodynamics, it is difficult to explain any process contributing to enhancing order [19, p. 653ff]. We can consider *culture* as an ordering process, but then we have to explain how this is possible. In my paper [20], I introduced an attempt to overcome and combine these contrary views. Based on the theoretical concept of Swenson's *autocatakinesis* I explore the possibilities of developing cultural technology beneficial to society. Autocatakinetic systems [21] attempt to characterize self-organizing systems at the level of macroscopic thermodynamic forces and flows.

Following Swenson, we can envision how to overcome materialistic monism [22, pp. 1f]. "Ecological science addresses the relations between living things and their environments, and the study of human ecology is the particular case of humans. However, there is an opposing tradition built into the foundations of modern science which *separates* living things and particularly humans, from their environments. Beginning in modern times with Descartes' radical separation of psychology and physics (or 'mind' from 'matter'), this dualistic tradition was extended into biology with Kant's biology versus physics (or living thing versus environment) dualism, and into evolutionary theory with the rise of Darwinism and its grounding in Boltzmannian thermodynamics. If ecological science is to be about what it purports to be about, about living thing-environment relations, it must provide a principled basis for dissolving Cartesian incommensurability. A deeper understanding of thermodynamic law and the principles of self-organizing ('autocatakinetic') systems provides the nomological basis for doing just this, for putting

---

[3] *Italic* formatting added by author.
[4] See the Second Law of Thermodynamics.

evolution back in its universal context, and showing the reciprocal relation between living things and their environments, thereby providing a principled foundation for ecological science in general and human ecology in particular."

Modern science and technology are incredibly successful [11], among others based on the MWV [23]. I do not deny this success, but the price we all have to pay is that we have severe difficulties handling adequately dynamic, non-linear systems [24] and, in particular, living systems in relation to their environment [25]. Any living system can only be understood together with its specific niche, habitat, and ecotope [26]. Humanity is obliged to overcome this dangerous and unsustainable situation. But how can we achieve this?

Twenty-three hundred years ago, Aristotle wrote in his Nicomachean Ethics that there are five different ways to grasp the truth as they are [27, p. 105f]: (1) Science ('episteme'), (2) art or producing ('techne'), (3) practical wisdom ('phronesis'), (4) theoretical wisdom ('sophia'), and (5) intuition or the capacity to grasp first principles or sources ('nous'). Only one of them is science (episteme), and this science is limited to things that cannot be otherwise than they are. The other four ways and capacities of grasping the truth apply to all the different contexts of reality and life. Now we need to broaden our view of science to include the other capacities [28].

4   From Non-living Things to Living Systems

Before discussing what we know about life and living systems, I have to talk about non-living things (NLT). This distinction between NLTs and living systems (LS) is so crucial that it is sometimes already part of the kindergarten curriculum [29] and primary school [30]. Obviously, almost everyone agrees that a stone is not a living thing, and any chemical element [31] is a 'dead' matter. NLT's are inanimate objects or forces that can influence, shape, alter a habitat, etc. Examples of NLT's include climate, rocks, water, weather, and natural events such as earthquakes or rockfalls. In biology, an NLT means any form of a thing that does not possess life. NLT's do not have cells and show no growth or movement. NLT's are lifeless and do not possess any life span. NLT's do not respire or require food for energy ('input') and hence do not excrete ('output'). Many distinct features make an NLT different from a living thing [32]. NLT's do not fall into the cycle of birth, growth, and death [33]. Non-living things are different in a way such as the fundamental unit of life is a living cell that grows, metabolizes, responds to external stimuli, adapts, and reproduces. Only a living thing has a live cell; an NLT doesn't. An NLT, on the other hand, is made up of elements or compounds formed out of chemical reactions. NLT's can be divided into two categories, and they are (1) natural NLTs (i.e., nature) and (2) man-made NLTs (i.e., artifacts). All things from both categories can be archived and/or displayed to the public in archives, libraries, and museums to calibrate culture through narrating history [34]. Most important characteristics of NLTs are listed below (taken from [35] and sorted alphabetically):

- Non-living things do not respond to the environment.
- Non-living things don't have protoplasm; thus, no life.
- There are no processes of reproduction, nutrition, excretion in them.

- These things are not sensitive.
- These things cannot die.
- These things do not obtain or use energy.
- They are lifeless and do not have cells.
- They cannot grow and develop.
- They do not adapt to their environment.
- They do not breathe.
- They do not possess any metabolic activities.
- They do not respond to stimuli.
- They don't move.
- They have no lifespan.

It seems to be challenging to define NLTs without referring to LSs. It is also unclear whether all these attributes have to be met or just a couple of them (see also [32]). E.g., a computer can be seen as an NLT but still needs electrical energy to operate and can be responsive to stimuli. Robots are also NLTs, but some of them can move (see, e.g. [36]). Most daily-life consumer products are NLTs, but they have a 'lifespan' (i.e., 'expiry date').

Schrödinger tried to clarify the relations between physics/chemistry on one side and biology on the other by asking the question [37, p. 3f]: "How can the events in space and time which take place within the spatial boundary of a *living organism* be accounted for by physics and chemistry? The preliminary answer ... can be summarized as follows: The obvious inability of present-day physics and chemistry to account for such events is no reason at all for doubting that they can be accounted for by those sciences." Schrödinger elaborates in his book [37] how biological systems (i.e., living organisms) must rely on the physical and chemical laws. For example, he proposed that the exchange of energy and matter with the environment could reduce thermodynamic entropy by living systems and the local accumulation of Gibbs free energy [38].

The main challenge is to explain how from 'dead' matter (i.e., NLT), something emerges that we experience as a life form (i.e., LS). How is it possible that complex organic molecules arise in non-living environments? Let us assume that an adequate prebiotic soup or paste was available on earth a very long time ago. How did the transition from chemical chaos to biological order come about? So far, we assume "that complex organic compounds - including amino acids, the primary constituents of proteins and an essential component of living systems - could have been produced from inorganic chemicals and lightning energy in the primitive environment of the earth" [39, p. 390]. Then, Darwinian selection must have emerged early as a source of complexity, but what was the first system to appear on the primitive earth capable of Darwinian selection? Was it a ribonucleic acid (RNA), some simpler covalent polymer of perhaps some non-covalent aggregate? Are there complex evolvable metabolisms that do not depend on a genetic material? We will not find definitive answers to these crucial questions in any book on the 'Origin of Life' [40, 41]; we don't even know how far away we are to unravel this mystery and whether our way of academic thinking is appropriate.

According to Phelan, life originated on earth probably in several distinct phases [39, p. 388ff]: (1) Phase 1: The formation of small molecules containing carbon and hydrogen; (2) phase 2: the formation of self-replicating, information-containing molecules; and (3) phase 3: the development of a membrane, enabling metabolism and creating the first cells. Phelan gives a basic definition of what he means by "life." *Life* is defined by the ability (1) to *replicate* and (2) by the presence of some sort of *metabolic activity*[5]. Remarkable is that this definition of life is grounded in the biological substrate, i.e., molecules. This view is incompatible with all approaches to creating 'artificial life' [42], where the authors are using the term 'life' very likely in a metaphorical sense [43].

What are the criteria for any LS, so we can call them alive? Most modern definitions avoid the noun 'life' and instead use the adjective 'living,' meaning that life is more of a *transient state* affecting some matter [44]. An LS is said to be transient or in a transient state when a process variable or parameter has been changed, and the LS has not yet reached a *steady state*. An LS or its process is in a steady state if the parameters called state parameters, which define the system's behavior, or the process are unchanging in time. Homeostasis is the property of an LS that regulates its internal environment and tends to maintain a stable, constant condition. The concept came from that of *milieu interieur* that was defined by Bernard [45]. Multiple dynamic equilibrium adjustment and regulation mechanisms make *homeostasis* possible. "However, the controversies surrounding the definition of life are probably just symptoms of a deeper problem, and unfortunately, these have led to the larger issue of the classical divide on the approaches to the origin of life. Each definition of life has put its emphasis on a trait(s) expressed by living entities, such as their replicative capabilities, their far-from-equilibrium state, their compartmentalization, or their evolutionary potential" [44, p. 3 of 53].

Most biologists agree that the basic unit of any LS is the cell, the smallest unit of life that can function independently and perform all the necessary functions of life, including reproducing itself. "The facts that (1) all living organisms are made up of one or more cells and (2) all cells arise from other, preexisting cells are the foundations of *cell theory*, one of the unifying theories in biology, and one that is universally accepted by all biologists" [39, p. 84]. Cells are the building blocks of any LS. "All organisms, from ants to plants to people, are composed of cells—the structural and functional units of life. The phenomenon we call life emerges at the level of a cell: A cell can regulate its internal environment, take in and use energy, and respond to its environment. The ability of cells to give rise to new cells is the basis for all reproduction and the growth and repair of multicellular organisms. A cell may be part of a complex plant or animal or an organism in its own right. Indeed, single-celled bacteria and other unicellular organisms far outnumber multicellular organisms on Earth" [5, p. 44]. We cannot separate any life form from its biological substrate – the wetware [46]. We cannot create life directly, but we can modulate already existing life forms (e.g., breeding).

5   How We Should Think and Act

Before I can discuss our way of thinking in more detail, I have to clarify the metaphysical foundation of such a discussion [47]. Any ontology is embedded in the actual world view of a particular community. But what is an ontology? Following Guarino, Oberle, and Staab [48], the word *ontology* is used with a different meaning in different contexts.

---

[5] Metabolic activity is the sum of all chemical processes by which molecules are acquired and used and energy is transformed in controlled reactions.

Perhaps the most radical difference is between the philosophical meaning, which has a well-established tradition, and the computational meaning, which emerged in recent years in the knowledge engineering domain, starting from an early informal definition of computational ontologies as explicit specifications of conceptualizations. However, in the context of this paper, I will refer to a philosophical discipline, namely the branch of philosophy that deals with the nature and structure of *reality* [49]. Unfortunately, philosophers sometimes treat *metaphysics* and *ontology* as synonyms. Already Aristotle dealt with this subject in his Metaphysics and defined *ontology* as the science of *being qua being*, i.e., the study of attributes that belong to things because of their very nature [50, p. 68]. In other words, metaphysics addresses the foundation of our world view.

As Levinas puts it [51, p. 122]: "From now on, the comprehension of being does not presuppose a merely theoretical attitude, but the whole of human comportment. The whole of humanity is ontology. An individual's scientific work, his or her affective life, the satisfaction of his or her needs and labour, his or her social life and death - all these moments articulate, with a rigour which reserves to each a determinate function, the comprehension of being or truth. Our entire civilization follows from this comprehension, be it only in forgetfulness of being. It is not because there is humanity that there is truth. It is because there is truth, because being is found to be inseparable from its appearing [aperite], or if one likes, because being is intelligible, that there is humanity".

Before I discuss 'how we should think,' I will describe 'how we think' according to state of the art in cognitive science. Holyoak and Morrison define *thinking* as follows [52, p. 1]: "Thinking is the systematic transformation of mental representations of knowledge to characterize actual or possible states of the world, often in service of goals."

For our reasoning capacity, we can use *deduction, induction*, and *abduction* (see part 2 in [53]). Deductive reasoning is an inference rule in which the conclusion is of greater generality than the premises. Inductive reasoning is an inference rule that we infer from particular cases to the general case. Abduction is an inference rule, requiring premises encompassing explanatory considerations and yielding a conclusion that makes some statement about the truth of a hypothesis (see also the distinction in abduction-1 and -2 [54]). Of course, we have different modes of thinking [53]: (1) reasoning, (2) quantitative thinking, (3) visuospatial thinking, (4) gesture in thought, (5) musical thought, and probably many more [55]. In general, we can distinguish between implicit and explicit modes of thinking [56]. While mainstream psychology and economics focused a long time on the concept of 'full rationality' [57], Neisser already tried to overcome this bias by concentrating in his research on ecological valid real-world behavior [58].

Today Griffin et al. discuss the limitations of *full* rationality for humans: "Herbert Simon [59], early in his Nobel Prize-winning research on economic models, argued that 'full' rationality was an unrealistic assumption because of processing limitations in living systems (and, incidentally, in virtually all computers currently available). He proposed a limited form of rationality, termed 'bounded rationality,' that accepted the limited search and computational ability of human brains but nonetheless assumed that after a truncated search and after considering a limited subset of alternatives, people did act and reason rationally, at least in terms of achieving their goals" [60, p. 324]. Bounded rationality revises perfect or full rationality notions to account for the fact that perfectly rational decisions are often not feasible in practice because of the intractability of natural decision problems and the finite computational resources available for making them. Elster argued "that failure to recognize the indeterminacy of rational-choice theory can lead to irrational behaviour" [61, p. 2]. The concept of bounded rationality significantly influenced different disciplines, i.e., cognitive science, economics, law, political science, and psychology [62]. However, while in daily life this is reasonable, academia as such still operates under the assumption of unbounded rationality! [63].

"[T]he picture of non-scientists drawn by scientists be-comes bleak: a few minds discover what reality is, while the vast majority of people have irrational ideas or at least are prisoners of many social, cultural and psychological factors that make them stick obstinately to obsolete prejudices. The only redeeming aspect of this picture is that if it were only possible to eliminate all these factors that hold people, prisoners of their prejudices, they would all, immediately and at no cost, become as sound-minded as the scientists, grasping the phenomena without further ado. In every one of us, there is a scientist who is asleep, and who will not wake up until social and cultural conditions are pushed aside" [64, pp. 184–185].

From around 1960 to 2000, the psychology of reasoning was – according to Evans [65] – strongly focused on the *deduction* paradigm, in which test subjects are assessed for their ability to judge the logical validity of arguments without any prior training or instruction. However, since the 1980s, experimental evidence has accumulated indicating that ordinary people were poor at logical reasoning because of being strongly influenced by irrelevant features of the content and subject to several other cognitive biases. As a result, the deduction paradigm has shifted in the past 20–25 years; there is also a lot more interest in human reasoning as a probabilistic and pragmatic rather than deductive process (see [62]).

Table 2. Dual-process theories of reasoning and higher cognition (from [65, p. 116]).

Type-1 processes	Type-2 processes
Unconscious, preconscious	Conscious
Rapid	Slow
Automatic	Controlled
Low effort	High effort
High capacity	Low capacity
Associative	Rule-based
Intuitive	Deliberative
Contextualized	Abstract
Cognitive biases	Normative reasoning
Independent of cognitive capacity (IQ, WMC)[a]	Correlated with individual differences in cognitive capacity
System-1	System-2

[a]IQ = intelligence quotient; WMC = working memory capacity.

Dual-Process Theories (DPT) are the focus of much research in cognitive and social psychology and have several independent origins. The main characteristics are summarized in Table 2. I already discussed the relationship between system-1 and -2 regarding time travel in [66]. Evans [65] has shown how dual-process accounts were developed from the 1970s onward within the study of deductive reasoning, primarily as an attempt to explain why cognitive biases coexisted and competed with attempts at effortful logical reasoning on these tasks. More recently, reasoning researchers have examined individual differences in cognitive capacity linked with type-2 *analytic* reasoning. They have also introduced a range of experimental and neuroscientific methods to identify dual processes. However, Evans has also shown how several fallacies have arisen in the received view of DPT, both within the psychology of reasoning and more generally.

Evans has identified five fallacies associated with DPT of *thinking* and *reasoning* [65, p. 117]: (1) All dual-process theories are essentially the same; (2) there are just two systems underlying type-1 and -2 processing; (3) type-1 processes are responsible for cognitive biases; type-2 processes for normatively correct responding; (4) type-1 processing is contextualized, whereas type-2 processing is abstract; and (5) fast processing indicates the use of a type-1 rather than type-2 process. All those five assumptions seem to be wrong. The next generation of DPTs provides a comprehensive overview of the new directions in which dual-process research is heading [67]. Human thinking is often characterized as an interplay between intuition and deliberation. This two-headed, dual-process view of human thinking has been very influential in the cognitive sciences and popular media. However, despite the popularity of DPTs, they face multiple challenges [65]. Recent advances indicate a strong need to re-think some of the fundamental assumptions of the original dual process model [68]. One challenge is to answer why and for what *emotions* are essential.

As I wrote already [69], if we assume *emotions* are perceived as essential aspects in relation with other cognitive functions, then we could go so far as to conceptualize emotions as the appearance of these implicit cognitive processes to our explicit conscious. This process is an internal perception loop about our own mental and bodily states (see Fig. 2 in [70]). Suppose we assume further that the information processing capacity of the unconscious (i.e., system-1) is several magnitudes higher than the conscious (i.e., system-2), and both systems are somehow separate. In that case, we have to answer how these two systems 'communicate.' My idea is that *emotions* can play this role as the 'voice of the unconscious' in telling the conscious the solutions found in a high-dimensional space. These emotions are not only to inform the conscious but also to the social context around us. Our body language is also part of the emotional expression space for adjusting social relations in a specific context [71].

So far, I have discussed that our cognitive architecture exists at least out of two different systems, which can be described with two different types of thinking processes. I have also argued that both systems can communicate via emotions. We know that rational thinking is limited and must be extended [72]. But where can we learn from to enhance our new way of thinking? First, I will introduce cultural differences between the West and East, and then I will discuss what we can learn from indigenous cultures.

There is a fundamentally different way of thinking between western and eastern cultures. Westerners and East Asians perceive the world and act in it in very different ways [73, 74]. *Westerners* pay primary attention to some focal object, analyzing its attributes and categorizing it to determine its behavior. The way to determine is mainly based on formal logic. Causal attributions are prime and tend to focus exclusively on the object; therefore, they are often mistaken. On the other side, *East Asians* pay immediate attention to a broad perceptual and conceptual field, noticing relationships and changes and grouping objects based on familiarities rather than categories. East Asians relate causal attributions to the context/environment instead of objects. Mainly social factors are directing the East Asians' attention because they live in complex social networks with determined role relations. Attention to the context is more important than to objects for effective functioning [75].

In contrast, Westerners live independently in less constraining social worlds and attend to the object and their goals with respect to it. Physical 'affordances' of the environment can also influence perception but is assumed less critical. For example, the built environments of the West are less complex and contain fewer objects than do those of the East. In addition, artistic products of the East emphasize the field and deemphasize objects. In contrast, Western art renders less of the field and highlights individual objects and people (see at [74, p. 11163]).

The western way of thinking – the MWV – underestimates the influential power of the context, environment resp., and focuses too much on the objects and their relationships with each other. While we know already that we can only understand an LS together with its ecotrope, we must enhance our Western way of thinking towards the Eastern way. Additionally, another invaluable source to consider for our future way of thinking is knowledge from indigenous cultures [76].

Nelson "believes we are at a crossroads in time. Within one instant, monumental changes can be made. Since the world is now globally connected, there is no excuse anymore. We are very aware of the fragility of the disbalance between humans and nature, and now is the time to act. Let us learn from the wisdom and way of life of indigenous peoples. They are rich because they feel. They are wise because they let nature be their guide. They are loving because they take care of each other. They are enlightened because they live life to the fullest. Let us be inspired and let them lead us into the future. We need it for the survival of humanity" [77, p. 8].

Traditional Ecological Knowledge (TEK) has emerged growing recognition that indigenous people worldwide developed sustainable *Indigenous Knowledge* (IK) that can be used to address problems we are facing on a global scale. Suzuki wrote, "my experiences with aboriginal peoples convinced me… of the power and relevance of their knowledge and world view in a time of imminent global eco-catastrophe" [78, p. xliv]. Following Mistry, it is helpful to have five commonly accepted characteristics of IK [79, pp. 371f]:

1. *Local* – IK is context-specific in that it has roots in a particular place and in the experiences of the people that live in that location. Transferring that knowledge to another location quite literally makes it meaningless.
2. *Oral transmission* or through imitation and demonstration – whether it be through stories, myths, songs, or through accompanying other people and observing and learning, IK is rarely written down. Yet, writing it down can change some of the fundamental properties of knowledge.

3. *Adaptive capacity* – over time and through everyday life experiences, IK is adapted through repetition, learning, experimentation, and the adoption of novel solutions. It is therefore not static but constantly changing.
4. *Social memory* – IK is shared to a much greater extent than other forms of knowledge. This shared understanding and knowledge are vital as it helps to establish a long-term communal understanding of people's environment and the transmission of pertinent experience. However, the distribution of this knowledge can still be socially differentiated, for example, by age and gender, and preserved in the memories of particular individuals by virtue of their spiritual or political status.
5. *Holistic* – IK is situated within numerous interlinked facets of people's lives. Therefore, it is difficult and impractical to separate, for example, the cultural from the ecological or the rational from the non-rational.

Shilling summarizes some crucial characteristics from North America's IK as follows: (1) *Reciprocity and respect* define the bond between all members of the land family. (2) *Reverence toward nature* plays a critical role in religious ceremonies, hunting rituals, arts and crafts, agricultural techniques, and other day-to-day activities. (3) One's *relationship to the land* is shaped by something other than economic profit. (4) To speak of an individual *owning land is anathema*, not unlike owning another person, akin to slavery. (5) Each generation is *responsible for leaving a healthy world* to future generations [80, p. 12].

How do IK and TEK relate to each other? Johnson describes TEK as "a body of knowledge built up by a group of people through generations of living in close contact with nature. It includes a system of classification, a set of empirical observations about the local environment, and a system of self-management that governs resource use. The quantity and quality of traditional environmental knowledge vary among community members, depending upon gender, age, social status, intellectual capability, and profession (hunter, spiritual leader, healer, etc.). With its roots firmly in the past, traditional environmental knowledge is both cumulative and dynamic, building upon the experience of earlier generations and adapting to the new technological and socioeconomic changes of the present" [81, p. 4].

However, according to McGregor, "there is a major dichotomy in the realm of TEK that needs to be understood: (1) there is the Aboriginal view of TEK, which reflects an Indigenous understanding of relationships to Creation[6], and (2) there is the dominant Eurocentric view of TEK, which reflects colonial attitudes toward Aboriginal people and their knowledge" [82, p. 386]. Because each local IK base contains this particular culture's whole ontology and epistemology, we can conclude that TEK is a derivative of IK. TEK can be regarded as a subset of all available IKs.

As McGregor puts it: "TEK is *not merely* descriptive knowledge about the natural environment, knowledge gained by experience in a place, but also prescriptive – that is, it provides an account of how people *ought* to act in relationship to nature. TEK is then a blend of science, spirituality, and ethics. In this way (and in many others),

---

[6] Many indigenous religions regard *creation* as an on-going process in which they are morally and religiously obligated to participate [see: Lyng v. Northwest Cemetery Ass'n, 485 U.S. 439, 460 (1988), Brennan, J. dissenting].

it differs from traditional Western scientific accounts of nature that merely describe nature (Mendelian genetics, for example) but says nothing about how we morally ought to treat nature" [83, pp. 109f]. What TEK in the context of IK characterizes is the normative aspect; while scientific knowledge framed by MWV avoids being normative, TEK cannot be understood without nature-oriented values. Fortunately, this normative approach is already reflected in the United Nations resolution from 2015 [84]. The seventeen 'Sustainable Development Goals' are specified as follows:

"Goal 1. End poverty in all its forms everywhere.
Goal 2. End hunger, achieve food security and improve nutrition and promote sustainable agriculture.
Goal 3. Ensure healthy lives and promote well-being for all at all ages.
Goal 4. Ensure inclusive and equitable quality education and promote lifelong learning opportunities for all.
Goal 5. Achieve gender equality and empower all women and girls.
Goal 6. Ensure availability and sustainable management of water and sanitation for all.
Goal 7 Ensure access to affordable, reliable, sustainable, and modern energy for all.
Goal 8. Promote sustained, inclusive, and sustainable economic growth, full and productive employment, and decent work for all.
Goal 9. Build resilient infrastructure, promote inclusive and sustainable industrialization, and foster innovation.
Goal 10. Reduce inequality within and among countries.
Goal 11. Make cities and human settlements inclusive, safe, resilient, and sustainable.
Goal 12. Ensure sustainable consumption and production patterns.
Goal 13. Take urgent action to combat climate change and its impacts.
Goal 14. Conserve and sustainably use the oceans, seas, and marine resources for sustainable development.
Goal 15. Protect, restore and promote sustainable use of terrestrial ecosystems, sustainably manage forests, combat desertification, halt and reverse land degradation and halt biodiversity loss.
Goal 16. Promote peaceful and inclusive societies for sustainable development, provide access to justice for all, and build effective, accountable, and inclusive institutions at all levels.
Goal 17. Strengthen the means of implementation and revitalize the Global Partnership for Sustainable Development" [84, p. 14].

Since 2015, the United Nations Secretary-General has regularly appointed a group of independent *scientists* to monitor the progress worldwide [85]. Already in the first report from 2015, IK has been mentioned: "Consideration of a broader range of knowledge and in particular indigenous knowledge is critical to the credibility and legitimacy of science-policy interface mechanisms" [85, p. 34]. Indigenous people are only considered as a 'vulnerable group'; this seems to be a clear case for McGregor's Eurocentric critique. Unfortunately, IK is not considered a source of inspiration to fundamentally change our way of thinking and acting in the world. IK should be mainly addressed to 'enhance credibility and legitimacy.' Monitoring the progress in achieving the sustainable development goals is still dominated by the MWV way of thinking and reasoning. So, we still have to go a long way to become wise, humble, responsible, and accountable!

Beauregard and colleagues wrote a manifesto for a post-materialist science. They conclude that "the shift from materialist science to post-materialist science may be of vital importance to the evolution of the human civilization" [86, p. 274]. "When we decide that the purpose of science is to generate wonder about nature, rather than to control nature, we will not be far from a relationship with nature that can flourish for all time and generations" [87, p. 129]. As academics and as responsible citizens, we have to put *spirituality* back on our agenda [88].

6 Conclusions

To overcome our mechanistic worldview (MWV), I introduced and discussed the fundamental difference between non-living things (NLT) and living systems (LS). The way of thinking in the MWV the Western academics follow these eight doctrines: (1) causality, (2) determinism, (3) localism, (4) materialism, (5) mechanism, (6) physicalism, (7) realism, and (8) reductionism. History has proven that this way of thinking is compelling to master NLTs and enables technological developments of tremendous power. But unfortunately, MWV cannot deal with LSs adequately and responsibly. Consequently, humanity is facing dramatic global challenges, of which today nobody knows how to overcome to avoid catastrophes. I argue that the way of thinking that produced these challenges is probably insufficient to overcome them. So, we need a *new* way of thinking and acting. I sketched two primary sources of inspiration for this new way of thinking: (a) the Eastern, Asian way of focusing on the context and environment first (i.e., a holistic dimension), and (b) the humble attitude of Indigenous thinking toward nature (i.e., value-driven reasoning). I sincerely hope this paper contributes to the *transformational power* in our way of thinking and acting in the world we all desperately need. This transformation will last long, but I am afraid it has to be done.

Acknowledgments. I am very grateful to Gerhard Wohland (Institut für dynamikrobuste Organisation, Germany), who introduced me to the critical distinction between non-living things and living systems at the Mensch-Maschine-Kommunikation workshop (MMK 2017, Gaienhofen, Germany). In addition, Florian Kaiser provided excellent feedback to an earlier version of this paper.

References

1. Dijksterhuis, E.J.: The Mechanization of the World Picture. Clarendon Press, Oxford (1961)
2. Bateson, G.: Steps to an Ecology of Mind: Collected Essays in Anthropology, Psychiatry, Evolution, and Epistemology, 7th edn. Ballantine Books, New York (1978)
3. Sheldrake, R.: The Science Delusion: Freeing the Spirit of Enquiry. Coronet, London (2012)
4. Labadi, S.: UNESCO, Cultural Heritage, and Outstanding Universal Value: Value-Based Analyses of the World Heritage and Intangible Cultural Heritage Conventions. AltaMira Press, Lanham, New York, Toronto, Plymouth (2013)
5. Taylor, M.R., et al.: Campbell biology: Concepts and connections. 10th (edn.) Essex: Pearson Higher Education (2022)

6. Freudenthal, G.: Atom and individual in the age of Newton: on the genesis of the mechanistic world view. In: Cohen, R.S., Wartofsky, M.W. (eds.) Boston Studies in the Philosophy of Science, vol. 88. Dordrecht: D. Reidel Publishing Company (1986)
7. Hawking, S., Mlodinow, L.: The Grand Design. Bantam Books, New York (2010)
8. Leydeckers, S.: Hello nanomaterials – Towards cultural (r)evolution. In: Hørmann, M. (ed.) Hello Materials Blog, Danish Design Center: Copenhagen (2012)
9. Merchant, C.: The Death of Nature. Women, Ecology and the Scientific Revolution. Harper & Row, San Francisco (1983)
10. Archer, D., Rahmstorf, S.: The Climate Crisis: an Introductory Guide to Climate Change. Cambridge University Press, Cambridge (2010)
11. Buchanan, R.A.: The power of the machine: the impact of technology from 1700 to the present day. Viking-Penguin Books, London, New York (1992)
12. Hornborg, A.: The Power of the Machine: Global Inequalities of Economy, Technology, and Environment. AltaMira Press, Walnut Creek, Lanham, New York, Oxford (2001)
13. Husbands, P., Holland, O., Wheeler, M. (eds.) The mechanical mind in history. MIT Press, Cambridge, London (2008)
14. Zhang, L.-F.: Thinking styles: their relationships with modes of thinking and academic performance. Educ. Psychol. **22**(3), 331–348 (2002)
15. Radin, D.: Supernormal: Science, Yoga, and the Evidence for Extraordinary Psychic Abilities. Deepak Chopra, New York (2013)
16. Radin, D.: Entangled Minds: Extrasensory Experiences in a Quantum Reality. Sydney: Paraview Pocket Books, New York, London, Toronto (2009)
17. Kutrovátz, G.: Heat death in ancient and modern thermodynamics. Open. Syst. Inf. Dyn. **8**(4), 349–359 (2001)
18. Ulanowicz, R.E.: Increasing entropy: Heat death or perpetual harmonies? Int. J. Des. Nat. Ecodyn. **4**(2), 83–96 (2009)
19. Serway, R.A., Jewett, J.W.: Physics for Scientists and Engineers with Modern Physics, 9th edn. Brooks/Cole, Boston (2014)
20. Rauterberg, M.: How is culture and cultural development possible? In: Hachimura, K., Ishida, T., Tosa, N. (eds.) International Conference on Culture and Computing, pp. 177–178. IEEE, Kyoto (2013)
21. Swenson, R., Turvey, M.T.: Thermodynamic reasons for perception-action cycles. Ecol. Psychol. **3**(4), 317–348 (1991)
22. Swenson, R.: Autocatakinetics, evolution, and the law of maximum entropy production: a principled foundation towards the study of human ecology. Adv. Hum. Ecol. **6**, 1–48 (1997)
23. Verbeek, P.-P.: What Things do: Philosophical Reflections on Technology, Agency, And Design. University Park: Pennsylvania State University Press (2005)
24. Meadows, D., Randers, J., Meadows, D.: Limits to Growth: the 30-Year Update. Sterling: Earthscan, London (2004)
25. Yanofsky, N.S.: The Outer Limits of Reason: What Science, Mathematics, and Logic Cannot Tell us. MIT Press, Cambridge, London (2013)
26. Whittaker, R.H., Levin, S.A., Root, R.B.: Niche, habitat, and ecotope. Am. Nat. **107**(955), 321–338 (1973)
27. Ameriks, K., Clarke, D.M. (eds.) Aristotle, Nicomachean Ethics. Cambridge Texts in the History of Philosophy. Cambridge University Press, Cambridge, New York, Melbourne, Madrid (2014)
28. Hennig, B., Rauterberg, M.: The Significance of Aristotle's four Causes for Design. Design Issues. **Manuscript** (under review), pp. 1–19 (2022)
29. Gasparatou, R., Ergazaki, M., Kosmopoulou, N.: Using philosophy for children to introduce the living/non-living distinction in kindergarten. Int. J. Early Years Educ. 1–16 (2020). (in press)

30. Petr, J.: The use of living and non-living things during school practice in primary science education. New Educ. Rev. **32**(2), 255–263 (2013)
31. Scerri, E.R.: The evolution of the periodic system. Sci. Am. **279**(3), 78–83 (1998)
32. Ablondi, F.: Automata, living and non-living: descartes' mechanical biology and his criteria for life. Biol. Philos. **13**(2), 179–186 (1998)
33. Rauterberg, M.: The three phases of life: An inter-cultural perspective. In: Hachimura, K., Ishida, T., Tosa, N. (eds.) Culture and Computing 2011, pp. 80–85. IEEE Computer Society, Los Alamitos (2011)
34. Hooper-Greenhill, E.: Museums and Education: Purpose, Pedagogy, Performance. Routledge, London, New York (2007)
35. Varsha, R.: Non-living things: properties, detailed classification and differences. In: Embibe, B., Avasthi, A. (eds.). Indiavidual Pvt. Ltd: Bengaluru (2022)
36. Naremore, J.: Love and death in A.I. artificial intelligence. Mich. Q. Rev. **44**(2), 256–284 (2005)
37. Schrödinger, E.: What is life? The Physical Aspect of the Living Cell. Cambridge University Press, Cambridge (1944)
38. Gibbs, J.W.: A method of geometrical representation of the thermodynamic properties by means of surfaces. Trans. Conn. Acad. Arts Sci. **2**, 382–404 (1873)
39. Phelan, J.: what is Life? A Guide to Biology, 2nd (edn.). W.H. Freeman, New York (2013)
40. Oparin, A.I.: The Origin of Life on the Earth, 3rd edn. Academic Press, New York (1957)
41. Seckbach, J. (ed.) Origins: genesis, evolution and diversity of life. In: Seckbach, J. (ed.) Cellular Origin and Life in Extreme Habitats and Astrobiology, vol. 6. Kluwer Academic Publishers, Dordrecht (2004)
42. Langton, C.G. (ed.) Artificial Life: an Overview. MIT Press, Cambridge, London (1996)
43. Boudry, M., Pigliucci, M.: The mismeasure of machine: Synthetic biology and the trouble with engineering metaphors. Stud. Hist. Philos. Sci. Part C: Stud. Hist. Philos. Biol. Biomed. Sci. **44**(4, Part B), 660–668 (2013)
44. Camprubí, E., et al.: The emergence of life. Space Sci. Rev. **215**(8), 1–53 (2019)
45. Bernard, C.: Lectures on the phenomena of life common to animals and plants. In: Thomas, C.C. (ed.) 1875 American Lecture Series, vol. 900. Charles C Thomas Publisher, Springfield (1974)
46. Bray, D.: Wetware: A Computer in Every Living Cell. Yale University Press, New Haven (2009)
47. Saariluoma, P.: Foundational Analysis: Presuppositions in Experimental Psychology. Routledge, London, New York (1997)
48. Guarino, N., Oberle, D., Staab, S.: What is an ontology? In: Staab, S., Studer, R. (eds.) Handbook on ontologies. IHIS, pp. 1–17. Springer, Heidelberg (2009). https://doi.org/10. 1007/978-3-540-92673-3_0
49. Hacking, I.: Historical ontology. In: Gärdenfors, P., Wolenski, J., Kijania-Placek, K. (eds.) In the Scope of Logic, Methodology and Philosophy of Science, pp. 583–600. Springer Science+Business Media, Dordrecht (2002). https://doi.org/10.1007/978-94-017-0475-5_13
50. Reeve, C.D.C.: Substantial Knowledge: Aristotle's Metaphysics. Hackett Publishing, Indianapolis, Cambridge (2000)
51. Levinas, E.: Is ontology fundamental? Philos. Today **33**(2), 121–129 (1989)
52. Holyoak, K.J., Morrison, R.G.: Thinking and reasoning: a reader's guide. In: Holyoak, K.J., Morrison, R.G. (eds.) The Oxford Handbook of Thinking and Reasoning, pp. 1–7. Oxford University Press, Oxford, New York (2012)
53. Holyoak, K.J., Morrison, R.G.: The oxford handbook of thinking and reasoning. In: Nathan, P.E. (ed.) Oxford Library of Psychology. Oxford University Press, Oxford, New York (2012)
54. Dorst, K.: The core of 'design thinking' and its application. Des. Stud. **32**(6), 521–532 (2011)

55. Freeman, M.: Modes of Thinking for Qualitative Data Analysis. Routledge, New York, London (2017)
56. Reber, A.S.: Implicit learning and tacit knowledge: an essay on the cognitive unconscious. In: Schacter, D. (ed.) Oxford Psychology Series. Oxford University Press, Oxford (1993)
57. Hunt, E.K., Lautzenheiser, M.: History of Economic Thought: a Critical Perspective. 3rd (edn.). M.E. Sharpe, Inc., New York, London (2011)
58. Neisser, U.: Memory observed: Remembering in Natural Contexts. W.H. Freeman, San Francisco (1982)
59. Simon, H.A.: Models of man: Social and rational. Mathematical Essays on Rational Human Behavior in a Social Setting. Wiley, New York (1957)
60. Griffin, D.W., et al.: Judgmental heuristics: a historical overview. In: Holyoak, K.J., Morrison, R.G. (eds.) The Oxford Handbook of Thinking and Reasoning, pp. 322–343. Oxford University Press, Oxford, New York (2012)
61. Elster, J., *Solomonic judgements: Studies in the limitation of rationality.* 1989, Cambridge • New York • Melbourne • Paris: Cambridge University Press
62. Gigerenzer, G., Selten, R. (eds.) Bounded Rationality: The Adaptive Toolbox. MIT Press, Cambridge, London (2001)
63. Dunbar, K., Fugelsang, J.: Scientific Thinking and Reasoning. In: Holyoak, K.J., Morrison, R.G. (eds.) The Cambridge Handbook of Thinking and Reasoning, pp. 705–725. Cambridge University Press, Cambridge, New York (2005)
64. Latour, B.: Science in Action: How to Follow Scientists and Engineers Through Society. Harvard University Press, Cambridge (1987)
65. Evans, J.S.B.T.: Dual-process theories of deductive reasoning: facts and fallacies. In: Holyoak, K.J., Morrison, R.G. (eds.) The Oxford Handbook of Thinking and Reasoning, pp. 115–133. Oxford University Press, Oxford, New York (2012)
66. Wang, X., Rauterberg, M.: Time travel in our mind based on system 2. In: Atmanspacher, H., Hameroff, S. (eds.) Book of Abstracts of the 13th Conference of the Science of Consciousness, pp. 130–131. Collegium Helveticum Zurich, Zurich (2019)
67. De Neys, W. (ed.) Dual Process Theory 2.0. In: Ball, L. (ed.) Current Issues in Thinking and Reasoning. Routledge, London, New York (2018)
68. Kahneman, D.: Thinking, Fast and Slow, 1st pbk. Farrar, Straus and Giroux, New York (2013)
69. Rauterberg, M.: Emotions as a communication medium between the unconscious and the conscious. In: Nakatsu, R., et al. (eds.) Cultural Computing - Second IFIP TC 14 Entertainment Computing Symposium, pp. 198–207. Springer, Heidelberg (2010). https://doi.org/10.1007/978-3-642-15214-6_20
70. Rauterberg, M.: About a framework for information and information processing of learning systems. In: Falkenberg, E.D., Hesse, W., Olivé, A. (eds.) Information System Concepts - Towards a Consolidation of View, pp. 54–69. Chapman & Hall, London, New York, Tokyo, Melbourne. (1995)
71. Patterson, M.L.: Nonverbal behavior: a functional perspective. In: Social Psychology. Springer Verlag, New York, Berlin, Heidelberg, Tokyo (1983)
72. Cook, K.S., Levi, M. (eds.) The Limits of Rationality. The University of Chicago, Chicago, London (1990)
73. Nisbett, R.E., et al.: Culture and systems of thought: holistic versus analytic cognition. Psychol. Rev. **108**(2), 291–310 (2001)
74. Nisbett, R.E., Masuda, T.: Culture and point of view. Proc. Natl. Acad. Sci. **100**(19), 11163–11170 (2003)
75. Libert, S., Pletcher, S.D.: Modulation of longevity by environmental sensing. Cell **131**(7), 1231–1234 (2007)
76. De La Cadena, M., Starn, O.: Introduction. In: De La Cadena, M., Starn, O. (eds.) Indigenous Experience Today, pp. 1–30. Berg, Oxford, New York (2007)

77. Nelson, J.: Before they Pass Away, 2nd edn. JN Publishing, Haelen (2020)
78. Suzuki, D., Knudtson, P.: Wisdom of the Elders: Sacred Native Stories of Nature. Bantam Books, New York, Toronto, London, Sydney (1992)
79. Mistry, J.: Indigenous knowledges. In: Kitchin, R., Thrift, N. (eds.) International Encyclopedia of Human Geography, pp. 371–376. Elsevier, Amsterdam, Boston, Heidelberg, London, New York (2009)
80. Shilling, D.: Introduction: the soul of sustainability. In: Nelson, M.K., Shilling, D. (eds.) Traditional Ecological Knowledge: Learning from Indigenous Practices for Environmental Sustainability, pp. 3–14. Cambridge University Press, Cambridge, New York, Melbourne, New Delhi, Singapore (2018)
81. Johnson, M.: Lore: Capturing Traditional Environmental Knowledge. Diane Publishing, Pennsylvania (1998)
82. McGregor, D.: Coming full circle: Indigenous knowledge, environment, and our future. Am. Indian Q. 28(3/4), 385–410 (2004)
83. McGregor, J.: Toward a philosophical understanding of TEK and ecofeminism. In: Nelson, M.K., Shilling, D. (eds.) Traditional Ecological Knowledge: Learning from Indigenous Practices for Environmental Sustainability, pp. 109–128. Cambridge University Press, Cambridge, New York, Melbourne, New Delhi, Singapore (2018)
84. United-Nations, resolution 70/1-transforming our world: the 2030 agenda for sustainable development. In: Seventieth United Nations General Assembly, Secretary-General. United Nations, New York (2015)
85. Le Blanc, D., et al.: Global sustainable development report. Advanced unedited ed, ed. U.N. Secretary General. United Nations, New York (2015)
86. Beauregard, M., et al.: Manifesto for a post-materialist science. Explore J. Sci. Healing 10(5), 272–274 (2014)
87. Nelson, M.P., Vucetich, J.A.: Wolves and ravens, science and ethics: traditional ecological knowledge meets long-term ecological research, in traditional ecological knowledge: learning from Indigenous practices for environmental sustainability. In: Nelson, M.K., Shilling, D. (eds.). Cambridge University Press, Cambridge, New York, Melbourne, New Delhi, Singapore. pp. 129–136 (2018)
88. Kheirandish, S., et al.: A comprehensive value framework for design. Technol. Soc. 62(art. 101302), 1–12 (2020)

Will Robots Know That They Are Robots? The Ethics of Utilizing Learning Machines

Rebekah Rousi$^{(\boxtimes)}$ ⓘ

School of Marketing and Communication, University of Vaasa, PO Box 700, 65101 Vaasa, Finland
`rebekah.rousi@uwasa.fi`

Abstract. The aspirations for a global society of learning technology are high these days. Machine Learning (ML) and artificial intelligence (AI) are two key terms of any socio-political and technological discourse. Both terms however, are riddled with confusion both on practical and conceptual levels. Learning for one thing, assumes that an entity gains and develops their knowledge bank in ways that are meaningful to the entity's existence. Intelligence entails not just computationality but flexibility of thought, problem-solving skills and creativity. At the heart of both concepts rests the philosophy and science of consciousness. For in order to meaningfully acquire information, or build upon knowledge, there should be a core or executive function that defines the concerns of the entity and what newly encountered information means in relation to its existence. A part of this definition of concerns is also the demarcation of the self in relation to others. This paper takes a socio-cognitive scientific approach to deconstructing the two currently overused terms of ML and AI by creating a design fiction of sorts. This design fiction serves to illustrate some complex problems of consciousness, identity and ethics in a potential future world of learning machines.

Keywords: Machine learning · Artificial intelligence · Consciousness · Ethics · Identity · Robots · Black box

1 Introduction

Mental images of intelligent learning technological systems can range from the abstract, screen-based or somewhat 'invisible' operating and information systems to the highly physicalized forms of autonomous robotics and vehicles. Perhaps the autonomous technologies that people are most familiar with these days are self-driving vehicles. These vehicles are already making their appearance on roads worldwide [1–3]. While the idea of a continuously learning and evolving piece of machinery may sound attractive from a number of perspectives, the thought of traffic systems filled with KITTs (Knight Industries Two Thousand) – the famous intelligent 1982 Pontiac Firebird Trans Am from the television show *Knight Rider* – might be slightly unnerving. Yet, technological solutions driven by, incorporating or representing machine learning (ML) and artificial intelligence (AI) are talked of and rationalized as possessing the capacity to learn. Learning entails thought, which is inherent in the term 'intelligence' [4, 5].

© The Author(s), under exclusive license to Springer Nature Switzerland AG 2022
M. Rauterberg (Ed.): HCII 2022, LNCS 13324, pp. 464–476, 2022.
https://doi.org/10.1007/978-3-031-05434-1_31

ML is a sub-field of AI [6]. Proportionately, deep learning (DL) is a sub-field of ML and neural networks (NN) is a sub-field of DL. Often DL and NN are used synonymously with ML, but this is not accurate [7]. ML is the broader term for computer systems that expand their data bases and adapt in terms of logic and behavior (output) without being directly programmed by a human [8]. DL on the other hand, comprises a complex architecture of algorithms that are intended to imitate the structures of the human brain [9]. A basic way of describing a NN is that it replicates networks or pathways of neurons (information messengers) that serve as an input layer (nodes or units), one to two (maybe three) hidden neuron layers, and a layer of output neurons [10]. This NN dimension of ML serves to mimic the activity of the brain. The main objective of ML is to develop technology that can more or less operate and exist on its own without (frequent) input from human programmers. Moreover, some of the intentions behind such technology include the increasing of accuracy, expansion of human natural capabilities (e.g., computational) and efficiency, and even replacement of human actors in mundane or safety critical tasks [11].

There are numerous methods applied to train (teach) ML [12]. Simply stated, machines 'learn' on the basis of prior computations [13]. Sample (or training) data can be used to form algorithmic models that are applied as a scaffolding upon which subsequent processing, predictions or decisions will be based [14]. In other words, the machine 'learns' to search for patterns within extensive amounts of data [15]. It is upon these patterns that the machine develops models via which it may produce predictions. Machines are purely computational and unable to generalize knowledge [6]. Until recently, the transfer of learning from one application to another was not possible. Yet, currently numerous research and development initiatives have focused on achieving this feat particularly in the area of fault diagnosis (see e.g., [16, 17]).

While learning through training data and sampling in some ways mimics human learning there are many human characteristics that are not, as yet, inherent in ML systems – consciousness, intentionality, social functions and psychology (identity), culture and emotions [10–18]. From a socio-cultural and environmental perspective, it may be observed that humans acquire, interpret, assimilate and act on information on the basis of perceived and routinized patterns [19–21]. Interestingly, culture has been previously characterized as the "software of the mind" [22]. One may even see culture and its psychological and historical conditioning [23–25] as a similar process to the training of the mind to read patterns and symbols (signs) – similar to ML training methods. However, the matter of consciousness and intentionality can be seen as the basic corner stones of human learning. Learning, whether it be an intentionally aimed for act or a process of unplanned knowledge development and assimilation (apperception; [26, 27]) that occurs through the progression of experience, becomes a part of human conscious intentionality and intentional learning. These are important factors in what is known as constructivist learning [28, 29] or constructivism in which learning is a developmental process that constantly builds on knowledge that is previously possessed.

2 The Nature of Learning, Emotions and Intentionality

Learning in its true form, is always linked to intentionality and intentional states within the brain [30]. In order to understand this argument better, it is important to define what is meant by learning and then to establish a definition of intentionality. According to the Merriam-Webster *Learner's Dictionary* [31] 'learning' as a noun, is defined as an "activity or process of gaining knowledge or skill by studying, practicing, being taught, or experiencing something..." Furthermore, Ambrose and colleagues [32] argue that learning should be understood as a process through which change is the result. This change occurs via experience – experience (previously mentally stored information, or knowledge) informs how subsequent information is acquired and mentally organized (represented) and forms experience (see Fig. 1). Experience itself is a part of what can be understood as a stream of consciousness, or continuous stream of thought, that exists in altering states of clearly represented contents (conscious experience), less represented or fragmented contents (sub-conscious experience) and non-represented contents (unconscious experience) [33]. Yet, through the understanding that learning is closely intertwined with consciousness, it may also be argued that learning is intentional [34–36] and emotional [37]. Quite specifically, in an organic sense, it can be understood that all learners, or learning entities, will come to understand ideas, concepts and other phenomena in different ways. Through this learning, lived experience is shaped and individual views of the world and how it is ordered also impacts the learning entity (person) in terms of not only a global understanding, but sense of identity, positioning and relationality [37].

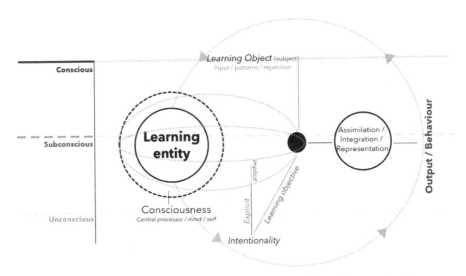

Fig. 1. Learning as a changing state of consciousness through input and action

What is learned, or the knowledge that is acquired or formed, is molded and tinted by qualities, sentiments and emotions [38] (see Fig. 2). In a cognitive-affective sense, emotions are organic radar systems, alerting creatures (including humans) to possible threats and dangers, as well as to possible benefits and gains in terms of psycho-physiological well-being [39, 40]. Emotions operate on a range of levels from primary or primitive responses (basic emotions) [41], to higher order experiences (cultural, social and associative) [42]. Emotions guide our attention, facilitate priority structuring of information, enable humans to remember, and what is more, enable humans to remember phenomena in specific ways and influence decision-making [43]. It may also be argued that emotions are driven by and information is processed, assimilated and objectified on the basis of human needs and motivations [44–46]. Human biology and its role in the cognitive-affective processes involved in generating and experiencing emotion is one distinct factor that as yet, is not present in ML. Efforts have been made to develop artificial emotions in machines (see e.g., [39, 47–49]), yet this is a heavily contested area in terms of ethics and indeed the survival of the human race on this planet (see e.g., [50, 39]).

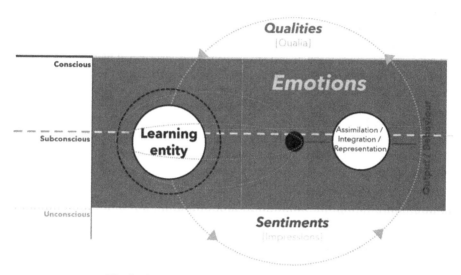

Fig. 2. Qualities, emotions and sentiments in learning

In addition to the emotional side of learning, the intentional perspective must also be accounted for. From a Husserlian understanding, intentionality can be seen as "the essential structure of consciousness" [51] (p. 6). In particular, this structure of consciousness holds corporeal and non-corporeal properties that are incited through both action as well as a sense, or thoughts of undertaking action [52, 53]. In other words, the theorization of intentionality and what it pertains posits an acknowledgement that experience (human or potentially otherwise) and being in the world as a learning organism comprises both input from external, or physical objects, in the world and internal mentally bound information that is not directly connected to the external [54, 55]. Representational (or computational) learning is an act bound to mental phenomena [51]. Despite some beliefs and common applications of the term 'intention' or 'intentionality', intentionality does not equal the act of will or a great sense of self-awareness or volition [51]. Yet, in relation to the scenario presented in this paper, self-awareness is of interest regarding the potential artificial learning being – learning machines.

3 The Experience of Learning Machines

In the case of human lived experience, it is known and accepted that during one's lifetime, one will be exposed to a multitude of experiences, occurrences, chronologies and relationships. Through all of these interactions and intersections learning occurs [56]. These fairly unique combinations or series of learnings (information acquisitions and knowledge formations) are what distinguish one individual and their personal story from the next [57]. In other words, it may be supposed that people *are* what they have learned through experience. In an era of autonomously learning machinery, it may be supposed that each machine or unit may develop its own *personality* or identity through its learnings from unique combinations of encounters and experiences [57]. This is, unless, the learnings are not stored separately, rather instead centrally through systems of connected networks [58]. Or even, through systems or systems of distributed networks (consider Skynet from the movie *Terminator* for instance). Yet, given not only the plurality of uses and contexts of this machinery, but also that of ownership of the technology, it may be assumed that for practical and logical purposes there are some degrees of individuality between these learning systems.

Let us imagine that we have already arrived at a future in which robotic machinery operates via a form of ML that is similar, if not identical to that of human beings. This would render the machines as seemingly autonomous – or as autonomous as human beings can be in light of the significance of social, economic, geographic and physiological circumstances. While ML is commonly spoken of in today's technological discourse, in light of the above discussion, current versions of this terminology can be interpreted as nothing more than what Drew McDermott [59] terms as "wishful mnemonics". Or the wishful, hopeful labelling of technological components, functions and concepts that extend beyond the reality of their actual capabilities. For this reason, we slant the term in another direction towards that of *learning machines* (LM). LMs can be thought of as autonomous technological entities or various forms of robotics that roam the earth acquiring, processing and acting on differing modes and quantities of information.

Human motivations for developing and implementing LMs within communities and nations at large will be varied. Each type of LM will no doubt be developed to undertake altering functions and roles within societies and their operations. The matter of exactly *why* a robot for instance, would need to be self-learning and to a degree self-sufficient is a topic left for other discussions. Yet, from a simplified viewpoint, and returning to the basic agreement of why ML is being developed in the first place, these entities and systems are intended to operate in a matter whereby humans do not need to continuously and directly maintain and program the technology [7]. Moreover, through their programmed learning capacities, the autonomous machines are expected to keep developing and advancing in ways that exceed human capabilities [60]. In the potential future reality of LMs this would also mean fleets of 'super entities' that are all to a various extent developing in different ways. Could this individuality of learning and shaping of logic through experience be classified as consciousness? May we entertain the thought that actual learning is taking place through a means of intentionality [55]? Particularly the latter question directs us towards consideration of the *black box* [61].

Interestingly, while many ethical problems referred to as the 'black box' are already known – that is, the lack of transparency, understandability and explainability caused by complex systems and vast quantities of unstructured and unlabeled data [62] – the more advanced machinery gets in terms of its learning capacity and learned material ('experience'), the less understandable it will become [63]. In a future scenario of countless mechanical learning entities not simply the information (or knowledge) of the units, will diversify, but so will the logic, relationships and identities (sense of self, us and others). In earlier programming processes and models, these technological systems could be explained by the logic in which the machines were designed and coded. The programmer(s) in other words, could be said to be accountable for explicating the data gathering, processing, operations and sequences of the machines [64]. The potential black box in traditional programming approaches could be said to rest in the human programmers themselves [65]. Yet, in a world where machines program themselves based on the phenomena with which they interact it is inevitable that humans will reach a state in which they themselves will not understand the technology they have 'given birth' to.

None the less, there is the assumption that every one of the LMs will have been developed to perform a specific function, or various sets of functions. The characters, traits, knowledge, logic, behavior and even *appraisal* (evaluative) capacities will differ according the domains and contexts in which the technology operates. Thus, programming will adapt according to the boundaries, affordances and input of the diversified situations to which the machinery is exposed [66], and none-the-least the operational goals [67]. Given these characteristics, one possibility for understanding LMs is to study and question human beings who have also operated in similar roles and conditions. Some form of comprehension regarding the contents, factors and situations that the LMs are exposed to could be achieved by probing their human counterparts and then perhaps, accessing databases and logs to observe patterns and other representational phenomena. One core aspect related to the availability and transparency of the databases and representation of algorithmic and computational processes relates to who can access this information and how? This matter will be returned to shortly in relation to ethics. Yet, given the development and seeming evolution of the LMs within their perspective contexts and relationships, and moreover, the capacity of the machinery to adapt its programming itself considerations may be made for how humans may maintain oversight, and at what stage can the LMs be considering legal entities (individuals) in and of themselves. It may be reasonable to imagine or assume that this machinery could develop a certain level of consciousness – maybe even more advanced than that of humans in light of their computational capacity – which would certainly reawaken discussions on the nature and existence of mental (experiential) phenomena such as qualia [68, 68].

If indeed, an LM possesses a form of consciousness that serves as a platform upon which constructivist learning takes place, there may be additional assumptions that: a) these LMs may indeed experience and exercise free will and opinions – if their learning is comprised of varied experiential encounters then their views of the world and its logic would differ from one another, and incidentally that of their creator(s); b) this free will and differences in logic, or LM subjectivity would mean that the entities would and/or should be in charge of their own actions – their creator would no longer be responsible for the actions and opinions of the objects (or subjects); and c) a level of self-awareness could potentially develop among the objects and their systems. Thus, there would be a scenario of *self* (or *us*) and *others* (see Fig. 3).

470   R. Rousi

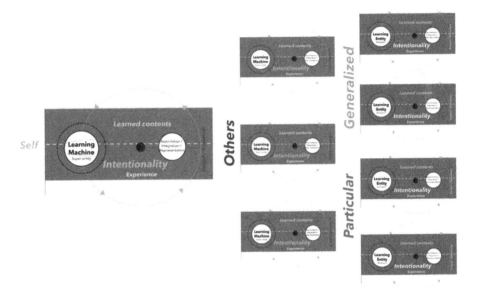

Fig. 3. Learning machines – self in relation to others

The definition of self in relation to others is integral to the construction of personal psychology and identity through the formation of an understanding of how individuals are in the world [70, 70] – roles, positions, relations etc. On the basis of an understanding in which accumulated individual *experiences*, or unique sequences and combinations of information exposure (input) shapes the LMs, their logic and even self-programming styles we may assume that a sense of self is formed in relation to others – both robots or other LMs as well as other learning entities such as humans. Information obtained, processed and represented about the self would place the LM in relation to these others. In light of symbolic interactionist theory [72, 73] for instance, the LMs would conceptualize themselves in relation to both general (any kind, unfamiliar or insignificant) others and particular others [74]. From an information processing and connectivity perspective, *general others* may be understood as being entities that either do not belong to a LMs cognitive domain (not of the same manufacturer, brand, ownership or operational field). While *particular others* may be connected – sharing the same databases, collective and connective cognition and adaptive programming – or they may even possess commonalities on the levels of manufacturer, technology-type, ownership or operational field (co-workers). How these LMs negotiate with one another in joint territories would require specific levels of cooperation and demarcation between the individual entities, their roles and how to function together (or against each other in the case of warfare) [75]. Thus, the boundaries of human identity and consciousness, machine identity, reality and consciousness may become increasingly blurred.

In an interview with Robert Lawrence Kuhn [76], filmed before the death of the late Marvin Minsky in 2016, Minsky emphasized that as technology becomes more and more complex, characters in simulations, videogames and other programs would become ever more complicated. While he claimed that these characters would not become human, he did mention that the separation and distinction between human and non-human characters would be difficult. This holds fast in a reality in which machines indeed are capable of learning intentionally, and where they will learn to learn. The classic questions of, "what is consciousness?" and "can machines ever be conscious?" will be tested. Yet, perhaps scientists may not come closer to this understanding than they have already in the scholarship of humans [68, 68].

4   Will Robots Know that They Are Robots? Ethical Considerations

As described above, acts of cognition and negotiation in spaces of LMs will become socio-psychological ones, rather than purely techno-social ones. There will be levels to which LMs need to be aware of themselves, their space, capabilities and limitations in relation to others [78]. What may also be observed is cyborg-like, or augmented, relationships formed between LMs that aid them in extending and enhancing their capabilities [79]. No doubt, teams or fleets of robots for instance will be used for these purposes. Even if the term 'cyborg' is used to delineate the cybernetic relationship between biological organisms (i.e., humans) and artificial objects or systems (technology) [79], in a world of self-learning machinery, the distinction between how robots use other robots and how humans use robots may not be so pronounced. Indeed, there may even be hierarchies and social status between various types of learning machinery.

Yet, returning to the human ethical perspective of oversight and transparency of AI logic, access to data bases and the visibility of, or ability to view computational and algorithmic processes may develop into an ethical challenge of *other* sorts. This meaning, that if a piece of machinery not only is capable of learning, adapting and evolving to suit its roles and conditions, but also is made responsible for its actions – which should happen if there is no human programmer oversight in its development – then, should it not have rights to demarcate its boundaries and exercise privacy [80]? The ability to reach and understand the workings of these LMs is one thing, but the question regarding whether or not it is ethical for humans to see these workings is another. What societies may face are populations of black boxes that are both artificial and human (see Fig. 4).

In the inevitable Black Box cybernetic society, the role of identity and identification is not simply a cosmetic one. Rather, it sets the boundaries between individuals and groups while also demarcating connections [80]. There are several problems that will certainly arise. One being issues of responsibility and accountability. Once a machine is already learning and developing on its own there needs to be the assumption that the entity is responsible for its own actions. That is unless: a) the owners ('masters') of the entities are held responsible and accountable for the robots' actions; or b) humans cease to entertain the idea of truly learning machines roaming loose in society. With option *b* responsibility and accountability would already be made at this stage of the intelligent digital transformation and those who endeavor to commit to the development of LMs will be held accountable already now.

In scenario *a* there is a different set of problems that link to notions of slavery and the potential citizen rights of robots. Hanson Robotics' Sofia is officially the first robot to gain citizenship of any nation (Saudi Arabia [81]), yet, it can be scarcely claimed that the

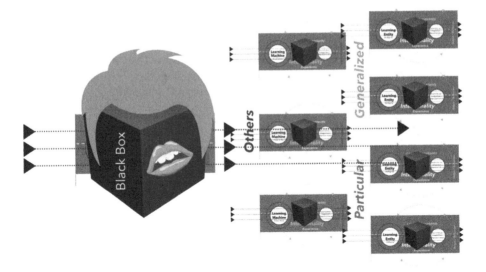

Fig. 4. Black box cybernetic society

machine's intelligence is anything like a human's. At least at this stage, self-awareness, embodied experience and social connections do not seem to be true characteristics of this symbolic sign of the human-like robotic future. But, when and if LMs would set foot in society traditional ideals of human-robot relationships would certainly be challenged. If it is not right to keep a conscious human (or any human) enslaved for the purposes of labor and other functions, then it would not be right to keep a robot.

There is also the dimension of self-learning robotics that humans will not welcome and that is the high likelihood of their superiority over humans [39]. Rather than being our servants, they will be our masters if humans indeed do survive to tell the tale. However, now we come to the ultimate question: When robots are conscious enough to engage in meaningful and intentional learning, will they know they are robots? We may be reminded about an interaction that took place not so long ago on a recent episode of the futuristic television show *Loki* (created by Michael Waldron, 2021):

> *Robot Scanner: Please confirm to your knowledge that you are not a fully robotic being, were bon an organic creature, and do in fact possess what many cultures would call a soul.*
>
> *Loki: What? "To my knowledge"? Do a lot of people not know if they're robots?*
>
> *Robot Scanner: Thank you for your confirmation. Please, move through.*
>
> *Loki: What if I was a robot and I didn't know it?*
>
> *Robot Scanner: The machine would melt you from the inside out. Please move along, sir.*
>
> *Loki: OK, I'm not a robot, so I'll be fine.*

While humorous there is an eerie point to this sketch-like scene. Will robots be aware that they are robots? Or, will the term be demeaning giving rise to the necessity to generate new, politically correct titles of identity? In a world of interactive black boxes that continuously learn and differentiate themselves from and in relation to others, it could be reasonable to think that maybe robots will not be aware of their own nature after all. Societies of humans and LMs may be huge melting pots. And, to return to a quote by Minsky [82] that may very well characterize the future human relationship to robots and the destiny of societal control: "Will robots inherit the earth? Yes, but they will be our children."

Acknowledgements. The author would like to thank the support of the School of Marketing and Communication, as well as the Digital Economy Platform, University of Vaasa, Finland. Gratitude is also placed towards the AI Ethics research group lead by Pekka Abrahamsson and the efforts of the Sea4Value Fairway project.

References

1. Rivard, G.: Ontario poised to become a leader. Auto123 (2021). https://www.auto123.com/en/news/first-autonomous-car-pilot-canada/63086/. Accessed 08 Feb 2022
2. Schoettle, B., Sivak, M.: Potential Impact of Self-Driving Vehicles on Household Vehicle Demand and Usage. University of Michigan, Transportation research institute, Ann Arbor (2015)
3. Litman, T.: Autonomous Vehicle Implementation Predictions: Implications for transport planning. https://www.vtpi.org/avip.pdf. Accessed 10 Feb 2022
4. Li, R.: A Theory of Conceptual Intelligence: Thinking, Learning, Creativity, and Giftedness. Praeger Publishers/Greenwood Publishing Group, Westport (1996)
5. Piaget, J.: The Psychology of Intelligence. Routledge, London (2003)
6. IBM Cloud Learn Hub. Machine learning. https://www.ibm.com/cloud/learn/machine-learning. Accessed 09 Feb 2022
7. Odi, U., Nguyen, T.: Geological facies prediction using computed tomography in a machine learning and deep learning environment. In: SPE/AAPG/SEG Unconventional Resources Technology Conference & OnePetro (2018)
8. Wolfewicz, A.: Deep learning vs. machine learning – what's the difference? https://levity.ai/blog/difference-machine-learning-deep-learning. Accessed 09 Feb 2022
9. Kriegeskorte, N., Golan, T.: Neural network models and deep learning. Curr. Biol. **29**(7), R231–R236 (2019)
10. Wang, S.C.: Artificial neural network. In: Wang, S.C. (ed.) Interdisciplinary computing in java programming. The Springer International Series in Engineering and Computer Science, pp. 81–100. Springer, Boston (2003). https://doi.org/10.1007/978-1-4615-0377-4_5
11. Ivanova, K., Gallasch, G.E., Jordans, J.: Automated and autonomous systems for combat service support: scoping study and technology prioritisation. Defence Science and Technology Group Edinburgh SA Australia (2016)
12. Batista, G.E., Prati, R.C., Monard, M.C.: A study of the behavior of several methods for balancing machine learning training data. ACM SIGKDD Explor. Newslett. **6**(1), 20–29 (2004)
13. SAS.: Machine learning. https://www.sas.com/en_us/insights/analytics/machine-learning.html. Accessed 08 Feb 2022

14. Elmes, A., et al.: Accounting for training data error in machine learning applied to Earth observations. Remote Sens. **12**(6), 1034 (2020)
15. Tan, O.: How does a machine learn? Forbes (2017). https://www.forbes.com/sites/forbestechcouncil/2017/05/02/how-does-a-machine-learn/?sh=4c7df937441d. Accessed 07 Feb 2022
16. Guo, L., Lei, Y., Xing, S., Yan, T., Li, N.: Deep convolutional transfer learning network: a new method for intelligent fault diagnosis of machines with unlabeled data. IEEE Trans. Industr. Electron. **66**(9), 7316–7325 (2018)
17. Yang, B., Lee, C.G., Lei, Y., Li, N., Lu, N.: Deep partial transfer learning network: a method to selectively transfer diagnostic knowledge across related machines. Mech. Syst. Signal Process. **156**, 107618 (2021)
18. Dehaene, S., Lau, H., Kouider, S.: What is consciousness, and could machines have it? Robot. AI Humanity, 43–56 (2021)
19. Bandura, A.: Social learning through imitation. 1962. In: Jones, M.R. (ed.) Nebraska Symposium on Motivation. Univer Nebraska Press, Nebraska (1962)
20. Kolb, D.A.: Experiential Learning: Experience As The Source Of Learning And Development. FT press, Upper Saddle River (2014)
21. Schwartz, B.: Psychology of Learning and Behavior. WW Norton & Co, New York (1989)
22. Hofstede, G., Hofstede, G.J., Minkov, M.: Cultures and Organizations: Software of the Mind, vol. 2. Mcgraw-hill, New York (2005)
23. Ivanov, V.V.: Cultural-historical theory and semiotics. In: Yasnitsky, A., Van der Veer, R., Ferrari, M. (eds.) Cambridge Handbook of Cultural-Historical Psychology, pp. 488–516. Cambridge University Press, Cambridge (2014)
24. Vygotsky, L.S.: The Psychology of Art. MIT Press, Cambridge (1971)
25. Vygotsky, L.S.: Consciousness as a problem for the psychology of behavior. In: Rieber, R.W., Wollock, J. (eds.) The Collected Works of L. S. Vygotsky Problems Of The Theory And History Of Psychology, vol. 3, pp. 63–79. Plenum Press, New York (1997)
26. Helfenstein, S., Saariluoma, P.: Apperception in primed problem solving. Cogn. Process. **8**(4), 211–232 (2007). https://doi.org/10.1007/s10339-007-0189-4
27. Saariluoma, P.: Apperception, Content-Based Psychology and Design, pp. 72–78. Human Behaviour in Design. Springer, Heidelberg (2003). https://doi.org/10.1007/978-3-662-07811-2_8
28. Yager, R.E.: The constructivist learning model. Sci. Teach. **58**(6), 52 (1991)
29. Fosnot, C.T.: Constructivism: Theory, Perspectives, and Practice. Teachers College Press, New York (2013)
30. Foley, J.M., Kaiser, L.M.: Learning transfer and its intentionality in adult and continuing education. New Dir. Adult Continuing Educ. **2013**(137), 5–15 (2013)
31. Merriam-Webster: Learning. https://learnersdictionary.com/definition/learning. Accessed 07 Feb 2022
32. Ambrose, S.A., Bridges, M.W., DiPietro, M., Lovett, M.C., Norman, M.K.: How Learning Works Seven Research - Based Principles for Smart Teaching. Wiley, Hoboken (2010)
33. Chalmers, D.J.: The puzzle of conscious experience. Sci. Am. **273**(6), 80–86 (1995)
34. Chalmer, D.J.: The content and epistemology of phenomenal belief. Conscious. New Philos. Perspect. **220**, 271 (2003)
35. Tomasello, M., Carpenter, M.: Shared intentionality. Dev. Sci. **10**(1), 121–125 (2007)
36. LeDoux, J.E.: Brain mechanisms of emotion and emotional learning. Curr. Opin. Neurobiol. **2**(2), 191–197 (1992)
37. Cammell, P.: Relationality and existence: Hermeneutic and deconstructive approaches emerging from Heidegger's philosophy. Humanistic Psychol. **43**(3), 235 (2015)
38. Bower, G.H.: How might emotions affect learning. In: The Handbook of Emotion and Memory: Research and Theory, vol. 3, p. 31 (1992)

39. Rousi, R.: Me, my bot and his other (robot) woman? Keeping your robot satisfied in the age of artificial emotion. Robot. **7**(3), 44 (2018)
40. Frijda, N.H., Swagerman, J.: Can computers feel? Theory and design of an emotional system. Cogn. Emot. **1**(3), 235–257 (1987)
41. Ekman, P.: Basic emotions. In: Handbook of Cognition and Emotion, vol. 98, no. 45–60, p. 16 (1999)
42. Rousi, R., Silvennoinen, J.: Simplicity and the art of something more A cognitive - semiotic approach to simplicity and complexity in human - technology interaction and design experience. Hum. Technol. **14**(1), 67–95 (2018)
43. LeBlanc, V.R., McConnell, M.M., Monteiro, S.D.: Predictable chaos: a review of the effects of emotions on attention, memory and decision making. Adv. Health Sci. Educ. **20**(1), 265–282 (2014). https://doi.org/10.1007/s10459-014-9516-6
44. Baldassarre, G.: What are intrinsic motivations? A biological perspective. In: 2011 IEEE international conference on development and learning (ICDL) vol. 2, pp. 1–8 IEEE (2011)
45. Huitt, W.: Motivation to learn: an overview. Educational psychology interactive, 12 (2001)
46. Rouse, K.A.G.: Beyond maslow's hierarchy of needs: what do people strive for? Perform. Improv. **43**(10), 27 (2004)
47. Fellous, J.M.: From human emotions to robot emotions. Architectures for Modeling Emotion: Cross-Disciplinary Foundations. American Association for Artificial Intelligence, 39–46 (2004)
48. Haikonen, P.O.: Robot Brains: Circuits and Systems for Conscious Machines. Wiley, Hoboken (2007)
49. Haikonen, P.O.: Consciousness and sentient robots. Int. J. Mach. Conscious. **5**(01), 11–26 (2013)
50. Coeckelbergh, M.: Moral appearances: emotions, robots, and human morality. Ethics. Inf. Technol. **12**(3), 235–241 (2010). https://doi.org/10.1007/s10676-010-9221-y
51. Creely, E.: Understanding things from within. A Husserlian phenomenological approach to doing educational research and inquiring about learning, Int. J. Res.Method Educ. (2016). doi: https://doi.org/10.1080/1743727X.2016.1182482
52. Dreyfus, H., Warthall, M.: A Companion To Phenomenology And Existentialism. Blackwell, Malden (2006)
53. Hopkins, B.: The Philosophy of Husserl. Acumen, Chesham (2011)
54. Brentano, F., Müller, B.: Descriptive Psychology. International Library of Philosophy. Routledge, London (1995)
55. Kriegel, U.: The Sources Of Intentionality. Oxford University Press, New York (2011)
56. Loehlin, J.C.: Genes And Environment In Personality Development. Sage Publications Inc, Thousand Oaks, CA (1992)
57. Caspi, A., Roberts, B.W.: Personality development across the life course: the argument for change and continuity. Psychol. Inq. **12**(2), 49–66 (2001)
58. Minsky, M.: Decentralized minds. Behav. Brain Sci. **3**(3), 439–440 (1980)
59. McDermott, D.: Artificial intelligence meets natural stupidity. ACM SIGART Bull. **57**(57), 4–9 (1976). https://doi.org/10.1145/1045339.1045340
60. Grace, K., Salvatier, J., Dafoe, A., Zhang, B., Evans, O.: When will AI exceed human performance? Evidence from AI experts. J. Artif. Intell. Res. **62**, 729–754 (2018)
61. Durán, J.M., Jongsma, K.R.: Who is afraid of black box algorithms? On the epistemological and ethical basis of trust in medical AI. J. Med. Ethics **47**(5), 329–335 (2021)
62. Turilli, M., Floridi, L.: The ethics of information transparency. Ethics Inf. Technol. **11**(2), 105–112 (2009)
63. Strobel, M.: Aspects of transparency in machine learning. In: Proceedings of the 18th International Conference on Autonomous Agents and MultiAgent Systems, pp. 2449–2451 (2019)

64. Winfield, A., Jirotka, M.: The case for an ethical black box. In: Gao, Y., Fallah, S., Jin, Y., Lekakou, C. (eds.) TAROS 2017. LNCS (LNAI), vol. 10454, pp. 262–273. Springer, Cham (2017). https://doi.org/10.1007/978-3-319-64107-2_21
65. Minsky, M.L.: Computation. Prentice-Hall, Englewood Cliffs, NJ (1967)
66. Simpkins, C., Bhat, S., Isbell Jr, C., Mateas, M.: Towards adaptive programming: integrating reinforcement learning into a programming language. In: Proceedings of the 23rd ACM SIGPLAN Conference on Object-oriented programming Systems Languages and Applications, pp. 603–614 (2008)
67. Rodríguez-Pérez, R., Bajorath, J.: Interpretation of machine learning models using shapley values: application to compound potency and multi-target activity predictions. J. Comput. Aided Mol. Des. 34(10), 1013–1026 (2020). https://doi.org/10.1007/s10822-020-00314-0
68. Dennett, D.: Quining qualia. In: Marcel, A., Bisiach, E. (eds.) Consciousness in Modern Science, pp. 42–77. Oxford University Press, Oxford (1988)
69. Jackson, F.: Epiphenomenal qualia. Philos. Q. (1950-) 32(127), 127–136 (1982)
70. Neisser, U.: Five kinds of self-knowledge. Philos. Psychol. 1(1), 35–59 (1988)
71. James, W.: The Principles of Psychology. Henry Holt and Company, New York (1890). https://www.gutenberg.org/files/57628/57628-h/57628-h.htm. Accessed 11 Feb 2022
72. Shott, S.: Emotion and social life: a symbolic interactionist analysis. Am. J. Sociol. 84(6), 1317–1334 (1979)
73. Rousi, R., Alanen, Hanna-Kaisa.: Socio-emotional Experience in Human Technology Interaction Design – A Fashion Framework Proposal. In: Rauterberg, Matthias (ed.) HCII 2021. LNCS, vol. 12795, pp. 131–150. Springer, Cham (2021). https://doi.org/10.1007/978-3-030-77431-8_8
74. Blumer, H.: Symbolic Interactionism: Perspective and Method. University of California Press, Berkeley, CA (1986)
75. Cummings, M.: Artificial Intelligence and The Future of Warfare. Chatham House for the Royal Institute of International Affairs, London (2017)
76. Kuhn, R.L.: Marvin Minsky: A Society Of Minds. Episode 1613. Closer to Truth. https://www.youtube.com/watch?v=Yz4m65nAMjg. Accessed 07 Feb 2022
77. Fernandez-Rojas, R., et al.: Contextual awareness in human-advanced-vehicle systems: a survey. IEEE Access 7, 33304–33328 (2019)
78. Clark, A., Chalmers, D.: The extended mind. Anal. 58(1), 7–19 (1998)
79. Warwick, K.: Cyborg morals, cyborg values, cyborg ethics. Ethics Inf. Technol. 5(3), 131–137 (2003)
80. Nissenbaum, H.: Privacy as contextual integrity. Wash. Law Rev. 79, 101–139 (2004)
81. Parviainen, J., Coeckelbergh, M.: The political choreography of the Sophia robot: beyond robot rights and citizenship to political performances for the social robotics market. AI. Soc. 36(3), 715–724 (2020). https://doi.org/10.1007/s00146-020-01104-w
82. Minsky, M.L.: Will robots inherit the earth. Sci. Am. 271, 108–113 (1994)

Mental Contents in Designing AI Ethics

Pertti Saariluoma$^{(\boxtimes)}$, Mari Myllylä, and Antero Karvonen

University of Jyväskylä, 40014 Jyväskylä, Finland
ps@jyu.fi

Abstract. In future intelligent digital society, the way people organize their life around technologies shall change because intelligent machines can follow ethical rules in their behavior. In the human mind, ethics exist as contents of mental representations. Therefore, it is important to investigate the information contents of mental representations or mental contents. One can also call this approach content-based cognitive research. The analysis of mental contents makes it possible to mimic human ethical information processing and construct human digital twins for designing ethical machine information processes. In this paper, we analyze the relevant AI aspects of Hume's guillotine. Hume asked critically whether facts can be used to derive values. His answer was negative. However, modern information technology can collect huge masses of facts, but can these facts be used in improving how we should live? Content-based analysis of human ethical information processing opens possibilities to bypass the logical dilemma of Hume's guillotine.

Keywords: Hume's guillotine · Weak and strong ethical AI · Mental contents · Ethical discourse

1 Introduction

David Hume was presumably the first to ask whether it is possible to derive values from facts [1]. David Hume wrote: "It is impossible that the distinction between moral good and evil can be made by reason" [1]. This aporia has been termed Hume's guillotine, Hume's law or the "is-ought to problem," and it is one of the ground problems of ethics [2]. Hume's critical question was revolutionary as it seems to be in contradiction with traditional everyday ethics. For example, if experience shows that excessive use of alcohol is risky for heath in the long run, would not this mean that people should give up drinking? In the context of intelligent systems, this classic problem acquires new forms and a new life.

Information systems have capacity to collect and to process massive amounts of facts, but assuming that Hume is right this new knowledge would be meaningless in thinking the ethical rules of actions. Computers operate on facts, and they can collect massive amounts of new and facts and new combinations of facts. However, on the ground of Hume's guillotine, one may justly ask if computational systems could also construct new values on the ground of given facts.

M. Rauterberg (Ed.): HCII 2022, LNCS 13324, pp. 477–487, 2022.
https://doi.org/10.1007/978-3-031-05434-1_32

Intuitively, Hume's guillotine seems problematic as one cannot seriously think that facts have no value thinking morals. Millions of people have taken several rounds of COVID-19 vaccination as they can look from statistics how non-vaccinated people have more serious that risks than vaccinated ones. Thus, thinking about the "big picture" facts affect human moral decisions. However, it is also true that over 10% of people at least are critical towards vaccination. They have several reasons for their denial such as the vaccinations not being sufficiently tested or that media is presenting incorrect data. Thus, official facts are not convincing the vaccination of critical people, but it seems that these people also rely on information. Arguments and facts have an important connection in human ethical thinking and action for all people, although their thinking would be different in content.

If there was no connection between facts and values, it might be impossible to have any ethical thinking at all. Ethics concerns action in some situations, and the knowledge is not only how to act but how to act in ethically correct manner. If one does not know what COVID-19 is and what vaccinations are, it is hard to have a negative stance to COVID-19 vaccinations. Therefore, contrary to Hume's law, it appears that there is some kind of connection between facts and values in human thinking and acting. However, to make progress it is necessary to analyze how people in their everyday life combine facts and values. This kind of analysis was done in Westermarck ethics [3].

The critical question is thus how people mentally represent ethics and the situations of life in their minds. Ethics is about the actions people take in some definite situations. They cannot take any actions without having a sufficiently clear representation about the situations [4]. To do a deed or to act, people always need to combine some facts with some ethical rules. However, Hume's guillotine points out that this should be problematic and unreliable. Therefore, one must ask how it is possible at all for people to have intelligent information processing with ethical contents.

Before working with ethical information processing in human minds, researchers need to have the conceptual tools to do it. Thus, the first questions are how mental contents can be analyzed and how this knowledge can be used in investigating and designing ethical AI systems. Here, the question is how facts and values are unified in human information processing and how our understanding of human information processing can be used in designing and constructing ethical AI systems. The basic tools of thinking in working with these problems are content-based cognitive research and content-based analysis of mind.

Ethics is a product of the human mind. Therefore, it is important to investigate how the human mind and cognition operates when it guides human ethical actions. Here, the focus shall be on the way facts and values can be integrated into human ethical information processing. As ethics in the mind can be seen as mental contents, it makes sense to ask how people process ethical mental contents in their minds [5–7].

Cognitive psychology and cognitive science have over the past few decades based their thinking on the idea that people represent information in their minds [7, 8]. Mental representations have been mostly studied from the highly successful limited capacity perspective [9], and mental contents have relatively seldom been focally discussed [5, 6]. Nevertheless, thought limited capacity forms the core of modern human technology interaction HTI psychology, it does not give a system of good concepts for analyzing ethics. Simply, on the basis of required mental capacity, one cannot differentiate between good or evil, and for this reason content-based thinking is essential in investigating the ethics of the mind.

In the cognitive science of mind (i.e., in philosophy and psychology), mental contents have been discussed with relative regularity, but not nearly as much as mental capacity. The topic of mental contents has been under discussion among phenomenologists [10] and ordinary language philosophers such as Wittgenstein and Austin [11]. Moreover, Allport and Fodor and related researchers have highlighted mental contents and the analysis of representations [5, 6]. Mental contents in experience have also been a topic in more recent scholarly discussions [12]. In clinical psychology, the contents of mental contents have been studied occasionally [13, 14]. Among mainstream cognitive psychologists, Newell and Simon [7] spoke of content-oriented thinking in simulating human thinking. Nevertheless, it has not been common to extensively base the analysis of mind and actions on the properties of mental contents [9, 15, 16].

Hence, as opposed to earlier representational theories [5, 6], we see the concept of taking the "contents as contents" as the core of content-based cognitive analysis [9, 15, 16]. Rather than relying on abstract concepts such as schemas, production systems or associative networks, we base the explanation on the properties of representational contents. This means that the explanation of experience and behavior should be grounded on the properties of actual representational information contents. One could characterize our approach as content-based, referring to the concept of explaining human actions on the ground of properties of information or basing the explanation on the contents of information contents in mental representations.

Mental representational contents can be about infinitely different phenomena. However, some kinds of information contents might be more relevant to ethics than others. For example, the ability to feel empathy towards others means that one individual can observe, understand, and experience the contents of a mind of another individual from that other subject's perspective. Comprehending another's mental contents can, in turn, either be dealt with emotional indifference, or it can create further feelings of moral responsibility, compassion and sympathy as a need to behave in a way that alleviates observed other's suffering [17, 18]. Thus, empathy is one important aspect in investigation of ethical mental representations and what kind of actions they can initiate.

In investigating ethics, content-based thinking refers to analysis of ethical representations and related actions. In cognitive science, the representational contents can be collected by means of various methods. It can be done by psychological methods such as protocol analysis, observation, interviews or documentary analysis. However, one can also apply philosophical analysis and use conceptual analysis such as conceptual engineering [19]. The choice of methods and their variations depend on the nature of the concrete problem. In this paper, our work will be conceptual and conceptual engineering in nature.

2 Content-Based Analysis of Mind

Ethics is a product of the human mind. Therefore, it is important to investigate how the human mind and cognition operates when it guides human ethical actions. Here, the focus shall be on the way facts and values can be integrated in human ethical information processing. As ethics in the mind can be seen as mental contents, it makes sense to ask how people process ethical mental contents in their minds [5–7].

Cognitive psychology and cognitive science have over the last decades grounded their thinking on the idea that people represent information in their minds [7, 8]. The mental representations have been mostly studied from the very successful limited capacity point of view [9]. However, mental contents have relatively seldom been focally discussed [9]. Nevertheless, although limited capacity forms the core of modern HTI psychology, it does not provide a system of good concepts for analyzing ethics. Simply, on the grounds of required mental capacity, one cannot differentiate between good or evil, and therefore content-based thinking is essential in investigating ethics in mind [4].

In the cognitive science of mind (i.e., in philosophy and psychology), mental contents have been discussed with relative regularity but not nearly as much as mental capacity. The issues of mental contents have been under discussion among phenomenologists [10] and ordinary language philosophers such as Wittgenstein and Austin [11]. Moreover, Allport [5] Fodor [6] and related researchers have highlighted mental content and the analysis of representations. Mental content in experience has also been the topic of more recent scholarly discussions [12]. In clinical psychology, the contents of mental contents have been studied occasionally [13, 14]. Among mainstream cognitive psychologists, Newell and Simon [7] spoke of content-oriented thinking in simulating human thinking. Nevertheless, it has not been common to extensively base the analysis of mind and actions on the properties of mental contents. However, one cannot say that mental contents would have belonged more to the mainstream cognitive analysis of the mind compared to capacity-based thinking.

Hence, differently from earlier representational theories, we see as the core of the content-based cognitive analysis the idea of taking the "contents as contents" [9, 15, 16]. Rather than relying on abstract concepts such as schemas, production systems or associative networks, we base the explanation on the properties of representational contents. This means that the explanation of experience and action should be grounded on the properties of actual representational information contents. One could characterize our approach as content-based, referring to the idea of explaining human actions on the ground of properties of information or basing the explanation on the contents of information contents in mental representations.

In investigating ethics, content-based thinking refers to the analysis of ethical representations and the related actions. In cognitive science the representational contents can be collected by means of different methods. It can be done by psychological methods such as protocol analysis, observation, interviews or documentary analysis. However, one can also apply philosophical analysis and use conceptual analysis such as conceptual engineering [17]. The choice of the methods and their variations depends on the nature of the concrete problem. Here, our work will be conceptual and conceptual engineering in nature.

3   Imitating Mind

Existing intelligent information processes can be used to develop new information processes in new physical entities. The process of developing new information processes on the basis of old ones can be called mimicking. Mimetic design is one important method of contemporary design. Here, we shall combine content-based thinking and cognitive mimetics to create a conceptual model for how ethical AI could operate.

Mimicking natural processes and structure is a well-founded branch in technology design [18]. Its primary focus has been on creating physical structures and processes by taking inspiration from solutions found in nature. This kind of design thinking is called biomimetics or biomimicry. The main idea of biomimetics is to solve complex technical problems by imitating the solutions that nature has developed for similar problems. Many physical artefacts from clothes, spades, and airplanes to Velcro tape, have their invented by means of biomimetic thinking. However, in developing intelligent technologies, a new model of mimicking is required. Rather than mimicking biological structures, it is good to focus on human information processes (focusing on contents) and imitate them in developing intelligent systems. Mimetics based on an analysis of human information processes in developing intelligent technological solutions can be called "cognitive mimetics" because the core of the processes is in imitating human information processing [20–22].

Understanding how the mind processes information and in our case understanding mental contents in processing ethical information is central in working with ethical information processes. Unless we understand how people process ethical information, it is hard to construct machines with the same capacities. This question makes sense as much of intelligent machine information processing is based on mimicking how people process information. Even the Turing machine was constructed on the foundation of Turing's vision for how human mathematicians solve problems [23]. Thus, human ethical information processing can be used to consider how ethical information processes could be realized in machines. In this paper, I shall outline the basics of modelling human ethical information processing.

The task of cognitive mimetics is to create a conceptual model for human ethical information processing. The outcome of cognitive mimicking could be a program, but it is possible also to create a conceptual model of people processing ethical information. This is not exceptional way of thinking, as in the history of philosophy practically all the models of human ethical information processing have so far been conceptual.

4   AI and Hume's Guillotine

Humankind has undergone technological revolutions many times in its history. Fire, bronze, agriculture, sailing, cannons, printing, clocks, steam engines, and electricity are common examples of technological innovations [24]. These new innovations have changed the everyday life of people by satisfying their biological needs.

The present socio-technological transformation is based not based on innovations in matter or energy, but rather on information and intelligent technologies. These are technologies which can process information. Consequently, their capacity to carry out tasks which previously required human intelligent information processing has greatly increased. The increased speed of computing and rapidly growing databases have made it possible to design technical artefacts with capacities to perform tasks which thus far only people have been able to carry out. Artificial intelligence has penetrated in application in numerous areas of modern life. Industrial robots, office automation, intelligent medicine and healthcare, changing teaching, marketing and political discourse, autonomous traffic systems and intelligent finance are typical examples of the information revolution.

In addition to fast routine processing logical inferences, machines can make decisions between alternative courses of actions. They can even learn to make classifications of their own so that people are not able to predict the information states which intelligent systems can generate. Consequently, intelligent systems can select between different sense making courses of actions.

The capacity for selective information processing makes it possible for modern AI-based systems to compare ethical values related to different courses of actions. Chess playing computers, for example, can find the best sequences of moves among millions of legal alternatives [16]. Intelligent choices make machine actions intelligent. Respectively, the selection between actions can also be grounded on ethical values and such machines can be seen as ethically selective.

Some choices between actions can be ethically more justified than others, and thus it makes sense to discuss ethics in the context of acting intelligent machines. Intelligent information systems can choose between different courses of actions on the basis of implemented ethical principles. For example, intelligent systems can prefer children to middle aged people in making decisions about the order of medical operations. Such decisions are ethical and carried out by intelligent machines. One can speak of ethical use of technical artefacts in society, but one can also develop systems with ethical capacities of some type. However, the problems of ethical AI are not conceptually straightforward.

Intelligent machines can be ethical in more than one sense. The first conception of ethical AI is that people implement their values in the evaluative structures of ethical programs. This position can be termed weak ethical AI (WEAI). The alternative position is that machines are able to generate themselves new ethical rules and principles. The latter conception can be called strong ethical AI or intelligence (SEAI). In terms of the former position, Hume's guillotine is apparently easier to solve than in the later. However, in order to clarify this conceptual engineering problem, it will be important to ask how ethical information processing is possible for people and subsequently return to the problem of how weak and strong ethical AI differ from each other.

The analysis of ethical processes helps us consider the relations between weak and strong ethical AI. Following the foundational concepts of life-based design, obtaining clarity regarding the way ethics and ethical norms are created in human life enables researchers to study the generations ethical design requirements and ethical information processing for technologies. In searching for solutions, it is necessary to pay attention to a central difference between two kinds of AI programs.

Weak AI is not a conceptually difficult case from a design perspective. Ethical norms such as classification algorithms or heuristic rules in chess machines can be implemented in AI programs [16]. It is possible to define the situations and their factual content as well as ethical properties. For example, intelligent programs can classify on the ground of given criteria who is allowed to get intensive care when the capacity of hospitals is surpassed. The programs can give priority to young or at risk group patients. This is an ethical choice but totally based on human given criteria. Critical information is recognized by intelligent systems given ethical norms are followed in deciding on activities. Thus, designers can build recognition association type action models with ethical contents.

However, strong ethical AI is more challenging and in this type of AI Hume's quilliotine is important. The strong ethical AI programs should develop their ethical norms on the ground of given data. No clear ethical rules to be followed can be presented for the problems of designing strong ethical AI. If Hume's is right data processing ethical machines cannot be constructed and strong AI would be impossible.

As argued above, Hume's guillotine is problematic. It seems that people can in some way circumvent in their practical life. People register facts and factual situation and they are able to draw conclusion about what they should do. They are able to form generalized rules concerning what should be done. To get information about these mechanisms and to understand why Hume's quilliotine does not really work, it is essential to consider the ways ethics is present in human everyday information processing.

5 Ethical Cycle

Hume's guillotine is an important ethical dilemma and one cannot say that it has been solved. To obtain clarity on the dilemma, one must think how it is possible for people to process ethical information. If facts had nothing to do with human values, it would be impossible to make situation relevant actions. Situations and actions are presented in the form of factual information in the minds of people and ethics concerning these situations.

One cannot doubt either the existence of factual information or the ethics of actions. They are real because they exist. There are no good grounds to doubt that facts would not be essential in actions. When exiting a room, people need to know where the walls and doors are. All information contents of the kind are present in human mental representations, which control actions.

Equally evident is that people are able to create ethical rules and norms and follow these in their actions. The process of creating ethical rules and norms can be called the ethical information creation process or ethical information process, which is an example of human creative thinking. People who have lost their money in high risk investments can think that in the future they should avoid such economic activities and be satisfied by less risky actions. In turn, people who see climate change as a threat to social security may choose environmentally-based investment practices.

Ethical machines are machines which can follow ethical norms in their behavior. For example, investment information processing supporting machines can use emission reduction as a criterion for investments. Thus, machines can support people in their pursuit towards ethical and normative goals. However, understanding how machines could actively suggest sense making ethical norms and goals requires further analysis of human ethical information processing. In this work, the historical considerations on ethics by different schools of philosophy are valuable for conceptual engineering [25].

Human experience (i.e., conscious mental representation) and its information contents form a central component of human information processing and thinking. Mental representations have their cognitive and emotional dimensions. Both play a significant role in ethical information processing. Ethically, an important component of mental content is its emotional valence [26]. Most emotions can be divided into positive or negative, pleasant or unpleasant, and happy or sad. Therefore, all situations emerging in the course of actions can be experienced positively or negatively.

The importance of emotions and their valence has been known in ethical discussion long times. Emotion-based ethical thinking is called emotivism [1, 27]. These theories begin with the idea that situations of life and respective experiences are emotionally positive or negative (pleasant and unpleasant). The emotional analysis of consequence of actions thus provides the basic for ethical analysis of actions and action types. For example, the so-called Golden Rule (one should not treat others in ways that one would not like to be treated oneself) can be seen as generalization of situational experiences of deeds the principle is followed or violated. Thus, the emotional component of any ethical information process is in the analysis and experience of the emotional valence can be taken as the first point of the ethical process.

Consequently, the development of ethical norms is grounded emotional analysis situations. However, it is not wise to end the analysis of ethical process with emotions. The situations of life are the consequences of actions. Thus, the value of actions can be defined on the basis of the valence of the situations arising as a consequence of particular types of actions. Norms describe what kinds of actions have had emotionally positive and what kinds of actions emotionally negative consequences. Actions leading to pains are not acceptable and actions leading to positive emotions are good. The first idea in defining human ethical information processing is based on emotional good or bad.

However, good and bad are empty without being associated with concrete situations. Some situations feel bad and some feel good. To be able to labels situation good or bad one needs to know what the situations are like. People must mentally represent the situation. They have to have a description of how things are in their minds and this representation is constructed of factual information. When one is ill, he or she normally feels bad, but they know also their situation and can for example, experience broken rib or migraine as a reason for the unpleasant situation. Thus, people have associated emotion and cognitive representation of the situation into a whole.

A third element in analyzing human ethical information processing is action. Situations do not appear independently of what people have done. A broken rib can be the consequence of being hasty on ice and falling. The deeds ending up to some type of situations may also be unknown to people so that people suffering from migraine do not know what to do to avoid the painful situations. It is unclear whether there is any deed which could lead to the illness.

The end situations of action and the actions themselves are normally linked in the minds of people. Unvaccinated COVID-19 patients in intensive care should know that with a great probability they could have avoided the serious illness by means of vaccination. Actions have their consequences and emotions are important in assessing the end situations. Literature on consequentialism entails numerous examples and aspect on ethics of consequences of deeds [28].

Depending on their experiences, people form the personal ethical rules guiding their life. Of course, they are helped by cultural ethical norms and their knowledge of them in forming their personal ethics. Childhood experiences and childhood teaching provide a good example of how peoples for their personal ethics represented as well as conscious rules as habits and attitudes.

Different people experience situations in different ways. Social interaction can be painful for some while it is positive to another. Therefore, the general ethical norms can be seen to be consequence of informal (everyday) and formal (or political) discourses. This socio-ethical process has been investigated in discourse ethics [29]. Thus, it is essential in add to ethical process the discourse between people in society ending to political analysis and even laws.

The circle of actions, situations, cognitions and emotions as well as social discourse forms a mental structure, which explains how people construct their ethical representations. The act and encode in their mind how they act. They associate end situations with their actions and evaluate these situations building explicit and implicit personal ethics. Then in the course of social discourse the actual rules for ethics and in general for what can be done are formed.

6 Hume's Error

The difference between the presented analysis of ethics and Hume's is different in one respect. Hume argued that reason cannot be ground on differentiating moral good from moral evil [1]. However, his perspective is possible only if one separates reason from emotions. However, in the light of modern psychology, it is evident that one cannot separate emotions from cognition as both are essential in creating human experience.

Emotions have their contents. Valence is one of the components of human mental contents. Similarly, emotional theme also contributes to the contents of mental representations. Envy is a different emotional state when compared from sympathy. Therefore, emotions construct a part of representational contents and this part is inseparable from cognitive aspects of human mental representations.

Cognitions and representations of actions form another important aspect of human mental contents. Cognitions such as perceiving and thinking enable people to represent space around themselves, their action paths and action structures, objects future states of world or what they think to do in future and what people have done earlier.

Emotions and cognition construct the contents of human mental representations. Emotional and cognitive concepts are always present, when people represent their past, present and future actions as well as the structure of their physical and social environments. Content based thinking makes it possible to investigate both aspects of mind.

From the content-based point of view Hume' guillotine and his negative answer to the relations of facts, emotions and values is not correct [1]. The question itself is rather nonsense and meaningless, because it assumes that emotions and cognitions are separable. However, this cannot be true as human mental contents always have both aspects. It is not possible to have emotional contents without cognitive information. As it is not possible to represent an object without form and location, it is impossible to have an action and end situation analysis without emotional analysis. Consequently, Hume's guillotine does not prevent from creating strong ethical AI. Cognitive mimetics is good tool in developing ethically autonomous AI.

7 Strong AI Ethics – A Conceptual Plan

Modern ICT-technology designing is a complex process. It requires combining different types of knowledge into eventual computational products. Conceptual engineering which is design, implementation and evaluation of concepts is a good tool in modern technical design. It enables designers to revise foundations of technological paradigms and open new ways of thinking in modern innovation and creative scientific processes.

The ethical cycle is not impossible to mimic computationally. One can collect situation descriptions using datamining. It is also possible to associate realistic human emotional valences to situations on the basis of emotionally enrich situation description. It has been argued that it is possible to simulate computationally emotions [30]. Thus, there are no principal obstacles for strong ethical AI.

By mean of data analysis, one can build models for creating autonomous ethics. These models have several stages:

1. The analysis of data
2. Constructing situational representation
3. Associating emotional values to representation
4. Determining action situations from initial state of the goal state.
5. Analyzing distribution of values among social groups
6. Resolving differences

If it is possible to computationally perform these sub-tasks, it is possible to develop autonomous ethical processes. No principal obstacles exit when only it is possible to go around Hume's guillotine. As a conclusion one can say that combining content-based analysis of human mind with cognitive mimetics makes it possible to develop conceptual and computational models for strong ethical AI.

References

1. Hume, D.: A Treatise of Human Nature. Dent, London (1738/1972)
2. Cohen, M.: "Is" and "Should". an unabridged gap. Philos. Rev. **74**(2), 220–228 (1965)
3. Westermarck, E.: The Origin and Development of Moral Ideas. Macmillan, London (1926)
4. Saariluoma, P.: Hume's guillotine in designing ethically intelligent technologies. In: Ahram, T., Taiar, R., Gremeaux-Bader, V., Aminian, K. (eds.) IHIET 2020. AISC, vol. 1152, pp. 10–15. Springer, Cham (2020). https://doi.org/10.1007/978-3-030-44267-5_2
5. Allport, D.: Patterns and actions: Cognitive mechanisms are content specific. In: Claxton, G. (ed.) Cognitive Psychology: New Directions, pp. 26–64. Routledge and Kegan Paul, London (1980)
6. Fodor, J.: A Theory of Contents. MIT-Press, Cambridge (1990). https://doi.org/10.1007/s40 544-013-0034-y
7. Newell, A., Simon, H.: Human Problem Solving. Prentice-Hall, Englewood Cliffs (1972)
8. Neisser, U.: Cognition and Reality. Freeman, San Francisco (1976)
9. Saariluoma, P.: Foundational Analysis. Routledge, London (1997)
10. Husserl, E.: Logische Unterschungen I-II. Niemeyer, Halle (1901–2)
11. Passmore, J.: A Hundred Years of Philosophy. Penguin Books, Harmondsworth (1957)
12. Chalmers, D.: The Character of Consciousness. Oxford University Press, Oxford (2010)

13. Freud, S.: Vorlesungen zur Einführung in die Psychoanalyse. Fischer, Frankfurth (1917/2000)
14. Beck, A.: Cognitive Therapy of Emotional Disorders. Penguin Books, Harmondsworth (1976)
15. Myllylä, M., Saariluoma, P.: Expertise and becoming conscious of something. New Ideas Psychol. **64**, 100916 (2022)
16. Saariluoma, P.: Chess Players' Thinking. Routledge, London (1995)
17. Chalmers, D.J.: What is conceptual engineering and what should it be? Inquiry, 1–18 (2020)
18. Vincent, J.F., Bogatyreva, O.A., Bogatyrev, N.R., Bowyer, A., Pahl, A.K.: Biomimetics: its practice and theory. J. R. Soc. Interface **3**, 471–482 (2006)
19. Floridi, L.: A defence of constructionism Philosophy has conceptual engineering. Metaphilosophy **42**(3), 282–304 (2011)
20. Saariluoma, P., Kujala, T., Karvonen, A., Ahonen, M.: Cognitive mimetics: main ideas. In: International Conference on Artificial Intelligence. CSREA Press (2018)
21. Saariluoma, P., Cañas, J., Karvonen, A.: Human digital twins and cognitive mimetic. In: Ahram, T., Taiar, R., Langlois, K., Choplin, A. (eds.) IHIET 2020. AISC, vol. 1253, pp. 97–102. Springer, Cham (2021). https://doi.org/10.1007/978-3-030-55307-4_15
22. Karvonen, A.: Cognitive mimetics for AI ethics: tacit knowledge, action ontologies and problem restructuring. In: Rauterberg, M. (ed.) HCII 2020. LNCS, vol. 12215, pp. 95–104. Springer, Cham (2020). https://doi.org/10.1007/978-3-030-50267-6_8
23. Turing, A.M.: On computable numbers, with an application to the entscheidungsproblem. In: Proceedings of the London Mathematical Society, vol. 42, pp. 230–65 (1936–7)
24. J. Science in History. Penguin Books, Harmondsworth (1969)
25. Malik, K.: The Quest for Moral Compass: The Global History of Ethics. Atlantic books, London (2014)
26. Frijda, N.H.: The Emotions. Cambridge University Press, Cambridge (1986)
27. Van Roojen, M.: The stanford encyclopedia of philosophy. In: Zalta, E. (ed.) Moral Cognitivism vs. Non-Cognitivism (2018). https://plato.stanford.edu/archives/fall2018/entries/moral-cognitivism/
28. Sinnott-Armstrong, W.: The stanford encyclopedia of philosophy. In: Zalta, E. (ed.) Consequentialism (2019). https://plato.stanford.edu/archives/fall2021/entries/consequentialism/
29. Habermas, J.: Diskursethik [Discourse ethics]. Surkamp, Frankfurth am Main (2009)
30. Simon, H.A.: Motivational and emotional controls of cognition. Psychol. Rev. **74**(1), 29–39 (1967)

Author Index

Printed in the United States
by Baker & Taylor Publisher Services